West's

ANNOTATED CALIFORNIA CODES

~~~~~~~

EDUCATION CODE

Sections 18000 to 22699

———

Official
California Education Code
Classification

———

WEST GROUP

A THOMSON COMPANY

MAT #40029170

West Group has created this publication to provide you with accurate and authoritative information concerning the subject matter covered. However, this publication was not necessarily prepared by persons licensed to practice law in a particular jurisdiction. West Group is not engaged in rendering legal or other professional advice, and this publication is not a substitute for the advice of an attorney. If you require legal or other expert advice, you should seek the services of a competent attorney or other professional.

 PRINTED ON 10% POST CONSUMER RECYCLED PAPER

PREFACE

This volume covers legislation relating to §§ 18000 to 22699 of the Education Code as supplemented through Chapter 51 of 2002 Regular Session urgency legislation and Chapter 3 of the Third Extraordinary Session and March 5, 2002 election.

The enactments, pertinent judicial constructions and other annotative materials that have accumulated in recent years have been integrated with existing provisions to simplify and facilitate the use of this volume.

All standard practice features of West's Annotated California Codes are continually updated for maximum utility. These valuable research features include:

Notes of Decisions—Court constructions setting forth the facts and the law.

Cross References—State laws of related subject matter, qualification or limitation are noted and listed.

Historical and Statutory Notes—Showing the source and tracing the development of the law.

California Code Forms—Time-saving references to these valuable code forms volumes.

Law Reviews—References to pertinent articles and commentaries.

Library References to:

Key Number Digests.

Corpus Juris Secundum.

Westlaw Topic Numbers.

Miscellaneous Digests, Books and Reports.

Law Revision Commission and other Comments.

United States Code Annotated—References to federal laws of related or qualifying matter.

Constitutional Provisions—References to related text of the state constitution.

Code of Regulations References.

Opinions of the Attorney General.

This volume contains those features appropriate to its contents.

An index, comprehensive and detailed, covering the complete text of the Education Code, appears in the last volume of the Code.

Annotations based on decisions of the State and Federal Courts, and Opinions of the Attorney General close with the following:

PREFACE

A Westlaw guide covering additional resources for use in your legal research is set out following this Preface. See Westlaw KeyCite® to update the case history information for opinions under Notes of Decisions.

The Publisher expresses its sincere appreciation to the State Officials, to the members of the Judiciary, to the Law Schools, and to the practicing Attorneys whose timely suggestions, supplementing the varied experience of the Publisher, have contributed materially to the successful planning and development of WEST'S ANNOTATED CALIFORNIA CODES.

THE PUBLISHER

July, 2002

COORDINATED RESEARCH
IN CALIFORNIA FROM WEST GROUP

ANNOTATED DESKTOP CODES

CA Civil Practice Statutes and Rules (Softbound)

CA Civil Practice Statutes and Rules (Hardbound)

CA Business Statutes Annotated

Blumberg CA Family Code Annotated

CA Commercial Code Annotated

DiMugno & Glad CA Insurance Laws Annotated

Dwyer & Bergsund CA Environmental Laws Annotated

Imwinkelried & Hallahan CA Evidence Code Annotated

McGovern CA Probate Code Annotated

Miller & Starr CA Real Estate Laws Annotated

UNANNOTATED DESKTOP CODES

California Civil Code

California Code of Civil Procedure

California Corporations Code

California Education Code

California Employment Laws

California Environment Laws

California Evidence Code

California Family Laws and Rules

California Insurance Code

California Juvenile Laws and Rules

California Penal Code

California Probate Code

California Revenue and Taxation Code

California Vehicle Code

California Water Code

COORDINATED RESEARCH

CALIFORNIA CIVIL PRACTICE:

Procedure

Torts

Business Litigation

Real Property Litigation

Family Law Litigation

Probate and Trust Proceedings

Employment Litigation

Workers' Compensation

Civil Rights Litigation

Environmental Litigation

CRIMINAL PRACTICE

West's California Criminal Law
Douglas Dalton

West's California Criminal Procedure
Laurie L. Levenson

California Criminal Defense Motions Forms Manual
Albert Menaster

California Criminal Forms and Instructions, 2d
Mark E. Overland and Edwards A. Rucker

California Drunk Driving Defense
Lawrence Tayler

California Criminal Trialbook
Harry M. Caldwell, Sue Steding and Gary Nichols

JURY SELECTION PRACTICE BOOKS

Bennett's Guide to Jury Selection and Trial Dynamics
California Civil Litigation

Bennett's Guide to Jury Selection and Trial Dynamics
California Criminal Litigation
Cathy E. Bennett, Robert B. Hirschhorn and Dr. Jo–Ellan Dimitruis

---

COORDINATED RESEARCH

WEST'S CALIFORNIA CODE FORMS

Business and Professions
Joel S. Primes

Civil
Jeanne P. Robinson

Civil Procedure
Gregory L. Ogden and Daryl Fisher–Ogden

Commercial
Stephen N. Hollman and Ray D. Henson

Corporations
Janet E. Kerr

Education
Jay E. Grenig

Elections, Fish & Game, Food & Agricultural, Insurance
Susan J. Orton

Family
Margaret McAllister

Government
Jay E. Grenig and H. Anthony Miller

Labor
W. Robert Morgan and Barbara Spector

Probate
Ann E. Stodden and Timothy A. Whitehouse

Public Utilities
Boris H. Lakusta

Revenue and Taxation
Publisher's Editorial Staff

JURY INSTRUCTIONS
[Also available in computer disk and looseleaf formats]

California Jury Instructions—Civil (BAJI)

California Jury Instructions—Criminal (CALJIC)

BARCLAY'S OFFICIAL CALIFORNIA CODE OF REGULATIONS
[Also available on CD–ROM]

WEST'S ANNOTATED CALIFORNIA CODES
[Also available on CD–ROM]

COORDINATED RESEARCH

CALIFORNIA OFFICIAL REPORTS, 4TH
[Also available on CD–ROM]

CALIFORNIA DIGEST OF OFFICIAL REPORTS, 3D
[Also available on CD–ROM]

WEST'S CALIFORNIA REPORTER
[Also available on CD–ROM]

WEST'S CALIFORNIA DIGEST, 2D
[Also available on CD–ROM]

———————

WEST'S CALIFORNIA JUDICIAL COUNCIL FORMS

CALIFORNIA REAL ESTATE, 3D
Harry Miller and Marvin Starr
[Also available on CD–ROM]

CALIFORNIA TRANSACTIONS FORMS

Business Entities

Business Transactions
[Also available on CD–ROM]

Estate Planning

Family Law

CALIFORNIA JURISPRUDENCE, 3D
[Also available on CD–ROM]

CALIFORNIA INSURANCE LAW HANDBOOK

CALIFORNIA AFFIRMATIVE DEFENSES
Ann Taylor Schwing

———————

CALIFORNIA COURT RULES

California Rules of Court, State and Federal
Bay Area Local Court Rules—Superior Courts
Central California Local Court Rules—Superior Courts
Los Angeles County Court Rules—Superior Court
Northern California Local Court Rules—Superior Courts
Southern California Local Court Rules—Superior Courts

———————

COORDINATED RESEARCH

THE RUTTER GROUP (TRG) PRACTICE GUIDES
[Also available on CD–ROM]

Alternative Dispute Resolution

Civil Appeals and Writs

Civil Procedure Before Trial

Civil Trials and Evidence

Corporations

Enforcing Judgments and Debts

Family Law

Federal Civil Procedure Before Trial

Federal Civil Procedure Before Trial, 9th Circuit

Insurance Litigation

Landlord-Tenant

Law Office Procedures Manual

Law Practice Management

Legal Secretary's Handbook

Personal Injury

Probate

Professional Responsibility

Real Property Transactions

THE WITKIN LIBRARY

Summary of California Laws, 9th
Bernard E. Witkin

California Procedure, 4th
Bernard E. Witkin

California Criminal Law, 3d
Bernard E. Witkin and Norman L. Epstein

California Evidence, 4th
Bernard E. Witkin
[Also available on CD–ROM]

COORDINATED RESEARCH

To order any of these California practice tools, call
your West Representative or **1–800–328–9352.**

NEED RESEARCH HELP?

You can get quality research results with free help—call the West
Reference Attorneys when you have questions concerning
Westlaw or West Publications at 1–800–733–2889.

NEED A NEW CASE TODAY?

You can get copies of new court cases faxed to you today—office, courthouse
or hotel, anywhere a fax machine is available. Call West*fax* at 1–800–562–2329.

INTERNET ACCESS

The new California print catalog is on the Internet at
http://www.westpub.com/Practice/CA–home.htm

Contact the West Editorial Department directly with your questions and
suggestions by e-mail at editor@westgroup.com. Visit West's home
page on the World Wide Web at http://www.westgroup.com.

WESTLAW ELECTRONIC RESEARCH GUIDE

Westlaw Computer Assisted Legal Research

Westlaw is part of the research system provided by West Group. With Westlaw, you find the same quality and integrity that you have come to expect from West books. For the most current and comprehensive legal research, combine the strengths of West books and Westlaw.

Westlaw Adds to Your Library

Whether you wish to expand or update your research, Westlaw can help. For instance, Westlaw is the most current source for case law, including slip opinions and unreported decisions. In addition to case law, the online availability of statutes, statutory indexes, legislation, court rules and orders, administrative materials, looseleaf publications, texts, periodicals, news and business information makes Westlaw an important asset to any library. Check the online Westlaw Directory or the print *Westlaw Database Directory* for a list of available databases and services. Following is a brief description of some of the capabilities that Westlaw offers.

Natural Language Searching

You can now search most Westlaw databases using WIN®, the revolutionary Natural Language search method. As an alternative to formulating a query using terms and connectors, WIN allows you to simply enter a description of your research issue in plain English:

> What is the government's obligation to warn military
> personnel of the danger of past exposure to radiation?

Westlaw then retrieves the set of documents that have the highest statistical likelihood of matching your description.

Retrieving a Specific Document

When you know the citation to a case or statute that is not in your library, use the Find service to retrieve the document on Westlaw. Access Find and type a citation like the following:

> find 639 p2d 939
> find ca elec s 7559

Updating Your Research

You can use Westlaw to update your research in many ways:

- Retrieve cases citing a particular statute.
- Update a state statute by accessing the Update service from the displayed statute using the jump marker, or by accessing the KeyCite service.

- Retrieve newly enacted legislation by searching in the appropriate legislative service database.

- Retrieve cases not yet reported by searching in case law databases.

- Read the latest U.S. Supreme Court opinions within an hour of their release.

- Update West digests by searching with topic and key numbers.

Determining Case History and Retrieving Citing Cases

KeyCite®: Cases and other legal materials listed in KeyCite Scope can be researched through West Group's KeyCite service on Westlaw®. Use KeyCite to check citations for form, parallel references, prior and later history, and comprehensive citator information, including citations to other decisions and secondary materials.

Additional Information

For more detailed information or assistance, contact your Westlaw Account Representative or call 1–800–REF–ATTY (1–800–733–2889).

CALIFORNIA CODES

The present system of Codes in California was anticipated by the enactment in 1872 of the Civil Code, the Code of Civil Procedure, the Penal Code, and the Political Code. The first three of these Codes are still in existence, but the subject matter of the Political Code is now largely covered by the Government Code.

The intensive codification program which produced the current set of Codes was launched in 1929 with the enactment of Stats.1929, c. 750, and was completed in 1953 with the enactment of the Unemployment Insurance Code. The set then consisted of twenty-five Codes including the three enacted in 1872. The total was increased to twenty-seven with the adoption of the Commercial Code in 1963, and the Evidence Code in 1965. In 1981, the twenty-eighth code was added when the Public Contract Code was enacted, and the twenty-ninth, the Family Code, was enacted in 1992, operative January 1, 1994.

Stats.1929, c. 750, which launched the codification program, created the California Code Commission, and charged it with the duty of revising all laws of the state. The work of revision was to comprehend the preparation of a statutory record showing the status and disposition of acts theretofore adopted, the codification, consolidation, compilation or revision of all statutes in force; and the express repeal of all statutes theretofore repealed by implication, held unconstitutional, or rendered obsolete by the revision. The final report of the Code Commission was submitted September 1, 1953.

An essential preliminary part of the Code Commission's work was the preparation of a statutory record showing origin, amendments, and repeals of state laws enacted since 1850. The first volume of Statutory Record was published in 1933. Thereafter supplementary records were published for the periods 1933–1948, 1949–1958, 1959–1968, and 1969–1978. The Record is supplemented and brought to date in each volume of the session laws.

The California Law Revision Commission was created in 1953 (Government Code § 8280) and charged with the duty of recommending changes deemed necessary to eliminate defects and anachronisms, to modify or eliminate antiquated and incquitable rules of law, and to bring the law into harmony with modern conditions (Government Code § 8289). The recommendations of the Commission have resulted in the enactment of numerous revisions of, as well as additions to, the law.

Publication of West's California Codes was announced in 1954. This is a completely annotated edition which is supplemented by means of pocket parts and pamphlets.

The official Codes incorporate all the general and permanent legislative law of California. West's Annotated Codes contain additionally the text of—

Initiative measures, for example,—

Chiropractic Act (Business and Professions Code § 1000–1 et seq.)

CALIFORNIA CODES

Daylight Savings Time Law (Government Code § 6807–1 et seq.

Gift and Inheritance Taxes (Revenue and Taxation Code)

Income Tax Indexing (Revenue and Taxation Code)

Insurance Rates and Regulation (Insurance Code § 1861.01 et seq. and Revenue and Taxation Code)

Osteopathic Law (Business and Professions Code § 3600–1 et seq.)

Political Reform Act of 1974 (Government Code § 81000 et seq.)

Safe Drinking Water and Toxic Enforcement Act of 1986 (Health and Safety Code)

Tax Limitation—Proposition 13, Jarvis–Gann (Constitutional Article 13A)

Tort Reform—Fair Responsibility Act of 1986 (Civil Code)

Usury Law (Civil Code § 1916–1 et seq.)

Victims' Bill of Rights, 1982 (Constitution, Penal and Welfare and Institutions Codes)

Uncodified laws of general interest—

See, for example, the Appendixes to the Public Utilities Code and the Harbors and Navigation Code

Water district laws—

See the Appendix to the Water Code

California Constitution

General and permanent laws are enacted currently in California as additions to or amendments of the Codes. The code section numbers, as well as Title, Division, Part, Chapter, and Article headings, where appropriate, are included in the laws as enacted. However, section headings for West's Codes are prepared by the West editorial staff, except for certain headings which are supplied by the Office of Legislative Counsel.

Subsequent to their original enactment several of the Codes have been repealed in their entirety and reenacted. These are—

Code	Originally enacted	Reenacted
Agricultural [1]	1933	1967
Education	1943	1976
Elections	1939	1961, 1994
Fish and Game	1933	1957
Probate	1931	1990
Vehicle	1935	1959

Research has been complicated in California by the enactment and reenactment of new Codes, Titles, Divisions, Parts, Chapters, and Articles in which subject matter is revised, transferred or repealed, and the same section num-

[1] Renamed the "Food and Agricultural Code" in 1972.

bers are used over again to identify different text. The problem thus created is solved in West's California Codes by the inclusion of tables, italicized notes, and historical and statutory notes containing explanatory matter and derivation credits, all of which combine to trace the law from its origin to the present, and from the present law to its source. Depending on their size and scope, the tables are inserted at the beginning of volumes or at the head of Divisions, Chapters, etc.

The means for finding a particular Code section are provided by—

General Index

Code Index

Analyses

  Code

  Title

  Division

  Part

  Chapter

  Article

Cross References

To update the case history information for California Supreme Court and Court of Appeal opinions, see the California Case History Table and California Cumulative Review, Rehearing and Hearing Table in West's California Reporter Advance Sheets or Westlaw's KeyCite®.

The pocket parts for West's California Codes supplement both the text and the annotative materials in the main volumes. Annotated pamphlets, normally issued twice a year, supplement only annotative features. Legislative service pamphlets, issued during legislative sessions as often as is necessary to provide prompt service, supplement the text of the Codes. Cumulative Tables and an Index in each legislative service pamphlet enable the user to find amendments of existing sections and to identify and locate newly enacted laws.

*

West's
ANNOTATED
CALIFORNIA CODES

BUSINESS AND PROFESSIONS
CIVIL
CIVIL PROCEDURE
COMMERCIAL
CORPORATIONS
EDUCATION
ELECTIONS
EVIDENCE
FAMILY
FINANCIAL
FISH AND GAME
FOOD AND AGRICULTURAL
GOVERNMENT
HARBORS AND NAVIGATION
HEALTH AND SAFETY
INSURANCE
LABOR
MILITARY AND VETERANS
PENAL
PROBATE
PUBLIC CONTRACT
PUBLIC RESOURCES
PUBLIC UTILITIES
REVENUE AND TAXATION
STREETS AND HIGHWAYS
UNEMPLOYMENT INSURANCE
VEHICLE
WATER
WELFARE AND INSTITUTIONS

*

TABLE OF CONTENTS

EDUCATION CODE

Analysis of Sections, see beginning of Chapters or Articles.

TITLE 1. GENERAL EDUCATION CODE PROVISIONS

DIVISION 1. GENERAL EDUCATION CODE PROVISIONS

PART 11. LIBRARIES

TABLE OF CONTENTS

TABLE OF CONTENTS

TABLE OF CONTENTS

INDEX

*A complete index to the Education Code
appears in the last volume of the Education Code*

ABBREVIATIONS

ABBREVIATIONS OF REPORTS, CODES AND OTHER PUBLICATIONS

A.B.A.J.	American Bar Association Journal
Agric.C.	Agricultural Code [1]
ALR 3d	American Law Reports Annotated, Third Series
ALR 4th	American Law Reports Annotated, Fourth Series
ALR 5th	American Law Reports Annotated, Fifth Series
ALR Fed	American Law Reports Federal Annotated
A.J.	Assembly Journal
Am.Dec.	American Decisions
Am Jur 2d	American Jurisprudence, Second Series
Am Jur Legal Forms	American Jurisprudence Legal Forms Annotated
Am Jur Legal Forms 2d	American Jurisprudence Legal Forms Annotated, Second Series
Am Jur Pl & Pr Forms (Rev)	American Jurisprudence Pleading and Practice Forms, Annotated, Revised
Am Jur Proof of Facts	American Jurisprudence Proof of Facts
Am Jur Trials	American Jurisprudence Trials
Am.L.Rev.	American Law Review
Am.L.T.	American Law Times United States Courts
Am.R.	American Reports
Am.St.R.	American State Reports
Ann.Cas.	American and English Annotated Cases
App.	California District Courts of Appeal
Bank.C.	Banking Code
Berk.Tech.L.J.	Berkeley Technology Law Journal
Beverly Hill B.Ass'n.J.	Beverly Hills Bar Association Journal
B.R.	Bankruptcy Reporter
Brief/Case (S.F. Bar)	Brief/Case (San Francisco Bar Law Review)
Bus. & Prof. C.	Business and Professions Code
B–W Cal Civil Practice	Bancroft–Whitney's California Civil Practice
C.A.	United States Court of Appeals
Cal.	California Reports
Cal.2d	California Reports, Second Series
Cal.3d	California Reports, Third Series
Cal.4th	California Reports, Fourth Series
Cal.Adm.Code	California Administrative Code (now California Code of Regulations)
Cal.App.	California Appellate Reports
Cal.App.2d	California Appellate Reports, Second Series
Cal.App.3d	California Appellate Reports, Third Series
Cal.App.4th	California Appellate Reports, Fourth Series

---

1 Renamed the "Food and Agricultural Code" in 1972.

ABBREVIATIONS

Cal.App.Supp.	California Appellate Reports Supplement
Cal.App.2d Supp.	California Appellate Reports, Second Series Supplement
Cal.App.3d Supp.	California Appellate Reports, Third Series Supplement
Cal.App.4th Supp.	California Appellate Reports, Fourth Series Supplement
Cal.Code of Regs.	California Code of Regulations
Cal.Comp.Cases	California Compensation Cases
Cal Forms	California Forms Annotated
Cal.Int'l Prac.	California International Practitioner
Cal Jur 3d	California Jurisprudence, Third Edition
Cal Jur 3d (Rev)	California Jurisprudence, Third Edition (Revised)
Cal.L.Rev.	California Law Review (University of California at Berkeley)
Cal.L.Rev.Comm.Reports	California Law Revision Commission Reports
Cal.Law.	California Lawyer
Cal.P.U.C.	Decisions of the California Public Utilities Commission
Cal.Reg.L.Rep.	California Regulatory Law Reporter
Cal.Rptr.	California Reporter
Cal.W.L.Rev.	California Western Law Review
C.C.	United States Circuit Court
C.C.A.	United States Circuit Court of Appeals
C.C.P.	Code of Civil Procedure
CEB	Continuing Education of the Bar
Civ.C.	Civil Code
Civ Litig Rep	Civil Litigation Reporter
C.J.S.	Corpus Juris Secundum
Cl.Ct.	Claims Court Reporter
C.Leg.Rec.	California Legal Record
C.L.J.	California Law Journal
C.L.J. & Lit.Rev.	California Law Journal and Literary Review
C.L.Rev.	California Law Review
Code Am.	Code Amendments
Cof.	Coffey's Probate Decisions
Com.C.	Commercial Code
Const.	Constitution
Corp.C.	Corporations Code
C.R.C.	Decisions of California Railroad Commission
C.U.	California Unreported Cases
D.C.	United States District Court
Deady	Deady's United States Circuit Court Reports
Dist.	California District Court
Ecology L.Q.	Ecology Law Quarterly
Educ.C.	Education Code
Elec.C.	Elections Code
Evid.C.	Evidence Code

ABBREVIATIONS

F. --------------------------------- Federal Reporter
F.2d ------------------------------- Federal Reporter, Second Series
F.3d ------------------------------- Federal Reporter, Third Series
Fam.C. ----------------------------- Family Code
Fed.Appx. -------------------------- Federal Appendix
Fed.Cas.No. ------------------------ Federal Cases
Fed.Cl. ---------------------------- Federal Claims Reporter
F.R.D. ----------------------------- Federal Rules Decisions
F.Supp. ---------------------------- Federal Supplement
Fin.C. ----------------------------- Financial Code
Fish & G.C. ------------------------ Fish and Game Code
Food & Agric.C. -------------------- Food and Agricultural Code
FPPC ------------------------------- Fair Political Practices Commission Opinions
Golden Gate U.L.Rev. --------------- Golden Gate University Law Review
Gov.C. ----------------------------- Government Code
Gov.Reorg.Plan --------------------- Governor's Reorganization Plan
Harb. & Nav.C. --------------------- Harbors and Navigation Code
Hastings Const.L.Q. ---------------- Hastings Constitutional Law Quarterly
Hastings Intl.L.Rev. --------------- Hastings International Law Review
Hastings L.J. ---------------------- Hastings Law Journal
Hastings Women's L.J. -------------- Hastings Women's Law Journal
Health & S.C. ---------------------- Health and Safety Code
Hoff.Dec. -------------------------- Hoffman's Decisions
Hoff.L.Cas. ------------------------ Hoffman's Land Cases
Hoff.Op. --------------------------- Hoffman's Opinions
How. ------------------------------- Howard's Reports, U.S.
I.A.C. ----------------------------- Industrial Accident Commission Decisions
Ins.C. ----------------------------- Insurance Code
Int.Rev.Rec. ----------------------- Internal Revenue Record
J.Juv.L. --------------------------- Journal of Juvenile Law
Lab. ------------------------------- Labatt's District Court Reports
Labor C. --------------------------- Labor Code
La Raza L.J. ----------------------- La Raza Law Journal
L.Ed. ------------------------------ United States Supreme Court Reports,
                                    Lawyers' Edition
L.Ed.2d ---------------------------- United States Supreme Court Reports,
                                    Lawyers' Edition, Second Series
Los Angeles B.Bull. ---------------- Los Angeles Bar Bulletin
Los Angeles B.J. ------------------- Los Angeles Bar Journal
L.A.Law. --------------------------- Los Angeles Lawyer
Loy.L.A.L.Rev. --------------------- Loyola of Los Angeles Law Review
L.R.A. ----------------------------- Lawyers' Reports Annotated
McAll ------------------------------ McAllister's United States Circuit Court Reports
Mil. & Vet.C. ---------------------- Military and Veterans Code
Morr.Min.Rep. ---------------------- Morrison's Mining Reports
Municipal Court Rule --------------- Rules for the Municipal Courts
Myr. ------------------------------- Myrick's Probate Reports
Op.Atty.Gen. ----------------------- Opinions Attorney General of California

ABBREVIATIONS

Op.Leg.Counsel	Opinions of Legislative Counsel
P.	Pacific Reporter
P.2d	Pacific Reporter, Second Series
Pac.L.J.	Pacific Law Journal
P.C.L.J.	Pacific Coast Law Journal
PEB	Permanent Editorial Board for the Uniform Commercial Code
Pen.C.	Penal Code
Pepperdine L.Rev.	Pepperdine Law Review
P.L.M.	Pacific Law Magazine
P.L.R.	Pacific Law Reporter
POF 2d	American Jurisprudence Proof of Facts, Second Series
POF 3d	American Jurisprudence Proof of Facts, Third Series
Pol.C.	Political Code
Prob.C.	Probate Code
Pub.Con.C.	Public Contract Code
Pub.Res.C.	Public Resources Code
Pub.Util.C.	Public Utilities Code
Rag.	Ragland California Superior Court Decisions
Rev. & T.C.	Revenue and Taxation Code
San Diego L.Rev.	San Diego Law Review
San Fernando Valley L.Rev.	San Fernando Valley Law Review
San Francisco Atty.	San Francisco Attorney
San Joaquin Agricultural L.Rev.	San Joaquin Agricultural Law Review
Santa Clara L.Rev.	Santa Clara Law Review
Santa Clara L.	Santa Clara Lawyer
S.Bar J.	Journal of the State Bar of California (California State Bar Journal)
SC–CDA Rule	Rules on Appeal to California Supreme Court and District Courts of Appeal
School C.	School Code
S.Ct.	Supreme Court Reporter
S.Cal.L.Rev.	Southern California Law Review
S.Cal.Rev.L. & Women's Studies	Southern California Review of Law and Women's Studies
Sw.U.L.Rev.	Southwestern University Law Review
Stan.L.Rev.	Stanford Law Review
Stats.	Statutes
Str. & H.C.	Streets and Highways Code
Super.	California Superior Court
Superior—App.Dept.	Rule Superior Court—Appellate Department Rules
Superior Court Rule	Rules for California Superior Courts
Superior—Mun. and Inf. Crim.App.Rule	Superior Court—Rules on Appeal from Municipal Courts and Inferior Courts in Criminal Cases
Superior—Mun.Civ.App.Rule	Superior Court—Rules on Appeal from Municipal Courts in Civil Cases
U.C.C.	Uniform Commercial Code

ABBREVIATIONS

U.C.Davis L.Rev.	University of California Davis Law Review
UCLA L.Rev.	University of California Los Angeles Law Review
U.La Verne L.Rev.	University of La Verne Law Review
U.L.A.	Uniform Laws Annotated
Un.Ins.C.	Unemployment Insurance Code
U.S.	United States Reports
U.S.C.A.	United States Code Annotated
U.S.C.A.Const.	United States Constitution
U.S.C.A.Const.Amend.	United States Constitution Amendment
U.S.Dept.Int.	United States Department of Interior
U.S.F.L.Rev.	University of San Francisco Law Review
U.S.F.Mar.L.J.	University of San Francisco Maritime Law Journal
U.West L.A.L.Rev.	University of West Los Angeles Law Review
Veh.C.	Vehicle Code
Water C.	Water Code
Water C.App.	Water Code Appendix
Welf. & Inst.C.	Welfare and Institutions Code
West.St.L.R.	Western State Law Review
West.St.U.L.Rev.	Western State University Law Review
Whittier L.Rev.	Whittier Law Review

ABBREVIATIONS

ABBREVIATIONS OF TOPICS IN
LIBRARY REFERENCES FEATURE

Actions	Actions
Admin Proc	Administrative Proceedings
Agency	Agency and Employment
Appeal	Appeal
Attack	Attack on Judgment in Trial Court
Attys	Attorneys
Com Prop	Community Property
Const Law	Constitutional Law
Contracts	Contracts
Corp	Corporations
Courts	Courts
Enf Judgm	Enforcement of Judgment
Equity	Equity
H & W	Husband and Wife
Judgm	Judgment
Jurisd	Jurisdiction
Neg Inst	Negotiable Instruments
Partn	Partnership
P & C	Parent and Child
Pers Prop	Personal Property
Plead	Pleading
Prov Rem	Provisional Remedies
PWT	Proceedings Without Trial
Real Prop	Real Property
Sales	Sales
Sec Trans–PP	Secured Transactions in Personal Property
Sec Trans–Real PP	Secured Transactions in Real Property
Tax	Taxation
Torts	Torts
Trial	Trial
Trusts	Trusts
Wills	Wills and Probate
Work Comp	Workers' Compensation
Writs	Extraordinary Writs

EFFECTIVE DATES OF LAWS

Constitution Article 4, Section 8, as amended effective June 6, 1990, provides, in subdivision (c):

"(1) Except as provided in paragraphs (2) and (3) of this subdivision, a statute enacted at a regular session shall go into effect on January 1 next following a 90–day period from the date of enactment of the statute and a statute enacted at a special session shall go into effect on the 91st day after adjournment of the special session at which the bill was passed.

"(2) A statute, other than a statute establishing or changing boundaries of any legislative, congressional, or other election district, enacted by a bill passed by the Legislature on or before the date the Legislature adjourns for a joint recess to reconvene in the second calendar year of the biennium of the legislative session, and in the possession of the Governor after that date, shall go into effect on January 1 next following the enactment date of the statute unless, before January 1, a copy of a referendum petition affecting the statute is submitted to the Attorney General pursuant to subdivision (d) of Section 10 of Article II, in which event the statute shall go into effect on the 91st day after the enactment date unless the petition has been presented to the Secretary of State pursuant to subdivision (b) of Section 9 of Article II.

"(3) Statutes calling elections, statutes providing for tax levies or appropriations for the usual current expenses of the state, and urgency statutes shall go into effect immediately upon their enactment."

See, also, Government Code § 9600.

Constitution Article 4, Section 10, as amended effective June 6, 1990, provides, in subd. (b):

"(1) Any bill, other than a bill which would establish or change boundaries of any legislative, congressional, or other election district, passed by the Legislature on or before the date the Legislature adjourns for a joint recess to reconvene in the second calendar year of the biennium of the legislative session, and in the possession of the Governor after that date, that is not returned within 30 days after that date becomes a statute.

"(2) Any bill passed by the Legislature before September 1 of the second calendar year of the biennium of the legislative session and in the possession of the Governor on or after September 1 that is not returned on or before September 30 of that year becomes a statute.

"(3) Any other bill presented to the Governor that is not returned within 12 days becomes a statute.

"(4) If the Legislature by adjournment of a special session prevents the return of a bill with the veto message, the bill becomes a statute unless the Governor vetoes the bill within 12 days after it is presented by depositing it and the veto message in the office of the Secretary of State.

"(5) If the 12th day of the period within which the Governor is required to perform an act pursuant to paragraph (3) or (4) of this subdivision is a Saturday, Sunday, or holiday, the period is extended to the next day that is not a Saturday, Sunday, or holiday."

See, also, Government Code § 9516.

Constitution Article 2, Section 10, and Article 18, Section 4, provide in part that an initiative statute or referendum (Article 2, Section 10), or an amendment or revision of the Constitution (Article 18, Section 4), "approved by a majority of votes thereon takes effect the day after the election unless the measure provides otherwise".

Government Code § 12080.5, as amended by Stats.1974, c. 1242, § 2, provides:

"Except as otherwise provided in this section, a reorganization plan submitted pursuant to this article [Executive Reorganization, § 12080 et seq.] shall become effective the first day after 60 calendar days of continuous session of the Legislature after the date on which the plan is transmitted to each house or at a later date as may be provided by the plan, unless, prior to the end of the 60–calendar-day period, either house of the Legislature adopts by a majority vote of the duly elected and qualified members thereof a resolution, as defined in subdivision (c) of Section 12080.

"As used in this section '60 calendar days of continuous session' shall be deemed broken only by an adjournment sine die, but in computing the 60 calendar days for the purposes of this provision days on which either house is not in session because of a recess of more than 10 days to a day certain shall not be included."

Constitution Article 4, Section 8, prior to the 1990 amendment, as amended November 7, 1972, provided, in subdivision (c):

"(1) Except as provided in paragraph (2) of this subdivision, a statute enacted at a regular session shall go into effect on January 1 next following a 90–day period from the date of enactment of the statute and a statute enacted at a special session shall go into effect on the 91st day after adjournment of the special session at which the bill was passed.

"(2) Statutes calling elections, statutes providing for tax levies or appropriations for the usual current expenses of the State, and urgency statutes shall go into effect immediately upon their enactment."

Prior to the 1972 amendment, Article 4, Section 8 of the Constitution, as adopted November 8, 1966, provided, in subd. (C):

"No statute may go into effect until the 61st day after adjournment of the regular session at which the bill was passed, or until the 91st day after adjournment of the special session at which the bill was passed, except statutes calling elections, statutes providing for tax levies or appropriations for the usual current expenses of the state, and urgency statutes."

Under former Section 1 of Article 4 of the Constitution no act became effective until "90 days after final adjournment of the session of the Legislature which passed such act" except acts calling elections, acts providing for tax levies or appropriations for the usual current expenses of the State, and urgency measures. The former section also provided that initiative and referendum measures approved by a majority of the votes cast thereon, at any election, took effect five days after the date of the official declaration of the vote by the Secretary of State. The former section was repealed November 8, 1966.

Under Constitution Article 4, Section 1A, adopted June 27, 1933, and repealed November 8, 1949, all acts passed at the 50th Regular Session on or before July 16, 1933, became effective 90 days after May 22, 1933, except urgency measures.

The following Table shows the date of adjournment or recess date and the effective date of non-urgency acts covering legislative sessions since 1933.

Year	Session	Adjournment or Recess Date	Effective Date
1933	Regular	July 26, 1933	August 21, 1933
1934	Extra	Sept. 15, 1934	Dec. 15, 1934
1935	Regular	June 16, 1935	Sept. 15, 1935
1936	Extra	May 26, 1936	Aug. 25, 1936
1937	Regular	May 28, 1937	Aug. 27, 1937
1938	Extra	March 12, 1938	June 11, 1938
1939	Regular	June 20, 1939	Sept. 19, 1939
1940	1st Extra	Dec. 5, 1940	March 6, 1941
1940	2nd Extra	May 24, 1940	†
1940	3rd Extra	Sept. 13, 1940	†
1940	4th Extra	Dec. 5, 1940	March 6, 1941
1940	5th Extra	Dec. 5, 1940	†
1941	Regular	June 14, 1941	Sept. 13, 1941
1941	1st Extra	Jan. 22, 1942	†
1942	2nd Extra	Jan. 18, 1942	†
1943	Regular	May 5, 1943	Aug. 4, 1943
1943	1st Extra	Jan. 30, 1943	May 1, 1943
1943	2nd Extra	March 25, 1943	June 24, 1943
1944	3rd Extra	Jan. 31, 1944	May 1, 1944
1944	4th Extra	June 13, 1944	Sept. 12, 1944
1945	Regular	June 16, 1945	Sept. 15, 1945
1946	1st Extra	Feb. 19, 1946	May 21, 1946
1946	2nd Extra	July 25, 1946	Oct. 24, 1946
1947	Regular	June 20, 1947	Sept. 19, 1947
1947	1st Extra	June 24, 1947	Sept. 23, 1947
1948	Regular	March 27, 1948	June 26, 1948
1949	Regular	July 2, 1949	Oct. 1, 1949
1949	1st Extra	Dec. 21, 1949	March 22, 1950
1950	Regular	April 4, 1950	July 4, 1950
1950	1st Extra	April 15, 1950	July 15, 1950
1950	2nd Extra	March 6, 1950	June 5, 1950
1950	3rd Extra	Sept. 26, 1950	Dec. 26, 1950
1951	Regular	June 23, 1951	Sept. 22, 1951

EFFECTIVE DATES OF LAWS

Year	Session	Adjournment or Recess Date	Effective Date
1952	Regular	April 1, 1952	July 1, 1952
1952	1st Extra	April 2, 1952	July 2, 1952
1952	2nd Extra	Aug. 13, 1952	Nov. 12, 1952
1953	Regular	June 10, 1953	Sept. 9, 1953
1954	Regular	March 30, 1954	June 29, 1954
1954	1st Extra	April 1, 1954	July 1, 1954
1955	Regular	June 8, 1955	Sept. 7, 1955
1956	Regular	April 3, 1956	July 3, 1956
1956	1st Extra	April 5, 1956	July 5, 1956
1957	Regular	June 12, 1957	Sept. 11, 1957
1958	Regular	March 30, 1958	June 29, 1958
1958	1st Extra	April 23, 1958	July 23, 1958
1958	2nd Extra	April 24, 1958	July 24, 1958
1959	Regular	June 19, 1959	Sept. 18, 1959
1960	Regular	March 26, 1960	June 25, 1960
1960	1st Extra	April 7, 1960	July 7, 1960
1960	2nd Extra	March 10, 1960	*
1961	Regular	June 16, 1961	Sept. 15, 1961
1962	Regular	April 3, 1962	July 3, 1962
1962	1st Extra	April 13, 1962	July 13, 1962
1962	2nd Extra	April 13, 1962	July 13, 1962
1962	3rd Extra	June 28, 1962	Sept. 27, 1962
1963	Regular	June 21, 1963	Sept. 20, 1963
1963	1st Extra	Aug. 1, 1963	Oct. 31, 1963
1964	Regular	March 26, 1964	June 25, 1964
1964	1st Extra	May 23, 1964	Aug. 22, 1964
1964	2nd Extra	May 23, 1964	Aug. 22, 1964
1965	Regular	June 18, 1965	Sept. 17, 1965
1965	1st Extra	July 6, 1965	Oct. 5, 1965
1965	2nd Extra	Nov. 4, 1965	Feb. 3, 1966
1966	Regular	April 4, 1966	July 4, 1966
1966	1st Extra	July 7, 1966	Oct. 6, 1966
1966	2nd Extra	July 8, 1966	Oct. 7, 1966
1967	Regular	Sept. 8, 1967	Nov. 8, 1967
1967	1st Extra	Sept. 7, 1967	Dec. 7, 1967
1967	2nd Extra	Dec. 8, 1967	March 8, 1968
1968	Regular	Sept. 13, 1968	Nov. 13, 1968
1968	1st Extra	Sept. 20, 1968	Dec. 20, 1968
1969	Regular	Sept. 10, 1069	Nov. 10, 1969
1970	Regular	Sept. 23, 1970	Nov. 23, 1970
1971	Regular	Jan. 3, 1972	March 4, 1972
1972	Regular	Jan. 5, 1973	March 7, 1973
1973	Regular	Dec. 7, 1973	Jan. 1, 1974
1973	1st Extra	Dec. 4, 1973	*
1974	Regular	Nov. 30, 1974	Jan. 1, 1975
1974	2nd Extra	Oct. 2, 1974	Jan. 1, 1975
1975	Regular	Sept. 12, 1975	Jan. 1, 1976

EFFECTIVE DATES OF LAWS

Year	Session	Adjournment or Recess Date	Effective Date
1975	1st Extra	June 27, 1975	Sept. 26, 1975
1975	2nd Extra	Sept. 12, 1975	Dec. 12, 1975
1975	3rd Extra	May 29, 1975	Aug. 28, 1975
1976	Regular	Nov. 30, 1976	Jan. 1, 1977
1977	Regular	Sept. 15, 1977	Jan. 1, 1978
1978	Regular	Nov. 30, 1978	Jan. 1, 1979
1978	1st Extra	April 24, 1978	April 20, 1978†
1979	Regular	Sept. 14, 1979	Jan. 1, 1980
1980	Regular	Nov. 30, 1980	Jan. 1, 1981
1981	Regular	Sept. 15, 1981	Jan. 1, 1982
1981–82	1st Extra	Feb. 25, 1982	May 27, 1982
1982	Regular	Nov. 30, 1982	Jan. 1, 1983
1983–84	1st Extra	July 19, 1983	Oct. 18, 1983
1983	Regular	Sept. 19, 1983	Jan. 1, 1984
1983–84	2nd Extra	Feb. 17, 1984	May 18, 1984
1984	Regular	Nov. 30, 1984	Jan. 1, 1985
1985	Regular	Sept. 13, 1985	Jan. 1, 1986
1985–86	1st Extra	Nov. 30, 1986	*
1986	Regular	Nov. 30, 1986	Jan. 1, 1987
1987	Regular	Sept. 11, 1987	Jan. 1, 1988
1987–88	1st Extra	Nov. 10, 1987	Nov. 16, 1987†
1988	Regular	Nov. 30, 1988	Jan. 1, 1989
1989	Regular	Sept. 15, 1989	Jan. 1, 1990
1989–90	1st Extra (c. 1 to 24)	Nov. 4, 1989	Nov. 7, 1989†
1989–90	1st Extra (c. 25 to 37)	Sept. 1, 1990	Dec. 1, 1990
1990	Regular	Nov. 30, 1990	Jan. 1, 1991
1991–92	1st Extra (c. 1 to 14)	Sept. 13, 1991	Jan. 1, 1992
1991	Regular	Sept. 14, 1991	Jan. 1, 1992
1991–92	1st Extra (c. 15 to 26)	Nov. 30, 1992	March 1, 1993
1991–92	2nd Extra	Nov. 30, 1992	*
1992	Regular	Nov. 30, 1992	Jan. 1, 1993
1993–94	1st Extra (c. 1 to 3)	Sept. 11, 1993	†
1993	Regular	Sept. 11, 1993	Jan. 1, 1994
1993–94	1st Extra (c. 4 to 60)	Aug. 31, 1994	Nov. 30, 1994
1994	Regular	Nov. 30, 1994	Jan. 1, 1995
1995–96	1st Extra (c. 1 to 10)	Sept. 15, 1995	Dec. 15, 1995
1995–96	2nd Extra (c. 1 to 7)	Sept. 15, 1995	†
1995	Regular	Sept. 15, 1995	Jan. 1, 1996
1995–96	1st Extra	Sept. 1, 1996	Dec. 1, 1996

EFFECTIVE DATES OF LAWS

Year	Session	Adjournment or Recess Date	Effective Date
	(c. 11)		
1995–96	2nd Extra	Sept. 1, 1996	*
1995–96	3rd Extra	March 15, 1996	June 14, 1996
1995–96	4th Extra	March 28, 1996	June 27, 1996
1996	Regular	Sept. 1, 1996	Jan. 1, 1997
1997–98	1st Extra	Sept. 13, 1997	Dec. 13, 1997
	(c. 1 to 8)		
1997	Regular	Sept. 13, 1997	Jan. 1, 1998
1997–98	1st Extra	Sept. 1, 1998	Dec. 1, 1998
	(c. 9)		
1998	Regular	Sept. 1, 1998	Jan. 1, 1999
1999–2000	1st Extra	March 26, 1999	June 25, 1999
	(c. 1 to 5)		
1999	Regular	Sept. 10, 1999	Jan. 1, 2000
2000	Regular	Aug. 31, 2000	Jan. 1, 2001
2001	Regular	Sept. 15, 2001	Jan. 1, 2002
2001–02	1st Extra	May 14, 2001	Aug. 13, 2001
	(c. 1 to 13)		
2001–02	2nd Extra	May 9, 2002	Aug. 8, 2002
	(c. 1 to 19)		

---

* No legislation was enacted which affected any code or law.

† Urgency only.

CITE THIS BOOK

Thus:

West's Ann.Cal.Educ. Code § _____

*

West's
ANNOTATED
CALIFORNIA CODES
EDUCATION CODE

AN ACT to repeal and reenact the Education Code, relating to education law

Enacted by Stats.1976, c. 1010

Amended by Stats.1976, c. 1011

Operative April 30, 1977

The people of the State of California do enact as follows:

Sections 18000 to 22699 appear in this volume

Title 1

GENERAL EDUCATION CODE PROVISIONS

Division 1

GENERAL EDUCATION CODE PROVISIONS

1

Westlaw Electronic Research

Westlaw supplements your legal research in many ways. Westlaw allows you to
- update your research with the most current information
- expand your library with additional resources
- retrieve current, comprehensive history and citing references to a case with KeyCite

For more information on using Westlaw to supplement your research, see the Westlaw Electronic Research Guide, which follows the Preface.

Part 11

LIBRARIES

LIBRARIES
Pt. 11

Part 11 was enacted by Stats.1976, c. 1010, § 2, operative April 30, 1977.

Cross References

California Library Services Act, see Education Code § 18700.
Community colleges, provision of library services, see Education Code § 78100.
Community recreation, see Education Code § 10900 et seq.
Conservation education library, see Education Code §§ 8722, 8730 et seq.
Consumer affairs, library, see Business and Professions Code §§ 313, 313.5.
County free libraries, see Government Code §§ 19100 et seq. and 26150 et seq.
County service areas, extended library facilities and services, authority of board of supervisors and funding, see Government Code § 25210.78 et seq.
County transactions and use tax for library programs, levy, ordinance and approval by voters, see Revenue and Taxation Code § 7286.59.
Credentials, types, see Education Code § 44250 et seq.
Disposal of books, see Education Code § 18133.
Distribution,
Laws, resolutions, and journals of the legislature, see Government Code § 9791.
State publications, see Government Code § 14900 et seq.
Foundations for institutions of arts and sciences, see Education Code § 21140 et seq.
Law libraries, see Business and Professions Code § 6300 et seq.
Law revision commission, access to State library, see Government Code § 8286.
Legislative counsel bureau, access to state library and other public records, see Government Code § 10209.
Legislative manuals, distribution, see Government Code § 9742.
Librarians, appointment of school district librarian, see Education Code § 18120.
Library districts,
Generally, see Education Code § 19400 et seq.
Unincorporated towns and villages, see Education Code § 19600 et seq.
Library of California Act, see Education Code § 18800 et seq.
Library service at county institution, see Government Code § 26151.
Municipal libraries, see Education Code § 18900 et seq.
Open meetings,
Bagley-Keene, actions of public agencies, see Government Code § 11120.
Ralph M. Brown Act, meetings of public commissions, boards and councils and other public agencies, see Government Code § 54950 et seq.
Public library finance, see Education Code § 18010 et seq.
Report of school district board on instructional materials, see Education Code § 60090.
School district librarian, appointment, see Education Code § 18120.
School libraries, see Education Code § 18100 et seq.
School library media teacher,
Qualification for employment, see Education Code § 44868.
Rank as teacher or instructor, see Education Code §§ 44869, 87436.
School obsolete instructional materials, donation or sale, see Education Code § 60510 et seq.
Shasta County Regional Library Facilities and Services Act, see Government Code § 26170 et seq.
State library, see Education Code § 19300 et seq.
State publications and documents, see Government Code § 14880 et seq.
Subdivisions, requirement for reservation of areas for libraries, see Government Code § 66479.
Taxes,
Exemptions for specified libraries, see Revenue and Taxation Code § 254; Const. Art. 13, § 3.
Special taxes imposed on behalf of public libraries, powers and duties relating to financial affairs of cities, counties, and other agencies, see Government Code § 53717 et seq.
Voluntary contributions, designations to the California Public School Library Protection Fund, see Revenue and Taxation Code § 18811 et seq.
Unified school districts and union high school districts public libraries, see Education Code § 18300 et seq.

Universities, libraries and related facilities in public universities, construction, renovation and equipment of libraries and related educational facilities for use as research and educational centers, see Government Code § 15820.

United States Code Annotated

Depository Library Program, generally, see 44 U.S.C.A. § 1901 et seq.

Library and information services, federal cooperation with state and local governments and public and private agencies to assure optimum provision of services, see 20 U.S.C.A. § 1501.

Literacy, improving literacy through school libraries, grants to states, see 20 U.S.C.A. § 6383.

Literary and scientific collections accessible to investigators and students, federal government collections and institutions for research and material for educational institutions, see 20 U.S.C.A. § 91.

Library of Congress, generally, see 2 U.S.C.A. § 131 et seq.

Museum and Library services, consolidation and administration of federal library programs, generally, see 20 U.S.C.A. § 9101 et seq.

National Commission on Libraries and Information Science, generally, see 20 U.S.C.A. § 1501 et seq.

National Library of Education, establishment within Department of Education, functions of library, see 20 U.S.C.A. § 6051 et seq.

National Library of Medicine, see 42 U.S.C.A. § 286 et seq.

Chapter 1

BOARD OF LIBRARY EXAMINERS [REPEALED]

Chapter 1, "Board of Library Examiners", enacted by Stats.1976, c. 1010, § 2, consisting of §§ 18000, 18001, was repealed by Stats.1981, c. 604, p. 2324, § 2.

§§ 18000, 18001. Repealed by Stats.1981, c. 604, p. 2324, § 2

Historical and Statutory Notes

The repealed sections, enacted by Stats.1976, c. 1010, § 2, established and set out powers and responsibilities of the board of library examiners.

Section 18000 was derived from Educ.C. 1959, § 27150, added by Stats.1970, c. 1048, p. 1876, § 1; Educ.C.1959, § 27251, enacted by Stats.1959, c. 2, p. 1458, § 27251; Educ.C. 1943, § 22161 (Stats.1943, c. 71, p. 735,

amended by Stats.1957, c. 1743, p. 3124, § 5); Stats.1911, c. 68, p. 82, § 6.

Section 18001 was derived from Educ.C. 1959, § 27150.1, added by Stats.1970, c. 1048, p. 1876, § 1; Educ.C.1959, § 27252, enacted by Stats.1959, c. 2, p. 1458, § 27252; Educ.C. 1943, § 22162 (Stats.1943, c. 71, p. 735); Stats. 1911, c. 68, p. 82, § 6.

Chapter 1.5

PUBLIC LIBRARY FINANCE

Chapter 1.5 was added by Stats.1982, c. 1498, p. 5805, § 1, operative July 1, 1983.

Cross References

County service areas, funding for extended library facilities and services, authority of board of supervisors, see Government Code § 25210.78 et seq.

County transactions and use tax for library programs, levy, ordinance and approval by voters, see Revenue and Taxation Code § 7286.59.

Finances,
Generally, see Education Code § 14000 et seq.
School funding priority and allocations to school state fund, see Const. Art. 16, § 8 et seq.

Franchise Tax Board,
Generally, see Government Code § 15700 et seq.
Powers and duties, see Revenue and Taxation Code § 19501 et seq.

School finances, generally, see Education Code § 41000 et seq.

State Department of Education, administration and finances, see Education Code § 33300 et seq.

State funds, general fund and special funds, investments and deposits, see Government Code § 16300 et seq.

State Librarian,
Generally, see Education Code § 19302 et seq.
Powers and duties, see Education Code § 19320 et seq.

Taxes,
Exemptions for libraries, see Revenue and Taxation Code § 254; Const. Art. 13, § 3.
Special taxes imposed on behalf of public libraries, powers and duties relating to financial affairs of cities, counties, and other agencies, see Government Code § 53717 et seq.
Voluntary contributions, designations to the California Public School Library Protection Fund, see Revenue and Taxation Code § 18811 et seq.

Treasurer, powers and duties, see Government Code § 12320 et seq.

Universities, libraries and related facilities in public universities, construction, renovation and equipment of libraries and related educational facilities for use as research and educational centers, see Government Code § 15820.

United States Code Annotated

Library and information services, federal cooperation with state and local governments and public and private agencies to assure optimum provision of services, see 20 U.S.C.A. § 1501.

Article 1

GENERAL PROVISIONS

Section
18010. Legislative findings and declarations.
18011. Legislative intent.
18012. Legislative policy and objective.
18013. Foundation program; appropriations.

Article 1 was added by Stats.1982, c. 1498, p. 5805, § 1, operative July 1, 1983.

Cross References

Administrative regulations and rulemaking, see Government Code § 11340 et seq.
Controller, powers and duties, see Government Code § 12410 et seq.
County free libraries, see Government Code § 26150 et seq.
State funds, see Government Code § 16300 et seq.
State Librarian,
Generally, see Education Code § 19302 et seq.
Powers and duties, see Education Code § 19320 et seq.
Statutes,
Construction and legislative intent, generally, see Code of Civil Procedure §§ 1858 and 1859.
Liberal construction of the Education Code, see Education Code § 3.
Rules of construction and definition for the Education Code, see Education Code § 10.

United States Code Annotated

Depository Library Program, generally, see 44 U.S.C.A. § 1901 et seq.
Library and information services, federal cooperation with state and local governments and public and private agencies to assure optimum provision of services, see 20 U.S.C.A. § 1501.
Library of Congress, generally, see 20 U.S.C.A. § 131.
Literary and scientific collections accessible to investigators and students, federal government collections and institutions for research and material for educational institutions, see 20 U.S.C.A. § 91.

§ 18010.   Legislative findings and declarations

The Legislature finds and declares that it is in the interest of the people and of the state that there be a general diffusion of information and knowledge through the continued operation of free public libraries. Such diffusion is a matter of general concern inasmuch as it is the duty of the state to provide encouragement to the voluntary lifelong learning of the people of the state.

The Legislature further declares that the public library is a supplement to the formal system of free public education, and a source of information and inspiration to persons of all ages, cultural backgrounds, and economic statuses, and a resource for continuing education and reeducation beyond the years of formal education, and as such deserves adequate financial support from government at all levels.

(Added by Stats.1982, c. 1498, p. 5805, § 1, operative July 1, 1983.)

Cross References

County free libraries, see Government Code § 26150 et seq.
County service areas, extended library facilities and services, authority of board of supervisors and funding, see Government Code § 25210.78 et seq.
Statutes,
  Construction and legislative intent, generally, see Code of Civil Procedure §§ 1858 and 1859.
  Liberal construction of the Education Code, Education Code § 3.
  Rules of construction and definition for the Education Code, Education Code § 10.

Library References

States ⊕123.
Westlaw Topic No. 360.
C.J.S. States § 226.

Legal Jurisprudences

Cal Jur 3d Muni § 295.

§ 18011.   Legislative intent

It is the intent of the Legislature under this chapter to initiate and examine a specific program providing equitable and adequate funds to the public libraries of the state which are established under various provisions of law, and which, historically dependent for their support on local property tax revenues, face a fiscal crisis as a result of ad valorem tax limitations imposed by Article XIII A of the California Constitution, which fiscal crisis has not been sufficiently resolved through application of existing statutes.

(Added by Stats.1982, c. 1498, p. 5805, § 1, operative July 1, 1983.)

Cross References

Statutes,
  Construction and legislative intent, generally, see Code of Civil Procedure §§ 1858 and 1859.
  Liberal construction of the Education Code, see Education Code § 3.

Statutes—Cont'd
    Rules of construction and definition for the Education Code, see Education Code § 10.

§ 18012. Legislative policy and objective

In adopting this chapter, the Legislature declares that its policy, and its objective in enacting the specific program prescribed in Section 18011, is to do all of the following:

(a) Assure the availability to every resident of the state of an adequate level of public library service regardless of the taxable wealth of the local jurisdiction providing the service.

(b) Provide permanent, stable, and predictable financing for public libraries of the state through a combination of state and local revenues.

(c) Provide state funds for public library service through application of a simple formula whose variable elements can be readily predicted and ascertained by both state and local officials, and which can be administered by the Controller and the State Librarian as ministerial functions.

(d) Reaffirm the principle of local control of the government and administration of public libraries under broad state policy determinations, and subject to the necessity for financial accounting to the state for the expenditure of state funds and required local matching funds.

(Added by Stats.1982, c. 1498, p. 5805, § 1, operative July 1, 1983.)

§ 18013. Foundation program; appropriations

The Legislature finds and declares that this chapter effects a state policy that each public library provide a minimum level of service, known as the foundation program, to the extent state funds are made available for that purpose as prescribed by this chapter. The Legislature, therefore, declares that state funds made available to each public library pursuant to this chapter, to the extent those funds are appropriations subject to limitation of a public library, shall be included in the appropriations limit of the state for purposes of Article XIII B of the California Constitution. However, this chapter does not mandate any new program or higher level of service on any local government for which state funds are not made available as prescribed by this chapter.

(Added by Stats.1982, c. 1498, p. 5805, § 1, operative July 1, 1983.)

Cross References

County free libraries, see Government Code § 26150 et seq.
County service areas, extended library facilities and services, authority of board of supervisors and
     funding, see Government Code § 25210.78 et seq.
State funds, see Government Code § 16300 et seq.
Statutes,
     Construction and legislative intent, generally, see Code of Civil Procedure §§ 1858 and 1859.
     Liberal construction of the Education Code, see Education Code § 3.
     Rules of construction and definition for the Education Code, see Education Code § 10.

Article 2

DEFINITIONS

Section
18015.   Public library; foundation program, fiscal officer.

*Article 2 was added by Stats.1982, c. 1498, p. 5806, § 1, operative July
1, 1983.*

Cross References

Rules of construction and definition for the Education Code, see Education Code § 3.
Words and phrases, general definitions, see Education Code § 70 et seq.

§ 18015.   Public library; foundation program, fiscal officer

As used in this chapter:

(a) "Public library" means a library, or two or more libraries, operated as a
single entity by one or more public jurisdictions and which serve the general
public without distinction.

(b) "Foundation program" means those elements of library service which are
basic to its function as a provider of information, education, and cultural
enrichment to all segments of the community, including, but not limited to,
collection development and maintenance, lending services, information services, facility maintenance, and administration. The foundation program shall
not include major capital improvements, which, for purposes of this chapter,
shall be defined as the purchase of real property, the construction or improvement of buildings, and the purchase of equipment and the payment of fees or
other costs in connection with the same.

(c) "Fiscal officer" means, for a municipal library, the chief fiscal officer of
the municipality; for a county library or a library district under the jurisdiction
of the county board of supervisors, the chief fiscal officer of the county; and for
an independent library district, the chief librarian of the district. In the case of
a public library which provides foundation program service by contract to one
or more jurisdictions in addition to the jurisdiction or jurisdictions with which
it is affiliated, the chief fiscal officer of the jurisdiction with which it is
primarily affiliated shall be deemed the fiscal officer for the public library for
the purposes of this chapter.

(Added by Stats.1982, c. 1498, p. 5806, § 1, operative July 1, 1983. Amended by
Stats.1984, c. 895, § 1.)

Article 3

FUNDING

Article 3 was added by Stats.1982, c. 1498, p. 5806, § 1, operative July 1, 1983.

§ 18020. Cost of program per capita; increases

For the fiscal year 1982–83, the cost of the foundation program is deemed to be twelve dollars ($12) per capita.

For the 1983–84 fiscal year and each fiscal year thereafter, the cost of the foundation program shall be increased by a percentage equal to the average statewide percentage increase in the total revenue limit for all unified school districts computed pursuant to Section 42238 from the prior fiscal year.

(Added by Stats.1982, c. 1498, p. 5806, § 1, operative July 1, 1983.)

§ 18021. Population served by each library; determination and certification

The State Librarian shall determine and certify, on or before June 1, 1982, and June 1 of each fiscal year thereafter, the population served by each public library of the state based upon census data compiled by the United States

Department of Commerce or estimates prepared by the California Department of Finance, whichever is more current. For such purposes, no person shall be deemed to be served by more than one public library.

(Added by Stats.1982, c. 1498, p. 5806, § 1, operative July 1, 1983.)

Cross References

Department of Finance, generally, see Government Code § 13000 et seq.
State Librarian,
 Generally, see Education Code § 19302 et seq.
 Powers and duties, see Education Code § 19320 et seq.

§ 18022. Total cost of program for each library

The total cost of the foundation program for each public library for the purposes of this chapter shall be the product of the per capita cost determined pursuant to Section 18020 multiplied by the population determined pursuant to Section 18021.

(Added by Stats.1982, c. 1498, p. 5807, § 1, operative July 1, 1983.)

§ 18023. Reports of revenue appropriated for program; local revenues

On or before August 31, 1982, and October 31 of each fiscal year thereafter, the fiscal officer of each public library shall report to the State Librarian the total revenue appropriated for the foundation program of the public library for that fiscal year and shall specify the amount of local revenue included in such total appropriation. For the purposes of this chapter, homeowner and business inventory exemption reimbursements, timber yield tax funds, and federal revenue sharing funds shall be deemed to be local revenues.

(Added by Stats.1982, c. 1498, p. 5807, § 1, operative July 1, 1983. Amended by Stats.1984, c. 831, § 1, eff. Aug. 31, 1984.)

Cross References

County transactions and use tax for library programs, see Revenue and Taxation Code § 7286.59.
State Librarian,
 Generally, see Education Code § 19302 et seq.
 Powers and duties, see Education Code § 19320 et seq.

§ 18024. Public library fund; creation; transfer of funds

(a) A fund is hereby created in the State Treasury to be known as the Public Library Fund.

(b) The Controller shall transfer on January 1, 1984, from the General Fund to the Public Library Fund the amount necessary to meet the state's obligations under this chapter for the remainder of the 1983–84 fiscal year.

(c) The Controller shall transfer on July 1, 1984, and on July 1 of each year thereafter, from the General Fund to the Public Library Fund the amount necessary to meet the state's obligation under this chapter for that particular fiscal year.

(Added by Stats.1982, c. 1498, p. 5807, § 1, operative July 1, 1983. Amended by Stats.1983, c. 323, § 9, eff. July 21, 1983.)

Historical and Statutory Notes

Stats.1983, c. 323, operative on July 21, 1983, and deemed to have become effective on July 1, 1983, unless otherwise provided, see Historical and Statutory Notes under Code of Civil Procedure § 1531.

Cross References

Allocation of tax revenues, see Revenue and Taxation Code § 95 et seq.
California Public School Library Protection Fund, see Education Code § 18178.
Controller, salary, powers and duties, see Government Code § 12400 et seq.
Public library facilities and services, special taxes, see Government Code § 53717.
State treasury, generally, see Government Code § 16300 et seq.
Use of library fund, see Education Code § 18170 et seq.

Library References

States ☞127.
Westlaw Topic No. 360.
C.J.S. States § 228.

§ 18025. Public library fund; disbursements; state allocations

(a) For the 1982–83 fiscal year and each fiscal year thereafter, the State Librarian shall determine the amount to which each public library is entitled for support of the library during the fiscal year. The amount shall be equal to 10 percent of the cost of the foundation program as determined pursuant to Section 18022.

(b) If local revenues appropriated for a public library for the 1982–83 fiscal year and each fiscal year thereafter, including tax revenues made available under Chapter 282 of the Statutes of 1979, total less than 90 percent of the cost of the foundation program as determined pursuant to Section 18022, the state allocation for that fiscal year shall be reduced proportionately. A proportional reduction in the state allocation as described in this subdivision shall not be made, however, commencing with the 1997–98 fiscal year and each fiscal year thereafter, if the amount appropriated to the Public Library Fund for that fiscal year is equal to or greater than the amount necessary to fund each public library in the amount it received for the prior fiscal year, thus providing the state's share of the cost of the foundation program to each library based only on its population served, as certified by the State Librarian. After the first fiscal year in which the proportional reduction is not made, no further reductions based on this subdivision shall be made in any future fiscal year . It is the intent of this subdivision to make this change without harm to any library currently receiving an unreduced share of the state's cost of the foundation program.

(c) If local revenues appropriated for a public library for the 1982–83 fiscal year and each fiscal year thereafter, including tax revenues made available under the provisions of Chapter 282 of the Statutes of 1979, total more than 90 percent of the cost of the foundation program as determined pursuant to Section 18022, the state allocation for that fiscal year shall remain at 10 percent of the cost of the foundation program as determined pursuant to Section 18022.

(d) In order for a public library to receive state funds under this chapter in the 1983–84 fiscal year and any fiscal year thereafter, the total amount of local revenues appropriated for the public library for that fiscal year, including tax revenues made available under Chapter 282 of the Statutes of 1979 and other revenues deemed to be local revenues according to Section 18023, shall be equal to at least the total amount of local revenues, as defined, appropriated for the public library in the previous fiscal year. State funds provided under this chapter shall supplement, but not supplant, local revenues appropriated for the public library.

(e)(1) Notwithstanding subdivision (d), or any other provision of law, in the 1993–94 fiscal year, any city, county, district, or city and county, that reduces local revenues appropriated for the public library for the 1993–94 fiscal year shall continue to receive state funds appropriated under this chapter for the 1993–94 fiscal year only, provided that the amount of the reduction to the appropriation to that public library for the 1993–94 fiscal year is no more than 20 percent of the 1992–93 fiscal year appropriation made to that public library as certified by the fiscal officer of the public library and transmitted to the State Librarian pursuant to Section 18023.

(2) Commencing with the 1993–94 fiscal year, and each fiscal year thereafter, any city, county, district, or city and county may request from the State Librarian a waiver of the requirements of subdivision (d) or of paragraph (1) by demonstrating that the percentage of the reduction in local revenues appropriated for the public library is no greater than the percentage of the reduction of local revenues received by the city, county, district, or city and county operating the public library as a result of changes made to Chapter 6 (commencing with Section 95) of Part 0.5 of the Revenue and Taxation Code by statutes enacted during or after the 1991–92 Regular Session having the effect of shifting property tax revenues from cities, counties, special districts, and redevelopment agencies to school districts and community colleges. Requests for the waiver and the substantiating documentation shall be submitted to the State Librarian along with the annual report of appropriation required by Section 18023 or any other report of appropriations applying to public libraries required by any other provision of law.

(3) Commencing with the 1997–98 fiscal year, and each fiscal year thereafter, any city, county, district, or city and county may request from the State Librarian a waiver of the requirements of subdivision (d) by demonstrating that the percentage of reduction in local revenues appropriated for the public library is no greater than the percentage of reduction of local revenues received by the city, county, district, or city and county operating the public library as a result of the addition of Article XIII D, otherwise known as the Right to Vote on Taxes Act, to the California Constitution as approved by the voters at the November 5, 1996, general election. Requests for the waiver and the substantiating documentation shall be submitted to the State Librarian along with the annual report of appropriation required by Section 18023 or any other report of appropriations applying to public libraries required by any other provision of law.

(4) Commencing with the 2000–01 fiscal year, and each fiscal year thereafter, any city, county, district, or city and county may request from the State Librarian a waiver of the requirements of subdivision (d) or of paragraph (1) by demonstrating that the reduction in local revenues appropriated for the public library is no greater than the reduction in local revenues received by the city, county, district, or city and county operating the public library as a result of the automatic termination of a locally approved special tax or benefit assessment for that public library. Requests for the waiver and substantiating documentation shall be submitted to the State Librarian along with the annual report of appropriation required by Section 18023 or any other report of appropriations applying to public libraries required by any other provision of law.

(f) If the state allocations computed pursuant to this section exceed the total amount of funds appropriated for purposes of this section in any fiscal year, the State Librarian shall adjust on a pro rata basis public library allocations prescribed by this section so that the total amount in each fiscal year does not exceed this amount.

(Added by Stats.1982, c. 1498, p. 5807, § 1, operative July 1, 1983. Amended by Stats.1984, c. 831, § 2, eff. Aug. 31, 1984; Stats.1993, c. 897 (S.B.544), § 1; Stats.1997, c. 167 (A.B.345), § 1; Stats.1997, c. 435 (S.B.1100), § 1, eff. Sept. 22, 1997; Stats.1997, c. 435 (S.B.1100), § 2, eff. Sept. 22, 1997, operative Jan. 1, 1998; Stats.2000, c. 506 (S.B.1350), § 5.)

Historical and Statutory Notes

Under the provisions of § 3 of Stats.1997, c. 435, the 1997 amendments of this section by c. 167 (A.B.345) and c. 435 (S.B.1100) were given effect and incorporated in the form set forth in § 1 of c. 435, operative until January 1, 1998, and then in the form set forth in § 2 of c. 435, operative on January 1, 1998.

Section affected by two or more acts at the same session of the legislature, see Government Code § 9605.

Section 4 of Stats.1997, c. 435 (S.B.1100), provides in part:

"In order to permit public libraries to take advantage of this legislation at the start of the 1997–98 fiscal year, it is necessary for this act to take effect immediately."

Short title and legislative findings, declarations and intent relating to Stats.2000, c. 506 (S.B.1350), see Historical and Statutory Notes under Business and Professions Code § 14482.

Cross References

Allocation of tax revenues, see Revenue and Taxation Code § 95 et seq.
California Public School Library Protection Fund, see Education Code § 18178.
Community colleges, generally, see Education Code § 70900 et seq.
Public library facilities and services, special taxes, see Government Code § 53717.
State funds, see Government Code § 16300 et seq.
State Librarian,
   Generally, see Education Code § 19302 et seq.
   Powers and duties, see Education Code § 19320 et seq.
Taxes, special taxes imposed on behalf of public libraries, authority of cities, counties and other
   agencies, see Government Code § 53717.
Use of library fund, see Education Code § 18170 et seq.

§ 18026. Distribution

Commencing with the 1984–85 fiscal year, the State Librarian shall certify to the Controller on or before November 15, 1984, and on or before each November 15 thereafter, the amounts determined in Section 18025. The Controller shall distribute to the fiscal officer of each public library 100 percent of the amount certified by the State Librarian on or before January 15 of the 1984–85 fiscal year, and on or before each January 15 thereafter.

(Added by Stats.1982, c. 1498, p. 5808, § 1, operative July 1, 1983. Amended by Stats.1984, c. 831, § 3, eff. Aug. 31, 1984.)

Cross References

Controller, salary, powers and duties, see Government Code § 12400 et seq.
State Librarian,
    Generally, see Education Code § 19302 et seq.
    Powers and duties, see Education Code § 19320 et seq.

Article 4

SERVICES

Article 4 was added by Stats.1982, c. 1498, p. 5808, § 1, operative July 1, 1983.

§ 18030. Availability of books and materials to other public libraries

Notwithstanding any other provision of law, books and other library materials acquired or maintained by a public library as a part of the foundation program supported in part by state funds under this chapter shall be made available upon request to other public libraries in the state without charge, subject to any restrictions which may apply to the use of the materials by residents of the area normally served by the library.

(Added by Stats.1982, c. 1498, p. 5808, § 1, operative July 1, 1983.)

Cross References

State funds, see Government Code § 16300 et seq.

§ 18030.5. Minors' access to Internet services

(a) Every public library that receives state funds pursuant to this chapter and that provides public access to the Internet shall, by a majority vote of the governing board, adopt a policy regarding access by minors to the Internet by January 1, 2000.

(b) Every public library that is required to adopt a policy pursuant to subdivision (a) shall make the policy available to members of the public at every library branch.

(Added by Stats.1998, c. 429 (S.B.1386), § 2.)

Cross References

State funds, see Government Code § 16300 et seq.

§ 18031. Operative date of chapter

The provisions of this chapter shall become operative July 1, 1983.

(Added by Stats.1982, c. 1498, p. 5808, § 1, operative July 1, 1983.)

§ 18032. Videotape access by minors; adoption of policy

(a) Every public library that receives state funds pursuant to this chapter and that provides public access to motion picture videotapes shall, by a majority vote of the governing board, adopt a policy regarding access by minors to motion picture videotapes by January 1, 2000.

(b) Every public library that is required to adopt a policy pursuant to subdivision (a) shall make that policy available to members of the public at every library branch.

(Added by Stats.1998, c. 462 (A.B.1886), § 1.)

Cross References

State funds, see Government Code § 16300 et seq.

Chapter 2

SCHOOL LIBRARIES

Chapter 2 was enacted by Stats.1976, c. 1010, § 2, operative April 30, 1977.

Cross References

Central library and repository, conservation education materials, see Education Code § 8730.
Federal aid to public libraries, see Education Code § 12130.
Governing boards,
    Generally, see Education Code §§ 78, 35010, 35012.
    Powers and duties, see Education Code §§ 17565 et seq., 35160 et seq., 72203.5, 81600 et seq.
Libraries and education, generally, see Government Code § 26150 et seq.
Library districts, see Education Code § 19400 et seq.
Library media teacher, qualifications, see Education Code § 44868.
State library, see Education Code § 19300 et seq.
Unified school district libraries and union high school district libraries, see Education Code
    § 18300 et seq.

Article 1

ESTABLISHMENT AND MAINTENANCE

Section
18100.   School library services required.
18101.   Standards.
18102.   Establishment and maintenance.
18103.   Libraries open to teachers and pupils.
18104.   Joint use library facility; Livermore Valley Joint Unified School District.

Article 1 was enacted by Stats.1976, c. 1010, § 2, operative April 30, 1977.

Cross References

Libraries and education, see Government Code § 26150 et seq.
Library districts, see Education Code § 19400 et seq.
Library media teacher, qualifications, see Education Code § 44868.
State library, see Education Code § 19300 et seq.
Unified districts, certain provisions, see Education Code § 35167.
Unified school district libraries and union high school district libraries, see Education Code
    § 18300 et seq.

Code of Regulations References

Applications for funds, see 5 Cal.Code of Regs. § 3900 et seq.

§ 18100.   School library services required

The governing board of each school district shall provide school library services for the pupils and teachers of the district by establishing and maintaining school libraries or by contractual arrangements with another public agency.

(Stats.1976, c. 1010, § 2, operative April 30, 1977. Amended by Stats.1990, c. 1372 (S.B.1854), § 153.)

Historical and Statutory Notes

Legislative findings in Stats.1990, c. 1372 (S.B.1854), regarding application of Education Code provisions to community colleges, and authority of community college districts under

Const. Art. 9, § 14, see Historical and Statutory Notes under Education Code § 40.

Derivation: Educ.C.1959, § 7050, added by Stats.1970, c. 1379, p. 2559, § 4.

Cross References

Governing boards,
    Generally, see Education Code §§ 78, 35010, 35012.
    Powers and duties, see Education Code §§ 17565 et seq., 35160 et seq., 72203.5, 81600 et seq.

Code of Regulations References

School library services, see 5 Cal.Code of Regs. § 16040 et seq.

Library References

Colleges and Universities ☞5.
Schools ☞76.
Westlaw Topic Nos. 81, 345.
C.J.S. Colleges and Universities § 8.
C.J.S. Schools and School Districts §§ 393, 395.

Legal Jurisprudences

Cal Jur 3d Sch §§ 98, 433.

Notes of Decisions

Librarians 1

_____

1. Librarians

School district, which reduced library services, was not required to retain any certificated librarians to provide required library services. San Jose Teachers Ass'n v. Allen (App. 1 Dist. 1983) 192 Cal.Rptr. 710, 144 Cal.App.3d 627.

§ 18101. Standards

The State Board of Education shall adopt standards, rules and regulations for school library services.

(Stats.1976, c. 1010, § 2, operative April 30, 1977. Amended by Stats.1990, c. 1372 (S.B.1854), § 154.)

Historical and Statutory Notes

Legislative findings in Stats.1990, c. 1372 (S.B.1854), regarding application of Education Code provisions to community colleges, and authority of community college districts under

Const. Art. 9, § 14, see Historical and Statutory Notes under Education Code § 40.

Derivation: Educ.C.1959, § 7050.1, added by Stats.1970, c. 1379, p. 2559, § 5.

Cross References

Administrative regulations and rulemaking, see Government Code § 11340 et seq.
Board of governors of community colleges, see Education Code § 71000 et seq.
Community colleges, similar provisions, see Education Code § 78101.
State board of education, see Education Code § 33000 et seq.; Const. Art. 9, § 7.

Code of Regulations References

Implementation of this section, see 5 Cal.Code of Regs. § 16040 et seq.

Library References

Legal Jurisprudences
Cal Jur 3d Sch § 98.

§ 18102. Establishment and maintenance

Libraries may be established and maintained under the control of the governing board of any school district.

(Stats.1976, c. 1010, § 2, operative April 30, 1977. Amended by Stats.1990, c. 1372 (S.B.1854), § 155.)

Historical and Statutory Notes

Legislative findings in Stats.1990, c. 1372 (S.B.1854), regarding application of Education Code provisions to community colleges, and authority of community college districts under Const. Art. 9, § 14, see Historical and Statutory Notes under Education Code § 40.

Derivation: Educ.C.1959, § 7051 (Stats.1959, c. 2, p. 808, § 7051).

Educ.C.1943, § 19051 (Stats.1943, c. 71, p. 685, amended by Stats.1955, c. 877, p. 1501, § 29).

School C. § 6.500.

Pol.C. § 1715, amended by Code Am.1880, c. 44, p. 40, § 34; Stats.1907, c. 6, p. 4, § 1; Stats.1909, c. 143, p. 245, § 1; Stats.1915, c. 469, p. 772, § 1.

Cross References

"Any school district", "all school districts", defined, see Education Code § 80.
Governing boards,
Generally, see Education Code §§ 78, 35010, 35012.
Powers and duties, see Education Code §§ 17565 et seq., 35160 et seq., 72203.5, 81600 et seq.

Libraries, books, see Education Code § 18110 et seq.
School library media teacher, qualifications, see Education Code § 44868.

Code of Regulations References

Records, see 5 Cal.Code of Regs. § 400 et seq.

Library References

Legal Jurisprudences
  Cal Jur 3d Sch § 98.

Notes of Decisions

Exemption from tax   1

_____

1. Exemption from tax
  School district's maintenance of free circulating library did not exempt property in district from tax for support of county library. Redman v. Weisenheimer (App. 2 Dist. 1929) 102 Cal. App. 488, 283 P. 363.

§ 18103.   Libraries open to teachers and pupils

The libraries shall be open to the use of the teachers and the pupils of the school district during the schoolday. In addition, the libraries may be open at other hours, including evenings and Saturdays, as the governing board may determine. Libraries open to serve students during evening and Saturday hours shall be under the supervision of certificated personnel. Certificated personnel employed to perform full-time services in an elementary, junior high, or high school during the regular schoolday, may supervise, but shall not without their consent be required to supervise, a school library on evenings or Saturdays. If a person agrees to supervise the school library during Saturday or evening hours, he or she shall be compensated in the amounts determined by the governing board of the district as indicated on the salary schedule.

(Stats.1976, c. 1010, § 2, operative April 30, 1977. Amended by Stats.1990, c. 1372 (S.B.1854), § 156.)

Historical and Statutory Notes

Legislative findings in Stats.1990, c. 1372 (S.B.1854), regarding application of Education Code provisions to community colleges, and authority of community college districts under Const. Art. 9, § 14, see Historical and Statutory Notes under Education Code § 40.

Derivation: Educ.C.1959, § 7052 (Stats.1959, c. 2, p. 808, § 7052, amended by Stats.1965, c. 1081, p. 2729, § 1).

Educ.C.1943, § 19052 (Stats.1943, c. 71, p. 685, amended by Stats.1955, c. 1552, p. 2833, § 2).

School C. § 6.501.

Pol.C. § 1715, amended by Code Am.1880, c. 44, p. 40, § 34; Stats.1907, c. 6, p. 4, § 1; Stats.1909, c. 143, p. 245, § 1; Stats.1915, c. 469, p. 772, § 1.

Cross References

Certificated and certified, defined, see Education Code § 90.
Certificated employees, generally, see Education Code § 44420 et seq.
Certificates and credentials, see Education Code §§ 44250 et seq., 44330 et seq.
Hours and supervision of community college libraries, see Education Code § 78103.

Library References

Legal Jurisprudences
  Cal Jur 3d Sch § 98.

§ 18104. Joint use library facility; Livermore Valley Joint Unified School District

(a) It is in the interest of the state to authorize the Livermore Valley Joint Unified School District to enter into a joint-use arrangement with another public entity for operation of a joint-use library facility located on land, in close proximity to a schoolsite, owned by the school district or by another public agency.

(b) Notwithstanding any other provision of law to the contrary, the Livermore Valley Joint Unified School District may enter into a contract with the county, the city, or other appropriate entity having responsibility for the provision of public library services, in which the district is located for the purpose of operating a joint-use library facility at a schoolsite owned by the district or at a site, within one mile of the schoolsite, owned by the school district, the county, the city, or other appropriate entity having responsibility for the provision of public library services in that area.

(c) The Livermore Valley Joint Unified School District may apply for the lease-purchase of a project that includes a library facility, funded entirely with local funds, which facility, if constructed, would be of sufficient size to accommodate the requirements of a joint-use library for which the district has entered into a contract, pursuant to subdivision (b).

(d) The contract specified in subdivision (b) shall contain at least all of the following:

(1) Agreement that the county, city, or other appropriate entity shall deposit with the school district an amount equal to the total cost of any space in the proposed library facility that is beyond the needs of the district, prior to the signing of the construction contract for the project. The deposit shall not be refundable, except to the extent that it may prove subsequently to be in excess of the actual total cost of the space that is beyond the needs of the district.

(2) Agreement between the district and the county, the city, or other appropriate entity regarding staffing, maintenance, materials acquisition, and other matters related to the administration and operating costs of the joint-use facility. The agreement shall provide that the school district shall not be responsible for any costs that are not related to the school use of the joint-use facility.

(3) Agreement between the district and the county, the city, or other appropriate entity regarding the procedure for amendment or termination of the contract, including the disposition of materials housed in the joint-use facility should termination of the contract occur.

(e) A joint-use facility constructed pursuant to this section shall comply with all requirements applicable to school facilities.

(Added by Stats.1998, c. 1034 (A.B.1995), § 1.)

Cross References

Contracts, generally, see Civil Code § 1549 et seq.

Article 2

BOOKS

Section
18110.　Adoption of book lists and other library materials.
18111.　Exclusion of books by governing board.

Article 2 was enacted by Stats.1976, c. 1010, § 2, operative April 30, 1977.

Cross References

County boards of education, see Education Code § 1000 et seq.; Const. Art. 9, §§ 3.3, 7.
Instructional materials, see Education Code § 60000 et seq.
Malicious cutting, tearing, etc. of books, see Education Code § 19910.
State libraries, books, see Education Code § 19330 et seq.
Vote required for adoption of books or supplies, see Education Code § 1014.
Wilful detention of books, see Education Code § 19911.

§ 18110.　Adoption of book lists and other library materials

County boards of education may adopt lists of books and other library materials for districts not employing a superintendent of schools or a librarian for full time.　The lists may be distributed to all school districts in a county for use in the selection of books and other library materials.

(Stats.1976, c. 1010, § 2, operative April 30, 1977.　Amended by Stats.1990, c. 1372 (S.B.1854), § 157.)

Historical and Statutory Notes

Legislative findings in Stats.1990, c. 1372 (S.B.1854), regarding application of Education Code provisions to community colleges, and authority of community college districts under Const. Art. 9, § 14, see Historical and Statutory Notes under Education Code § 40.

Derivation: Educ.C.1959, § 7101 (Stats.1959, c. 2, p. 808, § 7101, amended by Stats.1970, c. 1379, p. 2559, § 6).

Educ.C.1943, § 19071 (Stats.1943, c. 71, p. 685, amended by Stats.1945, c. 1078, p. 2075, § 1).

School C. § 6.510.

Pol.C. § 1771, amended by Code Am.1875–6, c. 523, p. 29, § 1; Code Am.1880, c. 44, p. 41, § 38; Stats.1881, c. 45, p. 44, § 15; Stats.1887, c. 107, p. 129, § 8; Stats.1889, c. 160, p. 192, § 32; Stats.1891, c. 129, p. 162, § 22; Stats. 1893, c. 193, p. 259, § 46; Stats.1901, c. 229, p. 671, § 5; Stats.1909, c. 644, p. 976, § 1; Stats. 1915, c. 470, p. 773, § 1; Stats.1917, c. 699, p. 1315, § 2; Stats.1919, c. 279, p. 454, § 1; Stats.1921, c. 574, p. 947, § 1; Stats.1927, c. 185, p. 335, § 1.

Cross References

"Any school district", "all school districts", defined, see Education Code § 80.
County boards of education, see Education Code § 1000 et seq.; Const. Art. 9, §§ 3.3, 7.
Instructional materials, see Education Code § 60000 et seq.
Malicious cutting, tearing, etc. of books, see Education Code § 19910.
Vote required for adoption of books or supplies, see Education Code § 1014.

Wilful detention of books, see Education Code § 19911.

Library References

Schools ☞76.
Westlaw Topic No. 345.
C.J.S. Schools and School Districts §§ 393, 395.

Legal Jurisprudences

Cal Jur 3d Sch § 98.
Am Jur 2d (Rev) Schools § 307.

§ 18111. Exclusion of books by governing board

The governing board of any school district may exclude from schools and school libraries all books, publications, or papers of a sectarian, partisan, or denominational character.

(Stats.1976, c. 1010, § 2, operative April 30, 1977. Amended by Stats.1990, c. 1372 (S.B.1854), § 158.)

Historical and Statutory Notes

Legislative findings in Stats.1990, c. 1372 (S.B.1854), regarding application of Education Code provisions to community colleges, and authority of community college districts under Const. Art. 9, § 14, see Historical and Statutory Notes under Education Code § 40.

Derivation: Educ.C.1959, § 7102 (Stats.1959, c. 2, p. 808, § 7102).

Educ.C.1943, § 19072 (Stats.1943, c. 71, p. 685).

School C. § 6.511.

Pol.C. § 1607, added by Stats.1917, c. 552, p. 736, § 6.

Cross References

"Any school district", "all school districts", defined, see Education Code § 80.
Governing boards,
    Generally, see Education Code §§ 78, 35010, 35012.
    Powers and duties, see Education Code §§ 17565 et seq., 35160 et seq., 72203.5, 81600 et seq.
Malicious cutting, tearing, etc. of books, see Education Code § 19910.
Public aid for sectarian purposes, prohibition, see Const. Art. 9, § 8, Art. 16, § 5.
State libraries, books, see Education Code § 19330 et seq.
Vote required for adoption of books or supplies, see Education Code § 1014.
Wilful detention of books, see Education Code § 19911.

Library References

ALR Library

Bible distribution or use in public schools—modern cases. 111 ALR Fed 121.
Propriety, under First Amendment, of school board's censorship of public school libraries or coursebooks. 64 ALR Fed 771.

Legal Jurisprudences

Cal Jur 3d Sch §§ 15, 98.
Am Jur 2d (Rev) Colleges and Universities § 34, Public Funds § 71, Schools §§ 307 et seq.
Am Jur 2d (Rev) Schools § 307.

Notes of Decisions

Bibles 3
Instructional materials 4
Sectarian 2
Validity 1

-----

1. Validity

Educ.C.1959, § 9012 did not conflict with provision of Const. Art. 9, § 8, that no sectarian or denominational doctrine shall be taught in any school. 35 Ops.Atty.Gen. 68 (1960).

2. Sectarian

Pol.C. § 1607, subd. 3, as added by Stats. 1917, p. 736, § 6, and § 1672 requiring exclusion of sectarian, partisan, or denominational publications from schools and school libraries, were intended, as indicated by their histories, to bar books and other publications of factional religion, but not all religious books not approved by all sects of a particular religion or the followers of all religions; the term "sectarian" being used in the sense of activities of the followers of one faith as related to those of adherents of another, rather than in accordance with the strict definition of the word "sect" as a body of persons distinguished by peculiarities of faith and practice from other bodies adhering to the same general system. Evans v. Selma Union High School Dist. of Fresno County (1924) 193 Cal. 54, 222 P. 801.

3. Bibles

The King James version of the Bible is not a sectarian book, the purchase of which for a school library would violate Const. Art. 1, § 4, as to religious freedom, Art. 4, § 30, or Art. 9, § 8, prohibiting appropriations of public money for sectarian purposes, or Pol.C. § 1607, subd. 3, as added by Stats.1917, p. 736, § 6 and § 1672 requiring exclusion of sectarian, partisan, or denominational publications from schools and school libraries, because there are differences between it and other versions, or because it is of protestant authorship, used in Protestant Churches, and not approved by the Roman Catholic Church; the mere act of purchasing it carrying no implication of adoption of the dogma therein. Evans v. Selma Union High School Dist. of Fresno County (1924) 193 Cal. 54, 222 P. 801.

The Bible may not be read in public school classes for religious purposes. 25 Ops.Atty.Gen. 316 (1955).

The Gideon Bible may not be distributed through the public school system. 25 Ops.Atty. Gen. 316 (1955).

4. Instructional materials

Where the overall purpose of the instruction has been previously approved, a school board may under appropriate rules and regulations delegate to school superintendent, principals or individual teachers the selection of specific instructional materials that are used in lectures or other school presentations and board's approval of the purposes of instruction is restricted by the explicit prohibitions contained in Educ.C. 1959, §§ 8451 to 8453, 8455. 49 Ops.Atty.Gen. 72, 4–26–67.

Pursuant to Educ.C.1959, §§ 8454, 9302, and 9551, instructional materials could only be used in the public schools if it had been approved by the state board of education or the county board of education or the local governing board, and inasmuch as instruction relating to fluorides had been approved by the state board of education, teachers in public schools might provide instruction in the facts relating to fluorides, fluoridation and prevention of dental disease. 43 Ops.Atty.Gen. 53 (1964).

Article 3

MANAGEMENT

Section
18120. Appointment and qualifications of district librarian.
18121. Rules and regulations.
18122. Annual report by governing board to Department of Education.

Article 3 was enacted by Stats.1976, c. 1010, § 2, operative April 30, 1977.

Cross References

Certificates and credentials, see Education Code §§ 44250 et seq., 44330 et seq.
Governing boards,
    Generally, see Education Code §§ 78, 35010, 35012.
    Powers and duties, see Education Code §§ 17565 et seq., 35160 et seq., 72203.5, 81600 et seq.
School library services, standards, see Education Code § 18101.
State board of education, see Education Code § 33000 et seq.; Const. Art. 9, § 7.
Superintendent of public instruction, see Education Code § 33100 et seq.; Const. Art. 9, §§ 2, 2.1.

§ 18120. Appointment and qualifications of district librarian

The governing board of a school district maintaining its own library or libraries may appoint a librarian or librarians to staff the libraries provided they qualify as librarians pursuant to Section 44868.

(Stats.1976, c. 1010, § 2, operative April 30, 1977. Amended by Stats.1990, c. 1372 (S.B.1854), § 159.)

Historical and Statutory Notes

Adoption of regulations incorporating text of specified Education Code sections repealed or amended by Stats.1990, c. 1372, legislative intent regarding continuation of the provisions of the sections, and operative effect of Stats.1990, c. 1372, see Historical and Statutory Notes under Education Code § 8070.

Legislative findings in Stats.1990, c. 1372 (S.B.1854), regarding application of Education Code provisions to community colleges, and authority of community college districts under Const. Art. 9, § 14, see Historical and Statutory Notes under Education Code § 40.

Derivation: Educ.C.1959, § 7151 (Stats.1959, c. 2, p. 808, § 7151, amended by Stats.1963, c. 1033, p. 2616, § 10; Stats.1970, c. 1379, p. 2559, § 8).

Educ.C.1943, § 19091 (Stats.1943, c. 71, p. 686, amended by Stats.1955, c. 1552, p. 2833, § 3).

School C. § 6.520.

Pol.C. § 1716, amended by Stats.1907, c. 6, p. 4, § 2; Stats.1909, c. 143, p. 246, § 2.

Cross References

Certificates and credentials, see Education Code §§ 44250 et seq., 44330 et seq.
County librarian, see Education Code § 19140 et seq.
Qualifications, see Education Code § 44868.
Service credential for library media teacher, see Education Code § 44269.

Library References

Schools ☞76.
Westlaw Topic No. 345.
C.J.S. Schools and School Districts §§ 393, 395.

Legal Jurisprudences

Cal Jur 3d Sch § 98.

§ 18121. Rules and regulations

The governing board of a school district is accountable for the proper care and preservation of the school libraries of the district, and may make all necessary rules and regulations not provided for by the State Board of Education, or the Superintendent of Public Instruction and not inconsistent therewith.

(Stats.1976, c. 1010, § 2, operative April 30, 1977. Amended by Stats.1990, c. 1372 (S.B.1854), § 160.)

Historical and Statutory Notes

Legislative findings in Stats.1990, c. 1372 (S.B.1854), regarding application of Education Code provisions to community colleges, and authority of community college districts under Const. Art. 9, § 14, see Historical and Statutory Notes under Education Code § 40.

Derivation: Educ.C.1959, § 7153 (Stats.1959, c. 2, p. 808, § 7153, amended by Stats.1970, c. 1379, p. 2559, § 10).

Educ.C.1943, § 19093 (Stats.1943, c. 71, p. 686).

School C. § 6.522.

Pol.C. § 1717, added by Code Am.1873–4, c. 543, p. 100, § 32.

Cross References

Administrative regulations and rulemaking, see Government Code § 11340 et seq.
Governing boards,
    Generally, see Education Code §§ 78, 35010, 35012.
    Powers and duties, see Education Code §§ 17565 et seq., 35160 et seq., 72203.5, 81600 et seq.
School library services, standards, see Education Code § 18101.
State board of education, see Education Code § 33000 et seq.; Const. Art. 9, § 7.
Superintendent of public instruction, see Education Code § 33100 et seq.; Const. Art. 9, §§ 2, 2.1.

Code of Regulations References

Records, see 5 Cal.Code of Regs. § 400 et seq.

Library References

Legal Jurisprudences

Cal Jur 3d Sch § 98.

Notes of Decisions

Library fines 1

_____

1. Library fines

Governing board of school district has authority to assess and collect fines against pupils for

failure to return library books in time, but such power may not be delegated to student body organization at the school. 25 Ops.Atty.Gen. 304 (1955).

§ 18122. Annual report by governing board to Department of Education

The governing board of a school district shall, on or before August 31st, in each year, report to the State Department of Education on the condition of school libraries, for the year ending June 30th preceding. The report shall, in addition to other matters deemed expedient by the governing board or the librarians, contain the statistical and other information as is deemed desirable by the State Department of Education. For this purpose the State Department of Education may send to the several districts under its supervision, instructions or question blanks so as to obtain the material for a comparative study of library conditions in the state.

(Stats.1976, c. 1010, § 2, operative April 30, 1977. Amended by Stats.1990, c. 1372 (S.B.1854), § 161.)

Historical and Statutory Notes

Adoption of regulations incorporating text of specified Education Code sections repealed or amended by Stats.1990, c. 1372, legislative intent regarding continuation of the provisions of the sections, and operative effect of Stats.1990, c. 1372, see Historical and Statutory Notes under Education Code § 8070.

Legislative findings in Stats.1990, c. 1372 (S.B.1854), regarding application of Education

Code provisions to community colleges, and authority of community college districts under Const. Art. 9, § 14, see Historical and Statutory Notes under Education Code § 40.

Derivation: Educ.C.1959, § 7154 (Stats.1959, c. 2, p. 809, § 7154, amended by Stats.1965, c. 1338, p. 3224, § 1).

Educ.C.1943, § 19094, added by Stats.1957, c. 2135, p. 3788, § 7.

Cross References

Board of governors of community colleges, see Education Code § 71000 et seq.
Governing boards,
 Generally, see Education Code §§ 78, 35010, 35012.
 Powers and duties, see Education Code §§ 17565 et seq., 35160 et seq., 72203.5, 81600 et seq.
State department of education, see Education Code § 33300 et seq.

Article 4

AFFILIATION WITH COUNTY AND CITY LIBRARIES

Article 4 was enacted by Stats.1976, c. 1010, § 2, operative April 30, 1977.

Cross References

County free libraries, see Education Code § 19100 et seq.
Governing boards,
    Generally, see Education Code §§ 78, 35010, 35012.
    Powers and duties, see Education Code §§ 17565 et seq., 35160 et seq., 72203.5, 81600 et seq.
Municipal libraries, see Education Code § 18900 et seq.
Provision of library services, see Education Code § 1770 et seq.

§ 18130. Contract with county library

Whenever the county in which a district is situated maintains a county library, the governing board of any school district or community college district may agree with the proper authorities of the county to contract for the provision of school library services by the county library. Either the governing board of the school district or community college district or the governing body of the county library may initiate proceedings for the provision of library services for the schools of the district. Such agreements shall be reviewed annually by contracting parties.

(Stats.1976, c. 1010, § 2, operative April 30, 1977.)

Historical and Statutory Notes

Derivation: Educ.C.1959, § 7201 (Stats.1959, c. 2, p. 809, § 7201, amended by Stats.1959, c. 754, p. 2741, § 1; Stats.1970, c. 1379, p. 2559, § 12).
    Educ.C.1943, § 19121 (Stats.1943, c. 71, p. 686).

School C. § 6.530.
    Pol.C. § 1715, amended by Code Am.1880, c. 44, p. 40, § 34; Stats.1907, c. 6, p. 4, § 1; Stats.1909, c. 143, p. 245, § 1; Stats.1915, c. 469, p. 772, § 1.

Cross References

"Any school district", "all school districts", defined, see Education Code § 80.
Contracts, generally, see Civil Code § 1549 et seq.
County free libraries, see Education Code § 19100 et seq.
Governing boards,
    Generally, see Education Code §§ 78, 35010, 35012.
    Powers and duties, see Education Code §§ 17565 et seq., 35160 et seq., 72203.5, 81600 et seq.
Provision of library services, see Education Code § 1770 et seq.

Library References

Schools ☞76.
Westlaw Topic No. 345.
C.J.S. Schools and School Districts §§ 393, 395.

Legal Jurisprudences
    Cal Jur 3d Sch § 99.

Notes of Decisions

Exemption from tax   1

---

1. Exemption from tax

School district's maintenance of free circulating library did not exempt property in district from tax for support of county library. Redman v. Weisenheimer (App. 2 Dist. 1929) 102 Cal. App. 488, 283 P. 363.

§ 18131. Purchase of books by school districts

Notwithstanding any other section of this article to the contrary, school districts may purchase textbooks, reference books, periodicals, and other publications approved by any board authorized to adopt these materials in addition to those furnished by the county library.

(Stats.1976, c. 1010, § 2, operative April 30, 1977. Amended by Stats.1990, c. 1372 (S.B.1854), § 163.)

Historical and Statutory Notes

Legislative findings in Stats.1990, c. 1372 (S.B.1854), regarding application of Education Code provisions to community colleges, and authority of community college districts under Const. Art. 9, § 14, see Historical and Statutory Notes under Education Code § 40.

Derivation: Educ.C.1959, § 7202.1, added by Stats.1963, c. 527, p. 1407, § 1.

Cross References

Exclusion of books by governing board, see Education Code § 18111.
Instructional materials, see Education Code § 60000 et seq.
Libraries, books, see Education Code § 18110 et seq.
School districts,
    Generally, see Education Code § 35000 et seq.
    Governing boards, see Education Code § 35100 et seq.
    Reorganization, see Education Code § 35500 et seq.
State libraries, books, see Education Code § 19330 et seq.

Code of Regulations References

Contents of school libraries, see 5 Cal.Code of Regs. § 16041.

Library References

Legal Jurisprudences

Am Jur 2d (Rev) Schools §§ 303 et seq.

§ 18132. Use of transferred funds

All funds transferred to a county library pursuant to this article shall be used by the county library only for: (a) the acquisition of books and other materials as are adopted by the body authorized to adopt courses of study for the school districts which have entered into an agreement for the provision of school library services by the county library, and (b) the care and distribution of the books and other materials to schools which are eligible to receive school library services from the county library.

(Stats.1976, c. 1010, § 2, operative April 30, 1977. Amended by Stats.1990, c. 1372 (S.B.1854), § 164.)

Historical and Statutory Notes

Legislative findings in Stats.1990, c. 1372 (S.B.1854), regarding application of Education Code provisions to community colleges, and authority of community college districts under Const. Art. 9, § 14, see Historical and Statutory Notes under Education Code § 40.

Derivation: Educ.C.1959, § 7203 (Stats.1959, c. 2, p. 809, § 7203, amended by Stats.1970, c. 1379, p. 2559, § 14).

Educ.C.1943, § 19123 (Stats.1943, c. 71, p. 686).

School C. § 6.531, amended by Stats.1937, c. 628, p. 1742, § 1; Stats.1939, c. 395, p. 1728, § 1.

Pol.C. § 1715, amended by Code Am.1880, c. 44, p. 40, § 34; Stats.1907, c. 6, p. 4, § 1; Stats.1909, c. 143, p. 245, § 1; Stats.1915, c. 469, p. 772, § 1.

Cross References

Exclusion of books by governing board, see Education Code § 18111.
Libraries, books, see Education Code § 18110 et seq.
Requirements for publishers and manufacturers, see Education Code § 60060 et seq.
State libraries, books, see Education Code § 19330 et seq.

§ 18133. Disposal of books and materials

The county librarian may (a) at his discretion dispose of books and other materials no longer fit for service, and (b) with the approval of the county board of education dispose of any books or other materials no longer needed by the course of study.

(Stats.1976, c. 1010, § 2, operative April 30, 1977.)

Historical and Statutory Notes

Derivation: Educ.C.1959, § 7204 (Stats.1959, c. 2, p. 809, § 7204).

Educ.C.1943, § 19124 (Stats.1943, c. 71, p. 686).

School C. § 6.531, amended by Stats.1937, c. 628, p. 1742, § 1; Stats.1939, c. 395, p. 1728, § 1.

Pol.C. § 1715, amended by Code Am.1880, c. 44, p. 40, § 34; Stats.1907, c. 6, p. 4, § 1; Stats.1909, c. 143, p. 245, § 1; Stats.1915, c. 469, p. 772, § 1.

Cross References

County boards of education, see Education Code § 1000 et seq.; Const. Art. 9, §§ 3.3, 7.
County librarian, see Education Code § 19140 et seq.
Destruction of obsolete instructional materials, see Education Code § 60530.
Donation or sale of obsolete instructional materials, see Education Code § 60510 et seq.
Exclusion of books by governing board, see Education Code § 18111.
Libraries, books, see Education Code § 18110 et seq.
Obsolete instructional materials, see Education Code § 60500 et seq.
State libraries, books, see Education Code § 19330 et seq.

§ 18134. Agreement with city

In any city conducting a public library owned and managed by the city, the governing board of any school district may enter into an arrangement with the governing body of the public library of the city similar to the arrangement authorized by this article between the governing boards of any school district and the county library.

(Stats.1976, c. 1010, § 2, operative April 30, 1977. Amended by Stats.1990, c. 1372 (S.B.1854), § 165.)

Historical and Statutory Notes

Legislative findings in Stats.1990, c. 1372 (S.B.1854), regarding application of Education Code provisions to community colleges, and authority of community college districts under Const. Art. 9, § 14, see Historical and Statutory Notes under Education Code § 40.

Derivation: Educ.C.1959, § 7205 (Stats.1959, c. 2, p. 809, § 7205).

Educ.C.1943, § 19125 (Stats.1943, c. 71, p. 686).

School C. § 6.532.

Pol.C. § 1715, amended by Code Am.1880, c. 44, p. 40, § 34; Stats.1907, c. 6, p. 4, § 1; Stats.1909, c. 143, p. 245, § 1; Stats.1915, c. 469, p. 772, § 1.

Cross References

"Any school district", "all school districts", defined, see Education Code § 80.
Governing boards,
    Generally, see Education Code §§ 78, 35010, 35012.
    Powers and duties, see Education Code §§ 17565 et seq., 35160 et seq., 72203.5, 81600 et seq.
Municipal libraries, see Education Code § 18900 et seq.

Notes of Decisions

Conflicts of interest   1
_____

1. Conflicts of interest
Contract between city and school district under this section could create a conflict of inter-

est making offices of city councilman and member of school district governing board incompatible. 48 Ops.Atty.Gen. 141, 12–13–66.

§ 18135. Transfer of fund

Whenever an agreement is made that school library services will be provided by a city, or county library, the county, or city and county, or city superintendent of schools may draw a warrant for the whole amount stipulated in the agreement, payable to the proper authorities of the library, upon the filing with him of a copy of the resolution of the governing board of the district embodying the agreement made with the library. The copy shall be duly certified as correct by the clerk of the district or other proper officer.

(Stats.1976, c. 1010, § 2, operative April 30, 1977.)

Historical and Statutory Notes

Derivation: Educ.C.1959, § 7207 (Stats.1959, c. 2, p. 809, § 7207, amended by Stats.1970, c. 1379, p. 2560, § 16).

Educ.C.1943, § 19127 (Stats.1943, c. 71, p. 687).

School C. § 6.534.

Pol.C. § 1716, amended by Stats.1907, c. 6, p. 4, § 2; Stats.1909, c. 143, p. 246, § 2.

Cross References

City superintendent of schools, see Education Code § 79.
County libraries, see Education Code § 19100 et seq.
Governing boards,
    Generally, see Education Code §§ 78, 35010, 35012.
    Powers and duties, see Education Code §§ 17565 et seq., 35160 et seq., 72203.5, 81600 et seq.
Municipal libraries, see Education Code § 18900 et seq.
Provision of library services, see Education Code § 1770 et seq.

Notes of Decisions

Exemption from tax 1

1. **Exemption from tax**

School district's maintenance of free circulating library did not exempt property in district from tax for support of county library. Redman v. Weisenheimer (App. 2 Dist. 1929) 102 Cal. App. 488, 283 P. 363.

§ 18136. High school district agreement with county for use of county free library

The governing board of any high school district lying wholly or partly within a county maintaining a county free library may enter into a contract or agreement with the board of supervisors of the county by which the high school district may secure the advantages of the county free library upon such terms and conditions as are fixed in the contract or agreement.

(Stats.1976, c. 1010, § 2, operative April 30, 1977.)

Historical and Statutory Notes

Derivation: Educ.C.1959, § 7208 (Stats.1959, c. 2, p. 810, § 7208).

Educ.C.1943, § 19128 (Stats.1943, c. 71, p. 687).

School C. § 6.535.

Pol.C. § 1741, amended by Stats.1909, c. 311, p. 486, § 1; Stats.1911, c. 176, p. 346, § 1; Stats.1915, c. 464, p. 769, § 1; Stats.1927, c. 412, p. 676, § 1.

Cross References

Board of supervisors,
    Generally, see Government Code §§ 25000, 25003 et seq.
    General powers, see Government Code § 25200 et seq.
Contracts, generally, see Civil Code § 1549 et seq.
County free libraries, see Education Code § 19100 et seq.; Government Code § 26150 et seq.
County service areas, extended library facilities and services, authority of board of supervisors and
    funding, see Government Code § 25210.78 et seq.
Governing boards,
    Generally, see Education Code §§ 78, 35010, 35012.
    Powers and duties, see Education Code §§ 17565 et seq., 35160 et seq., 72203.5, 81600 et seq.
High school district, defined, see Education Code 85.
Provision of library services, see Education Code § 1770 et seq.
School districts,
    Generally, see Education Code § 35000 et seq.
    Governing boards, see Education Code § 35100 et seq.
    Reorganization, see Education Code § 35500 et seq.

Library References

Legal Jurisprudences
    Cal Jur 3d Sch § 99.

§ 18137. Care of property

Whenever the governing board of a school district enters into an agreement with a county or city library for school library services the district shall provide for the care and custody of and assume responsibility for the books and other property delivered to it subject to the rules and regulations of the county or city library and the terms of the agreement.

(Stats.1976, c. 1010, § 2, operative April 30, 1977. Amended by Stats.1990, c. 1372 (S.B.1854), § 166.)

Historical and Statutory Notes

Legislative findings in Stats.1990, c. 1372 (S.B.1854), regarding application of Education Code provisions to community colleges, and authority of community college districts under Const. Art. 9, § 14, see Historical and Statutory Notes under Education Code § 40.

Derivation: Educ.C.1959, § 7209 (Stats.1959, c. 2, p. 810, § 7209, amended by Stats.1970, c. 1379, p. 2560, § 17).

Educ.C.1943, § 19129, added by Stats.1943, c. 700, p. 2459.

Cross References

County free libraries, see Education Code § 19100 et seq.
Governing boards,
    Generally, see Education Code §§ 78, 35010, 35012.
    Powers and duties, see Education Code §§ 17565 et seq., 35160 et seq., 72203.5, 81600 et seq.
Libraries, books, see Education Code § 18110 et seq.
Municipal libraries, see Education Code § 18900 et seq.

§ 18138. Termination of affiliation

With the consent of the county superintendent of schools the governing board of the school district may agree with the proper authorities of the county or city to terminate the affiliation of the district with the county or city library. Either the governing board of the school district or the governing body of the county library may initiate termination proceedings. The proceedings shall be terminated prior to the first day of February of the school year in which begun and may provide for either of the following:

(a) The complete withdrawal of affiliation effective on the first day of July next succeeding.

(b) A gradual withdrawal over a period of not to exceed three years beginning on the first day of July next succeeding the termination of proceedings.

The governing board of the school district shall enter into a written agreement with the proper authorities of the city or county providing for the terms of the gradual withdrawal, including the period to be covered, not to exceed three years, the amount of payment for each year, and the amount of service to be rendered.

Unless otherwise provided in the withdrawal agreement, the books purchased by a district during the period of the withdrawal become the property of the district.

All books purchased by a district shall be approved by the body authorized to adopt courses of study for the school districts of the county.

(Stats.1976, c. 1010, § 2, operative April 30, 1977. Amended by Stats.1990, c. 1372 (S.B.1854), § 167.)

Historical and Statutory Notes

Legislative findings in Stats.1990, c. 1372 (S.B.1854), regarding application of Education Code provisions to community colleges, and authority of community college districts under Const. Art. 9, § 14, see Historical and Statutory Notes under Education Code § 40.

Derivation: Educ.C.1959, § 7210 (Stats.1959, c. 2, p. 810, § 7210, amended by Stats.1959, c. 754, p. 2742, § 2; Stats.1961, c. 1911, p. 4032, § 1).

Educ.C.1943, § 19130, added by Stats.1943, c. 700, p. 2459.

§ 18139. Proceedings for termination of library services

With the consent of the county board of education, in those counties in which the county superintendent of schools performs library services for the school library of any district, the governing board of the school district may agree with the proper authorities of the county to terminate the affiliation of the district with the county superintendent of schools with respect to library services. The proceedings shall be terminated prior to the first day of February of the school year in which begun and may provide for either of the following:

(a) The complete withdrawal of affiliation effective on the first day of July next succeeding.

(b) A gradual withdrawal over a period of not to exceed five years beginning on the first day of July next succeeding the termination of proceedings.

The county board of education shall adopt rules and regulations governing a gradual withdrawal, including the period to be covered, not to exceed five years, the amount of payment for each year, and the amount of service to be rendered. The terms of the gradual withdrawal shall comply with the rules and regulations.

(Stats.1976, c. 1010, § 2, operative April 30, 1977. Amended by Stats.1990, c. 1372 (S.B.1854), § 168.)

Municipal libraries, see Education Code § 18900 et seq.

Library References

Legal Jurisprudences
Cal Jur 3d Sch § 99.
Am Jur 2d (Rev) Schools §§ 87 et seq.

Article 5

USE OF LIBRARY FUND

Section
18170.   Expenditure of library fund.
18171.   Warrant requirements; itemized bill.
18172.   Approval required prior to purchase.

Article 5 was enacted by Stats.1976, c. 1010, § 2, operative April 30, 1977.

§ 18170.   Expenditure of library fund

The governing board of any school district shall expend the library fund, together with the money that is added thereto by donation, in the purchase of school apparatus and books for a school library, including books for supplementary work.

(Stats.1976, c. 1010, § 2, operative April 30, 1977. Amended by Stats.1990, c. 1372 (S.B.1854), § 169.)

Historical and Statutory Notes

Legislative findings in Stats.1990, c. 1372 (S.B.1854), regarding application of Education Code provisions to community colleges, and authority of community college districts under Const. Art. 9, § 14, see Historical and Statutory Notes under Education Code § 40.

Derivation: Educ.C.1959, § 7351 (Stats.1959, c. 2, p. 812, § 7351).

Educ.C.1943, § 19201 (Stats.1943, c. 71, p. 688).

School C. § 6.560.

Pol.C. § 1712, amended by Code Am. 1873–4, c. 543, p. 99, § 31; Code Am. 1880, c. 44, p. 40, § 33; Stats.1881, c. 45, p. 44, § 12; Stats.1889, c. 160, p. 190, § 29; Stats.1893, c. 193, p. 256, § 41.

Cross References

"Any school district", "all school districts", defined, see Education Code § 80.
Governing boards,
     Generally, see Education Code §§ 78, 35010, 35012.
     Powers and duties, see Education Code §§ 17565 et seq., 35160 et seq., 72203.5, 81600 et seq.
Libraries, books, see Education Code § 18110 et seq.

Code of Regulations References

Contents of school libraries, see 5 Cal.Code of Regs. § 16041.

Library References

Legal Jurisprudences
Cal Jur 3d Sch § 87.
Am Jur 2d (Rev) Schools §§ 303 et seq.

Notes of Decisions

Exemption from tax 1

_____

1. Exemption from tax

School district's maintenance of free circulating library did not exempt property in district from tax for support of county library. Redman v. Weisenheimer (App. 2 Dist. 1929) 102 Cal. App. 488, 283 P. 363.

§ 18171. Warrant requirements; itemized bill

No warrant shall be drawn by the superintendent of schools upon the order of any governing board of any school district against the library fund of any district unless the order is accompanied by an itemized bill, showing the books and apparatus, and the price of each in payment of which the order is drawn, and unless the books and apparatus, except in the case of library books and apparatus purchased by a district employing a district superintendent of schools or a school librarian for full time, have been adopted by the county, city, or city and county board of education.

(Stats.1976, c. 1010, § 2, operative April 30, 1977. Amended by Stats.1990, c. 1372 (S.B.1854), § 170.)

Historical and Statutory Notes

Legislative findings in Stats.1990, c. 1372 (S.B.1854), regarding application of Education Code provisions to community colleges, and authority of community college districts under Const. Art. 9, § 14, see Historical and Statutory Notes under Education Code § 40.

Derivation: Educ.C.1959, § 7352 (Stats.1959, c. 2, p. 812, § 7352).

Educ.C.1943, § 19202 (Stats.1943, c. 71, p. 688, amended by Stats.1945, c. 1078, p. 2075, § 2).

School C. § 6.561.

Pol.C. § 1712, amended by Code Am. 1873–4, c. 543, p. 99, § 31; Code Am. 1880, c. 44, p. 40, § 33; Stats.1881, c. 45, p. 44, § 12; Stats.1889, c. 160, p. 190, § 29; Stats.1893, c. 193, p. 256, § 41.

Cross References

"Any school district", "all school districts", defined, see Education Code § 80.
County Boards of Education,
    Generally, see Education Code § 1000 et seq.
    Appointment or election, see Const. Art. 9, § 7 and Education Code § 1000 et seq., and § 5000 et seq.
    Duties and responsibilities, see Education Code § 1040 et seq.
    Jurisdiction, organization and procedure, see Education Code § 1000 et seq.
    Salaries and expenses, see Education Code § 1090 et seq.
County superintendent of schools, see Education Code § 1200 et seq.; Const. Art. 9, §§ 3, 3.1.
Governing boards,
    Generally, see Education Code §§ 78, 35010, 35012.
    Powers and duties, see Education Code §§ 17565 et seq., 35160 et seq., 72203.5, 81600 et seq.
Libraries, books, see Education Code § 18110 et seq.
Purchase without taking estimates or advertising for bids, see Education Code § 81651.
Requirements for publishers and manufacturers, see Education Code § 60060 et seq.

Library References

Legal Jurisprudences

Cal Jur 3d Sch § 87.
Am Jur 2d (Rev) Schools §§ 303 et seq.

§ 18172. Approval required prior to purchase

All orders of the governing board of any school district for books or apparatus shall in every case be submitted to the superintendent of schools of the county, city, or city and county, respectively, for his or her approval, before the books or apparatus shall be purchased.

(Stats.1976, c. 1010, § 2, operative April 30, 1977. Amended by Stats.1990, c. 1372 (S.B.1854), § 171.)

Historical and Statutory Notes

Legislative findings in Stats.1990, c. 1372 (S.B.1854), regarding application of Education Code provisions to community colleges, and authority of community college districts under Const. Art. 9, § 14, see Historical and Statutory Notes under Education Code § 40.

Derivation: Educ.C.1959, § 7353 (Stats.1959, c. 2, p. 812, § 7353).

Educ.C.1943, § 19203 (Stats.1943, c. 71, p. 688).

School C. § 6.562.

Pol.C. § 1712, amended by Code Am. 1873–4, c. 543, p. 99, § 31; Code Am. 1880, c. 44, p. 40, § 33; Stats.1881, c. 45, p. 44, § 12; Stats.1889, c. 160, p. 190, § 29; Stats.1893, c. 193, p. 256, § 41.

Cross References

"Any school district", "all school districts", defined, see Education Code § 80.
County superintendent of schools, see Education Code § 1200 et seq.; Const. Art. 9, §§ 3, 3.1.
Governing boards,
  Generally, see Education Code §§ 78, 35010, 35012.
  Powers and duties, see Education Code §§ 17565 et seq., 35160 et seq., 72203.5, 81600 et seq.
Libraries, books, see Education Code § 18110 et seq.

Library References

Legal Jurisprudences
  Cal Jur 3d Sch § 87.
  Am Jur 2d (Rev) Schools §§ 303 et seq.

Article 6

LIBRARY EDUCATION

Article 6 was added by Stats.1993, c. 1212 (A.B.323), § 1.

Repeal

For repeal of Article 6, see Education Code § 18179.

§ 18175. Short title

This article shall be known and may be cited as the "California Public School Library Protection Act."

(Added by Stats.1993, c. 1212 (A.B.323), § 1.)

Repeal

For repeal of Article 6, see Education Code § 18179.

Historical and Statutory Notes

Section 3 of Stats.1993, c. 1212 (A.B.323) provides:

"This bill shall become operative only if Senate Bill 170 of the 1993–94 Regular Session

[Stats.1993, c. 1228, eff. Jan. 1, 1994] is enacted and becomes effective on or before January 1, 1994."

Cross References

California Library Construction and Renovation Program, see Education Code § 19955 et seq.
Management of libraries, see Education Code § 18120 et seq.
Public library finance, see Education Code § 18010 et seq.

§ 18176. Legislative findings and declaration

(a) The Legislature finds and declares that a need exists to ensure that all schools have libraries with adequate and up-to-date resource materials and to assist school districts in staffing their library media centers, in order to achieve equity in learning opportunity in all school districts in this state. A 1987 study of California's public school libraries conducted by the State Department of Education and entitled "The Crisis in California School Libraries—A Special Study," concluded that declining support for school libraries over the last decade has resulted in inadequate and outdated book collections and support materials to meet the scholastic needs of pupils. Further, the study revealed that 68 percent of California's public school libraries have no certificated library media center teacher on staff.

(b) Whereas the study, identified in subdivision (a), concluded that the "school library is the neglected stepchild of educational reform," it is the intent of the Legislature to ensure that services and materials in public school library media programs and centers in kindergarten and grades 1 to 12, inclusive, be maintained at a level sufficient to enable pupils to become independent learners during their school years and as adults, and to enhance inservice training to public school teachers under the direction of certificated library media teachers. The Legislature intends that, by encouraging literacy in the elementary grades under this article, the high rate of pupils who drop out of school prior to graduation from high school will be reduced.

(Added by Stats.1993, c. 1212 (A.B.323), § 1.)

Repeal

For repeal of Article 6, see Education Code § 18179.

Historical and Statutory Notes

Section 3 of Stats.1993, c. 1212 (A.B.323) provides:

"This bill shall become operative only if Senate Bill 170 of the 1993–94 Regular Session

[Stats.1993, c. 1228, eff. Jan. 1, 1994] is enacted and becomes effective on or before January 1, 1994."

Cross References

"Any school district", "all school districts", defined, see Education Code § 80.
Certificated and certified, defined, see Education Code § 90.

Certificated employees, generally, see Education Code § 44420 et seq.
Public library finance, see Education Code § 18010 et seq.
Qualifications for employment as library media teacher, see Education Code § 44868.
Statutes,
  Construction and legislative intent, see Code of Civil Procedure §§ 1858 and 1859.
  Liberal construction of Education Code, see Education Code § 3.
  Rules of construction and definition for the Education Code, see Education Code § 10.

§ 18177. Qualification for funding; necessary showing; distribution of funding

(a) In order to qualify for funding under this article on behalf of any school, a school district shall demonstrate to the State Department of Education all of the following:

(1) That a school library improvement plan has been developed by the school library media teacher, classroom teachers, and the school principal, that has been approved by the local governing board. If a school library media teacher is not employed at a school, a school library media teacher employed by the district or county office of education shall be involved in the development of the plan. The plan shall provide for the selection and procurement of library materials and technology-based materials so as to conform the school's library media program to the California Curriculum Standards and Frameworks, as adopted by the State Department of Education, or to a comparable standard that is designed to use library media program materials and resources to improve teaching strategies, enhance staff development, and implement curriculum objectives in each subject area described in Chapter 2 (commencing with Section 51200) of Part 28.

(2) A proposed budget showing current and proposed expenditures for both the funding of library media technology, and the purchase of materials, including books, reference materials, periodicals, laser discs, CD-ROMs, maps, charts, globes, and other media, that are designed to meet the information needs appropriate to the grade level of pupils at the school. For the purposes of this section, the term "library media technology" includes any automated library management program or system designed to enhance the efficiency and delivery of library services to pupils.

(b) Of the total amount available in the fund created pursuant to Section 18178, 50 percent shall be made available to schools where a credentialed library media teacher is or will be employed at least one-half time. The other 50 percent of the money in that fund shall be available for schools that do not have a credentialed library media teacher that is or will be employed at least one-half time, but that have a school library improvement plan that includes provisions for appropriate maintenance of the materials collection and for supervision of pupils using the materials.

(Added by Stats.1993, c. 1212 (A.B.323), § 1.)

Repeal

For repeal of Article 6, see Education Code § 18179.

Historical and Statutory Notes

Section 3 of Stats.1993, c. 1212 (A.B.323) provides:

"This bill shall become operative only if Senate Bill 170 of the 1993–94 Regular Session [Stats.1993, c. 1228, eff. Jan. 1, 1994] is enacted and becomes effective on or before January 1, 1994."

Cross References

Designation on tax returns to California Public School Library Protection Fund, see Revenue and Taxation Code § 18812.
Franchise and income tax laws, allocations of money transferred to California Public School Library Protection Fund, see Revenue and Taxation Code § 18814.

United States Code Annotated

Technology for education, strengthening and improvement of elementary and secondary schools, federal assistance to develop and support a comprehensive system for the acquisition and use of technology and technology-enhanced curricula, instruction, and administrative support resources and services to improve the delivery of educational services, see 20 U.S.C.A. § 6812 et seq.

§ 18178. California Public School Library Protection Fund; grants; funding allocation; priorities

(a) The State Department of Education shall issue to applicant school districts, from the California Public School Library Protection Fund created under subdivision (d), grants for the benefit of schools that qualify for funding under Section 18177. The funds deposited in any fiscal year into the California Public School Library Protection Fund, other than those funds applied to administrative costs in accordance with subdivision (d), shall be allocated as follows:

(1) An amount of no more than 30 percent of the moneys available in the fund, on behalf of schools that currently do not have a school library. No more than ten thousand dollars ($10,000) shall be allocated to any one school pursuant to this paragraph. The funding allocated under this paragraph shall be used to purchase, for the school library, core literature or other library materials that are directly related to courses of study offered by the school.

(2) At least 70 percent of the moneys available in the fund, to replace outdated library materials. No more than five thousand dollars ($5,000) shall be allocated to any one school pursuant to this paragraph.

(b) Schoolsites shall not be eligible to receive more than one grant every five years from the fund. This restriction may be waived by the Superintendent of Public Instruction if all eligible applicant districts have been funded and funds remain in the California Public School Library Protection Fund.

(c) In apportioning grant funding under this section, the department shall accord highest priority to those schools for which the greatest funding need is demonstrated in the plan adopted pursuant to Section 18177. The department shall look to the following criteria to demonstrate need:

(1) Age of nonfiction materials in the current library.

(2) Size of the collection. The smaller the collection, the greater the funding need.

(3) Ability of pupils to use the education technology materials.

(d) The California Public School Library Protection Fund is hereby created in the State Treasury. It is the intent of the Legislature, that all money in the fund, including any money deposited in the fund from any source whatsoever, shall be appropriated by the Budget Act each fiscal year for expenditure pursuant to this article. The State Department of Education may apportion funds to school districts from the fund as authorized under this article.

(e) The funding provided under this section shall be expended as provided for in the school library improvement plan, and shall supplement, and not supplant, other expenditures by a school district for the support of a school library.

(f) The sole source of funding for this article shall be the fund created pursuant to subdivision (d).

(Added by Stats.1993, c. 1212 (A.B.323), § 1.)

Repeal

For repeal of Article 6, see Education Code § 18179.

Historical and Statutory Notes

Section 3 of Stats.1993, c. 1212 (A.B.323) provides:

"This bill shall become operative only if Senate Bill 170 of the 1993–94 Regular Session [Stats.1993, c. 1228, eff. Jan. 1, 1994] is enacted and becomes effective on or before January 1, 1994."

Cross References

California Library Construction and Renovation Program, see Education Code § 19955 et seq.
Designation on tax returns to California Public School Library Protection Fund, see Revenue and Taxation Code § 18812.
Franchise and income tax laws, allocations of money transferred to California Public School Library Protection Fund, see Revenue and Taxation Code § 18814.
Public library finance, see Education Code § 18010 et seq.
State treasury, generally, see Government Code § 16300 et seq.
Taxes, voluntary contributions, designations to the California Public School Library Protection Fund, see Revenue and Taxation Code § 18811 et seq.

United States Code Annotated

Technology for education, strengthening and improvement of elementary and secondary schools, federal assistance to develop and support a comprehensive system for the acquisition and use of technology and technology-enhanced curricula, instruction, and administrative support resources and services to improve the delivery of educational services, see 20 U.S.C.A. § 6812 et seq.

§ 18179. Duration of article

This article shall remain in effect only until January 1, 2004, and as of that date is repealed, unless a later enacted statute, which is enacted before January 1, 2004, deletes or extends that date.

(Added by Stats.1993, c. 1212 (A.B.323), § 1. Amended by Stats.1998, c. 665 (S.B. 1389), § 1.)

Historical and Statutory Notes

Section 3 of Stats.1993, c. 1212 (A.B.323) provides:

"This bill shall become operative only if Senate Bill 170 of the 1993–94 Regular Session

[Stats.1993, c. 1228, eff. Jan. 1, 1994] is enacted and becomes effective on or before January 1, 1994."

Article 7

CALIFORNIA PUBLIC SCHOOL LIBRARY ACT OF 1998

Article 7 was added by Stats.1998, c.332 (A.B.862), § 1, eff. Aug. 21, 1998.

§ 18180. Legislative findings and declarations

The Legislature finds and declares that school libraries that are staffed by qualified librarians and have adequate numbers of up-to-date library books, resource materials, and media centers, are a valuable resource for teachers and pupils. School libraries provide pupils access to resources that help them meet the academic standards established for them and to become independent and lifelong learners. School libraries also provide teachers access to resources that can help to improve teaching strategies, enhance staff development, and implement curriculum objectives in core subject areas.

(Added by Stats.1998, c. 332 (A.B.862), § 1, eff. Aug. 21, 1998.)

§ 18181. Establishment; districtwide school library plan; funding

(a) The California Public School Library Act of 1998 is hereby established to be administered by the Superintendent of Public Instruction. As a condition of receiving funding under this article, school districts shall develop a districtwide school library plan and the local school district governing board shall certify approval of the plan. In developing the plan, school districts are encouraged to include school library media teachers. If a school library media teacher is not employed at a school, schools are encouraged to involve a school library media teacher employed by the district or county office of education in the development of the plan. Charter schools may apply for funding on their own behalf or through their chartering entity. Notwithstanding Section 47610, charter schools applying on their own behalf are required to develop and certify approval of a school library plan.

(b) A county office of education that complies with this section may receive funding under the article commencing in the 1999–2000 fiscal year.

(Added by Stats.1998, c. 332 (A.B.862), § 1, eff. Aug. 21, 1998. Amended by Stats.1999, c. 646 (A.B.1600), § 9.2.)

Cross References

Charter schools, generally, see Education Code § 47600 et seq.

§ 18182. California Public School Library Protection Fund; appropriations

If the annual Budget Act contains an appropriation for purposes of this article, those funds shall be transferred to the California Public School Library Protection Fund by the Controller to augment the funds appropriated for the California Public Library Protection Act (Art. 6 (commencing with Sec. 18175)). Notwithstanding Article 6 (commencing with Section 18175), the combined appropriation shall be apportioned to school districts and county offices of education on an equal amount per unit of regular average daily attendance reported in the second principal apportionment of the prior fiscal year. The funds shall be expended to support the districtwide school library plan as required by Section 18181.

(Added by Stats.1998, c. 332 (A.B.862), § 1, eff. Aug. 21, 1998. Amended by Stats.1999, c. 646 (A.B.1600), § 9.4.)

Cross References

Attendance for computing apportionments, generally, see Education Code § 46000 et seq.
Taxes, voluntary contributions, designations to the California Public School Library Protection Fund, see Revenue and Taxation Code § 18811 et seq.

§ 18183. Funding; materials and resources for purchase

The funds transferred to the California Public School Library Protection Fund pursuant to Section 18182 are hereby appropriated for purposes of this article and may be expended for library resources, including books, periodicals, microforms, AV materials, computer software, CD ROMs, to purchase equipment necessary to provide access to school library resources within the school library and on-line resources. Materials purchased pursuant to this article shall be circulated from, or used in, the school library media center.

(Added by Stats.1998, c. 332 (A.B.862), § 1, eff. Aug. 21, 1998.)

Cross References

Taxes, voluntary contributions, designations to the California Public School Library Protection Fund, see Revenue and Taxation Code § 18811 et seq.

§ 18184. Curriculum standards and frameworks

The materials purchased with funds apportioned pursuant to Section 18182 shall conform to the California curriculum standards and frameworks, and to standards for the use of library media program materials and resources.

(Added by Stats.1998, c. 332 (A.B.862), § 1, eff. Aug. 21, 1998.)

§ 18185. Repealed by Stats.2000, c. 1058 (A.B.2907), § 14

Historical and Statutory Notes

The repealed section, added by Stats.1999, c. 646 (A.B.1600), § 8, related to the county office of education.

Article 8

CALIFORNIA CLASSROOM LIBRARY MATERIALS ACT OF 1999

Section
18200.   Legislative findings and declaration.
18201.   Establishment; application for funding; conditions for receipt of funds.
18202.   Business Organizations and Opportunities for Kids Fund.
18203.   Apportionment and use of funds.

Article 8 was added by Stats.1999, c. 78 (A.B.1115), § 19, eff. July 7, 1999.

§ 18200. Legislative findings and declaration

The Legislature finds and declares that the availability of grade-level appropriate reading materials in the classroom provides an intellectually stimulating environment for early readers and an opportunity to develop beginning reading skills; promotes an appreciation for reading; and helps to establish the conditions in which children become independent readers and lifelong learners. The Legislature further finds and declares that classroom libraries make resources available to teachers that help them to motivate pupils and to enhance their skill and enjoyment in reading.

(Added by Stats.1999, c. 78 (A.B.1115), § 19, eff. July 7, 1999.)

§ 18201. Establishment; application for funding; conditions for receipt of funds

(a) The California Classroom Library Materials Act of 1999 is hereby established, and shall be administered by the Superintendent of Public Instruction.

(b) Any school district that maintains a kindergarten or any of grades 1 to 4, inclusive, may apply for funding to the Superintendent of Public Instruction under this article. A charter school may apply for funding on its own behalf or through its chartering entity. Notwithstanding Section 47610, a charter school applying on its own behalf is required to develop and certify approval of a classroom library plan.

(c)(1) As a condition of receiving funding under this article, a school district shall develop a districtwide kindergarten and grade 1 to grade 4, inclusive, classroom library plan and shall receive certification of the plan from the governing board of the school district. A school district shall include in the plan a means of preventing loss, damage, or destruction of the materials.

41

(2) In developing the plan required by paragraph (1), school districts are encouraged to include school library media teachers, primary grade teachers, and to consider selections included in the list of recommended books established pursuant to Section 19336. If a school library media teacher is not employed by the school district, the district is encouraged to involve a school library media teacher employed by the county office of education in the development of the plan.

(Added by Stats.1999, c. 78 (A.B.1115), § 19, eff. July 7, 1999.)

Cross References

"Any school district", "all school districts", defined, see Education Code § 80.
Charter schools, generally, see Education Code § 47600 et seq.

§ 18202. Business Organizations and Opportunities for Kids Fund

(a) A fund is hereby established in the State Treasury to be known as the Business Organizations and Opportunities for Kids Fund. Moneys donated by private entities for the purchase of classroom reading materials pursuant to this article shall be deposited into this fund. These donations shall be tax exempt and treated as a charitable contribution to the extent allowed under both federal and state law.

(b) All moneys in the Business Organizations and Opportunities for Kids Fund are available for expenditure only upon an appropriation in the annual Budget Act or other act. The fund shall be administered by the State Librarian in consultation with the Superintendent of Public Instruction. The allocation and expenditure of money in the fund shall be consistent with Section 18203.

(Added by Stats.1999, c. 78 (A.B.1115), § 19, eff. July 7, 1999.)

Cross References

State Librarian,
    Generally, see Education Code § 19302 et seq.
    Powers and duties, see Education Code § 19320 et seq.
State treasury, generally, see Government Code § 16300 et seq.

§ 18203. Apportionment and use of funds

(a) Funds appropriated for the purposes of this article shall be apportioned to eligible school districts in an equal amount per enrollment reported in the second principal apportionment of the prior fiscal year for kindergarten or any of grades 1 to 4, inclusive. Upon receiving an apportionment, a school district shall allocate these funds to each schoolsite that maintains a kindergarten or any of grades 1 to 4, inclusive. The schoolsite shall expend the funds for the purchase of grade-level appropriate reading materials in accordance with the districtwide kindergarten and grade 1 to grade 4, inclusive, classroom library plan required by Section 18201.

(b) For the purposes of this article, "grade-level appropriate reading materials" means nontextbook fiction and nonfiction books and periodicals.

(Added by Stats.1999, c. 78 (A.B.1115), § 19, eff. July 7, 1999.)

Chapter 3

UNIFIED SCHOOL DISTRICTS AND UNION HIGH SCHOOL DISTRICTS PUBLIC LIBRARIES

Chapter 3 was enacted by Stats.1976, c. 1010, § 2, operative April 30, 1977.

Cross References

Unified school district, defined, see Education Code § 83.
Union high school district, defined, see Education Code § 86.

Article 1

DEFINITIONS

Section
18300. Trustees; library trustees.
18301. Library; library district; library districts.

Article 1 was enacted by Stats.1976, c. 1010, § 2, operative April 30, 1977.

Cross References

Library districts, generally, see Education Code § 19400 et seq.
Library districts in unincorporated towns and villages, see Education Code § 19600 et seq.

§ 18300. Trustees; library trustees

"Trustees," or "library trustees" as used in this chapter mean the regularly elected union high school trustees who reside within the library district.

(Stats.1976, c. 1010, § 2, operative April 30, 1977.)

Historical and Statutory Notes

Derivation: Educ.C.1959, § 28001 (Stats. 1959, c. 2, p. 1482, § 28001).

Educ.C.1943, § 22081 (Stats.1943, c. 71, p. 757).

School C. § 6.580, amended by Stats.1939, c. 291, p. 1545, § 1; Stats.1911, c. 279, p. 473, § 27.

Library References

Schools ☞76.
Westlaw Topic No. 345.

C.J.S. Schools and School Districts §§ 393, 395.

Notes of Decisions

Construction with other laws 1
Tax levy 2

1. Construction with other laws

Educ.C.1943, § 22801, construed with Educ. C.1943, §§ 22851, 22903, could only be interpreted to mean that the governing board of the union high school district, as a body, constitut-

ed the board of library trustees. 27 Ops.Atty. Gen. 161 (1956).

2. Tax levy

Educ.C.1959, § 28351 provided for the levy of a special tax for library funds by the board of supervisors if the school district public library was formed pursuant to Educ.C.1959, § 28001 et seq. 57 Ops.Atty.Gen. 447, 9–12–74.

§ 18301. Library; library district; library districts

"Library," "library district," or "library districts" as used in this chapter mean "union high school library district."

(Stats.1976, c. 1010, § 2, operative April 30, 1977.)

Historical and Statutory Notes

Derivation: Educ.C.1959, § 28002 (Stats. 1959, c. 2, p. 1482, § 28002).

Educ.C.1943, § 22802 (Stats.1943, c. 71, p. 757).

School C. § 6.580, amended by Stats.1939, c. 291, p. 1545, § 1; Stats.1911, c. 279, p. 473, § 27.

Library References

Legal Jurisprudences

Am Jur 2d (Rev) Special or Local Assessments §§ 114 et seq.

Article 2

UNIFIED SCHOOL DISTRICTS

Article 2 was enacted by Stats.1976, c. 1010, § 2, operative April 30, 1977.

Cross References

Unified school district, defined, see Education Code § 83.

§ 18310. Establishment of library district in unified district

For the purposes of this chapter a unified school district has all of the powers and duties of a union high school district. A library district may be formed upon the application of 50 or more taxpayers and residents of any unified district, and after an election, in the manner prescribed by this chapter for the formation of a library district upon the application of taxpayers and residents of a union high school district. If the requisite number of votes cast at the election are in favor of a unified school district library district the board of supervisors shall by resolution establish the library district and place the district in the control of the governing board of the unified school district.

(Stats.1976, c. 1010, § 2, operative April 30, 1977.)

Historical and Statutory Notes

Derivation: Educ.C.1959, § 28021, added by Stats.1959, c. 14, p. 1857, § 3.

Educ.C.1943, § 22811, added by Stats.1959, c. 14, p. 1862, § 2.

Cross References

Board of supervisors, see Government Code §§ 25000, 25003 et seq.
Governing boards,
   Generally, see Education Code §§ 78, 35010, 35012.
   Powers and duties, see Education Code §§ 17565 et seq., 35160 et seq., 72203.5, 81600 et seq.
Library districts, see Education Code § 19400 et seq.
Unified school district, defined, see Education Code § 83.
Union high school district, defined, see Education Code § 86.

Library References

Schools ☜76.
Westlaw Topic No. 345.
C.J.S. Schools and School Districts §§ 393, 395.

Additional References

Cal Digest of Official Reports 3d Series, Schools § 6.2.

Legal Jurisprudences
Cal Jur 3d Sch § 141.

§ 18311. Definitions

As used in this chapter the words "union high school district" mean union high school district or unified school district and the words "union high school" mean union high school or unified school district. Whenever the provisions of this chapter are being exercised by, or are being made applicable in, a unified school district, the words "union high school district" and "union high school" shall be deemed to mean unified school district.

(Stats.1976, c. 1010, § 2, operative April 30, 1977.)

Historical and Statutory Notes

Derivation: Educ.C.1959, § 28022, added by Stats.1959, c. 14, p. 1857, § 3.

Educ.C.1943, § 22812, added by Stats.1959, c. 14, p. 1862, § 2.

Cross References

Unified school district, defined, see Education Code § 83.
Union high school district, defined, see Education Code § 86.

Library References

Legal Jurisprudences
Cal Jur 3d Sch § 141.

§ 18312. Unified school district library district

If there are formed substantially within the territory of a union high school library district two or more unified school districts, the library district shall become a unified school district library district which shall be governed by the governing board of the unified school district whose territory includes the largest portion of the territory of the library district.

(Stats.1976, c. 1010, § 2, operative April 30, 1977.)

Historical and Statutory Notes

Derivation: Educ.C.1959, § 28023, added by Stats.1963, c. 1159, p. 2650, § 1.

Cross References

Governing boards,
    Generally, see Education Code §§ 78, 35010, 35012.
    Powers and duties, see Education Code §§ 17565 et seq., 35160 et seq., 72203.5, 81600 et seq.
Library districts, see Education Code § 19400 et seq.
Unified school district, defined, see Education Code § 83.

Library References

Legal Jurisprudences
Cal Jur 3d Sch § 141.

Additional References
Cal Digest of Official Reports 3d Series, Schools § 6.2.

Article 3

ESTABLISHMENT

Article 3 was enacted by Stats.1976, c. 1010, § 2, operative April 30, 1977.

§ 18320. Authority to establish library

Any union high school district may establish, equip, and maintain a public library for the dissemination of knowledge of the arts, sciences, and general literature, in accordance with this chapter.

(Stats.1976, c. 1010, § 2, operative April 30, 1977.)

Historical and Statutory Notes

Derivation: Educ.C.1959, § 28051 (Stats. 1959, c. 2, p. 1482, § 28051).

Educ.C.1943, § 22821 (Stats.1943, c. 71, p. 757).

School C. § 6.570.

Stats.1911, c. 279, p. 467, § 1.

Cross References

Union high school district, defined, see Education Code § 86.

Library References

Schools ☜76.
Westlaw Topic No. 345.
C.J.S. Schools and School Districts §§ 393, 395.

Legal Jurisprudences

Cal Jur 3d Sch § 141.

§ 18321. Title to property

The title to all property acquired for the purposes of the library, when not inconsistent with the terms of its acquisition, or not otherwise designated, vests in the district in which the library is, or is to be, situated.

(Stats.1976, c. 1010, § 2, operative April 30, 1977.)

Historical and Statutory Notes

Derivation: Educ.C.1959, § 28032 (Stats. 1959, c. 2, p. 1482, § 28052).
  Educ.C.1943, § 22822 (Stats.1943, c. 71, p. 757).

School C. § 6.571.
Stats.1911, c. 279, p. 471, § 17.

Cross References

Modification of ownership, interests in property, see Civil Code § 678 et seq.

§ 18322. Library free to inhabitants; violation of rules, regulations and bylaws

Every union high school library established under this chapter shall be forever free to the inhabitants and nonresident taxpayers of the library district, subject always to such rules, regulations, and bylaws as may be made by the board of library trustees. For violations of any rule, regulation, or bylaw a person may be fined or excluded from the privileges of the library.

(Stats.1976, c. 1010, § 2, operative April 30, 1977.)

Historical and Statutory Notes

Derivation: Educ.C.1959, § 28053 (Stats. 1959, c. 2, p. 1482, § 28053).
  Educ.C.1943, § 22823 (Stats.1943, c. 71, p. 757).

School C. § 6.572.
Stats.1911, c. 279, p. 470, § 15.

Cross References

Administrative regulations and rulemaking, see Government Code § 11340 et seq.

Library References

Additional References

Cal Digest of Official Reports 3d Series, Schools § 6.2.

Notes of Decisions

Fees   1

_____

1. Fees

Fees may not be charged to local residents for "library services", defined as the satisfaction with library materials of the patron's informational needs, by libraries that are organized under §§ 18300 et seq., 18900 et seq., 19100 et seq., 19400 et seq., 19600 et seq., or Gov.C. § 39732. 61 Ops.Atty.Gen. 512, 11–21–78.

Article 4

FORMATION OF DISTRICT

Section
18330.   Petition and election.
18331, 18332.   Repealed.
18333.   Conduct of election.
18334.   Repealed.
18335.   Report of election results.
18336.   Establishment of district.
18337.   Unfavorable vote.
18338.   Proceedings entered in the minutes of the board of supervisors.
18339.   Designation of district.
18340.   Actions; authority to hold and convey property in name of district.
18341.   Term of trustees.
18342.   Blanchard/Santa Paula Library District; governing board; terms; revenues.

Article 4 was enacted by Stats.1976, c. 1010, § 2, operative April 30, 1977.

§ 18330.   Petition and election

Upon the application by petition of 50 or more taxpayers and residents of any union high school district to the board of supervisors in the county in which the union high school district is located, for the formation of a library district, and setting forth the boundaries of the proposed district, the board of supervisors shall, within 10 days after receiving the petition, by resolution, order that an election be held in the proposed district for the determination of the question and shall conduct the election.

(Stats.1976, c. 1010, § 2, operative April 30, 1977. Amended by Stats.1987, c. 1452, § 89.)

Historical and Statutory Notes

Legislative findings, declarations and intent relating to Stats.1987, c. 1452, see Historical and Statutory Notes under Education Code § 1007.

Derivation: Educ.C.1959, § 28101 (Stats. 1959, c. 2, p. 1482, § 28101).

Educ.C.1943, § 22841 (Stats.1943, c. 71, p. 758).

School C. § 6.590.

Stats.1911, c. 279, p. 467, § 2.

West's California Code Forms

See West's Cal. Code Forms, Educ. § 18330—FORM 1.

Cross References

Board of supervisors, see Government Code §§ 25000, 25003 et seq.

Computation of time,
Generally, see Code of Civil Procedure §§ 12 and 12a and Government Code § 6800 et seq.
Time in which any act provided by the Education Code is to be done, see Education Code § 9.
Consolidation of elections, see Elections Code § 10400 et seq.
Continuation of statutes relating to subjects covered by provisions of this Code, see Education Code § 3.
Electors or voters, see Education Code § 5390; Const. Art. 2, §§ 2, 4; Elections Code §§ 321, 359, 2000 et seq.
Measures submitted to voters, see Elections Code § 9000 et seq.
Petitions and petition signers, see Elections Code § 100 et seq.
Uniform District Election Law, see Elections Code § 10500 et seq.
Union high school district, defined, see Education Code § 86.

Library References

Schools ☞76.
Westlaw Topic No. 345.
C.J.S. Schools and School Districts §§ 393, 395.

Legal Jurisprudences

Cal Jur 3d Sch § 141.

§§ 18331, 18332.   Repealed by Stats.1987, c. 1452, §§ 90, 91

Historical and Statutory Notes

The repealed sections, enacted by Stats.1976, c. 1010, § 2, derived from Educ.C.1959, §§ 28102, 28103 (Stats.1959, c. 2, pp. 1482, 1483, §§ 28102, 28103); Educ.C.1943, §§ 22842, 22843 (Stats.1943, c. 71, p. 758); School C. §§ 6.591, 6.592; Stats.1911, c. 279, p. 467, § 3, related to election notices and to hours for polls to be open.

Legislative findings, declarations and intent relating to Stats.1987, c. 1452, see Historical and Statutory Notes under Education Code § 1007.

§ 18333.   Conduct of election

The election shall be conducted in accordance with the general election laws of this state, where applicable, without reference to form of ballot or manner of voting, except that the ballots shall contain the words, "For Union High School Library District." The voter shall write or print after the words on his ballot the word "Yes" or the word "No."

(Stats.1976, c. 1010, § 2, operative April 30, 1977.)

Historical and Statutory Notes

Derivation: Educ.C.1959, § 28104 (Stats. 1959, c. 2, p. 1483, § 28104).
Educ.C.1943, § 22844 (Stats.1943, c. 71, p. 758).

School C. § 6.593.
Stats.1911, c. 279, p. 468, § 4.

Cross References

Library districts, see Education Code § 19400 et seq.
Measures submitted to voters, see Elections Code § 9000 et seq.

Library References

Legal Jurisprudences

Am Jur 2d Elections §§ 221, 225 et seq.

Additional References
Cal Digest of Official Reports 3d Series, Elections § 15.

§ 18334.   Repealed by Stats.1987, c. 1452, § 92

Historical and Statutory Notes

Section 18334, enacted by Stats.1976, c. 1010, § 2, derived from Educ.C.1959, § 28105 (Stats.1959, c. 2, p. 1483, § 28105); Educ.C. 1943, § 22845 (Stats.1943, c. 71, p. 758); School C. § 6.594; Stats.1911, c. 279, p. 468, § 5, related to electors entitled to vote.

Legislative findings, declarations and intent relating to Stats.1987, c. 1452, see Historical and Statutory Notes under Education Code § 1007.

§ 18335.   Report of election results

The election officers shall report the result of the election to the board of supervisors within five days subsequent to the holding thereof.

(Stats.1976, c. 1010, § 2, operative April 30, 1977.)

Historical and Statutory Notes

Derivation: Educ.C.1959, § 28106   (Stats. 1959, c. 2, p. 1483, § 28106).

Educ.C.1943, § 22846 (Stats.1943, c. 71, p. 758).

School C. § 6.595.

Stats.1911, c. 279, p. 468, § 6.

Cross References

Board of supervisors, see Government Code §§ 25000, 25003 et seq.
Computation of time,
    Generally, see Code of Civil Procedure §§ 12 and 12a and Government Code § 6800 et seq.
    Time in which any act provided by the Education Code is to be done, see Education Code § 9.
Continuation of statutes relating to subjects covered by provisions of this Code, see Education Code
    § 3.
Library districts, see Education Code § 19400 et seq.
Measures submitted to voters, see Elections Code § 9000 et seq.

Library References

Additional References
    Cal Digest of Official Reports 3d Series, Elections § 15.

§ 18336.   Establishment of district

If two-thirds of the votes cast at the election are in favor of a union high school library district, the board of supervisors shall, by resolution, establish the library district, and place the district in the control of the governing board of the union high school district.

(Stats.1976, c. 1010, § 2, operative April 30, 1977.)

Historical and Statutory Notes

Derivation: Educ.C.1959, § 28107   (Stats. 1959, c. 2, p. 1483, § 28107).

Educ.C.1943, § 22847 (Stats.1943, c. 71, p. 758).

School C. § 6.596.

Stats.1911, c. 279, p. 468, § 7.

Cross References

Board of supervisors, see Government Code §§ 25000, 25003 et seq.
Governing boards,
    Generally, see Education Code §§ 78, 35010, 35012.
    Powers and duties, see Education Code §§ 17565 et seq., 35160 et seq., 72203.5, 81600 et seq.

Library districts, see Education Code § 19400 et seq.
Measures submitted to voters, see Elections Code § 9000 et seq.
Union high school district, defined, see Education Code § 86.

Library References

Legal Jurisprudences

Cal Jur 3d Sch § 141.

Am Jur 2d (Rev) Special or Local Assessments
§ 138.

Am Jur 2d Elections § 309.

Additional References

Cal Digest of Official Reports 3d Series, Elections § 15.

§ 18337. Unfavorable vote

If more than one-third of the votes cast in the election is against a library district, the board of supervisors shall, by order, so declare and no other proceedings shall be taken in relation thereto until the expiration of one year from the date of presentation of the petition.

(Stats.1976, c. 1010, § 2, operative April 30, 1977.)

Historical and Statutory Notes

Derivation: Educ.C.1959, § 28108 (Stats. 1959, c. 2, p. 1483, § 28108).

Educ.C.1943, § 22848 (Stats.1943, c. 71, p. 758).

School C. § 6.601.

Stats.1911, c. 279, p. 468, § 8.

Cross References

Board of supervisors, see Government Code §§ 25000, 25003 et seq.
Library districts, see Education Code § 19400 et seq.
Measures submitted to voters, see Elections Code § 9000 et seq.

Library References

Additional References

Cal Digest of Official Reports 3d Series, Elections § 15.

§ 18338. Proceedings entered in the minutes of the board of supervisors

The fact of the presentation of the petition and the order establishing the library district shall be entered on the minutes of the board of supervisors, and shall be conclusive evidence of the due presentation of a proper petition, and that each of the petitioners was, at the time of signature and presentation of the petition a taxpayer and resident of the proposed district, and of the fact and regularity of all prior proceedings of every kind and nature provided for by this article, and of the existence and validity of the district.

(Stats.1976, c. 1010, § 2, operative April 30, 1977.)

Historical and Statutory Notes

Derivation: Educ.C.1959, § 28109 (Stats. 1959, c. 2, p. 1483, § 28109).

Educ.C.1943, § 22849 (Stats.1943, c. 71, p. 758).

School C. § 6.597.

Stats.1911, c. 279, p. 468, § 9.

Cross References

Library districts, see Education Code § 19400 et seq.

§ 18339. Designation of district

Every library district shall be designated by the name and style of "_____ Library District (using the name of the district) of _____ County (using the name of the county in which the district is situated)." A number shall not be used as a part of the designation of any library district.

(Stats.1976, c. 1010, § 2, operative April 30, 1977.)

Historical and Statutory Notes

Derivation: Educ.C.1959, § 28110 (Stats. 1959, c. 2, p. 1483, § 28110).

Educ.C.1943, § 22850 (Stats.1943, c. 71, p. 759).

School C. § 6.598.

Stats.1911, c. 279, p. 471, § 17.

Cross References

Library districts, see Education Code § 19400 et seq.

§ 18340. Actions; authority to hold and convey property in name of district

In the name of the library district, the governing board may sue and be sued, and may hold and convey property for the use and benefit of the district.

(Stats.1976, c. 1010, § 2, operative April 30, 1977.)

Historical and Statutory Notes

Derivation: Educ.C.1959, § 28111 (Stats. 1959, c. 2, p. 1483, § 28111).

Educ.C.1943, § 22851 (Stats.1943, c. 71, p. 759).

School C. § 6.599.

Stats.1911, c. 279, p. 471, § 17.

Cross References

Governing boards,
    Generally, see Education Code §§ 78, 35010, 35012.
    Powers and duties, see Education Code §§ 17565 et seq., 35160 et seq., 72203.5, 81600 et seq.

Library References

Legal Jurisprudences
    Am Jur 2d (Rev) Schools §§ 16 et seq.

Notes of Decisions

Governing board 1
───────────

1. Governing board
    Educ.C.1943, § 22801, construed with Educ. C.1943, §§ 22851, 22903, may only be interpret-

ed to mean that the governing board of the union high school district, as a body, constitute the board of library trustees. 27 Ops.Atty.Gen. 161 (1956).

§ 18341. Term of trustees

The trustees in whose control the library district has been placed shall severally hold office during the term for which they have been elected as trustees of the union high school district.

(Stats.1976, c. 1010, § 2, operative April 30, 1977.)

Historical and Statutory Notes

Derivation: Educ.C.1959, § 28112 (Stats. 1959, c. 2, p. 1483, § 28112).
Educ.C.1943, § 22852 (Stats.1943, c. 71, p. 759).

School C. § 6.600.
Stats.1911, c. 279, p. 468, § 7.

Cross References

Biennial election of trustees, see Education Code § 19510 et seq.
Term of offices for public officers and employees and continuation thereof, see Government Code §§ 1301 and 1302.
Union high school district, defined, see Education Code § 86.

Library References

Legal Jurisprudences
Cal Jur 3d Sch § 141.

Am Jur 2d (Rev) Public Officers and Employees § 163.

§ 18342. Blanchard/Santa Paula Library District; governing board; terms; revenues

(a) The Board of Trustees of the Santa Paula Union High School District in Ventura County may, by resolution, provide that the Santa Paula Union High School Public Library District shall be governed by a separate board of trustees. Upon adoption, the resolution shall be filed with the County Clerk of the County of Ventura. The effective date of the resolution shall not be earlier than January 1, 1996.

(b) Upon the effective date of the resolution adopted pursuant to subdivision (a), the name of the Santa Paula Union High School Public Library District shall be the Blanchard/Santa Paula Library District.

(c) The governing board shall consist of five members, each of whom shall be a registered voter residing within the library district.

(d) Except for the initial board, members appointed pursuant to paragraph (1) of subdivision (f), and members described in subdivision (h), of the governing board shall hold office for a fixed term of four years, beginning on the last Friday in November next succeeding their appointment or election.

(e) Within 60 days after filing with the County Clerk of the County of Ventura of the resolution adopted pursuant to subdivision (a), the Board of Supervisors of the County of Ventura shall appoint the initial governing board of the library district. The appointments shall be made from the membership of the Library Commission of the Santa Paula Union High School Public Library District.

(f) The first board of trustee shall, at their first meeting, so classify themselves by lot that their terms shall expire:

(1) Two on the last Friday in November of the first even-numbered calendar year succeeding his or her appointment.

(2) Three on the last Friday of November of the second succeeding even-numbered calendar year.

(g) The district shall continue to receive revenues, including apportioned property taxes and authorized special taxes as if it were still the Santa Paula

Union High School Public Library District. There shall be no change in district powers or responsibilities.

(h) Notwithstanding any other provision of law, those persons elected to the board of trustees in 1997 shall hold office for a fixed five-year term.

(Added by Stats.1995, c. 529 (S.B.614), § 2, eff. Oct. 4, 1995. Amended by Stats.1998, c. 829 (S.B.1652), § 21.)

Historical and Statutory Notes

Section 1 of Stats.1995, c. 529 (S.B.614), provides:

"This act shall be known and may be cited as the Local Government Omnibus Act of 1995. The Legislature finds and declares that Californians desire their governments to be run efficiently and economically and that public officials should avoid waste and duplication whenever possible. The Legislature further finds and declares that it desires to reduce its own operating costs by reducing the number of separate bills affecting related topics.

"Therefore, in enacting this act, it is the intent of the Legislature to combine several minor, noncontroversial statutory changes relating to public agencies into a single measure."

Cross References

Computation of time,
    Generally, see Code of Civil Procedure §§ 12 and 12a and Government Code § 6800 et seq.
    Time in which any act provided by the Education Code is to be done, see Education Code § 9.
Continuation of statutes relating to subjects covered by provisions of this Code, see Education Code
    § 3.
Governing board, defined, see Education Code § 78.

Article 5

DISSOLUTION OF DISTRICTS

Section
18370.   Election upon question of dissolution.
18371.   Call and conduct of election.
18372.   Vesting of property upon dissolution.
18373.   Outstanding bonded indebtedness.

Article 5 was enacted by Stats.1976, c. 1010, § 2, operative April 30, 1977.

§ 18370.   Election upon question of dissolution

The district may at any time be dissolved if two-thirds of the votes cast at an election called by the library trustees upon the question of dissolution are in favor of the dissolution.

(Stats.1976, c. 1010, § 2, operative April 30, 1977.)

Historical and Statutory Notes

Derivation: Educ.C.1959, § 28151 (Stats. 1959, c. 2, p. 1484, § 28151, amended by Stats. 1967, c. 92, p. 1008, § 1).

Educ.C.1943, § 22871 (Stats.1943, c. 71, p. 759).

School C. § 6.610.

Stats.1911, c. 279, p. 473, § 25.

Cross References

Measures submitted to voters, see Elections Code § 9000 et seq.

§ 18371. Call and conduct of election

The election shall be called and conducted in the same manner as other elections of the district.

(Stats.1976, c. 1010, § 2, operative April 30, 1977.)

Historical and Statutory Notes

Derivation: Educ.C.1959, § 28152 (Stats. 1959, c. 2, p. 1484, § 28152).

Educ.C.1943, § 22872 (Stats.1943, c. 71, p. 759).

School C. § 6.611.

Stats.1911, c. 279, p. 473, § 25.

Cross References

Measures submitted to voters, see Elections Code § 9000 et seq.

§ 18372. Vesting of property upon dissolution

Upon dissolution, the property of the district shall vest in any union high school district in which the library is situated.

(Stats.1976, c. 1010, § 2, operative April 30, 1977.)

Historical and Statutory Notes

Derivation: Educ.C.1959, § 28153 (Stats. 1959, c. 2, p. 1484, § 28153).

Educ.C.1943, § 22873 (Stats.1943, c. 71, p. 759).

School C. § 6.612.

Stats.1911, c. 279, p. 473, § 25.

Cross References

Union high school district, defined, see Education Code § 86.

§ 18373. Outstanding bonded indebtedness

If at the time of the election to dissolve the district, there is any outstanding bonded indebtedness of the district, the vote to dissolve the district shall dissolve it for all purposes excepting only the levy and collection of taxes for the payment of the indebtedness. From the time the district is dissolved until the bonded indebtedness, with the interest thereon, is fully paid, satisfied, and discharged, the board of supervisors is ex officio the library board of the district. The board shall levy such taxes and perform such other acts as are necessary in order to raise money for the payment of the indebtedness and the interest thereon.

(Stats.1976, c. 1010, § 2, operative April 30, 1977.)

Historical and Statutory Notes

Derivation: Educ.C.1959, § 28154 (Stats. 1959, c. 2, p. 1484, § 28154).

Educ.C.1943, § 22874 (Stats.1943, c. 71, p. 759).

School C. § 6.613.

Stats.1911, c. 279, p. 473, § 25.

Cross References

Board of supervisors, see Government Code §§ 25000, 25003 et seq.
Collection of taxes, see Revenue and Taxation Code § 2501 et seq.
Tax levies, see Government Code § 29100 et seq. and Revenue and Taxation Code § 2151 et seq.

Article 6

MEETINGS OF BOARDS OF TRUSTEES

Section
18380. Quarterly meetings.
18381. Special meetings.
18382. Quorum.
18383. Organizational meeting; terms of members.
18384. Record of proceedings.
18385. Certificate of establishment.

Article 6 was enacted by Stats.1976, c. 1010, § 2, operative April 30, 1977.

Cross References

Powers of board of trustees under this part, see Education Code § 18400 et seq.

§ 18380. Quarterly meetings

A board of library trustees shall meet at least quarterly, at the time and place that it may fix by resolution.

(Stats.1976, c. 1010, § 2, operative April 30, 1977. Amended by Stats.1995, c. 579 (A.B.1566), § 4, eff. Oct. 4, 1995, operative Jan. 1, 1996.)

Historical and Statutory Notes

Derivation: Educ.C.1959, § 28201 (Stats. 1959, c. 2, p. 1484, § 28201).

Educ.C.1943, § 22901 (Stats.1943, c. 71, p. 759).

School C. § 6.620.

Stats.1911, c. 279, p. 468, § 10.

Library References

Schools ☞76.
Westlaw Topic No. 345.
C.J.S. Schools and School Districts §§ 393, 395.

Legal Jurisprudences
Cal Jur 3d Sch § 141.

Am Jur 2d (Rev) Schools §§ 61 et seq.

Additional References

Cal Digest of Official Reports 3d Series, Schools § 15.

§ 18381. Special meetings

Special meetings may be called at any time by two trustees, by written notices served upon each member at least 12 hours before the time specified for the meeting.

(Stats.1976, c. 1010, § 2, operative April 30, 1977.)

Historical and Statutory Notes

Derivation: Educ.C.1959, § 28202 (Stats. 1959, c. 2, p. 1484, § 28202).

Educ.C.1943, § 22902 (Stats.1943, c. 71, p. 759).

School C. § 6.621.

Stats.1911, c. 279, p. 468, § 10.

West's California Code Forms

See West's Cal. Code Forms, Educ. § 18381—FORM 1.

Library References

Legal Jurisprudences

Am Jur 2d (Rev) Schools §§ 61 et seq.

Additional References

Cal Digest of Official Reports 3d Series, Schools § 15.

§ 18382. Quorum

Three members constitute a quorum for the transaction of business.

(Stats.1976, c. 1010, § 2, operative April 30, 1977.)

Historical and Statutory Notes

Derivation: Educ.C.1959, § 28203 (Stats. 1959, c. 2, p. 1484, § 28203).

Educ.C.1943, § 22903 (Stats.1943, c. 71, p. 759).

School C. § 6.622.

Stats.1911, c. 279, p. 468, § 10.

Library References

Legal Jurisprudences

Am Jur 2d (Rev) Schools §§ 61 et seq.

Additional References

Cal Digest of Official Reports 3d Series, Schools § 15.

Notes of Decisions

Construction with other laws 1

_____

1. Construction with other laws

Educ.C.1943, § 22801, construed with Educ. C.1943, §§ 22851, 22903, could only be inter-

preted to mean that the governing board of the union high school district, as a body, constitutes the board of library trustees. 27 Ops.Atty.Gen. 161 (1956).

§ 18383. Organizational meeting; terms of members

The board shall hold an annual organizational meeting. In a year in which a regular election for board members is conducted, the meeting shall be held on a day within a 15-day period that commences with the date upon which a board member elected at that election takes office. Organizational meetings in years in which no such regular election for board members is conducted shall be held during the same 15-day period on the calendar. At each of such meetings, the board shall elect one of its number president, and another one of its number secretary. They shall serve as such for one year or until their successors are elected and qualified.

(Stats.1976, c. 1010, § 2, operative April 30, 1977. Amended by Stats.1977, c. 36, § 73, eff. April 29, 1977.)

Historical and Statutory Notes

Derivation: Educ.C.1959, § 28204 (Stats. 1959, c. 2, p. 1484, § 28204, amended by Stats. 1976, c. 175, § 1).

Educ.C.1943, § 22904 (Stats.1943, c. 71, p. 759).

School C. § 6.623.

Stats.1911, c. 279, p. 468, § 10.

Cross References

Computation of time,
  Generally, see Code of Civil Procedure §§ 12 and 12a and Government Code § 6800 et seq.
  Time in which any act provided by the Education Code is to be done, see Education Code § 9.
Continuation of statutes relating to subjects covered by provisions of this Code, see Education Code
  § 3.

Library References

Legal Jurisprudences

Am Jur 2d (Rev) Schools §§ 61 et seq.

Additional References

Cal Digest of Official Reports 3d Series, Schools § 15.

§ 18384. Record of proceedings

The board shall cause a proper record of its proceedings to be kept.

(Stats.1976, c. 1010, § 2, operative April 30, 1977.)

Historical and Statutory Notes

Derivation: Educ.C.1959, § 28205 (Stats. 1959, c. 2, p. 1484, § 28205).

Educ.C.1943, § 22905 (Stats.1943, c. 71, p. 760).

School C. § 6.624.

Stats.1911, c. 279, p. 468, § 10.

Library References

Legal Jurisprudences

Am Jur 2d (Rev) Schools §§ 61 et seq.

Additional References

Cal Digest of Official Reports 3d Series, Schools § 15.

§ 18385. Certificate of establishment

At the first meeting of the board of trustees of any library district formed under this chapter it shall immediately cause to be made out and filed with the State Librarian a certificate showing that the library has been established, with the date thereof, the names of the trustees, and the officers of the board chosen for the current fiscal year.

(Stats.1976, c. 1010, § 2, operative April 30, 1977. Amended by Stats.1987, c. 1452, § 93.)

Historical and Statutory Notes

Legislative findings, declarations and intent relating to Stats.1987, c. 1452, see Historical and Statutory Notes under Education Code § 1007.

Derivation: Educ.C.1959, § 28206 (Stats. 1959, c. 2, p. 1484, § 28206).

Educ.C.1943, § 22906 (Stats.1943, c. 71, p. 760).

School C. § 6.624.

Stats.1911, c. 279, p. 468, § 10.

Cross References

State department of education, see Education Code § 33300 et seq.

State Librarian,
  Generally, see Education Code § 19302 et seq.
  Powers and duties, see Education Code § 19320 et seq.

Library References

Legal Jurisprudences

Am Jur 2d (Rev) Schools §§ 61 et seq.

Additional References

Cal Digest of Official Reports 3d Series, Schools § 15.

Article 7

POWERS OF BOARDS OF TRUSTEES

Section
18400. Rules, regulations, and bylaws.
18401. Administration of trusts; receipt of gifts; disposal of property.
18402. Officers and employees.
18403. Purchase of personal property.
18404. Real property purchased; buildings; rooms.
18405. State publications.
18406. Borrowing and lending arrangements with other libraries; nonresident borrowing.
18407. Incidental powers of board.
18408. Annual report to State Librarian.
18409. Hours.
18410. Library to be open at reasonable times.
18411. Contracts with other libraries.

Article 7 was enacted by Stats.1976, c. 1010, § 2, operative April 30, 1977.

Cross References

Appointment of library commission, see Education Code § 18440.
Delegation of powers to library commission, see Education Code § 18449.
Meetings of board of trustees, see Education Code § 18380 et seq.

§ 18400. Rules, regulations, and bylaws

The board of library trustees shall make and enforce all rules, regulations, and bylaws necessary for the administration, government, and protection of the library under its management, and all property belonging to the library.

(Stats.1976, c. 1010, § 2, operative April 30, 1977.)

Historical and Statutory Notes

Derivation: Educ.C.1959, § 28251 (Stats. 1959, c. 2, p. 1485, § 28251).
  Educ.C.1943, § 22921 (Stats.1943, c. 71, p. 760).

School C. §§ 6.630, 6.631.

Stats.1911, c. 279, p. 469, § 11.

Cross References

Administrative regulations and rulemaking, see Government Code § 11340 et seq.

Library References

Schools ⟶76.
Westlaw Topic No. 345.

C.J.S. Schools and School Districts §§ 393, 395.

§ 18401. Administration of trusts; receipt of gifts; disposal of property

The board of library trustees shall administer any trust declared or created for the library and receive by gift, devise, or bequest, and hold in trust or otherwise, property situated in this state or elsewhere, and where not otherwise provided, dispose of the property for the benefit of the library.

(Stats.1976, c. 1010, § 2, operative April 30, 1977.)

Historical and Statutory Notes

Derivation: Educ.C.1959, § 28252 (Stats. 1959, c. 2, p. 1485, § 28252).

Educ.C.1943, § 22922 (Stats.1943, c. 71, p. 760).

School C. § 6.632.

Stats.1911, c. 279, p. 469, § 11.

Cross References

Consent of trustees to exercise of powers under this section by library commission, see Education Code § 18449.

Library References

Legal Jurisprudences

Am Jur 2d (Rev) Schools §§ 65 et seq.

Additional References

Cal Digest of Official Reports 3d Series, Schools §§ 13 et seq.

§ 18402. Officers and employees

The board of library trustees shall prescribe the duties and powers of the librarian, secretary, and other officers and employees of the library, determine the number of and appoint all officers and employees, and fix their compensation. The officers and employees shall hold their offices and positions at the pleasure of the boards.

(Stats.1976, c. 1010, § 2, operative April 30, 1977.)

Historical and Statutory Notes

Derivation: Educ.C.1959, § 28253 (Stats. 1959, c. 2, p. 1485, § 28253).

Educ.C.1943, § 22923 (Stats.1943, c. 71, p. 760).

School C. § 6.633.

Stats.1911, c. 279, p. 469, § 11.

Library References

Legal Jurisprudences

Am Jur 2d (Rev) Schools §§ 65 et seq.

Additional References

Cal Digest of Official Reports 3d Series, Schools §§ 13 et seq.

§ 18403. Purchase of personal property

The board of library trustees shall purchase necessary books, journals, publications, and other personal property.

(Stats.1976, c. 1010, § 2, operative April 30, 1977.)

Historical and Statutory Notes

Derivation: Educ.C.1959, § 28254 (Stats. 1959, c. 2, p. 1485, § 28254).

Educ.C.1943, § 22924 (Stats.1943, c. 71, p. 760).

School C. § 6.634.

Stats.1911, c. 279, p. 469, § 11.

Library References

Legal Jurisprudences

Am Jur 2d (Rev) Schools §§ 65 et seq.

Additional References

Cal Digest of Official Reports 3d Series, Schools §§ 13 et seq.

§ 18404.   Real property purchased; buildings; rooms

The board of library trustees shall purchase such real property, and erect or rent and equip such buildings or rooms, as in its judgment are necessary to properly carry out the provisions of this chapter.

(Stats.1976, c. 1010, § 2, operative April 30, 1977.)

Historical and Statutory Notes

Derivation: Educ.C.1959, § 28255 (Stats. 1959, c. 2, p. 1485, § 28255).

Educ.C.1943, § 22925 (Stats.1943, c. 71, p. 760).

School C. § 6.635.

Stats.1911, c. 279, p. 469, § 11.

Cross References

Consent of trustees to exercise of powers under this section by library commission, see Education Code § 18449.

Library References

Legal Jurisprudences

Am Jur 2d (Rev) Schools §§ 65 et seq.

Additional References

Cal Digest of Official Reports 3d Series, Schools §§ 13 et seq.

§ 18405.   State publications

The board of library trustees may request the appropriate state officials to furnish the library with copies of any and all reports, laws, and other publications of the state not otherwise disposed of by law.

(Stats.1976, c. 1010, § 2, operative April 30, 1977.)

Historical and Statutory Notes

Derivation: Educ.C.1959, § 28256 (Stats. 1959, c. 2, p. 1485, § 28256, amended by Stats. 1959, c. 1214, p. 3301, § 3).

Educ.C.1943, § 22926 (Stats.1943, c. 71, p. 760).

School C. § 6.636.

Stats.1911, c. 279, p. 469, § 11.

Library References

Legal Jurisprudences

Am Jur 2d (Rev) Schools §§ 65 et seq.

Additional References

Cal Digest of Official Reports 3d Series, Schools §§ 13 et seq.

§ 18406.   Borrowing and lending arrangements with other libraries; non-resident borrowing

The board of library trustees shall borrow books from, lend books to, and exchange books with other libraries, and shall allow nonresidents to borrow books upon such conditions as it may prescribe.

(Stats.1976, c. 1010, § 2, operative April 30, 1977.)

Historical and Statutory Notes

Derivation: Educ.C.1959, § 28257 (Stats. 1959, c. 2, p. 1485, § 28257).

Educ.C.1943, § 22927 (Stats.1943, c. 71, p. 760).

School C. § 6.637.

Stats.1911, c. 279, p. 469, § 11.

Library References

Legal Jurisprudences

Am Jur 2d (Rev) Schools §§ 65 et seq.

Additional References

Cal Digest of Official Reports 3d Series, Schools §§ 13 et seq.

§ 18407. Incidental powers of board

The board of library trustees shall do and perform any and all other acts and things necessary or proper to carry out the provisions of this chapter.

(Stats.1976, c. 1010, § 2, operative April 30, 1977.)

Historical and Statutory Notes

Derivation: Educ.C.1959, § 28258 (Stats. 1959, c. 2, p. 1485, § 28258).

Educ.C.1943, § 22928 (Stats.1943, c. 71, p. 760).

School C. § 6.638.

Stats.1911, c. 279, p. 469, § 11.

Library References

Legal Jurisprudences

Am Jur 2d (Rev) Schools §§ 65 et seq.

Additional References

Cal Digest of Official Reports 3d Series, Schools §§ 13 et seq.

§ 18408. Annual report to State Librarian

The board of library trustees shall file through the librarian on or before the last day in August of each year, a report with the State Librarian at Sacramento, giving the condition of its library and the number of volumes contained therein on the 30th day of June preceding. The report shall, in addition to other matters deemed expedient by the board of trustees or the district librarian, contain such statistical and other information as is deemed desirable by the State Librarian. For this purpose the State Librarian may send to the several district librarians instructions or question blanks so as to obtain the material for a comparative study of library conditions in the state.

(Stats.1976, c. 1010, § 2, operative April 30, 1977.)

Historical and Statutory Notes

Derivation: Educ.C.1959, § 28259 (Stats. 1959, c. 2, p. 1485, § 28259).

Educ.C.1943, § 22929 (Stats.1943, c. 71, p. 760, amended by Stats.1957, c. 2135, p. 3788, § 5).

School C. § 6.639.

Stats.1911, c. 279, p. 469, § 11.

Cross References

State librarian, see Education Code § 19302 et seq.

Library References

§ 18409. Hours

The board of library trustees shall designate the hours during which the library will be open for the use of the public.

(Stats.1976, c. 1010, § 2, operative April 30, 1977.)

Historical and Statutory Notes

Derivation: Educ.C.1959, § 28260 (Stats. 1959, c. 2, p. 1485, § 28260, amended by Stats. 1959, c. 1210, p. 3299, § 1).

Educ.C.1943, § 22930 (Stats.1943, c. 71, p. 761).

School C. § 6.640.

Stats.1911, c. 279, p. 469, § 11.

§ 18410. Library to be open at reasonable times

All public libraries established under this chapter shall be open for the use of the public at all reasonable times.

(Stats.1976, c. 1010, § 2, operative April 30, 1977.)

Historical and Statutory Notes

Derivation: Educ.C.1959, § 28261 (Stats. 1959, c. 2, p. 1486, § 28261, amended by Stats. 1959, c. 1210, p. 3299, § 2).

Educ.C.1943, § 22931 (Stats.1943, c. 71, p. 761).

School C. § 6.641.

Stats.1911, c. 279, p. 469, § 11.

Library References

§ 18411. Contracts with other libraries

Boards of library trustees and the boards of trustees of neighboring library districts, or the legislative bodies of neighboring municipalities, or boards of supervisors of the counties in which public libraries are situated, may contract to lend the books of the libraries to residents of the counties, neighboring municipalities, or library districts, upon a reasonable compensation to be paid by the counties, neighboring municipalities, or library districts.

(Stats.1976, c. 1010, § 2, operative April 30, 1977.)

Historical and Statutory Notes

Derivation: Educ.C.1959, § 28262 (Stats. 1959, c. 2, p. 1486, § 28262).

Educ.C.1943, § 22932 (Stats.1943, c. 71, p. 761).

School C. § 6.641.

Stats.1911, c. 279, p. 470, § 16.

Cross References

Board of supervisors, see Government Code §§ 25000, 25003 et seq.
Contracts, generally, see Civil Code § 1549 et seq.

Library commission not to exercise powers granted under this section, see Education Code § 18449.

Library References

Legal Jurisprudences
Cal Jur 3d Sch § 141.

Article 8

LIBRARY COMMISSION

Article 8 was enacted by Stats.1976, c. 1010, § 2, operative April 30, 1977.

§ 18440.   Appointment of library commission

A board of library trustees may appoint, by resolution or other order entered in the minutes of the board of library trustees, a library commission consisting of five members to manage and operate the library or libraries of the district. Before any board of library trustees appoints a library commission as provided herein, the board of library trustees shall hold at least one public hearing on the matter of the creation of a library commission; notice of such hearing shall be given by publication pursuant to Section 6066 of the Government Code, in a newspaper designated by the board of library trustees and circulated throughout the district, and by posting of the notice in three public places in the district at least 15 days prior to the date of the public hearing.

(Stats.1976, c. 1010, § 2, operative April 30, 1977.)

Historical and Statutory Notes

Derivation: Educ.C.1959, § 28275, added by Stats.1968, c. 822, p. 1586, § 1.

Cross References

Newspapers, publications and official advertising, see Government Code § 6000 et seq.

Library References

Schools ⚬⚬76.
Westlaw Topic No. 345.

C.J.S. Schools and School Districts §§ 393, 395.

§ 18441. Terms of members

The members of the library commission shall hold office for three years from the first day of July next succeeding their appointment and until their successors are appointed and qualified, and shall serve without compensation.

(Stats.1976, c. 1010, § 2, operative April 30, 1977.)

Historical and Statutory Notes

Derivation: Educ.C.1959, § 28276, added by Stats.1968, c. 822, p. 1586, § 1.

§ 18442. Classification

The members of the first commission appointed shall be so classified by the board of library trustees at the time of their appointment that the term of office of one of the members shall expire on the first day of July one year after the first day of July next succeeding his appointment, two at the end of one additional year thereafter, and two at the end of two additional years thereafter.

(Stats.1976, c. 1010, § 2, operative April 30, 1977.)

Historical and Statutory Notes

Derivation: Educ.C.1959, § 28277, added by Stats.1968, c. 822, p. 1586, § 1.

Cross References

Term of offices for public officers and employees and continuation thereof, see Government Code §§ 1301 and 1302.

§ 18443. Vacancies

Vacancies shall be filled by the board of library trustees by appointment for the unexpired term.

(Stats.1976, c. 1010, § 2, operative April 30, 1977.)

Historical and Statutory Notes

Derivation: Educ.C.1959, § 28278, added by Stats.1968, c. 822, p. 1586, § 1.

§ 18444. Meetings

Within 30 days after their first appointment, and whenever vacancies in any office may occur and are filled, the commission shall meet and organize as a commission, electing a president and a secretary from their number, after which they may transact business. The commission shall meet at least once a month at such time and place as they may fix by resolution. Regular and special meetings shall be called and conducted as prescribed in Chapter 9 (commencing with Section 54950), Part 1, Division 2, Title 5 of the Government Code.

(Stats.1976, c. 1010, § 2, operative April 30, 1977.)

Historical and Statutory Notes

Derivation: Educ.C.1959, § 28279, added by Stats.1968, c. 822, p. 1586, § 1.

Cross References

Computation of time,
    Generally, see Code of Civil Procedure §§ 12 and 12a and Government Code § 6800 et seq.
    Time in which any act provided by the Education Code is to be done, see Education Code § 9.
Continuation of statutes relating to subjects covered by provisions of this Code, see Education Code
    § 3.

§ 18445. Quorum

A majority of the commission shall constitute a quorum for the transaction of business.

(Stats.1976, c. 1010, § 2, operative April 30, 1977.)

Historical and Statutory Notes

Derivation: Educ.C.1959, § 28280, added by Stats.1968, c. 822, p. 1586, § 1.

§ 18446. Action by resolution or motion; votes

The commission shall act only by resolution or motion. A majority vote of the members of the commission is required on each action taken, and the vote thereon shall be recorded.

(Stats.1976, c. 1010, § 2, operative April 30, 1977.)

Historical and Statutory Notes

Derivation: Educ.C.1959, § 28281, added by Stats.1968, c. 822, p. 1586, § 1.

§ 18447. Record of proceedings

The commission shall cause a proper record of its proceedings to be kept and maintained.

(Stats.1976, c. 1010, § 2, operative April 30, 1977.)

Historical and Statutory Notes

Derivation: Educ.C.1959, § 28282, added by Stats.1968, c. 822, p. 1586, § 1.

§ 18448. Traveling and incidental expenses

Members of the commission may be allowed actual necessary traveling and incidental expenses incurred in the performance of official business of the district as approved by the commission.

(Stats.1976, c. 1010, § 2, operative April 30, 1977.)

Historical and Statutory Notes

Derivation: Educ.C.1959, § 28283, added by Stats.1968, c. 822, p. 1586, § 1.

§ 18449. Powers and duties

The commission shall do and perform any and all powers and duties authorized or required of the board of library trustees in Article 7 (commencing with Section 18400) of this chapter with the exception of Section 18411, provided that the consent of the board of library trustees shall be necessary before the commission may dispose of property pursuant to Section 18401 and before the purchase, erection, rental, and equipment of buildings or rooms pursuant to Section 18404.

(Stats.1976, c. 1010, § 2, operative April 30, 1977.)

Historical and Statutory Notes

Derivation: Educ.C.1959, § 28284, added by Stats.1968, c. 822, p. 1586, § 1.

§ 18450. Warrant on county treasurer

Upon the receipt by the county auditor of an order of the library commission of the district, he shall issue his warrant upon the county treasurer for the amount stated in the order if sufficient funds be on deposit in the account of the district with the county treasurer.

(Stats.1976, c. 1010, § 2, operative April 30, 1977.)

Historical and Statutory Notes

Derivation: Educ.C.1959, § 28285, added by Stats.1968, c. 822, p. 1587, § 1.

Cross References

County auditor, see Government Code § 26900 et seq.
County treasurer, see Government Code § 27000 et seq.

§ 18451. Budget

Annually, and on or before the first day of June of each and every year, the commission shall submit or cause to be submitted to the board of library trustees its proposed budget for the operating and maintaining of the library or libraries of the district for the ensuing fiscal year. The proposed budget shall include an estimate of the cost of any or all of the following:

(a) Leasing of temporary quarters;

(b) Purchasing of suitable real property;

(c) Procuring plans and specifications, and erecting a suitable building or buildings;

(d) Furnishing and equipping the library building, and fencing and ornamenting the grounds for the accommodation of the public library.

(Stats.1976, c. 1010, § 2, operative April 30, 1977.)

Historical and Statutory Notes

Derivation: Educ.C.1959, § 28286, added by Stats.1968, c. 822, p. 1587, § 1.

§ 18452.   Dissolution of commission

The board of library trustees may dissolve the library commission created under the provisions of this article effective as of the 30th day of June next succeeding.   Before taking action to dissolve a library commission, the board of library trustees shall hold at least one public hearing on the matter;   notice of such hearing shall be given by publication pursuant to Section 6066 of the Government Code, in a newspaper designated by the board of library trustees and circulated throughout the district, and by posting of the notice in three public places in the district at least 15 days prior to the date of the public hearing.

(Stats.1976, c. 1010, § 2, operative April 30, 1977.)

Historical and Statutory Notes

Derivation: Educ.C.1959, § 28287, added by Stats.1968, c. 822, p. 1587, § 1.

Cross References

Newspapers, publications and official advertising, see Government Code § 6000 et seq.

Article 9

ESTIMATES OF FUNDS NEEDED

Section
18480.   Time for estimate of costs; costs to be estimated.

Article 9 was enacted by Stats.1976, c. 1010, § 2, operative April 30, 1977.

§ 18480.   Time for estimate of costs; costs to be estimated

In any library district formed under this chapter which maintains a public library, or which has petitioned for and has been granted permission to establish, and intends to maintain, a public library in accordance with this chapter, the board of library trustees shall furnish to the board of supervisors of the county in which the library district is situated, each and every year, on or before the first day of September, an estimate of the cost of any or all of the following:

(a) Leasing temporary quarters.

(b) Purchasing a suitable lot.

(c) Procuring plans and specifications and erecting a suitable building.

(d) Furnishing and equipping the building, and fencing and ornamenting the grounds for the accommodation of the public library.

(e) Conducting and maintaining the library for the ensuing fiscal year.

(Stats.1976, c. 1010, § 2, operative April 30, 1977.)

Historical and Statutory Notes

Derivation: Educ.C.1959, § 28301 (Stats. 1959, c. 2, p. 1486, § 28301).

Educ.C.1943, § 22951 (Stats.1943, c. 71, p. 761).

School C. § 6.650.

Stats.1911, c. 279, p. 469, § 12.

Cross References

Board of supervisors, see Government Code §§ 25000, 25003 et seq.

Library References

Schools ☞76.
Westlaw Topic No. 345.
C.J.S. Schools and School Districts §§ 393, 395.

Legal Jurisprudences

Cal Jur 3d Sch § 141.

Article 10

TAX LEVY

Section
18490 to 18492. Repealed.
18493. Library fund.
18494. Safety, preservation, and application of fund not payable into treasury.

Article 10 was enacted by Stats.1976, c. 1010, § 2, operative April 30, 1977.

Cross References

Tax levies, see Government Code § 29100 et seq. and Revenue and Taxation Code § 2151 et seq.
Taxes, special taxes imposed on behalf of public libraries, authority of cities, counties and other agencies, see Government Code § 53717.

§§ 18490 to 18492. Repealed by Stats.1994, c. 922 (A.B.2587), §§ 28 to 30

Historical and Statutory Notes

Section 18940, enacted by Stats.1976, c. 1010, § 2, derived from Educ.C.1959, § 28351 (Stats.1959, c. 2, p. 1486, § 28351); Educ.C. 1943, § 22971 (Stats.1943, c. 71, p. 761); School C. § 6.660; and Stats.1911, c. 279, p. 470, § 13, authorized a levy of a special tax.

Section 18941, enacted by Stats.1976, c. 1010, § 2, derived from Educ.C.1959, § 28352 (Stats.1959, c. 2, p. 1486, § 28352); Educ.C. 1943, § 22972 (Stats.1943, c. 71, p. 761); School C. § 6.661; and Stats.1911, c. 279, p. 470, § 13, set forth the amount of the tax levy.

Section 18942, enacted by Stats.1976, c. 1010, § 2, derived from Educ.C.1959, § 28353 (Stats.1959, c. 2, p. 1486, § 28353); Educ.C. 1943, § 22973 (Stats.1943, c. 71, p. 761); School C. § 6.662; and Stats.1911, c. 279, p. 470, § 13, related to computation, entry and collection of taxes levied.

Subordination of legislation by Stats.1994, c. 922 (A.B.2587), see Historical and Statutory Notes under Education Code § 2550.

§ 18493. Library fund

The revenue derived from the tax, together with all money acquired by gift, devise, bequest, or otherwise for the purposes of the library, shall be paid into the county treasury to the credit of the library fund of the district in which the tax was collected, subject only to the order of the library trustees of the district.

(Stats.1976, c. 1010, § 2, operative April 30, 1977.)

Historical and Statutory Notes

Derivation: Educ.C.1959, § 28354 (Stats. 1959, c. 2, p. 1486, § 28354).

Educ.C.1943, § 22974 (Stats.1943, c. 71, p. 761).

School C. § 6.663.

Stats.1911, c. 279, p. 470, § 14.

Cross References

County treasurer, see Government Code § 27000 et seq.
Expenditure of library fund, see Education Code § 18170.
Public library fund, creation, see Education Code § 18024.
Tax levies, see Government Code § 29100 et seq. and Revenue and Taxation Code § 2151 et seq.
Taxes, special taxes imposed on behalf of public libraries, authority of cities, counties and other agencies, see Government Code § 53717.

§ 18494. Safety, preservation, and application of fund not payable into treasury

If the payment into the treasury is inconsistent with the terms or conditions of any gift, devise, or bequest, the board of library trustees shall provide for the safety and preservation of the fund, and the application thereof to the use of the library, in accordance with the terms and conditions of the gift, devise, or bequest.

(Stats.1976, c. 1010, § 2, operative April 30, 1977.)

Historical and Statutory Notes

Derivation: Educ.C.1959, § 28355 (Stats. 1959, c. 2, p. 1487, § 28355).

Educ.C.1943, § 22975 (Stats.1943, c. 71, p. 762).

School C. § 6.664.

Stats.1911, c. 279, p. 470, § 14.

Cross References

Tax levies, see Government Code § 29100 et seq. and Revenue and Taxation Code § 2151 et seq.
Taxes, special taxes imposed on behalf of public libraries, authority of cities, counties and other agencies, see Government Code § 53717.

Article 11

CLAIMS

Section
18500. Claims for money or damages.

Article 11 was enacted by Stats.1976, c. 1010, § 2, operative April 30, 1977.

§ 18500. Claims for money or damages

All claims for money or damages against the district are governed by Part 3 (commencing with Section 900) and Part 4 (commencing with Section 940) of

Division 3.6 of Title 1 of the Government Code except as provided therein, or by other statutes or regulations expressly applicable thereto.

(Stats.1976, c. 1010, § 2, operative April 30, 1977.)

Historical and Statutory Notes

Derivation: Educ.C.1959, § 28381, added by Stats.1959, c. 1727, p. 4145, § 6, amended by Stats.1963, c. 1715, pp. 3396, 3397, § 14.

Cross References

Money or damages claims, see Education Code § 19500.

Library References

Schools ⟨key⟩112.
Westlaw Topic No. 345.
C.J.S. Schools and School Districts §§ 669 to 673, 679 to 681.

Additional References

Cal Digest of Official Reports 3d Series, Municipalities §§ 99 et seq.

Legal Jurisprudences

Am Jur 2d Municipal Corporations, Counties, and Other Political Subdivisions §§ 680 et seq.

Article 12

ELECTION FOR ISSUANCE OF BONDS

Article 12 was enacted by Stats.1976, c. 1010, § 2, operative April 30, 1977.

Cross References

Ballot requirements, see Education Code § 15123.
Bonds,
    Generally, see Education Code § 15100 et seq.
    Elections, inclusions in elections costs, see Education Code § 5420.
    Issuance by school districts, see Const. Art. 9, § 6 1/2.
    Tax exemption of bonds, see Const. Art. 13, § 3.
Consolidation of elections, see Elections Code § 10400 et seq.
Necessity of compliance with this article before issue of bonds, see Education Code § 18530.
Unsold bonds, issuance and sale for purposes of this section, see Education Code § 18555.

§ 18510. Calling election and submission of proposition as to issuance and sale of bonds

The board of trustees of any union high school library district may, when in its judgment it is deemed advisable, and shall upon a petition of 50 or more taxpayers and residents of the library district, call an election and submit to the electors of the district the proposition of whether the bonds of the district shall be issued and sold for the purpose of raising money for any or all of the following purposes:

(a) The purchase of suitable lots.

(b) Procuring plans and specifications and erecting a suitable building.

(c) Furnishing and equipping the building and fencing and ornamenting the grounds, for the accommodation of the union high school library.

(d) Any or all of the purposes of this chapter.

(e) Liquidating any indebtedness incurred for the purposes.

(f) Refunding any outstanding valid indebtedness evidenced by bonds or warrants of the district.

(Stats.1976, c. 1010, § 2, operative April 30, 1977.)

Historical and Statutory Notes

Derivation: Educ.C.1959, § 28401 (Stats. 1959, c. 2, p. 1487, § 28401).

Educ.C.1943, § 23001 (Stats.1943, c. 71, p. 762).

School C. § 6.670.

Stats.1911, c. 279, p. 471, § 18.

West's California Code Forms

See West's Cal. Code Forms, Educ. § 18510—FORM 1.

Cross References

Ballot requirements, see Education Code § 15123.
Bonds,
    Generally, see Education Code § 15100 et seq.
    Elections, inclusions in elections costs, see Education Code § 5420.
    Issuance by school districts, see Const. Art. 9, § 6 1/2.
    Tax exemption of bonds, see Const. Art. 13, § 3.
Consolidation of elections, see Elections Code § 10400 et seq.
Unsold bonds, issuance and sale for purposes of this section, see Education Code § 18555.

Library References

Schools ☞97.
Westlaw Topic No. 345.
C.J.S. Schools and School Districts §§ 522 to 524, 527 to 529.

Additional References

Cal Digest of Official Reports 3d Series, Public Securities and Obligations § 4.

§ 18511. Costs included in determining the amount of bonds to be issued and sold

In determining the amount of bonds to be issued and sold, the board of trustees may include:

(a) Legal or other fees incidental to or connected with the authorization, issuance and sale of the bonds.

(b) The costs of printing the bonds and other costs and expenses incidental to or connected with the authorization, issuance and sale of the bonds.

If such a determination is made, the proceeds of the sale of the bonds may be used to pay such costs and fees.

(Stats.1976, c. 1010, § 2, operative April 30, 1977.)

Historical and Statutory Notes

Derivation: Educ.C.1959, § 28401.1, added by Stats.1968, c. 220, p. 528, § 1, eff. May 29, 1968.

Cross References

Ballot requirements, see Education Code § 15123.
Bonds,
    Generally, see Education Code § 15100 et seq.
    Elections, inclusions in elections costs, see Education Code § 5420.
    Issuance by school districts, see Const. Art. 9, § 6 1/2.
    Tax exemption of bonds, see Const. Art. 13, § 3.
Consolidation of elections, see Elections Code § 10400 et seq.
Unsold bonds, issuance and sale for purposes of this section, see Education Code § 18555.

Library References

Additional References
Cal Digest of Official Reports 3d Series, Public Securities and Obligations § 4.

§ 18512. Repealed by Stats.1987, c. 1452, § 94

Historical and Statutory Notes

The repealed section, enacted by Stats.1976, c. 1010, § 2, derived from Educ.C.1959, § 28402, enacted by Stats.1959, c. 2, § 28402, amended by Stats.1968, c. 220, § 2; Educ.C. 1943, § 23002, enacted by Stats.1943, c. 71; School C. § 6.680; and Stats.1911, c. 279, § 19, related to the hours the poll must be open.

Legislative findings, declarations and intent relating to Stats.1987, c. 1452, see Historical and Statutory Notes under Education Code § 1007.

§ 18513. Method of voting

Voting shall be by ballot, without reference to the general election law in regard to form of ballot or manner of voting, except that the words to appear on the ballot shall be "Bonds—Yes" and "Bonds—No." Persons voting at the bond election shall put a cross (+) upon their ballot with pencil or ink, after the words "Bonds—Yes" or "Bonds—No," as the case may be, to indicate whether they have voted for or against the issuance of the bonds. The ballot shall be handed by the elector voting to the inspector, who shall then, in his presence, deposit it in the ballot box, and the judges shall enter the elector's name on the poll list.

(Stats.1976, c. 1010, § 2, operative April 30, 1977.)

Historical and Statutory Notes

Derivation: Educ.C.1959, § 28403 (Stats. 1959, c. 2, p. 1487, § 28403).
Educ.C.1943, § 23003 (Stats.1943, c. 71, p. 762).

School C. § 6.681.
Stats.1911, c. 279, p. 471, § 19.

Cross References

Ballot requirements, see Education Code § 15123.
Bonds,
    Generally, see Education Code § 15100 et seq.
    Elections, inclusions in elections costs, see Education Code § 5420.

Bonds—Cont'd
    Issuance by school districts, see Const. Art. 9, § 6 1/2.
    Tax exemption of bonds, see Const. Art. 13, § 3.
Consolidation of elections, see Elections Code § 10400 et seq.
Unsold bonds, issuance and sale for purposes of this section, see Education Code § 18555.

Library References

Additional References

Cal Digest of Official Reports 3d Series, Public Securities and Obligations § 4.

§ 18514.   Repealed by Stats.1987, c. 1452, § 95

Historical and Statutory Notes

The repealed section, enacted by Stats.1976, c. 1010, § 2, derived from Educ.C.1959, § 28404, enacted by Stats.1959, c. 2, § 28404; Educ.C.1943, § 23004, enacted by Stats.1943, c. 71; School C. § 6.682; and Stats.1911, c. 279, § 20, related to canvassing the returns the seventh day after the election.

Legislative findings, declarations and intent relating to Stats.1987, c. 1452, see Historical and Statutory Notes under Education Code § 1007.

§ 18515.   Favorable vote

If it appears that two-thirds of the votes cast at the election are in favor of issuing the bonds, the board shall cause an entry of the fact to be made upon its minutes and shall certify to the board of supervisors of the county all the proceedings had in the premises.

(Stats.1976, c. 1010, § 2, operative April 30, 1977.)

Historical and Statutory Notes

Derivation: Educ.C.1959, § 28405 (Stats. 1959, c. 2, p. 1487, § 28405).

Educ.C.1943, § 23005 (Stats.1943, c. 71, p. 762).

School C. § 6.683.

Stats.1911, c. 279, p. 471, § 20.

Cross References

Ballot requirements, see Education Code § 15123.
Board of supervisors, see Government Code §§ 25000, 25003 et seq.
Bonds,
    Generally, see Education Code § 15100 et seq.
    Elections, inclusions in elections costs, see Education Code § 5420.
    Issuance by school districts, see Const. Art. 9, § 6 1/2.
    Tax exemption of bonds, see Const. Art. 13, § 3.
Consolidation of elections, see Elections Code § 10400 et seq.
Unsold bonds, issuance and sale for purposes of this section, see Education Code § 18555.

Library References

Additional References

Cal Digest of Official Reports 3d Series, Public Securities and Obligations § 4.

§§ 18516, 18517. Repealed by Stats.1987, c. 1452, §§ 96, 97

Historical and Statutory Notes

Section 18516, enacted by Stats.1976, c. 1010, § 2, derived from Educ.C.1959, § 28406, added by Stats.1968, c. 220, § 2.5, related to notice of elections.

Section 18517, enacted by Stats.1976, c. 1010, § 2, amended by Stats.1977, c. 1205, § 20, derived from Educ.C.1959, § 28407, add-ed by Stats.1968, c. 220, § 3, related to consolidated elections.

Legislative findings, declarations and intent relating to Stats.1987, c. 1452, see Historical and Statutory Notes under Education Code § 1007.

§ 18518. Taxpayers' substantial rights affected to invalidate election

No error, irregularity, or omission which does not affect the substantial rights of the taxpayers within the district or the electors voting at any election at which bonds of any district are authorized to be issued shall invalidate the election or any bonds authorized by such election.

(Stats.1976, c. 1010, § 2, operative April 30, 1977.)

Historical and Statutory Notes

Derivation: Educ.C.1959, § 28408, added by Stats.1968, c. 220, p. 529, § 4.

Cross References

Ballot requirements, see Education Code § 15123.
Bonds,
    Generally, see Education Code § 15100 et seq.
    Elections, inclusions in elections costs, see Education Code § 5420.
    Issuance by school districts, see Const. Art. 9, § 6 1/2.
    Tax exemption of bonds, see Const. Art. 13, § 3.
Consolidation of elections, see Elections Code § 10400 et seq.
Unsold bonds, issuance and sale for purposes of this section, see Education Code § 18555.

Library References

Additional References

Cal Digest of Official Reports 3d Series, Public Securities and Obligations § 4.

Article 13

ISSUANCE AND SALE OF BONDS

Section
18530.	Issuance of bonds.
18531.	Restriction on total amount of bonds issued.
18532.	Interest.
18533.	Form of bonds and interest coupons.
18534.	Time of payment.
18534.3.	Division into series bonds.
18534.5.	Redemption prior to maturity.
18535.	Sale of bonds.
18536.	Deposits and withdrawal of proceeds.

Article 13 was enacted by Stats.1976, c. 1010, § 2, operative April 30, 1977.

Cross References

Bonds,
> Generally, see Education Code § 15100 et seq.
> Issuance by school districts, see Const. Art. 9, § 6 1/2.
> Tax exemption of bonds, see Const. Art. 13, § 3.

§ 18530. Issuance of bonds

After the provisions of Sections 18510 to 18515, inclusive, have been complied with, the board of supervisors shall issue the bonds of the district, to the number and amount provided in the proceedings, payable out of the building fund of the district, naming it, and the money shall be raised by taxation upon the taxable property in the district, for the redemption of the bonds and the payment of the interest thereon.

(Stats.1976, c. 1010, § 2, operative April 30, 1977.)

Historical and Statutory Notes

Derivation: Educ.C.1959, § 28451 (Stats. 1959, c. 2, p. 1488, § 28451).

Educ.C.1943, § 23021 (Stats.1943, c. 71, p. 762).

School C. § 6.690.

Stats.1911, c. 279, p. 471, § 20.

Cross References

Board of supervisors, see Government Code §§ 25000, 25003 et seq.
Bonds,
> Generally, see Education Code § 15100 et seq.
> Issuance by school districts, see Const. Art. 9, § 6 1/2.
> Tax exemption of bonds, see Const. Art. 13, § 3.

Library References

Schools ⊂⇒97.
Westlaw Topic No. 345.

C.J.S. Schools and School Districts §§ 522 to 524, 527 to 529.

§ 18531. Restriction on total amount of bonds issued

The total amount of bonds issued, shall not exceed 5 percent of the taxable property of the district, as shown by the last equalized assessment book of the county.

(Stats.1976, c. 1010, § 2, operative April 30, 1977.)

Historical and Statutory Notes

Derivation: Educ.C.1959, § 28452 (Stats. 1959, c. 2, p. 1488, § 28452).

Educ.C.1943, § 23022 (Stats.1943, c. 71, p. 763).

School C. § 6.691.

Stats.1911, c. 279, p. 471, § 20.

Cross References

Bonds,
> Generally, see Education Code § 15100 et seq.
> Issuance by school districts, see Const. Art. 9, § 6 1/2.
> Tax exemption of bonds, see Const. Art. 13, § 3.

Notes of Decisions

Purpose 1

_____

1. **Purpose**

The purpose of statutes limiting debts which may be incurred by governmental units is to protect taxpayers from confiscatory taxation, and such statutes must be construed with reference to evil which legislature sought to remedy in enacting them. Pacific Gas & Elec. Co. v. Shasta Dam Area Public Utility Dist. (App. 1955) 135 Cal.App.2d 463, 287 P.2d 841.

§ 18532. Interest

The bonds shall not bear a rate of interest greater than 8 percent, payable annually or semiannually.

(Stats.1976, c. 1010, § 2, operative April 30, 1977.)

Historical and Statutory Notes

Derivation: Educ.C.1959, § 28453 (Stats. 1959, c. 2, p. 1488, § 28453, amended by Stats. 1969, c. 600, p. 1231, § 3; Stats.1975, c. 130, p. 213, § 4).

Educ.C.1943, § 23023 (Stats.1943, c. 71, p. 763).

School C. § 6.691.

Stats.1911, c. 279, p. 471, § 20.

Library References

Additional References

Cal Digest of Official Reports 3d Series, Public Securities and Obligations § 9.

§ 18533. Form of bonds and interest coupons

The board of supervisors by an order entered upon its minutes shall prescribe the form of the bonds and of the interest coupons attached thereto.

(Stats.1976, c. 1010, § 2, operative April 30, 1977.)

Historical and Statutory Notes

Derivation: Educ.C.1959, § 28454 (Stats. 1959, c. 2, p. 1488, § 28454).

Educ.C.1943, § 23024 (Stats.1943, c. 71, p. 763).

School C. § 6.693.

Stats.1911, c. 279, p. 472, § 21.

Cross References

Board of supervisors, see Government Code §§ 25000, 25003 et seq.
Bonds,
    Generally, see Education Code § 15100 et seq.
    Issuance by school districts, see Const. Art. 9, § 6 1/2.
    Tax exemption of bonds, see Const. Art. 13, § 3.

§ 18534. Time of payment

The board of supervisors by an order entered upon its minutes shall fix the time when the whole or any part of the principal of the bonds will be payable, which shall not be more than 40 years from the date thereof.

(Stats.1976, c. 1010, § 2, operative April 30, 1977.)

Historical and Statutory Notes

Derivation: Educ.C.1959, § 28455 (Stats. 1959, c. 2, p. 1488, § 28455).

Educ.C.1943, § 23025 (Stats.1943, c. 71, p. 763).

School C. § 6.694.

Stats.1911, c. 279, p. 472, § 21.

Cross References

Board of supervisors, see Government Code §§ 25000, 25003 et seq.

§ 18534.3.   Division into series bonds

The board of supervisors may divide the principal amount of any issue into two or more series and fix different dates for the bonds of each series. The bonds of one series may be made payable at different times from those of any other series.

(Added by Stats.1977, c. 36, § 408, eff. April 29, 1977.)

Historical and Statutory Notes

Derivation: Educ.C.1959, § 28455.1, added by Stats.1976, c. 422, § 1.

Cross References

Board of supervisors, see Government Code §§ 25000, 25003 et seq.
Bonds,
    Generally, see Education Code § 15100 et seq.
    Issuance by school districts, see Const. Art. 9, § 6 1/2.
    Tax exemption of bonds, see Const. Art. 13, § 3.

§ 18534.5.   Redemption prior to maturity

The board of supervisors may provide for redemption of bonds before maturity at prices determined by it. A bond shall not be subject to call or redemption prior to maturity unless it contains a recital to that effect.

(Added by Stats.1977, c. 36, § 409, eff. April 29, 1977.)

Historical and Statutory Notes

Derivation: Educ.C.1959, § 28455.2, added by Stats.1976, c. 422, § 2.

Cross References

Board of supervisors, see Government Code §§ 25000, 25003 et seq.

§ 18535.   Sale of bonds

The bonds shall be sold in the manner prescribed by the board of supervisors, but for not less than 95 percent of par.

(Stats.1976, c. 1010, § 2, operative April 30, 1977. Amended by Stats.1977, c. 36, § 74, eff. April 29, 1977.)

Historical and Statutory Notes

Derivation: Educ.C.1959, § 28456 (Stats. 1959, c. 2, p. 1488, § 28456).

Educ.C.1943, § 23026 (Stats.1943, c. 71, p. 763).

School C. § 6.695.

Stats.1911, c. 279, p. 472, § 22.

Cross References

Board of supervisors, see Government Code §§ 25000, 25003 et seq.
Bonds,
Generally, see Education Code § 15100 et seq.
Issuance by school districts, see Const. Art. 9, § 6 1/2.
Tax exemption of bonds, see Const. Art. 13, § 3.

Library References

Schools ⟨key⟩97.
Westlaw Topic No. 345.

C.J.S. Schools and School Districts §§ 522 to 524, 527 to 529.

§ 18536. Deposits and withdrawal of proceeds

The proceeds of the sale of the bonds shall be deposited in the county treasury to the credit of the building fund of the library district, and shall be drawn out for the purposes for which the bonds were issued as other library money is drawn out.

(Stats.1976, c. 1010, § 2, operative April 30, 1977.)

Historical and Statutory Notes

Derivation: Educ.C.1959, § 28457 (Stats. 1959, c. 2, p. 1488, § 28457).

Educ.C.1943, § 23027 (Stats.1943, c. 71, p. 763).

School C. § 6.696.

Stats.1911, c. 279, p. 472, § 22.

Cross References

County treasurer, see Government Code § 27000 et seq.
Disbursement of library funds, see Education Code § 18493.

Article 14

CANCELLATION OF BONDS

Section
18550. Petition for withdrawal and cancellation of unsold bonds.
18551. Notice of hearing on petition.
18552. Hearing and order for cancellation.
18553. Effect of cancellation order.

Article 14 was enacted by Stats.1976, c. 1010, § 2, operative April 30, 1977.

Cross References

Bonds,
Generally, see Education Code § 15100 et seq.
Issuance by school districts, see Const. Art. 9, § 6 1/2.
Tax exemption of bonds, see Const. Art. 13, § 3.

§ 18550. Petition for withdrawal and cancellation of unsold bonds

Whenever any bonds issued under the provisions of this chapter remain unsold for the period of six months after having been offered for sale in the manner prescribed by the board of supervisors, the board of trustees of the library district for or on account of which the bonds were issued, or of any library district composed wholly or partly of territory which, at the time of holding the election authorizing the issuance of the bonds, was embraced within the district for or on account of which the bonds were issued, may petition the board of supervisors to cause the unsold bonds to be withdrawn from market and canceled.

(Stats.1976, c. 1010, § 2, operative April 30, 1977.)

Historical and Statutory Notes

Derivation: Educ.C.1959, § 28501 (Stats. 1959, c. 2, p. 1488, § 28501).

Educ.C.1943, § 23051 (Stats.1943, c. 71, p. 763).

School C. § 6.720.

Stats.1911, c. 279, p. 472, § 24.

Cross References

Board of supervisors, see Government Code §§ 25000, 25003 et seq.
Bonds,
    Generally, see Education Code § 15100 et seq.
    Issuance by school districts, see Const. Art. 9, § 6 1/2.
    Tax exemption of bonds, see Const. Art. 13, § 3.

Library References

Schools ☞97.
Westlaw Topic No. 345.

C.J.S. Schools and School Districts §§ 522 to 524, 527 to 529.

§ 18551. Notice of hearing on petition

Upon receiving the petition, signed by a majority of the members of the board of trustees, the supervisors shall fix a time for hearing the petition, which shall not be more than 30 days thereafter, and shall cause a notice, stating the time and place of hearing, and the object of the petition in general terms, to be published for 10 days prior to the day of hearing in a newspaper published in the library district, if there is one, and if there is no newspaper published in the library district, then in a newspaper published at the county seat of the county in which the library district or part thereof is situated.

(Stats.1976, c. 1010, § 2, operative April 30, 1977.)

Historical and Statutory Notes

Derivation: Educ.C.1959, § 28502 (Stats. 1959, c. 2, p. 1488, § 28502).

Educ.C.1943, § 23052 (Stats.1943, c. 71, p. 763).

School C. § 6.721.

Stats.1911, c. 279, p. 472, § 24.

Cross References

Library districts, see Education Code § 19400 et seq.
Publication, generally, see Government Code § 6000 et seq.

§ 18552. Hearing and order for cancellation

At the time and place designated in the notice for hearing the petition, or at any subsequent time to which the hearing may be postponed, the supervisors shall hear any reasons that may be submitted for or against the granting of the petition, and if they deem it for the best interests of the library district named in the petition that the unsold bonds be canceled, they shall make and enter an order in the minutes of their proceedings that the unsold bonds be canceled.

(Stats.1976, c. 1010, § 2, operative April 30, 1977.)

Historical and Statutory Notes

Derivation: Educ.C.1959, § 28503 (Stats. 1959, c. 2, p. 1489, § 28503).

Educ.C.1943, § 23053 (Stats.1943, c. 71, p. 763).

School C. § 6.722.

Stats.1911, c. 279, p. 472, § 24.

Cross References

Library districts, see Education Code § 19400 et seq.

§ 18553. Effect of cancellation order

Thereupon the bonds and the vote by which they were authorized to be issued, shall cease to be of any validity whatever.

(Stats.1976, c. 1010, § 2, operative April 30, 1977.)

Historical and Statutory Notes

Derivation: Educ.C.1959, § 28504 (Stats. 1959, c. 2, p. 1489, § 28504).

Educ.C.1943, § 23054 (Stats.1943, c. 71, p. 764).

School C. § 6.723.

Stats.1911, c. 279, p. 472, § 24.

Cross References

Publication, generally, see Government Code § 6000 et seq.

Article 14.5

SALE OF UNSOLD BONDS

Section
18555.   Issuance of unsold bonds.
18556.   Notice of hearing.
18557.   Hearing and granting request.
18558.   Submission to voters.

Article 14.5 was added by Stats.1977, c. 36, § 410, eff. April 29, 1977.

Cross References

Board of supervisors, see Government Code §§ 25000, 25003 et seq.
Bonds,
    Generally, see Education Code § 15100 et seq.
    Issuance by school districts, see Const. Art. 9, § 6 1/2.
    Tax exemption of bonds, see Const. Art. 13, § 3.

§ 18555. Issuance of unsold bonds

When the board of trustees of the library district determines that the purpose and object of the bonds has been accomplished, it may request the board of

supervisors to cause any unsold bonds to be issued and sold and the proceeds thereof used for any or all of the purposes set forth in Section 18510.
(Added by Stats.1977, c. 36, § 410, eff. April 29, 1977.)

Historical and Statutory Notes

Derivation: Educ.C.1959, § 28520, added by Stats.1976, c. 422, § 4.

Cross References

Bonds,
    Generally, see Education Code § 15100 et seq.
    Issuance by school districts, see Const. Art. 9, § 6 1/2.
    Tax exemption of bonds, see Const. Art. 13, § 3.

§ 18556. Notice of hearing

Upon receiving the request, signed by a majority of the members of the board of trustees, the supervisors shall fix a time for hearing the request, which shall not be more than 30 days thereafter, and shall cause a notice, stating the time and place of hearing, and the object of the request in general terms, to be published for 10 days prior to the day of hearing in a newspaper published in the library district, if there is one, and if there is no newspaper published in the library district, then in a newspaper published at the county seat of the county in which the library district or part thereof is situated.
(Added by Stats.1977, c. 36, § 410, eff. April 29, 1977.)

Historical and Statutory Notes

Derivation: Educ.C.1959, § 28521, added by Stats.1976, c. 422, § 4.

Cross References

Publication, generally, see Government Code § 6000 et seq.

§ 18557. Hearing and granting request

At the time and place designated in the notice for hearing the request, or at any subsequent time to which the hearing may be postponed, the supervisors shall hear any reasons that may be submitted for or against the granting of the request. If, before the conclusion of the hearing, a petition signed by registered voters within the district equal to not less than 10 percent of the vote cast within the boundaries of the district for all candidates for governor at the last gubernatorial election requesting an election is not filed, the board of supervisors may, if they determine it to be for the best interests of the library district, grant the request. In such event, they shall make and enter an order in the minutes of their proceedings that the unsold bonds shall be sold and the proceeds used for the purposes specified in the request.
(Added by Stats.1977, c. 36, § 410, eff. April 29, 1977.)

Historical and Statutory Notes

Derivation: Educ.C.1959, § 28522, added by Stats.1976, c. 422, § 4.

§ 18558. Submission to voters

In the event a petition, as set forth in Section 18557, is filed, the board of supervisors shall not grant the request without first submitting the question to the voters in the same manner and with the same effect as provided for a referendum by the electors of a district pursuant to Section 9340 of the Elections Code.

(Added by Stats.1977, c. 36, § 410, eff. April 29, 1977. Amended by Stats.1994, c. 923 (S.B.1546), § 24.)

Historical and Statutory Notes

Subordination of legislation by Stats.1994, c. 923 (S.B.1546), see Historical and Statutory Notes under Code of Civil Procedure § 203.

Derivation: Educ.C.1959, § 28523, added by Stats.1976, c. 422, § 4.

Cross References

Initiative and referendum, generally, see Const. Art. 2, §§ 8 to 11, Const. Art. 4, § 1 and Election Code § 9000 et seq.

Article 15

TAX FOR INTEREST AND REDEMPTION OF BONDS

Section
18560.   Tax levy.
18561.   Amount of tax.
18562.   Deposit and use of money collected.

Article 15 was enacted by Stats.1976, c. 1010, § 2, operative April 30, 1977.

§ 18560. Tax levy

The board of supervisors, at the time of making a levy of taxes for county purposes, shall levy a tax for that year upon the taxable property in the district, at the equalized assessed value thereof for that year, for the interest and redemption of the bonds.

(Stats.1976, c. 1010, § 2, operative April 30, 1977.)

Historical and Statutory Notes

Derivation: Educ.C.1959, § 28551 (Stats. 1959, c. 2, p. 1489, § 28551).
Educ.C.1943, § 23071 (Stats.1943, c. 71, p. 764).

School C. § 6.700.
Stats.1911, c. 279, p. 472, § 23.

Cross References

Board of supervisors, see Government Code §§ 25000, 25003 et seq.
Tax levies, see Government Code § 29100 et seq. and Revenue and Taxation Code § 2151 et seq.

Library References

Schools ☜99.
Westlaw Topic No. 345.

C.J.S. Schools and School Districts §§ 558 to 560, 571.

§ 18561. Amount of tax

The tax shall not be less than sufficient to pay the interest of the bonds for that year, and such portion of the principal as is to become due during the year. In any event the tax shall be high enough to raise, annually, for the first half of the term the bonds have to run, a sufficient sum to pay the interest thereon, and, during the balance of the term, high enough to pay the annual interest, and to pay annually, a proportion of the principal of the bonds equal to a sum produced by taking the whole amount of the bonds outstanding and dividing it by the number of years the bonds then have to run.

(Stats.1976, c. 1010, § 2, operative April 30, 1977.)

Historical and Statutory Notes

Derivation: Educ.C.1959, § 28552 (Stats. 1959, c. 2, p. 1489, § 28552).

Educ.C.1943, § 23072 (Stats.1943, c. 71, p. 764).

School C. § 6.701.

Stats.1911, c. 279, p. 472, § 23.

Cross References

Tax levies, see Government Code § 29100 et seq. and Revenue and Taxation Code § 2151 et seq.
Taxes, special taxes imposed on behalf of public libraries, authority of cities, counties and other agencies, see Government Code § 53717.

§ 18562. Deposit and use of money collected

All money levied, when collected, shall be paid into the county treasury to the credit of the library district, and be used for the payment of principal and interest on the bonds, and for no other purpose.

(Stats.1976, c. 1010, § 2, operative April 30, 1977.)

Historical and Statutory Notes

Derivation: Educ.C.1959, § 28553 (Stats. 1959, c. 2, p. 1489, § 28553).

Educ.C.1943, § 23073 (Stats.1943, c. 71, p. 764).

School C. § 6.702.

Stats.1911, c. 279, p. 472, § 23.

Cross References

County treasurer, see Government Code § 27000 et seq.

Article 16

PAYMENT OF INTEREST AND BONDS

Section
18570. Payment of principal and interest.
18571. Cancellation of bonds.

Article 16 was enacted by Stats.1976, c. 1010, § 2, operative April 30, 1977.

Bonds,
   Generally, see Education Code § 15100 et seq.
   Issuance by school districts, see Const. Art. 9, § 6 1/2.
   Tax exemption of bonds, see Const. Art. 13, § 3.
County auditor, see Government Code § 26900 et seq.
County treasurer, see Government Code § 27000 et seq.

§ 18570.   Payment of principal and interest

The principal and interest on the bonds shall be paid by the county treasurer, upon the warrant of the county auditor, out of the fund provided therefor. (Stats.1976, c. 1010, § 2, operative April 30, 1977.)

Historical and Statutory Notes

Derivation: Educ.C.1959,   § 28651   (Stats. 1959, c. 2, p. 1489, § 28651).
   Educ.C.1943, § 23101 (Stats.1943, c. 71, p. 764).

School C. § 6.710.

Stats.1911, c. 279, p. 472, § 23.

Cross References

County warrants, see Government Code § 29800 et seq.
Issuance of warrant by auditor, see Government Code § 29742.

Library References

Legal Jurisprudences
   Am Jur 2d Public Securities and Obligations
      §§ 399 et seq.

§ 18571.   Cancellation of bonds

The county auditor shall cancel and file with the county treasurer the bonds and coupons as rapidly as they are paid. (Stats.1976, c. 1010, § 2, operative April 30, 1977.)

Historical and Statutory Notes

Derivation: Educ.C.1959,   § 28652   (Stats. 1959, c. 2, p. 1489, § 28652).
   Educ.C.1943, § 23102 (Stats.1943, c. 71, p. 764).

School C. § 6.711.

Stats.1911, c. 279, p. 472, § 23.

Cross References

Bonds,
   Generally, see Education Code § 15100 et seq.
   Issuance by school districts, see Const. Art. 9, § 6 1/2.
   Tax exemption of bonds, see Const. Art. 13, § 3.
Hearing and order for cancellation, see Education Code § 19532.
Petition for withdrawal and cancellation of unsold bonds, see Education Code § 19530.

Chapter 4

CALIFORNIA LIBRARY SERVICES ACT

Chapter 4 was added by Stats.1977, c. 1255, § 2.

Former Chapter 4, Public Library Services, consisting of §§ 18700 to 18772, enacted by Stats.1976, c. 1010, § 2, was repealed by Stats.1977, c. 1255, § 1.

Repeal

Chapter 4, California Library Services Act, is repealed upon replacement of its provisions by Chapter 4.5, Library of California Act, under the terms of Education Code § 18870.

Code of Regulations References

Library services, detailed analysis, see 5 Cal. Code of Regs. § 20100 et seq.
Public library affiliation with an existing system, see 5 Cal. Code of Regs. § 20190.

Article 1

GENERAL PROVISIONS

Section
18700.   Short title.
18701.   Legislative findings and declarations.
18702.   Legislative intent.
18703.   Legislative policy.

Article 1 was added by Stats.1977, c. 1255, § 2.

Repeal

Chapter 4, California Library Services Act, is repealed upon replacement of its provisions by Chapter 4.5, Library of California Act, under the terms of Education Code § 18870.

Code of Regulations References

Library services, detailed analysis, see 5 Cal. Code of Regs. § 20100 et seq.
Public library affiliation with an existing system, see 5 Cal. Code of Regs. § 20190.

§ 18700.   Short title

This chapter shall be known as the California Library Services Act.

(Added by Stats.1977, c. 1255, § 2.)

Historical and Statutory Notes

Former § 18700, enacted by Stats.1976, c. 1010, § 2, which stated the legislative declaration, was repealed by Stats.1977, c. 1255, § 1. See Education Code § 18701.

Code of Regulations References

Library services, detailed analysis, see 5 Cal. Code of Regs. § 20100 et seq.
Public library affiliation with an existing system, see 5 Cal. Code of Regs. § 20190.

Library References

Legal Jurisprudences
Cal Jur 3d Sch § 333.

§ 18701. Legislative findings and declarations

The Legislature finds and declares that it is in the interest of the people of the state to insure that all people have free and convenient access to all library resources and services that might enrich their lives, regardless of where they live or of the tax base of their local government.

This finding is based on the recognition that:

(a) The public library is a primary source of information, recreation, and education to persons of all ages, any location or any economic circumstance.

(b) The expansion of knowledge and the increasing complexity of our society create needs for materials and information which go beyond the ability of any one library to provide.

(c) The public libraries of California are supported primarily by local taxes. The ability of local governments to provide adequate service is dependent on the taxable wealth of each local jurisdiction and varies widely throughout the state.

(d) Public libraries are unable to bear the greater costs of meeting the exceptional needs of many residents, including the handicapped, non-English and limited English-speaking persons, those who are confined to home or in an institution, and those who are economically disadvantaged.

(e) The effective sharing of resources and services among the libraries of California requires an ongoing commitment by the state to compensate libraries for services beyond their clientele.

(f) The sharing of services and resources is most efficient when a common data base is available to provide information on where materials can be found.

(Added by Stats.1977, c. 1255, § 2.)

Historical and Statutory Notes

Former § 18701, enacted by Stats.1976, c. 1010, § 2, specifying legislative intent, was repealed by Stats.1977, c. 1255, § 1. See Education Code § 18702.

Derivation: Former § 18700, enacted by Stats.1976, c. 1010, § 2.

Educ.C.1959, § 27111, added by Stats.1963, c. 1802, p. 3630, § 1.

Educ.C.1959, § 27111.5, added by Stats.1966, 1st Ex.Sess., c. 97, p. 545, § 1.

Code of Regulations References

Library services, detailed analysis, see 5 Cal. Code of Regs. § 20100 et seq.
Public library affiliation with an existing system, see 5 Cal. Code of Regs. § 20190.

§ 18702. Legislative intent

It is the intent of the Legislature to provide all residents with the opportunity to obtain from their public libraries needed materials and informational services by facilitating access to the resources of all libraries in this state.

This policy shall be accomplished by assisting public libraries to improve service to the underserved of all ages, and by enabling public libraries to provide their users with the services and resources of all libraries in this state. (Added by Stats.1977, c. 1255, § 2.)

Repeal

Chapter 4, California Library Services Act, is repealed upon replacement of its provisions by Chapter 4.5, Library of California Act, under the terms of Education Code § 18870.

Historical and Statutory Notes

Former § 18702, enacted by Stats.1976, c. 1010, § 2, specifying legislative policy, was repealed by Stats.1977, c. 1255, § 1. See Education Code § 18703.

Derivation: Former § 18701, enacted by Stats.1976, c. 1010, § 2.

Cross References

Statutes,
   Construction and legislative intent, see Code of Civil Procedure §§ 1858 and 1859.
   Liberal construction of Education Code, see Education Code § 3.
   Rules of construction and definition for the Education Code, see Education Code § 10.

Code of Regulations References

Library services, detailed analysis, see 5 Cal. Code of Regs. § 20100 et seq.
Public library affiliation with an existing system, see 5 Cal. Code of Regs. § 20190.

§ 18703. Legislative policy

In adopting this chapter, the Legislature declares that its policy shall be:

(a) To reaffirm the principle of local control of the government and administration of public libraries, and to affirm that the provisions of this chapter apply only to libraries authorized by their jurisdictions to apply to participate in the programs authorized by this act.

(b) To require no library, as a condition for receiving funds or services under this chapter, to acquire or exclude any specific book, periodical, film, recording, picture, or other material, or any specific equipment, or to acquire or exclude any classification of books or other material by author, subject matter, or type.

(c) To encourage adequate financing of libraries from local sources, with state aid to be furnished to supplement, not supplant, local funds.

(d) To encourage service to the underserved of all ages.

(e) To encourage and enable the sharing of resources between libraries.

(f) To reimburse equitably any participating library for services it provides beyond its jurisdiction if a public library, or, if not a public library, beyond its normal clientele.

(g) To ensure public participation in carrying out the intent of this act.
(Added by Stats.1977, c. 1255, § 2.)

Repeal

Chapter 4, California Library Services Act, is repealed upon replacement of its provisions by Chapter 4.5, Library of California Act, under the terms of Education Code § 18870.

Historical and Statutory Notes

Derivation: Former § 18702, enacted by Stats.1976, c. 1010, § 2.

Educ.C.1959, §§ 27112, 27121, added by Stats.1963, c. 1802, pp. 3631, 3632 § 1.

Cross References

Local public library services, see Education Code § 18730.

Code of Regulations References

Library services, detailed analysis, see 5 Cal. Code of Regs. § 20100 et seq.
Public library affiliation with an existing system, see 5 Cal. Code of Regs. § 20190.

Article 2

DEFINITIONS

Section
18710. Definitions.

Article 2 was added by Stats.1977, c. 1255, § 2.

Repeal

Chapter 4, California Library Services Act, is repealed upon replacement of its provisions by Chapter 4.5, Library of California Act, under the terms of Education Code § 18870.

§ 18710. Definitions

As used in this chapter, unless the context otherwise indicates or unless specific exception is made:

(a) "Academic library" means a library established and maintained by a college or university to meet the needs of its students and faculty, and others by agreement.

(b) "Act" means the California Library Services Act.

(c) "Cooperative Library System" means a public library system that consists of two or more jurisdictions entering into a written agreement to implement a regional program in accordance with this chapter, and which, as of the effective date of this chapter, was designated a library system under the Public Library Services Act of 1963 or was a successor to such a library system.

(d) "Direct loan" means the lending of a book or other item directly to a borrower.

(e) "Equal access" means the right of the residents of jurisdictions that are members of a Cooperative Library System to use on an equal basis with one another the services and loan privileges of any and all other members of the same system.

(f) "Independent public library" means a public library not a member of a system.

(g) "Interlibrary loan" means the lending of a book or other item from one library to another as the result of a user request for the item.

(h) "Interlibrary reference" means the providing of information by one library or reference center to another library or reference center as the result of a user request for the information.

(i) "Jurisdiction" means a county, city and county, city, or any district that is authorized by law to provide public library services and that operates a public library.

(j) "Libraries for institutionalized persons" means libraries maintained by institutions for the purpose of serving their resident populations.

(k) "Net imbalance" means the disproportionate cost incurred under universal borrowing or equal access when a library directly lends a greater number of items to users from outside its jurisdiction than its residents directly borrow from libraries of other jurisdictions.

(*l*) "Public library" means a library, or two or more libraries, that is operated by a single public jurisdiction and that serves its residents free of charge.

(m) "School library" means an organized collection of printed and audiovisual materials that satisfies all of the following criteria:

(1) Is administered as a unit.

(2) Is located in a designated place.

(3) Makes printed, audiovisual, and other materials as well as necessary equipment and services of a staff accessible to elementary and secondary school students and teachers.

(n) "Special library" means one maintained by an association, government service, research institution, learned society, professional association, museum, business firm, industrial enterprise, chamber of commerce, or other organized group, the greater part of their collections being in a specific field or subject, e.g., natural sciences, economics, engineering, law, and history.

(*o*) "Special Services Programs" means a project establishing or improving service to the underserved of all ages.

(p) "State board" means the California Library Services Board.

(q) "System" means a cooperative library system.

(r) "Underserved" means any population segment with exceptional service needs not adequately met by traditional library service patterns; including, but not limited to, those persons who are geographically isolated, economically disadvantaged, functionally illiterate, of non-English-speaking or limited-English-speaking ability, shut-in, institutionalized, or handicapped.

(s) "Universal borrowing" means the extension by a public library of its direct loan privileges to the eligible borrowers of all other public libraries. (Added by Stats.1977, c. 1255, § 2. Amended by Stats.1987, c. 1452, § 98.)

Repeal

Chapter 4, California Library Services Act, is repealed upon replacement of its provisions by Chapter 4.5, Library of California Act, under the terms of Education Code § 18870.

Historical and Statutory Notes

Legislative findings, declarations and intent relating to Stats.1987, c. 1452, see Historical and Statutory Notes under Education Code § 1007.

Former § 18710, enacted by Stats.1976, c. 1010, § 2, listing definitions, was repealed by Stats.1977, c. 1255, § 1. See this section.

Derivation: Former § 18710, enacted by Stats.1976, c. 1010, § 2.

Educ.C.1959, § 27113, added by Stats.1963, c. 1802, p. 3631, § 1, amended by Stats.1972, c. 618, p. 1114, § 56.

Cross References

Crimes against public decency and good morals, distribution or exhibition to minors, public libraries, see Penal Code § 313.1.

Code of Regulations References

Interlibrary reference, see 5 Cal. Code of Regs. § 20157.
Library services, detailed analysis, see 5 Cal. Code of Regs. § 20100 et seq.
Public library affiliation with an existing system, see 5 Cal. Code of Regs. § 20190.
System reference, service components, see 5 Cal. Code of Regs. § 20154.

Notes of Decisions

Cooperative library systems   1
———

1. Cooperative library systems

Upon replacement of the California Library Services Act cooperative library system programs, a cooperative library system may continue to operate, with or without state funding, depending upon the particular circumstances present. Ops.Atty.Gen. No. 01–301 (July 11, 2001).

Article 3

ADMINISTRATION

Article 3 was added by Stats.1977, c. 1255, § 2.

Repeal

Chapter 4, California Library Services Act, is repealed upon replacement of its provisions by Chapter 4.5, Library of California Act, under the terms of Education Code § 18870.

§ 18720. California Library Services Board; establishment; members; terms of office

There is hereby established in the state government the California Library Services Board, to consist of 13 members. The Governor shall appoint nine members of the state board. Three of the Governor's appointments shall be representative of laypersons, one of whom shall represent the handicapped, one representing limited- and non-English-speaking persons, and one representing economically disadvantaged persons.

The Governor shall also appoint six members of the board, each of whom shall represent one of the following categories: school libraries, libraries for institutionalized persons, public library trustees or commissioners, public libraries, special libraries, and academic libraries.

The Legislature shall appoint the remaining four public members from persons who are not representative of categories mentioned in this section. Two shall be appointed by the Senate Rules Committee and two shall be appointed by the Speaker of the Assembly.

The terms of office of members of the state board shall be for four years and shall begin on January 1 of the year in which the respective terms are to start.

(Added by Stats.1977, c. 1255, § 2. Amended by Stats.1987, c. 1452, § 99.)

Repeal

Chapter 4, California Library Services Act, is repealed upon replacement of its provisions by Chapter 4.5, Library of California Act, under the terms of Education Code § 18870.

Historical and Statutory Notes

Legislative findings, declarations and intent relating to Stats.1987, c. 1452, see Historical and Statutory Notes under Education Code § 1007.

Former § 18720, enacted by Stats.1976, c. 1010, § 2, providing that the state librarian was to administer the chapter and prescribe rules and regulations, was repealed by Stats.1977, c. 1255, § 1. See Education Code § 18726.

Cross References

Appointments by Governor, public officers and employees, see Government Code § 1300 et seq.
Term of offices for public officers and employees and continuation thereof, see Government Code §§ 1301 and 1302.

Library board procedures, see 5 Cal. Code of Regs. § 20116 et seq.

§ 18721. Repealed by Stats.1987, c. 1452, § 100

Historical and Statutory Notes

The repealed section, added by Stats.1977, c. 1255, § 2, related to appointment of members to the board and their terms.

Legislative findings, declarations and intent relating to Stats.1987, c. 1452, see Historical and Statutory Notes under Education Code § 1007.

Former § 18721, enacted by Stats.1976, c. 1010, § 2, authorizing the state library to expend appropriated funds, was repealed by Stats. 1977, c. 1255, § 1. See Education Code § 18724.

§ 18722. Validation of board's acts

The concurrence of seven members of the state board shall be necessary to the validity of any of its acts.

(Added by Stats.1977, c. 1255, § 2.)

Repeal

Chapter 4, California Library Services Act, is repealed upon replacement of its provisions by Chapter 4.5, Library of California Act, under the terms of Education Code § 18870.

§ 18723. Compensation of members

Members of the state board shall serve without pay. They shall receive their actual and necessary traveling expenses while on official business.

(Added by Stats.1977, c. 1255, § 2.)

Repeal

Chapter 4, California Library Services Act, is repealed upon replacement of its provisions by Chapter 4.5, Library of California Act, under the terms of Education Code § 18870.

Cross References

Traveling expenses, state agency officers and employees, see Government Code § 11030 et seq.

§ 18724. Duties of the board

The duties of the state board shall be to adopt rules, regulations, and general policies for the implementation of this chapter. In addition, the state board, consistent with the terms and provisions of this chapter, shall have the following powers and duties:

(a) To direct the State Librarian in the administration of this chapter.

(b) To review for its approval all annual proposals submitted under this chapter.

(c) To annually submit budget proposals as part of the annual budget of the Department of Education.

(d) To expend the funds appropriated for the purpose of implementing the provisions of this chapter.

(e) To require participating libraries and systems to prepare and submit any reports and information which are necessary to carry out the provisions of this chapter, and to prescribe the form and manner for providing such reports and information.

(f) To develop formulas for the equitable allocation of reimbursements under Sections 18731, 18743, 18744, and 18765. Such formulas shall be submitted to the Department of Finance for approval.

(g) To require that any public library participating in programs authorized by this chapter provide access to its bibliographic records and materials location information consistent with the legislative policy of encouraging the sharing of resources between libraries.

(Added by Stats.1977, c. 1255, § 2. Amended by Stats.1978, c. 331, p. 680, § 2, eff. June 30, 1978; Stats.1979, c. 395, p. 1470, § 1, eff. July 27, 1979.)

Repeal

Chapter 4, California Library Services Act, is repealed upon replacement of its provisions by Chapter 4.5, Library of California Act, under the terms of Education Code § 18870.

Historical and Statutory Notes

Derivation: Former § 18721, enacted by Stats.1976, c. 1010, § 2.

Educ.C.1959, § 27114.1, added by Stats.1963, c. 1802, p. 3631, § 1.

Cross References

Administrative regulations and rulemaking, see Government Code § 11340 et seq.
Department of Finance, generally, see Government Code § 13000 et seq.
State librarian, see Education Code § 19302 et seq.

Code of Regulations References

Appropriating funds for each library system, see 5 Cal. Code of Regs. § 20158.
Definitions of reporting terms, see 5 Cal. Code of Regs. § 20235.
Library services, detailed analysis, see 5 Cal. Code of Regs. § 20100 et seq.

§ 18725.   State Advisory Council on Libraries

The state board shall serve as the State Advisory Council on Libraries for the purpose of meeting the requirements of the federal Library Services and Construction Act.

(Added by Stats.1977, c. 1255, § 2.)

Repeal

Chapter 4, California Library Services Act, is repealed upon replacement of its provisions by Chapter 4.5, Library of California Act, under the terms of Education Code § 18870.

United States Code Annotated

Library and information services, federal cooperation with State and local governments and public and private agencies to assure optimum provision of services, see 20 U.S.C.A. § 1501.

§ 18726. State Librarian; chief executive officer

The State Librarian shall be the chief executive officer of the state board for purposes of this chapter and shall:

(a) Make such reports and recommendations as may be required by the state board.

(b) Administer the provisions of this chapter.

(c) Review all claims to insure programmatic and technical compliance with the provisions of this chapter.

(Added by Stats.1977, c. 1255, § 2.)

Repeal

Chapter 4, California Library Services Act, is repealed upon replacement of its provisions by Chapter 4.5, Library of California Act, under the terms of Education Code § 18870.

Historical and Statutory Notes

Derivation: Former § 18720, enacted by Stats.1976, c. 1010, § 2.   Educ.C.1959, § 27114, added by Stats.1963, c. 1802, p. 3631, § 1.

Cross References

State librarian, see Education Code § 19302 et seq.

Article 4

LOCAL PUBLIC LIBRARY SERVICES

Article 4 was added by Stats.1977, c. 1255, § 2.

Repeal

Chapter 4, California Library Services Act, is repealed upon replacement of its provisions by Chapter 4.5, Library of California Act, under the terms of Education Code § 18870.

§ 18730. Applications for special services programs

Any public library or combination of public libraries may submit proposals to the state board for Special Services Programs within the service area. Applications shall identify the needs of the target service group, assess the capacity of the applicant library or libraries to respond to those needs, and shall identify the activities and timelines necessary to achieve those objectives. Funds may be expended for the development of collections to meet the needs of the underserved, together with the employment or retraining of staff necessary to properly utilize the collections, and to provide appropriate services to the underserved.

(Added by Stats.1977, c. 1255, § 2.)

Repeal

Chapter 4, California Library Services Act, is repealed upon replacement of its provisions by Chapter 4.5, Library of California Act, under the terms of Education Code § 18870.

Historical and Statutory Notes

Former § 18730, enacted by Stats.1976, c. 1010, § 2, derived from Educ.C.1959, § 27121, added by Stats.1963, c. 1802, p. 3632, § 1, specifying that there were no requirements of libraries to receive certain grants, was repealed by Stats.1977, c. 1255, § 1.

§ 18731. Universal borrowing

Any California public library may participate in universal borrowing. Public libraries participating in universal borrowing may not exclude the residents of any jurisdiction maintaining a public library. Public libraries that incur a net imbalance shall be reimbursed for the handling costs of the net loans according to the allocation formula developed pursuant to subdivision (f) of Section 18724. Reimbursement shall be incurred only for imbalances between:

(a) System member libraries and independent public libraries.

(b) Independent public libraries with each other.

(c) Member libraries of one system with member libraries of other systems.

(Added by Stats.1977, c. 1255, § 2. Amended by Stats.1987, c. 1452, § 101.)

Repeal

Chapter 4, California Library Services Act, is repealed upon replacement of its provisions by Chapter 4.5, Library of California Act, under the terms of Education Code § 18870.

Historical and Statutory Notes

Legislative findings, declarations and intent relating to Stats.1987, c. 1452, see Historical and Statutory Notes under Education Code § 1007.

Code of Regulations References

Direct loans, see 5 Cal. Code of Regs. § 20200.
Reimbursement for net direct loans, see 5 Cal. Code of Regs. § 20215.

§ 18732. Consolidation of two or more jurisdictions into a single library agency; establishment grants

If two or more public library jurisdictions wish to consolidate their libraries into a single library agency, an establishment grant in the annual maximum amount of twenty-thousand dollars ($20,000) shall be made to the newly consolidated library jurisdiction for each of two years, provided that notice of such consolidation is filed with the State Librarian within one year after the consolidation.

(Added by Stats.1977, c. 1255, § 2. Amended by Stats.1979, c. 395, p. 1471, § 2, eff. July 27, 1979.)

Repeal

Chapter 4, California Library Services Act, is repealed upon replacement of its provisions by Chapter 4.5, Library of California Act, under the terms of Education Code § 18870.

Historical and Statutory Notes

Derivation: Former § 18770, enacted by Stats.1976, c. 1010, § 2.   Educ.C.1959, § 27144, added by Stats.1963, c. 1802, § 1.

Cross References

Computation of time,
    Generally, see Code of Civil Procedure §§ 12 and 12a and Government Code § 6800 et seq.
    Time in which any act provided by the Education Code is to be done, see Education Code § 9.
Continuation of statutes relating to subjects covered by provisions of this Code, see Education Code
    § 3.
State Librarian,
    Generally, see Education Code § 19302 et seq.
    Powers and duties, see Education Code § 19320 et seq.

Code of Regulations References

Public library consolidations, see 5 Cal. Code of Regs. § 20180.

Article 4.2

CALIFORNIA LIBRARY LITERACY SERVICE

Section
18733.   Establishment; purpose.
18733.1. Eligibility for funding.
18733.2. Identification of program costs; apportionment of funds.
18733.3. Administrative support; technical services.

Article 4.2 was added by Stats.1990, c. 1095 (A.B.3381), § 2, eff. Sept. 20, 1990.

Repeal

Chapter 4, California Library Services Act, is repealed upon replacement of its provisions by Chapter 4.5, Library of California Act, under the terms of Education Code § 18870.

§ 18733. Establishment; purpose

The California Library Literacy Service is hereby established, as a public library services program designed to reduce adult illiteracy by providing English language literacy instruction and related services to adults and youth who are not enrolled in school. For purposes of this article, "English language literacy instruction" means the development of basic skills of reading and writing in the English language.

(Added by Stats.1990, c. 1095 (A.B.3381), § 2, eff. Sept. 20, 1990.)

Repeal

Chapter 4, California Library Services Act, is repealed upon replacement of its provisions by Chapter 4.5, Library of California Act, under the terms of Education Code § 18870.

§ 18733.1.　Eligibility for funding

(a) In order to be eligible for state funding under this article, a public library shall establish an adult literacy instructional program in accordance with this article, which shall provide adult basic literacy instruction and related services. Participant learning shall be evaluated on the basis of statewide guidelines established by the State Librarian.

(b) The public library shall do all of the following in establishing and implementing the program:

(1) Seek community and local government awarenes [1] of and support for the program and develop a local commitment of resources for the program's continuation.

(2) Develop cooperative relationships with other local literacy service providers and participate in existing community adult literacy coalitions, in order to address the wide variety of literacy needs of the community and ensure an effective utilization of resources. The public library shall assist in the establishment of a community adult literacy coalition where none currently exists.

(3) Recruit and train volunteers to provide tutoring and other services in public library and other community settings.

(Added by Stats.1990, c. 1095 (A.B.3381), § 2, eff. Sept. 20, 1990.)

[1] So in chaptered copy.

Repeal

Chapter 4, California Library Services Act, is repealed upon replacement of its provisions by Chapter 4.5, Library of California Act, under the terms of Education Code § 18870.

Cross References

State Librarian,
　Generally, see Education Code § 19302 et seq.
　Powers and duties, see Education Code § 19320 et seq.

§ 18733.2.　Identification of program costs; apportionment of funds

(a) Annually, the state board shall identify the program costs for which state funding apportioned under this article is authorized to be expended, based upon the stated purposes of this article and the amount of funding for those purposes made available by the Legislature. Annually, each public library seeking funding under this article for the subsequent fiscal year shall submit to the state board, for its review and approval, a plan of service describing its proposed operation of the adult literacy instructional program for the subsequent year, and a proposed budget for that program. The state board shall approve any submitted budget only to the extent the expenditures proposed by that budget qualify as program costs authorized under this subdivision.

(b) To the extent funding is made available by the Legislature for the purposes of this article, the State Librarian shall annually apportion, to each public library for which a plan of service and proposed budget are approved pursuant to subdivision (a), an amount equal to the following:

(1) For the first fiscal year of operation, 75 percent of the base operating budget for the program.

(2) For the second fiscal year of operation, 100 percent of the base operating budget for the program.

(3) For the third fiscal year of operation, 100 percent of the base operating budget for the program.

(4) For the fourth fiscal year of operation, 75 percent of the base operating budget for the program.

(5) For the fifth fiscal year of operation, 50 percent of the base operating budget for the program.

(6) For the sixth, and each subsequent, fiscal year of operation, a percentage, not to exceed 100 percent, of the amount of private and local public moneys available to that public library for the purposes of this article. To determine that percentage for any fiscal year, the state board shall divide the result of subparagraph (A) by the result of subparagraph (B), as follows:

(A) The amount of the state funding appropriated for the fiscal year for the purposes of this article that remains after the apportionment of state funding for that fiscal year under paragraphs (1) to (5), inclusive.

(B) The total amount of private and local public moneys available for the purposes of this article for that fiscal year that are identified in the budgets submitted for that fiscal year by all public libraries seeking state funding under this article for their sixth, or subsequent, fiscal year of operation.

(c) For purposes of this section, "base operating budget" means the program budget approved by the state board for a public library for the initial year of operating that program. For the purposes of any of paragraphs (2) to (5), inclusive, of subdivision (b), the state board, at the request of any public library, may adjust the amount of the "base operating budget" for that library to the extent the board deems necessary, pursuant to documentation provided by that library, to appropriately reduce adult illiteracy in that community in accordance with this article.

(Added by Stats.1990, c. 1095 (A.B.3381), § 2, eff. Sept. 20, 1990.)

Repeal

Chapter 4, California Library Services Act, is repealed upon replacement of its provisions by Chapter 4.5, Library of California Act, under the terms of Education Code § 18870.

§ 18733.3. Administrative support; technical services

The State Library shall provide administrative support and technical assistance to public libraries in the development and operation of the adult literacy instructional programs conducted by public libraries pursuant to this article. In addition, the State Library shall conduct and coordinate services in support of those programs, including, but not limited to, the following:

(a) Research, and dissemination of research, on the prevalence and characteristics of adult illiteracy and the efficacy of various basic literacy instructional strategies and methodologies.

(b) Enhancement of public education and awareness regarding adult literacy.

(c) Training of tutors and of persons who train tutors.

(d) Training of public library literacy staff in volunteer recruitment and the management of volunteer programs.

(Added by Stats.1990, c. 1095 (A.B.3381), § 2, eff. Sept. 20, 1990.)

Repeal

Chapter 4, California Library Services Act, is repealed upon replacement of its provisions by Chapter 4.5, Library of California Act, under the terms of Education Code § 18870.

Article 4.5

FAMILIES FOR LITERACY PROGRAM

Article 4.5 was added by Stats.1987, c. 1359, § 2.

Repeal

Chapter 4, California Library Services Act, is repealed upon replacement of its provisions by Chapter 4.5, Library of California Act, under the terms of Education Code § 18870.

Historical and Statutory Notes

Legislative findings, declarations and intent relating to Stats.1987, c. 1359, see Historical and Statutory Notes under Education Code § 18735.

§ 18735. Creation of program; purpose; provision of specified services and assistance

There is hereby created the Families for Literacy Program, a library services program with the purpose of preventing illiteracy through coordinated literacy and preliteracy services to families that include illiterate adults and young children. The program shall provide reading preparation services for young children in public library settings and shall instruct parents in reading to their children. In addition, the program shall provide technical assistance, parent support, and any resources and materials necessary for its implementation.
(Added by Stats.1987, c. 1359, § 2.)

Repeal

Chapter 4, California Library Services Act, is repealed upon replacement of its provisions by Chapter 4.5, Library of California Act, under the terms of Education Code § 18870.

Historical and Statutory Notes

Section 1 of Stats.1987, c. 1359, provides:

"(a) The Legislature finds and declares that there are an estimated 4.8 million California adults who are functionally illiterate. The Legislature further finds that illiteracy tends to be perpetuated in a cycle from parents to children and, therefore, that without intervention many children of illiterate adults in California are likely to become functionally illiterate.

"(b) The Legislature recognizes that a strong and frequent reason for illiterate adults to begin literacy training programs is to learn to read to their children so that they can prevent the probable illiteracy of their children.

"(c) In addition, the Legislature recognizes that between 1980 and 1985, the population of infants and young children under six increased by 25 percent from 2.04 to 2.55 million. Of these, 800,000 live in families below or near the poverty line.

"(d) The Legislature further recognizes that illiteracy can be prevented and that reading preparation activities, whereby young children are read to and exposed to books by their parents are effective measures toward preventing future reading difficulties. Illiterate parents can also improve their own reading skills through reading to their children. In addition, parents and children learning together can provide units of mutual support. The Legislature further recognizes that the public library literacy services of the California Literacy Campaign are currently reaching thousands of illiterate adults throughout California, and the habit of public library use as children is the most significant correlate of adult library use.

"(e) It is the intent of the Legislature in enacting this article to establish a library services program that is directed to breaking the "cycle of illiteracy" through coordinated literacy and preliteracy services to families that include illiterate adults and young children."

§ 18735.1. Eligible libraries; eligible families

To be eligible to receive funding for the Families for Literacy Program, a public library shall meet all of the following requirements:

(a) Is currently offering literacy services.

(b) Agrees to offer new services to families with young children with the goal of helping the children become successful readers by increasing their general competence, self-confidence, and positive emotional associations with reading as a family experience and familiarity with the lifelong use of library resources.

Recruitment of parents not previously included in public library literacy programs is a high priority.

(c) Families eligible for the program shall include, but not be limited to, young children up to the age of five years.

(d) Program meetings shall be held in public library settings.

(e) The public library literacy program staff and children's services staff shall work in close coordination with the State Library in administering the Families for Literacy Program to assure maximum integration of literacy services to parents and preliteracy services to their children.

(Added by Stats.1987, c. 1359, § 2.)

Repeal

Chapter 4, California Library Services Act, is repealed upon replacement of its provisions by Chapter 4.5, Library of California Act, under the terms of Education Code § 18870.

Historical and Statutory Notes

Legislative findings, declarations and intent relating to Stats.1987, c. 1359, see Historical and Statutory Notes under Education Code § 18735.

Cross References

State Library, generally, see Education Code § 19300 et seq.

§ 18735.2. Services offered by a public library under the Families for Literacy Program

Services offered by a public library under this article shall include the following:

(a) Acquisition of books, of appropriate reading levels for, and containing subjects of interest to, children for ownership by young children of families participating in the program.

(b) Regular meetings of parents and children in public library settings during hours that are suitable for parents and their children.

(c) Storytelling, word games, and other exercises designed to promote enjoyment of reading in adults and children.

(d) Use of children's books and language experience stories from the meetings as material for adult literacy instruction.

(e) Instruction for parents in book selection and reading aloud to children.

(f) Services to enhance full family participation and to foster a family environment conducive to reading.

(g) Assistance to parents in using services in order to access books and other materials on such topics as parenting, child care, health, nutrition, and family life education.

(h) Other services, as necessary to enable families to participate in the Families for Literacy Program.

(Added by Stats.1987, c. 1359, § 2.)

Historical and Statutory Notes

Legislative findings, declarations and intent relating to Stats.1987, c. 1359, see Historical and Statutory Notes under Education Code § 18735.

§ 18735.3. Administrative support and technical assistance provided by State Library; award of project grants

The State Library shall provide administrative support and technical assistance to public libraries in the development and operation of local projects. The California Library Services Board shall award project grants for the Families for Literacy Program on a competitive basis to eligible public libraries and monitor the activities and progress of these projects once established.

(Added by Stats.1987, c. 1359, § 2.)

Historical and Statutory Notes

Legislative findings, declarations and intent relating to Stats.1987, c. 1359, see Historical and Statutory Notes under Education Code § 18735.

Cross References

State Library, generally, see Education Code § 19300 et seq.

§ 18735.4. Program planning and evaluation; coordination of research

The State Library shall coordinate research to support program planning and evaluation of the Families for Literacy Program. Research activities shall include all of the following:

(a) Collection and interpretation of demographic data on children and families, including the number and ages of children, the location of children within rural and urban areas, the family characteristics of these children, and the ethnicity and primary language of these children.

(b) Formative evaluation of the program's effectiveness submitted to the Legislature by January 2, 1990, to determine: (1) if the program has been successful in engaging parents and children positively in reading together, (2) if the program has resulted in measurable literacy progress for adults and reading preparation for children, (3) the number of families served, and (4) the number of adults that have obtained basic literary skills through the program. The State Library shall include with its annual formative evaluation to the Legislature any recommendations it may have for changes in the program.

(c) Development of applications of the results of the program, as well as the collective experiences of other library programs, to teacher development and training.

(d) Review of public library children's services to identify key factors in the design and development of programs that enhance full family participation in reading and learning activities, especially those that are suitable to the needs of the disadvantaged child.

(Added by Stats.1987, c. 1359, § 2.)

Repeal

Chapter 4, California Library Services Act, is repealed upon replacement of its provisions by Chapter 4.5, Library of California Act, under the terms of Education Code § 18870.

Historical and Statutory Notes

Legislative findings, declarations and intent relating to Stats.1987, c. 1359, see Historical and Statutory Notes under Education Code § 18735.

Cross References

State Library, generally, see Education Code § 19300 et seq.

Article 5

LIBRARY SYSTEM SERVICES

Section

Article 5 was added by Stats.1977, c. 1255, § 2.

Repeal

Chapter 4, California Library Services Act, is repealed upon replacement of its provisions by Chapter 4.5, Library of California Act, under the terms of Education Code § 18870.

Code of Regulations References

Budget request upon submitting plan of service, see 5 Cal. Code of Regs. § 20135.

§ 18740. Systems eligible for funds

A library system, eligible for funds under this article, may consist of the following systems:

(a) A cooperative library system that, as of the effective date of this act, was designated a system under the Public Library Services Act of 1963.

(b) A library system in which two or more systems consolidate to form a library system.

(c) A library system that is formed by adding independent public library jurisdictions to an existing system.

(d) A library system formed by any combination of the above.

(Added by Stats.1977, c. 1255, § 2. Amended by Stats.1987, c. 1452, § 102.)

Repeal

Chapter 4, California Library Services Act, is repealed upon replacement of its provisions by Chapter 4.5, Library of California Act, under the terms of Education Code § 18870.

Historical and Statutory Notes

Legislative findings, declarations and intent relating to Stats.1987, c. 1452, see Historical and Statutory Notes under Education Code § 1007.

Former § 18740, enacted by Stats.1976, c. 1010, § 2, relating to systems eligible for funds, was repealed by Stats.1977, c. 1255, § 1.

Derivation: Former § 18740, enacted by Stats.1976, c. 1010, § 2.

Educ.C.1959, § 27125, added by Stats.1963, c. 1802, p. 3632, § 1.

Cross References

Legislative policy, see Education Code § 18703.

§ 18741. Annual reference allowance

(a) Each system described in Section 18740 shall receive an annual allowance for the improvement and maintenance of coordinated reference service support to the members of the system. Following the effective date of this chapter, if there occurs a consolidation among individual public libraries that, as of the effective date of this chapter, are members of a system, the per member allowance to the system shall continue at the same level as if the consolidation had not taken place.

(b) After identifying the needs of the underserved, each system shall use a fair and equitable portion of its reference allowance to improve the system's reference service to its underserved population through appropriate collection development, provision of reference specialists, and staff training. Funds for the reference grant may also be used for general and specialized reference collection development, employment of reference specialists, and system-wide reference training.

(Added by Stats.1977, c. 1255, § 2. Amended by Stats.1987, c. 1452, § 103.)

Repeal

Chapter 4, California Library Services Act, is repealed upon replacement of its provisions by Chapter 4.5, Library of California Act, under the terms of Education Code § 18870.

Historical and Statutory Notes

Section 3 of Stats.1977, c. 1255, provided:

"For each fiscal year, the state board may adjust both the formula allowance prescribed by Section 18741 of the Education Code and the standard unit costs of reimbursable transactions prescribed by Sections 18731, 18743, 18744, and 18765 of the Education Code to reflect differences in costs due to fluctuations in the value of money."

Legislative findings, declarations and intent relating to Stats.1987, c. 1452, see Historical and Statutory Notes under Education Code § 1007.

Former § 18741, enacted by Stats.1976, c. 1010, § 2, derived from Educ.C.1959, § 27126, added by Stats.1963, c. 1802, p. 3633, § 1, amended by Stats.1966, 1st Ex.Sess., c. 97, p. 546, § 1.5; Stats.1972, c. 618, p. 1114, § 57, relating to formation of library system, was repealed by Stats.1977, c. 1255, § 1.

Derivation: Former § 18771, enacted by Stats.1976, c. 1010, § 2.

Educ.C.1959, § 27145.5, added by Stats.1965, c. 1820, p. 4198, § 3, amended by Stats.1966, 1st Ex.Sess., c. 97, p. 548, § 11.

Code of Regulations References

System reference, rules and regulations, see 5 Cal. Code of Regs. § 20150 et seq.

Notes of Decisions

Cooperative library systems 1

_____

1. Cooperative library systems

Upon replacement of the California Library Services Act cooperative library system pro-grams, a cooperative library system may continue to operate, with or without state funding, depending upon the particular circumstances present. Ops.Atty.Gen. No. 01–301 (July 11, 2001).

§ 18742. System-wide applications for Special Services Programs

Any system may apply to the state board for funds for Special Service Programs on a system-wide basis. Proposals shall identify the needs of the target service group, assess the capacity of the applicant system to respond to those needs, and shall identify the activities and timelines necessary to achieve those objectives. Systems may also apply for funds for other system-wide programs, but such programs shall include a component for serving the underserved on a system-wide basis.

(Added by Stats.1977, c. 1255, § 2.)

Repeal

Chapter 4, California Library Services Act, is repealed upon replacement of its provisions by Chapter 4.5, Library of California Act, under the terms of Education Code § 18870.

Historical and Statutory Notes

Former § 18742, enacted by Stats.1976, c. 1010, § 2, derived from Educ.C.1959, § 27127, added by Stats.1963, c. 1802, p. 3633, § 1, requiring the state librarian to assist public agencies in applications for inclusion in existing library system, was repealed by Stats.1977, c. 1255, § 1.

Notes of Decisions

Cooperative library systems 1

1. **Cooperative library systems**
   Upon replacement of the California Library Services Act cooperative library system pro-

grams, a cooperative library system may continue to operate, with or without state funding, depending upon the particular circumstances present. Ops.Atty.Gen. No. 01–301 (July 11, 2001).

§ 18743. Equal access to all residents of the system

Each member library of a system shall provide equal access to all residents of the area served by the system. Member libraries that incur a net imbalance shall be reimbursed through the system for the handling costs of the net loans according to the allocation formula developed pursuant to subdivision (f) of Section 18724.

(Added by Stats.1977, c. 1255, § 2. Amended by Stats.1987, c. 1452, § 104.)

Repeal

Chapter 4, California Library Services Act, is repealed upon replacement of its provisions by Chapter 4.5, Library of California Act, under the terms of Education Code § 18870.

Historical and Statutory Notes

Legislative findings, declarations and intent relating to Stats.1987, c. 1452, see Historical and Statutory Notes under Education Code § 1007.

Former § 18743, enacted by Stats.1976, c. 1010, § 2, derived from Educ.C.1959, § 27128, added by Stats.1966, 1st Ex.Sess., c. 97, p. 546, § 2, authorizing the state librarian to determine

final date for grant requests and authorizing pro rata distribution of certain grants, was repealed by Stats.1977, c. 1255, § 1.

Derivation: Former § 18751, enacted by Stats.1976, c. 1010, § 2.

Educ.C.1959, § 27131, added by Stats.1963, c. 1802, p. 3633, § 1, amended by Stats.1966, 1st Ex.Sess., c. 97, p. 547, § 4.

Cross References

Library system, see Education Code §§ 18710, 18740.

Code of Regulations References

Direct loans, see 5 Cal. Code of Regs. § 20200.
Reimbursement for net direct loans, see 5 Cal. Code of Regs. § 20215.

§ 18744. Interlibrary loans

Each member library of a system shall be reimbursed through the system to cover handling costs, excluding communication and delivery costs, of each interlibrary loan between member libraries of the system according to the allocation formula developed pursuant to subdivision (f) of Section 18724.

(Added by Stats.1977, c. 1255, § 2. Amended by Stats.1987, c. 1452, § 105.)

Repeal

Chapter 4, California Library Services Act, is repealed upon replacement of its provisions by Chapter 4.5, Library of California Act, under the terms of Education Code § 18870.

Historical and Statutory Notes

Legislative findings, declarations and intent relating to Stats.1987, c. 1452, see Historical and Statutory Notes under Education Code § 1007.

Former § 18744, enacted by Stats.1976, c. 1010, § 2, derived from Educ.C.1959, § 27129, added by Stats.1969, c. 535, p. 1162, § 1, authorizing school districts to contract with public agencies for services, was repealed by Stats. 1977, c. 1255, § 1.

Code of Regulations References

Interlibrary loans, rules and regulations, see 5 Cal. Code of Regs. § 20251 et seq.

Notes of Decisions

Cooperative library systems   1

_____

1. Cooperative library systems

Upon replacement of the California Library Services Act cooperative library system pro-

grams, a cooperative library system may continue to operate, with or without state funding, depending upon the particular circumstances present. Ops.Atty.Gen. No. 01–301 (July 11, 2001).

§ 18745.   Intrasystem communications and delivery

Each system shall annually apply to the state board for funds for intrasystem communications and delivery. Proposals shall be based upon the most cost-effective methods of exchanging materials and information among the member libraries.

(Added by Stats.1977, c. 1255, § 2. Amended by Stats.1987, c. 1452, § 106.)

Repeal

Chapter 4, California Library Services Act, is repealed upon replacement of its provisions by Chapter 4.5, Library of California Act, under the terms of Education Code § 18870.

Historical and Statutory Notes

Legislative findings, declarations and intent relating to Stats.1987, c. 1452, see Historical and Statutory Notes under Education Code § 1007.

Code of Regulations References

Definitions of reporting terms, see 5 Cal. Code of Regs. § 20235.

Notes of Decisions

Cooperative library systems   1

_____

1. Cooperative library systems

Upon replacement of the California Library Services Act cooperative library system pro-

grams, a cooperative library system may continue to operate, with or without state funding, depending upon the particular circumstances present. Ops.Atty.Gen. No. 01–301 (July 11, 2001).

§ 18746.   Funds for planning, coordination and evaluation of overall systemwide services

Each system shall annually apply to the state board for funds for planning, coordination, and evaluation of the overall systemwide services authorized by this chapter.

(Added by Stats.1977, c. 1255, § 2. Amended by Stats.1987, c. 1452, § 107.)

Repeal

Chapter 4, California Library Services Act, is repealed upon replacement of its provisions by Chapter 4.5, Library of California Act, under the terms of Education Code § 18870.

Historical and Statutory Notes

Legislative findings, declarations and intent relating to Stats.1987, c. 1452, see Historical and Statutory Notes under Education Code § 1007.

Notes of Decisions

Cooperative library systems 1

_____

1. Cooperative library systems

Upon replacement of the California Library Services Act cooperative library system programs, a cooperative library system may continue to operate, with or without state funding, depending upon the particular circumstances present. Ops.Atty.Gen. No. 01–301 (July 11, 2001).

§ 18747. Administrative council; advisory board

(a) Each system shall establish an administrative council whose membership consists of the head librarians of each jurisdiction in the system. Duties of the administrative council shall include general administrative responsibility for the system, adopting a system plan of service, and submitting annual proposals to the state board for implementation of the provisions of this article.

(b) Each system shall establish an advisory board consisting of as many members as there are member jurisdictions of the system. The governing body of each member jurisdiction shall appoint one member to the advisory board from among its residents.

(Added by Stats.1977, c. 1255, § 2. Amended by Stats.1987, c. 1452, § 108.)

Repeal

Chapter 4, California Library Services Act, is repealed upon replacement of its provisions by Chapter 4.5, Library of California Act, under the terms of Education Code § 18870.

Historical and Statutory Notes

Legislative findings, declarations and intent relating to Stats.1987, c. 1452, see Historical and Statutory Notes under Education Code § 1007.

Similar provisions were formerly contained at Education Code § 18748.

Code of Regulations References

System advisory board, see 5 Cal. Code of Regs. § 20145.

§ 18748. Repealed by Stats.1987, c. 1452, § 109

Historical and Statutory Notes

The repealed section, added by Stats.1977, c. 1255, § 2, related to establishment of an advisory board. Similar provisions were added at Education Code § 18747.

Legislative findings, declarations and intent relating to Stats.1987, c. 1452, see Historical and Statutory Notes under Education Code § 1007.

§ 18749. Advisory board; terms of members

The term of any member of a system advisory board shall be for two years, and each member shall serve no more than two consecutive terms. Staggered terms shall be established by drawing of lots at the first meeting of the advisory board so that a simple majority of the members shall initially serve a two-year term, and the remainder initially a one-year term.

The appointing jurisdiction shall ensure that members of a system advisory board are representative of the public-at-large and of the underserved residents in the system service area.

(Added by Stats.1977, c. 1255, § 2.)

Repeal

Chapter 4, California Library Services Act, is repealed upon replacement of its provisions by Chapter 4.5, Library of California Act, under the terms of Education Code § 18870.

§ 18750. Duties of Advisory board

The duties of each system advisory board shall include, but are not limited to, the following:

(a) Assisting the Administrative Council in the development of the system plan of service.

(b) Advising the Administrative Council on the need for services and programs.

(c) Assisting in the evaluation of the services provided by the system.

(Added by Stats.1977, c. 1255, § 2.)

Repeal

Chapter 4, California Library Services Act, is repealed upon replacement of its provisions by Chapter 4.5, Library of California Act, under the terms of Education Code § 18870.

Historical and Statutory Notes

Former § 18750, enacted by Stats.1976, c. 1010, § 2, derived from Educ.C.1959, § 27130, added by Stats.1963, c. 1802, p. 3633, § 1, amended by Stats.1966, 1st Ex.Sess., c. 97, p. 546, § 3, providing for establishment and per capita grants, was repealed by Stats.1977, c. 1255, § 1.

Code of Regulations References

System advisory board, see 5 Cal. Code of Regs. § 20145.

§ 18751. System consolidation grant

When any system or systems consolidate, a grant of ten thousand dollars ($10,000) for each of the two years following the consolidation shall be made to the newly consolidated system.

(Added by Stats.1977, c. 1255, § 2.)

Repeal

Chapter 4, California Library Services Act, is repealed upon replace-
ment of its provisions by Chapter 4.5, Library of California Act, under
the terms of Education Code § 18870.

Historical and Statutory Notes

Former § 18751, enacted by Stats.1976, c. 1010, § 2, specifying requirements of library system for grants, was repealed by Stats.1977, c. 1255, § 1. See Education Code § 18743.

Derivation: Former § 18770, enacted by Stats.1976, c. 1010, § 2.

Educ.C.1959, § 27144, added by Stats.1963, c. 1802, § 1.

Code of Regulations References

System consolidations, see 5 Cal. Code of Regs. § 20185.

§ 18752. Repealed by Stats.1987, c. 1452, § 110

Historical and Statutory Notes

The repealed section, added by Stats.1977, c. 1255, § 2, related to grants made when a jurisdiction joined an existing system.

Legislative findings, declarations and intent relating to Stats.1987, c. 1452, see Historical and Statutory Notes under Education Code § 1007.

Former § 18752, enacted by Stats.1976, c. 1010, § 2, derived from Educ.C.1959, § 27132, added by Stats.1963, c. 1802, p. 3634, § 1, amended by Stats.1965, c. 1820, p. 4197, § 1, relating to contracts between the state librarian and public agencies for grants, was repealed by Stats.1977, c. 1255, § 1.

§ 18753. Repealed by Stats.1977, c. 1255, § 1

Historical and Statutory Notes

The repealed section, enacted by Stats.1976, c. 1010, § 2, derived from Educ.C.1959, § 27133, added by Stats.1963, c. 1802, p. 3634,

§ 1, amended by Stats.1966, 1st Ex.Sess., c. 97, p. 548, § 1; Stats.1972, c. 590, p. 1043, § 14, related to limitations on establishment grants.

Article 6

STATEWIDE SERVICES

Article 6 was added by Stats.1977, c. 1255, § 2.

Repeal

Chapter 4, California Library Services Act, is repealed upon replace-
ment of its provisions by Chapter 4.5, Library of California Act, under
the terms of Education Code § 18870.

111

§ 18760.   State reference centers; establishment

The state board shall establish and administer two or more state reference centers. The centers shall be responsible for answering reference requests that cannot be met by systems and libraries participating in the programs authorized by this chapter.

(Added by Stats.1977, c. 1255, § 2.)

Repeal

Chapter 4, California Library Services Act, is repealed upon replacement of its provisions by Chapter 4.5, Library of California Act, under the terms of Education Code § 18870.

§ 18761.   Services provided by state reference centers

Each reference center established by the state shall provide statewide service. Such service shall include the handling of reference requests that cannot be met locally and regionally.

(Added by Stats.1977, c. 1255, § 2.)

Repeal

Chapter 4, California Library Services Act, is repealed upon replacement of its provisions by Chapter 4.5, Library of California Act, under the terms of Education Code § 18870.

§ 18762.   Reciprocal or contractual agreements; authority of state reference centers

Each reference center established pursuant to Section 18760 may enter into reciprocal or contractual agreements with libraries or any other information source for the purpose of making available their materials and informational services for the benefit of the library users of this state. Each California public library participating in any program under this chapter shall make materials and services available, as needed, to state reference centers.

(Added by Stats.1977, c. 1255, § 2.)

Repeal

Chapter 4, California Library Services Act, is repealed upon replacement of its provisions by Chapter 4.5, Library of California Act, under the terms of Education Code § 18870.

§ 18763.   Budget of state reference centers

The budget of any reference center established pursuant to Section 18760 may include funds for the general operations of such centers, including funds for collection development and use.

(Added by Stats.1977, c. 1255, § 2.)

Repeal

Chapter 4, California Library Services Act, is repealed upon replacement of its provisions by Chapter 4.5, Library of California Act, under the terms of Education Code § 18870.

§ 18764. Repository for collections relevant to economically disadvantaged and non-English-speaking persons

The state board shall designate one or more of the reference centers established pursuant to Section 18760 as a repository for collections specially relevant to economically disadvantaged persons and non-English-speaking persons.

(Added by Stats.1977, c. 1255, § 2.)

Repeal

Chapter 4, California Library Services Act, is repealed upon replacement of its provisions by Chapter 4.5, Library of California Act, under the terms of Education Code § 18870.

§ 18765. State interlibrary loan program; reimbursement

Each California library eligible to be reimbursed under this section for participation in the statewide interlibrary loan program shall be reimbursed according to the allocation formula developed pursuant to subdivision (f) of Section 18724 to cover the handling costs of each interlibrary loan whenever the borrowing library is a public library, except for the interlibrary loans made between members of a cooperative library system as provided in Section 18744. Libraries eligible for interlibrary loan reimbursement under this section shall include public libraries, libraries operated by public schools or school districts, libraries operated by public colleges or universities, libraries operated by public agencies for institutionalized persons, and libraries operated by nonprofit private educational or research institutions. Loans to eligible libraries by public libraries shall also be reimbursed according to the allocation formula developed pursuant to subdivision (f) of Section 18724.

(Added by Stats.1977, c. 1255, § 2. Amended by Stats.1987, c. 1452, § 111.)

Repeal

Chapter 4, California Library Services Act, is repealed upon replacement of its provisions by Chapter 4.5, Library of California Act, under the terms of Education Code § 18870.

Historical and Statutory Notes

Legislative findings, declarations and intent relating to Stats.1987, c. 1452, see Historical and Statutory Notes under Education Code § 1007.

Code of Regulations References

Interlibrary loans, rules and regulations, see 5 Cal. Code of Regs. § 20251 et seq.

§ 18766. Statewide communications and delivery network

The state board shall establish and maintain a statewide communications and delivery network between and among systems, state reference centers, independent public libraries and all other libraries participating in the programs authorized by this act.

(Added by Stats.1977, c. 1255, § 2.)

Repeal

Chapter 4, California Library Services Act, is repealed upon replacement of its provisions by Chapter 4.5, Library of California Act, under the terms of Education Code § 18870.

§ 18767. Computerized data base; bibliographic records and location of materials

The state board shall establish and maintain a computerized data base of bibliographic records and locations of all materials acquired by public libraries in this state, for the purpose of carrying out the legislative policy of enabling libraries to share resources efficiently.

(Added by Stats.1978, c. 331, p. 680, § 1, eff. June 30, 1978.)

Repeal

Chapter 4, California Library Services Act, is repealed upon replacement of its provisions by Chapter 4.5, Library of California Act, under the terms of Education Code § 18870.

Library References

Schools ☞47.
Westlaw Topic No. 345.

C.J.S. Schools and School Districts §§ 81 to 92, 174.

§§ 18770 to 18772. Repealed by Stats.1977, c. 1255, § 1

Historical and Statutory Notes

Section 18770, enacted by Stats.1976, c. 1010, § 2, related to establishment grants. See Education Code §§ 18732, 18751.

Section 18771, enacted by Stats.1976, c. 1010, § 2, related to per capita grants. See Education Code § 18741.

Section 18772, enacted by Stats.1976, c. 1010, § 2, derived from Educ.C.1959, § 27146, added by Stats.1963, c. 1802, § 1, amended by Stats.1965, c. 204, § 20; Stats.1965, c. 1820, § 5; Stats.1966, 1st Ex.Sess., c. 97, § 11.5, related to per capita grants.

Chapter 4.5

LIBRARY OF CALIFORNIA ACT

Chapter 4.5 was added by Stats.1998, c. 948 (S.B.409), § 1.

Operative Effect

Chapter 4, California Library Services Act, comprising §§ 18700 to 18767, is repealed upon replacement of its provisions by Chapter 4.5, Library of California Act, under the terms of Education Code § 18870.

Article 1

GENERAL PROVISIONS

Section
18800. Short title.
18801. Legislative findings, declarations and intent.
18802. Declaration of legislative policy.

Article 1 was added by Stats.1998, c. 948 (S.B.409), § 1.

Operative Effect

Chapter 4, California Library Services Act, comprising §§ 18700 to 18767, is repealed upon replacement of its provisions by Chapter 4.5, Library of California Act, under the terms of Education Code § 18870.

§ 18800. Short title

This chapter shall be known as the Library of California Act.

(Added by Stats.1998, c. 948 (S.B.409), § 1.)

Library References

Legal Jurisprudences
  Cal Jur 3d Sch § 333.

§ 18801. Legislative findings, declarations and intent

(a) The Legislature finds all of the following:

(1) Our economy is information based. Because libraries are information providers, they have a primary responsibility for the collection, organization, and dissemination of information supporting the economic development of California.

(2) Resource sharing, cooperation, and collaboration among all California libraries of all types creates a whole that is greater than the sum of its parts. Each library can serve as a gateway to the resources and services of every other California library.

(3) The state's economic and democratic vitality depends upon the education of all Californians and their equitable access to information in an effective,

115

timely fashion. Public and private partnerships enhance information access and delivery.

(4) Access to information is increasingly technology based. Technology is vital to the libraries serving Californians. The sharing of resources and services among libraries is most cost-effective when appropriate technology is utilized effectively.

(5) Our multicultural and complex society creates needs for materials, information, and services that go beyond the ability of any one library or any one type of library to provide.

(6) The academic library is a primary source of curriculum-related educational and research information for higher education.

(7) The public library is a primary source of information, enrichment, and lifelong learning for persons of any age, location, or economic circumstance.

(8) The school library is a primary source of curriculum-related resources and instructional reading materials in elementary and secondary schools.

(9) The special library is a primary source of information and research resources related to its specific mission or the purpose of its parent organization which may be a corporation, hospital, legal organization or other institution.

(10) No single library is able to meet all the diverse needs of all of its primary clientele, including people with disabilities, non-English-speaking and limited-English-speaking persons, those who are confined to home or an institution, those who are geographically isolated, and those who are economically disadvantaged. Highly specialized information needs often surpass the resources of any single library in the state.

(11) The effective sharing of resources and services among the libraries of California requires a structure and an ongoing commitment by the state to compensate libraries for services provided to Californians other than their primary clientele.

(b) The Legislature therefore finds and declares the following:

(1) It is in the interest of the people of the state to ensure that all Californians have free and convenient access to all library resources and services that could provide essential information and enrich their lives.

(2) To respond fully and successfully to these information needs and to the diversity of California's population, libraries of all types and in all parts of the state must be enabled to interact, cooperate, and share resources.

(c)(1) It is the intent of the Legislature to provide all Californians with the opportunity to obtain from a local library all their needed materials and informational services by facilitating, and supporting through that library, access to the resources of all libraries in the state.

(2) It is the intent of the Legislature to accomplish this goal by enabling libraries of all types and in all parts of the state to provide their users with the services and resources of all libraries in this state, and by assisting libraries to provide and improve service to the underserved.

(Added by Stats.1998, c. 948 (S.B.409), § 1.)

§ 18802. Declaration of legislative policy

In adopting this chapter, the Legislature declares that its policy is as follows:

(a) To reaffirm the principle of local control of the government or administration, or both, of libraries and to affirm that the provisions of this chapter apply only to libraries authorized by their jurisdictions or institutions to apply to participate in the programs authorized by this chapter.

(b) To enable the users of all libraries, regardless of the library type, size, or geographic location, to benefit from some or all of the services authorized by this chapter.

(c) To require that no library, as a condition for receiving funds or services under this chapter, acquire, provide access to, or exclude any specific book, periodical, film, recording, data base, picture, or other material or medium, or acquire, provide access to, or exclude any classification of books or other material by author, subject matter, or type.

(d) To encourage adequate funding of libraries from local or other sources, with state aid under this program to be furnished as a supplement to, rather than a replacement for, other funds.

(e) To ensure that the necessary technological infrastructure is provided.

(f) To ensure library service to the underserved of all ages.

(g) To encourage and enable the sharing of resources among libraries of all types.

(h) To reimburse equitably any participating library for services it provides to Californians other than its primary clientele.

(i) To assure that no existing library service programs, funded at the local or state level, are diminished as a result of the resource sharing authorized by this chapter.

(Added by Stats.1998, c. 948 (S.B.409), § 1.)

Article 2

DEFINITIONS

Section
18810. Definitions.

Article 2 was added by Stats.1998, c. 948 (S.B.409), § 1.

Operative Effect

Chapter 4, California Library Services Act, comprising §§ 18700 to 18767, is repealed upon replacement of its provisions by Chapter 4.5, Library of California Act, under the terms of Education Code § 18870.

§ 18810. Definitions

As used in this chapter, unless the context otherwise indicates or unless specific exception is made, the following definitions apply:

(a) "Academic library" means a library established and maintained by a college or university or other postsecondary institution to meet the educational needs of its students, faculty, staff, and others by agreement.

(b) "Act" means the Library of California Act.

(c) "Direct loan" means the lending of a book or other item, or furnishing a copy directly to a borrower, in person or through electronic means.

(d) "Document delivery" means the transmission, in response to a request, of information from one library to another, in either a physical or digital format.

(e) "Electronic direct access" means the provision of electronic borrowing, or electronic document delivery services directly to library users, or both.

(f) "Information agencies" means institutions that provide or preserve, or both, information resources, such as archives, historical societies, libraries, and museums.

(g) "Institution" means a business or corporation, college, correctional facility, education agency, governmental agency, hospital, not-for-profit organization, professional association, school district, or other organized group that is authorized by law and that operates one or more libraries. These libraries would be academic, school, or special libraries located in California. For the purposes of this act, if an institution is a member of a regional library network and a library of that institution decides to participate in a regional library network and meets the eligibility standards, but is located within the geographic boundaries of a network that is different from the network within which the institution is located, that library shall be a participating library in the regional network within which it is located.

(h) "Interlibrary loan" means the lending or providing of a book or other item, or furnishing a copy, from one library to another library that is under a different jurisdictional or institutional administration as the result of a request for the item from its primary clientele.

(i) "Interlibrary reference" means the providing of information by one library or reference center to another library or reference center that is under a different jurisdictional or institutional administration as the result of a request from its primary clientele for information that is beyond that library's mission and resources.

(j) "Library user" means a Californian who is part of the primary clientele of a library but does not work for that library.

(k) "Network region" means a geographic subdivision of California within which libraries organize as a regional library network under this act for the purpose of resource sharing and mutual cooperation. Boundaries of network regions are determined on the basis of the following criteria: public library jurisdictional boundaries; commonality with boundaries of educational institutions; recognition of current transportation, marketing, and communication patterns; location of and access to library resources; adequacy of resources for resource sharing purposes; and population.

(*l*) "Participating library" means the libraries of a public library jurisdiction that is a member of a regional library network or a library of an institution that is a member of a regional library network if that library decides to participate in a regional library network and meets the eligibility standards set forth in Section 18830.

(m) "Patron referral" means the accepted procedure among libraries by which onsite services are made available in an appropriate format to people who would otherwise not be able to utilize them.

(n) "Preservation" means the prevention or delay of deterioration of, and damage to, archival and library materials through the appropriate environmental controls or treatment, or both. For the purposes of this chapter, preservation encompasses conservation, digitization, and duplication of endangered materials in a different format.

(o) "Primary clientele" means the people for whom the library has been established to provide services. It includes people served by different outlets of its jurisdiction or institution. A person may be a member of the primary clientele of more than one type of library.

(p) "Public library" means a library, or two or more libraries, operated by a single public jurisdiction to meet the needs of its primary clientele and others by agreement.

(q) "Public library jurisdiction" means a county, city and county, city or any district that is authorized by law to provide public library services and that operates a public library.

(r) "Regional library council" means the administrative body over each regional library network, on which all members are represented.

(s) "Regional library network" means a not-for-profit, cooperative organization established by the Library of California Board composed of libraries within the public library jurisdictions or institutions that choose to become members and agree to share resources and services with, or to provide resources and services to, or both, other members of the regional library network.

(t) "Resources" are library materials that include, but are not limited to, print, nonprint materials and microformats; network resources such as software, hardware, and equipment; electronic and magnetic records; data bases; communication technology; facilities; and human expertise.

(u) "School library" means a library that is established to support the curriculum-related research and instructional reading needs of pupils and teachers and provides the collections, related equipment, and instructional services of a staff for an elementary or secondary school.

(v) "Special library" means a library that is maintained by a parent organization to serve a specialized clientele; or an independent library that may provide specialized materials or services, or both, in a specific subject to the public, a segment of the public, or other libraries. It is maintained by an association, business or corporation, government agency, research institution, learned society, not-for-profit organization, professional association, museum, industrial enterprise, chamber of commerce, or other organized group and is characterized by its depth of subject coverage.

(w) "Statewide resource library group" means those libraries in California that have the most comprehensive or specialized resources, or both, in topics needed by people statewide or regionally and that agree to provide access to their resources to all members of all regional library networks.

(x) "State board" means the Library of California Board.

(y) "Type of library" means academic, public, school, or special library.

(z) "Underserved" means any population segment with service needs not adequately met by traditional library service patterns; including, but not limited to: children, disabled, economically displaced, ethnic and culturally diverse populations, geographically isolated, illiterate, institutionalized, non-English speaking, and young adults.

(Added by Stats.1998, c. 948 (S.B.409), § 1.)

Notes of Decisions

Cooperative library systems   1

_____

1. Cooperative library systems
  Upon replacement of the California Library Services Act cooperative library system programs, a cooperative library system may continue to operate, with or without state funding, depending upon the particular circumstances present. Ops.Atty.Gen. No. 01–301 (July 11, 2001).

Article 3

ADMINISTRATION

Article 3 was added by Stats.1998, c. 948 (S.B.409), § 1.

Operative Effect

Chapter 4, California Library Services Act, comprising §§ 18700 to 18767, is repealed upon replacement of its provisions by Chapter 4.5, Library of California Act, under the terms of Education Code § 18870.

§ 18820. Library of California Board; establishment; membership

(a) There is hereby established in the state government the Library of California Board. The state board shall consist of 13 members.

(b) It is the intent of the Legislature that members of the state board be broadly representative of the people served by libraries statewide and that members reflect the cultural traditions of California's people and the diverse geographic areas of the state.

(c) The Governor shall appoint nine members to the state board. The Governor shall appoint two members to represent academic libraries, two members to represent public libraries, two members to represent school libraries, and two members to represent special libraries. At the time of their appointment and throughout their tenure, these eight members must work for, or be part of, or be associated with, the governance structure of the type of library they represent, and that library must be a member of a regional library network. The Governor shall also appoint one member representing the general public.

(d) The Senate Rules Committee shall appoint two members representing the general public. The Speaker of the Assembly shall also appoint two members representing the general public.

(e) The initial members of the state board shall be those persons serving on the California Library Services Board at the time of the enactment of this chapter. As new members are appointed, the composition of the board shall reflect the provisions of this section. The terms of office of members of the state board is four years or the remainder of the term for a position filled after a vacancy. No individual shall serve for more than two consecutive four-year terms.

(f) The concurrence of seven members of the state board is necessary for the validity of any of its acts.

(g) Members of the state board shall serve without pay. They shall receive their actual and necessary traveling expenses while conducting official business.

(Added by Stats.1998, c. 948 (S.B.409), § 1.)

Cross References

Appointments by Governor, public officers and employees, see Government Code § 1300 et seq.
Statutes,
    Construction and legislative intent, see Code of Civil Procedure §§ 1858 and 1859.
    Liberal construction of Education Code, see Education Code § 3.
    Rules of construction and definition for the Education Code, see Education Code § 10.
Term of offices for public officers and employees and continuation thereof, see Government Code
    §§ 1301 and 1302.
Traveling expenses, state agency officers and employees, see Government Code § 11030 et seq.

§ 18821. Powers and duties of board; rules and regulations

The state board shall adopt rules, regulations, and general policies for the implementation of this chapter and, consistent with this chapter, shall have the following powers and duties:

(a) To direct the State Librarian in the administration of this chapter.

(b) To review for its approval all proposals submitted under this chapter.

(c) To submit budget proposals as part of the annual budget of the State Library.

(d) To expend the funds appropriated for the purpose of implementing this chapter.

(e) To establish regional library networks.

(f) To require participating libraries, member institutions, public library jurisdictions, and regional library networks to prepare and submit any reports and information necessary to carry out the provisions of this chapter, and to prescribe the form and manner for providing the reports and information.

(g) To develop formulas for the equitable allocation of reimbursements.

(h) To administer an appeals process for membership eligibility in a regional library network.

(i) To work with and support the work of the regional library networks and the statewide resource libraries group.

(j) To administer the California Library Services Act, California Literacy Campaign, and Families for Literacy program.

(k) To serve as the State Advisory Council on Libraries on matters related to the federal Library Services and Technology Act.

(Added by Stats.1998, c. 948 (S.B.409), § 1.)

§ 18822. State librarian; duties

The State Librarian is the chief executive officer of the state board for the purposes of this chapter and shall do all of the following:

(a) Make reports and recommendations that may be required by the state board.

(b) Administer and monitor the provisions of this chapter.

(c) Review all claims to ensure the programmatic and technical compliance with the provisions of this chapter.

(Added by Stats.1998, c. 948 (S.B.409), § 1.)

Cross References

State Librarian,
    Generally, see Education Code § 19302 et seq.
    Powers and duties, see Education Code § 19320 et seq.

Article 4

ELIGIBLE LIBRARIES

Section
18830. Regional library network members; standards; duties.
18831. State-supported services; state funds.

Article 4 was added by Stats.1998, c. 948 (S.B.409), § 1.

Operative Effect

Chapter 4, California Library Services Act, comprising §§ 18700 to 18767, is repealed upon replacement of its provisions by Chapter 4.5, Library of California Act, under the terms of Education Code § 18870.

§ 18830. Regional library network members; standards; duties

(a) Libraries in public library jurisdictions that are members of a regional library network and libraries in institutions that are members of a regional library network are eligible to receive services under this chapter and to become participating libraries. The board of governance or the appropriate administrative authority for each academic library, public library, school library, and special library that decides to join a regional library network shall take official action to approve network membership. That local governing agency or appropriate administrative authority shall agree not to reduce funding for library services as a result of network participation. Each public library jurisdiction, school district, university or college, and institution or corporation, or agency or branch thereof, may become a member of a regional library network. A public library jurisdiction not a member of the California Library Service Act public library system on the effective date of this section, and an institution, shall have at least one library that agrees to be a participating library and meets the following eligibility standards:

(1) A written explicit mission statement and service objectives.

(2) A fixed location in California.

(3) Established hours of service.

(4) An organized collection of information and materials accessible for use by its primary clientele.

(5) Designated, onsite, paid staff for library services. At least one staff person shall have a master's degree in library or information science or a

California library media teacher credential issued by the Commission on Teacher Credentialing, but equivalent graduate education or demonstrated professional experience may be substituted for this requirement. The eligibility determination will be made by the regional library network.

(6) An established funding base.

(b) Participating libraries must agree to all of the following:

(1) To share resources and services with other members of the regional library network.

(2) To provide resources and services for other members of the regional library network.

(3) To meet the minimum resource-sharing performance standards of the regional library network.

(c) Participating libraries may not obtain services provided under this act on behalf of nonparticipating libraries. No membership fees or service fees may be assessed for access to services delivered by state funds under this chapter. Regional library networks may provide their members with increased or enhanced services for a fee, at the option of each member.

(d) Library jurisdictions that are members of the California Library Services Act public library systems on the effective date of this section are deemed to meet the eligibility standards in subdivision (a), and shall not be required to certify that they meet these eligibility standards.

(Added by Stats.1998, c. 948 (S.B.409), § 1.)

Cross References

State funds, see Government Code § 16300 et seq.
Teacher credentialing, generally, see Education Code § 44200 et seq.

Notes of Decisions

Cooperative library systems 1

1. Cooperative library systems

Upon replacement of the California Library Services Act cooperative library system programs, a cooperative library system may continue to operate, with or without state funding, depending upon the particular circumstances present. Ops.Atty.Gen. No. 01–301 (July 11, 2001).

§ 18831. State-supported services; state funds

(a) Each participating library shall receive state-supported services from a single regional library network. Geographical boundaries determine which regional library network a public library jurisdiction or institution, and its participating libraries, may join; exceptions may be made by the state board. Realignment of membership from one regional library network to another is permissible. A public library jurisdiction or an institution that is a member of a regional library network may also subscribe to services offered by other regional library networks.

(b) Eligible libraries may receive state funds for services delivered under this chapter.

(Added by Stats.1998, c. 948 (S.B.409), § 1.)

Cross References

State funds, see Government Code § 16300 et seq.

Article 5

REGIONAL LIBRARY NETWORK SERVICES

Article 5 was added by Stats.1998, c. 948 (S.B.409), § 1.

Operative Effect

Chapter 4, California Library Services Act, comprising §§ 18700 to 18767, is repealed upon replacement of its provisions by Chapter 4.5, Library of California Act, under the terms of Education Code § 18870.

§ 18840.   Eligibility for funds; submission of plan; contents

To be eligible for funds under this article, a regional library network shall submit a plan to the state board for its approval. The plan shall include all of the following:

(a) An organizational structure.

(b) Bylaws.

(c) Membership policies, assuring that all eligible libraries in eligible public library jurisdictions and in eligible institutions in the geographic region will be enabled to participate.

(d) A long-range plan, including the transition of services from the California Library Services Act to the Library of California Act, the criteria and functions for regional resource libraries, and the linkages with information agencies in the region.

(e) The endorsement of the charter members. The charter members shall include more than one type of library.

(f) Geographical contiguity.

(Added by Stats.1998, c. 948 (S.B.409), § 1.)

§ 18841.   Regional library council; establishment; membership; representative board

(a) Each regional library network shall establish a regional library council. Every eligible public library jurisdiction is designated as a member of the

125

regional library network and its library director or designee is its representative on the regional network council. Every eligible institution of which one or more libraries is a participating library, as described in Section 18830, is designated as a member of the regional library network and shall designate its representative on the regional network council from among the directors of those participating libraries and its chief library coordinator. In addition, the regional library council shall include one library user from each type of member library. There shall be one vote per person on the regional network council. Duties of the regional network council include overall administrative responsibility for the network, adopting an annual plan of service, assuring the appropriate expenditure of funds, and submitting annual budget proposals to the state board for implementation of the provisions of this article.

(b) Each regional network council shall elect from its membership a representative board to carry out its policies. The board shall include at least one representative from each type of library elected by representatives of that type of library and at least one library user. There shall be one vote per person on the representative board.

(c) Administration and management of the regional library network shall provide the vision and leadership necessary to perform the functions and deliver the services in a timely and satisfactory manner.

(Added by Stats.1998, c. 948 (S.B.409), § 1.)

§ 18842. Duties of regional library network

Each regional library network shall do all of the following:

(a) Make available a telecommunications system for the transfer of information and communications among its members.

(b) Provide regional communications based upon the most effective methods of exchanging information among its members.

(c) Provide intraregional delivery service based upon the most cost-effective methods for moving materials among its members.

(d) Provide online access to the information files, resources, and bibliographic records of its members which may be accessed regionally and statewide.

(Added by Stats.1998, c. 948 (S.B.409), § 1.)

Notes of Decisions

Cooperative library systems 1

------

1. Cooperative library systems

Upon replacement of the California Library Services Act cooperative library system programs, a cooperative library system may continue to operate, with or without state funding, depending upon the particular circumstances present. Ops.Atty.Gen. No. 01–301 (July 11, 2001).

§ 18843. Funding for electronic online resources

Any eligible library or combination of eligible libraries may receive funds from a regional library network for the provision of public access to the range of library resources and services available statewide through electronic online resources.

(Added by Stats.1998, c. 948 (S.B.409), § 1.)

Notes of Decisions

Cooperative library systems 1
_____

1. **Cooperative library systems**
    Upon replacement of the California Library Services Act cooperative library system pro-grams, a cooperative library system may continue to operate, with or without state funding, depending upon the particular circumstances present. Ops.Atty.Gen. No. 01–301 (July 11, 2001).

§ 18844. Access services components; participation; reimbursement

Each eligible library may participate in one or more of the access services components through its regional library network and be reimbursed fully for its service to Californians who do not constitute its primary clientele. Reimbursement rates shall be equitable. The state board shall develop the reimbursement rate formulas. All of the following are access services components:

(a) Interlibrary loan. Each eligible library shall be reimbursed fully to cover the handling costs of each interlibrary loan among members of the regional library networks. Participants shall provide, as well as utilize, interlibrary loan services and may not charge handling fees to other members.

(b) Patron referral and onsite services. Each eligible library shall be reimbursed fully for services and resources that are provided to Californians who would otherwise be ineligible for services from that public library jurisdiction or that institution. These persons must be referred by another member of a regional library network. Information agencies that are not libraries may also participate in this component and be reimbursed if they are the only source for the information.

(c) Direct loan. Each eligible library may provide access to Californians by providing direct borrowing privileges to the primary clientele of other libraries. They shall be reimbursed fully for the handling costs of all loans according to an allocation formula. Each public library jurisdiction that is a member of a regional library network shall provide direct borrowing privileges to all residents of the area served by the regional library network.

(d) Electronic direct access. Each eligible library may provide access to Californians by providing electronic borrowing privileges or electronic document delivery privileges, or both, to the primary clientele of other participating libraries. They shall be reimbursed fully for the handling costs of each transaction. Members participating in the electronic direct access component shall provide and utilize electronic direct access services and may not charge handling fees for this service to other members participating in this program or to their primary clientele.

(e) Document delivery. Each eligible library shall be reimbursed fully to cover the costs of document delivery resulting from an interlibrary loan transaction and electronic loan transaction as defined in this section.

(Added by Stats.1998, c. 948 (S.B.409), § 1.)

Notes of Decisions

Cooperative library systems   1

———

1. Cooperative library systems

Upon replacement of the California Library Services Act cooperative library system pro-

grams, a cooperative library system may continue to operate, with or without state funding, depending upon the particular circumstances present. Ops.Atty.Gen. No. 01–301 (July 11, 2001).

§ 18845.   Training and continuing education activities

Each regional library network shall provide opportunities for training and continuing education activities that encourage the most effective use of the resources and services authorized under this chapter, and that respond to the needs of its members in the effective delivery of services.

(Added by Stats.1998, c. 948 (S.B.409), § 1.)

Notes of Decisions

Cooperative library systems   1

———

1. Cooperative library systems

Upon replacement of the California Library Services Act cooperative library system pro-

grams, a cooperative library system may continue to operate, with or without state funding, depending upon the particular circumstances present. Ops.Atty.Gen. No. 01–301 (July 11, 2001).

§ 18846.   Referral of information requests

(a) Each regional library network shall provide information and referrals to answer requests that are beyond the capacity or capability of its members by accessing the resources and expertise of other libraries, improving general reference service in participating libraries, and improving reference service to respond to the needs of the underserved populations in the region.

(b) Any eligible library or combination of eligible libraries or regional library network may receive funds from the state board for information service enhancement within the service area.

(Added by Stats.1998, c. 948 (S.B.409), § 1.)

§ 18847.   Public relations packages

Each regional library network shall augment the public awareness programs of its members by providing public relations packages to them for customization and dissemination.

(Added by Stats.1998, c. 948 (S.B.409), § 1.)

Notes of Decisions

Cooperative library systems   1

———

1. Cooperative library systems

Upon replacement of the California Library Services Act cooperative library system pro-

grams, a cooperative library system may continue to operate, with or without state funding, depending upon the particular circumstances present. Ops.Atty.Gen. No. 01–301 (July 11, 2001).

§ 18848.   Cooperative, coordinated resource development programs; funding

Any combination of eligible libraries may receive funds from the regional library network for cooperative, coordinated resource development programs of benefit to the local service area and to the region as a whole. Each library participating in this program shall already be capable of meeting the basic, recurring needs of its primary clientele through its locally supported collection. Library resources purchased, in whole or in part, under this program shall be widely accessible to Californians for the useful life of those resources.

(Added by Stats.1998, c. 948 (S.B.409), § 1.)

§ 18849.   Funding for services to the underserved programs; application

Any regional library network may apply to the state board for funds for services to the underserved programs on a region-wide basis. Regional library networks may also apply for funds for other region-wide programs, but these programs shall include a component for serving the underserved on a region-wide basis.

(Added by Stats.1998, c. 948 (S.B.409), § 1.)

Article 6

STATEWIDE SERVICES

Article 6 was added by Stats.1998, c. 948 (S.B.409), § 1.

Operative Effect

Chapter 4, California Library Services Act, comprising §§ 18700 to 18767, is repealed upon replacement of its provisions by Chapter 4.5, Library of California Act, under the terms of Education Code § 18870.

§ 18850.   Telecommunications infrastructure; statewide communications system; statewide delivery system

The state board shall make available all of the following:

(a) A telecommunications infrastructure to ensure that all participating libraries have equitable access to the resources and services of all other California libraries.

(b) A statewide communications system between and among regional library networks, statewide resource libraries, information agencies, and all other organizations or institutions participating in the programs authorized by this chapter.

(c) A statewide delivery system between and among regional library networks, statewide resource libraries, information agencies, and all other organizations or institutions participating in the programs authorized by this chapter.

(Added by Stats.1998, c. 948 (S.B.409), § 1.)

§ 18851. Bibliographic records and communication protocols

(a) The state board shall promote and support standard bibliographic records and communication protocols in participating libraries to ensure statewide access to their resources.

(b) The state board shall make available online access to bibliographic records and locations of serial publications held by participating libraries and statewide online access to library information files, resources, and bibliographic records statewide, as facilitated by the regional library networks.

(Added by Stats.1998, c. 948 (S.B.409), § 1.)

Library References

Legal Jurisprudences
  Cal Jur 3d Sch § 44.

§ 18852. Continuing education clearinghouse

(a) The state board shall make available a continuing education clearinghouse related to library services and encourage the coordination of activities among the continuing education providers statewide.

(b) The state board shall provide for training and continuing education opportunities that encourage the most effective use of the resources and services authorized under this chapter.

(Added by Stats.1998, c. 948 (S.B.409), § 1.)

§ 18853. Access to statewide specialized information expertise and resources; facilitation and support

(a) The state board shall facilitate and support access to specialized information expertise and resources statewide to answer information requests generated by its primary clientele that are beyond the capacity or capability of a member institution or public library jurisdiction and its regional library network. The information may be provided by libraries, information agencies, and other regional library networks; and it shall be provided through electronic or physical means. Provision shall be made for information formats specially relevant to culturally diverse populations and persons with disabilities.

(b) Any eligible library or combination of libraries or regional library networks may receive funds from the state board for information service enhancement within the service area.

(Added by Stats.1998, c. 948 (S.B.409), § 1.)

Notes of Decisions

Cooperative library systems 1
_____

1. **Cooperative library systems**
   Upon replacement of the California Library Services Act cooperative library system pro-

grams, a cooperative library system may continue to operate, with or without state funding, depending upon the particular circumstances present. Ops.Atty.Gen. No. 01–301 (July 11, 2001).

§ 18854. Expansion of public awareness

The state board shall expand public awareness of the value, services, and resources of the participating library of whatever type, emphasizing its ability to serve as a gateway to all other California libraries.

(Added by Stats.1998, c. 948 (S.B.409), § 1.)

§ 18855. Cooperative, coordinated resource development; voluntary transfer clearinghouse; funding

(a) The state board shall encourage, promote and support cooperative, coordinated resource development among member institutions and member public library jurisdictions.

(b) The state board shall make available a clearinghouse to facilitate the voluntary transfer of a participating library's resources to another participating library in response to changes in that library's mission or location.

(c) Any combination of eligible libraries may receive funds from the state board for cooperative, coordinated resource development programs of benefit to people in their local area and in the state as a whole. Each library participating in this program shall already be capable of meeting the basic, recurring needs of its primary clientele through its locally supported collection. Library resources purchased, in whole or in part, under this program shall be widely accessible to Californians for the useful life of those resources.

(Added by Stats.1998, c. 948 (S.B.409), § 1.)

Notes of Decisions

Cooperative library systems 1
_____

1. **Cooperative library systems**
   Upon replacement of the California Library Services Act cooperative library system pro-

grams, a cooperative library system may continue to operate, with or without state funding, depending upon the particular circumstances present. Ops.Atty.Gen. No. 01–301 (July 11, 2001).

§ 18856. Preservation information center; funding for preservation of, and access to, documentation of California's heritage

(a) The state board shall make available a preservation information center to provide preservation information, coordinate preservation activities, and conduct preservation training for participating libraries and information agencies statewide.

(b) Any eligible library or combination of eligible libraries may receive funds from the state board for the preservation of, and widespread access to, materials that document California's heritage, enhance its educational opportunities and economic future, and portray its cultural diversity. Materials in all formats may be preserved.

(Added by Stats.1998, c. 948 (S.B.409), § 1.)

Notes of Decisions

Cooperative library systems   1

————

1. Cooperative library systems

Upon replacement of the California Library Services Act cooperative library system pro-

grams, a cooperative library system may continue to operate, with or without state funding, depending upon the particular circumstances present. Ops.Atty.Gen. No. 01–301 (July 11, 2001).

§ 18857. Services to the underserved programs; submission of proposals

Any eligible library or combination of eligible libraries may submit proposals to the state board for services to the underserved programs within the service area. Funds may be expended for the development of collections to meet the needs of the underserved, together with the employment or retraining of staff necessary to promote and utilize the collections effectively, and to provide appropriate services to the underserved.

(Added by Stats.1998, c. 948 (S.B.409), § 1.)

Notes of Decisions

Cooperative library systems   1

————

1. Cooperative library systems

Upon replacement of the California Library Services Act cooperative library system pro-

grams, a cooperative library system may continue to operate, with or without state funding, depending upon the particular circumstances present. Ops.Atty.Gen. No. 01–301 (July 11, 2001).

§ 18858. Administration and management

Administration and management shall provide the vision and leadership necessary to perform the functions and deliver the services in a timely and satisfactory manner. Statewide coordination includes linkages with national and international library networks and participation in initiatives related to library services and development that cross state and national boundaries.

(Added by Stats.1998, c. 948 (S.B.409), § 1.)

§ 18859. Participation by major resource libraries statewide

Major resource libraries statewide may participate in these programs through the statewide resource libraries group, developing protocols whereby their resources may be accessed appropriately by people throughout California. Each library must be a member or a participating library in a regional library network.

(a) Funds may be allocated to some or all libraries in this group for services delivered and performed under this article.

(b) Collaborative and cooperative projects advancing library services to the people of California may be undertaken and supported by some or all members of this group.

(Added by Stats.1998, c. 948 (S.B.409), § 1.)

Article 7

STATE FUNDING

Section

Article 7 was added by Stats.1998, c. 948 (S.B.409), § 1.

Operative Effect

Chapter 4, California Library Services Act, comprising §§ 18700 to 18767, is repealed upon replacement of its provisions by Chapter 4.5, Library of California Act, under the terms of Education Code § 18870.

§ 18860. Regional level planning; duties of state

(a) Planning shall occur at the regional level for the development of library service programs responsive to the needs of people within each network region. Some or all of these service programs may be supported by the state.

(b) It is the intent of the Legislature that the state do all of the following:

(1) Reimburse all participating libraries for services provided to Californians who do not constitute their primary clientele.

(2) Support the necessary infrastructure enabling the interlibrary resource sharing to occur.

(3) Assure equitable access to the rich resources of its many libraries to all Californians.

(Added by Stats.1998, c. 948 (S.B.409), § 1.)

Cross References

Statutes,
    Construction and legislative intent, see Code of Civil Procedure §§ 1858 and 1859.
    Liberal construction of Education Code, see Education Code § 3.
    Rules of construction and definition for the Education Code, see Education Code § 10.

§ 18861. Allocation of funds; reimbursement formulas; criteria

Funds shall be allocated to member institutions and member public library jurisdictions in accordance with reimbursement formulas adopted by the state board and with criteria adopted by the state board to carry out the provisions of this chapter.

(Added by Stats.1998, c. 948 (S.B.409), § 1.)

Notes of Decisions

Cooperative library systems   1

---

1. Cooperative library systems

Upon replacement of the California Library Services Act cooperative library system pro-

grams, a cooperative library system may continue to operate, with or without state funding, depending upon the particular circumstances present. Ops.Atty.Gen. No. 01–301 (July 11, 2001).

§ 18862. Basic funding allocation; three year establishment period; yearly appropriation components

(a) During the first three years of operation, each regional library network shall receive a basic funding allocation for service delivery as it establishes services and expands its membership.

(b) After its three-year establishment period, each regional library network shall receive an appropriation that contains a base component that is a uniform statewide minimum allocation, a component related to demographic variables including population, geography, population demographics and cost of living, and a component related to the amount of service delivered in the preceding fiscal year.

(Added by Stats.1998, c. 948 (S.B.409), § 1.)

§ 18863. Allocation of funds for support of statewide services

Funds appropriated for the support of statewide services shall be allocated to those services in accordance with criteria adopted by the state board to carry out the provisions of this chapter.

(Added by Stats.1998, c. 948 (S.B.409), § 1.)

§ 18864. Transition period

There shall be a transition period from California Library Services Act services and funding to the Library of California Act services and funding.

(Added by Stats.1998, c. 948 (S.B.409), § 1.)

§ 18865. Requirement that funding support cost of administration and services

Funding provided under this chapter shall support the costs of administering its provisions and delivering its services.

(Added by Stats.1998, c. 948 (S.B.409), § 1.)

Article 8

TRANSITION

Section
18870. Transition period; duration; controlling law; notice of full implementation.

Article 8 was added by Stats.1998, c. 948 (S.B.409), § 1.

§ 18870. Transition period; duration; controlling law; notice of full implementation

(a) The transition period from the California Library Services Act to the Library of California Act shall begin on the effective date of this chapter.

(b) As new program elements and state funds are phased in to implement this chapter, they will replace and augment the corresponding program elements and funds in the California Library Services Act.

(c) When all program elements of the California Library Services Act have been replaced and augmented under the provisions of this chapter, the California Library Services Act as set forth in Chapter 4 (commencing with Section 18700) is hereby repealed unless a subsequent act of the Legislature continues it in full force and effect. During the transition period this chapter shall control in case of conflicts between this chapter and the California Library Services Act. The state board shall file a written notice with the Secretary of the Senate and the Chief Clerk of the Assembly notifying the Legislature of the fact, and date, of full implementation of this chapter.

(Added by Stats.1998, c. 948 (S.B.409), § 1.)

Cross References

State funds, see Government Code § 16300 et seq.

Notes of Decisions

Cooperative library systems   1

---

1. Cooperative library systems

Upon replacement of the California Library Services Act cooperative library system programs, a cooperative library system may continue to operate, with or without state funding, depending upon the particular circumstances present. Ops.Atty.Gen. No. 01–301 (July 11, 2001).

Chapter 5

MUNICIPAL LIBRARIES

Chapter 5 was enacted by Stats.1976, c. 1010, § 2, operative April 30, 1977.

Article 1

ESTABLISHMENT

Section
18900. Authority of specified legislative bodies to establish public libraries.
18901. Petition of electors.

Article 1 was enacted by Stats.1976, c. 1010, § 2, operative April 30, 1977.

Cross References

Affiliation of school libraries with city libraries, see Education Code § 18134 et seq.
Annexation by municipality of territory served by county free library, see Education Code § 19114.
Civil service for municipal library employees, see Government Code § 45002.
Contracts to lend books to neighboring areas, see Education Code § 18411.
Contracts with county boards, see Education Code § 19112.

Library References

Library problems. Reports of Assembly Interim Committee on Education, 1955 to 1957, vol. 10, No. 9. Vol. 2 of Appendix to Journal of the Assembly, Reg.Sess., 1957.

§ 18900. Authority of specified legislative bodies to establish public libraries

The common council, board of trustees, or other legislative body of any city in the state may, and upon being requested to do so by one-fourth of the electors of the municipal corporation in the manner provided in this article, shall, by ordinance, establish in and for the municipality a public library if there is none already established therein.
(Stats.1976, c. 1010, § 2, operative April 30, 1977.)

Historical and Statutory Notes

Derivation: Educ.C.1959, § 27301 (Stats. 1959, c. 2, p. 1461, § 27301, amended by Stats. 1971, c. 438, p. 880, § 83).

Educ.C.1943, § 22201 (Stats.1943, c. 71, p. 738).

Stats.1901, c. 170, p. 557, § 1, amended by Stats.1909, c. 481, p. 823, § 1.

Library References

Legal Jurisprudences
Cal Jur 3d Muni § 295.

Notes of Decisions

Civil service   2
Employees' status   1
Rental of city space   3

_____

1. Employees' status

Under Educ.C.1959, § 27301 and §§ 27360, 27362, 27368, 27401, 27402, 27453, and 27455 and Gov.C. §§ 45002, 45005, a municipal library, although autonomous as to its internal operations, was not independent of the city and

its employees were city employees. City of Ukiah v. Board of Trustees of Municipal Library of City of Ukiah (App. 3 Dist. 1961) 15 Cal.Rptr. 811, 195 Cal.App.2d 344.

2. Civil service

A library employee was an employee of the city, and subject to its civil service ordinance, by virtue of provision therein that it shall be applicable to all employees of the city, even though the ordinance did not specifically designate library employees, and Gov.C. § 45002 provided for separate designation of library employees. City of Ukiah v. Board of Trustees of Municipal Library of City of Ukiah (App. 3 Dist. 1961) 15 Cal.Rptr. 811, 195 Cal.App.2d 344.

3. Rental of city space

A city maintaining a "Carnegie" library under Stats.1901, p. 557, as amended, Stats.1905, p.

296, Stats.1909, p. 823, could charge the county which used part of the library to maintain its county free library under County Free Library Act, Stats.1911, p. 80, as amended, for rent for the use of such space, and the county could pay for such space. 4 Ops.Atty.Gen. 343 (1944).

§ 18901. Petition of electors

The request may be by a single petition, or by several petitions. The several petitions shall be substantially in the same form. The single petition, or several petitions in the aggregate, shall have, the signatures of the requisite number of electors.

(Stats.1976, c. 1010, § 2, operative April 30, 1977.)

Historical and Statutory Notes

Derivation: Educ.C.1959, § 27302 (Stats. 1959, c. 2, p. 1461, § 27302).

Educ.C.1943, § 22202 (Stats.1943, c. 71, p. 738).

Stats.1901, c. 170, p. 558, § 2, amended by Stats.1909, c. 481, p. 824, § 1.

Cross References

Electors and voters, see Education Code § 5390; Const. Art. 2, §§ 2, 4; Elections Code §§ 321, 359, 2000 et seq.

Library References

Legal Jurisprudences
Cal Jur 3d Fam Law § 68.

Article 2

TRUSTEES

Article 2 was enacted by Stats.1976, c. 1010, § 2, operative April 30, 1977.

Cross References

Library districts, trustees, see Education Code § 19420 et seq.

§ 18910. Appointment of board of trustees

The public library shall be managed by a board of library trustees, consisting of five members, to be appointed by the mayor, president of the board of trustees, or other executive head of the municipality, with the consent of the legislative body of the municipality.

(Stats.1976, c. 1010, § 2, operative April 30, 1977.)

Historical and Statutory Notes

Derivation: Educ.C.1959, § 27351 (Stats. 1959, c. 2, p. 1461, § 27351).

Educ.C.1943, § 22212 (Stats.1943, c. 71, p. 738).

Stats.1901, c. 170, p. 558, § 3, amended by Stats.1909, c. 481, p. 824, § 1.

Cross References

Library districts, trustees, see Education Code § 19420 et seq.

Notes of Decisions

Library management and control   1

_____

1.   Library management and control

In proceedings to determine the right to manage and control a public library, it appeared that, prior to March 28, 1878, there had been a private voluntary association which had established and maintained in L. a library for the use of its members, and in 1874, Stats.1874, p. 274, an act was passed providing for the establishment of a public library in L., and by its provisions the library was controlled by nine regents, who were elected by the city council, and on March 28, 1878, the act was repealed by the city charter, and the mayor and council were constituted trustees of the library, and on March 28, 1878, the city council elected a board of regents, and April 6th the board duly organized, and the same day the library association made over to the public library thus organized all the books belonging to the association, this library did not come under Stats.1880, p. 231, which put in the charge of trustees therein provided for all libraries established by authority of that act. People v. Howard (1892) 94 Cal. 73, 29 P. 485.

§ 18911. Term of office and compensation

The trustees shall hold office for three years. The members of the first board appointed shall so classify themselves by lot that one of their number shall go out of office at the end of the current fiscal year, two at the end of one year thereafter, and two at the end of two years thereafter.

The legislative body of the municipality may, by ordinance, provide for the compensation of such trustees; provided that the respective compensation for such trustees shall not exceed fifty dollars ($50) per month.

(Stats.1976, c. 1010, § 2, operative April 30, 1977.)

Historical and Statutory Notes

Derivation: Educ.C.1959, § 27352 (Stats. 1959, c. 2, p. 1461, § 27352, amended by Stats. 1974, c. 509, p. 1188, § 1).

Educ.C.1943, § 22213 (Stats.1943, c. 71, p. 738).

Stats.1901, c. 170, p. 558, § 3, amended by Stats.1909, c. 481, p. 824, § 1.

Cross References

Term of offices for public officers and employees and continuation thereof, see Government Code §§ 1301 and 1302.

Notes of Decisions

Discharge 1
Extension of term 2

2. Extension of term

Trial court's extending terms of incumbent members of board of library trustees by approximate length of time trustees were deprived of their offices by city's unlawful action was a reasonable means of rectifying wrong caused by city and was not an abuse of discretion. Friends of the Library of Monterey Park v. City of Monterey Park (App. 2 Dist. 1989) 259 Cal. Rptr. 358, 211 Cal.App.3d 358.

1. Discharge

City council could not discharge board of library trustees without cause or hearing. Friends of the Library of Monterey Park v. City of Monterey Park (App. 2 Dist. 1989) 259 Cal. Rptr. 358, 211 Cal.App.3d 358.

§ 18912. Eligibility of men and women

Men and women are equally eligible to appointment as trustees.

(Stats.1976, c. 1010, § 2, operative April 30, 1977.)

Historical and Statutory Notes

Derivation: Educ.C.1959, § 27353 (Stats. 1959, c. 2, p. 1461, § 27353).

Educ.C.1943, § 22214 (Stats.1943, c. 71, p. 738).

Stats.1901, c. 170, p. 558, § 3, amended by Stats.1909, c. 481, p. 824, § 1.

§ 18913. Vacancies

Vacancies shall be filled by appointment for the unexpired term in the same manner as the original appointments are made.

(Stats.1976, c. 1010, § 2, operative April 30, 1977.)

Historical and Statutory Notes

Derivation: Educ.C.1959, § 27354 (Stats. 1959, c. 2, p. 1461, § 27354).

Educ.C.1943, § 22215 (Stats.1943, c. 71, p. 738).

Stats.1901, c. 170, p. 558, § 3, amended by Stats.1909, c. 481, p. 824, § 1.

§ 18914. Monthly meetings

Boards of library trustees shall meet at least once a month at such times and places as they may fix by resolution.

(Stats.1976, c. 1010, § 2, operative April 30, 1977.)

Historical and Statutory Notes

Derivation: Educ.C.1959, § 27355 (Stats. 1959, c. 2, p. 1461, § 27355).

Educ.C.1943, § 22216 (Stats.1943, c. 71, p. 738).

Stats.1901, c. 170, p. 558, § 4, amended by Stats.1905, c. 292, p. 296, § 1; Stats.1909, c. 481, p. 824, § 1.

§ 18915. Special meetings

Special meetings may be called at any time by three trustees, by written notice served upon each member at least three hours before the time specified for the proposed meeting.

(Stats.1976, c. 1010, § 2, operative April 30, 1977.)

Historical and Statutory Notes

Derivation: Educ.C.1959, § 27356 (Stats. 1959, c. 2, p. 1461, § 27356).

Educ.C.1943, § 22217 (Stats.1943, c. 71, p. 738).

Stats.1901, c. 170, p. 558, § 4, amended by Stats.1905, c. 292, p. 296, § 1; Stats.1909, c. 481, p. 824, § 1.

§ 18916. Quorum

A majority of the board shall constitute a quorum for the transaction of business.

(Stats.1976, c. 1010, § 2, operative April 30, 1977.)

Historical and Statutory Notes

Derivation: Educ.C.1959, § 27357 (Stats. 1959, c. 2, p. 1461, § 27357).

Educ.C.1943, § 22218 (Stats.1943, c. 71, p. 738).

Stats.1901, c. 170, p. 558, § 4, amended by Stats.1905, c. 292, p. 296, § 1; Stats.1909, c. 481, p. 824, § 1.

§ 18917. President

The board shall appoint one of its number president, who shall serve for one year and until his successor is appointed, and in his absence shall select a president pro tem.

(Stats.1976, c. 1010, § 2, operative April 30, 1977.)

Historical and Statutory Notes

Derivation: Educ.C.1959, § 27358 (Stats. 1959, c. 2, p. 1462, § 27358).

Educ.C.1943, § 22219 (Stats.1943, c. 71, p. 738).

Stats.1901, c. 170, p. 558, § 4, amended by Stats.1905, c. 292, p. 296, § 1; Stats.1909, c. 481, p. 824, § 1.

§ 18918. Record of proceedings

The board shall cause a proper record of its proceedings to be kept.

(Stats.1976, c. 1010, § 2, operative April 30, 1977.)

Historical and Statutory Notes

Derivation: Educ.C.1959, § 27359 (Stats. 1959, c. 2, p. 1462, § 27359).

Educ.C.1943, § 22220 (Stats.1943, c. 71, p. 738).

Stats.1901, c. 170, p. 558, § 4, amended by Stats.1905, c. 292, p. 296, § 1; Stats.1909, c. 481, p. 824, § 1.

§ 18919. Rules, regulations and by-laws

The board of library trustees may make and enforce all rules, regulations, and bylaws necessary for the administration, government, and protection of the libraries under its management, and all property belonging thereto.

(Stats.1976, c. 1010, § 2, operative April 30, 1977.)

Historical and Statutory Notes

Derivation: Educ.C.1959, § 27360 (Stats. 1959, c. 2, p. 1462, § 27360).

Educ.C.1943, § 22221 (Stats.1943, c. 71, p. 738).

Stats.1901, c. 170, p. 558, § 5, amended by Stats.1909, c. 481, p. 824, § 1.

Cross References

Administrative regulations and rulemaking, see Government Code § 11340 et seq.
Violation of rules, regulations or bylaws, penalty, see Education Code § 18960.

§ 18920. Administration of trusts; receipt, holdings and disposal of property

The board of library trustees may administer any trust declared or created for the library, and receive by gift, devise, or bequest and hold in trust or otherwise, property situated in this state or elsewhere, and where not otherwise provided, dispose of the property for the benefit of the library.

(Stats.1976, c. 1010, § 2, operative April 30, 1977.)

Historical and Statutory Notes

Derivation: Educ.C.1959, § 27361 (Stats. 1959, c. 2, p. 1462, § 27361).

Educ.C.1943, § 22222 (Stats.1943, c. 71, p. 738).

Stats.1901, c. 170, p. 558, § 5, amended by Stats.1909, c. 481, p. 824, § 1.

Cross References

Foundations for institutions of arts and sciences, see Education Code § 21140 et seq.

Notes of Decisions

Funds donated to city   1

---

1. Funds donated to city

Stats.1901, p. 557, c. 170, providing for the establishment of free public libraries and reading rooms, creating a board of trustees, and prescribing their duties, did not embrace the construction of a library to be erected with funds donated to a city unless the gift by its terms and conditions, either expressly or by proper implication, so provided. Board of Library Trustees of City of Hanford v. Board of Trustees of City of Hanford (App. 1906) 2 Cal. App. 760, 84 P. 227.

§ 18921. Officers and employees

The board of library trustees may prescribe the duties and powers of the librarian, secretary, and other officers and employees of the library; determine the number of and appoint all officers and employees, and fix their compensation. The officers and employees shall hold their offices or positions at the pleasure of the board.

(Stats.1976, c. 1010, § 2, operative April 30, 1977.)

Historical and Statutory Notes

Derivation: Educ.C.1959, § 27362 (Stats. 1959, c. 2, p. 1462, § 27362).

Educ.C.1943, § 22223 (Stats.1943, c. 71, p. 739).

Stats.1901, c. 170, p. 558, § 5, amended by Stats.1909, c. 481, p. 824, § 1.

Cross References

Civil service, see Government Code § 45002.

Notes of Decisions

Civil service   2
Employees' status   1

1. Employees' status

Under Educ.C.1959, § 27362 and §§ 27301, 27360, 27368, 27401, 27402, 27453, and 27455 and Gov.C. §§ 45002, 45005, a municipal library, although autonomous as to its internal operations, was not independent of the city and its employees were city employees. City of Ukiah v. Board of Trustees of Municipal Library of City of Ukiah (App. 3 Dist. 1961) 15 Cal.Rptr. 811, 195 Cal.App.2d 344.

2. Civil service

A library employee was an employee of the city, and subject to its civil service ordinance, by virtue of provision therein that it shall be applicable to all employees of the city, even though the ordinance did not specifically designate library employees, and Gov.C. § 45002 provided for separate designation of library employees. City of Ukiah v. Board of Trustees of Municipal Library of City of Ukiah (App. 3 Dist. 1961) 15 Cal.Rptr. 811, 195 Cal.App.2d 344.

§ 18922.   Purchase of personal property

The board of library trustees may purchase necessary books, journals, publications, and other personal property.

(Stats.1976, c. 1010, § 2, operative April 30, 1977.)

Historical and Statutory Notes

Derivation: Educ.C.1959, § 27363 (Stats. 1959, c. 2, p. 1462, § 27363).

Educ.C.1943, § 22224 (Stats.1943, c. 71, p. 739).

Stats.1901, c. 170, p. 558, § 5, amended by Stats.1909, c. 481, p. 824, § 1.

§ 18923.   Authority to purchase real property, and to erect or rent and equip building

The board of library trustees may purchase real property, and erect or rent and equip, such buildings or rooms, as may be necessary, when in its judgment a suitable building, or portion thereof, has not been provided by the legislative body of the municipality for the library.

(Stats.1976, c. 1010, § 2, operative April 30, 1977.)

Historical and Statutory Notes

Derivation: Educ.C.1959, § 27364 (Stats. 1959, c. 2, p. 1462, § 27364).

Educ.C.1943, § 22225 (Stats.1943, c. 71, p. 739).

Stats.1901, c. 170, p. 558, § 5, amended by Stats.1909, c. 481, p. 824, § 1.

§ 18924. State publications

The board of library trustees may request the appropriate state officials to furnish the library with copies of any and all reports, laws, and other publications of the state not otherwise disposed of by law.

(Stats.1976, c. 1010, § 2, operative April 30, 1977.)

Historical and Statutory Notes

Derivation: Educ.C.1959, § 27365 (Stats. 1959, c. 2, p. 1462, § 27365, amended by Stats. 1959, c. 1214, p. 3300, § 1).

Educ.C.1943, § 22226 (Stats.1943, c. 71, p. 739).

Stats.1901, c. 170, c. 558, § 5, amended by Stats.1909, c. 481, p. 825, § 1.

Cross References

Distribution of state publications, see Government Code §§ 9791, 14900 et seq.

§ 18925. Exchanging with other libraries; nonresident borrowing

The board of library trustees may borrow books from, lend books to, and exchange books with other libraries, and may allow nonresidents to borrow books upon such conditions as the board may prescribe.

(Stats.1976, c. 1010, § 2, operative April 30, 1977.)

Historical and Statutory Notes

Derivation: Educ.C.1959, § 27366 (Stats. 1959, c. 2, p. 1462, § 27366).

Educ.C.1943, § 22227 (Stats.1943, c. 71, p. 738).

Stats.1901, c. 170, p. 558, § 5, amended by Stats.1909, c. 481, p. 825, § 1.

§ 18926. Incidental powers of board

The board of library trustees may do and perform any and all other acts and things necessary or proper to carry out the provisions of this chapter.

(Stats.1976, c. 1010, § 2, operative April 30, 1977.)

Historical and Statutory Notes

Derivation: Educ.C.1959, § 27367 (Stats. 1959, c. 2, p. 1462, § 27367).

Educ.C.1943, § 22228 (Stats.1943, c. 71, p. 739).

Stats.1901, c. 170, p. 558, § 5, amended by Stats.1909, c. 481, p. 825, § 1.

§ 18927. Annual report to legislative body and to State Librarian

The board of library trustees, or if there is no board of trustees, then the administrative head of the library shall, on or before August 31st, in each year, report to the legislative body of the municipality and to the State Librarian on the condition of the library, for the year ending the 30th day of June preceding. The reports shall, in addition to other matters deemed expedient by the board of trustees or administrative head of the library, contain such statistical and other information as is deemed desirable by the State Librarian. For this purpose the State Librarian may send to the several boards of trustees or administrative heads of the library instructions or question blanks so as to obtain the material for a comparative study of library conditions in the state.

(Stats.1976, c. 1010, § 2, operative April 30, 1977.)

Historical and Statutory Notes

Derivation: Educ.C.1959, § 27368 (Stats. 1959, c. 2, p. 1462, § 27368).

Educ.C.1943, § 22229 (Stats.1943, c. 71, p. 739, amended by Stats.1957, c. 2135, p. 3787, § 2).

Stats.1901, c. 170, p. 559, § 6, amended by Stats.1905, c. 292, p. 296, § 2; Stats.1909, c. 481, p. 825, § 1.

Cross References

State librarian, see Education Code § 19302 et seq.

Article 3

SUPPORT OF LIBRARIES

Section
18950. Repealed.
18951. Library fund.
18952. Safety, preservation, and application of fund not payable into treasury.
18953. Payments from the library fund.

Article 3 was enacted by Stats.1976, c. 1010, § 2, operative April 30, 1977.

§ 18950. Repealed by Stats.1977, c. 309, § 1, eff. July 8, 1977

Historical and Statutory Notes

The repealed section, enacted by Stats.1976, c. 1010, § 2, authorized a municipality to levy a tax for the construction and maintenance of the library and purchasing property therefor. The repealed section was derived from Educ.C.1959, § 27401, enacted by Stats.1959, c. 2, p. 1463,

§ 27401, amended by Stats.1959, c. 1082, p. 3147, § 1; Stats.1965, c. 1561, p. 3652, § 1; Educ.C.1943, § 22241 (Stats.1943, c. 71, p. 739); Stats.1901, c. 170, p. 559, § 7, amended by Stats.1909, c. 481, p. 825, § 1.

§ 18951. Library fund

All money acquired by gift, devise, bequest, or otherwise, for the purposes of the library, shall be apportioned to a fund to be designated the library fund, and shall be applied to the purposes authorized in this chapter.

(Stats.1976, c. 1010, § 2, operative April 30, 1977. Amended by Stats.1977, c. 309, § 1.1, eff. July 8, 1977.)

Historical and Statutory Notes

Derivation: Educ.C.1959, § 27402 (Stats. 1959, c. 2, p. 1463, § 27402).

Educ.C.1943, § 22242 (Stats.1943, c. 71, p. 739).

Stats.1901, c. 170, p. 559, § 8, amended by Stats.1909, c. 481, p. 825, § 1.

Library References

States ⬖127.
Westlaw Topic No. 360.
C.J.S. States § 228.

§ 18952. Safety, preservation, and application of fund not payable into treasury

If payment into the treasury is inconsistent with the conditions or terms of any gift, devise, or bequest, the board shall provide for the safety and preservation of the fund, and the application thereof to the use of the library, in accordance with the terms and conditions of the gift, devise, or bequest.

(Stats.1976, c. 1010, § 2, operative April 30, 1977.)

Historical and Statutory Notes

Derivation: Educ.C.1959, § 27403 (Stats. 1959, c. 2, p. 1463, § 27403).

Educ.C.1943, § 22243 (Stats.1943, c. 71, p. 740).

Stats.1901, c. 170, p. 559, § 8, amended by Stats.1909, c. 481, p. 825, § 1.

§ 18953. Payments from the library fund

Payments from the fund shall be made upon warrants issued after due audit by, and an order from, the library trustees. The warrants shall be signed by the president and secretary of the board of library trustees. The treasurer of the municipality shall pay such warrants without any further order or warrant from any other authority.

(Stats.1976, c. 1010, § 2, operative April 30, 1977.)

Historical and Statutory Notes

Derivation: Educ.C.1959, § 27404 (Stats. 1959, c. 2, p. 1463, § 27404).

Educ.C.1943, § 22244 (Stats.1943, c. 71, p. 740).

Stats.1901, c. 170, p. 559, § 8, amended by Stats.1909, c. 481, p. 825, § 1.

Article 4

GOVERNMENT

Article 4 was enacted by Stats.1976, c. 1010, § 2, operative April 30, 1977.

§ 18960. Library free to inhabitants; violation of rules, regulations or by-laws

Every library established pursuant to this chapter shall be forever free to the inhabitants and nonresident taxpayers of the municipality, subject always to such rules, regulations, and bylaws as may be made by boards of library

145

trustees. Any person who violates any rule, regulations, or bylaw may be fined or excluded from the privileges of the library.

(Stats.1976, c. 1010, § 2, operative April 30, 1977.)

Historical and Statutory Notes

Derivation: Educ.C.1959, § 27451 (Stats. 1959, c. 2, p. 1463, § 27451).

Educ.C.1943, § 22261 (Stats.1943, c. 71, p. 740).

Stats.1901, c. 170, p. 559, § 9, amended by Stats.1909, c. 481, p. 825, § 1.

Cross References

Administrative regulations and rulemaking, see Government Code § 11340 et seq.
Rules, regulations and bylaws of board of library trustees, see Education Code § 18919.

Library References

Legal Jurisprudences
Am Jur 2d Municipal Corporations, Counties, and Other Political Subdivisions § 542.

Notes of Decisions

Fees   1

_____

1. Fees

Fees may not be charged to local residents for "library services", defined as the satisfaction with library materials of the patron's informational needs, by libraries that are organized under §§ 18300 et seq., 18900 et seq., 19100 et seq., 19400 et seq., 19600 et seq., or Gov.C. § 39732. 61 Ops.Atty.Gen. 512, 11–21–78.

§ 18961.   Contracts with neighboring municipalities or county

The board of library trustees and the legislative body of any neighboring municipality or the board of supervisors of the county in which the public library is situated, may contract for lending the books of the library to residents of the county or neighboring municipality, upon a reasonable compensation to be paid by the county or neighboring municipality.

(Stats.1976, c. 1010, § 2, operative April 30, 1977.)

Historical and Statutory Notes

Derivation: Educ.C.1959, § 27452 (Stats. 1959, c. 2, p. 1463, § 27452).

Educ.C.1943, § 22262 (Stats.1943, c. 71, p. 740).

Stats.1901, c. 170, p. 560, § 10, amended by Stats.1909, c. 481, p. 826, § 1.

Cross References

Affiliation with school libraries, see Education Code § 18134 et seq.
Contracts, generally, see Civil Code § 1549 et seq.
Contracts with counties, see Education Code § 19112.

Notes of Decisions

Rental of city space   1

_____

1.   Rental of city space

A city maintaining a "Carnegie" library under Stats.1901, p. 557, as amended, Stats.1905, p. 296, Stats.1909, p. 823, could charge the county which used part of the library to maintain its county free library under County Free Library Act, Stats.1911, p. 80, as amended, for rent for the use of such space, and the county could pay for such space. 4 Ops.Atty.Gen. 343 (1944).

§ 18962. Title to property

The title to all property acquired for the purposes of the library, when not inconsistent with the terms of its acquisition, or otherwise designated, vests in the municipality in which the library is situated, and in the name of the municipal corporation may be sued for and defended by action at law or otherwise.

(Stats.1976, c. 1010, § 2, operative April 30, 1977.)

Historical and Statutory Notes

Derivation: Educ.C.1959, § 27453 (Stats. 1959, c. 2, p. 1464, § 27453).

Educ.C.1943, § 22263 (Stats.1943, c. 71, p. 740).

Stats.1901, c. 170, p. 560, § 11, amended by Stats.1909, c. 481, p. 826, § 1.

§ 18963. Application of chapter to prior municipal libraries and libraries governed by city charter

Any municipal library which was established and existed on June 11, 1909, under the provisions of an act entitled "An act to establish free public libraries and reading rooms," approved April 26, 1880,[1] is continued under the provisions of this chapter and shall be considered the same as if established under the provisions of this chapter. This chapter has no application to any library established or governed by a city charter, and any city charter is in no manner affected by this chapter.

(Stats.1976, c. 1010, § 2, operative April 30, 1977.)

[1] Stats.1880, c. 126, p. 231.

Historical and Statutory Notes

Derivation: Educ.C.1959, § 27454 (Stats. 1959, c. 2, p. 1464, § 27454).

Educ.C.1943, § 22264 (Stats.1943, c. 71, p. 740).

Stats.1901, c. 170, p. 560, § 12, amended by Stats.1909, c. 481, p. 826, § 1.

§ 18964. Disestablishment of library

Any ordinance establishing a library adopted pursuant to this chapter shall be repealed by the body which adopted it upon being requested to do so by 51 percent of the electors of the municipal corporation, as shown by the great register. Upon the repeal of the ordinance the library is disestablished in the municipal corporation.

(Stats.1976, c. 1010, § 2, operative April 30, 1977.)

Historical and Statutory Notes

Derivation: Educ.C.1959, § 27455 (Stats. 1959, c. 2, p. 1464, § 27455).

Educ.C.1943, § 22265 (Stats.1943, c. 71, p. 740).

Stats.1901, c. 170, p. 560, § 13, amended by Stats.1909, c. 481, p. 826, § 1.

Library References

Legal Jurisprudences
Cal Jur 3d Muni § 295.

§ 18965. Government of public library services upon consolidation

Whenever the governing bodies of two or more cities or counties consolidate their existing public library services, as a joint exercise of powers under Chapter 5 (commencing with Section 6500), Division 7, Title 1 of the Government Code, and the ownership or management of the cities' and counties' library facilities and other library assets are turned over to a newly formed joint agency, any boards of public library trustees existing prior to the consolidation, may be dissolved by ordinance.

(Stats.1976, c. 1010, § 2, operative April, 30, 1977.)

Historical and Statutory Notes

Derivation: Educ.C.1959, § 27456, added by Stats.1963, c. 1143, p. 2623, § 1.

Chapter 6

COUNTY FREE LIBRARIES

Chapter 6 was enacted by Stats.1976, c. 1010, § 2, operative April 30, 1977.

Cross References

Board of supervisors, see Government Code §§ 25000, 25003 et seq.
Construction,
    Lease and construction, generally, see Government Code § 26150.
    Repair and construction of buildings only from taxes on property part of county free library system, see Government Code § 25351.
County free libraries, see Government Code § 26150 et seq.
County service areas, extended library facilities and services, authority of board of supervisors and funding, see Government Code § 25210.78 et seq.
County libraries, contracts to provide school library services, see Education Code § 1773.
Library service at county institutions, see Government Code § 26151.
Reimbursement for costs mandated by state, inclusion of county free libraries as special districts, see Revenue and Taxation Code § 2216.
Supervision by state librarian, see Education Code § 19167.

Article 1

ESTABLISHMENT

Section
19100. Power to establish and maintain.

Section

Article 1 was enacted by Stats.1976, c. 1010, § 2, operative April 30, 1977.

Cross References

Construction, lease, etc., see Government Code § 26150.
County libraries, contracts to provide school library services, see Education Code § 1773.
Library service at county institutions, see Government Code § 26151.
Supervision by state librarian, see Education Code § 19167.

§ 19100. Power to establish and maintain

The boards of supervisors of the several counties may establish and maintain, within their respective counties, county free libraries pursuant to this chapter.

(Stats.1976, c. 1010, § 2, operative April 30, 1977.)

Historical and Statutory Notes

Derivation: Educ.C.1959, § 27151 (Stats. 1959, c. 2, p. 1454, § 27151).

Educ.C.1943, § 22101 (Stats.1943, c. 71, p. 732).

Stats.1911, c. 68, p. 80, § 1.

Cross References

Board of supervisors, see Government Code §§ 25000, 25003 et seq.
Construction and repair of buildings only from taxes on property part of county free library system, see Government Code § 25351.
County free libraries, see Government Code § 26150 et seq.
County service areas, extended library facilities and services, authority of board of supervisors and funding, see Government Code § 25210.78 et seq.

Library References

Counties ☞47.
Westlaw Topic No. 104.
C.J.S. Counties §§ 70 to 73.

Legal Jurisprudences

Cal Jur 3d Sch § 47.

Notes of Decisions

Exemption from tax 1
Fees 2

1. Exemption from tax

School district's maintenance of free circulating library did not exempt property in district from tax for support of county library. Redman v. Weisenheimer (App. 2 Dist. 1929) 102 Cal. App. 488, 283 P. 363.

2. Fees

Fees may not be charged to local residents for "library services", defined as the satisfaction with library materials of the patron's informational needs, by libraries that are organized under §§ 18300 et seq., 18900 et seq., 19100 et seq., 19400 et seq., 19600 et seq., or Gov.C. § 39732. 61 Ops.Atty.Gen. 512, 11–21–78.

§ 19101. Establishment at the county seat or elsewhere in the county

The board of supervisors of any county may establish at the county seat or elsewhere in the county, a county free library for that part of the county lying outside of cities maintaining free public libraries, and outside of library districts maintaining district libraries, and for all such additional portions of the county as may elect to become a part of, or to participate in, the county free library system as provided in this chapter.

(Stats.1976, c. 1010, § 2, operative April 30, 1977.)

Historical and Statutory Notes

Derivation: Educ.C.1959, § 27152 (Stats. 1959, c. 2, p. 1454, § 27152).

Educ.C.1943, § 22102 (Stats.1943, c. 71, p. 732, amended by Stats.1957, c. 653, p. 1852, § 1).

Stats.1911, c. 68, p. 80, § 2.

Cross References

Board of supervisors, see Government Code §§ 25000, 25003 et seq.
County free libraries, see Government Code § 26150 et seq.
County service areas, extended library facilities and services, authority of board of supervisors and funding, see Government Code § 25210.78 et seq.

Library References

Legal Jurisprudences

Cal Jur 3d Sch § 47.

Notes of Decisions

Eligibility to vote 2
Free library services 1

1. Free library services

Under this section, a county free library service may be provided in absence of notice or contract in a city which does not maintain a free public library. 22 Ops.Atty.Gen. 9 (1953).

2. Eligibility to vote

Electors residing in a library district and in cities maintaining free public libraries are eligible to vote in proposed referendum election on question whether to establish a county free library, even though the county free library may be established only for that part of the county lying outside of the cities maintaining free public libraries and outside library districts maintaining district libraries. 28 Ops.Atty.Gen. 100 (1956).

§ 19102. Publication of notice of contemplated action

At least once a week for two successive weeks prior to taking any action, the board of supervisors shall publish, in a newspaper designated by it and published in the county, notice of the contemplated action, giving the date of the meeting at which the action is proposed to be taken.

(Stats.1976, c. 1010, § 2, operative April 30, 1977.)

Historical and Statutory Notes

Derivation: Educ.C.1959, § 27153 (Stats. 1959, c. 2, p. 1454, § 27153).

Educ.C.1943, § 22103 (Stats.1943, c. 71, p. 732).

Stats.1911, c. 68, p. 80, § 2.

Cross References

Board of supervisors, see Government Code §§ 25000, 25003 et seq.
Publication, generally, see Government Code § 6000 et seq.

§ 19103. Participation by city or library districts in the county library system

After the establishment of a county free library, the board of trustees, common council, or other legislative body of any city in the county maintaining a free public library, or the board of trustees of any library district maintaining a district library, may notify the board of supervisors that the city or library district desires to become a part of the county free library system. Thereafter the city or library district shall be a part of the system and its inhabitants shall be entitled to the benefits of the county free library, and the property within the city or library district shall be liable to taxes levied for county free library purposes.

(Stats.1976, c. 1010, § 2, operative April 30, 1977.)

Historical and Statutory Notes

Derivation: Educ.C.1959, § 27154 (Stats. 1959, c. 2, p. 1454, § 27154).

Educ.C.1943, § 22104 (Stats.1943, c. 71, p. 732).

Stats.1911, c. 68, p. 80, § 3, amended by Stats.1939, c. 234, p. 1492, § 1.

Cross References

Board of supervisors, see Government Code §§ 25000, 25003 et seq.
County free libraries, see Government Code § 26150 et seq.
County service areas, extended library facilities and services, authority of board of supervisors and funding, see Government Code § 25210.78 et seq.
School districts, affiliation with county and city libraries, see Education Code § 18130 et seq.
Tax levies, see Government Code § 29100 et seq. and Revenue and Taxation Code § 2151 et seq.
Taxes, special taxes imposed on behalf of public libraries, authority of cities, counties and other agencies, see Government Code § 53717.

Library References

Legal Jurisprudences

Cal Jur 3d Sch § 47.

Notes of Decisions

Absence of notice   1
Taxable property   2

1. Absence of notice

Under Educ.C.1943, § 22102, a county free library service might be provided in absence of notice or contract in a city which did not main-

tain a free public library. 22 Ops.Atty.Gen. 9 (1953).

2. Taxable property

Property in a library district is subject to taxation for county free library purposes to the same extent as property in the remainder of the county, just as though the library district had not been created. 28 Ops.Atty.Gen. 100 (1956).

§ 19104. Withdrawal of city or library district from county library system

The board of trustees, common council, or other legislative body of any city or the board of trustees of any library district may on or before January 1st of any year, notify the board of supervisors that the city or library district no longer desires to be a part of the county free library system. The notice shall be accompanied by a statement complying with the requirements of Chapter 8 (commencing with Section 54900) of Part 1 of Division 2 of Title 5 of the Government Code. The clerk of the board of supervisors shall file the statement with the county assessor and the State Board of Equalization. Thereafter the city or library district shall cease to participate in the benefits of the county free library, and the property situated in the city or library district shall not be liable to taxes for county free library purposes.

(Stats.1976, c. 1010, § 2, operative April 30, 1977.)

Historical and Statutory Notes

Derivation: Educ.C.1959, § 27155 (Stats. 1959, c. 2, p. 1454, § 27155, amended by Stats. 1972, c. 1135, p. 2190, § 2; Stats.1973, c. 842, p. 1506, § 1).

Educ.C.1943, § 22105 (Stats.1943, c. 71, p. 732).

Stats.1911, c. 68, p. 80, § 3, amended by Stats.1939, c. 234, p. 1492, § 1.

Cross References

County free libraries, see Government Code § 26150 et seq.
County service areas, extended library facilities and services, authority of board of supervisors and funding, see Government Code § 25210.78 et seq.
Taxes, special taxes imposed on behalf of public libraries, authority of cities, counties and other agencies, see Government Code § 53717.

§ 19105. Effective date of withdrawal

If the notice is given after January 1st of any year, the property situated in the city or library district shall be liable to taxes for county free library purposes during the immediately succeeding year, and the notice shall not be effective until the next succeeding year, and library service shall be rendered in the city or library district during the year for which taxes are levied for library purposes in the city or library district.

(Stats.1976, c. 1010, § 2, operative April 30, 1977.)

Historical and Statutory Notes

Derivation: Educ.C.1959, § 27156 (Stats. 1959, c. 2, p. 1455, § 27156, amended by Stats. 1972, c. 1135, p. 2190, § 3).

Educ.C.1943, § 22106 (Stats.1943, c. 71, p. 732).

Stats.1911, c. 68, p. 80, § 3, amended by
Stats.1939, c. 234, p. 1492, § 1.

Cross References

County free libraries, see Government Code § 26150 et seq.
County service areas, extended library facilities and services, authority of board of supervisors and
    funding, see Government Code § 25210.78 et seq.
Tax levies, see Government Code § 29100 et seq. and Revenue and Taxation Code § 2151 et seq.
Taxes, special taxes imposed on behalf of public libraries, authority of cities, counties and other
    agencies, see Government Code § 53717.

§ 19106. Publication of notice of contemplated participation in, or withdrawal from, county library system

Before any board of trustees, common council, or other legislative body of
any city, or the board of trustees of any library district gives notice that the city
or library district desires to become a part of the county free library system, or
gives notice of withdrawal from the system, the board of trustees, common
council, or other legislative body of the city or the board of trustees of the
library district shall publish at least once a week for two successive weeks prior
to the giving of either notice, in a newspaper designated by the board of
trustees, common council, or other legislative body of the city or the board of
library trustees of the library district, and circulating throughout the city or
library district, notice of the contemplated action, giving the date and the place
of the meeting at which the contemplated action is proposed to be taken.

(Stats.1976, c. 1010, § 2, operative April 30, 1977.)

Historical and Statutory Notes

Derivation: Educ.C.1959, § 27157 (Stats.
1959, c. 2, p. 1455, § 27157).
    Educ.C.1943, § 22107 (Stats.1943, c. 71, p.
733).

Stats.1911, c. 68, p. 80, § 3, amended by
Stats.1939, c. 234, p. 1492, § 1.

Cross References

County free libraries, see Government Code § 26150 et seq.
County service areas, extended library facilities and services, authority of board of supervisors and
    funding, see Government Code § 25210.78 et seq.
Publication, generally, see Government Code § 6000 et seq.

§ 19107. Contracts with cities

The board of supervisors of any county in which a county free library has
been established may enter into contracts with any city maintaining a free
public library, and any such city, through its board of trustees or other
legislative body, may enter into contracts with the county to secure to the
residents of the city the same privileges of the county free library as are granted
to, or enjoyed by, the residents of the county outside of the city, or such
privileges as are agreed upon in the contract, upon such consideration named
in the contract as is agreed upon, to be paid into the county free library fund.
Thereupon the residents of the city shall have the same privileges with regard to
the county free library as the residents of the county outside of the city, or such
privileges as are agreed upon by the contract.

(Stats.1976, c. 1010, § 2, operative April 30, 1977.)

Historical and Statutory Notes

Derivation: Educ.C.1959, § 27158 (Stats. 1959, c. 2, p. 1455, § 27158).

Educ.C.1943, § 22108 (Stats.1943, c. 71, p. 733).

Stats.1911, c. 68, p. 81, § 4.

Cross References

Board of supervisors, see Government Code §§ 25000, 25003 et seq.
Contracts, generally, see Civil Code § 1549 et seq.
County free libraries, see Government Code § 26150 et seq.
County service areas, extended library facilities and services, authority of board of supervisors and funding, see Government Code § 25210.78 et seq.

Notes of Decisions

Absence of contract 1

_____

1. Absence of contract

Under Educ.C.1943, § 22102 (repealed) a county free library service may be provided in

absence of notice or contract in a city which did not maintain a free public library. 2 Ops.Atty. Gen. 9 (1943).

§ 19108. Contracts with other counties

The board of supervisors of any county in which a county free library has been established may enter into a contract with the board of supervisors of any other county to secure to the residents of the other county such privileges of the county free library as are agreed upon by the contract and upon such considerations as are agreed upon in the contract to be paid into the county free library fund. Thereupon the inhabitants of the other county shall have such privileges of the county free library as are agreed upon by the contract.

(Stats.1976, c. 1010, § 2, operative April 30, 1977.)

Historical and Statutory Notes

Derivation: Educ.C.1959, § 27159 (Stats. 1959, c. 2, p. 1455, § 27159).

Educ.C.1943, § 22109 (Stats.1943, c. 71, p. 733).

Stats.1911, c. 68, p. 81, § 5.

Cross References

Board of supervisors, see Government Code §§ 25000, 25003 et seq.
Contracts, generally, see Civil Code § 1549 et seq.
County free libraries, see Government Code § 26150 et seq.
County service areas, extended library facilities and services, authority of board of supervisors and funding, see Government Code § 25210.78 et seq.

§ 19109. Authority to contract and to levy library tax to carry out contract

The board of supervisors of any county may enter into a contract with the board of supervisors of another county in which a county free library has been established, and may levy a library tax, for the purpose of carrying out the contract.

(Stats.1976, c. 1010, § 2, operative April 30, 1977.)

Historical and Statutory Notes

Derivation: Educ.C.1959, § 27160 (Stats. 1959, c. 2, p. 1456, § 27160).

Educ.C.1943, § 22110 (Stats.1943, c. 71, p. 733).

Stats.1911, c. 68, p. 81, § 5.

Cross References

Board of supervisors, see Government Code §§ 25000, 25003 et seq.
Contracts, generally, see Civil Code § 1549 et seq.
County free libraries, see Government Code § 26150 et seq.
County service areas, extended library facilities and services, authority of board of supervisors and funding, see Government Code § 25210.78 et seq.
Tax levies, see Government Code § 29100 et seq. and Revenue and Taxation Code § 2151 et seq.
Taxes, special taxes imposed on behalf of public libraries, authority of cities, counties and other agencies, see Government Code § 53717.

Library References

Counties ☜111(1), 190.1.
Westlaw Topic No. 104.
C.J.S. Counties §§ 150, 227.

§ 19110. Contracts with other counties for services of librarian

The board of supervisors of any county may contract with the board of supervisors of any other county or two or more other counties to provide for the services of a single qualified librarian to serve simultaneously as the county librarian of each county.

(Stats.1976, c. 1010, § 2, operative April 30, 1977. Amended by Stats.1991, c. 52 (A.B.490), § 1.)

Historical and Statutory Notes

Derivation: Educ.C.1959, § 27161 (Stats. 1959, c. 2, p. 1456, § 27161).

Educ.C.1943, § 22110.5, added by Stats.1957, c. 2151, p. 3809, § 1.

Cross References

Board of supervisors, see Government Code §§ 25000, 25003 et seq.
Contracts, generally, see Civil Code § 1549 et seq.
County librarian, see Education Code § 19140 et seq.; Government Code § 24000 et seq.

§ 19111. Termination of contract upon the establishment of county library

The making of the contract shall not bar the board of supervisors of the county during the continuance of the contract from establishing a county free library under the provisions of this chapter if none is already established. Upon the establishment of any county free library, the contract may be terminated upon such terms as may be agreed upon by the parties thereto, or may continue for the term thereof.

(Stats.1976, c. 1010, § 2, operative April 30, 1977.)

Historical and Statutory Notes

Derivation: Educ.C.1959, § 27162 (Stats. 1959, c. 2, p. 1456, § 27162).

Educ.C.1943, § 22111 (Stats.1943, c. 71, p. 733).

Stats.1911, c. 68, p. 81, § 59.

§ 19112. Contract that city library assume functions of county library

Instead of establishing a separate county free library, the board of supervisors may enter into a contract with the board of library trustees or other authority in charge of the free public library of any city and the board of library trustees, or other authority in charge of the free public library, may make such a contract. The contract may provide that the free public library of the city shall assume the functions of a county free library within the county with which the contract is made, including cities in the county. The board of supervisors may agree to pay annually into the library fund of the city such sum as may be agreed upon. Either party to the contract may terminate the contract by giving six months' notice of intention to do so.

(Stats.1976, c. 1010, § 2, operative April 30, 1977.)

Notes of Decisions

Rental of city space   1

———

1. **Rental of city space**

A city maintaining a "Carnegie" library under Stats.1905, p. 296, Stats.1909, p. 823, could charge the county which used part of the library to maintain its county free library under County Free Library Act, Stats.1911, p. 80, as amended, for rent for the use of such space, and the county could pay for such space. 4 Ops.Atty. Gen. 343 (1944).

§ 19113. Disestablishment of county library

After a county free library has been established, it may be disestablished in the same manner as it was established. At least once a week for two successive weeks prior to taking any action, the board of supervisors shall publish, in a newspaper designated by them, and published in the county, notice of the contemplated action, giving therein the date of the meeting at which the contemplated action is proposed to be taken.

(Stats.1976, c. 1010, § 2, operative April 30, 1977.)

Historical and Statutory Notes

Derivation: Educ.C.1959, § 27164 (Stats.   Stats.1911, c. 68, p. 85, § 15.
1959, c. 2, p. 1456, § 27164).

Educ.C.1943, § 22113 (Stats.1943, c. 71, p.
734).

Cross References

Board of supervisors, see Government Code §§ 25000, 25003 et seq.
County free libraries, see Government Code § 26150 et seq.
County service areas, extended library facilities and services, authority of board of supervisors and
     funding, see Government Code § 25210.78 et seq.
Publication, generally, see Government Code § 6000 et seq.

§ 19114. Annexation of territory by municipal corporation not served by county library

Whenever any of the territory being served by a county free library is annexed to, or otherwise included within, any municipal corporation not served by the county free library, the board of supervisors of the county shall order the county free library to continue to serve the territory annexed to, or otherwise included within the municipality, until the end of the fiscal year or years for which a tax has been levied upon the property of the annexed territory for the support of the county free library.

(Stats.1976, c. 1010, § 2, operative April 30, 1977.)

Historical and Statutory Notes

Derivation: Educ.C.1959, § 27165 (Stats.   Stats.1927, c. 592, p. 1028, § 1.
1959, c. 2, p. 1456, § 27165).

Educ.C.1943, § 22114 (Stats.1943, c. 71, p.
734).

Cross References

Board of supervisors, see Government Code §§ 25000, 25003 et seq.
County free libraries, see Government Code § 26150 et seq.
County service areas, extended library facilities and services, authority of board of supervisors and
     funding, see Government Code § 25210.78 et seq.
Tax levies, see Government Code § 29100 et seq. and Revenue and Taxation Code § 2151 et seq.
Taxes, special taxes imposed on behalf of public libraries, authority of cities, counties and other
     agencies, see Government Code § 53717.

§ 19115. Use of library by nonresidents of territory taxed for library purposes

The board of supervisors may establish a reasonable fee to be collected from persons who desire to participate in the services and benefits of the county free library and who are not residents of the territory in the county which is liable for taxes for county free library purposes. In establishing the fee, the board may also prescribe such regulations or limitations applicable to the use of the county free library by such persons as may reasonably be necessary.

(Stats.1976, c. 1010, § 2, operative April 30, 1977.)

§ 19115

GENERAL PROVISIONS
Div. 1

Historical and Statutory Notes

Derivation: Educ.C.1959, § 27166, added by
Stats.1961, c. 1165, p. 2907, § 1.

Cross References

Board of supervisors, see Government Code §§ 25000, 25003 et seq.
County free libraries, see Government Code § 26150 et seq.
County service areas, extended library facilities and services, authority of board of supervisors and
 funding, see Government Code § 25210.78 et seq.
Taxes, special taxes imposed on behalf of public libraries, authority of cities, counties and other
 agencies, see Government Code § 53717.

§ 19116. Los Angeles County or Riverside County; withdrawal of city or library district from county library system

(a) Sections 19104 and 19105 are not applicable to the withdrawal of a city or library district from the county free library system in Los Angeles County or Riverside County. The legislative body of any city or the board of trustees of any library district, whose jurisdiction is within the County of Los Angeles or the County of Riverside, may notify the board of supervisors for Los Angeles County or Riverside County, as appropriate, that the city or library district no longer desires to be a part of the county free library system. The notice shall state whether the city or library district intends to acquire property pursuant to subdivision (c). The board of supervisors shall transmit a copy of the notice to the Los Angeles County Assessor or Riverside County Assessor, as appropriate, the Los Angeles County Auditor or Riverside County Auditor, as appropriate, and the State Board of Equalization.

(b) When a city or library district files a notice pursuant to subdivision (a), it shall remain a member of the county free library system until July 1 of the base year or the date on which property is transferred pursuant to subdivision (c), whichever date is later. Upon ceasing to be a member of the county free library system, the city or library district shall not participate in any benefits of the county free library system, and shall assume the responsibility for the provision of library services within its jurisdiction. Unless otherwise agreed by July 1 of the base year in writing by the Board of Supervisors of Los Angeles County or the Board of Supervisors of Riverside County, as appropriate, and the withdrawing city or library district, an amount of property tax revenue equal to the property tax revenues allocated to the county free library pursuant to Article 2 (commencing with Section 96) of Chapter 6 of Part 0.5 of Division 1 of the Revenue and Taxation Code in the fiscal year prior to the base year and that were derived from property situated within the boundaries of the withdrawing entity shall be allocated to and used to maintain library services by the withdrawing entity in the base year and, adjusted forward, in each fiscal year thereafter at the same time allocations are made pursuant to Article 2 (commencing with Section 96) of Chapter 6 of Part 0.5 of Division 1 of the Revenue and Taxation Code. This subdivision shall not apply to property tax revenues that have been pledged to repay bonded indebtedness of the county free library.

(c) If there are one or more county library facilities within the territorial boundaries of the withdrawing entity at the time the withdrawing entity provides notice pursuant to subdivision (a), the withdrawing entity shall have the right to acquire any or all of those facilities from the county and the county shall, no later than July 1 of the base year, transfer to the withdrawing entity each facility to be acquired and the personal property therein related to the provision of library services. If the facility or personal property was purchased with bond proceeds or other forms of indebtedness, acquisition shall only take place if the withdrawing entity assumes any remaining indebtedness and in no way impairs the repayment thereof. If the withdrawing entity opts not to acquire any facilities or personal property, the county at its discretion may dispose of the facilities or personal property or convert the use of those facilities or personal property, including transferring collections and other personal property to other sites and converting facilities to other purposes. If the withdrawing entity opts to acquire any facilities or personal property, the acquisition prices shall be as follows unless otherwise provided for by statute or contract:

(1) Each county library facility which, for the purposes of this section, shall include the real property upon which the facility is located and any fixtures therein and shall not include computer systems and software, shall be transferred for the lesser of:

(A) No cost, if the facility was donated to the county by the withdrawing entity.

(B) The price paid to the withdrawing entity by the county for the facility, if the county bought the facility from the withdrawing entity. However, if the county constructed capital improvements to the facility after it was bought from the withdrawing entity, the county's total out-of-pocket costs for the capital improvement excluding any costs for routine repairs, restoration or maintenance, shall be added to the price.

(C) The fair market value of the facility. However, if any portion of the facility was donated to the county by the withdrawing entity or if any moneys were donated by the withdrawing entity towards the county's construction or acquisition of the facility or any portion thereof, the value of the donation shall be subtracted from the fair market value.

(2) Any personal property within the facility related to the provision of library services, including books and resource materials, computer systems and software, furniture, and furnishings, shall be transferred for the lesser of:

(A) No cost, if the property was donated to the county by the withdrawing entity.

(B) The fair market value of the personal property. However, on or before the March 1 preceding the July 1 of the base year, the county librarian may designate collections of resource books and materials that are unique in, and integral to, the county free library system to be special collections. The special collections shall be acquired by the withdrawing entity only upon mutually agreeable terms and conditions.

(d) If a facility transferred pursuant to subdivision (c) serves residents of surrounding jurisdictions, the board of supervisors governing the county free library system may require, as a condition of transferring the facility, that the library services provided by the withdrawing entity to its residents also be available on the same basis to the residents of the surrounding jurisdictions. However, if the withdrawing entity contributes to the provision of library services from other city funds, or through taxes, assessments, or fees of its residents, the withdrawing entity may provide additional services to its residents. If the requirement to provide regional services is imposed and, unless otherwise agreed in writing by the county and the withdrawing entity by July 1 of the base year, an amount of property tax revenues equal to the property tax revenues derived from property situated in the surrounding jurisdictions which were, in the fiscal year prior to the base year, allocated to the county free library system pursuant to Article 2 (commencing with Section 96) of Chapter 6 of Part 0.5 of Division 1 of the Revenue and Taxation Code shall be allocated to and used to maintain library services by the withdrawing entity in the base year and, adjusted forward, in each fiscal year thereafter at the same time other allocations are made pursuant to Article 2 (commencing with Section 96) of Chapter 6 of Part 0.5 of Division 1 of the Revenue and Taxation Code. This subdivision shall not apply to property tax revenues that have been pledged to repay bonded indebtedness. If a surrounding jurisdiction subsequently provides notice of its intent to withdraw from the county free library system pursuant to subdivision (a), on the date the surrounding jurisdiction ceases to participate in the benefits of the county free library system pursuant to subdivision (b), the withdrawing entity shall no longer be required to make library services available to the residents of the surrounding jurisdiction and property tax revenues derived from property situated in the surrounding jurisdiction shall no longer be allocated to the withdrawing entity pursuant to this subdivision.

(e) For purposes of this section, the following terms are defined as follows:

(1) "Base year" means the fiscal year commencing on the July 1 following the December 2 following the date of the notice given pursuant to subdivision (a) of this section.

(2) "Fair market value" means:

(A) Any value agreed upon by the withdrawing entity and the county.

(B) If no agreement as to value is reached by the March 1 preceding the July 1 of the base year, the value assigned by an appraiser agreed upon by the withdrawing entity and the county.

(C) If no agreement as to the appointment of an appraiser is reached pursuant to subparagraph (B) by the April 1 preceding the July 1 of the base year, the value assigned by an appraiser agreed upon between the withdrawing entity's appraiser and the county's appraiser.

(D) If no agreement as to the appointment of an appraiser is reached pursuant to subparagraph (C) by the May 1 preceding the July 1 of the base year, the value assigned by a state certified appraiser designated by the withdrawing entity. The designated appraiser shall provide the appraisal in writing to the county no later than the June 1 preceding the July 1 of the base year.

(E) The withdrawing entity shall reimburse the county for any appraisal costs the county incurs in determining the fair market value pursuant to this section.

(3) "Surrounding jurisdictions" means cities and library districts that are adjacent to the withdrawing entity and tax rate areas in unincorporated areas of the county which tax rate areas are wholly or partially within the withdrawing entity's sphere of influence, which cities, libraries, and tax rate areas are within the county free library system and have no facility within their territorial boundaries providing library services at the time the withdrawing entity provides notice pursuant to subdivision (a).

(Added by Stats.1996, c. 522 (S.B.1998), § 1, operative July 1, 1997. Amended by Stats.1996, c. 523 (A.B.1767), § 1, operative July 1, 1997; Stats.1997, c. 248 (A.B.927), § 1, eff. Aug. 8, 1997; Stats.1998, c. 485 (A.B.2803), § 49.)

Historical and Statutory Notes

Section 2 of Stats.1996, c. 523 (A.B.1767), provides:

"(a) This bill shall become operative only if Senate Bill 1998 of the 1995–96 Regular Session [Stats.1996, c. 522] is enacted and becomes effective on or before January 1, 1997, and adds Section 19116 to the Education Code.

"(b) If the condition set forth in subdivision (a) is satisfied, this bill shall become operative on July 1, 1997."

Section affected by two or more acts at the same session of the legislature, see Government Code § 9605.

Section 2 of Stats.1997, c. 248 (A.B.927), provides:

"Due to unique facts and circumstances applicable to Riverside County, insofar as the withdrawal of cities and libraries from the Riverside County free library system, the Legislature finds and declares that a general statute cannot be made applicable within the meaning of Section 16 of Article IV of the California Constitution."

Cross References

Allocation of property tax revenue,
    Jurisdictional changes and negotiated transfers, see Revenue and Taxation Code § 99.
    Revenue allocation shifts for education, reductions in revenue deemed allocated in prior fiscal year, see Revenue and Taxation Code § 97.37.
    Tax equity allocations for certain cities, counties other than Ventura with qualifying cities within boundaries, see Revenue and Taxation Code § 98.
County free libraries, see Government Code § 26150 et seq.
County service areas, extended library facilities and services, authority of board of supervisors and funding, see Government Code § 25210.78 et seq.
Taxes, special taxes imposed on behalf of public libraries, authority of cities, counties and other agencies, see Government Code § 53717.

Article 2

COUNTY LIBRARIAN

Section
19150.   Qualifications for acting or assistant librarian.

Article 2 was enacted by Stats.1976, c. 1010, § 2, operative April 30, 1977.

Cross References

County librarian as county officer, see Government Code § 24000.
County librarian serving two or more counties, see Education Code § 19110.

§ 19140.   Appointment of county librarian

Upon the establishment of a county free library, the board of supervisors shall appoint a county librarian.

(Stats.1976, c. 1010, § 2, operative April 30, 1977.)

Historical and Statutory Notes

Derivation: Educ.C.1959, § 27201 (Stats. 1959, c. 2, p. 1457, § 27201, amended by Stats. 1959, c. 911, p. 2945, § 1).

Educ.C.1943, § 22131 (Stats.1943, c. 71, p. 734).

Stats.1911, c. 68, p. 82, § 7.

Cross References

Board of supervisors, see Government Code §§ 25000, 25003 et seq.
County free libraries, see Government Code § 26150 et seq.
County librarian as a county officer, see Government Code § 24000.
County service areas, extended library facilities and services, authority of board of supervisors and
   funding, see Government Code § 25210.78 et seq.

Library References

Counties ☞61.
Westlaw Topic No. 104.
C.J.S. Counties § 97.

Legal Jurisprudences

Cal Jur 3d Sch § 49.

Notes of Decisions

Salary   1

————

1. Salary

   Under Educ.C.1943, § 22131 and Educ.C. 1943, §§ 22132 to 22138 and Gov.C. § 24000, if

salary of county librarian was fixed at $2700 it could not be increased during a fixed four year term of office even when the term ran with the office and not with the officer. 14 Ops.Atty. Gen. 234 (1949).

§ 19141.   Civil service

If any county adopts a civil service system or a limited civil service system for county officers and employees, the county librarian shall be entitled to the benefits of such civil service system.

This section does not limit any powers conferred on any county by charter.

(Stats.1976, c. 1010, § 2, operative April 30, 1977.)

Historical and Statutory Notes

Derivation: Educ.C.1959, § 27201.5, added
by Stats.1959, c. 911, p. 2946, § 2.

§ 19142. Qualifications

No person may be appointed to the office of county librarian on or after January 1, 1987, unless he or she possesses both of the following qualifications:

(a) Graduation from a graduate library school program accredited by the American Library Association.

(b) Demonstrated knowledge of principles and practices of public administration, including county government, and of the laws applicable to library service in this state.

(Stats.1976, c. 1010, § 2, operative April 30, 1977. Amended by Stats.1986, c. 269, § 1.)

Historical and Statutory Notes

Derivation: Educ.C.1959, § 27202 (Stats. 1959, c. 2, p. 1457, § 27207).

Educ.C.1943, § 22132 (Stats.1943, c. 71, p. 734).

Stats.1911, c. 68, p. 82, § 7.

Library References

Legal Jurisprudences

Cal Jur 3d Sch § 49.

§ 19143. State citizenship

At the time of his or her appointment, the county librarian need not be a citizen of the State of California.

(Stats.1976, c. 1010, § 2, operative April 30, 1977. Amended by Stats.1987, c. 1452, § 112; Stats.1991, c. 52 (A.B.490), § 2.)

Historical and Statutory Notes

Legislative findings, declarations and intent relating to Stats.1987, c. 1452, see Historical and Statutory Notes under Education Code § 1007.

Derivation: Educ.C.1959, § 27203 (Stats. 1959, c. 2, p. 1457, § 27203).

Educ.C.1943, § 22133 (Stats.1943, c. 71, p. 734).

Stats.1911, c. 68, p. 82, § 7.

§ 19144. Repealed by Stats.1987, c. 1452, § 113

Historical and Statutory Notes

The repealed section, enacted by Stats.1976, c. 1010, § 2, derived from Educ.C.1959, § 27204 (Stats.1959, c. 2, p. 1457, § 27204); Educ.C.1943, § 22134 (Stats.1943, c. 71, p. 734); and Stats.1911, c. 68, p. 82, § 6, related to eligibility of persons of either sex for office of county librarian.

Legislative findings, declarations and intent relating to Stats.1987, c. 1452, see Historical and Statutory Notes under Education Code § 1007.

§ 19145. Oath and bond

The county librarian shall, prior to entering upon his duties, file the usual oath, and he shall be required to file an official bond in an amount determined by the board of supervisors, unless he is covered by a master bond pursuant to Section 1481 of the Government Code.

(Stats.1976, c. 1010, § 2, operative April 30, 1977.)

Historical and Statutory Notes

Derivation: Educ.C.1959, § 27205 (Stats. 1959, c. 2, p. 1457, § 27205, amended by Stats. 1973, c. 112, p. 173, § 2).

Educ.C.1943, § 22135 (Stats.1943, c. 71, p. 734).

Stats.1911, c. 68, p. 83, § 9, amended by Stats.1921, c. 40, p. 52, § 1.

Cross References

Board of supervisors, see Government Code §§ 25000, 25003 et seq.
Oath,
    Administration and certification of oaths, see Education Code § 60.
    Defined, see Education Code § 76.
    Oath of office, public officers and employees, see Const. Art. 20, § 3 and Government Code
        § 1360 et seq.
Official bonds, see Government Code § 1450 et seq.

Library References

Legal Jurisprudences
    Am Jur 2d (Rev) Public Officers and Employ-
        ees § 131.

§ 19146. Duties

The county librarian shall, subject to the general rules adopted by the board of supervisors, build up and manage, according to accepted principles of library management, a library for the use of the people of the county, and shall determine what books and other library equipment shall be purchased.

(Stats.1976, c. 1010, § 2, operative April 30, 1977.)

Historical and Statutory Notes

Derivation: Educ.C.1959, § 27206 (Stats. 1959, c. 2, p. 1457, § 27206).

Educ.C.1943, § 22136 (Stats.1943, c. 71, p. 735).

Stats.1911, c. 68, p. 83, § 9, amended by Stats.1921, c. 40, p. 52, § 1.

Cross References

Board of supervisors, see Government Code §§ 25000, 25003 et seq.

Notes of Decisions

Purchase or destruction of books   1

———

1. Purchase or destruction of books

Under Educ.C.1959, § 27253 and § 27206 limiting board of supervisors to adoption of general rules and regulations regarding policy of county free library, such board may not order purchase or destruction of certain book for the county library, because this function is vested in certified county librarian. 42 Ops.Atty.Gen. 18 (1963).

§ 19147. Payment of salary

The salary of the county librarians shall be paid by each of the counties in equal monthly installments, at the same time and in the same manner and out of the same fund as the salaries of other county officers are paid.

(Stats.1976, c. 1010, § 2, operative April 30, 1977.)

Historical and Statutory Notes

Derivation: Educ.C.1959, § 27207 (Stats. 1959, c. 2, p. 1457, § 27207).

Educ.C.1943, § 22137 (Stats.1943, c. 71, p. 735).

Stats.1911, c. 68, p. 83, § 9, amended by Stats.1921, c. 40, p. 52, § 1.

§ 19148. Payment of salary in county with more than 400,000 population

The board of supervisors of a county over 400,000 population, as determined by the 1960 decennial census, maintaining a county free library may provide that the salary of the county librarian be paid from the same fund used for maintaining and operating the county free library.

Nothing in this section shall be construed as modifying the status of the county librarian as a county official pursuant to Section 24000 of the Government Code.

(Stats.1976, c. 1010, § 2, operative April 30, 1977.)

Historical and Statutory Notes

Derivation: Educ.C.1959, § 27207.1, added by Stats.1967, c. 363, p. 1592, § 1.

Cross References

Board of supervisors, see Government Code §§ 25000, 25003 et seq.
County free libraries, see Government Code § 26150 et seq.
County librarian as a county officer, see Government Code § 24000.
County service areas, extended library facilities and services, authority of board of supervisors and funding, see Government Code § 25210.78 et seq.

§ 19149. Traveling expenses

The county librarian and his assistant shall be allowed actual and necessary traveling expenses incurred on the business of the office.

(Stats.1976, c. 1010, § 2, operative April 30, 1977.)

Historical and Statutory Notes

Derivation: Educ.C.1959, § 27208 (Stats. 1959, c. 2, p. 1457, § 27208).

Educ.C.1943, § 22138 (Stats.1943, c. 71, p. 735).

Stats.1911, c. 68, p. 83, § 9, amended by Stats.1921, c. 40, p. 52, § 1.

Cross References

Traveling expenses, state agency officers and employees, see Government Code § 11030 et seq.

§ 19150. Qualifications for acting or assistant librarian

Except when the county librarian is temporarily absent, no person shall serve in the position of county librarian under the title of acting county librarian, or assistant librarian in charge, or any other such title, unless the person meets the qualifications set forth in Section 19142.

In the event qualified candidates for the position of the county librarian cannot be found, the county supervisors shall secure a written permission from the State Librarian to appoint an unqualified person to the position. This written permission may be granted by the State Librarian for a period of time up to but not exceeding one year. The State Librarian may from time to time in his or her discretion renew the permit.

(Stats.1976, c. 1010, § 2, operative April 30, 1977. Amended by Stats.1986, c. 269, § 2.)

Historical and Statutory Notes

Derivation: Educ.C.1959,   § 27209   (Stats.   Educ.C.1943, § 22139, added by Stats.1957,
1959, c. 2, p. 1457, § 27209).   c. 2151, p. 3809, § 2.

Cross References

State Librarian,
    Generally, see Education Code § 19302 et seq.
    Powers and duties, see Education Code § 19320 et seq.

Article 3

GOVERNMENT

Article 3 was enacted by Stats.1976, c. 1010, § 2, operative April 30, 1977.

§ 19160. Powers and duties of board of supervisors

The county free library is under the general supervision of the board of supervisors, which may:

(a) Make general rules and regulations regarding the policy of the county free library.

(b) Establish, upon the recommendation of the county librarian, branches and stations throughout the county and may locate the branches and stations in cities wherever deemed advisable.

(c) Determine the number and kind of employees of the library.

(Stats.1976, c. 1010, § 2, operative April 30, 1977. Amended by Stats.1989, c. 406, § 1.)

Historical and Statutory Notes

Derivation: Educ.C.1959, § 27253 (Stats. 1959, c. 2, p. 1458, § 27253).

Educ.C.1943, § 22163 (Stats.1943, c. 71, p. 735).

Stats.1911, c. 68, p. 82, § 8.

Cross References

Administrative regulations and rulemaking, see Government Code § 11340 et seq.
Board of supervisors, see Government Code §§ 25000, 25003 et seq.
County free libraries, see Government Code § 26150 et seq.
County librarian, see Education Code § 19140 et seq.; Government Code § 24000.
County service areas, extended library facilities and services, authority of board of supervisors and funding, see Government Code § 25210.78 et seq.

Library References

Counties ⊶47.
Westlaw Topic No. 104.
C.J.S. Counties §§ 70 to 73.

Legal Jurisprudences

Cal Jur 3d Sch § 47.

Notes of Decisions

Purchase or destruction of books 1

---

1. Purchase or destruction of books

Under Educ.C.1959, § 27206 and § 27253, limiting board of supervisors to adoption of general rules and regulations regarding policy of county free library, such board may not order purchase or destruction of certain book for the county library, because this function is vested in certified county librarian. 42 Ops.Atty.Gen. 18 (1963).

§§ 19161 to 19166. Repealed by Stats.1989, c. 406, §§ 2 to 7

Historical and Statutory Notes

Section 19161, enacted by Stats.1976, c. 1010, § 2, derived from Educ.C.1959, § 27254 (Stats.1959, c. 2, p. 1458, § 27254); Educ.C. 1943, § 22164 (Stats.1943, c. 71, p. 735); and Stats.1911, c. 68, p. 82, § 8, related to the removal of employees.

Section 19162, enacted by Stats.1976, c. 1010, § 2, derived from Educ.C.1959, § 27255 (Stats.1959, c. 2, p. 1458, § 27255); Educ.C. 1943, § 22165 (Stats.1943, c. 71, p. 735); and Stats.1911, c. 68, p. 82, § 8, related to removed employees' rights of re-employment.

Section 19163, enacted by Stats.1976, c. 1010, § 2, derived from Educ.C.1959, § 27256 (Stats.1959, c. 2, p. 1458, § 27256); Educ.C. 1943, § 22166 (Stats.1943, c. 71, p. 735); and Stats.1911, c. 68, p. 82, § 8, provided for employment for a definite time.

Section 19164, enacted by Stats.1976, c. 1010, § 2, derived from Educ.C.1959, § 27257 (Stats.1959, c. 2, p. 1458, § 27257); Educ.C. 1943, § 22167 (Stats.1943, c. 71, p. 735); and Stats.1911, c. 68, p. 82, § 8, related to grading of employees.

Section 19165, enacted by Stats.1976, c. 1010, § 2, derived from Educ.C.1959, § 27258 (Stats.1959, c. 2, p. 1458, § 27258); Educ.C. 1943, § 22168 (Stats.1943, c. 71, p. 736); and Stats.1911, c. 68, p. 82, § 8, related to the qualifications for appointment to positions in graded service.

Section 19166, enacted by Stats.1976, c. 1010, § 2, derived from Educ.C.1959, § 27259 (Stats.1959, c. 2, p. 1458, § 27259); Educ.C. 1943, § 22169 (Stats.1943, c. 71, p. 736); and

Stats.1911, c. 68, p. 82, § 8, related to apprentices.

§ 19167. Supervision by State Librarian

The county free libraries are under the general supervision of the State Librarian, who shall from time to time, either personally or by one of his or her assistants, visit the county free libraries and inquire into their condition. The actual and necessary expenses of the visits shall be paid out of the moneys appropriated for the support of the California State Library.

(Stats.1976, c. 1010, § 2, operative April 30, 1977. Amended by Stats.1987, c. 1452, § 114.)

Historical and Statutory Notes

Legislative findings, declarations and intent relating to Stats.1987, c. 1452, see Historical and Statutory Notes under Education Code § 1007.

Derivation: Educ.C.1959, § 27260 (Stats. 1959, c. 2, p. 1459, § 27260).

Educ.C.1943, § 22170 (Stats.1943, c. 71, p. 736, amended by Stats.1957, c. 1743, p. 3124, § 6).

Stats.1911, c. 68, p. 83, § 10.

Cross References

County free libraries, see Government Code § 26150 et seq.
County service areas, extended library facilities and services, authority of board of supervisors and funding, see Government Code § 25210.78 et seq.
State librarian, see Education Code § 19302 et seq.
State Library, generally, see Education Code § 19300 et seq.

Library References

Legal Jurisprudences
Cal Jur 3d Sch § 47.

§ 19168. Annual convention by county librarians

The State Librarian shall annually call a convention of county librarians, to assemble at such time and place as he deems most convenient, for the discussion of questions pertaining to the supervision and administration of the county free libraries, the laws relating thereto, and such other subjects affecting the welfare and interest of the county free libraries as are properly brought before it. All county librarians shall attend and take part in the proceedings of the convention. The actual and necessary expenses of the county librarians attending the convention shall be paid out of the county free library fund.

(Stats.1976, c. 1010, § 2, operative April 30, 1977.)

Historical and Statutory Notes

Derivation: Educ.C.1959, § 27261 (Stats. 1959, c. 2, p. 1459, § 27261).

Educ.C.1943, § 22171 (Stats.1943, c. 71, p. 736).

Stats.1911, c. 68, p. 83, § 10.

Cross References

County free libraries, see Government Code § 26150 et seq.
County librarian, see Education Code § 19140 et seq.; Government Code § 24000.
County service areas, extended library facilities and services, authority of board of supervisors and funding, see Government Code § 25210.78 et seq.

State Librarian,
　　Generally, see Education Code § 19302 et seq.
　　Powers and duties, see Education Code § 19320 et seq.

Library References

Legal Jurisprudences
　Cal Jur 3d Sch § 49.

§ 19169. Annual report of county librarian

The county librarian shall, on or before August 31st, in each year, report to the board of supervisors and to the State Librarian on the condition of the county free library, for the year ending June 30th preceding. The reports shall, in addition to other matters deemed expedient by the county librarian, contain such statistical and other information as is deemed desirable by the State Librarian. For this purpose the State Librarian may send to the several county librarians instructions or question blanks so as to obtain the material for a comparative study of library conditions in the state.

(Stats.1976, c. 1010, § 2, operative April 30, 1977.)

Historical and Statutory Notes

Derivation: Educ.C.1959, § 27262 (Stats. 1959, c. 2, p. 1459, § 27262).

Educ.C.1943, § 22172 (Stats.1943, c. 71, p. 736, amended by Stats.1957, c. 2135, p. 3787, § 1).

Stats.1911, c. 68, p. 83, § 11.

Cross References

County free libraries, see Government Code § 26150 et seq.
County librarian, see Education Code § 19140 et seq.; Government Code § 24000.
County service areas, extended library facilities and services, authority of board of supervisors and
　　funding, see Government Code § 25210.78 et seq.
State librarian, see Education Code § 19302 et seq.

§ 19170. Repealed by Stats.1980, c. 1208, p. 4081, § 29

Historical and Statutory Notes

The repealed section, enacted by Stats.1976, c. 1010, § 2, derived from Educ.C.1959, § 27263 (Stats.1959, c. 2, p. 1459, § 27263); Educ.C.1943, § 22173 (Stats.1943, c. 71, p. 736, amended by Stats.1951, c. 1681, p. 3879, § 3; Stats.1957, c. 1456, p. 2780, § 1); and Stats. 1911, c. 68, p. 84, § 12, provided for tax levies for the county free library.

§ 19171. Allocations of federal funds

The county board of supervisors of any county may in its discretion allocate and appropriate any funds received by the county under the State and Local Fiscal Assistance Act of 1972 (Public Law 92–512) [1] for the purpose of establishing, maintaining, and purchasing property for the county free library.

(Stats.1976, c. 1010, § 2, operative April 30, 1977.)

[1] 31 U.S.C.A. § 6701 et seq., (repealed).

Historical and Statutory Notes

Derivation: Educ.C.1959, § 27263.5, added by Stats.1974, c. 459, p. 1082, § 1, eff. July 11, 1974.

Cross References

County boards of supervisors, generally, see Education Code § 1400 et seq.
County free libraries, see Government Code § 26150 et seq.
County or counties, defined, see Education Code § 92.
County service areas, extended library facilities and services, authority of board of supervisors and funding, see Government Code § 25210.78 et seq.

United States Code Annotated

Library and information services, federal cooperation with State and local governments and public and private agencies to assure optimum provision of services, see 20 U.S.C.A. § 1501.

§ 19172. Repealed by Stats.1994, c. 922 (A.B.2587), § 31

Historical and Statutory Notes

The repealed section, enacted by Stats.1976, c. 1010, § 2, derived from Educ.C.1959, § 27264 (Stats.1959, c. 2, p. 1459, § 27264), Educ.C.1943, § 22174 (Stats.1943, c. 71, p. 737), amended by Stats.1951, c. 1681, p. 3879, § 4, and Stats.1911, c. 68, p. 84, § 12, authorized the board to levy a tax where districts elected not to become part of the system.

§ 19173. Creation of special taxing zones

The board of supervisors may create special taxing zones within the territory of the county subject to taxation for county free library purposes for the purpose of levying special taxes within the zones when it is found by the board that the territory within the zones require special services or special facilities in addition to those provided generally by the county free library system and that the special tax levy is commensurate with the special benefits to be provided in the zones.

Taxes levied pursuant to this section, together with taxes levied pursuant to Section 19170, shall not exceed the higher of the limit provided by Section 19170 or the applicable provisions of Section 2263 of the Revenue and Taxation Code.

(Stats.1976, c. 1010, § 2, operative April 30, 1977.)

Historical and Statutory Notes

Derivation: Educ.C.1959, § 27264.5, added by Stats.1961, c. 978, p. 2619, § 1, amended by Stats.1974, c. 847, p. 1813, § 1.

Cross References

Board of supervisors, see Government Code §§ 25000, 25003 et seq.
County free libraries, see Government Code § 26150 et seq.
County service areas, extended library facilities and services, authority of board of supervisors and funding, see Government Code § 25210.78 et seq.
Special districts defined, see Revenue and Taxation Code §§ 2215, 2216.
Tax levies, see Government Code § 29100 et seq. and Revenue and Taxation Code § 2151 et seq.
Taxes, special taxes imposed on behalf of public libraries, authority of cities, counties and other agencies, see Government Code § 53717.

§ 19174. Receipt of gifts, bequests or devises

The board of supervisors may receive, on behalf of the county, any gift, bequest, or devise for the county free library, or for any branch or subdivision of the library.

(Stats.1976, c. 1010, § 2, operative April 30, 1977.)

Historical and Statutory Notes

Derivation: Educ.C.1959, § 27265 (Stats. 1959, c. 2, p. 1460, § 27265).

Educ.C.1943, § 22175 (Stats.1943, c. 71, p. 737).

Stats.1911, c. 68, p. 84, § 12.

Cross References

Board of supervisors, see Government Code §§ 25000, 25003 et seq.
County free libraries, see Government Code § 26150 et seq.
County service areas, extended library facilities and services, authority of board of supervisors and funding, see Government Code § 25210.78 et seq.

Library References

Counties ☞104.
Westlaw Topic No. 104.
C.J.S. Counties §§ 144, 148.

§ 19174.5. County general fund; use

Notwithstanding any other provision of law, funds from the county general fund may be used to support the county free library.

(Added by Stats.1978, c. 331, p. 681, § 3, eff. June 30, 1978.)

Historical and Statutory Notes

Section 4 of Stats.1978, c. 331, p. 681, provides:

"The addition of Section 19174.5 to the Education Code made by Section 3 of this act does not constitute a change in, but is declaratory of, the existing law."

Cross References

County free libraries, see Government Code § 26150 et seq.
County service areas, extended library facilities and services, authority of board of supervisors and funding, see Government Code § 25210.78 et seq.

§ 19175. Property, collection of taxes, and funds

The title to all property belonging to the county free library is vested in the county. All laws applicable to the collection of county taxes shall apply to the collection of the taxes provided in Section 19170. All moneys of the county free library, whether derived from taxation or otherwise, shall be in the custody of the county treasurer.

(Stats.1976, c. 1010, § 2, operative April 30, 1977. Amended by Stats.1994, c. 922 (A.B.2587), § 32.)

§ 19176. Claims against the county free library fund

Each claim against the county free library fund shall be authorized and approved by the county librarian, or in his absence from the county by his assistant. It shall then be acted upon in the same manner as other claims against the county.

(Stats.1976, c. 1010, § 2, operative April 30, 1977.)

§ 19177. Contracts or agreements with county law libraries

In any county of this state where a law library exists under the provisions of Chapter 5 (commencing with Section 6300) of Division 3 of the Business and Professions Code, the board of supervisors of the county may enter into contracts, or agreements with the board of law library trustees of the law library for the cooperation of the law library and the county free library, and, in that connection, may contract or agree with the board of law library trustees of the law library that the county librarian and other employees of the county free library perform the duties required to be done or performed by the officers and employees of the law library for a compensation to be named in the contract or agreement, and to be paid into the county free library fund.

(Stats.1976, c. 1010, § 2, operative April 30, 1977.)

Historical and Statutory Notes

Derivation: Educ.C.1959, § 27268 (Stats.   Stats.1911, c. 68, p. 84, § 13.
1959, c. 2, p. 1460, § 27268).

Educ.C.1943, § 22178 (Stats.1943, c. 71, p.
737).

Cross References

Board of supervisors, see Government Code §§ 25000, 25003 et seq.
Contracts, generally, see Civil Code § 1549 et seq.
County free libraries, see Government Code § 26150 et seq.
County librarian, see Education Code § 19140 et seq.; Government Code § 24000.
County service areas, extended library facilities and services, authority of board of supervisors and
    funding, see Government Code § 25210.78 et seq.
State librarian, see Education Code § 19302 et seq.

Library References

Legal Jurisprudences
   Cal Jur 3d Sch § 48.

Notes of Decisions

Compensation of county librarian 1

_____

1. Compensation of county librarian

   If the board of supervisors enters into a new contract for compensation between the county free library and the county law library, additional compensation may be paid to the county librarian for the performance of such additional duties in view of this section. 14 Ops.Atty.Gen. 234 (1949).

§ 19178. School and teachers' libraries

The board of supervisors may accept on behalf of the county free library, all books and other property of school libraries and of the teachers' library, and may manage and maintain them as a part of the county free library.

(Stats.1976, c. 1010, § 2, operative April 30, 1977.)

Historical and Statutory Notes

Derivation: Educ.C.1959, § 27269 (Stats.   Stats.1911, c. 68, p. 85, § 14.
1959, c. 2, p. 1460, § 27269).

Educ.C.1943, § 22179 (Stats.1943, c. 71, p.
737).

Cross References

Board of supervisors, see Government Code §§ 25000, 25003 et seq.
County free libraries, see Government Code § 26150 et seq.
County service areas, extended library facilities and services, authority of board of supervisors and
    funding, see Government Code § 25210.78 et seq.
School libraries, see Education Code § 18100 et seq.

§ 19179. Application of chapter to prior county libraries and to contracts between counties and cities

Any county library which was established and existed on April 26, 1911, under the provisions of an act entitled "An act to provide county library systems," approved April 12, 1909,[1] is continued under the provisions of this chapter and shall be considered the same as if established under the provisions of this chapter. If a contract has been entered into between any county board of supervisors and any city pursuant to this article, the contract shall continue in force, and the provisions of Section 19112 shall be applicable thereto, until the establishment and equipment of a county free library under the provisions of this chapter, unless sooner terminated.

(Stats.1976, c. 1010, § 2, operative April 30, 1977.)

[1] Stats.1909, c. 479, p. 811.

Historical and Statutory Notes

Derivation: Educ.C.1959, § 27270 (Stats. 1959, c. 2, p. 1460, § 27270).

Educ.C.1943, § 22180 (Stats.1943, c. 71, p. 737).

Stats.1911, c. 68, p. 85, § 17.

Cross References

Contracts, generally, see Civil Code § 1549 et seq.
County boards of supervisors, generally, see Education Code § 1400 et seq.
County free libraries, see Government Code § 26150 et seq.
County or counties, defined, see Education Code § 92.
County service areas, extended library facilities and services, authority of board of supervisors and funding, see Government Code § 25210.78 et seq.

§ 19180. Financing of buildings for county free library purposes

The board of supervisors of any county in which there has been established a county free library which does not serve the entire county may, on behalf of the county free library, construct, build, repair or refurnish buildings to be used for county free library purposes, payment for which may be made from the general fund of the county. If payment is made from the county's general fund, the county auditor shall each fiscal year thereafter transfer from the county free library fund to the county's general fund as a prior claim against the county free library fund for as many years as are determined by the board of supervisors but not to exceed 20, an equal annual installment in such amount that over the designated period of years the entire payment from the county's general fund will be completely repaid. Payment of the costs of the construction of a county free library building may also be made from the employees retirement fund of a retirement system established under the authority of the County Employees Retirement Law of 1937 [1] as an investment of that fund and under the conditions specified in that law.

(Stats.1976, c. 1010, § 2, operative April 30, 1977.)

[1] Government Code § 31450 et seq.

Historical and Statutory Notes

Derivation: Educ.C.1959, § 27271, added by Stats.1959, c. 1197, p. 3286, § 1.

Cross References

Board of supervisors, see Government Code §§ 25000, 25003 et seq.
County free libraries, see Government Code § 26150.

Chapter 7

STATE LIBRARY

Chapter 7 was enacted by Stats.1976, c. 1010, § 2, operative April 30, 1977.

Historical and Statutory Notes

Stats.1852, c. 5, p. 44, §§ 1 to 6, was an act providing a fund for the use of a state library. By the terms of the act, each state officer commissioned by the governor was required to contribute $5 to the state library fund before entering on the duties of his office and provision was made for a withholding tax of $5 for library purposes directed to the pay by the members of the legislature. Provision was made for the government of the state library, for the acceptance of contributions, and for the appointment of a librarian to perform specified duties.

Stats.1853, c. 101, p. 148, §§ 1, 2, supplemented the 1852 act with respect to the collection of fees by the secretary of state to constitute a portion of the library fund.

The acts of 1852 and 1853 remained in effect until their repeal by Stats.1943, c. 71, p. 788, § 4005, although their provisions were largely superseded, if not entirely so, by the adoption of the Political Code in 1872, particularly §§ 2292 to 2305 thereof.

Stats.1871–72, c. 563, p. 824, §§ 1 to 4, provided for the establishment of a cabinet department in the state library for the purpose of maintaining a display cabinet of minerals, precious metals, mineralogical, geological, and fossiliferous specimens, and precious stones. This statute also remained unchanged until its repeal by Stats.1943, c. 71, p. 789, § 40005.

Constitutional Provisions

Article 9, § 1, provides that a general diffusion of knowledge and intelligence being essential to preservation of the rights and liberties of the people, the legislature shall encourage by all suitable means the promotion of intellectual, scientific, moral, and agricultural improvement.

Cross References

Access to state library,
    Law revision commission, see Government Code § 8286.
    Legislative counsel bureau, see Government Code § 10209.
County historical records commissions, advice of state library, see Government Code § 12232.
Open central registry of appointive offices, maintenance in state libraries, see Government Code § 12033.1.
School libraries, see Education Code § 18100 et seq.
State libraries, annual report by governing board, see Education Code § 18122.

Article 1

DIVISION OF LIBRARIES IN DEPARTMENT OF EDUCATION

Section
19300. Legislative declaration.
19301. California State Library.
19302. State Librarian.
19303. Appointment.
19304, 19305. Repealed.

Section
19306. Appointment of assistant.

Article 1 was enacted by Stats.1976, c. 1010, § 2, operative April 30, 1977.

§ 19300. Legislative declaration

The Legislature hereby declares that it is in the interest of the people and of the state that there be a general diffusion of knowledge and intelligence through the establishment and operation of public libraries. Such diffusion is a matter of general concern inasmuch as it is the duty of the state to provide encouragement to the voluntary lifelong learning of the people of the state.

The Legislature further declares that the public library is a supplement to the formal system of free public education, and a source of information and inspiration to persons of all ages, and a resource for continuing education and reeducation beyond the years of formal education, and as such deserves adequate financial support from government at all levels.

(Stats.1976, c. 1010, § 2, operative April 30, 1977.)

Historical and Statutory Notes

Derivation: Educ.C.1959, § 27000, added by Stats.1959, c. 755, p. 2742, § 1.

§ 19301. California State Library

There is in the State Department of Education a division known as the California State Library.

(Stats.1976, c. 1010, § 2, operative April 30, 1977. Amended by Stats.1987, c. 1452, § 115.)

Historical and Statutory Notes

Legislative findings, declarations and intent relating to Stats.1987, c. 1452, see Historical and Statutory Notes under Education Code § 1007.

Derivation: Educ.C.1959, § 27001 (Stats. 1959, c. 2, p. 1452, § 27001).

Educ.C.1943, § 22001 (Stats.1943, c. 71, p. 729).

Pol.C. § 362g, added by Stats.1927 Cal. 579, p. 968. § 1.

School C. § 2.1450.

Cross References

Establishment of divisions in department of education, see Education Code § 33309.
State department of education, see Education Code § 33300 et seq.

Library References

States ☞45.
Westlaw Topic No. 360.
C.J.S. States §§ 79 to 80, 82, 136.

Legal Jurisprudences
Cal Jur 3d Sch § 36.

§ 19302. State Librarian

The division shall be in charge of a chief who shall be a technically trained librarian and shall be known as the "State Librarian."

(Stats.1976, c. 1010, § 2, operative April 30, 1977.)

Historical and Statutory Notes

Derivation: Educ.C.1959, § 27002 (Stats. 1959, c. 2, p. 1452, § 27002).

Educ.C.1943, § 22002 (Stats.1943, c. 71, p. 729).

School C. § 2.1451.

Library References

States ⚷44.
Westlaw Topic No. 360.
C.J.S. States §§ 80, 82.

§ 19303. Appointment

The State Librarian shall be appointed by and hold office at the pleasure of the Governor, subject to confirmation by the Senate.

(Stats.1976, c. 1010, § 2, operative April 30, 1977.)

Historical and Statutory Notes

Derivation: Educ.C.1959, § 27003 (Stats. 1959, c. 2, p. 1452, § 27003, amended by Stats. 1961, c. 603, p. 1750, § 5; Stats.1967, c. 645, p. 1991, § 1).

Educ.C.1943, § 22003 (Stats.1943, c. 71, p. 729, amended by Stats.1945, c. 1185, p. 2237,

§ 8; Stats.1949, c. 1005, p. 1851, § 5; Stats. 1951, c. 1613, p. 3629, § 24).

School C. § 2.1452.

Cross References

Appointment, confirmation by senate, see Government Code § 1322.
Governor, see Const. Art. 5, § 1 et seq.

Library References

Legal Jurisprudences

Cal Jur 3d Sch § 36.

§§ 19304, 19305. Repealed by Stats.1987, c. 1452, §§ 116, 117

Historical and Statutory Notes

Section 19304, enacted by Stats.1976, c. 1010, § 2, derived from Educ.C.1959, § 27004 (Stats.1959, c. 2, p. 1452, § 27004); Educ.C. 1943, § 22004 (Stats.1943, c. 71, p. 730, § 22004); and School C. § 2.1453, related to the duties of the state librarian.

Section 19305, enacted by Stats.1976, c. 1010, § 2, derived from Educ.C.1959, § 27005 (Stats.1959, c. 2, p. 1452, § 27005); Educ.C. 1943, § 22005 (Stats.1943, c. 71, p. 730) and

Pol.C. § 2295, amended by Code Am. 1873–4, c. 610, p. 37, § 66; Stats.1903, c. 74, p. 82, § 2; Stats.1913, c. 617, p. 1150, § 2; Stats.1929, c. 206, p. 367, § 2, related to the state librarian's duty to be in attendance at the library.

Legislative findings, declarations and intent relating to Stats.1987, c. 1452, see Historical and Statutory Notes under Education Code § 1007.

§ 19306. Appointment of assistant

The State Librarian may appoint an assistant who shall be a civil executive officer.

(Stats.1976, c. 1010, § 2, operative April 30, 1977.)

Historical and Statutory Notes

Derivation: Educ.C.1959, § 27006 (Stats. 1959, c. 2, p. 1452, § 27006).

Educ.C.1943, § 22006 (Stats.1943, c. 71, p. 730).

Pol.C. § 2293, amended by Stats.1899, c. 31, p. 30, § 2; Stats.1903, c. 74, p. 81, § 1; Stats. 1909, c. 251, p. 384, § 1; Stats.1913, c. 617, p. 1149, § 1.

Article 2

POWERS AND DUTIES

Article 2 was enacted by Stats.1976, c. 1010, § 2, operative April 30, 1977.

§ 19320. Powers and duties of state librarian

The State Librarian may do all of the following:

(a) Make rules and regulations, not inconsistent with law, for the government of the State Library.

(b) Appoint assistants as necessary.

(c) Sell or exchange duplicate copies of books.

(d) Keep in order and repair the books and property in the library.

(e) Prescribe rules and regulations permitting persons other than Members of the Legislature and other state officers to have the use of books from the library.

(f) Collect and preserve statistics and other information pertaining to libraries, which shall be available to other libraries within the state applying for the information.

(g) Establish, in his or her discretion, deposit stations in various parts of the state, under the control of an officer or employee of the State Library. No book shall be kept permanently away from the main library, which may be required for official use. Books and other library materials from public libraries of the state may be accepted for deposit, under agreements entered into by the State Librarian and the public libraries concerned, whereby materials that should be preserved but are rarely used in the region may be stored and made available for use under the same conditions that apply to materials in the State Library.

(h) Collect, preserve, and disseminate information regarding the history of the state.

(i) Authorize the State Library to serve as regional library for the blind, in cooperation with the Library of Congress.

(j) Give advisory, consultive, and technical assistance with respect to public libraries to librarians and library authorities, and assist all other authorities, state and local, in assuming their full responsibility for library services.

(k) Authorize the State Library to serve as the central reference and research library for the departments of state government and maintain adequate legislative reference and research library services for the Legislature.

(*l*) Acquire, organize and supply books and other library informational and reference materials to supplement the collections of other public libraries of the state with the more technical, scientific and scholarly works, to the end that through an established interlibrary loan system, the people of the state shall have access to the full range of reference and informational materials.

(m) Make studies and surveys of public library needs and adopt rules and regulations for the allocation of federal funds to public libraries.

(n) Contract, at his or her discretion, with other public libraries in the state to give public services of the types referred to in subdivisions (g) and (*l*) of this section, when service by contract appears to be a needed supplement to the facilities and services carried on directly by the State Library.

(Stats.1976, c. 1010, § 2, operative April 30, 1977. Amended by Stats.1987, c. 1452, § 118.)

Historical and Statutory Notes

Legislative findings, declarations and intent relating to Stats.1987, c. 1452, see Historical and Statutory Notes under Education Code § 1007.

Derivation: Educ.C.1959, § 27051 (Stats. 1959, c. 2, p. § 27051, amended by Stats.1959, c. 1955, p. 4560, § 1).

Educ.C.1943, § 22021 (Stats.1943, c. 71, p. 730, amended by Stats.1957, c. 1742, p. 3123, § 1; Stats.1957, c. 1743, p. 3123, § 1).

Pol.C. § 2293, amended by Stats.1899, c. 31, p. 30, § 2; Stats.1903, c. 74, p. 81, § 1; Stats. 1909, c. 251, p. 384, § 1; Stats.1913, c. 617, p. 1149, § 1.

Cross References

Administrative regulations and rulemaking, see Government Code § 11340 et seq.
Contracts, generally, see Civil Code § 1549 et seq.
State department of education, see Education Code § 33300 et seq.

Code of Regulations References

Library services provided by the state, rules and regulations, see 5 Cal.Code of Regs. § 20000 et seq.
Persons authorized to use books, see 5 Cal.Code of Regs. §§ 20020, 20021.

Library References

Legal Jurisprudences
Cal Jur 3d Sch § 36.

United States Code Annotated

Library of Congress, generally, see 2 U.S.C.A. § 131 et seq.
Museum and Library services, consolidation and administration of federal library programs, generally, see 20 U.S.C.A. § 9101 et seq.

§ 19320.5. Library services to children and youth; consultant

The State Librarian shall employ a consultant to provide technical assistance to public libraries in the development and enhancement of library services to children and youth.

(Added by Stats.1987, c. 1359, § 3.)

Library References

§ 19321. Additional powers and duties of state librarian

The State Librarian shall also do all of the following:

(a) Purchase books, maps, engravings, paintings, furniture, and other materials and equipment necessary to carry out State Library programs and services.

(b) Number and stamp all books and maps belonging to the library, or otherwise indicate ownership of them, and keep a catalog thereof.

(c) Have bound all books and papers that require binding.

(d) Keep a register of all books taken from the library.

(Stats.1976, c. 1010, § 2, operative April 30, 1977. Amended by Stats.1987, c. 1452, § 119.)

Historical and Statutory Notes

Legislative findings, declarations and intent relating to Stats.1987, c. 1452, see Historical and Statutory Notes under Education Code § 1007.

Derivation: Educ.C.1959, § 27052 (Stats. 1959, c. 2, p. 1453, 27052).

Educ.C.1943, § 22022 (Stats.1943, c. 71, p. 730).

Pol.C. § 2295, amended by Code Am. 1873–4, c. 610, § 66; Stats.1903, c. 74, § 2; Stats.1913, c. 617, § 2; Stats.1929, c. 206, § 2.

Cross References

State department of education, see Education Code § 33300 et seq.

§ 19322. Powers of department; library services

The Department of Education may:

(a) Contract with counties, cities, or districts within this state, agencies of the state, and agencies of the United States government for the purpose of providing library services.

(b) Establish and operate library service centers.

(Stats.1976, c. 1010, § 2, operative April 30, 1977.)

Historical and Statutory Notes

Derivation: Educ.C.1959, § 27054 (Stats.   Educ.C.1943, § 22024, added by Stats.1957,
1959, c. 2, p. 1453, § 27054).   c. 1744, p. 3125, § 1.

Cross References

Contracts, generally, see Civil Code § 1549 et seq.
State department of education, see Education Code § 33300 et seq.

§ 19323. Tape recordings of books

The State Librarian shall make available on a loan basis to legally blind persons, or to persons who are visually or physically handicapped to such an extent that they are unable to read conventional printed materials, in the state tape recordings of books and other related materials. The tape recordings shall be selected by the State Library on the same basis as the State Library's general program for providing library materials to legally blind readers.

(Stats.1976, c. 1010, § 2, operative April 30, 1977.)

Historical and Statutory Notes

Derivation: Educ.C.1959, § 27055, added by
Stats.1968, c. 1355, p. 2588, § 1.

§ 19324. Braille materials; duplication

The State Librarian may duplicate any braille book master, other than textbook masters, presented by any legally blind person directly to the State Librarian for duplication. The State Librarian may duplicate any braille book master, other than textbook masters, presented by any other person or agency directly to the State Librarian for duplication.

(Stats.1976, c. 1010, § 2, operative April 30, 1977.)

Historical and Statutory Notes

Derivation: Educ.C.1959, § 27056, added by
Stats.1970, c. 1162, p. 2066, § 1.

§ 19325. Toll-free telephone service; regional libraries for the blind and physically handicapped

The State Librarian may provide the following:

(a) Toll-free telephone services for registered patrons of the federally designated regional libraries for the blind and physically handicapped, in order to enable those persons to have direct patron access to library services.

(b) Toll-free telephone access to telephonic reading systems for individuals with print disabilities who are registered patrons of the federally designated regional libraries for the blind and physically handicapped.

(Added by Stats.1978, c. 606, p. 2045, § 1. Amended by Stats.1987, c. 1452, § 120; Stats.2001, c. 654 (A.B.1723), § 3.)

Historical and Statutory Notes

Legislative findings, declarations and intent relating to Stats.1987, c. 1452, see Historical and Statutory Notes under Education Code § 1007.

Sections 1, 2 and 5 of Stats.2001, c. 654 (A.B.1723), provide:

"SECTION 1. The Legislature finds and declares all of the following:

"(a) Thousands of California citizens have disabilities that prevent them from directly accessing conventional print material due to visual impairments, dyslexia, and orthopedic disabilities, which prevent the physical manipulation of print materials.

"(b) For decades there have been governmental and nonprofit organizations dedicated to providing access to reading materials on a wide variety of subjects by way of Braille, large print, or audio tape recordings.

"(c) Access to time-sensitive or local or regional publications, or both, is not feasible to produce through these traditional means and formats.

"(d) Lack of direct and prompt access to these materials, such as newspapers, magazines, newsletters, broadcast media schedules, and other time-sensitive materials has a detrimental effect on the educational opportunities, literacy, and opportunity for full participation in governmental and community forums by people with print disabilities.

"(e) The California State Library, through the leadership of State Librarian Dr. Kevin Starr, has caused to be established in five locations throughout California high technology systems that provide access to previously inaccessible material by use of a standard telephone.

"(f) These telephonic reading systems are currently underutilized because they are capable of serving many more people than can call without incurring long distance telephone charges.

"(g) It is not cost-effective to establish the hundreds of locations necessary to give print disabled Californians local telephone call access to those locations.

"(h) Toll-free access to current and future telephonic reading systems operated by governmental or nonprofit organizations in California will provide meaningful access to this important print material for all Californians with print disabilities.

"SEC. 2. This bill may be known and shall be cited as the Kevin Starr Access to Information Act of 2001."

"SEC. 5. The sum of eight hundred thirty thousand dollars ($830,000) is hereby appropriated from the California Teleconnect Fund Administrative Committee Fund to the California State Library to fund the seven existing telephonic reading centers in Los Angeles, San Diego, Fresno, San Francisco, and Sacramento until July 1, 2002. Any funds appropriated to the California State Library pursuant to this section, which are not encumbered on or before July 1, 2002, shall revert to the California Teleconnect Fund Administrative Committee Fund."

Code of Regulations References

Toll-free telephone service, see 5 Cal.Code of Regs. § 20400.

§ 19325.1. Telephonic reading systems; operation or funding of the operation by qualifying entities; authority of State Librarian

(a) The State Librarian may operate a telephonic reading system, fund the operation of telephonic reading systems operated by qualifying entities, or both.

(b) As used in this section, the following terms have the following meanings, unless otherwise indicated:

(1) "Telephonic reading system" means a system operated by the State Librarian or a qualifying entity, whereby a caller can hear the reading of material such as newspapers, magazines, newsletters, broadcast media schedules, transit route and schedule information, and other reference or time-sensitive materials, as determined by the operator of the system.

(2) "Qualifying entity" means any agency, instrumentality, or political subdivision of the state or any nonprofit organization whose primary mission is to provide services to people who are blind or visually impaired.

(c) Qualifying entities that were eligible, as of January 1, 2001, to receive funds from the State Librarian relating to the operation of a telephonic reading system may continue to receive funding from the State Librarian.

(d) The State Librarian, in cooperation with qualifying entities, may expand the type and scope of materials available on telephonic reading systems in order to meet the local, regional, or foreign language needs of print-disabled residents of this state. The State Librarian may also expand the scope of services and availability of telephonic reading services by current methods and technologies or by methods and technologies that may be developed. The State Librarian may inform current and potential patrons of the availability of telephonic reading service through appropriate means, including, but not limited to, direct mailings, direct telephonic contact, and public service announcements.

(f) The State Librarian may enter into contracts or other agreements that he or she determines to be appropriate to provide telephonic reading services pursuant to this section.

(Added by Stats.2001, c. 654 (A.B.1723), § 4.)

Historical and Statutory Notes

Sections 1, 2 and 5 of Stats.2001, c. 654 (A.B.1723), provide:

"SECTION 1. The Legislature finds and declares all of the following:

"(a) Thousands of California citizens have disabilities that prevent them from directly accessing conventional print material due to visual impairments, dyslexia, and orthopedic disabilities, which prevent the physical manipulation of print materials.

"(b) For decades there have been governmental and nonprofit organizations dedicated to providing access to reading materials on a wide variety of subjects by way of Braille, large print, or audio tape recordings.

"(c) Access to time-sensitive or local or regional publications, or both, is not feasible to produce through these traditional means and formats.

"(d) Lack of direct and prompt access to these materials, such as newspapers, magazines, newsletters, broadcast media schedules, and other time-sensitive materials has a detrimental effect on the educational opportunities, literacy, and opportunity for full participation in governmental and community forums by people with print disabilities.

"(e) The California State Library, through the leadership of State Librarian Dr. Kevin Starr, has caused to be established in five locations throughout California high technology systems that provide access to previously inaccessible material by use of a standard telephone.

"(f) These telephonic reading systems are currently underutilized because they are capable of serving many more people than can call without incurring long distance telephone charges.

"(g) It is not cost-effective to establish the hundreds of locations necessary to give print disabled Californians local telephone call access to those locations.

"(h) Toll-free access to current and future telephonic reading systems operated by governmental or nonprofit organizations in California will provide meaningful access to this important print material for all Californians with print disabilities.

"SEC. 2. This bill may be known and shall be cited as the Kevin Starr Access to Information Act of 2001."

"SEC. 5. The sum of eight hundred thirty thousand dollars ($830,000) is hereby appropriated from the California Teleconnect Fund Administrative Committee Fund to the California State Library to fund the seven existing telephonic reading centers in Los Angeles, San Diego, Fresno, San Francisco, and Sacramento until July 1, 2002. Any funds appropriated to the California State Library pursuant to this section, which are not encumbered on or before July 1, 2002, shall revert to the California Teleconnect Fund Administrative Committee Fund."

Cross References

Contracts, generally, see Civil Code § 1549 et seq.

§ **19326.** **Gold medal for excellence in humanities and sciences; advisory panel; selection; private contributions**

(a) The State Librarian may annually award a gold medal for excellence in the humanities and science to an individual or organization for publication of a work that has enriched the collection of the State Library and enriched the state by significantly contributing to the intellectual, cultural, and scientific knowledge of the people of the state.

(b) The award shall formally be known as the "California State Library Gold Medal for Excellence in the Humanities and Science."

(c) To assist in making the selection of a recipient of the California State Library Gold Medal for Excellence in the Humanities and Science, the State Librarian shall consult an advisory panel consisting of one representative from each of the following:

(1) The Governor.

(2) The President pro Tempore of the Senate.

(3) The Speaker of the Assembly.

(4) The Chief Justice of the California Supreme Court.

(d) The State Librarian is authorized to seek private contributions to defray the cost of awarding the California State Library Gold Medal for Excellence in the Humanities and Science and related expenses.

(Added by Stats.1996, c. 213 (S.B.1605), § 1.)

§ **19327.** **State library foundation; operating agreements; fees**

(a) In order to protect and preserve valuable and irreplaceable treasures of the state, the State Librarian may enter into an operating agreement with a private, nonprofit, tax-exempt organization, currently known as the California State Library Foundation, as follows:

(1) The California State Library Foundation may be designated by the State Librarian as the only authorized provider of copies and reproductions of rare and valuable State Library materials.

(2) The California State Library Foundation may be authorized by the State Librarian to provide copies and reproductions of documents and other information found in the collection of the State Library, as requested by members of the public.

(3) The California State Library Foundation may be authorized by the State Librarian to use State Library facilities and equipment designated by the State Librarian as necessary for the California State Library Foundation to provide services to the State Library efficiently and economically.

(b) The State Librarian may establish an agreement with the California State Library Foundation to collect fees from the public for providing the services specified in subdivision (a). Fees for copying, reproduction, and other services provided by the California State Library Foundation shall be at a level consistent with the cost of providing these services.

(Added by Stats.1996, c. 213 (S.B.1605), § 2.)

§ 19328. Bernard E. Witkin State Law Library of California; designation

(a) The Legislature hereby finds and declares that Bernard E. Witkin's legendary contribution to California law is deserving of a lasting tribute and an expression of gratitude from the state whose legal system, he, more than any other single individual in the 20th century, helped to shape.

(b) The law library of the California State Library, located in the Library and Courts Building in the City and County of Sacramento, is hereby designated as the Bernard E. Witkin State Law Library of California.

(c) The State Librarian, in cooperation with the Department of General Services, may install appropriate plaques and markers showing this special designation upon receiving donations from nonstate resources to cover any costs.

(Added by Stats.1997, c. 411 (S.B.605), § 1.)

Article 3

BOOKS

Article 3 was enacted by Stats.1976, c. 1010, § 2, operative April 30, 1977. The heading of Article 3 was added by Stats.1976, c. 1011, § 21, operative April 30, 1977.

§ 19330. Withdrawal of books by state officers

Books may be taken from the library by the Members of the Legislature and by other state officers during regular office hours.

(Stats.1976, c. 1010, § 2, operative April 30, 1977. Amended by Stats.1987, c. 1452, § 121.)

Historical and Statutory Notes

Legislative findings, declarations and intent relating to Stats.1987, c. 1452, see Historical and Statutory Notes under Education Code § 1007.

Derivation: Educ.C.1959, § 27101 (Stats. 1959, c. 2, p. 1453, § 27101).

Educ.C.1943, § 22042 (Stats.1943, c. 71, p. 731, amended by Stats.1957, c. 1743, p. 3124, § 2).

Pol.C. § 2296.

Code of Regulations References

Library services provided by the State, rules and regulations, see 5 Cal.Code of Regs. § 20000 et seq.

§ 19331. Failure to return books; officers or employees of state; salary deductions

The Controller, when notified by the State Librarian that any officer or employee of the state for whom he or she draws a warrant for salary has failed to return any book taken by him or her, or for which he or she has given an order, within the time prescribed by the rules, or the time within which it was agreed to be returned, and which notice shall give the value of the book, shall, after first informing the officer or employee of the notice, upon failure by him or her to return the book, deduct from the warrant for the salary of the officer or employee, twice the value of the book, and place the amount deducted in the General Fund.

(Stats.1976, c. 1010, § 2, operative April 30, 1977. Amended by Stats.1987, c. 1452, § 122.)

Historical and Statutory Notes

Legislative findings, declarations and intent relating to Stats.1987, c. 1452, see Historical and Statutory Notes under Education Code § 1007.

Derivation: Educ.C.1959, § 27102 (Stats. 1959, c. 2, p. 1453, § 27102).

Educ.C.1943, § 22044 (Stats.1943, c. 71, p. 731, amended by Stats.1957, c. 1743, p. 3124, § 3).

Pol.C. § 2298, amended by Stats.1889, c. 31, p. 30, § 3; Stats.1903, c. 74, p. 82, § 3.

Cross References

State controller, see Government Code § 12400 et seq.; Const. Art. 5, § 11.
State department of education, see Education Code § 33300 et seq.

§ 19332. Failure to return books; officers or employees of state; purchase of duplicates; salary deductions

In case of the neglect or refusal on the part of any officer or employee of the state to return a book for which he or she has given an order or a receipt or has in his or her possession, the State Librarian may purchase for the library a duplicate of the book, and notify the Controller of the purchase, together with the cost of the book. Upon the receipt of the notice from the department, the Controller shall deduct twice the cost of the duplicate book from the warrant for the salary of the officer or employee, and place the amount deducted in the General Fund.

(Stats.1976, c. 1010, § 2, operative April 30, 1977. Amended by Stats.1987, c. 1452, § 123.)

Historical and Statutory Notes

Legislative findings, declarations and intent relating to Stats.1987, c. 1452, see Historical and Statutory Notes under Education Code § 1007.

Derivation: Educ.C.1959, § 27103 (Stats. 1959, c. 2, p. 1453, § 27103).

Educ.C.1943, § 22045 (Stats.1943, c. 71, p. 731, amended by Stats.1957, c. 1743, p. 3124, § 4).

Pol.C. § 2298, amended by Stats.1899, c. 31, p. 30, § 3; Stats.1903, c. 74, p. 82, § 3.

§ 19333. Suit for the recovery of book, or three times its value

The State Librarian may bring suit in his or her official capacity for the recovery of any book, or for three times the value thereof, together with costs of suit, against any person who has the book in his or her possession or who is responsible therefor. If the department has purchased a duplicate of any book, it may bring suit for three times the amount expended for the duplicate, together with costs of suit.

(Stats.1976, c. 1010, § 2, operative April 30, 1977.   Amended by Stats.1987, c. 1452, § 124.)

Historical and Statutory Notes

Legislative findings, declarations and intent relating to Stats.1987, c. 1452, see Historical and Statutory Notes under Education Code § 1007.

Derivation: Educ.C.1959, § 27104, (Stats. 1959, c. 2, p. 1454, § 27104).

Educ.C.1943, § 22046 (Stats.1943, c. 71, p. 731).

Pol.C. § 2298, amended by Stats.1899, c. 31, p. 30, § 3; Stats.1903, c. 74, p. 82, § 3.

§ 19334. Liability of person who injures or fails to return books

Every person who injures or fails to return any book taken is liable in three times its value.

(Stats.1976, c. 1010, § 2, operative April 30, 1977.)

Historical and Statutory Notes

Derivation: Educ.C.1959, § 27105 (Stats. 1959, c. 2, p. 1454, § 27105).

Educ.C.1943, § 22047 (Stats.1943, c. 71, p. 732).

Pol.C. § 2299.

Article 4

READING INITIATIVE PROGRAM

Article 4 was added by Stats.1994, c. 787 (S.B.1993), § 1.

§ 19335. Short title

This act shall be known and may be cited as the Reading Initiative Program.

(Added by Stats.1994, c. 787 (S.B.1993), § 1.)

§ 19336.   Reading Initiative Program;   administration by State Librarian;
        duties

The State Librarian shall establish the Reading Initiative Program with funds appropriated for that purpose and with funds received from private sources. The State Librarian shall administer the program, for which purpose he or she shall do all of the following:

(a) Develop a list of recommended books, in consultation with various groups, including, but not limited to, teachers, librarians, parents, writers, publishers, and employees of the State Department of Education. The recommended books shall supplement the state-recommended English/language arts curriculum framework, and shall include recreational reading selections for children.

(b) Develop a method of involving pupils enrolled in kindergarten and grades 1 to 12, inclusive, in the program and an appropriate form of recognition for pupils who volunteer to participate in the program and who succeed in the program.   Rewards and related recognition activities shall be funded with amounts received from private sources.

(c) To the extent private funds are available, and consistent with subdivision (b), expend private funds received by the State Librarian for the purposes of this article to obtain and make available to the public the books on the list developed pursuant to subdivision (a) .

(Added by Stats.1994, c. 787 (S.B.1993), § 1.   Amended by Stats.1996, c. 124 (A.B. 3470), § 19.)

Chapter 8

LIBRARY DISTRICTS

Chapter 8 was enacted by Stats.1976, c. 1010, § 2, operative April 30, 1977.

Article 1

FORMATION, ANNEXATION, DISSOLUTION

Article 1 was enacted by Stats.1976, c. 1010, § 2, operative April 30, 1977.

Cross References

Library districts in unincorporated towns and villages, see Education Code § 19600 et seq.
Unified school district public libraries, see Education Code § 18300 et seq.

§ 19400.   Organization and powers of district ·

A library district may be organized, as provided in this chapter. The library district may establish, equip, and maintain a public library for the dissemination of knowledge of the arts, sciences, and general literature and may exercise the powers granted or necessarily implied pursuant to this chapter.

(Stats.1976, c. 1010, § 2, operative April 30, 1977.)

Historical and Statutory Notes

Derivation: Educ.C.1959, § 27751 (Stats. 1959, c. 2, p. 1474, § 27751).

Educ.C.1943, § 22601 (Stats.1943, c. 71, p. 749).

Stats.1935, c. 337, p. 1165, § 2.

Library References

Municipal Corporations ⊕1.
Westlaw Topic No. 268.
C.J.S. Municipal Corporations §§ 2 to 7.

Legal Jurisprudences

Cal Jur 3d Sch § 140.

§ 19401.   Territory includable in district

The library district may include incorporated or unincorporated territory, or both, in any one or more counties, so long as the territory of the district consists of contiguous parcels and the territory of no city is divided.

(Stats.1976, c. 1010, § 2, operative April 30, 1977.)

Historical and Statutory Notes

Derivation: Educ.C.1959, § 27752 (Stats. 1959, c. 2, p. 1474, § 27752).

Educ.C.1943, § 22602 (Stats.1943, c. 71, p. 750).

Stats.1935, c. 337, p. 1165, § 3.

Library References

Legal Jurisprudences
Cal Jur 3d Sch § 140.

§ 19402.   Petition to form district

Whenever the formation of a library district is desired, a petition which may consist of any number of instruments, may be presented at a regular meeting of

189

the board of supervisors of the county in which is located the largest proportionate value of the lands within the proposed district as shown by the last equalized county assessment roll.   The petition shall specify whether the proposed library district shall be governed by a three-member board of library trustees or by a five-member board of library trustees.   The board of supervisors to whom the petition is presented is designated in this chapter as the supervising board of supervisors.

(Stats.1976, c. 1010, § 2, operative April 30, 1977.   Amended by Stats.1982, c. 354, p. 1666, § 1.)

Historical and Statutory Notes

Derivation: Educ.C.1959,   § 27753   (Stats.   Stats.1935, c. 337, p. 1165, § 4.
1959, c. 2, p. 1474, § 27753).

Educ.C.1943,   § 22603   (Stats.1943,   c. 71,   p.
750).

West's California Code Forms

See West's Cal. Code Forms, Educ. § 19402—FORM 1.

Library References

Legal Jurisprudences

Cal Jur 3d Sch § 140.

§ 19403.   Qualifications of signers and number required

The petition shall be signed by registered voters residing within the proposed library district equal in number to at least 5 percent of the number of votes cast in the territory comprising the proposed district at the last preceding general state election at which a Governor was elected.

(Stats.1976, c. 1010, § 2, operative April 30, 1977.)

Historical and Statutory Notes

Derivation: Educ.C.1959,   § 27754   (Stats.   Stats.1935, c. 337 p. 1165, § 4.
1959, c. 2, p. 1474, § 27754).

Educ.C.1943,   § 22604   (Stats.1943,   c. 71,   p.
750).

§ 19404.   Proceedings for filing and hearing

The proceedings for the filing and hearing of the petition are governed and controlled by the provisions of Sections 58032, 58033, 58034, 58060, and 58061 of the Government Code.

(Stats.1976, c. 1010, § 2, operative April 30, 1977.)

Historical and Statutory Notes

Derivation: Educ.C.1959,   § 27755   (Stats.   Stats.1935, c. 337, p. 1166, § 5.
1959, c. 2, p. 1474, § 27755).

Educ.C.1943,   § 22605   (Stats.1943,   c. 71,   p.
750, amended by Stats.1957, c. 59, p. 628, § 5).

§ 19405. Proceedings for final hearing

The proceedings for final hearing of the petition and the formation of the district are governed and controlled by the provisions of Article 4 (commencing with Section 58090), Article 5 (commencing with Section 58130), and Article 7 (commencing with Section 58200) of Chapter 1 of Title 6 of the Government Code.

(Stats.1976, c. 1010, § 2, operative April 30, 1977.)

Historical and Statutory Notes

Derivation: Educ.C.1959, § 27756 (Stats. 1959, c. 2, p. 1474, § 27756).

Educ.C.1943, § 22606 (Stats.1943, c. 71, p. 750, amended by Stats.1957, c. 59, p. 628, § 6).

Stats.1935, c. 337, p. 1166, § 6.

§ 19406. Written protests

On the filing of written protests by registered voters residing in the proposed district equal in number to at least 50 percent of the number of votes cast in the territory comprising the proposed district at the last preceding general state election at which a Governor was elected, the proceeding for the formation of the district shall be terminated as provided in Sections 58103 and 58104 of the Government Code.

(Stats.1976, c. 1010, § 2, operative April 30, 1977.)

Historical and Statutory Notes

Derivation: Educ.C.1959, § 27757 (Stats. 1959, c. 2, p. 1474, § 27757).

Educ.C.1943, § 22607 (Stats.1943, c. 71, p. 750, amended by Stats.1957, c. 59, p. 628, § 7).

Stats.1935, c. 337, p. 1166, § 7.

Cross References

State department of education, see Education Code § 33300 et seq.

§ 19407. Organization of districts in more than one county

No library district including territory in more than one county shall be organized under this chapter without the concurrent consent by resolution of each board of supervisors involved, as well as the consent of the governing body of each city to be included.

(Stats.1976, c. 1010, § 2, operative April 30, 1977.)

Historical and Statutory Notes

Derivation: Educ.C.1959, § 27758 (Stats. 1959, c. 2, p. 1474, § 27758).

Educ.C.1943, § 22608 (Stats.1943, c. 71, p. 750).

Stats.1935, c. 337, p. 1172, § 39.

Library References

Legal Jurisprudences

Cal Jur 3d Sch § 140.

Article 2

TRUSTEES

Article 2 was enacted by Stats.1976, c. 1010, § 2, operative April 30, 1977.

§ 19420.   Appointment of trustees

Within 30 days after the filing with the county clerk or county board of supervisors of the resolution declaring the organization of the district, the supervising board of supervisors shall appoint the required number of library trustees from the district at large.

(Stats.1976, c. 1010, § 2, operative April 30, 1977. Amended by Stats.1982, c. 354, p. 1666, § 2; Stats.1998, c. 829 (S.B.1652), § 22.)

Historical and Statutory Notes

Derivation: Educ.C.1959, § 27801 (Stats. 1959, c. 2, p. 1475, § 27801).

Educ.C.1943, § 22626 (Stats.1943, c. 71, p. 751).

Stats.1935, c. 337, p. 1166, § 8.

Cross References

Board of supervisors, see Government Code §§ 25000, 25003 et seq.
Computation of time,
     Generally, see Code of Civil Procedure §§ 12 and 12a and Government Code § 6800 et seq.
     Time in which any act provided by the Education Code is to be done, see Education Code § 9.
Continuation of statutes relating to subjects covered by provisions of this Code, see Education Code
     § 3.
County boards of supervisors, generally, see Education Code § 1400 et seq.
County or counties, defined, see Education Code § 92.

Library References

Legal Jurisprudences
   Cal Jur 3d Sch § 140.

§ 19421. Designation of governing board

The governing board of the district shall be called "the Board of Library Trustees of _____ Library District" (inserting the name of the particular district).

(Stats.1976, c. 1010, § 2, operative 30, 1977.)

Historical and Statutory Notes

Derivation: Educ.C.1959, § 27802 (Stats. 1959, c. 2, p. 1475, § 27802).

Educ.C.1943, § 22627 (Stats.1943, c. 71, p. 751).

Stats.1935, c. 337, p. 1166, § 10.

Cross References

Governing board, defined, see Education Code § 78.

§ 19422. Term of office

The trustee shall hold office for the term of four years beginning on the last Friday in November next succeeding their appointment or election.

(Stats.1976, c. 1010, § 2, operative April 30, 1977. Amended by Stats.1977, c. 36, § 75, eff. April 29, 1977; Stats.1978, c. 1376, p. 4561, § 4.)

Historical and Statutory Notes

1978 activity relating to notices, filings, calls and conduct of the 1979 March elections not required upon change of the March elections to the first Tuesday after the first Monday in November in odd-numbered years, see Historical and Statutory Notes under Education Code § 1007.

Expiration of terms of office of trustees of library districts, school districts and community college districts effected by the legislature at the

1977–78 Regular Session of the Legislature, see Historical and Statutory Notes under Education Code § 1007.

Derivation: Educ.C.1959, § 27803 (Stats. 1959, c. 2, p. 1475, § 27803, amended by Stats. 1965, c. 1098, p. 2745, § 1; Stats.1976, c. 151, § 1).

Educ.C.1943, § 22628 (Stats.1943, c. 71, p. 651).

Stats.1935, c. 337, p. 1166, § 10.

Cross References

Term of offices for public officers and employees and continuation thereof, see Government Code §§ 1301 and 1302.

§ 19423. Classification of members of first board

The first board of library trustees appointed or elected in a district shall at their first meeting so classify themselves by lot that their terms shall expire:

(a) For three-member boards, one on the last Friday in November of the first odd-numbered calendar year next succeeding his or her appointment or election, and two on the last Friday in November of the second succeeding odd-numbered calendar year.

(b) For five-member boards, two on the last Friday in November of the first odd-numbered calendar year next succeeding his or her appointment or elec-

193

tion, and three on the last Friday in November of the second succeeding odd-numbered calendar year.

(Stats.1976, c. 1010, § 2, operative April 30, 1977. Amended by Stats.1977, c. 36, § 76, eff. April 29, 1977; Stats.1978, c. 1376, p. 4561, § 5; Stats.1982, c. 354, p. 1666, § 3; Stats.1987, c. 56, § 38.)

Historical and Statutory Notes

1978 activity relating to notices, filing, calls and conduct of the 1979 March elections not required upon change of the March elections to the first Tuesday after the first Monday in November in odd-numbered years, see Historical and Statutory Notes under Education Code § 1007.

Expiration of terms of office of trustees of library districts, school districts and community college districts effected by the legislature at the

1977–78 Regular Session of the Legislature, see Historical and Statutory Notes under Education Code § 1007.

Derivation: Educ.C.1959, § 27804 (Stats. 1959, c. 2, p. 1475, § 27804, amended by Stats. 1976, c. 151, § 2.)

Educ.C.1943, § 22629 (Stats.1943, c. 71, p. 751).

Stats.1935, c. 337, p. 1166, § 10.

§ 19424. Organization of board

At its first meeting called after the original appointment of the board, and annually thereafter at its first meeting called after the last Friday in November in odd-numbered years, the board shall organize by electing one of its number president, and another one of its number secretary. They shall serve as such for one year or until their successors are elected and qualified.

(Stats.1976, c. 1010, § 2, operative April 30, 1977. Amended by Stats.1977, c. 36, § 77, eff. April 29, 1977; Stats.1978, c. 1376, p. 4561, § 6.)

Historical and Statutory Notes

1978 activity relating to notices, filings, calls and conduct of the 1979 March elections not required upon change of the March elections to the first Tuesday after the first Monday in November in odd-numbered years, see Historical and Statutory Notes under Education Code § 1007.

Derivation: Educ.C.1959, § 27805 (Stats. 1959, c. 2, p. 1475, § 27805, amended by Stats. 1976, c. 151, § 3).

Educ.C.1943, § 22630 (Stats.1943, c. 71, p. 751).

Stats.1935, c. 337, p. 1166, § 13.

§ 19425. Record of proceedings and filing of certificate of establishment

The board shall cause a proper record of its proceedings to be kept, and at the first meeting of the board of trustees of the library district, it shall immediately cause to be made out and filed with the State Librarian a certificate showing that the library district has been established, with the date thereof, the names of the trustees, and the officers of the board chosen for the current fiscal year.

(Stats.1976, c. 1010, § 2, operative April 30, 1977. Amended by Stats.1987, c. 1452, § 125.)

Historical and Statutory Notes

Legislative findings, declarations and intent relating to Stats.1987, c. 1452, see Historical and Statutory Notes under Education Code § 1007.

Derivation: Educ.C.1959, § 27806 (Stats. 1959, c. 2, p. 1476, § 27806).

Educ.C.1943, § 22631 (Stats.1943, c. 71, p. 751).

Stats.1935, c. 337, p. 1167, § 13.

§ 19426. Vacancies

A vacancy in the board of library trustees shall be filled for the unexpired term by appointment of the supervising board of supervisors.

(Stats.1976, c. 1010, § 2, operative April 30, 1977.)

Historical and Statutory Notes

Derivation: Educ.C.1959, § 27807 (Stats. 1959, c. 2, p. 1476, § 27807).

Educ.C.1943, § 22632 (Stats.1943, c. 71, p. 751).

Stats.1935, c. 337, p. 1166, § 9.

§ 19427. Holding office until successor is elected and qualified

Each library trustee shall hold office until his successor is elected and qualified.

(Stats.1976, c. 1010, § 2, operative April 30, 1977.)

Historical and Statutory Notes

Derivation: Educ.C.1959, § 27808 (Stats. 1959, c. 2, p. 1476, § 27808).

Educ.C.1943, § 22633 (Stats.1943, c. 71, p. 751).

Stats.1935, c. 337, p. 1166, § 9.

§ 19428. Monthly meetings

The board of library trustees shall meet at least once a month, at such time and place as it may fix by resolution.

(Stats.1976, c. 1010, § 2, operative April 30, 1977.)

Historical and Statutory Notes

Derivation: Educ.C.1959, § 27809 (Stats. 1959, c. 2, p. 1476, § 27809).

Educ.C.1943, § 22634 (Stats.1943, c. 71, p. 752).

Stats.1935, c. 337, p. 1167, § 14.

§ 19429. Special meetings

Special meetings may be called at any time, as follows:

(a) A special meeting of a three-member board of library trustees may be called by two trustees, by written notices served upon each member at least 12 hours before the time specified for the meeting.

(b) A special meeting of a five-member board of library trustees may be called by three trustees, by written notices served upon each member at least 12 hours before the time specified for the meeting.

(Stats.1976, c. 1010, § 2, operative April 30, 1977. Amended by Stats.1982, c. 354, p. 1666, § 4.)

Historical and Statutory Notes

Derivation: Educ.C.1959, § 27810 (Stats. 1959, c. 2, p. 1476, § 27810).

Educ.C.1943, § 22635 (Stats.1943, c. 71, p. 752).

Stats.1935, c. 337, p. 1167, § 14.

§ 19430. Quorum

(a) For three-member boards, two members constitute a quorum for the transaction of business.

(b) For five-member boards, three members constitute a quorum for the transaction of business.

(Stats.1976, c. 1010, § 2, operative April 30, 1977. Amended by Stats.1982, c. 354, p. 1667, § 5.)

Historical and Statutory Notes

Derivation: Educ.C.1959, § 27811 (Stats. 1959, c. 2, p. 1476, § 27811).

Educ.C.1943, § 22636 (Stats.1943, c. 71, p. 752).

Stats.1935, c. 337, p. 1167, § 14.

§ 19431. Proposal to increase number of trustees; procedure

A proposal to increase the number of seats on the board of library trustees from three to five may be initiated in either of the following alternative ways:

(a) By a petition signed by registered voters residing within the library district equal in number to at least 5 percent of the total number of votes cast in the library district at the last preceding general state election at which a Governor was elected, and filed with the supervising board of supervisors of the library district.

(b) By a resolution adopted by the board of trustees and filed with the supervising board of supervisors.

(Added by Stats.1982, c. 354, p. 1667, § 6.)

West's California Code Forms

See West's Cal. Code Forms, Educ. § 19431—FORM 1.

§ 19432. Petitions or resolutions to increase number of trustees; hearings; notice; appointment of additional trustees

(a) The supervising board of supervisors, at its option, may conduct a public hearing on a petition or resolution filed pursuant to Section 19431. Notice of the hearing shall be published pursuant to Sections 6060 and 6061. At the hearing, any interested person shall be given an opportunity to present his or her views on the proposal. At the conclusion of the hearing, the supervising board of supervisors may increase the board of library trustees to a five member board.

(b) If the board of library trustees is increased from three to five members, the supervising board of supervisors shall appoint the two additional trustees from the district at large, and the trustees shall classify themselves by lot so that their terms shall expire as provided in subdivision (b) of Section 19423.

(Added by Stats.1982, c. 354, p. 1667, § 7.)

Article 3

POWERS

Article 3 was enacted by Stats.1976, c. 1010, § 2, operative April 30, 1977.

§ 19460. Rules, regulations, and bylaws

The board of library trustees shall make and enforce all rules, regulations, and bylaws necessary for the administration, government, and protection of the library under its management, and all property belonging to the district.

(Stats.1976, c. 1010, § 2, operative April 30, 1977.)

Historical and Statutory Notes

Derivation: Educ.C.1959, § 27851 (Stats.   Stats.1935, c. 337, p. 1167, § 15.
1959, c. 2, p. 1476, § 27851).

Educ.C.1943, § 22651 (Stats.1943, c. 71, p. 752).

Cross References

Administrative regulations and rulemaking, see Government Code § 11340 et seq.
Violations of rules, regulations and bylaws, see Education Code § 19479.

Library References

Legal Jurisprudences
Cal Jur 3d Sch § 140.

§ 19461. Administration of trust

The board of library trustees shall administer any trust declared or created for the library, and received by gift, devise, or bequest, and hold in trust or otherwise, property situated in this state or elsewhere, and where not otherwise provided, dispose of the property for the benefit of the library.
(Stats.1976, c. 1010, § 2, operative April 30, 1977.)

Historical and Statutory Notes

Derivation: Educ.C.1959, § 27852 (Stats.   Stats.1935, c. 337, p. 1167, § 15.
1959, c. 2, p. 1476, § 27852).

Educ.C.1943, § 22652 (Stats.1943, c. 71, p. 752).

Cross References

Foundations for institutions of arts and sciences, see Education Code § 21140 et seq.

§ 19462. Officers and employees

The board of library trustees shall prescribe the duties and powers of the librarian, secretary, and other officers and employees of the library, determine the number of and appoint all officers and employees, and fix their compensation. The officers and employees shall hold their offices and positions at the pleasure of the board.
(Stats.1976, c. 1010, § 2, operative April 30, 1977.)

Historical and Statutory Notes

Derivation: Educ.C.1959, § 27853 (Stats.   Stats.1935, c. 337, p. 1167, § 15.
1959, c. 2, p. 1476, § 27853).

Educ.C.1943, § 22653 (Stats.1943, c. 71, p. 752).

Notes of Decisions

Compensation and benefits   1

———

1. Compensation and benefits

Longevity salary increase, fifth week of vacation for full-time professional employees, and four-month fully paid sabbatical for librarians were correctly found important to employees, to have been an inducement for them to remain employed with district, and were form of compensation which they had earned by remaining in employment, and thus it would be grossly unfair to allow library district to eliminate such benefits without payment of compensation for such service. California League of City Employee Associations v. Palos Verdes Library Dist. (App. 2 Dist. 1978) 150 Cal.Rptr. 739, 87 Cal.App.3d 135.

§ 19463.   Purchase of personal property

The board of library trustees shall purchase necessary books, journals, publications, and other personal property.

(Stats.1976, c. 1010, § 2, operative April 30, 1977.)

Historical and Statutory Notes

Derivation: Educ.C.1959, § 27854 (Stats. 1959, c. 2, p. 1476, § 27854).

Educ.C.1943, § 22654 (Stats.1943, c. 71, p. 752).

Stats.1935, c. 337, p. 1167, § 15.

§ 19464.   Purchase of real property

The board of library trustees shall purchase real property, and erect or rent and equip, such buildings or rooms, as in its judgment are necessary properly to carry out the provisions of this chapter.

(Stats.1976, c. 1010, § 2, operative April 30, 1977.)

Historical and Statutory Notes

Derivation: Educ.C.1959, § 27855 (Stats. 1959, c. 2, p. 1476, § 27855).

Educ.C.1943, § 22655 (Stats.1943, c. 71, p. 752).

Stats.1935, c. 337, p. 1167, § 15.

§ 19465.   State publications

The board of library trustees shall require the Secretary of State and other state officials to furnish the library with copies of any and all reports, laws, and other publications of the state not otherwise disposed of by law.

(Stats.1976, c. 1010, § 2, operative April 30, 1977.)

Historical and Statutory Notes

Derivation: Educ.C.1959, § 27856 (Stats. 1959, c. 2, p. 1476, § 27856).

Educ.C.1943, § 22656 (Stats.1943, c. 71, p. 752).

Stats.1935, c. 337, p. 1167, § 15.

Cross References

Secretary of State, powers and duties, see Government Code § 12159 et seq.

§ 19466.   Exchanging with other libraries; nonresident borrowing

The board of library trustees shall borrow books from, lend books to, and exchange books with other libraries, and may allow nonresidents of the district to borrow books upon such conditions as the board may prescribe.

(Stats.1976, c. 1010, § 2, operative April 30, 1977.)

Historical and Statutory Notes

Derivation: Educ.C.1959, § 27857 (Stats.   Stats.1935, c. 337, p. 1167, § 15.
1959, c. 2, p. 1476, § 27857).

Educ.C.1943, § 22657 (Stats.1943, c. 71, p.
752).

§ 19467.   Powers of board

The board of library trustees shall borrow money, give security therefor, purchase on contract, and do and perform any and all other acts and things necessary or proper to carry out the provisions of this chapter.

(Stats.1976, c. 1010, § 2, operative April 30, 1977.)

Historical and Statutory Notes

Derivation: Educ.C.1959, § 27858 (Stats.   Stats.1935, c. 337, p. 1167, § 15.
1959, c. 2, p. 1477, § 27858).

Educ.C.1943, § 22658 (Stats.1943, c. 71, p.
752).

Cross References

Contracts, generally, see Civil Code § 1549 et seq.

§ 19468.   Annual report to State Librarian

The board of library trustees shall file, through the librarian, on or before the last day of August of each year, a report with the State Librarian at Sacramento giving the condition of its library and the number of volumes contained therein on the 30th day of June preceding. The report shall, in addition to other matters deemed expedient by the board of trustees or the district librarian, contain such statistical and other information as is deemed desirable by the State Librarian. For this purpose the State Librarian may send to the several district librarians instructions or question blanks so as to obtain the material for a comparative study of library conditions in the state.

(Stats.1976, c. 1010, § 2, operative April 30, 1977.)

Historical and Statutory Notes

Derivation: Educ.C.1959, § 27859 (Stats.   Stats.1935, c. 337, p. 1167, § 15.
1959, c. 2, p. 1477, § 27859).

Educ.C.1943, § 22659 (Stats.1943, c. 71, p.
752, amended by Stats.1957, c. 2135, p. 3787,
§ 4).

Cross References

State librarian, see Education Code § 19302 et seq.

§ 19469.   Hours open for public use

The board of library trustees shall designate the hours during which the library shall be open for the use of the public.

(Stats.1976, c. 1010, § 2, operative April 30, 1977. Amended by Stats.1982, c. 354, p. 1667, § 8.)

Historical and Statutory Notes

Derivation: Educ.C.1959, § 27860 (Stats. 1959, c. 2, p. 1477, § 27860).

Educ.C.1943, § 22660 (Stats.1943, c. 71, p. 753).

Stats.1935, c. 337, p. 1167, § 15.

§ 19470. Annual estimate of costs

Annually, at least 15 days before the first day of the month in which county taxes are levied, the board of library trustees of each library district shall furnish to the board of supervisors of the county in which the district or any part thereof is situated, an estimate in writing of the amount of money necessary for all purposes required under this chapter during the next ensuing fiscal year.

(Stats.1976, c. 1010, § 2, operative April 30, 1977.)

Historical and Statutory Notes

Derivation: Educ.C.1959, § 27861 (Stats. 1959, c. 2, p. 1477, § 27861).

Educ.C.1943, § 22661 (Stats.1943, c. 71, p. 753).

Stats.1935, c. 337, p. 1168, § 16.

Cross References

Board of supervisors, see Government Code §§ 25000, 25003 et seq.
Tax levies, see Government Code § 29100 et seq. and Revenue and Taxation Code § 2151 et seq.

§§ 19471, 19472. Repealed by Stats.1994, c. 922 (A.B.2587), §§ 33 and 34

Historical and Statutory Notes

Section 19471, enacted by Stats.1976, c.1010, § 2, derived from Educ.C.1959, § 27862 (Stats. 1959, c. 2, p. 1477, § 27862), Educ.C.1943, § 22662 (Stats.1943, c. 71, p. 753), Stats.1935, c. 337, p. 1168, § 16, authorized the board to levy a special tax.

Section 19472, enacted by Stats.1976, c.1010, § 2, derived from Educ.C.1959, § 27863 (Stats. 1959, c. 2, p. 1477, § 27863), Educ.C.1943, § 22663 (Stats.1943, c. 71, p. 753), Stats.1935, c. 337, p. 1168, § 16, authorized the board to levy a special tax.

§ 19473. Computation and collection of tax; payment into county treasury

The tax shall be computed, entered upon the tax rolls, and collected in the same manner as county taxes are computed, entered, and collected. All money collected shall be paid into the county treasury to the credit of the particular library district fund and shall be paid out on the order of the district board, signed by the president and secretary.

(Stats.1976, c. 1010, § 2, operative April 30, 1977.)

Historical and Statutory Notes

Derivation: Educ.C.1959, § 27864 (Stats. 1959, c. 2, p. 1477, § 27864).

Educ.C.1943, § 22664 (Stats.1943, c. 71, p. 753).

Stats.1935, c. 337, p. 1168, § 16.

§ 19474. Repealed by Stats.1994, c. 922 (A.B.2587), § 35

Historical and Statutory Notes

Section 19474, enacted by Stats.1976, c.1010, § 2, derived from Educ.C.1959, § 27865 (Stats. 1959, c. 2, p. 1477, § 27865), Educ.C.1943, § 22665 (Stats.1943, c. 71, p. 753), Stats.1935, c. 337, p. 1168, § 17, related to taxes in districts in more than one county.

§ 19475. Deposit of money from gifts, bequests, devises, or otherwise, to credit of library fund

All money acquired by gift, devise, bequest, or otherwise, for the purposes of the library, shall be paid into the county treasury to the credit of the library fund of the district, subject only to the order of the library trustees of the district.

(Stats.1976, c. 1010, § 2, operative April 30, 1977.)

Historical and Statutory Notes

Derivation: Educ.C.1959, § 27866 (Stats. 1959, c. 2, p. 1478, § 27866).

Educ.C.1943, § 22666 (Stats.1943, c. 71, p. 753).

Stats.1935, c. 337, p. 1169, § 18.

§ 19476. Safety, preservation, and application of fund not payable into treasury

If the payment into the treasury is inconsistent with the terms or conditions of any gift, devise, or bequest, the board of library trustees shall provide for the safety and preservation of the fund, and the application thereof to the use of the library, in accordance with the terms and conditions of the gift, devise, or bequest.

(Stats.1976, c. 1010, § 2, operative April 30, 1977.)

Historical and Statutory Notes

Derivation: Educ.C.1959, § 27867 (Stats. 1959, c. 2, p. 1478, § 27867).

Educ.C.1943, § 22667 (Stats.1943, c. 71, p. 753).

Stats.1935, c. 337, p. 1169, § 18.

§ 19477. Warrants

Upon the receipt by the county auditor of an order of the library trustees of the district, he shall issue his warrant upon the county treasurer for the amount stated in the order.

(Stats.1976, c. 1010, § 2, operative April 30, 1977.)

§ 19478. Nonpayment for want of funds

When any warrant is presented to the treasurer for payment and it is not paid for want of funds, the treasurer shall endorse thereon "not paid for want of funds" with the date of presentation and sign his name thereto, and from that time the warrant bears interest at the rate of 6 percent per annum until it is paid or until funds are available for its payment and the county treasurer gives notice to the warrant holder that funds are available for the payment. The giving of the notice is deemed complete upon deposit thereof in the United States mail in a sealed envelope addressed to the warrant holder at his address given by him at the time of presentation of the warrant to the treasurer, with postage thereon fully prepaid and registered.
(Stats.1976, c. 1010, § 2, operative April 30, 1977.)

§ 19479. Library free to inhabitants; violation of rules, regulations and bylaws

Every library established under this chapter shall be forever free to the inhabitants and nonresident taxpayers of the library district, subject always to such rules, regulations, and bylaws as may be made by the board of library trustees. For violation of any rule, regulation, or bylaw a person may be fined or excluded from the privileges of the library.
(Stats.1976, c. 1010, § 2, operative April 30, 1977.)

Notes of Decisions

Fees   1

_____

1. Fees

Fees may not be charged to local residents for "library services", defined as the satisfaction with library materials of the patron's informational needs, by libraries that are organized under §§ 18300 et seq., 18900 et seq., 19100 et seq., 19400 et seq., 19600 et seq., or Gov.C. § 39732. 61 Ops.Atty.Gen. 512, 11–21–78.

§ 19480.   Title to property

The title to all property acquired for the purposes of the library, when not inconsistent with the terms of its acquisition, or not otherwise designated, vests in the district in which the library is or is to be situated.

(Stats.1976, c. 1010, § 2, operative April 30, 1977.)

Historical and Statutory Notes

Derivation: Educ.C.1959, § 27871 (Stats. 1959, c. 2, p. 1478, § 27871).

Educ.C.1943, § 22671 (Stats.1943, c. 71, p. 754).

Stats.1935, c. 337, p. 1170, § 22.

§ 19481.   Designation of district

Every library district shall be designated by the name and style of _____ Library District (using the name of the district) of _____ County (using the name of the county or counties in which the district is situated). In that name the trustees may sue and be sued, and may hold and convey property for the use and benefit of the district. A number shall not be used as a part of the designation of any library district.

(Stats.1976, c. 1010, § 2, operative April 30, 1977.)

Historical and Statutory Notes

Derivation: Educ.C.1959, § 27872 (Stats. 1959, c. 2, p. 1478, § 27872).

Educ.C.1943, § 22672 (Stats.1943, c. 71, p. 754).

Stats.1935, c. 337, p. 1170, § 22.

§ 19482.   Contracts with other libraries

The board of library trustees and the boards of trustees of neighboring library districts, or the governing bodies of neighboring cities, or boards of supervisors of counties in which public libraries are situated, may contract to lend the books of libraries created under this chapter to residents of the counties, neighboring cities, or library districts, upon a reasonable compensation to be paid by the counties, neighboring cities, or library districts.

(Stats.1976, c. 1010, § 2, operative April 30, 1977.)

Historical and Statutory Notes

Derivation: Educ.C.1959, § 27873 (Stats. 1959, c. 2, p. 1479, § 27873).

Educ.C.1943, § 22673 (Stats.1943, c. 71, p. 754).

Stats.1935, c. 337, p. 1169, § 21.

Contracts, generally, see Civil Code § 1549 et seq.

§ 19483. Property liable to taxation for county free library

Anything in Sections 19100 to 19179, inclusive, to the contrary, notwithstanding, the property in any library district created under this chapter subsequent to the establishment of a county free library is subject to taxation for county free library purposes as though the library district had not been created. This section shall not apply to any adjustments in property tax allocations made pursuant to Section 19116.

(Stats.1976, c. 1010, § 2, operative April 30, 1977. Amended by Stats.1996, c. 522 (S.B.1998), § 2, operative July 1, 1997.)

Historical and Statutory Notes

Derivation: Educ.C.1959, § 27874 (Stats. 1959, c. 2, p. 1479, § 27874, amended by Stats. 1959, c. 595, p. 2572, § 13).

Educ.C.1943, § 22674 (Stats.1943, c. 71, p. 754, amended Stats.1957, c. 1985, p. 3532, § 1). Stats.1935, c. 337, p. 1172, § 40.

Cross References

County free libraries, see Government Code § 26150 et seq.
County service areas, extended library facilities and services, authority of board of supervisors and funding, see Government Code § 25210.78 et seq.
Taxes, special taxes imposed on behalf of public libraries, authority of cities, counties and other agencies, see Government Code § 53717.

Article 4

CLAIMS

Section
19500.   Money or damages claims.

Article 4 was enacted by Stats.1976, c. 1010, § 2, operative April 30, 1977.

§ 19500. Money or damages claims

All claims for money or damages against the district are governed by Part 3 (commencing with Section 900) and Part 4 (commencing with Section 940) of Division 3.6 of Title 1 of the Government Code except as provided therein, or by other statutes or regulations expressly applicable thereto.

(Stats.1976, c. 1010, § 2, operative April 30, 1977.)

Historical and Statutory Notes

Derivation: Educ.C.1959, § 27891, added by Stats.1959, c. 1727, p. 4145, § 5, amended by Stats.1963, c. 1715, p. 3396, § 13.

Article 5

BIENNIAL ELECTION OF TRUSTEES

Article 5 was enacted by Stats.1976, c. 1010, § 2, operative April 30, 1977. The heading of Article 5, "Annual Election of Trustees", was amended by Stats.1977, c. 36, § 77.5, eff. April 29, 1977.

§ 19510.   Biennial election of trustees

An election shall be held biennially in each library district for the election of one or more library trustees who shall hold office for four years beginning on the last Friday in November next succeeding his election. This election shall be held in the district on the same day as the school district election as specified in Section 5000 in the odd-numbered years. Trustees shall be nominated in the manner prescribed in Section 5012.

(Stats.1976, c. 1010, § 2, operative April 30, 1977. Amended by Stats.1977, c. 36, § 78, eff. April 29, 1977; Stats.1978, c. 1376, p. 4561, § 7.)

Historical and Statutory Notes

1978 activity relating to notices, filings, calls and conduct of the 1979 March elections not required upon change of the March elections to the first Tuesday after the first Monday in November in odd-numbered years, see Historical and Statutory Notes under Education Code § 1007.

Expiration of terms of office of trustees of library districts, school districts and community college districts effected by the legislature at the 1977–78 Regular Session of the Legislature, see Historical and Statutory Notes under Education Code § 1007.

Derivation: Educ.C.1959, § 27901 (Stats. 1959, c. 2, p. 1479, § 27901, amended by Stats. 1965, c. 1098, p. 2745, § 2; Stats.1976, c. 151, § 5).

Educ.C.1943, § 22691 (Stats.1943, c. 71, p. 754).

Stats.1935, c. 337, p. 1167, § 11.

§ 19511.   Electors qualified to vote

To be qualified to vote at any library district election a person shall be registered to vote in the library district, at least 29 days before the election.

(Stats.1976, c. 1010, § 2, operative April 30, 1977. Amended by Stats.1977, c. 36, § 79, eff. April 29, 1977; Stats.1978, c. 1376, p. 4561, § 8.)

Historical and Statutory Notes

Derivation: Educ.C.1959, § 27902 (Stats. 1959, c. 2, p. 1479, § 27902, amended by Stats. 1976, c. 151, § 6).

Educ.C.1943, § 22692 (Stats.1943, c. 71, p. 755, amended by Stats.1949, c. 5, p. 12, § 11).

Stats.1935, c. 337, p. 1167, § 12.

Cross References

Electors and voters, see Education Code § 5390; Const. Art. 2, §§ 2, 4; Elections Code §§ 321, 359, 2000 et seq.

§§ 19512, 19513. Repealed by Stats.1979, c. 334, p. 1193, §§ 13, 14, eff. July 27, 1979

Historical and Statutory Notes

Section 19512, enacted by Stats.1976, c. 1010, § 2, amended by Stats.1977, c. 36, § 80, derived from Educ.C.1959, § 27902.1, added by Stats.1965, c. 1098, p. 2746, § 3, amended by Stats.1976, c. 151, § 7, related to conditions for dispensing with elections.

Section 19513, enacted by Stats.1976, c. 1010, § 2, derived from Educ.C.1959, § 27902.2, added by Stats.1965, c. 1098, p. 2746, § 4, related to publication of appointments of nominees.

§ 19514. Appointment of nominee or any qualified voter

If pursuant to Section 5327 a district election is not held, the board of supervisors of the county in which the district, or the largest part thereof in area, is situated shall at its next regular meeting appoint to the positions of trustee those persons nominated, and such persons shall qualify, take office, and serve exactly as if elected at a general district election. If no person has been nominated, the board of supervisors shall appoint any qualified voter of the district to the position.

(Stats.1976, c. 1010, § 2, operative April 30, 1977. Amended by Stats.1979, c. 334, p. 1193, § 15, eff. July 27, 1979.)

Historical and Statutory Notes

Derivation: Educ.C.1959, § 27902.3, added by Stats.1965, c. 1098, p. 2746, § 5.

Cross References

Board of supervisors, see Government Code §§ 25000, 25003 et seq.
Electors and voters, see Education Code § 5390; Elections Code §§ 321, 359; Const. Art. 2, §§ 2, 4.

§ 19515. Provisions governing elections

Except as otherwise provided in this article, Chapter 3 (commencing with Section 5300) of Part 4 of this division shall govern and control the conduct of elections pursuant to this chapter.

(Stats.1976, c. 1010, § 2, operative April 30, 1977. Amended by Stats.1977, c. 36, § 81, eff. April 29, 1977.)

Historical and Statutory Notes

Derivation: Educ.C.1959, § 27903, added by Stats.1976, c. 151, § 9.

Educ.C.1959, § 27903 (Stats.1959, c. 2, p. 1479, § 27903).

Educ.C.1943, § 22693 (Stats.1943, c. 71, p. 755, amended by Stats.1955, c. 877, p. 1504, § 39).

Stats.1935, c. 337, p. 1170, § 23.

Library References

Legal Jurisprudences

Am Jur 2d Public Securities and Obligations §§ 131 et seq.

Article 6

BONDS

Section

19520. Calling election and submission of questions as to issuance and sale of bonds.
19521. Bond election.
19522. Contents of resolution calling election.
19523. Repealed.
19524. Favorable vote.
19525. Limitation on total amount of bonds issued.
19526. Form and term of bonds.
19527. Maximum interest and sale price of bonds; proceeds of sale.
19528. Tax levy for interest and redemption.
19529. Deposit and use of money collected.
19530. Petition for withdrawal and cancellation of unsold bonds.
19531. Notice of hearing on petition.
19532. Hearing and order for cancellation.

Article 6 was enacted by Stats.1976, c. 1010, § 2, operative April 30, 1977.

Cross References

Bonds,
Generally, see Education Code § 15100 et seq.
Issuance by school districts, see Const. Art. 9, § 6 1/2.
Tax exemption of bonds, see Const. Art. 13, § 3.

§ 19520. Calling election and submission of questions as to issuance and sale of bonds

The board of trustees of any library district may, when in their judgment it is deemed advisable, and shall, upon a petition of 50 or more taxpayers and residents of the library district, call an election and submit to the electors of the district, the proposition of whether the bonds of the district will be issued and sold for the purpose of raising money for any or all of the following:

(a) The purchase of suitable lots.

(b) Procuring plans and specifications and erecting a suitable building.

(c) Furnishing and equipping the building and fencing and ornamenting the grounds, for the accommodation of the public library.

(d) Any or all of the purposes of this chapter.

(e) Liquidating any indebtedness incurred for the purposes.

(f) Refunding any outstanding valid indebtedness, evidenced by bonds or warrants of the district.

(Stats.1976, c. 1010, § 2, operative April 30, 1977.)

Historical and Statutory Notes

Derivation: Educ.C.1959, § 27951 (Stats. 1959, c. 2, p. 1479, § 27951).

Educ.C.1943, § 22721 (Stats.1943, c. 71, p. 755).

Stats.1935, c. 337, p. 1170, § 24.

Cross References

Bonds,
 Generally, see Education Code § 15100 et seq.
 Issuance by school districts, see Const. Art. 9, § 6 1/2.
 Tax exemption of bonds, see Const. Art. 13, § 3.
Electors and voters, see Education Code § 5390; Const. Art. 2, §§ 2, 4; Elections Code §§ 321, 359, 2000 et seq.

Library References

Municipal Corporations ⊕906.
Westlaw Topic No. 268.
C.J.S. Municipal Corporations §§ 1645 to 1646, 1702.

Legal Jurisprudences
Cal Jur 3d Sch § 140.
Am Jur 2d Public Securities and Obligations 131 et seq.

§ 19521. Bond election

The bond election shall be called and conducted and the results thereof canvassed, returned, and declared in the manner provided in Chapter 3 (commencing with Section 5300) of Part 4 of this division.

(Stats.1976, c. 1010, § 2, operative April 30, 1977. Amended by Stats.1977, c. 36, § 82, eff. April 29, 1977.)

Historical and Statutory Notes

Derivation: Educ.C.1959, § 27952 (Stats. 1959, c. 2, p. 1480, § 27952, amended by Stats. 1976, c. 151, § 10).

Educ.C.1943, § 22722 (Stats.1943, c. 71, p. 755, amended by Stats.1955, c. 877, p. 1504, § 40).

Stats.1935, c. 337, p. 1170, § 25.

Cross References

Bonds,
 Generally, see Education Code § 15100 et seq.
 Issuance by school districts, see Const. Art. 9, § 6 1/2.
 Tax exemption of bonds, see Const. Art. 13, § 3.

Library References

Legal Jurisprudences
Am Jur 2d Public Securities and Obligations 131 et seq.

§ 19522. Contents of resolution calling election

The board of trustees shall set forth in the resolution calling for a bond election the amount and denomination of the bonds, the rate of interest, and the number of years that all or any part of the bonds are to run.

(Stats.1976, c. 1010, § 2, operative April 30, 1977. Amended by Stats.1977, c. 36, § 83, eff. April 29, 1977.)

Historical and Statutory Notes

Derivation: Educ.C.1959, § 27953 (Stats. 1959, c. 2, p. 1480, § 27953, amended by Stats. 1976, c. 151, § 11).

Educ.C.1943, § 22723 (Stats.1943, c. 71, p. 755, amended by Stats.1955, c. 877, p. 1504, § 41).

Stats.1935, c. 337, p. 1170, § 26.

Library References

Legal Jurisprudences

Am Jur 2d Public Securities and Obligations 131 et seq.

§ 19523. Repealed by Stats.1987, c. 1452, § 126

Historical and Statutory Notes

The repealed section, enacted by Stats.1976, c. 1010, § 2, derived from Educ.C.1959, § 27954 (Stats.1959, c. 2, p. 1480, § 27954); Educ.C.1943, § 22724 (Stats.1943, c. 71, p. 755); and Stats.1935, c. 337, p. 1170, § 27, related to voting methods.

Legislative findings, declarations and intent relating to Stats.1987, c. 1452, see Historical and Statutory Notes under Education Code § 1007.

§ 19524. Favorable vote

If it appears that two-thirds of the votes cast at the election were cast in favor of issuing the bonds, the board shall enter the fact upon its minutes and shall certify all the proceedings to the supervising board of supervisors. Thereupon the board of supervisors shall issue the bonds of the district, in the number and amount provided in the proceedings, and the district shall be named on the bonds. The bonds shall be paid out of the building fund of the district.

The money for the redemption of the bonds and the payment of interest thereon shall be raised by taxation upon the taxable property in the district.

(Stats.1976, c. 1010, § 2, operative April 30, 1977. Amended by Stats.1987, c. 1452, § 127.)

Historical and Statutory Notes

Legislative findings, declarations and intent relating to Stats.1987, c. 1452, see Historical and Statutory Notes under Education Code § 1007.

Derivation: Educ.C.1959, § 27955 (Stats. 1959, c. 2, p. 1480, § 27955).

Educ.C.1943, § 22725 (Stats.1943, c. 71, p. 755, amended by Stats.1955, c. 877, p. 1504, § 42).

Stats.1935, c. 337, p. 1170, § 28.

Cross References

Board of supervisors, see Government Code §§ 25000, 25003 et seq.

§ 19525. Limitation on total amount of bonds issued

The total amount of bonds issued shall not exceed 5 percent of the assessed value of the property of the district, prior to the 1980–81 fiscal year and shall not exceed 1.25 percent of the assessed value of the district beginning after the 1981–82 fiscal year, as shown by the last equalized assessment roll of the county or counties in which the district is situated.

(Stats.1976, c. 1010, § 2, operative April 30, 1977. Amended by Stats.1980, c. 1208, p. 4081, § 30.)

Historical and Statutory Notes

Derivation: Educ.C.1959, § 27956 (Stats. 1959, c. 2, p. 1480, § 27956).

Educ.C.1943, § 22726 (Stats.1943, c. 71, p. 756).

Stats.1935, c. 337, p. 1170, § 28.

Cross References

Bonds,
    Generally, see Education Code § 15100 et seq.
    Issuance by school districts, see Const. Art. 9, § 6 1/2.
    Tax exemption of bonds, see Const. Art. 13, § 3.

§ 19526. Form and term of bonds

The supervising board of supervisors by an order entered upon its minutes shall prescribe the form of the bonds and of the interest coupons attached thereto, and shall fix the time when the whole or any part of the principal of the bonds shall be payable, which shall not be more than 40 years from the date thereof.

(Stats.1976, c. 1010, § 2, operative April 30, 1977.)

Historical and Statutory Notes

Derivation: Educ.C.1959, § 27957 (Stats. 1959, c. 2, p. 1480, § 27957).

Educ.C.1943, § 22727 (Stats.1943, c. 71, p. 756).

Stats.1935, c. 337, p. 1171, § 29.

Cross References

Bonds,
    Generally, see Education Code § 15100 et seq.
    Issuance by school districts, see Const. Art. 9, § 6 1/2.
    Tax exemption of bonds, see Const. Art. 13, § 3.

Library References

§ 19527.   Maximum interest and sale price of bonds; proceeds of sale

The bonds shall not bear a greater amount of interest than 6 percent, to be payable annually or semiannually. The bonds shall be sold in the manner prescribed by the board of supervisors, but for not less than par, and the proceeds of the sale thereof shall be deposited in the county treasury to the credit of the building fund of the library district, and shall be drawn out for the purposes for which the bonds were issued as other library money is drawn out.

(Stats.1976, c. 1010, § 2, operative April 30, 1977.)

Historical and Statutory Notes

Derivation: Educ.C.1959,   § 27958   (Stats.   Stats.1935, c. 337, p. 1171, § 30.
1959, c. 2, p. 1480, § 27958).

Educ.C.1943, § 22728 (Stats.1943, c. 71, p.
756).

Cross References

Board of supervisors, see Government Code §§ 25000, 25003 et seq.
Bonds,
    Generally, see Education Code § 15100 et seq.
    Issuance by school districts, see Const. Art. 9, § 6 1/2.
    Tax exemption of bonds, see Const. Art. 13, § 3.

Library References

§ 19528.   Tax levy for interest and redemption

The board of supervisors of each county in which any part of the district is situated, at the time of making the levy of taxes for county purposes, shall levy a tax for that year upon the taxable property in the district, at the equalized assessed value thereof for that year, for the interest and redemption of the bonds. The tax shall not be less than sufficient to pay the interest of the bonds for that year, and such portion of the principal as is to become due during the year. In any event the tax shall be high enough to raise, annually, for the first half of the term the bonds are to run, a sufficient sum to pay the interest thereon, and during the balance of the term, high enough to pay the annual interest and to pay, annually, a proportion of the principal of the bonds equal to a sum produced by taking the whole amount of the bonds outstanding and dividing it by the number of years the bonds then have to run.

(Stats.1976, c. 1010, § 2, operative April 30, 1977.)

Historical and Statutory Notes

Derivation: Educ.C.1959,   § 27959   (Stats.   Educ.C.1943, § 22729 (Stats.1943, c. 71, p.
1959, c. 2, p. 1481, § 27959).   756).

Stats.1935, c. 337 p. 1171, § 31.

§ 19529. Deposit and use of money collected

All money levied, when collected, shall be paid into the county treasury to the credit of the library district, and shall be used for the payment of principal and interest on the bonds, and for no other purpose. The principal and interest on the bonds shall be paid by the county treasurer, upon the warrant of the county auditor, out of the fund provided therefor. The county auditor shall cancel and file with the county treasurer the bonds and coupons as rapidly as they are paid.

(Stats.1976, c. 1010, § 2, operative April 30, 1977.)

§ 19530. Petition for withdrawal and cancellation of unsold bonds

Whenever any bonds issued under this article remain unsold for the period of six months after having been offered for sale in the manner prescribed by the supervising board of supervisors, the board of trustees of the library district for or on account of which the bonds were issued, or of any library district composed wholly or partly of territory which, at the time of holding the election authorizing the issuance of the bonds, was embraced within the district for or on account of which the bonds were issued, may petition the supervising board of supervisors to cause the unsold bonds to be withdrawn from the market and canceled.

(Stats.1976, c. 1010, § 2, operative April 30, 1977.)

Historical and Statutory Notes

Derivation: Educ.C.1959, § 27961 (Stats. 1959, c. 2, p. 1481, § 27961).

Educ.C.1943, § 22731 (Stats.1943, c. 71, p. 756).

Stats.1935, c. 337, p. 1171, § 33.

Cross References

Bonds,
> Generally, see Education Code § 15100 et seq.
> Issuance by school districts, see Const. Art. 9, § 6 1/2.
> Tax exemption of bonds, see Const. Art. 13, § 3.

Library References

Legal Jurisprudences
> Am Jur 2d Public Securities and Obligations 131 et seq.

§ 19531. Notice of hearing on petition

Upon receiving the petition, signed by a majority of the members of the board of trustees, the supervising board of supervisors shall fix a time for hearing the petition, which shall be not more than 30 days thereafter, and shall cause a notice, stating the time and place of hearing, and the object of the petition in general terms, to be published as provided in this chapter.

(Stats.1976, c. 1010, § 2, operative April 30, 1977.)

Historical and Statutory Notes

Derivation: Educ.C.1959, § 27962 (Stats. 1959, c. 2, p. 1481, § 27962).

Educ.C.1943, § 22732 (Stats.1943, c. 71, p. 757).

Stats.1935, c. 337, p. 1172, § 34.

Library References

Legal Jurisprudences
> Am Jur 2d Public Securities and Obligations 131 et seq.

§ 19532. Hearing and order for cancellation

At the time and place designated in the notice for hearing the petition, or at any subsequent time to which the hearing is postponed, the supervising board of supervisors shall hear any reasons that are submitted for or against the granting of the petition, and if they deem it for the best interests of the library district named in the petition that the unsold bonds be canceled, they shall make and enter an order in the minutes of their proceedings that the unsold bonds be canceled. Thereupon the bonds, and the vote by which they were authorized to be issued, shall cease to be of any validity whatever.

(Stats.1976, c. 1010, § 2, operative April 30, 1977.)

Historical and Statutory Notes

Derivation: Educ.C.1959, § 27963 (Stats. 1959, c. 2, p. 1481, § 27963).

Educ.C.1943, § 22733 (Stats.1943, c. 71, p. 757).

Stats.1935, c. 337, p. 1172, § 35.

Library References

Legal Jurisprudences
Am Jur 2d Public Securities and Obligations
131 et seq.

Chapter 9

LIBRARY DISTRICTS AND MUSEUMS IN UNINCORPORATED TOWNS AND VILLAGES

Chapter 9 was enacted by Stats.1976, c. 1010, § 2, operative April 30, 1977. The heading of Chapter 9, "Library Districts in Unincorporated Towns and Villages", was amended by Stats.1978, c. 988, p. 3052, § 1.

Article 1

FORMATION

Article 1 was enacted by Stats.1976, c. 1010, § 2, operative April 30, 1977.

§ 19600. Authority to establish, equip, and maintain library and museum

Any unincorporated town or village of this state may establish, equip, and maintain a public library for the dissemination of knowledge of the arts, sciences, and general literature, in accordance with this chapter. Any unincorporated town or village of this state may also establish, equip, and maintain a public museum in accordance with this chapter.

(Stats.1976, c. 1010, § 2, operative April 30, 1977. Amended by Stats.1978, c. 988, p. 3052, § 2.)

Historical and Statutory Notes

Derivation: Educ.C.1959, § 27501 (Stats. 1959, c. 2, p. 1464, § 27501).

Educ.C.1943, § 22301 (Stats.1943, c. 71, p. 741).

Stats.1909, c. 480, p. 815, § 1.

Library References

Municipal Corporations ☞57.
Westlaw Topic No. 268.
C.J.S. Municipal Corporations §§ 104, 106, 108, 110 to 115, 117 to 118, 122, 137 to 138, 143, 145 to 146.

Legal Jurisprudences

Cal Jur 3d Sch § 142.

Notes of Decisions

Exemption from tax   3
Nature of library district   2
Validity   1

_____

1. Validity

Statute authorizing organization of library districts did not deny due process because not providing opportunity for objection to inclusion in district. Palos Verdes Library Dist. of Los Angeles County v. McClellan (App. 2 Dist. 1929) 97 Cal.App. 769, 276 P. 600.

As, in view of Const. Art. 9, § 1, and Stats. 1909, p. 815, §§ 1, 15, relative to establishment of libraries, library district organized under such act was an educational district, statute did not deprive taxpayers of property without due process of law because providing for including their property without notice and opportunity to object to its inclusion. Palos Verdes Library

Dist. of Los Angeles County v. McClellan (App. 2 Dist. 1929) 97 Cal.App. 769, 276 P. 600.

Statute authorizing organization of library districts was valid. Palos Verdes Library Dist. of Los Angeles County v. McClellan (App. 2 Dist. 1929) 97 Cal.App. 769, 276 P. 600.

2. Nature of library district

Library districts are conducted for the general diffusion of knowledge and intelligence and are educational as well as quasi municipal. Palos Verdes Library Dist. of Los Angeles County v. McClellan (App. 2 Dist. 1929) 97 Cal.App. 769, 276 P. 600.

3. Exemption from tax

School district's maintenance of free circulating library did not exempt property in district from tax for support of county library. Redman v. Weisenheimer (App. 2 Dist. 1929) 102 Cal. App. 488, 283 P. 363.

§ 19601. Petition and election

Upon the application, by petition, of 50 or more taxpayers and residents of any unincorporated town or village to the board of supervisors in the county in which the town or village is located, for the formation of a library district, and setting forth the boundaries of the proposed district, the board of supervisors shall, within 10 days after receiving the petition, by resolution, order that an election be held in the proposed district for the determination of the question and shall conduct the election.

(Stats.1976, c. 1010, § 2, operative April 30, 1977. Amended by Stats.1987, c. 1452, § 128.)

Historical and Statutory Notes

Legislative findings, declarations and intent relating to Stats.1987, c. 1452, see Historical and Statutory Notes under Education Code § 1007.

Derivation: Educ.C.1959, § 27502 (Stats. 1959, c. 2, p. 1464, § 27502).

Educ.C.1943, § 22302 (Stats.1943, c. 71, p. 741).

Stats.1909, c. 480, p. 815, § 2.

West's California Code Forms

See West's Cal. Code Forms, Educ. § 19601—FORM 1.
See West's Cal. Code Forms, Educ. § 19601—FORM 2.

Cross References

Computation of time,
    Generally, see Code of Civil Procedure §§ 12 and 12a and Government Code § 6800 et seq.
    Time in which any act provided by the Education Code is to be done, see Education Code § 9.
Continuation of statutes relating to subjects covered by provisions of this Code, see Education Code
    § 3.
County board of supervisors, see Government Code §§ 25000, 25003 et seq.
Electors and voters, see Education Code § 5390; Const. Art. 2, §§ 2, 4; Elections Code §§ 321,
    359, 2000 et seq.
Residence, as person's domicile,
    Generally, see Elections Code § 349.
    Determination of domicile, see Elections Code § 2020 et seq.
Taxpayer, defined, personal income tax, see Revenue and Taxation Code § 17004.

Library References

Legal Jurisprudences
Cal Jur 3d Sch § 142.

Am Jur 2d Elections §§ 193 et seq.; 291 et seq.

§ 19602. Repealed by Stats.1987, c. 1452, § 129

Historical and Statutory Notes

The repealed section, enacted by Stats.1976, c. 1010, § 2, derived from Educ.C.1959, § 27503 (Stats.1959, c. 2, p. 1464, § 27503); Educ.C.1943, § 22303 (Stats.1943, c. 71, p. 741); and Stats.1909, c. 480, p. 815, § 3, related to notices of election.

Legislative findings, declarations and intent relating to Stats.1987, c. 1452, see Historical and Statutory Notes under Education Code § 1007.

§ 19603. Transmittal of notification of election call; action by local agency formation commission

Within five days after the district formation election has been called, the legislative body which has called the election shall transmit, by registered mail, a written notification of the election call to the executive officer of the local agency formation commission of the county or principal county in which the territory or major portion of the territory of the proposed district is located. Such written notice shall include the name and a description of the proposed district, and may be in the form of a certified copy of the resolution adopted by the legislative body calling the district formation election.

The executive officer, within five days after being notified that a district formation election has been called, shall submit to the commission, for its approval or modification, an impartial analysis of the proposed district formation.

The impartial analysis shall not exceed 500 words in length and shall include a specific description of the boundaries of the district proposed to be formed.

The local agency formation commission, within five days after the receipt of the executive officer's analysis, shall approve or modify the analysis and submit it to the officials in charge of conducting the district formation election.

(Stats.1976, c. 1010, § 2, operative April 30, 1977.)

Historical and Statutory Notes

Derivation: Educ.C.1959, § 27503.1, added by Stats.1970, c. 736, p. 1366, § 1.

Cross References

Computation of time,
 Generally, see Code of Civil Procedure §§ 12 and 12a and Government Code § 6800 et seq.
 Time in which any act provided by the Education Code is to be done, see Education Code § 9.
Continuation of statutes relating to subjects covered by provisions of this Code, see Education Code
 § 3.
Registered mail, defined, see Education Code § 70.
Restatements and continuation of statutes, generally, see Government Code § 9604.

Library References

Legal Jurisprudences
 Am Jur 2d Elections §§ 193 et seq.; 291 et
 seq.

§ 19604. Filing of arguments for and against district formation

The board of supervisors or any member or members of the board authorized by the board, or any individual voter or bona fide association of citizens entitled to vote on the district formation proposition, or any combination of such voters and associations of citizens, may file a written argument for or a written argument against the proposed district formation.

Arguments shall not exceed 300 words in length and shall be filed with the officials in charge of conducting the election not less than 54 days prior to the date of the district formation election.

(Stats.1976, c. 1010, § 2, operative April 30, 1977.)

Historical and Statutory Notes

Derivation: Educ.C.1959, § 27503.2, added by Stats.1970, c. 736, p. 1366, § 2.

§ 19605. Selection of arguments; preferences and priorities

If more than one argument for or more than one argument against the proposed district formation is filed with the election officials within the time prescribed, such election officials shall select one of the arguments for printing and distribution to the voters.

In selecting the arguments, the election officials shall give preference and priority in the order named to the arguments of the following:

(a) The board of supervisors or any member or members of the board authorized by the board.

(b) Individual voters or bona fide associations of citizens or a combination of such voters and associations.

(Stats.1976, c. 1010, § 2, operative April 30, 1977.)

Historical and Statutory Notes

Derivation: Educ.C.1959, § 27503.3, added by Stats.1970, c. 736, p. 1366, § 3.

§§ 19606, 19607. Repealed by Stats.1987, c. 1452, §§ 130, 131

Historical and Statutory Notes

Section 19606, enacted by Stats.1976, c. 1010, § 2, amended by Stats.1977, c. 1205, § 20.5, derived from Educ.C.1959, § 27503.4, added by Stats.1970, c. 736, p. 1367, § 4, related to ballot pamphlets.

Section 19607, enacted by Stats.1976, c. 1010, § 2, derived from Educ.C.1959, § 27504 (Stats.1959, c. 2, p. 1465, § 27504); Educ.C.

1943, § 22304 (Stats.1943, c. 71, p. 741); and Stats.1909, c. 480, p. 815, § 3, related to poll hours.

Legislative findings, declarations and intent relating to Stats.1987, c. 1452, see Historical and Statutory Notes under Education Code § 1007.

§ 19608. Conduct of election

The election shall be conducted in accordance with the general election laws of this state, where applicable, without reference to form of ballot or manner of voting, except that the ballots shall contain the words, "For library district," and the voter shall write or print after the words on his ballot the word "Yes," or the word "No."

(Stats.1976, c. 1010, § 2, operative April 30, 1977.)

Historical and Statutory Notes

Derivation: Educ.C.1959, § 27505 (Stats. 1959, c. 2, p. 1465, § 27505).

Educ.C.1943, § 22305 (Stats.1943, c. 71, p. 741).

Stats.1909, c. 480, p. 815, § 4.

Cross References

Elections, conduct of elections, generally, see Education Code § 5300 et seq.; Elections Code § 10240 et seq.

§ 19609. Repealed by Stats.1987, c. 1452, § 132

Historical and Statutory Notes

The repealed section, enacted by Stats.1976, c. 1010, § 2, derived from Educ.C.1959, § 27506 (Stats.1959, c. 2, p. 1465, § 27506);

Educ.C.1943, § 22306 (Stats.1943, c. 71, p. 741); and Stats.1909, c. 480, p. 815, § 5, provided that qualified electors were entitled to vote.

Legislative findings, declarations and intent relating to Stats.1987, c. 1452, see Historical and Statutory Notes under Education Code § 1007.

§ 19610. Report of election results

The election officers shall report the result of the election to the board of supervisors within five days after the election.

(Stats.1976, c. 1010, § 2, operative April 30, 1977.)

Historical and Statutory Notes

Derivation: Educ.C.1959, § 27507 (Stats. 1959, c. 2, p. 1465, § 27507).

Educ.C.1943, § 22307 (Stats.1943, c. 71, p. 741).

Stats.1909, c. 480, p. 816, § 6.

Cross References

Board of supervisors, see Government Code §§ 25000, 25003 et seq.
Computation of time,
  Generally, see Code of Civil Procedure §§ 12 and 12a and Government Code § 6800 et seq.
  Time in which any act provided by the Education Code is to be done, see Education Code § 9.
Continuation of statutes relating to subjects covered by provisions of this Code, see Education Code
  § 3.

Library References

Legal Jurisprudences

Am Jur 2d Elections §§ 193 et seq.; 291 et seq.

§ 19611. Establishment of district; appointment and qualifications of board of library trustees

If a majority of the votes at the election is in favor of a library district, the board of supervisors shall by resolution, establish the library district, and shall appoint five trustees, who shall be qualified electors and residents within the limits of the district, to be known as a board of library trustees of the town or village for which they are appointed.

(Stats.1976, c. 1010, § 2, operative April 30, 1977.)

Historical and Statutory Notes

Derivation: Educ.C.1959, § 27508 (Stats. 1959, c. 2, p. 1465, § 27508, amended by Stats. 1965, c. 179, p. 1146, § 2).

Educ.C.1943, § 22308 (Stats.1943, c. 71, p. 741).

Stats.1909, c. 480, p. 816, § 7.

§ 19612. Vacancies

Vacancies shall be filled by the board of supervisors by appointment for the unexpired term.

(Stats.1976, c. 1010, § 2, operative April 30, 1977.)

Historical and Statutory Notes

Derivation: Educ.C.1959, § 27511 (Stats. Stats.1909, c. 480, p. 816, § 7.
1959, c. 2, p. 1465, § 27511).

Educ.C.1943, § 22311 (Stats.1943, c. 71, p. 742).

§ 19613. Unfavorable vote

If a majority of the votes cast is against a library district, the board of supervisors shall, by order, so declare, and no other proceedings shall be taken in relation thereto until the expiration of one year from the date of presentation of the petition.

(Stats.1976, c. 1010, § 2, operative April 30, 1977.)

Historical and Statutory Notes

Derivation: Educ.C.1959, § 27512 (Stats. Stats.1909, c. 480, p. 816, § 8.
1959, c. 2, p. 1465, § 27512).

Educ.C.1943, § 22312 (Stats.1943, c. 71, p. 742).

§ 19614. Entries in minutes of board of supervisors

The fact of the presentation of the petition, and the order establishing the library district and making the appointment of the five library trustees, shall be entered in the minutes of the board of supervisors and shall be conclusive evidence of the due presentation of a proper petition, and that each of the petitioners was, at the time of signature and presentation of the petition, a taxpayer and resident of the proposed district, and of the fact and regularity of all prior proceedings of every kind and nature provided for by this article and of the existence and validity of the district.

(Stats.1976, c. 1010, § 2, operative April 30, 1977.)

Historical and Statutory Notes

Derivation: Educ.C.1959, § 27513 (Stats. Educ.C.1943, § 22313 (Stats.1943, c. 71, p.
1959, c. 2, p. 1465, § 27513, amended by Stats. 742).
1965, c. 179, p. 1146, § 4). Stats.1909, c. 480, p. 816, § 9.

Article 2

POWERS

Section
19650. State publications.
19651. Borrowing from, lending to, and exchanging with other libraries; nonresident
          borrowing.
19652. Incidental power of board.
19653. Annual report to State Librarian.
19654. Hours open to public.
19655. Annual estimate of costs.
19656. Board elections.
19657. Repealed.
19658. Library and safety, preservation and application of fund not payable to trea-
          sury.
19659. Warrants.
19660. Nonpayment of warrants.
19661. Library free to inhabitants; violations of rules, regulations or by-laws.
19662. Contracts with other libraries.
19663. Title to property.
19664. Designation of district.

> *Article 2 was enacted by Stats.1976, c. 1010, § 2, operative April 30,*
> *1977.*

§ 19640. Monthly meetings of board of library trustees

The board of library trustees shall meet at least once a month, at such time
and place as it may fix by resolution.

(Stats.1976, c. 1010, § 2, operative April 30, 1977.)

Historical and Statutory Notes

Derivation: Educ.C.1959, § 27551 (Stats.   Stats.1909, c. 480, p. 816, § 10.
1959, c. 2, p. 1466, § 27551).

Educ.C.1943, § 22331 (Stats.1943, c. 71, p.
742).

Library References

Legal Jurisprudences   Am Jur 2d (Rev) Administrative Law §§ 52 et
  Cal Jur 3d Sch § 142.   seq., 99 et seq.

§ 19641. Special meetings

Special meetings may be called at any time by three trustees, by written
notices served upon each member at least 12 hours before the time specified for
the meeting.

(Stats.1976, c. 1010, § 2, operative April 30, 1977.)

Historical and Statutory Notes

Derivation: Educ.C.1959, § 27552 (Stats.   Educ.C.1943, § 22332 (Stats.1943, c. 71, p.
1959, c. 2, p. 1466, § 27552, amended by Stats.   742).
1965, c. 179, p. 1147, § 5).   Stats.1909, c. 480, p. 816, § 10.

West's California Code Forms

See West's Cal. Code Forms, Educ. § 19641—FORM 1.

§ 19642. Quorum

Three members constitute a quorum for the transaction of business.

(Stats.1976, c. 1010, § 2, operative April 30, 1977.)

Historical and Statutory Notes

Derivation: Educ.C.1959, § 27553 (Stats. 1959, c. 2, p. 1466, § 27553, amended by Stats. 1965, c. 179, p. 1147, § 6).

Educ.C.1943, § 22333 (Stats.1943, c. 71, p. 742).

Stats.1909, c. 480, p. 816, § 10.

§ 19643. Organization of board

At its first meeting held after the general district election the board shall organize by electing one of its number president, and another one of its number secretary. They shall serve as such for one year or until their successors are elected and qualified.

(Stats.1976, c. 1010, § 2, operative April 30, 1977.)

Historical and Statutory Notes

Derivation: Educ.C.1959, § 27554 (Stats. 1959, c. 2, p. 1466, § 27554, amended by Stats. 1967, c. 29, p. 889, § 2.2).

Educ.C.1943, § 22334 (Stats.1943, c. 71, p. 742).

Stats.1909, c. 480, p. 816, § 10.

§ 19644. Record of proceedings and filing of certificate of establishment

The board shall cause a proper record of its proceedings to be kept, and at the first meeting of the board of trustees, it shall immediately cause to be made out and filed with the State Librarian a certificate showing that the library has been established, with the date thereof, the names of the trustees, and the officers of the board chosen for the current fiscal year.

(Stats.1976, c. 1010, § 2, operative April 30, 1977. Amended by Stats.1987, c. 1452, § 133.)

Historical and Statutory Notes

Legislative findings, declarations and intent relating to Stats.1987, c. 1452, see Historical and Statutory Notes under Education Code § 1007.

Derivation: Educ.C.1959, § 27555 (Stats. 1959, c. 2, p. 1466, § 27555).

Educ.C.1943, § 22335 (Stats.1943, c. 71, p. 742).

Stats.1909, c. 480, p. 816, § 10.

Cross References

State department of education, see Education Code § 33300 et seq.
State Librarian,
    Generally, see Education Code § 19302 et seq.
    Powers and duties, see Education Code § 19320 et seq.

§ 19645. Rules, regulations and bylaws

The board of library trustees shall make and enforce all rules, regulations, and bylaws necessary for the administration, government, and protection of the library under its management, and all property belonging to it.

(Stats.1976, c. 1010, § 2, operative April 30, 1977.)

Historical and Statutory Notes

Derivation: Educ.C.1959, § 27556 (Stats. 1959, c. 2, p. 1466, § 27556).

Educ.C.1943, § 22336 (Stats.1943, c. 71, p. 742).

Stats.1909, c. 480, p. 817, § 11, amended by Stats.1939, c. 368, p. 1706, § 1.

Cross References

Administrative regulations and rulemaking, see Government Code § 11340 et seq.
Violation of rules, regulations and bylaws, penalty, see Education Code § 19661.

§ 19646. Administration of trusts, receipts, holdings and disposal of property

The board of library trustees shall administer any trust declared or created for the library, and receive by gift, devise, or bequest, and hold in trust or otherwise, property situated in this state or elsewhere, and where not otherwise provided, dispose of the property for the benefit of the library.

(Stats.1976, c. 1010, § 2, operative April 30, 1977.)

Historical and Statutory Notes

Derivation: Educ.C.1959, § 27557 (Stats. 1959, c. 2, p. 1466, § 27557).

Educ.C.1943, § 22337 (Stats.1943, c. 71, p. 742).

Stats.1909, c. 480, p. 817, § 11, amended by Stats.1939, c. 368, p. 1706, § 1.

Cross References

Foundations for institutions of arts and sciences, see Education Code § 21140 et seq.

§ 19647. Officers and employees

The board of library trustees shall prescribe the duties and powers of the librarian, secretary, and other officers and employees of the library, determine the number of and appoint all officers and employees, and fix their compensation. The officers and employees shall hold their offices and positions at the pleasure of the board.

(Stats.1976, c. 1010, § 2, operative April 30, 1977.)

Historical and Statutory Notes

Derivation: Educ.C.1959, § 27558 (Stats. 1959, c. 2, p. 1466, § 27558).

Educ.C.1943, § 22338 (Stats.1943, c. 71, p. 743).

Stats.1909, c. 480, p. 817, § 11, amended by Stats.1939, c. 368, p. 1706, § 1.

§ 19648. Purchase of personal property

The board of library trustees shall purchase necessary books, journals, publications, and other personal property.

(Stats.1976, c. 1010, § 2, operative April 30, 1977.)

Historical and Statutory Notes

Derivation: Educ.C.1959, § 27559 (Stats. 1959, c. 2, p. 1466, § 27559).

Educ.C.1943, § 22339 (Stats.1943, c. 71, p. 743).

Stats.1909, c. 480, p. 817, § 11, amended by
Stats.1939, c. 368, p. 1706, § 1.

§ 19649. Purchase of real property, and erection or rental and equipment of building or rooms

The board of library trustees shall also purchase such real property, and erect or rent and equip, such building or rooms, as in its judgment is necessary to properly carry out the provisions of this chapter.

(Stats.1976, c. 1010, § 2, operative April 30, 1977.)

Historical and Statutory Notes

Derivation: Educ.C.1959, § 27560 (Stats. 1959, c. 2, p. 1466, § 27560).

Educ.C.1943, § 22340 (Stats.1943, c. 71, p. 743).

Stats.1909, c. 480, p. 817, § 11, amended by Stats.1939, c. 368, p. 1706, § 1.

§ 19650. State publications

The board of library trustees may request the appropriate state officials to furnish the library with copies of any and all reports, laws, and other publications of the state not otherwise disposed of by law.

(Stats.1976, c. 1010, § 2, operative April 30, 1977.)

Historical and Statutory Notes

Derivation: Educ.C.1959, § 27561 (Stats. 1959, c. 2, p. 1466, § 27561, amended by Stats. 1959, c. 1214, p. 3301, § 2).

Educ.C.1943, § 22341 (Stats.1943, c. 71, p. 743).

Stats.1909, c. 480, p. 817, § 11, amended by Stats.1939, c. 368, p. 1706, § 1.

Cross References

Distribution of state publications, see Government Code §§ 9791, 14900 et seq.

§ 19651. Borrowing from, lending to, and exchanging with other libraries; nonresident borrowing

The board of library trustees shall borrow books from, lend books to, and exchange books with other libraries. It shall allow nonresidents to borrow books upon such conditions as it may prescribe.

(Stats.1976, c. 1010, § 2, operative April 30, 1977.)

Historical and Statutory Notes

Derivation: Educ.C.1959, § 27562 (Stats. 1959, c. 2, p. 1467, § 27562).

Educ.C.1943, § 22342 (Stats.1943, c. 71, p. 743).

Stats.1909, c. 480, p. 817, § 11, amended by Stats.1939, c. 368, p. 1706, § 1.

Library References

Legal Jurisprudences

Cal Jur 3d Sch § 142.

§ 19652.   Incidental power of board

The board of library trustees shall do and perform any and all other acts and things necessary or proper to carry out the provisions of this chapter.

(Stats.1976, c. 1010, § 2, operative April 30, 1977.)

Historical and Statutory Notes

Derivation: Educ.C.1959, § 27563 (Stats. 1959, c. 2, p. 1467, § 27563).

Educ.C.1943, § 22343 (Stats.1943, c. 71, p. 743).

Stats.1909, c. 480, p. 817, § 11, amended by Stats.1939, c. 368, p. 1706, § 1.

§ 19653.   Annual report to State Librarian

The board of library trustees shall file, through the librarian, on or before the last day in the month of August of each year, a report with the State Librarian at Sacramento giving the condition of the library and the number of volumes contained therein on the 30th day of June preceding. The report shall, in addition to other matters deemed expedient by the board of trustees or the librarian, contain such statistical and other information as is deemed desirable by the State Librarian. For this purpose the State Librarian may send to the several district librarians instructions or question blanks so as to obtain the material for a comparative study of library conditions in the state.

(Stats.1976, c. 1010, § 2, operative April 30, 1977.)

Historical and Statutory Notes

Derivation: Educ.C.1959, § 27564 (Stats. 1959, c. 2, p. 1467, § 27564).

Educ.C.1943, § 22344 (Stats.1943, c. 71, p. 743, amended by Stats.1957, c. 2135, p. 3787, § 3).

Stats.1909, c. 480, p. 817, § 11, amended by Stats.1939, c. 368, p. 1706, § 1.

Cross References

State librarian, see Education Code § 19302.

§ 19654.   Hours open to public

The board of library trustees shall designate the hours during which the library is open for the use of the public. All public libraries established under this chapter shall be open for the use of the public during every day in the year except on such legal holidays as may be determined by the board of library trustees.

(Stats.1976, c. 1010, § 2, operative April 30, 1977.)

Historical and Statutory Notes

Derivation: Educ.C.1959, § 27565 (Stats. 1959, c. 2, p. 1467, § 27565).

Educ.C.1943, § 22345 (Stats.1943, c. 71, p. 743).

Stats.1909, c. 480, p. 817, § 11, amended by Stats.1939, c. 368, p. 1706, § 1.

§ 19655. Annual estimate of costs

In any library district formed under the provisions of this chapter, which maintains a public library, or which has petitioned for and been granted permission to establish, and intends to maintain a public library in accordance with this chapter, the board of library trustees shall furnish to the board of supervisors of the county in which the library district is situated, each and every year, on or before the first day of September, an estimate of the cost of any or all of the following:

(a) Leasing temporary quarters.

(b) Purchasing a suitable lot.

(c) Procuring plans and specifications and erecting a suitable building.

(d) Furnishing and equipping the building and fencing and ornamenting the grounds, for the accommodation of the public library.

(e) Conducting and maintaining the library for the ensuing fiscal year.

(Stats.1976, c. 1010, § 2, operative April 30, 1977.)

Historical and Statutory Notes

Derivation: Educ.C.1959, § 27566 (Stats. 1959, c. 2, p. 1467, § 27566).

Educ.C.1943 § 22346 (Stats.1943, c. 71, p. 743).

Stats.1909, c. 480, p. 817, § 12.

Cross References

Board of supervisors, see Government Code §§ 25000, 25003 et seq.

§ 19656. Board elections

The board of library trustees may, when in its judgment it is deemed advisable, and upon the petition of 50 or more taxpayers residing within the library district shall, call an election and submit to the electors of the library district the question of whether the bonds of the library district shall be issued and sold for any or all the purposes of this chapter.

(Stats.1976, c. 1010, § 2, operative April 30, 1977.)

Historical and Statutory Notes

Derivation: Educ.C.1959, § 27567 (Stats. 1959, c. 2, p. 1467, § 27567).

Educ.C.1943, § 22347 (Stats.1943, c. 71, p. 744).

Stats.1909, c. 480, p. 817, § 12.

227

West's California Code Forms

See West's Cal. Code Forms, Educ. § 19656—FORM 1.

Library References

Legal Jurisprudences

Am Jur 2d Elections §§ 193 et seq.; 291 et seq.

§ 19657. Repealed by Stats.1994, c. 922 (A.B.2587), § 36

Historical and Statutory Notes

The repealed section, enacted by Stats.1976, c. 1010, § 2, derived from Educ.C.1959, § 27567 (Stats.1959, c. 2, p. 1467, § 27567); Educ.C.1943, § 22347 (Stats.1943, c. 71, p. 744); Stats.1909, c. 480, p. 817, § 12, authorized a special tax levy.

§ 19658. Library and safety, preservation and application of fund not payable to treasury

The revenue derived from the tax, together with all money acquired by gift, devise, bequest, or otherwise, for the purposes of the library, shall be paid into the county treasury, to the credit of the library fund of the district in which the tax is collected, subject only to the order of the library trustees of the district. If payment into the treasury is inconsistent with the terms or conditions of any gift, devise, or bequest, the board of library trustees shall provide for the safety and preservation of the fund, and the application thereof to the use of the library, in accordance with the terms and conditions of the gift, devise, or bequest.

(Stats.1976, c. 1010, § 2, operative April 30, 1977.)

Historical and Statutory Notes

Derivation: Educ.C.1959, § 27569 (Stats. 1959, c. 2, p. 1468, § 27569).

Educ.C.1943, § 22349 (Stats.1943, c. 71, p. 744).

Stats.1909, c. 480, p. 818, § 14, amended by Stats.1931, c. 998, p. 2002, § 1.

Cross References

Foundations for institutions of arts and sciences, see Education Code § 21140 et seq.
Taxes, special taxes imposed on behalf of public libraries, authority of cities, counties and other agencies, see Government Code § 53717.

§ 19659. Warrants

Upon the receipt by the county auditor of an order of the library trustees of the district he shall issue his warrant upon the county treasurer for the amount stated in the order.

(Stats.1976, c. 1010, § 2, operative April 30, 1977.)

Historical and Statutory Notes

Derivation: Educ.C.1959, § 27570 (Stats. 1959, c. 2, p. 1468, § 27570).

Educ.C.1943, § 22350 (Stats.1943, c. 71, p. 744).

Stats.1909, c. 480, p. 818, § 14, amended by Stats.1931, c. 998, p. 2002 § 1.

Cross References
County auditor, see Government Code § 26900 et seq.
County treasurer, see Government Code § 27000 et seq.

§ 19660.   Nonpayment of warrants

When any warrant is presented to the treasurer for payment and it is not paid for want of funds the treasurer shall endorse thereon "not paid for want of funds" with the date of presentation and sign his name thereto and from that time the warrant bears interest at the rate of 6 percent per annum until it is paid or until funds are available for its payment and the county treasurer gives notice to the warrant holder that funds are available for payment. The giving of the notice is deemed complete upon deposit thereof in the United States mail in a sealed envelope addressed to the warrant holder at his address given by him at the time of presentation of the warrant to the treasurer, with postage thereon fully prepaid and registered.

(Stats.1976, c. 1010, § 2, operative April 30, 1977.)

Historical and Statutory Notes

Derivation: Educ.C.1959, § 27571 (Stats. 1959, c. 2, p. 1468, § 27571).

Educ.C.1943, § 22351 (Stats.1943, c. 71, p. 744).

Stats.1909, c. 480, p. 818, § 14, amended by Stats.1931, c. 998, p. 2002, § 1.

Cross References

County treasurer, see Government Code § 27000 et seq.

§ 19661.   Library free to inhabitants; violations of rules, regulations or by-laws

Every library established under this chapter shall be forever free to the inhabitants and nonresident taxpayers of the library district, subject always to such rules, regulations, and bylaws as may be made by the board of library trustees. For any violation of the rules, regulations, or bylaws a person may be fined or excluded from the privileges of the library.

(Stats.1976, c. 1010, § 2, operative April 30, 1977.)

Historical and Statutory Notes

Derivation: Educ.C.1959, § 27572 (Stats. 1959, c. 2, p. 1468, § 27572).

Educ.C.1943, § 22352 (Stats. 1943, c. 71, p. 744).

Stats.1909, c. 480, p. 818, § 15.

Cross References

Administrative regulations and rulemaking, see Government Code § 11340 et seq.
Rules, regulations and bylaws of board of library trustees, see Education Code § 19645.

Library References

Legal Jurisprudences

Cal Jur 3d Sch § 142.

Notes of Decisions

Fees 2
Validity 1

to object to its inclusion. Palos Verdes Library Dist. of Los Angeles County v. McClellan (App. 2 Dist. 1929) 97 Cal.App. 769, 276 P. 600.

1. Validity

As, in view of Const. Art. 9, § 1, and Stats. 1909, p. 815, §§ 1, 15, relative to establishment of libraries, library district organized under such act was an educational district, statute did not deprive taxpayers of property without due process of law because providing for inclusion of their property without notice and opportunity

2. Fees

Fees may not be charged to local residents for "library services", defined as the satisfaction with library materials of the patron's informational needs, by libraries that are organized under §§ 18300 et seq., 18900 et seq., 19100 et seq., 19400 et seq., 19600 et seq., or Gov.C. § 39732. 61 Ops.Atty.Gen. 512, 11–21–78.

§ 19662. Contracts with other libraries

Boards of library trustees and the boards of trustees of neighboring library districts, or the legislative bodies of neighboring municipalities, or boards of supervisors of the counties in which public libraries are situated, may contract to lend the books of the libraries to residents of the counties or neighboring municipalities, or library districts, upon a reasonable compensation to be paid by the counties, neighboring municipalities, or library districts.

(Stats.1976, c. 1010, § 2, operative April 30, 1977.)

Historical and Statutory Notes

Derivation: Educ.C.1959, § 27573 (Stats. 1959, c. 2, p. 1468, § 27573).

Educ.C.1943, § 22353 (Stats.1943, c. 71, p. 745).

Stats. 1909, c. 480, p. 818, § 16.

Cross References

Contracts, generally, see Civil Code § 1549 et seq.

Library References

Legal Jurisprudences
Cal Jur 3d Sch § 142.

§ 19663. Title to property

The title to all property acquired for the purposes of the libraries, when not inconsistent with the terms of its acquisition, or not otherwise designated, vests in the district in which libraries are, or are to be situated.

(Stats.1976, c. 1010, § 2, operative April 30, 1977.)

Historical and Statutory Notes

Derivation: Educ.C.1959, § 27574 (Stats. 1959, c. 2, p. 1469, § 27574).

Educ.C.1943, § 22354 (Stats.1943, c. 71, p. 745).

Stats.1909, c. 480, p. 819, § 17.

§ 19664. Designation of district

Every library district shall be designated by the name and style of _____ Library District, (using the name of the district), of

_____ County, (using the name of the county in which the district is situated). In that name the trustees may sue and be sued, and may hold and convey property for the use and benefit of the district. A number shall not be used as a part of the designation of any library district.

(Stats.1976, c. 1010, § 2, operative April 30, 1977.)

Historical and Statutory Notes

Derivation: Educ.C.1959, § 27575 (Stats. 1959, c. 2, p. 1469, § 27575).

Educ.C.1943, § 22355 (Stats.1943, c. 71, p. 745).

Stats.1909, c. 480, p. 819, § 17.

Article 2.5

MUSEUMS

Article 2.5 was added by Stats.1978, c. 988, p. 3052, § 3.

§ 19670. Power to establish; board of museum trustees

The board of library trustees may vote to establish a public museum in the library district and to constitute the board of library trustees as the board of museum trustees for the purposes of managing such museum in accordance with the provisions of this chapter.

(Added by Stats.1978, c. 988, p. 3052, § 3.)

Library References

Municipal Corporations ☞57.
Westlaw Topic No. 268.

C.J.S. Municipal Corporations §§ 104, 106, 108, 110 to 115, 117 to 118, 122, 137 to 138, 143, 145 to 146.

§ 19671. Monthly meetings

The board of museum trustees shall meet at least once a month, at such time and place as it may fix by resolution.

(Added by Stats.1978, c. 988, p. 3052, § 3.)

§ 19672. Special meetings

Special meetings may be called at any time by three trustees, by written notices served upon each member at least 12 hours before the time specified for the meeting.

(Added by Stats.1978, c. 988, p. 3052, § 3.)

West's California Code Forms

See West's Cal. Code Forms, Educ. § 19672—FORM 1.

§ 19673. Quorum

Three members constitute a quorum for the transaction of business.

(Added by Stats.1978, c. 988, p. 3052, § 3.)

§ 19674. President; secretary

At its first meeting held after being constituted, the board shall organize by electing one of its number president, and another one of its number secretary. They shall serve as such for one year or until their successors are elected and qualified.

(Added by Stats.1978, c. 988, p. 3052, § 3.)

§ 19675. Record of proceedings; certificate

The board shall cause a proper record of its proceedings to be kept, and at the first meeting of the board of trustees, it shall immediately cause to be made out and filed with the Department of Education at Sacramento a certificate showing that the museum has been established, with the date thereof, the names of the trustees, and the officers of the board chosen for the current fiscal year.

(Added by Stats.1978, c. 988, p. 3052, § 3.)

Library References

Municipal Corporations ⚖61.
Westlaw Topic No. 268.

C.J.S. Municipal Corporations §§ 134, 136, 150, 156 to 158, 160 to 161.

§ 19676. Rules, regulations and bylaws

The board of museum trustees shall make and enforce all rules, regulations, and bylaws necessary for the administration, government, and protection of the museum under its management, and all property belonging to it.

(Added by Stats.1978, c. 988, p. 3052, § 3.)

§ 19677. Administration of trusts; receipt, holdings and disposal of property; deposit of funds

The board of museum trustees shall administer any trust declared or created for the museum, and receive by gift, devise, or bequest, and hold in trust or otherwise, property situated in this state or elsewhere, and where not otherwise provided, dispose of the property for the benefit of the museum.

Any funds from private sources which are used for the support of any public museum established pursuant to this chapter shall be deposited in a special fund in the county treasury of the county in which the public museum is located. Such fund shall be under the control of and administered by the board of museum trustees.

(Added by Stats.1978, c. 988, p. 3052, § 3.)

§ 19678. Officers and employees

The board of museum trustees shall prescribe the duties and powers of the curator, secretary, and other officers and employees of the museum, determine the number of and appoint all officers and employees, and fix their compensation. The officers and employees shall hold their offices and positions at the pleasure of the board.

(Added by Stats.1978, c. 988, p. 3052, § 3.)

§ 19679. Purchase of personal property

The board of museum trustees shall purchase necessary objects of artistic, scientific, or historical interest, and other personal property.

(Added by Stats.1978, c. 988, p. 3052, § 3.)

§ 19680. Purchase of real property, and erection of rental and equipment of buildings or rooms

The board of museum trustees shall also purchase such real property, and erect or rent and equip, such building or rooms, as in its judgment is necessary to properly carry out the provisions of this chapter.

(Added by Stats.1978, c. 988, p. 3052, § 3.)

§ 19681. Incidental powers of board

The board of museum trustees shall do and perform any and all other acts and things necessary or proper to carry out the provisions of this chapter.
(Added by Stats.1978, c. 988, p. 3052, § 3.)

§ 19682. Hours open for public use

The board of museum trustees shall designate the hours during which the museum is open for the use of the public. All public museums established under this chapter shall be open for the use of the public during every day in the year except on legal holidays as may be determined by the board of museum trustees.
(Added by Stats.1978, c. 988, p. 3052, § 3.)

§ 19683. Annual estimate of costs

In any library district formed under the provisions of this chapter, which maintains a public museum, in accordance with this chapter, the board of museum trustees shall furnish to the board of supervisors of the county in which the library district is situated, each and every year, on or before the first day of September, an estimate of the cost of any or all of the following:

(a) Leasing temporary quarters.

(b) Purchasing a suitable lot.

(c) Procuring plans and specifications and erecting a suitable building.

(d) Furnishing and equipping the building and fencing and ornamenting the grounds, for the accommodation of the public museum.

(e) Conducting and maintaining the museum for the ensuing fiscal year.
(Added by Stats.1978, c. 988, p. 3052, § 3.)

§ 19684. Title to property

The title to all property acquired for the purposes of the museum, when not inconsistent with the terms of its acquisition, or not otherwise designated, vests in the district in which museums are, or are to be situated.
(Added by Stats.1978, c. 988, p. 3052, § 3.)

§ 19685. Legislative intent; private funding

It is the intent of the Legislature that public museums established pursuant to this chapter shall be funded primarily by private funds. The board of supervisors of the county in which such a public museum is located is authorized, but not required, to allocate county funds for the support of such museum.
(Added by Stats.1978, c. 988, p. 3052, § 3.)

Article 3

CLAIMS

Section
19690. Claims for moneys or damages.

Article 3 was enacted by Stats.1976, c. 1010, § 2, operative April 30, 1977.

§ 19690. Claims for moneys or damages

All claims for money or damages against the district are governed by Part 3 (commencing with Section 900) and Part 4 (commencing with Section 940) of Division 3.6 of Title 1 of the Government Code except as provided therein, or by other statutes or regulations expressly applicable thereto.

(Stats.1976, c. 1010, § 2, operative April 30, 1977.)

Historical and Statutory Notes

Derivation: Educ.C.1959, § 27591, added by Stats.1959, c. 1727, p. 4144, § 4, amended by Stats.1963, c. 1715, p. 3396, § 12.

Library References

Legal Jurisprudences
 Am Jur 2d Municipal Corporations, Counties, and Other Political Subdivisions §§ 680 et seq.

Article 4

BIENNIAL ELECTION OF TRUSTEES

Section
19700. Conduct of elections; terms of trustees.
19701. Number of trustees.
19702. Eligibility to vote.

Article 4 was enacted by Stats.1976, c. 1010, § 2, operative April 30, 1977. The heading of Article 4, "Annual Election of Trustees", was amended by Stats.1981, c. 714, p. 2606, § 79.

§ 19700. Conduct of elections; terms of trustees

(a) Except as otherwise provided in this article, the Uniform District Election Law (Part 4 (commencing with Section 10500) of Division 10 of the Elections

Code) shall govern and control the conduct of elections pursuant to this chapter. Elections shall be held biennially in the district on the same day as the school district election as specified in Section 5000 in the odd-numbered years.

(b) The trustees shall hold office for the term of four years beginning on the first Friday in December next succeeding their appointment or election.

(c) The members of the first board of library trustees appointed or elected in a district shall, at their first meeting, so classify themselves by lot that their terms shall expire: two on the first Friday in December of the first odd-numbered calendar year next succeeding their appointment or election, and three on the first Friday in December of the second succeeding odd-numbered calendar year.

(Stats.1976, c. 1010, § 2, operative April 30, 1977. Amended by Stats.1977, c. 1205, § 21; Stats.1978, c. 1376, p. 4561, § 9; Stats.1992, c. 970 (S.B.1260), § 2; Stats.1994, c. 923 (S.B.1546), § 25.)

Historical and Statutory Notes

1978 activity relating to notices, filings, calls and conduct of the 1979 March elections not required upon change of the March elections to the first Tuesday after the first Monday in November in odd-numbered years, see Historical and Statutory Notes under Education Code § 1007.

Expiration of terms of office of trustees of library districts, school districts and community college districts effected by the legislature at the 1977–78 Regular Session of the Legislature see Historical and Statutory Notes under Education Code § 1007.

Derivation: Educ.C.1959, § 27601, added by Stats.1967, c. 29, p. 887, § 2.4, amended by Stats.1974, c. 116, p. 232, § 2; Stats.1974, c. 509, p. 1188, § 2.

Cross References

Term of offices for public officers and employees and continuation thereof, see Government Code §§ 1301 and 1302.
Uniform District Election Law, see Elections Code § 10500 et seq.

§ 19701. Number of trustees

The number of library trustees for any library district established under the provisions of this chapter is five.

(Stats.1976, c. 1010, § 2, operative April 30, 1977.)

Historical and Statutory Notes

Derivation: Educ.C.1959, § 27602, added by Stats.1963, c. 394, p. 1200, § 2, amended by Stats.1965, c. 179, p. 1147, § 8.
Educ.C.1959, § 27602, enacted by Stats.1959, c. 2, p. 1469, § 27602.

Educ.C.1943, § 22372 (Stats.1943, c. 71, p. 745).

Stats.1909, c. 480, p. 819, § 19.

§ 19702. Eligibility to vote

Every person who is registered to vote in the library district where the election is held at least 29 days before the election, may vote at the election.

(Stats.1976, c. 1010, § 2, operative April 30, 1977. Amended by Stats.1978, c. 1376, p. 4562, § 10.)

Historical and Statutory Notes

Derivation: Educ.C.1959, § 27610, added by
Stats.1963, c. 394, p. 1201, § 2.

Library References

Legal Jurisprudences
Am Jur 2d Public Securities and Obligations
§§ 131 et seq.

Article 5

BONDS

Article 5 was enacted by Stats.1976, c. 1010, § 2, operative April 30, 1977.

Cross References

Bonds,
Generally, see Education Code § 15100 et seq.
Issuance by school districts, see Const. Art. 9, § 6 1/2.
Tax exemption of bonds, see Const. Art. 13, § 3.

§ 19720. Calling election and submission of questions as to issuance and sale of bonds

The board of trustees of any library district may, when in their judgment it is deemed advisable, and shall upon a petition of 50 or more taxpayers and residents of the library district, call an election and submit to the electors of the district the question of whether the bonds of the district shall be issued and sold for the purpose of raising money for any or all of the following:

(a) The purchase of suitable lots.

(b) Procuring plans and specifications and erecting a suitable building.

(c) Furnishing and equipping the building, and fencing and ornamenting the grounds, for the accommodation of the public library.

(d) Any or all of the purposes of this chapter.

(e) Liquidating any indebtedness incurred for the purposes.

(f) Refunding any outstanding valid indebtedness, evidenced by bonds or warrants of the district.

(Stats.1976, c. 1010, § 2, operative April 30, 1977.)

Historical and Statutory Notes

Derivation: Educ.C.1959, § 27651 (Stats. 1959, c. 2, p. 1470, § 27651).

Educ.C.1943, § 22401 (Stats.1943, c. 71, p. 746).

Stats.1909, c. 480, p. 820, § 28.

West's California Code Forms

See West's Cal. Code Forms, Educ. § 19720—FORM 1.

Cross References

Bonds,
    Generally, see Education Code § 15100 et seq.
    Issuance by school districts, see Const. Art. 9, § 6 1/2.
    Tax exemption of bonds, see Const. Art. 13, § 3.
School bond elections, see Education Code § 15120 et seq.

Library References

Municipal Corporations ⟷906.
Westlaw Topic No. 268.

C.J.S. Municipal Corporations §§ 1645 to 1646, 1702.

Notes of Decisions

Election validity   1

_____

1. Election validity

Library district bond election was not invalid because statutory hours were not observed, when votes cast within statutory hours were largely in favor of bonds. Palos Verdes Library Dist. of Los Angeles County v. McClellan (App. 2 Dist. 1929) 97 Cal.App. 769, 276 P. 600.

§ 19721.   Notice of election

The election shall be called by posting notices, signed by the board, in three of the most public places in the district, for not less than 20 days before the election, and by publishing the notice not less than once a week for three successive weeks in a newspaper published in the district if there is one, or if there is none, in a newspaper published in the county.

(Stats.1976, c. 1010, § 2, operative April 30, 1977.)

Historical and Statutory Notes

Derivation: Educ.C.1959, § 27652 (Stats. 1959, c. 2, p. 1470, § 27652).

Educ.C.1943, § 22402 (Stats.1943, c. 71, p. 747).

Stats.1909, c. 480, p. 820, § 29.

West's California Code Forms

See West's Cal. Code Forms, Educ. § 19721—FORM 1.

Cross References

Publication, generally, see Government Code § 6000 et seq.

§ 19722.   Contents of notice

The notice shall contain:

(a) Time and place of holding the election.

(b) The names of inspectors and judges to conduct the election.

(c) The hours during the day in which the polls will be open.

(d) The amount and denomination of the bonds, the rate of interest, and the number of years, not exceeding 40, the whole or any part of the bonds are to be run.

(Stats.1976, c. 1010, § 2, operative April 30, 1977.)

Historical and Statutory Notes

Derivation: Educ.C.1959, § 27653 (Stats. 1959, c. 2, p. 1470, § 27653).

Educ.C.1943, § 22403 (Stats.1943, c. 71, p. 747).

Stats.1909, c. 480, p. 820, § 30.

§ 19723.   Conduct of election

The election shall be conducted in accordance with the provisions relating to the election of trustees, insofar as they are applicable to the election for bonds.

(Stats.1976, c. 1010, § 2, operative April 30, 1977.)

Historical and Statutory Notes

Derivation: Educ.C.1959, § 27654 (Stats. 1959, c. 2, p. 1471, § 27654, amended by Stats. 1967, c. 29, p. 890, § 15.7).

Educ.C.1943, § 22404 (Stats.1943, c. 71, p. 747).

Stats.1909, c. 480, p. 820, § 31.

Cross References

Election of trustees, see Education Code § 19700 et seq.
Uniform District Election Law, see Elections Code § 10500 et seq.

§ 19724.   Method of voting

Voting shall be by ballot, without reference to the general election law in regard to form of ballot, or manner of voting, except that the words to appear on the ballot shall be, "Bonds—Yes," and "Bonds—No." Persons voting at the bond election shall put a cross (+) upon their ballots, with pencil or ink, after the words, "Bonds—Yes," or "Bonds—No," as the case may be, to indicate whether they have voted for or against the issuance of the bonds. The ballot shall be handed by the elector voting to the inspector, who shall then, in his presence, deposit the ballot in the ballot box, and the judges shall enter the elector's name on poll list.

(Stats.1976, c. 1010, § 2, operative April 30, 1977.)

Historical and Statutory Notes

Derivation: Educ.C.1959, § 27655 (Stats. 1959, c. 2, p. 1471, § 27655).

Educ.C.1943, § 22405 (Stats.1943, c. 71, p. 747).

Stats.1909, c. 480, p. 821, § 32.

§ 19725. Favorable vote

On the seventh day after the election, at 8 o'clock p.m., the returns having been made to the board of trustees, the board shall meet and canvass the returns, and if it appears that more than one-half of the votes cast at the election are in favor of issuing the bonds, then the board shall cause an entry of the fact to be made upon its minutes and shall certify to the board of supervisors, all the proceedings had in the premises. Thereupon the board of supervisors shall issue the bonds of the district, to the number and amount provided in the proceedings, payable out of the building fund of the district, naming the district.

(Stats.1976, c. 1010, § 2, operative April 30, 1977.)

Historical and Statutory Notes

Derivation: Educ.C.1959, § 27656 (Stats. 1959, c. 2, p. 1471, § 27656, amended by Stats. 1963, c. 1293, p. 2819, § 1).

Educ.C.1943, § 22406 (Stats.1943, c. 71, p. 747).

Stats.1909, c. 480, p. 821, § 33, amended by Stats.1911, c. 172, p. 343, § 1.

§ 19726. Taxation for redemption and payment of interest

The money shall be raised by taxation upon the taxable property in the district, for the redemption of the bonds and the payment of the interest thereon.

(Stats.1976, c. 1010, § 2, operative April 30, 1977.)

Historical and Statutory Notes

Derivation: Educ.C.1959, § 27657 (Stats. 1959, c. 2, p. 1471, § 27657).

Educ.C.1943, § 22407 (Stats.1943, c. 71, p. 747).

Stats.1909, c. 480, p. 821, § 33, amended by Stats. 1911, c. 172, p. 343, § 1.

Cross References

Assessments, generally, see Revenue and Taxation Code § 401 et seq.

§ 19727. Limitation on total amount of bonds issued

The total amount of bonds issued shall not exceed 5 percent of the taxable property of the district, as shown by the last equalized assessment book of the county.

(Stats.1976, c. 1010, § 2, operative April 30, 1977.)

Historical and Statutory Notes

Derivation: Educ.C.1959, § 27658 (Stats. 1959, c. 2, p. 1471, § 27658).

Educ.C.1943, § 22408 (Stats.1943, c. 71, p. 747).

Stats.1909, c. 480, p. 821, § 33, amended by Stats.1911, c. 172, p. 343, § 1.

Cross References

Bonds,
    Generally, see Education Code § 15100 et seq.

Bonds—Cont'd
    Issuance by school districts, see Const. Art. 9, § 6 1/2.
    Tax exemption of bonds, see Const. Art. 13, § 3.
Equalized county assessment roll, see Revenue and Taxation Code § 2050 et seq.

Library References

Municipal Corporations ⚯914.
Westlaw Topic No. 268.

C.J.S. Municipal Corporations §§ 1654, 1656
    to 1657.

Notes of Decisions

Purpose 1

---

1. Purpose

The purpose of statutes limiting debts which may be incurred by governmental units is to protect taxpayers from confiscatory taxation, and such statutes must be construed with reference to evil which legislature sought to remedy in enacting them. Pacific Gas & Elec. Co. v. Shasta Dam Area Public Utility Dist. (App. 1955) 135 Cal.App.2d 463, 287 P.2d 841.

§ 19728. Form of bonds and coupons; time when principal payable

The board of supervisors by an order entered upon its minutes shall prescribe the form of the bonds and of the interest coupons attached thereto, and shall fix the time when the whole or any part of the principal of the bonds shall be payable, which shall not be more than 40 years from the date thereof.

(Stats.1976, c. 1010, § 2, operative April 30, 1977.)

Historical and Statutory Notes

Derivation: Educ.C.1959, § 27659 (Stats. 1959, c. 2, p. 1471, § 27659).
    Educ.C.1943, § 22409 (Stats.1943, c. 71, p. 747).

Stats.1909, c. 480, p. 821, § 34.

Cross References

Bonds,
    Generally, see Education Code § 15100 et seq.
    Issuance by school districts, see Const. Art. 9, § 6 1/2.
    Tax exemption of bonds, see Const. Art. 13, § 3.

§ 19729. Maximum interest and sale price of bonds; proceeds of sale

The bonds shall not bear a greater amount of interest than 6 percent, to be payable annually or semiannually. The bonds shall be sold in the manner prescribed by the board of supervisors, but for not less than par, and the proceeds of the sale thereof shall be deposited in the county treasury to the credit of the building fund of the library district, and shall be drawn out for the purposes for which the bonds were issued as other library moneys are drawn out.

(Stats.1976, c. 1010, § 2, operative April 30, 1977.)

Historical and Statutory Notes

Derivation: Educ.C.1959, § 27660 (Stats. 1959, c. 2, p. 1471, § 27660).
    Educ.C.1943, § 22410 (Stats.1943, c. 71, p. 748).

Stats.1909, c. 480, p. 821, § 35.

Cross References

Bonds,
    Generally, see Education Code § 15100 et seq.
    Issuance by school districts, see Const. Art. 9, § 6 1/2.
    Tax exemption of bonds, see Const. Art. 13, § 3.

§ 19730. Tax levy for interest and redemption

The board of supervisors, at the time of making the levy of taxes for county purposes, shall levy a tax for that year upon the taxable property in the district, at the equalized assessed value thereof for that year, for the interest and redemption of the bonds. The tax shall not be less than sufficient to pay the interest of the bonds for that year, and such portion of the principal as is to become due during the year. In any event the tax shall be high enough to raise, annually, for the first half of the term the bonds have to run, a sufficient sum to pay the interest thereon, and during the balance of the term, high enough to pay the annual interest and to pay, annually, a proportion of the principal of the bonds equal to a sum produced by taking the whole amount of the bonds outstanding and dividing it by the number of years the bonds then have to run.

(Stats.1976, c. 1010, § 2, operative April 30, 1977.)

Historical and Statutory Notes

Derivation: Educ.C.1959, § 27661 (Stats. 1959, c. 2, p. 1472, § 27661).

Educ.C.1943, § 22411 (Stats.1943, c. 71, p. 748).

Stats.1909, c. 480, p. 821, § 36.

Cross References

Tax levies, see Government Code § 29100 et seq. and Revenue and Taxation Code § 2151 et seq.

Library References

Municipal Corporations ⚖956(1).
Westlaw Topic No. 268.

C.J.S. Municipal Corporations §§ 1725 to 1731, 1734.

§ 19731. Deposit and use of money collected

All money levied, when collected, shall be paid into the county treasury to the credit of the library district, and shall be used for the payment of principal and interest on the bonds, and for no other purpose. The principal and interest on the bonds shall be paid by the county treasurer, upon the warrant of the county auditor, out of the fund provided therefor. The county auditor shall cancel and file with the county treasurer the bonds and coupons as rapidly as they are paid.

(Stats.1976, c. 1010, § 2, operative April 30, 1977.)

Historical and Statutory Notes

Derivation: Educ.C.1959, § 27662 (Stats. 1959, c. 2, p. 1472, § 27662).

Educ.C.1943, § 22412 (Stats.1943, c. 71, p. 748).

Stats.1909, c. 480, p. 821, § 36.

§ 19732. Petition for withdrawal and cancellation of unsold bonds

Whenever any bonds issued under this article remain unsold for the period of six months after having been offered for sale in the manner prescribed by the board of supervisors, the board of trustees of the library district for or on account of which the bonds were issued, or of any library district composed wholly or partly of territory which, at the time of holding the election authorizing the issuance of the bonds, was embraced within the district for or on account of which the bonds were issued, may petition the board of supervisors to cause the unsold bonds to be withdrawn from market and canceled.

(Stats.1976, c. 1010, § 2, operative April 30, 1977.)

Historical and Statutory Notes

Derivation: Educ.C.1959, § 27663 (Stats. 1959, c. 2, 1472, § 27663).

Educ.C.1943, § 22413 (Stats.1943, c. 71, p. 748).

Stats.1909, c. 480, p. 822, § 37.

Cross References

Bonds,
  Generally, see Education Code § 15100 et seq.
  Issuance by school districts, see Const. Art. 9, § 6 1/2.
  Tax exemption of bonds, see Const. Art. 13, § 3.

§ 19733. Notice of hearing on petition

Upon receiving the petition, signed by a majority of the members of the board of trustees, the supervisors shall fix a time for hearing the petition, which shall be not more than 30 days thereafter, and shall cause a notice, stating the time and place of hearing, and the object of the petition in general terms, to be published for 10 days prior to the day of hearing, in some newspaper published in the library district, if there is one, and if there is no newspaper published in the library district, then in a newspaper published at the county seat of the county in which the library district or part thereof is situated.

(Stats.1976, c. 1010, § 2, operative April 30, 1977.)

Historical and Statutory Notes

Derivation: Educ.C.1959, § 27664 (Stats. 1959, c. 2, p. 1472, § 27664).

Educ.C.1943, § 22414 (Stats.1943, c. 71, p. 748).

Stats.1909, c. 480, p. 822, § 37.

§ 19734. Hearing and order for cancellation

At the time and place designated in the notice for hearing the petition, or at any subsequent time to which the hearing is postponed, the supervisors shall hear any reasons that are submitted for or against the granting of the petition, and if they deem it for the best interests of the library district that the unsold bonds be canceled, they shall make and enter an order in the minutes of their proceedings that the unsold bonds be canceled. Thereupon the bonds, and the vote by which they were authorized to be issued, shall cease to be of any validity whatever.

(Stats.1976, c. 1010, § 2, operative April 30, 1977.)

Historical and Statutory Notes

Derivation: Educ.C.1959, § 27665 (Stats. 1959, c. 2, p. 1472, § 27665).

Educ.C.1943, § 22415 (Stats.1943, c. 71, p. 749).

Stats.1909, c. 480, p. 822, § 37.

Chapter 10

CORPORATIONS TO ADMINISTER
LIBRARIES [REPEALED]

Chapter 10, "Corporations to Administer Libraries", was added by Stats.1978, c. 1305, p. 4278, § 21, operative Jan. 1, 1980, and comprised § 19800. The heading of Chapter 10 was repealed by Stats.1989, c. 1360, § 19.

Former Chapter 10, "Corporations to Administer Libraries", enacted by Stats.1976, c. 1010, § 2, comprising §§ 19800 to 19811, was repealed by Stats.1978, c. 1305, p. 4278, § 20, operative Jan. 1, 1980.

§ 19800. Repealed by Stats.1987, c. 1452, § 134

Historical and Statutory Notes

The repealed section, added by Stats.1978, c. 1305, § 21, provided for corporations existing under the chapter to be subject to and to be deemed organized under nonprofit public benefit corporation law.

Legislative findings, declarations and intent relating to Stats.1987, c. 1452, see Historical and Statutory Notes under Education Code § 1007.

Former § 19800, enacted by Stats.1976, c. 1010, § 2, derived from Educ.C.1959, § 28701 (Stats.1959, c. 2, p. 1489, § 28701); Educ.C. 1943, § 23201 (Stats.1943, c. 71, p. 764); and Civ.C. § 653ab, added by Stats.1927, c. 722, p. 1323, § 1, amended by Stats.1929, c. 711, p. 1286, § 43, relating to the authority to incorporate to establish a library, was repealed by Stats.1978, c. 1305, § 20, operative Jan. 1, 1980.

§§ 19801 to 19811. Repealed by Stats.1978, c. 1305, p. 4278, § 20, operative Jan. 1, 1980

Historical and Statutory Notes

Section 19801, enacted by Stats.1976, c. 1010, § 2, derived from Educ.C.1959, § 28702 (Stats.1959, c. 2, p. 1490, § 28702); Educ.C. 1943, § 23202 (Stats.1943, c. 71, p. 764); and Civ.C. § 653ac, added by Stats.1927, c. 722, p. 1324, § 1, amended by Stats.1931, c. 114, p. 154, § 1, related to the capacity of the nonprofit business to receive gifts.

Section 19802, enacted by Stats.1976, c. 1010, § 2, derived from Educ.C.1959, § 28703 (Stats.1959, c. 2, p. 1490, § 28703); Educ.C. 1943, § 23203 (Stats.1943, c. 71, p. 765); and Civ.C. § 653ac, added by Stats.1927, c. 722, p.

1324, § 1, amended by Stats.1931, c. 114, p. 154, § 1, related to the powers and duties of trustees and directors of the corporation.

Section 19803, enacted by Stats.1976, c. 1010, § 2, derived from Educ.C.1959, § 28704 (Stats.1959, c. 2, p. 1490, § 28704); Educ.C. 1943, § 23204 (Stats.1943, c. 71, p. 765, amended by Stats.1955, c. 877, p. 1504, § 43); and Civ.C. § 653ad, added by Stats.1927, c. 722, p. 1324, § 1, related to the powers of the corporation.

Section 19804, enacted by Stats.1976, c. 1010, § 2, derived from Educ.C.1959, § 28705

(Stats.1959, c. 2, p. 1490, § 28705); Educ.C. 1943, § 23205 (Stats.1943, c. 71, p. 765); and Civ.C. § 643ad, added by Stats.1927, c. 722, p. 1324, § 1, related to the appointment of agents and officers of the corporation.

Section 19805, enacted by Stats.1976, c. 1010, § 2, derived from Educ.C.1959, § 28706 (Stats.1959, c. 2, p. 1490, § 28706); Educ.C. 1943, § 23206 (Stats.1943, c. 71, p. 765); and Civ.C. § 653ad, added by Stats.1927, c. 722, p. 1324, § 1, related to powers of the corporation relating to property.

Section 19806, enacted by Stats.1976, c. 1010, § 2, derived from Educ.C.1959, § 28707 (Stats.1959, c. 2, p. 1490, § 28707); Educ.C. 1943, § 23207 (Stats.1943, c. 71, p. 765); and Civ.C. § 653ad, added by Stats.1927, c. 722, p. 1324, § 1, related to corporation business transactions.

Section 19807, enacted by Stats.1976, c. 1010, § 2, derived from Educ.C.1959, § 28708 (Stats.1959, c. 2, p. 1490, § 28708); Educ.C. 1943, § 23208 (Stats.1943, c. 71, p. 765, amended by Stats.1955, c. 877, p. 1505, § 44); and Civ.C. § 653ad, added by Stats.1927, c. 722, p. 1324, § 1, related to the sale of securities by the corporation.

Section 19808, enacted by Stats.1976, c. 1010, § 2, derived from Educ.C.1959, § 28709

(Stats.1959, c. 2, p. 1490, § 28709); Educ.C. 1943, § 23209 (Stats.1943, c. 71, p. 765); and Civ.C. § 653ae, added by Stats.1927, c. 722, p. 1324, § 1, related to adoption of bylaws by the corporation.

Section 19809, enacted by Stats.1976, c. 1010, § 2, derived from Educ.C.1959, § 28710 (Stats.1959, c. 2, p. 1491, § 28710); Educ.C. 1943, § 23210 (Stats.1943, c. 71, p. 765); and Civ.C. § 653ae, added by Stats.1927, c. 722, p. 1324, § 1, related to provisions allowed in the corporations bylaws.

Section 19810, enacted by Stats.1976, c. 1010, § 2, derived from Educ.C.1959, § 28711 (Stats.1959, c. 2, p. 1491, § 28711); Educ.C. 1943, § 23211 (Stats.1943, c. 71, p. 766); and Civ.C. § 653af, added by Stats.1927, c. 722, p. 1325, § 1, related to the attorney general's authority to inquire into the corporation's right to do business.

Section 19811, enacted by Stats.1976, c. 1010, § 2, derived from Educ.C.1959, § 28712 (Stats.1959, c. 2, p. 1491, § 28712, amended by Stats.1974, c. 1103, p. 2362, § 9); Educ.C.1943, § 23212 (Stats.1943, c. 71, p. 766); and Civ.C. § 653ag, added by Stats.1927, c. 722, p. 1325, § 1, related to filing of the articles of incorporation.

Chapter 11

MISCELLANEOUS PROVISIONS

Chapter 11 was enacted by Stats.1976, c. 1010, § 2, operative April 30, 1977.

Explanatory Note

For another Chapter 11, "California Library Construction and Renovation Bond Act of 1988", see Education Code § 19950 et seq.

Article 1

DEPOSIT OF NEWSPAPERS IN LIBRARIES

Article 1 was enacted by Stats.1976, c. 1010, § 2, operative April 30, 1977.

§ 19900. Authority to deposit newspaper files

The board of supervisors of any county may authorize the county recorder to deposit with any free public library maintained at the county seat, or with the State Library, such newspaper files, or portions thereof, as may be in the custody of the recorder by virtue of Chapter 110 of the Statutes of 1862, relating to the purchase and preservation of newspapers, or by virtue of any other act.

(Stats.1976, c. 1010, § 2, operative April 30, 1977.)

Historical and Statutory Notes

Derivation: Educ.C.1959, § 28751 (Stats. 1959, c. 2, p. 1491, § 28751).

Educ.C.1943, § 23301 (Stats.1943, c. 71, p. 766).

Stats.1909, c. 289, p. 436, § 1, amended by Stats.1919, c. 186, p. 278, § 1.

Cross References

Board of supervisors, see Government Code §§ 25000, 25003 et seq.
County recorder, see Government Code § 27201 et seq.
State Library, generally, see Education Code § 19300 et seq.

Library References

Legal Jurisprudences
Cal Jur 3d Sch § 333.

§ 19901. Agreement for preservation, care and accessibility of files

Before making the deposit, the board of supervisors shall obtain from the board of trustees or authorities in charge of the free public library, or the State Librarian, as the case may be, an agreement that it will properly preserve and care for the newspaper files, and make them accessible to the public.

(Stats.1976, c. 1010, § 2, operative April 30, 1977. Amended by Stats.1987, c. 1452, § 135; Stats.1990, c. 1372 (S.B.1854), § 172.)

Historical and Statutory Notes

Legislative findings, declarations and intent relating to Stats.1987, c. 1452, see Historical and Statutory Notes under Education Code § 1007.

Legislative findings in Stats.1990, c. 1372 (S.B.1854), regarding application of Education Code provisions to community colleges, and authority of community college districts under

Const. Art. 9, § 14, see Historical and Statutory Notes under Education Code § 40.

Derivation: Educ.C.1959, c. 28752 (Stats. 1959, c. 2, p. 1491, § 28752).

Educ.C.1943, § 23302 (Stats.1943, c. 71, p. 766).

Stats.1909, c. 289, p. 436, § 2, amended by Stats.1919, c. 186, p. 278, § 2.

Cross References

State department of education, see Education Code § 33300 et seq.
State Librarian,
   Generally, see Education Code § 19302 et seq.
   Powers and duties, see Education Code § 19320 et seq.

§ 19902. Deposit in State Library

The board of supervisors of any county may authorize the boards of trustees or other authorities in charge of any free public library with which newspaper files have been deposited in accordance with Section 19900 to deposit the newspaper files with the State Library.

(Stats.1976, c. 1010, § 2, operative April 30, 1977.)

Historical and Statutory Notes

Derivation: Educ.C.1959, § 28753 (Stats. 1959, c. 2, p. 1491, § 28753).

Educ.C.1943, § 23303 (Stats.1943, c. 71, p. 766).

Stats.1909, c. 289, p. 436, § 3, added by Stats.1919, c. 186, p. 278, § 3.

Cross References

Board of supervisors, see Government Code §§ 25000, 25003 et seq.
State Library, generally, see Education Code § 19300 et seq.

Library References

Article 2

OFFENSES AGAINST LIBRARIES

Section
19910.   Malicious cutting, tearing, defacing, breaking, or injuring.
19911.   Willful detention of property.

Article 2 was enacted by Stats.1976, c. 1010 § 2 operative April 30, 1977.

§ 19910. Malicious cutting, tearing, defacing, breaking, or injuring

Any person who maliciously cuts, tears, defaces, breaks, or injures any book, map, chart, picture, engraving, statue, coin, model, apparatus, or other work of literature, art, mechanics, or object of curiosity, deposited in any public library, gallery, museum, collection, fair, or exhibition, is guilty of a misdemeanor.

The parent or guardian of a minor who willfully and maliciously commits any act within the scope of this section shall be liable for all damages so caused by the minor.

(Stats.1976, c. 1010, § 2, operative April 30, 1977.)

Historical and Statutory Notes

Derivation: Educ.C.1959, § 28801 (Stats. 1959, c. 2, p. 1492, § 28801, amended by Stats. 1963, c. 375, p. 1165, § 1).

Educ.C.1943, § 23321 (Stats.1943, c. 71, p. 766).

Pen.C. § 623, amended by Stats.1901, c. 84, p. 99, § 1.

Cross References

Liability of parents and guardians for willful misconduct of minor, see Civil Code § 1714.1.
Malicious mischief, see Penal Code § 594 et seq.
Misdemeanors, definition and penalties, see Penal Code §§ 17, 19 and 19.1.

Library References

Malicious Mischief ⇔1.
Westlaw Topic No. 248.

C.J.S. Malicious or Criminal Mischief or Damage to Property §§ 2 to 5.

Legal Jurisprudences
 Cal Jur 3d Fam Law § 543; Sch § 334.
 Am Jur 2d Malicious Mischief §§ 10, 11.

Treatises and Practice Aids
 Witkin & Epstein, Criminal Law (2d ed)
  § 687.

Forms
 B-W Cal Civil Practice: Torts § 3:34.

§ 19911. Willful detention of property

Any person who willfully detains any book, newspaper, magazine, pamphlet, manuscript, or other property belonging to any public or incorporated library, reading room, museum, or other educational institution, for 30 days after notice in writing to return the article or property, given after the expiration of the time for which by the rules of the institution the article or property may be kept, is guilty of a misdemeanor.

The parent or guardian of a minor who willfully and maliciously commits any act within the scope of this section shall be liable for all damages so caused by the minor.

(Stats.1976, c. 1010, § 2, operative April 30, 1977.)

Historical and Statutory Notes

Derivation: Educ.C.1959, § 28802 (Stats. 1959, c. 2, p. 1492, § 28802, amended by Stats. 1963, c. 375, p. 1165, § 2).
 Educ.C.1943, § 23322 (Stats.1943, c. 71, p. 766).

Pen.C. § 623½ added by Stats.1899, c. 81, p. 97, § 1.

Cross References

Liability of parents and guardians for willful misconduct of minor, see Civil Code § 1714.1.
Misdemeanors, definition and penalties, see Penal Code §§ 17, 19 and 19.1.

Library References

Legal Jurisprudences
 Cal Jur 3d Sch § 334.

Treatises and Practice Aids
 Witkin & Epstein, Criminal Law (2d ed)
  §§ 64, 1124.

Chapter 11

CALIFORNIA LIBRARY CONSTRUCTION AND RENOVATION BOND ACT OF 1988

Chapter 11, added by Stats.1988, c. 49, § 1, eff. March 18, 1988, subject to adoption by the electors of Prop. 85, was approved by the electors at the statewide election Nov. 8, 1988.

Article 1

GENERAL PROVISIONS

Section
19950.   Short title.
19951.   Legislative findings and declaration; funding for library facilities.
19952.   Definitions.

Article 1, added by Stats.1988, c. 49, § 1, eff. March 18, 1988, subject to adoption by the voters, was approved by the voters at the statewide election Nov. 8, 1988.

§ 19950. Short title

This chapter shall be known and may be cited as the California Library Construction and Renovation Bond Act of 1988.

(Added by Stats.1988, c. 49, § 1, eff. March 18, 1988, approved (Prop.85), Nov. 8, 1988.)

Historical and Statutory Notes

Sections 2 and 3 of Stats.1988, c. 49, provides:

"Sec. 2. Section 1 of this act shall take effect upon the adoption by the voters of the California Library Construction and Renovation Bond Act of 1988, as set forth in Section 1 of this act.

"Sec. 3. Section 1 of this act shall be submitted to the voters at the statewide general election in November 1988, in accordance with provisions of the Government Code and the Elections Code governing submission of statewide measures to the voters."

See Prop. 85, approved at the Nov. 8, 1988 election.

§ 19951. Legislative findings and declaration; funding for library facilities

The Legislature finds and declares all of the following:

(a) The public library is a supplement to the formal system of free public education, a source of information and inspiration to persons of all ages, cultural backgrounds, and economic statuses, and a resource for continuing education and reeducation beyond the years of formal education, and therefore deserves adequate financial support from government at all levels.

(b) It is in the interest of the people and of the state that there be a general diffusion of information and knowledge through the continued operation of free public libraries. This diffusion is a matter of general concern inasmuch as it is the duty of the state to provide encouragement to the voluntary lifelong learning of the people of the state.

(c) Many existing public library facilities are not safe, efficient, or accessible for use, adequate for the size of the communities they serve, or otherwise capable of providing the public library services needed by the communities they serve.

(d) Many communities that are populous enough to require a public library facility do not have one.

(e) Local public library authorities do not have sufficient funds to construct or rehabilitate necessary public library facilities.

(f) Funding to meet the need for public library facilities, which is beyond the ability of local government to supply, is most appropriately met by a partnership of state and local governments.

(Added by Stats.1988, c. 49, § 1, eff. March 18, 1988, approved (Prop.85), Nov. 8, 1988.)

§ 19952. Definitions

As used in this chapter, the following terms have the following meanings:

(a) "Committee" means the California Library Construction and Renovation Finance Committee created pursuant to Section 19972.

(b) "Fund" means the California Library Construction and Restoration Fund created pursuant to Section 19955.

(c) "Board" means the California Library Construction and Renovation Board. The board includes the State Librarian, the Treasurer, the Director of Finance, the Assembly Member appointed by the Speaker of the Assembly, and the Senator appointed by the Senate Rules Committee.

Legislative members of the board shall meet with, and participate in, the work of the board to the extent that their participation is not incompatible with their duties as Members of the Legislature. For the purposes of this chapter, Members of the Legislature who are members of the board shall constitute a joint legislative committee on the subject matter of this chapter.

(Added by Stats.1988, c. 49, § 1, eff. March 18, 1988, approved (Prop.85), Nov. 8, 1988.)

Cross References

State Librarian,
    Generally, see Education Code § 19302 et seq.
    Powers and duties, see Education Code § 19320 et seq.

Article 2

CALIFORNIA LIBRARY CONSTRUCTION
AND RENOVATION PROGRAM

*Article 2, added by Stats.1988, c. 49, § 1, eff. March 18, 1988, subject
to adoption by the voters, was approved by the voters at the statewide
election Nov. 8, 1988.*

§ 19955. California library construction and renovation fund; creation; deposit of proceeds; continuous appropriation

The proceeds of bonds issued and sold pursuant to this chapter shall be
deposited in the California Library Construction and Renovation Fund, which
is hereby created. Notwithstanding Section 13340 of the Government Code,
the fund shall be continuously appropriated without regard to fiscal year.
(Added by Stats.1988, c. 49, § 1, eff. March 18, 1988, approved (Prop.85), Nov. 8, 1988.)

Code of Regulations References

Library Construction and Renovation Board, see 5 Cal. Code of Regs. § 20410 et seq.

Library References

States ☞127.
Westlaw Topic No. 360.
C.J.S. States § 228.

§ 19956. Availability of moneys for grants to local public entities

All moneys deposited in the fund shall be available for grants to any city,
county, city and county, or district that is empowered at the time of the project
application to own and maintain a facility for the acquisition, construction,
remodeling, or rehabilitation of facilities for public library services.
(Added by Stats.1988, c. 49, § 1, eff. March 18, 1988, approved (Prop.85), Nov. 8, 1988.)

Code of Regulations References

California State Library, construction and renovation,
    Application for grants, see 5 Cal. Code of Regs. § 20420.
    Eligibility for grants, see 5 Cal. Code of Regs. § 20412.
    Facility dedicated to direct public library service, see 5 Cal. Code of Regs. § 20424.

§ 19957. Grant and matching funds; use; purposes

The grant funds authorized pursuant to Section 19956 and the matching funds provided pursuant to Section 19962 shall be used by the recipient for any of the following purposes:

(a) Acquisition or construction of new facilities or additions to existing facilities.

(b) Acquisition of land necessary for purposes of subdivision (a).

(c) Remodeling of existing facilities for energy conservation purposes.

(d) Remodeling of existing facilities to provide access for the disabled.

(e) Rehabilitation of existing facilities to bring them into compliance with current health and safety requirements for public facilities.

(f) Procurement and installation of shelving fastened to the structure, and built-in equipment required to make a facility fully operable.

(g) Payment of fees charged by architects, engineers, and other design professionals whose services are required to plan and execute a project authorized pursuant to this chapter.

(Added by Stats.1988, c. 49, § 1, eff. March 18, 1988, approved (Prop.85), Nov. 8, 1988.)

Code of Regulations References

California State Library, construction and renovation,
    Application for grants, see 5 Cal. Code of Regs. § 20420.
    Audits and state payments, see 5 Cal. Code of Regs. § 20422.
    Facility dedicated to direct public library service, see 5 Cal. Code of Regs. § 20424.
    Matching funds, see 5 Cal. Code of Regs. § 20416.
    Normal public construction costs and excessive costs, see 5 Cal. Code of Regs. § 20418.
    Purposes of grants, see 5 Cal. Code of Regs. § 20414.

§ 19957.5. Grant applicants; eligibility; order for possession; purchase of land; acquisition of land

(a) An applicant for a grant for the acquisition, construction, remodeling, or rehabilitation of public library facilities under this chapter, as opposed to an application for a grant to acquire land pursuant to subdivision (b) of Section 19957, shall be eligible to apply for that grant if that applicant has an order issued by a court for possession of property in an eminent domain action pursuant to Section 1255.410 of the Code of Civil Procedure.

(b) The terms "purchase of land" or "acquisition of land," as used in this chapter, or in any rule, regulation, or policy adopted by the state librarian pursuant to Section 19960, shall include, but shall not be limited to, the acquisition of land by eminent domain and the eligible cost of acquisition of land by eminent domain shall be the fair market value of the property as defined by Sections 1263.310 to 1263.330, inclusive, of the Code of Civil Procedure. However, the eligible cost of the land for a library project's site acquired by eminent domain, if title to the land will not be transferred until after the grant application is submitted, shall be limited to the appraised value of the land.

(Added by Stats.1991, c. 45 (S.B.1252), § 1, eff. June 3, 1991.)

Cross References

Administrative regulations and rulemaking, see Government Code § 11340 et seq.
State Librarian,
    Generally, see Education Code § 19302 et seq.
    Powers and duties, see Education Code § 19320 et seq.

§ 19958. Grant and matching funds; restrictions on use

No grant funds authorized pursuant to Section 19956 or matching funds provided pursuant to Section 19962 shall be used by a recipient for any of the following purposes:

(a) Books and other library materials.

(b) Administration costs of the project, including, but not limited to, the costs of all of the following:

(1) Preparation of the grant application.

(2) Procurement of matching funds.

(3) Conducting an election for obtaining voter approval of the project.

(4) Plan checking and code compliance inspections.

(c) Interest or other carrying charges for financing the project, including, but not limited to, costs of loans or lease-purchase agreements in excess of the direct costs of any of the authorized purposes specified in Section 19957.

(d) Any ongoing operating expenses for the facility, its personnel, supplies, or any other library operations.

(Added by Stats.1988, c. 49, § 1, eff. March 18, 1988, approved (Prop.85), Nov. 8, 1988.)

Code of Regulations References

California State Library, construction and renovation,
    Audits and state payments, see 5 Cal. Code of Regs. § 20422.
    Purposes of grants, see 5 Cal. Code of Regs. § 20414.

Library References

States ☞123.
Westlaw Topic No. 360.
C.J.S. States § 226.

§ 19959. Construction projects funded in part by grants; competitive bidding; law governing

All construction contracts for projects funded in part through grants awarded pursuant to this chapter shall be awarded through competitive bidding pursuant to Part 3 (commencing with Section 20100) of the Public Contract Code.

(Added by Stats.1988, c. 49, § 1, eff. March 18, 1988, approved (Prop.85), Nov. 8, 1988.)

Cross References

Contracts, generally, see Civil Code § 1549 et seq.

§ 19960. State librarian; administration of chapter

This chapter shall be administered by the State Librarian, who shall adopt rules, regulations, and policies for the implementation of this chapter.

(Added by Stats.1988, c. 49, § 1, eff. March 18, 1988, approved (Prop.85), Nov. 8, 1988.)

Cross References

Administrative regulations and rulemaking, see Government Code § 11340 et seq.
State Librarian,
    Generally, see Education Code § 19302 et seq.
    Powers and duties, see Education Code § 19320 et seq.

Code of Regulations References

California State Library, construction and renovation, application for grants, see 5 Cal. Code of
    Regs. § 20420.

§ 19961. Applications for grants by local public entities

A city, county, city and county, or district may apply to the State Librarian
for a grant pursuant to this chapter, as follows:

(a) Each application shall be for a project for a purpose authorized by
Section 19957.

(b) The applicant shall request not less than thirty-five thousand dollars
($35,000) per project.

(c) No application shall be submitted for a project for which construction
bids already have been advertised.

(Added by Stats.1988, c. 49, § 1, eff. March 18, 1988, approved (Prop.85), Nov. 8, 1988.)

Cross References

State Librarian,
    Generally, see Education Code § 19302 et seq.
    Powers and duties, see Education Code § 19320 et seq.

Code of Regulations References

California State Library, construction and renovation,
    Application for grants, see 5 Cal. Code of Regs. § 20420.
    Eligibility for grants, see 5 Cal. Code of Regs. § 20412.
    Matching funds, see 5 Cal. Code of Regs. § 20416.

§ 19962. Matching funds by grant recipients; amount; cash expenditures, land donations or plans and drawings or credit toward matching percentage

(a) Each grant recipient shall provide matching funds from any available
source in an amount equal to 35 percent of the costs of the project. The
remaining 65 percent of the costs of the project shall be provided through
allocations from the fund.

(b) Qualifying matching funds shall be cash expenditures in the categories
specified in Section 19957 which are made no earlier than three years prior to
the submission of the application to the State Librarian. Except as otherwise
provided in subdivision (c), in-kind expenditures shall not qualify as matching
funds.

(c) Land donated or otherwise acquired for use as a site for the facility,
including, but not limited to, land purchased more than three years prior to the
submission of the application to the State Librarian, may be credited towards
the 35 percent matching funds requirement at its appraised value as of the date
of the application.

(d) Cash expenditures not to exceed 10 percent for furnishings required to make the facility fully operable may be credited towards the 35 percent matching funds requirement. The recipient shall certify to the board that these furnishings have an estimated useful life of not less than 10 years.

(e) Architect fees for plans and drawings for library renovation and new construction, including plans and drawings purchased more than three years prior to the submission of the application to the State Librarian, may be credited towards the 35 percent matching funds requirement.

(Added by Stats.1988, c. 49, § 1, eff. March 18, 1988, approved (Prop.85), Nov. 8, 1988.)

Cross References

State Librarian,
    Generally, see Education Code § 19302 et seq.
    Powers and duties, see Education Code § 19320 et seq.

Code of Regulations References

California State Library, construction and renovation,
    Application for grants, see 5 Cal. Code of Regs. § 20420.
    Audits and state payments, see 5 Cal. Code of Regs. § 20422.
    Facility dedicated to direct public library service, see 5 Cal. Code of Regs. § 20424.
    Matching funds, see 5 Cal. Code of Regs. § 20416.
    Normal public construction costs and excessive costs, see 5 Cal. Code of Regs. § 20418.
    Purposes of grants, see 5 Cal. Code of Regs. § 20414.

§ 19963. Works of art; restriction on expenditure

An amount not to exceed 1 percent of the cost of construction of the project may be used for appropriate works of art to enhance the facility.

(Added by Stats.1988, c. 49, § 1, eff. March 18, 1988, approved (Prop.85), Nov. 8, 1988.)

Code of Regulations References

California State Library, construction and renovation,
    Application for grants, see 5 Cal. Code of Regs. § 20420.
    Audits and state payments, see 5 Cal. Code of Regs. § 20422.
    Normal public construction costs and excessive costs, see 5 Cal. Code of Regs. § 20418.
    Purposes of grants, see 5 Cal. Code of Regs. § 20414.

§ 19964. Consistency of estimated costs with normal area construction costs; grant for excess costs

(a) The estimated costs of a project for which an application is submitted shall be consistent with normal public construction costs in the applicant's area.

(b) An applicant wishing to construct a project with costs which exceed normal public construction costs in the applicant's area may apply for a grant in an amount not to exceed 65 percent of the normal costs if the applicant certifies that it is capable of financing the remainder of the project costs from other sources.

(Added by Stats.1988, c. 49, § 1, eff. March 18, 1988, approved (Prop.85), Nov. 8, 1988.)

§ 19965. No increase in funding after approval; applicant responsible for cost changes; return of funding in excess of costs

Once an application has been approved by the board and included in the State Librarian's request to the committee, the amount of funding to be provided to the applicant shall not be increased. Any actual changes in project costs shall be the full responsibility of the applicant. In the event that the amount of funding which is provided is greater than the cost of the project, the applicant shall return that portion of the funding which exceeds the cost of the project to the State Librarian.

(Added by Stats.1988, c. 49, § 1, eff. March 18, 1988, approved (Prop.85), Nov. 8, 1988.)

§ 19966. Review of applications; considerations by board

In reviewing applications, the board shall consider all of the following factors:

(a) Needs of urban and rural areas.

(b) Projected population growth.

(c) Changing concepts of public library service.

(d) Distance of the proposed project from other existing and proposed facilities.

(e) Age and condition of the facility.

(Added by Stats.1988, c. 49, § 1, eff. March 18, 1988, approved (Prop.85), Nov. 8, 1988.)

§ 19967. Dedication of facility to public library direct service; time period; effect of early cessation of use; release of maintenance obligation; awards for other projects

(a) A facility, or the part thereof, acquired, constructed, remodeled, or rehabilitated with grants received pursuant to this chapter shall be dedicated to public library direct service use for a period of not less than 20 years following completion of the project, or the useful life of the building, whichever is longer.

(b) If the facility, or part thereof, acquired, constructed, remodeled, or rehabilitated with grants received pursuant to this chapter ceases to be used for public library direct service prior to the expiration of the period specified in subdivision (a), the board shall be entitled to recover from the grant recipient or the recipient's successor in the maintenance of the facility, an amount which bears the same ratio to the value of the facility, or the appropriate part thereof, at the time it ceased to be used from public library direct service as the amount of the grant bore to the cost of the facility or appropriate part thereof. For purposes of this subdivision, the value of the facility, or the appropriate part thereof, shall be determined by the mutual agreement of the parties, or through an action brought for that purpose in the superior court.

(c) The board may release the grant recipient or the recipient's successor in the maintenance of the facility from its obligation under subdivision (a), and waive the requirements of subdivision (b), if the board determines that so doing would not diminish the quality of public library service in the community served by the facility.

(d) Notwithstanding subdivision (f) of Section 16724 of the Government Code, moneys recovered pursuant to subdivision (b) shall be deposited in the fund, and shall be available for the purpose of awarding grants for other projects.

(Added by Stats.1988, c. 49, § 1, eff. March 18, 1988, approved (Prop.85), Nov. 8, 1988.)

Code of Regulations References

California State Library, construction and renovation,
    Application for grants, see 5 Cal. Code of Regs. § 20420.
    Audits and state payments, see 5 Cal. Code of Regs. § 20422.
    Facility dedicated to direct public library service, see 5 Cal. Code of Regs. § 20424.
    Matching funds, see 5 Cal. Code of Regs. § 20416.
    Purposes of grants, see 5 Cal. Code of Regs. § 20414.

Article 3

FISCAL PROVISIONS

Article 3, added by Stats.1988, c. 49, § 1, eff. March 18, 1988, subject to adoption by the voters, was approved by the voters at the statewide election Nov. 8, 1988.

Cross References

Bonds,
Generally, see Education Code § 15100 et seq.
Issuance by school districts, see Const. Art. 9, § 6 1/2.
Tax exemption of bonds, see Const. Art. 13, § 3.

§ 19970. Issuance and sale of bonds; amount; reimbursement of fund; bonds as general obligation of state

Bonds in the total amount of seventy-five million dollars ($75,000,000) (exclusive of refunding bonds), or so much thereof as is necessary, may be issued and sold to provide a fund to be used for carrying out the purposes expressed in this chapter and to be used to reimburse the General Obligation Bond Expense Revolving Fund pursuant to Section 16724.5 of the Government Code. The bonds shall, when sold, be and constitute a valid and binding obligation of the State of California, and the full faith and credit of the State of California is hereby pledged for the punctual payment of both principal of, and interest on, the bonds as the principal and interest become due and payable.

(Added by Stats.1988, c. 49, § 1, eff. March 18, 1988, approved (Prop.85), Nov. 8, 1988.)

Cross References

Bonds,
Generally, see Education Code § 15100 et seq.
Issuance by school districts, see Const. Art. 9, § 6 1/2.
Tax exemption of bonds, see Const. Art. 13, § 3.

Library References

States ☞148.
Westlaw Topic No. 360.
C.J.S. States § 252.

Legal Jurisprudences
Am Jur 2d Public Securities and Obligations
§§ 131 et seq.

§ 19971. State general obligation bond law; applicability

The bonds authorized by this chapter shall be prepared, executed, issued, sold, paid, and redeemed as provided in the State General Obligation Bond Law (Chapter 4 (commencing with Section 16720) of Part 3 of Division 4 of Title 2 of the Government Code), and all of the provisions of that law apply to the bonds and to this chapter and are hereby incorporated in this chapter as though set forth in full in this chapter.

(Added by Stats.1988, c. 49, § 1, eff. March 18, 1988, approved (Prop.85), Nov. 8, 1988.)

Cross References

Bonds,
Generally, see Education Code § 15100 et seq.

Bonds—Cont'd
    Issuance by school districts, see Const. Art. 9, § 6 1/2.
    Tax exemption of bonds, see Const. Art. 13, § 3.

Library References

Legal Jurisprudences
    Am Jur 2d Public Securities and Obligations
      §§ 131 et seq.

§ 19972. Finance committee; creation; membership; board

(a) Solely for the purpose of authorizing the issuance and sale, pursuant to the State General Obligation Bond Law, of the bonds authorized by this chapter, the California Library Construction and Renovation Finance Committee is hereby created. For purposes of this chapter, the California Library Construction and Renovation Finance Committee is the "committee" as that term is used in the State General Obligation Bond Law. The committee consists of the Treasurer, the State Librarian, the Director of Finance, or their designated representatives. The Treasurer shall serve as chairperson of the committee. A majority of the committee may act for the committee.

(b) For purposes of the State General Obligation Bond Law, the California Library Construction and Renovation Board is designated the "board."

(Added by Stats.1988, c. 49, § 1, eff. March 18, 1988, approved (Prop.85), Nov. 8, 1988.)

Cross References

State Librarian,
    Generally, see Education Code § 19302 et seq.
    Powers and duties, see Education Code § 19320 et seq.

Library References

Legal Jurisprudences
    Am Jur 2d Public Securities and Obligations
      §§ 131 et seq.

§ 19973. Determination of need for bonds; amount

The committee shall determine whether or not it is necessary or desirable to issue bonds authorized pursuant to this chapter in order to carry out the actions specified in Article 2 (commencing with Section 19955), and, if so, the amount of bonds to be issued and sold. Successive issues of bonds may be authorized and sold to carry out those actions progressively, and it is not necessary that all of the bonds authorized to be issued be sold at any one time.

(Added by Stats.1988, c. 49, § 1, eff. March 18, 1988, approved (Prop.85), Nov. 8, 1988.)

Cross References

Bonds,
    Generally, see Education Code § 15100 et seq.
    Issuance by school districts, see Const. Art. 9, § 6 1/2.
    Tax exemption of bonds, see Const. Art. 13, § 3.

Library References

Legal Jurisprudences
Am Jur 2d Public Securities and Obligations
§§ 131 et seq.

§ 19974. Collection of revenue; payment of principal and interest; duties of officers

There shall be collected each year and in the same manner and at the same time as other state revenue is collected, in addition to the ordinary revenues of the state, a sum in an amount required to pay the principal of, and interest on, the bonds each year, and it is the duty of all officers charged by law with any duty in regard to the collection of the revenue to do and perform each and every act which is necessary to collect that additional sum.

(Added by Stats.1988, c. 49, § 1, eff. March 18, 1988, approved (Prop.85), Nov. 8, 1988.)

Library References

Legal Jurisprudences
Am Jur 2d Public Securities and Obligations
§§ 131 et seq.

§ 19975. Appropriation from general fund

Notwithstanding Section 13340 of the Government Code, there is hereby appropriated from the General Fund in the State Treasury, for the purposes of this chapter, an amount that will equal the total of the following:

(a) The sum annually necessary to pay the principal of, and interest on, bonds issued and sold pursuant to this chapter, as the principal and interest become due and payable.

(b) The sum which is necessary to carry out the provisions of Section 19976, appropriated without regard to fiscal years.

(Added by Stats.1988, c. 49, § 1, eff. March 18, 1988, approved (Prop.85), Nov. 8, 1988.)

Cross References

State treasury, generally, see Government Code § 16300 et seq.

§ 19976. Withdrawal from general fund; deposit; return to fund with interest

For the purposes of carrying out this chapter, the Director of Finance may authorize the withdrawal from the General Fund of an amount or amounts not to exceed the amount of the unsold bonds which have been authorized to be sold for the purpose of carrying out this chapter. Any amounts withdrawn shall be deposited in the fund. Any money made available under this section shall be returned to the General Fund, with interest at the rate earned by the money in the Pooled Money Investment Account during the time the money was withdrawn from the General Fund pursuant to this section from money received from the sale of bonds for the purpose of carrying out this chapter.

(Added by Stats.1988, c. 49, § 1, eff. March 18, 1988, approved (Prop.85), Nov. 8, 1988.)

§ 19976.5. Bonds including opinion on exclusion of interest from federal tax; separate accounts for proceeds and earnings; use

Notwithstanding any other provision of this bond act, or of the State General Obligation Bond Law (Chapter 4 (commencing with Section 16720) of Part 3 of Division 4 of Title 2 of the Government Code), if the Treasurer sells bonds pursuant to this bond act that include a bond counsel opinion to the effect that the interest on the bonds is excluded from gross income for federal tax purposes under designated conditions, the Treasurer may maintain separate accounts for the bond proceeds invested and the investment earnings on those proceeds, and may use or direct the use of those proceeds or earnings to pay any rebate, penalty, or other payment required under federal law, or take any other action with respect to the investment and use of those bond proceeds, as may be required or desirable under federal law in order to maintain the tax-exempt status of those bonds and to obtain any other advantage under federal law on behalf of the funds of this state.

(Added by Stats.1991, c. 652 (S.B.822), § 6.)

Cross References

Bonds,
    Generally, see Education Code § 15100 et seq.
    Issuance by school districts, see Const. Art. 9, § 6 1/2.
    Tax exemption of bonds, see Const. Art. 13, § 3.

§ 19977. Request for loan from pooled money investment account; documents; repayment of loan

The board may request the Pooled Money Investment Board to make a loan from the Pooled Money Investment Account, in accordance with Section 16312 of the Government Code, for the purposes of carrying out this chapter. The amount of the request shall not exceed the amount of the unsold bonds which the committee has by resolution authorized to be sold for the purpose of carrying out this chapter. The board shall execute any documents required by the Pooled Money Investment Board to obtain and repay the loan. Any amounts loaned shall be deposited in the fund to be allocated by the board in accordance with this chapter.

(Added by Stats.1988, c. 49, § 1, eff. March 18, 1988, approved (Prop.85), Nov. 8, 1988.)

§ 19978. Refunding bonds

Any bonds issued and sold pursuant to this chapter may be refunded by the issuance of refunding bonds in accordance with Article 6 (commencing with Section 16780) of Chapter 4 of Part 3 of Division 2 of Title 2 of the Government Code. Approval by the electors of the state for the issuance of bonds shall include the approval of the issuance of any bonds issued to refund any bonds originally issued or any previously issued refunding bonds.

(Added by Stats.1988, c. 49, § 1, eff. March 18, 1988, approved (Prop.85), Nov. 8, 1988.)

Cross References

Bonds,
    Generally, see Education Code § 15100 et seq.
    Issuance by school districts, see Const. Art. 9, § 6 1/2.
    Tax exemption of bonds, see Const. Art. 13, § 3.

Library References

Legal Jurisprudences
Am Jur 2d Public Securities and Obligations
    §§ 131 et seq.

§ 19979. Transfer to general fund; premium and accrued interest

All money deposited in the fund which is derived from premium and accrued interest on bonds sold shall be reserved in the fund and shall be available for transfer to the General Fund as a credit to expenditures for bond interest.

(Added by Stats.1988, c. 49, § 1, eff. March 18, 1988, approved (Prop.85), Nov. 8, 1988.)

§ 19980. Proceeds from bond sales not subject to constitutional limitations

The Legislature hereby finds and declares that, inasmuch as the procee ds [1] from the sale of bonds authorized by this chapter are not "proceeds of taxes" as that term is used in Article XIII B of the California Constitution, the disbursement of these proceeds is not subject to the limitations imposed by that article.

(Added by Stats.1988, c. 49, § 1, eff. March 18, 1988, approved (Prop.85), Nov. 8, 1988.)

[1] So in chaptered copy.

Cross References

Bonds,
    Generally, see Education Code § 15100 et seq.
    Issuance by school districts, see Const. Art. 9, § 6 1/2.
    Tax exemption of bonds, see Const. Art. 13, § 3.

§ 19981. Costs for administration of chapter

An amount not to exceed 1 percent of the fund may be used by the State Librarian for costs of administering this chapter.

(Added by Stats.1988, c. 49, § 1, eff. March 18, 1988, approved (Prop.85), Nov. 8, 1988.)

Cross References

State Librarian,
    Generally, see Education Code § 19302 et seq.
    Powers and duties, see Education Code § 19320 et seq.

Chapter 12

CALIFORNIA READING AND LITERACY IMPROVEMENT AND PUBLIC LIBRARY CONSTRUCTION AND RENOVATION BOND ACT OF 2000

Chapter 12 was added by Stats.1999, c. 726 (S.B.3), § 1, eff. Oct. 10, 1999, (Prop. 14, approved March 7, 2000).

Historical and Statutory Notes

Effective date, submission of provisions to voters, and ballot requirements relating to Stats. 1999, c. 726 (S.B.3), (Prop. 14), see Historical and Statutory Notes under Education Code § 19985.

Article 1

GENERAL PROVISIONS

Section
19985.   Short title.
19985.5.   Legislative findings and declarations.
19986.   Definitions.

Article 1 was added by Stats.1999, c. 726 (S.B.3), § 1, eff. Oct. 10, 1999, (Prop. 14, approved March 7, 2000).

Historical and Statutory Notes

Effective date, submission of provisions to voters, and ballot requirements relating to Stats. 1999, c. 726 (S.B.3), (Prop. 14), see Historical and Statutory Notes under Education Code § 19985.

§ 19985.   Short title

This chapter shall be known and may be cited as the California Reading and Literacy Improvement and Public Library Construction and Renovation Bond Act of 2000.

(Added by Stats.1999, c. 726 (S.B.3), § 1, eff. Oct. 10, 1999, (Prop. 14, approved March 7, 2000).)

Historical and Statutory Notes

Sections 2, 3, and 4 of Stats.1999, c. 726, provide:

"SEC. 2.   Section 1 of this act shall take effect upon the adoption by the voters of the California Library Construction and Renovation Bond Act of 2000, as set forth in Section 1 of this act. [As introduced, § 1 of S.B. 3 added Chapter 12, 'California Library Construction and Renovation Bond Act of 2000', and § 19985 provided that Chapter 12 be known and cited as 'the California Library Construction and Renovation Bond Act of 2000'. The chapter heading and its citation in § 19985 were changed to 'California Reading and Literacy Improvement and Public Library Construction and Renovation Bond Act of 2000' in S.B. 3 as amended by the Senate on April 6, 1999.]

"SEC. 3.   Section 1 of this act shall be submitted to the voters at the March 7, 2000, statewide primary election in accordance with provisions of the Elections Code and the Government Code governing submission of statewide measures to voters.

"SEC. 4.   Notwithstanding any other provisions of law, all ballots of the election shall have printed thereon and in a square thereof, the words: "California Reading and Literacy Improvement and Public Library Construction and Renovation Bond Act of 2000" and in the same square under those words, the following in 8–point type: "This act provides for a bond issue of three hundred fifty million dollars ($350,000,000) to provide funds for the construction and renovation of public library facilities in order to expand access to reading and literacy programs in California's public education system and to expand access to public library services for all residents of California." Opposite the square, there shall be left spaces in which the voters may place a cross in the manner required by law to indicate whether they vote for or against the act.

"Where the voting in the election is done by a means of voting machines used pursuant to law in the manner that carries out the intent of this section, the use of the voting machines and the expression of the voters' choice by means thereof are in compliance with this section."

Proposition 14 (Stats.1999, c. 726 (S.B.3), § 1) was approved by the voters at the March 7, 2000, election.

§ 19985.5. Legislative findings and declarations

The Legislature finds and declares the following:

(a) Reading and literacy skills are fundamental to success in our economy and our society.

(b) The Legislature and Governor have made enormous strides in improving the quality of reading instruction in public schools.

(c) Public libraries are an important resource to further California's reading and literacy goals both in conjunction with the public schools and for the adult population.

(d) The construction and renovation of public library facilities is necessary to expand access to reading and literacy programs in California's public education system and to expand access to public library services for all residents of California.

(Added by Stats.1999, c. 726 (S.B.3), § 1, eff. Oct. 10, 1999 (Prop. 14, approved March 7, 2000).)

Historical and Statutory Notes

Effective date, submission of provisions to voters, and ballot requirements relating to Stats. 1999, c. 726 (S.B.3), (Prop. 14), see Historical and Statutory Notes under Education Code § 19985.

§ 19986. Definitions

As used in this chapter, the following terms have the following meanings:

(a) "Committee" means the California Library Construction and Renovation Finance Committee established pursuant to Section 19972.

(b) "Fund" means the California Public Library Construction and Renovation Fund.

(c) "Board" means the California Public Library Construction and Renovation Board. This board is comprised of the State Librarian, the Treasurer, the Director of Finance, an Assembly Member appointed by the Speaker of the Assembly, a Senator appointed by the Senate Rules Committee, and a member appointed by the Governor.

Legislative members of the board shall meet with, and participate in, the work of the board to the extent that their participation is not incompatible with their duties as Members of the Legislature. For the purposes of this chapter,

Members of the Legislature who are members of the board shall constitute a joint legislative committee on the subject matter of this chapter.

(Added by Stats.1999, c. 726 (S.B.3), § 1, eff. Oct. 10, 1999 (Prop.14, approved March 7, 2000).)

Historical and Statutory Notes

Effective date, submission of provisions to voters, and ballot requirements relating to Stats. 1999, c. 726 (S.B.3), (Prop. 14), see Historical and Statutory Notes under Education Code § 19985.

Cross References

State Librarian,
    Generally, see Education Code § 19302 et seq.
    Powers and duties, see Education Code § 19320 et seq.

Article 2

PROGRAM PROVISIONS

Article 2 was added by Stats.1999, c. 726 (S.B.3), § 1, eff. Oct. 10, 1999, (Prop. 14, approved March 7, 2000).

Historical and Statutory Notes

Effective date, submission of provisions to voters, and ballot requirements relating to Stats. 1999, c. 726 (S.B.3), (Prop. 14), see Historical and Statutory Notes under Education Code § 19985.

§ 19987. California Public Library Construction and Renovation Fund

The proceeds of bonds issued and sold pursuant to this chapter shall be deposited in the California Public Library Construction and Renovation Fund, which is hereby established.

(Added by Stats.1999, c. 726 (S.B.3), § 1, eff. Oct. 10, 1999 (Prop.14, approved March 7, 2000).)

Historical and Statutory Notes

Effective date, submission of provisions to voters, and ballot requirements relating to Stats. 1999, c. 726 (S.B.3), (Prop. 14), see Historical and Statutory Notes under Education Code § 19985.

§ 19988. Continuous appropriation

All moneys deposited in the fund, except as provided in Section 20011, are continuously appropriated to the State Librarian, notwithstanding Section 13340 of the Government Code, and shall be available for grants to any city, county, city and county, or district that is authorized at the time of the project application to own and maintain a public library facility for the purposes set forth in Section 19989.

(Added by Stats.1999, c. 726 (S.B.3), § 1, eff. Oct. 10, 1999 (Prop.14, approved March 7, 2000).)

Historical and Statutory Notes

Effective date, submission of provisions to voters, and ballot requirements relating to Stats. 1999, c. 726 (S.B.3), (Prop. 14), see Historical and Statutory Notes under Education Code § 19985.

Cross References

State Librarian,
   Generally, see Education Code § 19302 et seq.
   Powers and duties, see Education Code § 19320 et seq.

§ 19989. Purposes for funds

The grant funds authorized pursuant to Section 19988, and the matching funds provided pursuant to Section 19995, shall be used by the recipient for any of the following purposes:

(a) Acquisition or construction of new facilities or additions to existing public library facilities.

(b) Acquisition of land necessary for the purposes of subdivision (a).

(c) Remodeling or rehabilitation of existing public library facilities or of other facilities for the purpose of their conversion to public library facilities. All remodeling and rehabilitation projects funded with grants authorized pursuant to this chapter shall include any necessary upgrading of electrical and telecommunications systems to accommodate Internet and similar computer technology.

(d) Procurement or installation, or both, of furnishings and equipment required to make a facility fully operable, if the procurement or installation is part of a construction or remodeling project funded pursuant to this section.

(e) Payment of fees charged by architects, engineers, and other professionals, whose services are required to plan or execute a project authorized pursuant to this chapter.

(Added by Stats.1999, c. 726 (S.B.3), § 1, eff. Oct. 10, 1999 (Prop.14, approved March 7, 2000).)

Historical and Statutory Notes

Effective date, submission of provisions to voters, and ballot requirements relating to Stats. 1999, c. 726 (S.B.3), (Prop. 14), see Historical and Statutory Notes under Education Code § 19985.

§ 19990. Impermissible purposes for funds

Any grant funds authorized pursuant to Section 19988, or matching funds provided pursuant to Section 19995, may not be used by a recipient for any of the following purposes:

(a) Books and other library materials.

(b) Administrative costs of the project, including, but not limited to, the costs of any of the following:

(1) Preparation of the grant application.

(2) Procurement of matching funds.

(3) Conduct of an election for obtaining voter approval of the project.

(c) Interest or other carrying charges for financing the project, including, but not limited to, costs of loans or lease-purchase agreements in excess of the direct costs of any of the authorized purposes specified in Section 19989.

(d) Any ongoing operating expenses for the facility, its personnel, supplies, or any other library operations.

(Added by Stats.1999, c. 726 (S.B.3), § 1, eff. Oct. 10, 1999 (Prop.14, approved March 7, 2000).)

Historical and Statutory Notes

Effective date, submission of provisions to voters, and ballot requirements relating to Stats. 1999, c. 726 (S.B.3), (Prop. 14), see Historical and Statutory Notes under Education Code § 19985.

§ 19991. Bids for construction contracts

All construction contracts for projects funded in part through grants awarded pursuant to this chapter shall be awarded through competitive bidding pursuant to Part 3 (commencing with Section 20100) of Division 2 of the Public Contract Code.

(Added by Stats.1999, c. 726 (S.B.3), § 1, eff. Oct. 10, 1999 (Prop.14, approved March 7, 2000).)

Historical and Statutory Notes

Effective date, submission of provisions to voters, and ballot requirements relating to Stats. 1999, c. 726 (S.B.3), (Prop. 14), see Historical and Statutory Notes under Education Code § 19985.

Cross References

Contracts, generally, see Civil Code § 1549 et seq.

Library References

States ☞98.
Westlaw Topic No. 360.
C.J.S. States §§ 160 to 167.

§ 19992.   Administration of chapter; rules, regulations, and policies

This chapter shall be administered by the State Librarian. The board shall adopt rules, regulations, and policies for the implementation of this chapter.

(Added by Stats.1999, c. 726 (S.B.3), § 1, eff. Oct. 10, 1999 (Prop.14, approved March 7, 2000).)

Historical and Statutory Notes

Effective date, submission of provisions to voters, and ballot requirements relating to Stats. 1999, c. 726 (S.B.3), (Prop. 14), see Historical and Statutory Notes under Education Code § 19985.

Cross References

Administrative regulations and rulemaking, see Government Code § 11340 et seq.
State Librarian,
    Generally, see Education Code § 19302 et seq.
    Powers and duties, see Education Code § 19320 et seq.

§ 19993.   Grant application

A city, county, city and county, or district may apply to the State Librarian for a grant pursuant to this chapter, as follows:

(a) Each application shall be for a project for a purpose authorized by Section 19989.

(b) An application may not be submitted for a project for which construction bids already have been advertised.

(c) The applicant shall request not less than fifty thousand dollars ($50,000) per project.

(Added by Stats.1999, c. 726 (S.B.3), § 1, eff. Oct. 10, 1999 (Prop.14, approved March 7, 2000).)

Historical and Statutory Notes

Effective date, submission of provisions to voters, and ballot requirements relating to Stats. 1999, c. 726 (S.B.3), (Prop. 14), see Historical and Statutory Notes under Education Code § 19985.

Cross References

State Librarian,
    Generally, see Education Code § 19302 et seq.
    Powers and duties, see Education Code § 19320 et seq.

§ 19994.   Priorities for construction, remodeling, or rehabilitation

(a) The State Librarian shall consider applications for construction of new public library facilities submitted pursuant to Section 19993 in the following priority order:

(1) First priority shall be given to joint use projects in which the agency that operates the library and one or more school districts have a cooperative agreement.

(2) Second priority shall be given to all other public library projects.

(b) The State Librarian shall consider applications for remodeling or rehabilitation of existing public library facilities pursuant to Section 19993 in the following priority order:

(1) First priority shall be given to public library projects in the attendance areas of public schools that are determined, pursuant to regulations adopted by the board, to have inadequate infrastructure to support access to computers and other educational technology.

(2) Second priority shall be given to all other projects.

(Added by Stats.1999, c. 726 (S.B.3), § 1, eff. Oct. 10, 1999 (Prop.14, approved March 7, 2000).)

Historical and Statutory Notes

Effective date, submission of provisions to voters, and ballot requirements relating to Stats. 1999, c. 726 (S.B.3), (Prop. 14), see Historical and Statutory Notes under Education Code § 19985.

Cross References

State Librarian,
    Generally, see Education Code § 19302 et seq.
    Powers and duties, see Education Code § 19320 et seq.

§ 19995. Matching funds

(a) Each grant recipient shall provide matching funds from any available source in an amount equal to 35 percent of the costs of the project. The remaining 65 percent of the costs of the project, up to a maximum of twenty million dollars ($20,000,000) per project, shall be provided through allocations from the fund.

(b) Qualifying matching funds shall be cash expenditures in the categories specified in Section 19989 which are made not earlier than three years prior to the submission of the application to the State Librarian. Except as otherwise provided in subdivision (c), in-kind expenditures do not qualify as matching funds.

(c) Land donated or otherwise acquired for use as a site for the facility, including, but not limited to, land purchased more than three years prior to the submission of the application to the State Librarian, may be credited towards the 35 percent matching funds requirement at its appraised value as of the date of the application. This subdivision shall not apply to land acquired with funds authorized pursuant to Part 68 (commencing with Section 100400).

(d) Architect fees for plans and drawings for library renovation and new construction, including, but not limited to, plans and drawings purchased more than three years prior to the submission of the application to the State Librarian, may be credited towards the 35 percent matching funds requirement.

(Added by Stats.1999, c. 726 (S.B.3), § 1, eff. Oct. 10, 1999 (Prop.14, approved March 7, 2000).)

Historical and Statutory Notes

Effective date, submission of provisions to voters, and ballot requirements relating to Stats. 1999, c. 726 (S.B.3), (Prop. 14), see Historical and Statutory Notes under Education Code § 19985.

Cross References

State Librarian,
Generally, see Education Code § 19302 et seq.
Powers and duties, see Education Code § 19320 et seq.

§ 19996. Normal public construction costs

(a) The estimated costs of a project for which an application is submitted shall be consistent with normal public construction costs in the applicant's area.

(b) An applicant wishing to construct a project having costs that exceed normal public construction costs in the area may apply for a grant in an amount not to exceed 65 percent of the normal costs up to a maximum of twenty million dollars ($20,000,000) per project if the applicant certifies that it is capable of financing the remainder of the project costs from other sources.

(Added by Stats.1999, c. 726 (S.B.3), § 1, eff. Oct. 10, 1999 (Prop.14, approved March 7, 2000).)

Historical and Statutory Notes

Effective date, submission of provisions to voters, and ballot requirements relating to Stats. 1999, c. 726 (S.B.3), (Prop. 14), see Historical and Statutory Notes under Education Code § 19985.

§ 19997. Costs exceeding funding; funding exceeding costs

Once an application has been approved by the board and included in the State Librarian's request to the committee, the amount of the funding to be provided to the applicant may not be increased. Any actual changes in project costs are the full responsibility of the applicant. If the amount of funding that is provided is greater than the cost of the project, the applicant shall return that portion of the funding that exceeds the cost of the project to the fund. If an applicant has been awarded funding by the board, but chooses not to proceed with the project, the applicant shall return all of the funding to the fund.

(Added by Stats.1999, c. 726 (S.B.3), § 1, eff. Oct. 10, 1999 (Prop.14, approved March 7, 2000).)

Historical and Statutory Notes

Effective date, submission of provisions to voters, and ballot requirements relating to Stats. 1999, c. 726 (S.B.3), (Prop. 14), see Historical and Statutory Notes under Education Code § 19985.

Cross References

State Librarian,
Generally, see Education Code § 19302 et seq.
Powers and duties, see Education Code § 19320 et seq.

§ 19998. Priorities; factors

(a) In reviewing applications, as part of establishing the priorities set forth in Section 19994 the board shall consider all of the following factors:

(1) Needs of urban and rural areas.

(2) Population growth.

(3) Age and condition of the existing library facility.

(4) The degree to which the existing library facility is inadequate in meeting the needs of the residents in the library service area and the degree to which the proposed project responds to the needs of those residents.

(5) The degree to which the library's plan of service integrates appropriate electronic technologies into the proposed project.

(6) The degree to which the proposed site is appropriate for the proposed project and its intended use.

(7) The financial capacity of the local agency submitting the application to open and maintain operation of the proposed library for applications for the construction of new public libraries.

(b) If, after an application has been submitted, material changes occur that would alter the evaluation of an application, the State Librarian may accept an additional written statement from the applicant for consideration by the board.

(Added by Stats.1999, c. 726 (S.B.3), § 1, eff. Oct. 10, 1999 (Prop.14, approved March 7, 2000).)

Historical and Statutory Notes

Effective date, submission of provisions to voters, and ballot requirements relating to Stats. 1999, c. 726 (S.B.3), (Prop. 14), see Historical and Statutory Notes under Education Code § 19985.

Cross References

State Librarian,
　　Generally, see Education Code § 19302 et seq.
　　Powers and duties, see Education Code § 19320 et seq.

§ 19999. Period of dedication to library use; transfer of state interest

(a) A facility, or the part thereof, acquired, constructed, or remodeled, or rehabilitated with grants received pursuant to this chapter shall be dedicated to public library direct service use for a period of not less than 20 years following completion of the project.

(b) The interest of the state in land or a facility, or both, pursuant to the funding of a project under this chapter, as described in subdivision (a), may be transferred by the State Librarian from the land or facility, or both, for which that funding was granted to a replacement site and facility acquired or constructed for the purpose of providing public library direct service.

(c) If the facility, or any part thereof, acquired, constructed, remodeled, or habilitated with grants received pursuant to this chapter ceases to be used for public library direct service prior to the expiration of the period specified in subdivision (a), the board is entitled to recover, from the grant recipient or the recipient's successor in the maintenance of the facility, an amount that bears the same ratio to the value of the facility, or the appropriate part thereof, at the time it ceased to be used for public library direct service as the amount of the grant bore to the cost of the facility or the appropriate part thereof. For purposes of this subdivision, the value of the facility, or the appropriate part thereof, is determined by the mutual agreement of the board and the grant recipient or successor, or through an action brought for that purpose in the superior court.

(d) Notwithstanding subdivision (f) of Section 16724 of the Government Code, any money recovered pursuant to subdivision (c) shall be deposited in the fund, and shall be available for the purpose of awarding grants for other projects.

(Added by Stats.1999, c. 726 (S.B.3), § 1, eff. Oct. 10, 1999 (Prop.14. approved March 7, 2000).)

Historical and Statutory Notes

Effective date, submission of provisions to voters, and ballot requirements relating to Stats. 1999, c. 726 (S.B.3), (Prop. 14), see Historical and Statutory Notes under Education Code § 19985.

Cross References

State Librarian,
  Generally, see Education Code § 19302 et seq.
  Powers and duties, see Education Code § 19320 et seq.

Article 3

FISCAL PROVISIONS

Section
20000. Bond amount; state obligation.
20001. State General Obligation Bond Law.
20002. California Library Construction and Renovation Finance Committee as "committee" for bond law; California Public Library Construction and Renovation Board as "board" for bond law.
20003. Issuance of bonds.
20004. State revenue collection.
20005. Appropriation.
20006. General Fund withdrawal.
20007. Pooled Money Investment Account loan.
20008. Refunding bonds.
20009. Fund deposits derived from premium and accrued interest.
20010. Constitution Article XIII B; application.
20011. Administration expenses; appropriation.

Article 3 was added by Stats.1999, c. 726 (S.B.3), § 1, eff. Oct. 10, 1999 (Prop. 14, approved March 7, 2000).

Historical and Statutory Notes

Effective date, submission of provisions to voters, and ballot requirements relating to Stats. 1999, c. 726 (S.B.3), (Prop. 14), see Historical and Statutory Notes under Education Code § 19985.

§ 20000. Bond amount; state obligation

Bonds in the amount of three hundred fifty million dollars ($350,000,000), exclusive of refunding bonds, or so much thereof as is necessary, may be issued and sold for deposit in the fund to be used in accordance with, and for carrying out the purposes expressed in, this chapter, including all acts amendatory thereof and supplementary thereto, and to be used to reimburse the General Obligation Bond Expense Revolving Fund pursuant to Section 16724.5 of the Government Code. The bonds, when sold, shall be and constitute a valid and binding obligation of the State of California, and the full faith and credit of the State of California is hereby pledged for the punctual payment of both principal of and interest on bonds as the principal and interest become due and payable.

(Added by Stats.1999, c. 726 (S.B.3), § 1, eff. Oct. 10, 1999 (Prop.14, approved March 7, 2000).)

Historical and Statutory Notes

Effective date, submission of provisions to voters, and ballot requirements relating to Stats. 1999, c. 726 (S.B.3), (Prop. 14), see Historical and Statutory Notes under Education Code § 19985.

Cross References

Bonds,
Generally, see Education Code § 15100 et seq.
Issuance by school districts, see Const. Art. 9, § 6 1/2.
Tax exemption of bonds, see Const. Art. 13, § 3.

§ 20001. State General Obligation Bond Law

The bonds authorized by this chapter shall be prepared, executed, issued, sold, paid, and redeemed as provided in the State General Obligation Bond Law (Chapter 4 (commencing with Section 16720) of Part 3 of Division 4 of Title 2 of the Government Code), and all of the provisions of that law apply to the bonds and to this chapter and are hereby incorporated in this chapter as though set forth in full in this chapter.

(Added by Stats.1999, c. 726 (S.B.3), § 1, eff. Oct. 10, 1999 (Prop.14, approved March 7, 2000).)

Historical and Statutory Notes

Effective date, submission of provisions to voters, and ballot requirements relating to Stats. 1999, c. 726 (S.B.3), (Prop. 14), see Historical and Statutory Notes under Education Code § 19985.

Cross References

Bonds,
Generally, see Education Code § 15100 et seq.
Issuance by school districts, see Const. Art. 9, § 6 1/2.
Tax exemption of bonds, see Const. Art. 13, § 3.

§ **20002.** California Library Construction and Renovation Finance Committee as "committee" for bond law; California Public Library Construction and Renovation Board as "board" for bond law

(a) For purposes of this chapter, the California Library Construction and Renovation Finance Committee established pursuant to Section 19972 is the "committee" as that term is used in the State General Obligation Bond Law.

(b) For purposes of the State General Obligation Bond Law, the California Public Library Construction and Renovation Board established pursuant to subdivision (c) of Section 19986 is designated the "board."

(Added by Stats.1999, c. 726 (S.B.3), § 1, eff. Oct. 10, 1999 (Prop.14, approved March 7, 2000).)

Historical and Statutory Notes

Effective date, submission of provisions to voters, and ballot requirements relating to Stats. 1999, c. 726 (S.B.3), (Prop. 14), see Historical and Statutory Notes under Education Code § 19985.

Cross References

Bonds,
   Generally, see Education Code § 15100 et seq.
   Issuance by school districts, see Const. Art. 9, § 6 1/2.
   Tax exemption of bonds, see Const. Art. 13, § 3.

§ 20003. Issuance of bonds

The committee shall determine whether or not it is necessary or desirable to issue bonds authorized pursuant to this chapter in order to carry out the actions specified in this chapter, including all acts amendatory thereof and supplementary thereto, and, if so, the amount of bonds to be issued and sold. Successive issues of bonds may be authorized and sold to carry out those actions progressively, and it is not necessary that all of the bonds authorized to be issued be sold at any one time.

(Added by Stats.1999, c. 726 (S.B.3), § 1, eff. Oct. 10, 1999 (Prop.14, approved March 7, 2000).)

Historical and Statutory Notes

Effective date, submission of provisions to voters, and ballot requirements relating to Stats. 1999, c. 726 (S.B.3), (Prop. 14), see Historical and Statutory Notes under Education Code § 19985.

Cross References

Bonds,
   Generally, see Education Code § 15100 et seq.
   Issuance by school districts, see Const. Art. 9, § 6 1/2.
   Tax exemption of bonds, see Const. Art. 13, § 3.

Library References

States ⚌147.
Westlaw Topic No. 360.
C.J.S. States § 252.

§ 20004. State revenue collection

There shall be collected each year and in the same manner and at the same time as other state revenue is collected, in addition to the ordinary revenues of the state, a sum in an amount required to pay the principal of and interest on the bonds each year. It is the duty of all officers charged by law with any duty in regard to the collection of the revenue to do and perform each and every act that is necessary to collect that additional sum.

(Added by Stats.1999, c. 726 (S.B.3), § 1, eff. Oct. 10, 1999 (Prop.14, approved March 7, 2000).)

Historical and Statutory Notes

Effective date, submission of provisions to voters, and ballot requirements relating to Stats. 1999, c. 726 (S.B.3), (Prop. 14), see Historical and Statutory Notes under Education Code § 19985.

§ 20005. Appropriation

Notwithstanding Section 13340 of the Government Code, there is hereby appropriated from the General Fund in the State Treasury, for the purposes of this chapter, an amount that will equal the total of the following:

(a) The sum annually necessary to pay the principal of and interest on bonds issued and sold pursuant to this chapter, as the principal and interest become due and payable.

(b) The sum necessary to carry out Section 20006, appropriated without regard to fiscal years.

(Added by Stats.1999, c. 726 (S.B.3), § 1, eff. Oct. 10, 1999 (Prop.14, approved March 7, 2000).)

Historical and Statutory Notes

Effective date, submission of provisions to voters, and ballot requirements relating to Stats. 1999, c. 726 (S.B.3), (Prop. 14), see Historical and Statutory Notes under Education Code § 19985.

Cross References

State treasury, generally, see Government Code § 16300 et seq.

§ 20006. General Fund withdrawal

For the purposes of carrying out this chapter, the Director of Finance may authorize the withdrawal from the General Fund of an amount or amounts not to exceed the amount of the unsold bonds that have been authorized to be sold for the purpose of carrying out this chapter. Any amounts withdrawn shall be deposited in the fund. Any money made available under this section shall be returned to the General Fund, with interest at the rate earned by the money in the Pooled Money Investment Account during the time the money was withdrawn from the General Fund pursuant to this section, from money received from the sale of bonds for the purpose of carrying out this chapter.

(Added by Stats.1999, c. 726 (S.B.3), § 1, eff. Oct. 10, 1999 (Prop.14, approved March 7, 2000).)

Historical and Statutory Notes

Effective date, submission of provisions to voters, and ballot requirements relating to Stats. 1999, c. 726 (S.B.3), (Prop. 14), see Historical and Statutory Notes under Education Code § 19985.

§ 20007. Pooled Money Investment Account loan

The board may request the Pooled Money Investment Board to make a loan from the Pooled Money Investment Account, in accordance with Section 16312 of the Government Code, for the purposes of carrying out this chapter. The amount of the request shall not exceed the amount of the unsold bonds that the committee has, by resolution, authorized to be sold for the purpose of carrying out this chapter. The board shall execute any documents required by the Pooled Money Investment Board to obtain and repay the loan. Any amounts loaned shall be deposited in the fund to be allocated by the board in accordance with this chapter.

(Added by Stats.1999, c. 726 (S.B.3), § 1, eff. Oct. 10, 1999 (Prop.14, approved March 7, 2000).)

Historical and Statutory Notes

Effective date, submission of provisions to voters, and ballot requirements relating to Stats. 1999, c. 726 (S.B.3), (Prop. 14), see Historical and Statutory Notes under Education Code § 19985.

§ 20008. Refunding bonds

Any bonds issued and sold pursuant to this chapter may be refunded by the issuance of refunding bonds in accordance with Article 6 (commencing with Section 16780) of Chapter 4 of Part 3 of Division 2 of Title 2 of the Government Code. Approval of the electors of the state for the issuance of bonds under this chapter shall include the approval of the issuance of any bonds issued to refund any bonds originally issued or any previously issued refunding bonds.

(Added by Stats.1999, c. 726 (S.B.3), § 1, eff. Oct. 10, 1999 (Prop.14, approved March 7, 2000).)

Historical and Statutory Notes

Effective date, submission of provisions to voters, and ballot requirements relating to Stats. 1999, c. 726 (S.B.3), (Prop. 14), see Historical and Statutory Notes under Education Code § 19985.

Cross References

Bonds,
    Generally, see Education Code § 15100 et seq.
    Issuance by school districts, see Const. Art. 9, § 6 1/2.
    Tax exemption of bonds, see Const. Art. 13, § 3.

§ 20009. Fund deposits derived from premium and accrued interest

All money deposited in the fund that is derived from premium and accrued interest on bonds sold pursuant to this chapter shall be reserved in the fund and shall be available for transfer to the General Fund as a credit to expenditures for bond interest.

(Added by Stats.1999, c. 726 (S.B.3), § 1, eff. Oct. 10, 1999 (Prop.14, approved March 7, 2000).)

Historical and Statutory Notes

Effective date, submission of provisions to voters, and ballot requirements relating to Stats. 1999, c. 726 (S.B.3), (Prop. 14), see Historical and Statutory Notes under Education Code § 19985.

§ 20010. Constitution Article XIII B; application

The Legislature hereby finds and declares that, inasmuch as the proceeds from the sale of bonds authorized by this chapter are not "proceeds of taxes" as that term is used in Article XIII B of the California Constitution, the disbursement of these proceeds is not subject to the limitations imposed by that article.

(Added by Stats.1999, c. 726 (S.B.3), § 1, eff. Oct. 10, 1999 (Prop.14, approved March 7, 2000).)

Historical and Statutory Notes

Effective date, submission of provisions to voters, and ballot requirements relating to Stats. 1999, c. 726 (S.B.3), (Prop. 14), see Historical and Statutory Notes under Education Code § 19985.

Library References

States ☞123.
Westlaw Topic No. 360.
C.J.S. States § 226.

§ 20011. Administration expenses; appropriation

Amounts deposited in the fund pursuant to this chapter may be appropriated in the annual Budget Act to the State Librarian for the actual amount of office, personnel, and other customary and usual expenses incurred in the direct administration of grant projects pursuant to this chapter, including, but not limited to, expenses incurred by the State Librarian in providing technical assistance to an applicant for a grant under this chapter.

(Added by Stats.1999, c. 726 (S.B.3), § 1, eff. Oct. 10, 1999 (Prop.14, approved March 7, 2000).)

Historical and Statutory Notes

Effective date, submission of provisions to voters, and ballot requirements relating to Stats. 1999, c. 726 (S.B.3), (Prop. 14), see Historical and Statutory Notes under Education Code § 19985.

Cross References

State Librarian,
  Generally, see Education Code § 19302 et seq.
  Powers and duties, see Education Code § 19320 et seq.

Part 12

FOUNDATIONS AND STATE COMMITTEES
AND COMMISSIONS

Part 12 was enacted by Stats.1976 c. 1010, § 2, operative April 30, 1977.

Cross References

Director of education, agreements for performance of services, see Education Code § 33117.
Incorporation of unincorporated associations, see Corporations Code § 5121, 7121, 9121.
Sabbatical leaves, break in continuity of service, see Education Code § 44967.

Law Review and Journal Commentaries

Enforcement of college trustees' fiduciary duties: Students and the problem of standing. Charles R. Berry and Gerald J. Buchwald (1974) 9 U.S.F.L.Rev. 1.

Chapter 1

FOUNDATIONS, TRUSTS, AND INSTITUTIONS
OF ARTS AND SCIENCES

The heading of Chapter 1, formerly Chapter 2, enacted by Stats.1976, c. 1010, § 2, operative April 30, 1977, was renumbered Chapter 1 and amended by Stats.1983, c. 142, § 10.

The heading of former Chapter 1, "State Committees and Commissions", enacted by Stats.1976, c. 1010, § 2, operative April 30, 1977, was repealed by Stats.1983, c. 142, § 9.

Article 1

FOUNDATIONS AND TRUSTS

Article 1 was enacted by Stats.1976, c. 1010, § 2, operative April 30, 1977.

§§ 21000, 21001.   Repealed by Stats.1981, c. 604, p. 2324, § 3

Historical and Statutory Notes

Section 21000, enacted by Stats.1976, c. 1010, § 2, derived from Educ.C.1959, § 501 (Stats.1959, c. 2, p. 609, § 501); Educ.C.1943, § 20201 (Stats.1943, c. 71, p. 703); and School C. § 2.1365, added Stats.1933, c. 812, p. 2153, § 1, related to the establishment and composition of the State Council of Educational Planning and Coordination.

Section 21001, enacted by Stats.1976, c. 1010, § 2, derived from Educ.C.1959, § 502 (Stats.1959, c. 2, p. 610, § 502); Educ.C.1943, § 20202 (Stats.1943, c. 71, p. 704); and School C. § 2.1366, added Stats.1933, c. 812, p. 2153, § 1, related to the function of the State Council of Educational Planning and Coordination.

§ 21100.   Authority for private grants of property to educational institutions

Any person desiring in his lifetime to promote the public welfare by founding, endowing, and maintaining within this state a university, college, school, seminary of learning, mechanical institute, museum, botanic garden, public park, or gallery of art, or any or all thereof, may, for such purposes, by grant in writing convey to a trustee, or any number of trustees, named in the grant, and to their successors, any property, real or personal, belonging to him and situated within this state.   If he is married and the property is community property, then both husband and wife shall join in the grant.

(Stats.1976, c. 1010, § 2, operative April 30, 1977.)

Historical and Statutory Notes

Derivation: Educ.C.1959, § 31051 (Stats. 1959, c. 2, p. 1507, § 31051).

Educ.C.1943, § 24001 (Stats.1943, c. 71, p. 767).

Stats.1885, c. 47, p. 50, § 2, amended by Stats.1891, c. 239, p. 454, § 1.

Cross References

Community property, see Family Code §§ 65 and 760.

Library References

Charities ⬡12.
Westlaw Topic No. 75.
C.J.S. Charities § 9.

Am Jur 2d (Rev) Charities §§ 32, 48, Colleges
and Universities § 37.

Legal Jurisprudences
Cal Jur 3d Sch § 335.

Notes of Decisions

Beneficiaries 3
Trust enforcement 2
Validity 1

1. Validity

The word "eleemosynary," in its modern and legal meaning, is interchangeable with "charitable," and the creation of a perpetuity by a conveyance of property in trust for the founding of an educational institution, as is authorized by Stats.1885, p. 49, was not in violation of the provision of Art. 20, § 9. People ex rel. Ellert v. Cogswell (1896) 113 Cal. 129, 45 P. 270.

2. Trust enforcement

The state, as representative of the public, could maintain an action to enforce, or prevent the mismanagement of, a public trust, such as was created by the conveyance of property to trustees, authorized by Stats.1885, p. 49, for the founding or maintenance of an institution of learning. People ex rel. Ellert v. Cogswell (1896) 113 Cal. 129, 45 P. 270.

3. Beneficiaries

It was essential to the validity of a charitable trust that the beneficiaries be designated as a class only, leaving the numbers and individuals to be determined by the trustees in its administration. People ex rel. Ellert v. Cogswell (1896) 113 Cal. 129, 45 P. 270.

§ 21101. Items which grantor may designate

The grantor may designate in the grant:

(a) The nature, object, and purposes of the institution to be founded, endowed, and maintained.

(b) The name by which it shall be known.

(c) The powers and duties of the trustees, and the manner in which they shall account, and to whom, if accounting is required. Such powers and duties shall not be exclusive of other powers and duties which may be necessary to enable the trustees to fully carry out the objects of the grant.

(d) The mode and manner, and by whom, the successors to the trustee or trustees named in the grant are to be appointed.

(e) Such rules and regulations for the management of the property conveyed as the grantor may elect to prescribe. Such rules shall, unless the grantor otherwise prescribes, be deemed advisory only, and shall not preclude the trustees from making such changes as new conditions may from time to time require.

(f) The place where and the time when the buildings necessary and proper for the institution shall be erected, and the character and extent thereof.

(Stats.1976, c. 1010, § 2, operative April 30, 1977.)

Historical and Statutory Notes

Derivation: Educ.C.1959, § 31052 (Stats. 1959, c. 2, p. 1507, § 31052).

Educ.C.1943, § 24002 (Stats.1943, c. 71, p. 767).

Stats.1885, c. 47, p. 50, § 3.

§ 21102. Other provisions which grantor may establish

The grantor may also provide for all other things necessary and proper to carry out the purposes of the grant, and especially may provide for the trades and professions which shall be taught in the institution, and the terms upon which deserving scholars of the public and private schools of the various counties of this state may be admitted to all the privileges of the institution, as a reward for meritorious conduct and good scholarship.

(Stats.1976, c. 1010, § 2, operative April 30, 1977.)

Historical and Statutory Notes

Derivation: Educ.C.1959, § 31053 (Stats. 1959, c. 2, p. 1508, § 31053).
 Educ.C.1943, § 24003 (Stats.1943, c. 71, p. 767).

Stats.1885, c. 47, p. 50, § 3.

§ 21103. Provisions allowed for scholarships

The grantor may also provide for maintaining free scholarships for children of persons who have rendered service to or who have died in the service of the state and for maintaining free scholarships for children of mechanics, tradesmen, and laborers, who have died without leaving means sufficient to give their children a practical education, fitting them for the useful trades or arts.

(Stats.1976, c. 1010, § 2, operative April 30, 1977.)

Historical and Statutory Notes

Derivation: Educ.C.1959, § 31054 (Stats. 1959, c. 2, p. 1508, § 31054).
 Educ.C.1943, § 24004 (Stats.1943, c. 71, p. 768).

Stats.1885, c. 47, p. 50, § 3.

§ 21104. Grantor's provision for attendance of students and others at lectures and other functions

The grantor may also provide the terms and conditions upon which students in the public and private schools, and other deserving persons, may, without cost to themselves, attend the lectures of any university established, and also the terms and conditions upon which the museums, art galleries, and conservatories of music, connected with any such institution, shall be open to all deserving persons without charge, and without their becoming students of the institution.

(Stats.1976, c. 1010, § 2, operative April 30, 1977.)

Historical and Statutory Notes

Derivation: Educ.C.1959, § 31055 (Stats. 1959, c. 2, p. 1508, § 31055).

Educ.C.1943, § 24005 (Stats.1943, c. 71, p. 768).

Stats.1885, c. 47, p. 50, § 3.

Library References

Legal Jurisprudences

Cal Jur 3d Char § 10.

§ 21105. Trustee's right to sue and defend in relation to trust matters

The trustee or trustees named in the grant, and their successors, may, in the name of the institution, as designated in the grant, sue and defend, in relation to the trust property, and in relation to all matters affecting the institution. (Stats.1976, c. 1010, § 2, operative April 30, 1977.)

Historical and Statutory Notes

Derivation: Educ.C.1959, § 31056 (Stats. 1959, c. 2, p. 1508, § 31056).

Educ.C.1943, § 24006 (Stats.1943, c. 71, p. 768).

Stats.1885, c. 47, p. 51, § 4.

Library References

Legal Jurisprudences

Am Jur 2d (Rev) Charities § 97.

§ 21106. Right of grantor to elect to exercise powers of trustee

The grantor, by a provision in the grant, may elect, in relation to the property conveyed, and in relation to the erection, maintenance, and management of the institution, to perform, during his life, all the duties and exercise all the powers which, by the terms of the grant, are enjoined upon and vested in the trustee or trustees. (Stats.1976, c. 1010, § 2, operative April 30, 1977.)

Historical and Statutory Notes

Derivation: Educ.C.1959, § 31057 (Stats. 1959, c. 2, p. 1508, § 31057).

Educ.C.1943, § 24007 (Stats.1943, c. 71, p. 768).

Stats.1885, c. 47, p. 51, § 5.

Library References

Legal Jurisprudences

Am Jur 2d (Rev) Charities § 97.

§ 21107. Right of grantor's surviving spouse to act as trustee

A grantor who is a married person may further provide that his or her surviving spouse during his or her life, may, in relation to the property conveyed, and in relation to the election, maintenance, and management of the institution, perform all the duties and exercise all the powers which, by the terms of the grant, are enjoined upon and vested in the trustee and trustees.

(Stats.1976, c. 1010, § 2, operative April 30, 1977. Amended by Stats.1977, c. 36, § 84, eff. April 29, 1977.)

Historical and Statutory Notes

Derivation: Educ.C.1959, § 31058 (Stats. 1959, c. 2, p. 1508, § 31058, amended by Stats. 1976, c. 1171, § 8).

Educ.C.1943, § 24008 (Stats.1943, c. 71, p. 768).

Stats.1885, c. 47, p. 51, § 5.

Library References

Legal Jurisprudences

Am Jur 2d (Rev) Charities § 97.

§ 21108. Succession of named trustees to management of trust after death of grantor or spouse

In the cases referred to in Sections 21106 and 21107, the powers and duties conferred and imposed upon the trustee or trustees shall be exercised and performed by the grantor, or by his or her spouse, during his or her life, as the case may be. Upon the death of the grantor, or the surviving spouse, as the case may be, the powers and duties shall devolve upon and shall be exercised by the trustees named in the grant, and their successors.

(Stats.1976, c. 1010, § 2, operative April 30, 1977. Amended by Stats.1977, c. 36, § 85, eff. April 29, 1977.)

Historical and Statutory Notes

Derivation: Educ.C.1959, § 31059 (Stats. 1959, c. 2, p. 1508, § 31059, amended by Stats. 1976, c. 1171, § 9).

Educ.C.1943, § 24009 (Stats.1943, c. 71, p. 768).

Stats.1885, c. 47, p. 51, § 5.

Library References

Legal Jurisprudences

Am Jur 2d (Rev) Charities § 97.

§ 21109. Grantor authorized to reserve right to alter, amend or modify terms and conditions of grant

The grantor may reserve the right to alter, amend, or modify the terms and conditions of the grant, and the trusts created, in respect to any of the matters mentioned or referred to in Sections 21101 to 21104, inclusive.

(Stats.1976, c. 1010, § 2, operative April 30, 1977.)

Historical and Statutory Notes

Derivation: Educ.C.1959, § 31060 (Stats. 1959, c. 2, p. 1509, § 31060).

Educ.C.1943, § 24010 (Stats.1943, c. 71, p. 768).

Stats.1885, c. 47, p. 51, § 6.

§ 21110. Grantor's right to reserve dominion over property without liability to account

The grantor may also reserve, during his or her life, the right of absolute dominion over the personal property conveyed, and also over the rents, issues, and profits of the real property conveyed, without liability to account therefor in any manner whatever, and without any liability over against his or her estate.

(Stats.1976, c. 1010, § 2, operative April 30, 1977. Amended by Stats.1977, c. 36, § 86, eff. April 29, 1977.)

Historical and Statutory Notes

Derivation: Educ.C.1959, § 31061 (Stats. 1959, c. 2, p. 1509, § 31061, amended by Stats. 1976, c. 1171, § 10).

Educ.C.1943, § 24011 (Stats.1943, c. 71, p. 768).

Stats.1885, c. 47, p. 51, § 6.

§ 21111. Grantor's right to convey life estate to spouse

A grantor who is a married person may further provide that his or her spouse, during his or her life, may have the same absolute dominion, over the personal property, and the rents, issues, and profits, without liability to account therefor in any manner whatever, and without liability over against the estate of either the grantor or his or her spouse.

(Stats.1976, c. 1010, § 2, operative April 30, 1977. Amended by Stats.1977, c. 36, § 87, eff. April 29, 1977.)

Historical and Statutory Notes

Derivation: Educ.C.1959, § 31062 (Stats. 1959, c. 2, p. 1509, § 31062, amended by Stats. 1976, c. 1171, § 11).

Educ.C.1943, § 24012 (Stats.1943, c. 71, p. 769).

Stats.1885, c. 47, p. 51, § 6.

§ 21112. Allowance for relinquishment of rights by founder, spouse or surviving spouse

The founder or founders, surviving founder, or spouse or surviving spouse of any founder, of a university, college, school, seminary of learning, mechanical institute, museum, gallery of art, library or any other institution, or any or all thereof, founded pursuant to this article, may, by an instrument in writing, resign, relinquish, and surrender all the rights, powers, privileges and duties reserved to or vesting in him or her, over, in, or concerning any of the property granted or given to the institution, or over or concerning the institution founded. Thereupon all estates, rights, powers, privileges, trusts, and duties which would otherwise vest in or devolve upon the trustee or trustees of the trusts and estates created upon the death of the person resigning, relinquishing, and surrendering, by the terms of the grant and amendments thereof, and by the terms of any grants, gifts, bequests, and devices supplementary thereto, or of any confirmatory grants, shall immediately vest in and devolve upon the trustee or trustees. Nothing herein contained shall prevent the person resigning, relinquishing and surrendering the rights, powers, privileges, or duties from thereafter becoming and serving as one of the trustees, or from becoming and serving as an officer of any board of trustees.

(Stats.1976, c. 1010, § 2, operative April 30, 1977. Amended by Stats.1977, c. 36, § 88, eff. April 29, 1977.)

Historical and Statutory Notes

Derivation: Educ.C.1959, § 31063 (Stats. 1959, c. 2, p. 1509, § 31063, amended by Stats. 1976, c. 1171, § 12).

Educ.C.1943, § 24013 (Stats.1943, c. 71, p. 769).

Stats.1903, c. 130, p. 140, § 1.

§ 21113. Grantor allowed to provide for trustees to become custodians of minors

The grantor may provide in the grant that the trustees and their successors, may, in the name of the institution, become the custodian of the person of minors. When any such provision is made in a grant, the trustees and their successors may take the custody and control in the manner and for the time and in accordance with the provisions of Chapter 4 (commencing with Section 3070) of Division 3 of the Labor Code.

(Stats.1976, c. 1010, § 2, operative April 30, 1977.)

Historical and Statutory Notes

Derivation: Educ.C.1959, § 31064 (Stats. 1959, c. 2, p. 1509, § 31064).

Educ.C.1943, § 24014 (Stats.1943, c. 71, p. 769).

Stats.1885, c. 47, p. 51, § 7.

Library References

Legal Jurisprudences

Am Jur 2d (Rev) Charities § 97.

§ 21114. Execution, acknowledgment and recording of grant

The grant shall be executed, acknowledged, and recorded in the same manner as is provided by law for the execution, acknowledgment, and recording of grants of real property.

(Stats.1976, c. 1010, § 2, operative April 30, 1977.)

Historical and Statutory Notes

Derivation: Educ.C.1959, § 31065 (Stats. 1959, c. 2, p. 1509, § 31065).

Educ.C.1943, § 24015 (Stats.1943, c. 71, p. 769).

Stats.1885, c. 47, p. 52, § 8.

Cross References

Recording,
  Constructive notice, conveyances or real property or estate for years, see Civil Code § 1213.
  Instruments or judgments, documents to be recorded and manner of recording, see Government Code § 27320 et seq., and § 7280 et seq.
  Property transfers, place of recordation, see Civil Code § 1169.

§ 21115. Limitation upon action or defense

No suit, action, or proceeding shall be commenced or maintained by any person to set aside, annul, or affect the conveyance, or to affect the title to the property conveyed, or the right to the possession, or to the rents, issues, and profits thereof, unless the action is commenced within two years after the date of filing the grant for record. No defense shall be made to any suit, action, or proceeding commenced by the trustee or trustees named in the grant, or their successors, privies, or persons holding under them, which involves the legality of the grant, or affects the title to the property conveyed, or the right to the possession, or the rents, issues, and profits thereof, unless the defense is made in a suit, action, or proceeding commenced within two years after the grant has been filed for record.

(Stats.1976, c. 1010, § 2, operative April 30, 1977.)

Historical and Statutory Notes

  Derivation: Educ.C.1959, § 31066 (Stats.   Stats.1885, c. 47, p. 52, § 9.
1959, c. 2, p. 1510, § 31066).
  Educ.C.1943, § 24016 (Stats.1943, c. 71, p.
769).

§ 21116. Limitation upon proceedings against property conveyed by grant

The property conveyed by the grant shall not, after a lapse of two years from the date of the filing for record of the grant, be subject to forced sale, under execution, or judicial proceedings of any kind, against the grantor or his privies, unless the action under which the execution is issued, or the proceedings under which the sale is ordered, has been commenced within two years after the grant has been filed for record. No property shall be subject to execution or forced sale under any judgment obtained in any proceedings instituted within two years, if there is other property of the grantor, subject to execution or forced sale sufficient to satisfy the judgment. Nothing in this section contained shall be construed to affect mechanics' or laborers' liens.

(Stats.1976, c. 1010, § 2, operative April 30, 1977.)

Historical and Statutory Notes

Derivation: Educ.C.1959, § 31067 (Stats. 1959, c. 2, p. 1510, § 31067).

Educ.C.1943, § 24017 (Stats.1943, c. 71, p. 770).

Stats.1885, c. 47, p. 52, § 10.

Cross References

Computation of time,
    Generally, see Code of Civil Procedure §§ 12 and 12a and Government Code § 6800 et seq.
    Time in which any act provided by the Education Code is to be done, see Education Code § 9.
Continuation of statutes relating to subjects covered by provisions of this Code, see Education Code
    § 3.
Mechanics lien, see Civil Code § 3110.

Library References

Legal Jurisprudences

Cal Jur 3d Sch § 335.

Treatises and Practice Aids

Witkin, Procedure (4th ed) Enf Judgm § 108.

§ 21117. Subsequent bequest to state of property previously granted to trust

Any person making the grant may, at any time thereafter, by last will or testament, devise and bequeath to the state all or any of the property, real and personal, mentioned in the grant, or in any supplemental grant, and the devise or bequest shall only take effect if, from any cause whatever, the grant is annulled or set aside, or the trusts therein declared for any reason fail. Such devise and bequest is permitted to be made by way of assurance that the wishes of the grantor shall be carried out, and in the faith that the state, if it succeeds to the property, or any part thereof, will, to the extent and value of the property, carry out, in respect to the objects and purposes of the grant, all the wishes and intentions of the grantor.

(Stats.1976, c. 1010, § 2, operative April 30, 1977.)

Historical and Statutory Notes

Derivation: Educ.C.1959, § 31068 (Stats. 1959, c. 2, p. 1510, § 31068).

Educ.C.1943, § 24018 (Stats.1943, c. 71, p. 770).

Stats.1885, c. 47, p. 52, § 11.

§ 21118. Conditions as to religious instruction not binding on state

No wish, direction, act, or condition expressed, made, or given by any grantor, under this article, as to religious instruction to be given in any school, college, seminary, mechanical institute, museum, or gallery of art, or in respect to the exercise of religious belief, on the part of any pupil of the school or institution of learning, shall be binding upon the state. The state shall not enforce, or permit to be enforced or carried out, any such wish, direction, act, or condition.

(Stats.1976, c. 1010, § 2, operative April 30, 1977.)

Historical and Statutory Notes

Derivation: Educ.C.1959, § 31069 (Stats. 1959, c. 2, p. 1510, § 31069).

Educ.C.1943, § 24019 (Stats.1943, c. 71, p. 770).

Stats.1885, c. 47, p. 52, § 11.

Library References

Legal Jurisprudences

Cal Jur 3d Char § 10.

§ 21119. Constructions of provisions of article

The provisions of this article shall be liberally construed with a view to effect its objects and promote its purposes.

(Stats.1976, c. 1010, § 2, operative April 30, 1977.)

Historical and Statutory Notes

Derivation: Educ.C.1959, § 31070 (Stats. 1959, c. 2, p. 1510, § 31070).

Educ.C.1943, § 24020 (Stats.1943, c. 71, p. 770).

Stats.1885, c. 47, p. 49, § 1.

Library References

Legal Jurisprudences

Am Jur 2d (Rev) Charities §§ 52, 53, Colleges and Universities § 37.

Article 2

INSTITUTIONS OF ARTS AND SCIENCES

Article 2 was enacted by Stats.1976, c. 1010, § 2, operative April 30, 1977.

§ 21140. Provision for private grant of property to library, museum or art gallery

Any person intending in his lifetime or by will or trust deed, to operate after his death, to found, maintain, and perpetuate in this state a public library, museum, gallery of art, or any or all thereof, for the diffusion of mechanical, scientific, artistic, and general knowledge, may for that purpose, convey in writing by words denoting a gift or grant to one or more trustees named in the gift or grant, and to their successors, any library or collection of books and works, for the public library, or any museum, or gallery of art in this state.

(Stats.1976, c. 1010, § 2, operative April 30, 1977.)

Historical and Statutory Notes

Derivation: Educ.C.1959, § 31101 (Stats. 1959, c. 2, p. 1511, § 31101).

Educ.C.1943, § 24041 (Stats.1943, c. 71, p. 770).

Stats.1887, c. 32, p. 26, § 1.

Library References

Charities ⌐14.
Westlaw Topic No. 75.
C.J.S. Charities § 7.

Legal Jurisprudences
Cal Jur 3d Char § 10; Sch §§ 10, 335.
Am Jur 2d (Rev) Charities §§ 52, 53.

§ 21141. Items which grantor may designate

The gift or grant may also express and shall be construed to be a conveyance of the future additions and accretions thereof.

(Stats.1976, c. 1010, § 2, operative April 30, 1977.)

Historical and Statutory Notes

Derivation: Educ.C.1959, § 31102 (Stats. 1959, c. 2, p. 1511, § 31102).

Educ.C.1943, § 24042 (Stats.1943, c. 71, p. 771).

Stats.1887, c. 32, p. 26, § 1.

§ 21142. Grant or conveyance of other property

The grantor may also in like manner, convey by grant to the trustee or trustees any real property within this state belonging to him, which may be necessary or proper for the erection and maintenance of buildings suitable to the institution, and the buildings erected thereon, with grounds, conveniently adjacent thereto, and other lands, tenements, and hereditaments for the purpose of producing an income for the support and maintenance of the institutions and any collateral burdens which may be imposed by the terms of the foundation as part and parcel of the regulations for its conduct, and also personal property of all descriptions, which may subserve the purposes of the institution and maintenance of the library, museum, or gallery of art.

(Stats.1976, c. 1010, § 2, operative April 30, 1977.)

Historical and Statutory Notes

Derivation: Educ.C.1959, § 31103 (Stats. 1959, c. 2, p. 1511, § 31103).

Educ.C.1943, § 24043 (Stats.1943, c. 71, p. 771).

Stats.1887, c. 32, p. 26, § 1.

§ 21143. Contributions and gifts by persons other than founder

Any contributions or gifts by any other person than the founder, of any property suitable to the general plan or support of any institution mentioned in this article, shall immediately vest in the trustees, and become incorporated into and subject to the trust, and to all its terms and conditions, and be managed under the rules and regulations prescribed therefor.

(Stats.1976, c. 1010, § 2, operative April 30, 1977.)

Historical and Statutory Notes

Derivation: Educ.C.1959, § 31104 (Stats. 1959, c. 2, p. 1511, § 31104).

Educ.C.1943, § 24044 (Stats.1943, c. 71, p. 771).

Stats.1887, c. 32, p. 26, § 2.

§ 21144. Other items which founder may designate

The person making the gift, grant, or conveyance, as founder may therein designate:

(a) The name by which the institution shall be known.

(b) Its nature, object, and purposes.

(c) The powers and duties of the trustees, which shall not be exclusive of other powers and duties that, in their judgment, may be necessary more effectually to carry out the purposes of the institution.

(d) The mode, manner, and by whom the successors to the trustees named in the gift or grant shall be appointed.

(e) Such rules and regulations for the management of the institution, and the furtherance of its purposes, as the grantor may elect to prescribe. Such rules and regulations shall, unless the grant shall otherwise prescribe, be deemed advisory only, and shall not preclude the trustees or their successors from making such changes as new conditions may, from time to time, require.

(f) The place or places where the necessary buildings shall be erected, and the general character thereof. The grantor may provide in the grant for all other things necessary or proper to carry out the purposes of the grant, or otherwise, by his last will or testament.

(Stats.1976, c. 1010, § 2, operative April 30, 1977.)

Historical and Statutory Notes

Derivation: Educ.C.1959, § 31105 (Stats. 1959, c. 2, p. 1511, § 31105).

Educ.C.1943, § 24045 (Stats.1943, c. 71, p. 771).

Stats.1887, c. 32, p. 26, § 3.

Library References

Legal Jurisprudences

Cal Jur 3d Char § 10.

§ 21145. Right of trustees to sue and defend in relation to trust matters

The trustees named in the gift or grant, and their successors, may, in the name of the institution, sue and defend in relation to the trust property, and to all matters affecting the institution.

(Stats.1976, c. 1010, § 2, operative April 30, 1977.)

Historical and Statutory Notes

Derivation: Educ.C.1959, § 31106 (Stats. 1959, c. 2, p. 1512, § 31106).

Educ.C.1943, § 24046 (Stats.1943, c. 71, p. 771).

Stats.1887, c. 32, p. 27, § 4.

Library References

Legal Jurisprudences
  Am Jur 2d (Rev) Charities § 97.

§ 21146. Right of founder to elect to reserve power to veto over acts of trustees

By a provision in the gift or grant, the founder may elect, in respect to the personal and real property conveyed, and the additions and increase thereof, and in respect to the erection, maintenance, and management of any buildings auxiliary thereto, and in respect to any property connected with the institution, to reserve to himself a veto and right of annulment or modification of any act of the trustees.

(Stats.1976, c. 1010, § 2, operative April 30, 1977.)

Historical and Statutory Notes

Derivation: Educ.C.1959, § 31107 (Stats. 1959, c. 2, p. 1512, § 31107).

Educ.C.1943, § 24047 (Stats.1943, c. 71, p. 771).

Stats.1887, c. 32, p. 27, § 5.

Library References

Legal Jurisprudences
  Am Jur 2d (Rev) Charities § 97.

§ 21147. Notice of veto in writing required

If he elects to veto, annul, or modify any act of the trustees, he shall, within 30 days after notice of the performance of the act, file in the office of the trustees, or deliver to their president or principal officer, a notice in writing, of the veto, annulment, or modification.

(Stats.1976, c. 1010, § 2, operative April 30, 1977.)

Historical and Statutory Notes

Derivation: Educ.C.1959, § 31108 (Stats. 1959, c. 2, p. 1512, § 31108).

Educ.C.1943, § 24048 (Stats.1943, c. 71, p. 772).

Stats.1887, c. 32, p. 27, § 5.

Computation of time,
    Generally, see Code of Civil Procedure §§ 12 and 12a and Government Code § 6800 et seq.
    Time in which any act provided by the Education Code is to be done, see Education Code § 9.
Continuation of statutes relating to subjects covered by provisions of this Code, see Education Code
    § 3.

§ 21148. Right of grantor to elect to exercise powers of trustee

Upon a like notice, in conformity with a provision in the gift or grant, he may elect to perform during his life all the powers which, by the terms of the grant, are vested in or enjoined upon the trustees, and their successors. Upon the death or disability to act of the founder and grantor, the powers and duties shall devolve upon, and be exercised by, the trustees, and their successors.

(Stats.1976, c. 1010, § 2, operative April 30, 1977.)

Historical and Statutory Notes

Derivation: Educ.C.1959, § 31109 (Stats.   Stats.1887, c. 32, p. 27, § 5.
1959, c. 2, p. 1512, § 31109).
    Educ.C.1943, § 24049 (Stats.1943, c. 71, p.
772).

Library References

Legal Jurisprudences
    Am Jur 2d (Rev) Charities § 97.

§ 21149. Grantor authorized to reserve right to alter, amend or modify terms and conditions of grant

The founder may also reserve the right to alter, amend, or modify, at any time during his life, or by his last will and testament, the terms and conditions of the grant, and the trust created in respect to the institution, its buildings, and the property conveyed.

(Stats.1976, c. 1010, § 2, operative April 30, 1977.)

Historical and Statutory Notes

Derivation: Educ.C.1959, § 31110 (Stats.   Stats.1887, c. 32, p. 27, § 5.
1959, c. 2, p. 1512, § 31110).
    Educ.C.1943, § 24050 (Stats.1943, c. 71, p.
772).

§ 21150. Specifications concerning officers

The founder may in the deed of trust name and describe the character and personality of any one or more of the immediate or future trustees, the librarian, and other officers, and name and impose any particular duty to be performed by any one or more trustees or other officers so described and characterized. He may declare and limit any compensation, and fix the character and method of the compensation he chooses to provide for the trustee or other officer whom the terms of his foundation may characterize, and upon whom specific or general duties are imposed.

(Stats.1976, c. 1010, § 2, operative April 30, 1977.)

Historical and Statutory Notes

Derivation: Educ.C.1959, § 31111 (Stats. 1959, c. 2, p. 1512, § 31111).

Stats.1887, c. 32, p. 27, § 6.

Educ.C.1943, § 24051 (Stats.1943, c. 71, p. 772).

§ 21151. Execution, acknowledgment and recording of grant

The gift or grant shall be executed, acknowledged, and recorded in the manner provided by law for the execution, acknowledgment, and recording of grants of real property.

(Stats.1976, c. 1010, § 2, operative April 30, 1977.)

Historical and Statutory Notes

Derivation: Educ.C.1959, § 31112 (Stats. 1959, c. 2, p. 1512, § 31112).

Stats.1887, c. 32, p. 28, § 7.

Educ.C.1943, § 24052 (Stats.1943, c. 71, p. 772).

Cross References

Recording transfers, see Civil Code § 1169 et seq.
Transfer of real property, see Civil Code § 1091 et seq.

§ 21152. Limitation upon action

No suit, action, or proceeding shall be commenced or maintained by any person to set aside, annul, or affect any gift, grant, or conveyance, or to affect the title to the property conveyed, or the right to the possession or to the rents, issues, and profits thereof, unless the action is commenced within two years after the date of the filing of the grant for record.

(Stats.1976, c. 1010, § 2, operative April 30, 1977.)

Historical and Statutory Notes

Derivation: Educ.C.1959, § 31113 (Stats. 1959, c. 2, p. 1512, § 31113).

Stats.1887, c. 32, p. 28, § 8.

Educ.C.1943, § 24053 (Stats.1943, c. 71, p. 772).

Cross References

Computation of time,
    Generally, see Code of Civil Procedure §§ 12 and 12a and Government Code § 6800 et seq.
    Time in which any act provided by the Education Code is to be done, see Education Code § 9.
Continuation of statutes relating to subjects covered by provisions of this Code, see Education Code
    § 3.

Library References

Legal Jurisprudences
    Cal Jur 3d Sch § 335.

§ 21153. Subsequent bequest to state of property previously granted to trust

Any founder, making a gift or grant for any of the purposes mentioned in this article, may, at any time thereafter, by last will or testament, devise or bequeath to the state all or any of the property, real and personal, mentioned in the gift or grant, or in any supplemental grant or gift, and the devise or bequest shall take effect if, from any cause whatever, the gift or grant is annulled or set aside, or the trusts therein declared for any reason fail. Such devise or bequest is suffered to be made by way of assurance that the intentions of the grantor shall be carried out, and in the faith that the state, if it succeeds to the property, or any part thereof, will, to the extent and value of the property carry out, in respect to the objects and purposes of the grant, all the wishes and intentions of the grantor.

(Stats.1976, c. 1010, § 2, operative April 30, 1977.)

Historical and Statutory Notes

Derivation: Educ.C.1959, § 31114 (Stats. 1959, c. 2, p. 1513, § 31114).

Educ.C.1943, § 24054 (Stats.1943, c. 71, p. 772).

Stats.1887, c. 32, p. 28, § 9.

Library References

Legal Jurisprudences
Cal Jur 3d Char §§ 10, 335.

§ 21154. Construction of article

The provisions of this article shall be liberally construed, with a view to effect its objects and purposes.

(Stats.1976, c. 1010, § 2, operative April 30, 1977.)

Historical and Statutory Notes

Derivation: Educ.C.1959, § 31115 (Stats. 1959, c. 2, p. 1513, § 31115).

Educ.C.1943, § 24055 (Stats.1943, c. 71, p. 773).

Stats.1887, c. 32, p. 28, § 10.

Library References

Legal Jurisprudences
Am Jur 2d (Rev) Charities §§ 180 et seq.,
  Colleges and Universities § 37.

Article 3

LEGAL VALIDATION PROCEEDINGS

Section

Article 3 was enacted by Stats.1976, c. 1010, § 2, operative April 30, 1977.

Cross References

Declaratory relief, see Code of Civil Procedure § 1060 et seq.
Uniform supervision of Trustees for Charitable Purposes Act, see Government Code § 12580 et seq.

§ 21180. Trustees authorized to commence special proceedings

The trustee or trustees of any trust or trusts created for the founding, endowment, and maintenance of a university, college, school, seminary of learning, mechanical institute, museum, gallery of art, library, or any other institution, or any or all thereof, pursuant to Article 1 (commencing with Section 21100) and Article 2 (commencing with Section 21140) of this chapter, may commence a special proceeding to determine all questions of law and fact affecting the existence of, and the due and voluntary execution and delivery, and the terms, validity, and legal effect of the grant founding the institution, and of all amendments or attempted amendments to the grant, and of any supplemental grants or gifts, and of any confirmatory conveyances, of the founder or surviving founder, or spouse or surviving spouse of the founder.

(Stats.1976, c. 1010, § 2, operative April 30, 1977. Amended by Stats.1977, c. 36, § 89, eff. April 29, 1977.)

Historical and Statutory Notes

Derivation: Educ.C.1959, § 31151 (Stats. 1959, c. 2, p. 1513, § 31151 amended by Stats. 1976, c. 1171, § 13).

Educ.C.1943, § 24076 (Stats.1943, c. 71, p. 773).

Stats.1903, c. 7, p. 9, § 1.

Library References

Charities ⚵50.
Westlaw Topic No. 75.
C.J.S. Charities §§ 52 to 57.

§ 21181. Validity of gifts or grants; additional purposes for special proceedings

The special proceeding may also be commenced to determine all questions of law and fact affecting the due and voluntary execution and delivery, and the validity and legal effect, of any gift or grant made in general terms for the benefit of the institution, or of any department of the institution, or of any gift or grant made in general terms for the benefit of the institution, or of any department of the institution, or of any gift or grant made in general terms for the benefit of the institution, or of any department of the institution, upon the trusts provided for in the grant founding the institution, and amendments thereof and grants, bequests, and devises supplementary thereto.

(Stats.1976, c. 1010, § 2, operative April 30, 1977.)

Historical and Statutory Notes

Derivation: Educ.C.1959, § 31152 (Stats. 1959, c. 2, p. 1513, § 31152).

Educ.C.1943, § 24077 (Stats.1943, c. 71, p. 773).

Stats.1903, c. 7, p. 9, § 1.

Library References

Legal Jurisprudences
Cal Jur 3d Sch § 336.

§ 21182. Title to property; additional purposes for special proceedings

The special proceeding may also be commenced to determine all questions bearing upon the passing to the trustee or trustees of the legal title to the properties, real and personal, conveyed or attempted to be conveyed, so far as the property or the proceeds thereof, or any property acquired in exchange therefor or with proceeds thereof, is described in the petition provided for in this article, and the interest or title of the trustee or trustees in or to any property described in the petition.

(Stats.1976, c. 1010, § 2, operative April 30, 1977.)

Historical and Statutory Notes

Derivation: Educ.C.1959, § 31153 (Stats. 1959, c. 2, p. 1513, § 31153).

Educ.C.1943, § 24078 (Stats.1943, c. 71, p. 773).

Stats.1903, c. 7, p. 9, § 1.

§ 21183. Grant or surrender of rights, powers, privileges, or duties; additional purposes

The special proceeding may also be commenced to determine all questions of law and fact affecting the due and voluntary execution and delivery, and the validity and legal effect, of any grant or surrender by any founder, surviving founder, or spouse or surviving spouse of any founder, to, or in favor of, the trustee or trustees, of any rights, powers, privileges, or duties reserved to or vesting in any such person over or concerning any property described in the petition, or over or concerning the institution, which would otherwise vest in or

296

devolve upon the trustee or trustees upon the death of the person granting or surrendering the right, powers, privileges, or duties, and of any relinquishment or release by the founder, surviving founder, or spouse or surviving spouse of any founder, of any other rights, powers, privileges, or duties reserved to or vesting in any such person.

(Stats.1976, c. 1010, § 2, operative April 30, 1977. Amended by Stats.1977, c. 36, § 90, eff. April 29, 1977.)

Historical and Statutory Notes

Derivation: Educ.C.1959, § 31154 (Stats. 1959, c. 2, p. 1514, § 31154, amended by Stats. 1976, c. 1171, § 14).

Educ.C.1943, § 24079 (Stats.1943, c. 71, p. 773).

Stats. 1903, c. 7, p. 9, § 1.

§ 21184. Petition in superior court

The trustee or trustees of any trust created pursuant to Article 1 (commencing with Section 21100) and Article 2 (commencing with Section 21140) of this chapter, in the name of the institution or institutions, or in the name of the trustee or trustees of the institution, or in the name of the board of trustees of the institution, may file, in the superior court of the county in which the lands described in the founding grant, or some portion thereof, are situated, or, if no real estate has been granted to the trustees, then in the county where the main part of the institution is situated, a petition in writing, signed by counsel for the trustee or trustees, or by counsel for a majority thereof.

(Stats.1976, c. 1010, § 2, operative April 30, 1977.)

Historical and Statutory Notes

Derivation: Educ.C.1959, § 31155 (Stats. 1959, c. 2, p. 1514, § 31155).

Educ.C.1943, § 24080 (Stats.1943, c. 71, p. 774).

Stats.1903, c. 7, p. 9, § 1.

Library References

Legal Jurisprudences
Cal Jur 3d Sch § 336.

Notes of Decisions

Attorney general 1
_____

1. **Attorney general**
Primary right to enforce a charitable trust resided in attorney general. Pratt v. Security

Trust & Savings Bank (App. 2 Dist. 1936) 15 Cal.App.2d 630, 59 P.2d 862.

§ 21185. Content of petition

The petition shall contain copies of all grants, amendments, attempted amendments, supplemental grants, instruments of gift, confirmatory conveyances, and grants and instruments of surrender, relinquishment or release, so far as known to the trustee or trustees.

(Stats.1976, c. 1010, § 2, operative April 30, 1977.)

Historical and Statutory Notes

Derivation: Educ.C.1959, § 31156 (Stats. 1959, c. 2, p. 1514, § 31156).

Educ.C.1943, § 24081 (Stats.1943, c. 71, p. 774).

Stats.1903, c. 7, p. 9, § 1.

§ 21186. Allegations concerning trust instruments

The petition shall allege in general terms the due and voluntary execution and delivery, and the validity, of any and all instruments, copies of which are set out in the petition, and shall describe all property, real and personal, the legal title to which is held or claimed to be held by the trustee or trustees under or by virtue of any or all of the instruments, whether or not the property is the original property conveyed, the proceeds thereof, or reinvested proceeds.

(Stats.1976, c. 1010, § 2, operative April 30, 1977.)

Historical and Statutory Notes

Derivation: Educ.C.1959, § 31157 (Stats. 1959, c. 2, p. 1514, § 31157).

Educ.C.1943, § 24082 (Stats.1943, c. 71, p. 774).

Stats.1903, c. 7, p. 9, § 1.

§ 21187. Allegation concerning estate or interest in trust

The petition shall allege in general terms the estate or interest which the trustee or trustees have or claim in or to the property described.

(Stats.1976, c. 1010, § 2, operative April 30, 1977.)

Historical and Statutory Notes

Derivation: Educ.C.1959, § 31158 (Stats. 1959, c. 2, p. 1514, § 31158).

Educ.C.1943, § 24083 (Stats.1943, c. 71, p. 774).

Stats.1903, c. 7, p. 9, § 1.

§ 21188. Content of petition

The petition shall pray, in effect, that the court:

(a) Examine and determine all questions of law and fact affecting the due and voluntary execution and delivery, and the terms, validity, and legal effect of all the instruments, copies of which are set out in the petition.

(b) Examine and determine all questions bearing upon the passing to the trustee or trustees, of the legal title to all the properties, real and personal, conveyed or attempted to be conveyed, so far as the property or the proceeds thereof, or any property acquired in exchange therefor or with the proceeds thereof, is described in the petition.

(c) Examine and determine the interest or title of the trustee or trustees in or to the property.

(d) Establish and determine that the trustee or trustees are rightfully vested with the legal title thereto.

(Stats.1976, c. 1010, § 2, operative April 30, 1977.)

Historical and Statutory Notes

Derivation: Educ.C.1959, § 31159 (Stats. 1959, c. 2, p. 1514, § 31159).

Educ.C.1943, § 24084 (Stats.1943, c. 71, p. 774).

Stats.1903, c. 7, p. 9, § 1.

§ 21189. Notice of hearing

The court or judge shall fix the time for hearing the petition, and shall order the clerk of the court to post in at least three public places in the county a notice of the filing of the petition, attached to a copy of the petition, and order a copy of the notice together with a copy of the petition to be personally served upon the founder, if living, and upon the spouse or surviving spouse of any founder, and upon any living grantor or donor of any other grant or gift set out in the petition, and may order such other or further notice to be given as the judge or court may deem proper. The notice shall be posted and served at least 10 days before the hearing.

(Stats.1976, c. 1010, § 2, operative April 30, 1977. Amended by Stats.1977, c. 36, § 91, eff. April 29, 1977; Stats.1977, c. 242, § 10, eff. July 7, 1977.)

Historical and Statutory Notes

The 1977 amendment of this section by c. 242 explicitly amended this section as proposed by Stats.1977, c. 36.

Subordination of 1977 legislation, see Historical and Statutory Notes under Education Code § 1.

Operative effect of Stats.1977, c. 242, see Historical and Statutory Notes under Education Code § 8367.

Derivation: Educ.C.1959, § 31160 (Stats. 1959, c. 2, p. 1515, § 31160, amended by Stats. 1976, c. 1171, § 15).

Educ.C.1943, § 24085 (Stats.1943, c. 71, p. 774).

Stats.1903, c. 7, p. 11, § 2.

Cross References

Notices and filing and service of papers, see Code of Civil Procedure § 1010 et seq.

§ 21190. Effect of lack of due and proper notice

If the court or judge finds upon the hearing that due and proper notice has not been given as provided in Section 21189, it shall reset the hearing and cause due and proper notice to be given.

(Stats.1976, c. 1010, § 2, operative April 30, 1977.)

Historical and Statutory Notes

Derivation: Educ.C.1959, § 31161 (Stats. 1959, c. 2, p. 1515, § 31161).

Educ.C.1943, § 24086 (Stats.1943, c. 71, p. 775).

Stats.1903, c. 7, p. 11, § 2.

Cross References

Notices and filing and service of papers, see Code of Civil Procedure § 1010 et seq.

§ 21191. Title of notice and proceedings

The notice and petition shall be entitled substantially in the following form:

299

In the Superior Court of the _____ County of _____, State of California.

In the matter of the petition of _____ (giving the name or names in which the petition is brought) for the ascertainment of the existence and terms of, and for the determination of the validity and legal effect of grants or other instruments creating, changing, or affecting trusts and estates for the founding, endowment, and maintenance of _____ (naming the institution or institutions founded).
(Stats.1976, c. 1010, § 2, operative April 30, 1977.)

Historical and Statutory Notes

Derivation: Educ.C.1959, § 31162 (Stats. 1959, c. 2, p. 1515, § 31162).

Educ.C.1943, § 24087 (Stats.1943, c. 71, p. 775).

Stats.1903, c. 7, p. 11, § 2.

Cross References

Notices and filing and service of papers, see Code of Civil Procedure § 1010 et seq.

§ 21192. Contents of notice

The notice shall state the time and place fixed for the hearing of the petition and shall be addressed to the founder or founders, if living, and to the spouse or surviving spouse of any deceased founder, and the living grantor or donor of any other grant or gift set out in the petition, and in general terms to all other persons having or claiming any interest in, or rights, powers, or duties over or concerning the property described in the petition; and shall direct that they and each of them appear and answer the petition on or before the time set for the hearing. The notice shall also state that unless they so appear and demur or answer, the petitioners will apply to the court to grant the prayer of the petition, and that each person failing to so appear and answer, shall be deemed to admit as true all the material allegations of the petition.
(Stats.1976, c. 1010, § 2, operative April 30, 1977. Amended by Stats.1977, c. 36, § 92, eff. April 29, 1977.)

Historical and Statutory Notes

Derivation: Educ.C.1959, § 31163 (Stats. 1959, c. 2, p. 1515, § 31163, amended by Stats. 1976, c. 1171, § 16).

Educ.C.1943, § 24088 (Stats.1943, c. 71, p. 775).

Stats.1903, c. 7, p. 11, § 2.

Cross References

Notices and filing and service of papers, see Code of Civil Procedure § 1010 et seq.

§ 21193. Waiver of notice

Any person required to be served, or any other person interested may waive notice by written waiver filed with the clerk of the court.
(Stats.1976, c. 1010, § 2, operative April 30, 1977.)

Historical and Statutory Notes

Derivation: Educ.C.1959, § 31164 (Stats. 1959, c. 2, p. 1515, § 31164).

Educ.C.1943, § 24089 (Stats.1943, c. 71, p. 775).

Stats.1903, c. 7, p. 11, § 2.

Cross References

Notices and filing and service of papers, see Code of Civil Procedure § 1010 et seq.

§ 21194. Interested persons authorized to demur to or answer petition

Any person interested in the determination of any of the questions presented by the petition may demur to or answer the petition and may set up any new matter affecting the determination of the questions.

(Stats.1976, c. 1010, § 2, operative April 30, 1977.)

Historical and Statutory Notes

Derivation: Educ.C.1959, § 31165 (Stats. Stats.1903, c. 7, p. 12, § 3.
1959, c. 2, p. 1516, § 31165).

Educ.C.1943, § 24090 (Stats.1943, c. 71, p. 775).

Cross References

Allowable pleadings, see Code of Civil Procedure § 422.10.
Contents of complaint, see Code of Civil Procedure § 429.30.
Demurrer to all or part of pleadings, see Code of Civil Procedure § 430.50.
Denials and defenses, see Code of Civil Procedure § 430.10 et seq.
Objections to pleadings, see Code of Civil Procedure § 430.10 et seq.
Pleadings, economic litigation for limited civil cases, see Code of Civil Procedure § 92.
Specification of grounds, demurrer, see Code of Civil Procedure § 430.60.

Library References

Legal Jurisprudences
Cal Jur 3d Sch § 336.

§ 21195. Information and belief as basis of allegation

Any allegation of the petition or answer may be made upon information and belief.

(Stats.1976, c. 1010, § 2, operative April 30, 1977.)

Historical and Statutory Notes

Derivation: Educ.C.1959, § 31166 (Stats. Stats.1903, c. 7, p. 12, § 3.
1959, c. 2, p. 1516, § 31166).

Educ.C.1943, § 24090 (Stats.1943, c. 71, p. 775).

§ 21196. Demurrer and answer; application of Code of Civil Procedure

The provisions of the Code of Civil Procedure respecting the demurrer and the answer to a verified complaint, shall be applicable to a demurrer or answer to the petition.

(Stats.1976, c. 1010, § 2, operative April 30, 1977.)

Historical and Statutory Notes

Derivation: Educ.C.1959, § 31167 (Stats. Educ.C.1943, § 24092 (Stats.1943, c. 71, p.
1959, c. 2, p. 1516, § 31167). 775).

Stats.1903, c. 7, p. 12, § 3.

Cross References

Allowable pleadings, see Code of Civil Procedure § 422.10.
Contents of complaint, see Code of Civil Procedure § 429.30.
Demurrer to all or part of pleadings, see Code of Civil Procedure § 430.50.
Denials and defenses, see Code of Civil Procedure § 430.10 et seq.
Objections to pleadings, see Code of Civil Procedure § 430.10 et seq.
Pleadings, economic litigation for limited civil cases, see Code of Civil Procedure § 92.
Specification of grounds, demurrer, see Code of Civil Procedure § 430.60.

§ 21197. Plaintiffs and defendants

The persons demurring to or answering the petition shall be the defendants to the special proceeding and the petitioners shall be the plaintiffs.

(Stats.1976, c. 1010, § 2, operative April 30, 1977.)

Historical and Statutory Notes

Derivation: Educ.C.1959, § 31168 (Stats. 1959, c. 2, p. 1516, § 31168).

Educ.C.1943, § 24093 (Stats.1943, c. 71, p. 775).

Stats.1903, c. 7, p. 12, § 3.

§ 21198. Uncontroverted material statements to be taken as true

Every material statement of the petition not specifically controverted by the answer shall, for the purposes of the special proceeding, be taken as true, and each person failing to answer the petition shall be deemed to admit as true all the material allegations of the petition.

(Stats.1976, c. 1010, § 2, operative April 30, 1977.)

Historical and Statutory Notes

Derivation: Educ.C.1959, § 31169 (Stats. 1959, c. 2, p. 1516, § 31169).

Educ.C.1943, § 24090 (Stats.1943, c. 71, p. 775).

Stats.1903, c. 7, p. 12, § 3.

§ 21199. Proceedings subject to provisions of Code of Civil Procedure

The rules of pleading and practice provided for by the Code of Civil Procedure, which are not inconsistent with this article, are applicable to the special proceeding provided for.

(Stats.1976, c. 1010, § 2, operative April 30, 1977.)

Historical and Statutory Notes

Derivation: Educ.C.1959, § 31170 (Stats. 1959, c. 2, p. 1516, § 31170).

Educ.C.1943, § 24095 (Stats.1943, c. 71, p. 776).

Stats.1903, c. 7, p. 12, § 3.

Cross References

Pleadings, generally, see Code of Civil Procedure § 420 et seq.

§ 21200. Hearing

Upon the hearing of the special proceeding, the court shall examine into and determine all questions of law and fact within the scope of the proceeding herein provided for, whether presented by the petition or answer, or by the proofs upon the hearing.

The court shall find and determine whether the notice of the filing of the petition has been duly given for the time and in the manner prescribed in this article.

(Stats.1976, c. 1010, § 2, operative April 30, 1977.)

Historical and Statutory Notes

Derivation: Educ.C.1959, § 31171 (Stats. 1959, c. 2, p. 1516, § 31171).

Educ.C.1943, § 24096 (Stats.1943, c. 71, p. 776).

Stats.1903, c. 7, p. 12, § 4.

Library References

Legal Jurisprudences

Cal Jur 3d Sch § 336.

§ 21201. Costs at discretion of court

The costs of the special proceeding may be allowed and apportioned between all parties, in the discretion of the court.

(Stats.1976, c. 1010, § 2, operative April 30, 1977.)

Historical and Statutory Notes

Derivation: Educ.C.1959, § 31172 (Stats. 1959, c. 2, p. 1516, § 31172).

Educ.C.1943, § 24097 (Stats.1943, c. 71, p. 776).

Stats.1903, c. 7, p. 12, § 4.

Library References

Legal Jurisprudences

Cal Jur 3d Sch § 336.

§ 21202. Recordation of judgment

A certified copy of the judgment of the court in the special proceeding shall be recorded in the office of the recorder of the county in which the action is brought and in the office of the recorder of every county in which any of the real property affected is situated.

(Stats.1976, c. 1010, § 2, operative April 30, 1977.)

Historical and Statutory Notes

Derivation: Educ.C.1959, § 31173 (Stats. 1959, c. 2, p. 1516, § 31173).

Educ.C.1943, § 24098 (Stats.1943, c. 71, p. 776).

Stats.1903, c. 7, p. 12, § 5.

§ 21203. Effect of judgment

The judgment of the court in the special proceeding is determinative of the terms and trusts upon which any property thereafter given for the benefit of the institution, or any department thereof, is held by the trustee or trustees, unless otherwise provided by the grantor or donor.

(Stats.1976, c. 1010, § 2, operative April 30, 1977.)

Historical and Statutory Notes

Derivation: Educ.C.1959, § 31174 (Stats. 1959, c. 2, p. 1516, § 31174).

Educ.C.1943, § 24099 (Stats.1943, c. 71, p. 776).

Stats.1903, c. 7, p. 13, § 6.

Library References

ALR Library

Construction and operation of private pension plan provision for distribution of pension funds upon termination of plan. 55 ALR3d 767.

Employer's liability for action of trustees or similar body administering employer's pension plan. 54 ALR3d 189.

Literature as to private pension plans: Statements in literature distributed to employees as controlling all the provisions of general plan. 50 ALR3d 1270.

Mandatory retirement of public officer or employee based on age. 81 ALR3d 811.

Legal Jurisprudences

Cal Jur 3d Sch § 336.

Am Jur 2d (Rev) Pensions and Retirement Funds §§ 1614 et seq.

Additional References

Cal Digest of Official Reports 3d Series, Pensions and Retirement Systems §§ 1 et seq., Schools § 35.

Chapter 2

[HEADING RENUMBERED]

The heading of Chapter 2, "Foundations, Trusts, and Institutions of Arts and Sciences", was renumbered Chapter 1 and amended by Stats. 1983, c. 142, § 10. See Education Code § 21100 et seq.

Part 13

STATE TEACHERS' RETIREMENT SYSTEM

STATE TEACHERS' RETIREMENT SYSTEM

Part 13 was added by Stats.1993, c. 893 (A.B.1796), § 2.

Former Part 13, "State Teachers' Retirement System", enacted by Stats.1976, c. 1010, § 2, consisting of §§ 22000 to 24944, was repealed by Stats.1993, c. 893 (A.B.1796), § 1.

Constitutional Provisions

Article 9, § 6, provides that amounts apportioned by the state are to be considered as derived from local taxes insofar as certain local retirement systems are concerned.

Historical and Statutory Notes

For legislative intent, continuing application, and subordination provisions relating to Stats. 1993, c. 893 (A.B.1796), see Historical and Statutory Notes under Education Code § 22000.

Cross References

Agreements for social security coverage, see Government Code § 22200 et seq.
Apportionment of funds, see Const. Art. 9, § 6.
Construction, effect on charter provisions concerning school employees, see Education Code §§ 44850, 87419.
Construction to preserve judicial rights and remedies, see Education Code §§ 44849, 87418.
Contributions made in carrying out contracts with governmental units, see Education Code § 33117.
County Employees Retirement Law of 1937, see Government Code § 31450 et seq.
County superintendents, retirement system contributions and benefits, see Education Code § 1204.
Deposits of public pension and retirement funds, see Government Code § 7520 et seq.

Exchange position, effect of acceptance on teacher's rights, see Education Code §§ 44854, 87423.

Exchange teachers, see Education Code §§ 44854, 44855, 87423, 87424.

Failure to present district system warrants on time, see Education Code §§ 42661, 85271.

Joint district salary retirement plans, see Education Code § 24900 et seq.

Public employees' retirement system, see Government Code § 20000 et seq.

Public pension and retirement plans, see Government Code § 7500 et seq.

Retiree benefit funds, see Education Code § 1350.

Retirement of employees of school districts as having effect of dismissal, see Education Code §§ 44907, 87467.

Teacher-assistant with temporary certificate, see Education Code § 44926.

Termination of school district employees, effect on retirement rights, see Education Code §§ 44956, 87744.

Waiver of provisions of code permissible except provisions of this part, see Education Code § 33050.

Code of Regulations References

Conflict of Interest Code, see 5 Cal. Code of Regs. § 22000.

Deposit of retirement annuity fund contributions, see 5 Cal. Code of Regs. § 20534.

Chapter 1

GENERAL PROVISIONS

Section

22000.   Short title.

22001.   Establishment of State Teachers' Retirement System.

22001.5. Finding and declaration; merger of plans; administration by board; short title.

22002.   Declaration of financing policies.

22003.   Revision of State Teachers' Retirement Law; construction.

22004.   Memorandum of understanding; conflict with provisions.

22004.1. Repealed.

22004.2. Repealed.

22005.   Tax exemption.

22006.   Rights or benefits not subject to execution or other process; exception; unassignability.

22007.   Duration of obligation.

22008.   Limitation of actions; collection of overpayments.

22009.   Severability of part.

22010.   Repealed.

22011 to 22013.   Repealed.

Chapter 1 was added by Stats.1993, c. 893 (A.B.1796), § 2.

§ 22000.   Short title

This part may be known and cited as the E. Richard Barnes Act and together with Part 14 (commencing with Section 26000) shall be known as the Teachers' Retirement Law.

(Added by Stats.1993, c. 893 (A.B.1796), § 2. Amended by Stats.1999, c. 939 (S.B. 1074), § 1.)

Historical and Statutory Notes

Sections 3 and 4 of Stats.1993, c. 893 (A.B. 1796), provide:

"Sec. 3.   It is the intent of the Legislature in enacting this act to reorganize and clarify the State Teachers' Retirement Law and thus facilitate its administration. It is not the intent of the Legislature to make any substantive change in the law. Thus, if, in the opinion of any court or administrative officer, a different result under any provision of the State Teachers' Retirement Law as it read on December 31, 1993, would occur because of the enactment of this act, the provision as it read on December 31, 1993, shall be followed and the result shall be as it would have been on December 31, 1993. Further, it is the intent of the Legislature that no new or additional rights vest in any member, retirant, or beneficiary as a result of the enactment of this act. No provision of this act may be interpreted to vest any such new or additional right. No dollar amount of any current or future benefit under this act shall be revised in any way because of the enactment of this act.

"Sec. 4. Any section of any act enacted in 1993 at the 1993–94 Regular Session of the Legislature that amends, adds, or repeals any section of the State Teachers' Retirement Law (Part 13 (commencing with Section 22000) of the Education Code) and that is chaptered either before or after this act is chaptered shall prevail over this act."

Section 90 of Stats.1999, c. 939 (S.B.1074), provides:

"SEC. 90. Any section of any act enacted by the Legislature during the 1999 calendar year that takes effect on or before January 1, 2000, and that amends, amends and renumbers, adds, repeals and adds, or repeals a section that is amended, amended and renumbered, repealed and added, or repealed by this act, shall prevail over this act, whether that act is enacted prior to, or subsequent to, the enactment of this act. The repeal, or repeal and addition, of any article, chapter, part, title, or division of any code by this act shall not become operative if any section or any other act that is enacted by the Legislature during the 1999 calendar year and takes effect on or before January 1, 2000, amends, amends and renumbers, adds, repeals and adds, or repeals any section contained in that article, chapter, part, title, or division."

Section affected by two or more acts at the same session of the legislature, see Government Code § 9605.

Former § 22000, enacted by Stats.1976, c. 1010, § 2, providing a short title for Part 13, was repealed by Stats.1993, c. 893 (A.B.1796), § 1. See, now, this section.

Derivation: Former § 22000, enacted by Stats.1976, c. 1010, § 2.

Educ.C.1959, § 13801, added by Stats.1969, c. 896, p. 1738, § 2, amended by Stats.1972, c. 361, p. 672, § 1.

Educ.C.1959, § 13802, enacted by Stats.1959, c. 2, p. 983, § 13802.

Educ.C.1943, § 14252, added by Stats.1944, 4th Ex.Sess., c. 13, p. 115, § 2.

Educ.C.1943, § 14276 (Stats.1943, c. 71, p. 591).

School C. § 5.879, added by Stats.1937, c. 626, p. 1740, § 4, amended by Stats.1939, c. 1040, p. 2868, § 16.

Cross References

Charter schools, participation in State Teacher's Retirement System, see Education Code § 47611. Exclusion from state retirement system of persons subject to teachers' retirement law, see Government Code § 20300.

Law Review and Journal Commentaries

Retirement Systems Act, proposed amendments to the act. (1945) 33 Cal.L.Rev. 434.

Library References

Schools ⚎146.
Westlaw Topic No. 345.
C.J.S. Schools and School Districts §§ 338, 340 to 343, 346.

Legal Jurisprudences
Cal Jur 3d Pens § 6; Sch § 368; Univ & C § 41.

Treatises and Practice Aids

Witkin, Procedure (4th ed) Admin Proc § 150.

Forms

B-W Cal Civil Practice: Family Law Litigation §§ 6:67, 6:84.

Notes of Decisions

Amendments 7
Contractual relationship 3
Obligation of state 4
Persons covered 6
Purpose 1
Rules 8

Transfer of general funds 5

Vested rights　2

_____

1. Purpose

State teachers' retirement law was aimed at ends of providing substantial or reasonable pension for retirees, while assuring adequate funding of entire system. O'Connor v. State Teachers' Retirement System (App. 2 Dist. 1996) 51 Cal.Rptr.2d 540, 43 Cal.App.4th 1610, rehearing denied, review denied.

Prime purpose of the retirement system is to enable a teacher satisfactorily to protect herself for years of retirement and to nominate anyone she so desires or her estate as beneficiaries upon her death. Lyles v. Teachers Retirement Bd. (App. 5 Dist. 1963) 33 Cal.Rptr. 328, 219 Cal.App.2d 523.

2. Vested rights

The obligation of the state being to pay benefits of retired teachers only so far as it had obligated itself to do so, there was an obligation as to teachers already retired to pay the benefits, because the rights were vested, but as to teachers still on the active list there was only an expectancy which the state could take away at any time, even though contributions were compulsory. 4 Ops.Atty.Gen. 185 (1944).

3. Contractual relationship

The original Teachers' Retirement Act adopted in 1913, amended in 1924 and again in 1935, did not constitute a contractual relationship between the state of California and the teachers of the state who were affected by the act. 4 Ops.Atty.Gen. 185 (1944).

4. Obligation of state

The state had an obligation to pay benefits, even though the act itself did not make provision for sufficient funds to meet the payments, only to the extent that it had made itself obligated. 4 Ops.Atty.Gen. 185 (1944).

5. Transfer of general funds

Transfer of funds from general fund to teachers' retirement fund was compelled by continuing appropriation statutes, notwithstanding appropriations for payments of lesser amounts in annual budget bills enacted subsequently, in view of principles prohibiting impairment of contract. California Teachers Ass'n v. Cory (Teachers' Retirement Bd. of State Teachers' Retirement Ass'n) (App. 3 Dist. 1984) 202 Cal. Rptr. 611, 155 Cal.App.3d 494.

6. Persons covered

The benefits of the former public school retirement salary law were not limited to those who were members of the teaching force of the state when the act went into effect, in view of § 18 of the Retirement Salary Act (Stats.1913, p. 1423) thereof, declaring the act binding upon all teachers elected or appointed after approval of the act and who, not being in the service of the public schools at the time of its approval, were not competent to sign or deliver the statutory notification. Dean v. Clarke (App. 2 Dist. 1921) 53 Cal.App. 30, 199 P. 857.

7. Amendments

Record established that construction placed by defendant teachers' retirement board on statutory provisions, including 1957 amendments, governing computation of part-time teaching service was warranted as opposed to plaintiff teacher's construction that her retirement allowance should be computed on basis of years of service to which she was entitled to be credited under law existing prior to July 1, 1956. Cummings v. California State Teachers' Retirement Bd. (App. 1 Dist. 1966) 50 Cal.Rptr. 391, 241 Cal.App.2d 149.

Since a successful teachers' retirement system must be on a compulsory basis, the legislature may change the law in any way before retirement and the teachers already employed have a mere expectancy in any particular pension law, and the legislature may make the plan compulsory in regard to teachers already employed. 4 Ops.Atty.Gen. 185 (1944).

8. Rules

A rule adopted by the state board of education concerning the right of teachers to a retirement salary was of no effect if it conflicted with an act of the legislature. Dean v. Clarke (App. 2 Dist. 1921) 53 Cal.App. 30, 199 P. 857.

§ 22001.　Establishment of State Teachers' Retirement System

In order to provide a financially sound plan for the retirement, with adequate retirement allowances, of teachers in the public schools of this state, teachers in schools supported by this state, and other persons employed in connection with the schools, the State Teachers' Retirement System is established. The system is a unit of the State and Consumer Services Agency.

(Added by Stats.1993, c. 893 (A.B.1796), § 2.)

Historical and Statutory Notes

Legislative intent regarding Stats.1993, c. 893 (A.B.1796), including possible continuing application of provisions of repealed State Teachers' Retirement Law, see Historical and Statutory Notes under Education Code § 22000.

Former § 22001, enacted by Stats.1976, c. 1010, § 2, amended by Stats.1979, c. 520, § 1, relating to establishment of a state teachers' retirement system, was repealed by Stats.1993, c. 893 (A.B.1796), § 1. See this section.

Derivation: Former § 22001, enacted by Stats.1976, c. 1010, § 2, amended by Stats. 1979, c. 520, § 1.

Educ.C.1959, § 13802, added by Stats.1969, c. 896, p. 1738, § 2.

Educ.C.1959, § 13801, enacted by Stats.1959, c. 2, p. 983, § 13801; Stats.1969, c. 138, p. 299, § 33.

Educ.C.1943, § 14251, added by Stats.1944, 4th Ex.Sess., c. 13, p. 115, § 2.

Cross References

Agencies in state government, State and Consumer Services Agency, see Government Code § 12800.

Eligibility of members of another retirement system, see Education Code § 22516.

Establishment and control of funds, see Education Code § 22400 et seq.

Exclusion of members from state system, see Government Code § 20300.

State and Consumer Services Agency, composition, see Government Code § 12804.

Library References

Schools ☞146(1).
Westlaw Topic No. 345.
C.J.S. Schools and School Districts §§ 338, 340 to 343, 346.

Legal Jurisprudences
Cal Jur 3d Pens § 11; Sch § 368.
Am Jur 2d (Rev) Pensions and Retirement Funds §§ 1604 et seq.

Notes of Decisions

Funds 1

---

1. Funds

Transfer of funds from general fund to teachers' retirement fund was compelled by continuing appropriation statutes, notwithstanding appropriations for payments of lesser amounts in annual budget bills enacted subsequently, in view of principles prohibiting impairment of contract. California Teachers Ass'n v. Cory (Teachers' Retirement Bd. of State Teachers' Retirement Ass'n) (App. 3 Dist. 1984) 202 Cal. Rptr. 611, 155 Cal.App.3d 494.

§ 22001.5. Finding and declaration; merger of plans; administration by board; short title

The Legislature hereby finds and declares that on July 1, 1996, the State Teachers' Retirement System Cash Balance Plan was created and established to provide a retirement plan for persons employed to perform creditable service for less than 50 percent of the full-time equivalent for the position. The persons eligible for the Cash Balance Plan were excluded from mandatory membership in the State Teachers' Retirement System Defined Benefit Plan. Both plans are administered by the Teachers' Retirement Board. Prior to the creation and establishment of the Cash Balance Plan, the State Teachers' Retirement System Defined Benefit Plan had been identified simply as the State Teachers' Retirement System. As a result, the system was identified as both the administrative body and the retirement plan. The State Teachers' Retirement Law was amended to identify the retirement plan as the State Teachers' Retirement System Defined Benefit Plan in order to distinguish that plan from the Cash Balance Plan. Because both plans were intended to provide for the retirement of teachers and other persons employed in connection with public schools of this state and schools supported by this state, a merger of these two plans is now hereby made for the purpose of establishing a single retirement plan that shall be known and may be cited as the State Teachers' Retirement Plan consisting of the different benefit programs set forth in this part and Part 14 (commencing with Section 26000). This plan shall be administered by the Teachers' Retirement Board as set forth in this part and Part 14 (commencing with Section 26000). This part, together with Part 14 (commencing with Section 26000) shall be known and may be cited as the Teachers' Retirement Law.

(Added by Stats.1998, c. 1048 (S.B.2085), § 1.)

§ 22002.   Declaration of financing policies

The Legislature recognizes that the assets of the State Teachers' Retirement Plan with respect to the Defined Benefit Program are insufficient to meet the obligations of that program already accrued or to accrue in the future with respect to service credited to members of that program prior to July 1, 1972. Therefore, the Legislature declares the following policies with respect to the financing of the Defined Benefit Program of the State Teachers' Retirement Plan:

(a) Members shall contribute a percentage of creditable compensation, unless otherwise specified in this part.

(b) Employers shall contribute a percentage of the total creditable compensation on which member contributions are based.

(c) The state shall contribute a sum certain for a given number of years for the purpose of payment of benefits under this part.

(Added by Stats.1993, c. 893 (A.B.1796), § 2. Amended by Stats.1996, c. 634 (S.B. 2041), § 1; Stats.1997, c. 482 (S.B.471), § 1; Stats.1998, c. 965 (A.B.2765), § 1.)

Historical and Statutory Notes

Legislative intent regarding Stats.1993, c. 893 (A.B.1796), including possible continuing application of provisions of repealed State Teachers' Retirement Law, see Historical and Statutory Notes under Education Code § 22000.

Former § 22002, enacted by Stats.1976, c. 1010, § 2, providing financing policies for the retirement system, was repealed by Stats.1993, c. 893 (A.B.1796), § 1. See this section.

Derivation: Former § 22002, enacted by Stats.1976, c. 1010, § 2.

Educ.C.1959, § 13804, added by Stats.1971, c. 1305, p. 2568, § 2.

Educ.C.1959, § 13804, added by Stats.1969, c. 896, p. 1738, § 2.

Educ.C.1959, § 14215, enacted by Stats.1959, c. 2, p. 1015, § 14215.

Educ.C.1943, § 14561, added by Stats.1944, 4th Ex.Sess., c. 13, p. 135, § 2.

Cross References

Eligibility of members of another retirement system, see Education Code § 22516.
Establishment and control of funds, see Education Code § 22400 et seq.
Exclusion of members from state system, see Government Code § 20300.
State and Consumer Services Agency, composition, see Government Code § 12804.

Library References

Legal Jurisprudences
Cal Jur 3d Pens § 11.

Am Jur 2d (Rev) Pensions and Retirement Funds §§ 1604 et seq.

Notes of Decisions

Salary scale 1

___

1. **Salary scale**

The state teachers' retirement system under Educ.C.1959, § 14109 could properly use a sal-ary scale which considered only seniority and merit increases in fixing member contributions under the state teachers' retirement law. 50 Ops.Atty.Gen. 43, 9–8–67.

§ 22003. Revision of State Teachers' Retirement Law; construction

The revision of the State Teachers' Retirement Law, enacted at the 1971 and 1972 Regular Sessions of the Legislature, shall not be construed to affect benefits of persons retired prior to July 1, 1972, or their beneficiaries, except as specifically provided.

(Added by Stats.1993, c. 893 (A.B.1796), § 2.)

Historical and Statutory Notes

Legislative intent regarding Stats.1993, c. 893 (A.B.1796), including possible continuing application of provisions of repealed State Teachers' Retirement Law, see Historical and Statutory Notes under Education Code § 22000.

Former § 22003, enacted by Stats.1976, c. 1010, § 2, relating to administrative costs, was repealed by Stats.1993, c. 893 (A.B.1796), § 1. See Education Code § 22304.

Derivation: Former § 22009, enacted by Stats.1976, c. 1010, § 2.

Educ.C.1959, § 13805, added by Stats.1971, c. 1305, p. 2568, § 4, amended by Stats.1974, c. 1293, p. 2805, § 1.

§ 22004. Memorandum of understanding; conflict with provisions

If the provisions of this part are in conflict with the provisions of a memorandum of understanding reached pursuant to Chapter 12 (commencing with Section 3560) of Division 4 of Title 1 of the Government Code, the memorandum of understanding shall be controlling without further legislative action, except that if the provisions of a memorandum of understanding require the expenditure of funds, the provisions shall not become effective unless approved by the Legislature in the annual Budget Act.

(Added by Stats.1993, c. 893 (A.B.1796), § 2.)

Historical and Statutory Notes

Legislative intent regarding Stats.1993, c. 893 (A.B.1796), including possible continuing application of provisions of repealed State Teachers' Retirement Law, see Historical and Statutory Notes under Education Code § 22000.

Former § 22004, enacted by Stats.1976, c. 1010, § 2, relating to tax exemptions, was re-pealed by Stats.1993, c. 893 (A.B.1796), § 1. See Education Code § 22005.

Derivation: Former § 22013, added by Stats. 1979, c. 1072, § 1.

Cross References

Higher education and employer-employee relations, see Government Code § 3560 et seq.

Library References

Legal Jurisprudences

Cal Jur 3d Death & G Tax § 63.

§ 22004.1. Repealed by Stats.1993, c. 893 (A.B.1796), § 1

Historical and Statutory Notes

The repealed section, added by Stats.1984, c. 683, § 1, amended by Stats.1988, c. 382, § 1, related to future tax liabilities. See Education Code § 22314.

Legislative intent regarding Stats.1993, c. 893 (A.B.1796), including possible continuing appli- cation of provisions of repealed State Teachers' Retirement Law, see Historical and Statutory Notes under Education Code § 22000.

§ 22004.2. Repealed by Stats.1994, c. 933 (A.B.3171), § 1, eff. Sept. 28, 1994

Historical and Statutory Notes

The repealed section, added by Stats.1991, c. 543 (S.B.1171), § 1, amended by Stats.1993, c. 1082 (A.B.2278), § 1, related to limitations im- posed by the Internal Revenue Code with re- spect to benefit enhancements for certain mem- bers. Similar provisions were added by Stats. 1993, c. 893, § 2, as Education Code § 22317.

Repeal of this section by Stats.1993, c. 893 (A.B.1796), § 1, failed to become operative.

See Stats.1993, c. 893 (A.B.1796), § 4, in the Historical and Statutory Notes under Education Code § 22000, and Government Code § 9605.

Legislative intent regarding Stats.1993, c. 893 (A.B.1796), including possible continuing appli- cation of provisions of repealed State Teachers' Retirement Law, see Historical and Statutory Notes under Education Code § 22000.

§ 22005. Tax exemption

The right of a person to a pension, retirement allowance, return of contribu- tions, any optional benefit, or any other right accrued or accruing to any person under this part is exempt from taxation, including any inheritance tax, whether state, county, municipal, or district.

(Added by Stats.1993, c. 893 (A.B.1796), § 2.)

Historical and Statutory Notes

Legislative intent regarding Stats.1993, c. 893 (A.B.1796), including possible continuing appli- cation of provisions of repealed State Teachers' Retirement Law, see Historical and Statutory Notes under Education Code § 22000.

Former § 22005, enacted by Stats.1976, c. 1010, § 2, amended by Stats.1980, c. 173, § 3; Stats.1981, c. 528, § 2; Stats.1982, c. 497, § 86, providing that retirement rights or benefits were not subject to process or attachment, was

repealed by Stats.1993, c. 893 (A.B.1796), § 1. See Education Code § 22006.

Derivation: Former § 22004, enacted by Stats.1976, c. 1010, § 2.

Educ.C.1959, § 13807, added by Stats.1969, c. 896, p. 1738, § 2.

Educ.C.1959, § 13836, enacted by Stats.1959, c. 2, p. 986, § 13836.

Educ.C.1943, § 14278, added by Stats.1955, c. 1506, p. 2747, § 2.

Library References

Legal Jurisprudences
Cal Jur 3d Pens § 16.

Treatises and Practice Aids
Miller & Starr, Cal Real Estate 2d § 31:25.

Additional References

Cal Digest of Official Reports 3d Series, Pen- sions and Retirement Systems § 7.

Notes of Decisions

Income tax   1

state income tax on their retirement benefits.
63 Ops.Atty.Gen. 213, 3–14–80.

1. Income tax

This section, does not exempt members of the state teachers' retirement system from paying

§ 22006. Rights or benefits not subject to execution or other process; exception; unassignability

The right of a person to an annuity or a retirement allowance, to the return of contributions, the annuity, or retirement allowance itself, any optional benefit, any other right or benefit accrued or accruing to any person under this part, and the moneys in the fund created under this part are not subject to execution or any other process whatsoever, except to the extent permitted by Section 704.110 of the Code of Civil Procedure, and are unassignable except as specifically provided in this part.

(Added by Stats.1993, c. 893 (A.B.1796), § 2. Amended by Stats.1996, c. 634 (S.B. 2041), § 2.)

Historical and Statutory Notes

Legislative intent regarding Stats.1993, c. 893 (A.B.1796), including possible continuing application of provisions of repealed State Teachers' Retirement Law, see Historical and Statutory Notes under Education Code § 22000.

Former § 22006, enacted by Stats.1976, c. 1010, § 2, amended by Stats.1977, c. 659, § 1; Stats.1982, c. 5, § 1, relating to the duration of obligations under the retirement system, was repealed by Stats.1993, c. (A.B.1796), § 1. See Education Code § 22007.

Derivation: Former § 22005, enacted by Stats.1976, c. 1010, § 2, amended by Stats.

1980, c. 173, § 3; Stats.1981, c. 528, § 2; Stats. 1982, c. 497, § 86.

Educ.C.1959, § 13808, added by Stats.1969, c. 896, p. 1738, § 2.

Educ.C.1959, § 14407, enacted by Stats.1959, c. 2, p. 1035, § 14407.

Educ.C.1943, § 14666, added by Stats.1944, 4th Ex.Sess., c. 13, p. 144, § 2.

Educ.C.1943, § 14503 (Stats.1943, c. 71, p. 611).

School C. § 5.865, added by Stats.1937, c. 626, p. 1736, § 4.

Library References

Treatises and Practice Aids
Witkin, Procedure (4th ed) Enf Judgm § 194.

§ 22007. Duration of obligation

The obligations of any member, or the member's beneficiaries, to this system and the Defined Benefit Program continue throughout membership, and thereafter until all of the obligations of this system and the Defined Benefit Program to or in respect to the member or the member's beneficiaries have been discharged.

(Added by Stats.1993, c. 893 (A.B.1796), § 2. Amended by Stats.1996, c. 634 (S.B. 2041), § 3; Stats.1999, c. 939 (S.B.1074), § 2.)

Historical and Statutory Notes

Legislative intent regarding Stats.1993, c. 893 (A.B.1796), including possible continuing appli-

cation of provisions of repealed State Teachers'

Retirement Law, see Historical and Statutory Notes under Education Code § 22000.

Former § 22007, added by Stats.1982, c. 5, § 3, amended by Stats.1988, c. 739, § 1; Stats. 1989, c. 118, § 1, relating to limitation of actions on collection of overpayments, was repealed by Stats.1993, c. 893 (A.B.1796), § 1. See Education Code § 22008.

Former § 22007, enacted by Stats.1976, c. 1010, § 2, amended by Stats.1977, c. 659, § 2,

relating to limitation of actions, was repealed by Stats.1982, c. 5, p. 5, § 2.

Derivation: Former § 22006, amended by Stats.1982, c. 5, § 1.

Educ.C.1959, § 13810, added by Stats.1969, c. 896, p. 1738, § 2.

Educ.C.1959, § 14127.1, added by Stats.1963, c. 1552, p. 3138, § 2, amended by Stats.1967, c. 1093, p. 2729, § 6.

Cross References

State Teachers' Retirement System, beneficiary designation, discharge of liability, see Education Code § 23302.

§ 22008. Limitation of actions; collection of overpayments

For the purposes of payments into or out of the retirement fund for adjustments of errors or omissions with respect to the Defined Benefit Program or the Defined Benefit Supplement Program, the period of limitation of actions shall be applied, except as provided in Sections 23302 and 24613, as follows:

(a) No action may be commenced by or against the board, the system, or the plan more than three years after all obligations to or on behalf of the member, former member, beneficiary, or annuity beneficiary have been discharged.

(b) If the system makes an error that results in incorrect payment to a member, former member, beneficiary, or annuity beneficiary, the system's right to commence recovery shall expire three years from the date the incorrect payment was made.

(c) If an incorrect payment is made due to lack of information or inaccurate information regarding the eligibility of a member, former member, beneficiary, or annuity beneficiary to receive benefits under the Defined Benefit Program or Defined Benefit Supplement Program, the period of limitation shall commence with the discovery of the incorrect payment.

(d) Notwithstanding any other provision of this section, if an incorrect payment has been made on the basis of fraud or intentional misrepresentation by a member, beneficiary, annuity beneficiary, or other party in relation to or on behalf of a member, beneficiary, or annuity beneficiary, the three-year period of limitation shall not be deemed to commence or to have commenced until the system discovers the incorrect payment.

(e) The collection of overpayments under subdivisions (b), (c), and (d) shall be made pursuant to Section 24617.

(Added by Stats.1993, c. 893 (A.B.1796), § 2. Amended by Stats.1996, c. 1165 (A.B. 3032), § 1; Stats.1999, c. 939 (S.B.1074), § 3; Stats.2000, c. 74 (A.B.1509), § 1.)

Historical and Statutory Notes

Legislative intent regarding Stats.1993, c. 893 (A.B.1796), including possible continuing application of provisions of repealed State Teachers' Retirement Law, see Historical and Statutory Notes under Education Code § 22000.

Former § 22008, enacted by Stats.1976, c. 1010, § 2, derived from Educ.C.1959, § 13812, added by Stats.1969, c. 896, § 2, amended by Stats.1971, c. 1305, § 5; Stats.1974, c. 1293, § 7; Educ.C.1959, § 13833, enacted by Stats.

1959, c. 2, § 13833; Educ.C.1943, § 14276.7, added by Stats.1955, c. 1395, § 4, amended by Stats.1956, 1st Ex.Sess., c. 55, § 3, relating to exclusion of overtime from compensation, was repealed by Stats.1981, c. 124, § 1.

Derivation: Former § 22007, added by Stats. 1982, c. 5, § 3, amended by Stats.1988, c. 739, § 1; Stats.1989, c. 118, § 1.

Former § 22007, enacted by Stats.1976, c. 1010, § 2, amended by Stats.1977, c. 659, § 2.

Educ.C.1959, § 13811, added by Stats.1969, c. 896, p. 1738, § 2, amended by Stats.1971, c. 1004, p. 1921, § 2; Stats.1974, c. 1293, p. 2805, § 6.

Educ.C.1959, § 14127.1, added by Stats.1963, c. 1552, p. 3138, § 2, amended by Stats.1967, c. 1093, p. 2729, § 6.

Cross References

State Teachers' Retirement System, beneficiary designation, discharge of liability, see Education Code § 23302.

Library References

Legal Jurisprudences
Am Jur 2d (Rev) Pensions and Retirement Funds §§ 1727 et seq.

§ 22009.   Severability of part

If any provision of this part or the application thereof to any person or circumstance is held invalid, that invalidity shall not affect other provisions or applications of this part that can be given effect without the invalid provision or application, and to this end the provisions of this part are severable.
(Added by Stats.1993, c. 893 (A.B.1796), § 2.)

Historical and Statutory Notes

Legislative intent regarding Stats.1993, c. 893 (A.B.1796), including possible continuing application of provisions of repealed State Teachers' Retirement Law, see Historical and Statutory Notes under Education Code § 22000.

Former § 22009, enacted by Stats.1976, c. 1010, § 2, relating to the effect of revision of the

retirement law, was repealed by Stats.1993, c. 893 (A.B.1796), § 1.   See Education Code § 22003.

Derivation: Former § 22011 enacted by Stats.1976, c. 1010, § 2.

Educ.C.1959, § 13815, added by Stats.1974, c. 1293, p. 2806, § 8.

Library References

Statutes ☞64(2).
Westlaw Topic No. 361.

C.J.S. Statutes §§ 87, 89 to 90, 94 to 97, 99, 102 to 104, 107.

§ 22010.   Repealed by Stats.1981, c. 124, p. 864, § 2

Historical and Statutory Notes

The repealed section, enacted by Stats.1976, c. 1010, § 2, derived from Educ.C.1959,

§ 13814, added by Stats.1973, c. 1029, § 1, related to benefits for surviving spouses.

§§ 22011 to 22013.   Repealed by Stats.1993, c. 893 (A.B.1796), § 1

Historical and Statutory Notes

Section 22011, enacted by Stats.1976, c. 1010, § 2, related to severability of provisions. See Education Code § 22009.

Section 22012, enacted by Stats.1976, c. 1010, § 2, provided authority of the retirement

board to enter into contracts with retirement systems of other states.   See Education Code § 22205.

Chapter 2

DEFINITIONS

Chapter 2 was added by Stats.1994, c. 933 (A.B.3171), § 3, eff. Sept. 28, 1994.

Former Chapter 2, "Definitions", added by Stats.1993, c. 893 (A.B. 1796), § 2, comprising §§ 22100 to 22174, was repealed by Stats.1994, c. 933 (A.B.3171), § 2, eff. Sept. 28, 1994. See Education Code § 22100 et seq.

§ 22100. Construction of chapter

Unless the context otherwise requires, the definitions set forth in this chapter govern the construction of this part.

(Added by Stats.1994, c. 933 (A.B.3171), § 3, eff. Sept. 28, 1994.)

Historical and Statutory Notes

Former § 22100, added by Stats.1993, c. 893 (A.B.1796), § 2, relating to construction of former Chapter 2, "Definitions", was repealed by Stats.1994, c. 933 (A.B.3171), § 2, eff. Sept. 28, 1994. See this section.

Former § 22100, enacted by Stats.1976, c. 1010, § 2, relating to the construction of former chapter 2, was repealed by Stats.1993, c. 893 (A.B.1796), § 1. See this section.

Derivation: Former § 22100, added by Stats. 1993, c. 893, § 2.

Former § 22100, enacted by Stats.1976, c. 1010, § 2.

Educ.C.1959, § 13820, added by Stats.1969, c. 896, p. 1738, § 2.

Educ.C.1959, § 13803 (Stats.1959, c. 2, p. 983, § 13803).

Educ.C.1943, § 14253, added by Stats.1944, 4th Ex.Sess., c. 13, p. 115, § 2.

Educ.C.1943, § 14251 (1943, c. 71, p. 590).

School C. § 5.801, added by Stats.1937, c. 626, p. 1717, § 4.

Library References

Legal Jurisprudences

Cal Jur 3d Sch § 368.

§ 22101. Accumulated annuity deposit contributions

"Accumulated annuity deposit contributions" means the sum of all the annuity deposits standing to the credit of the member's account, together with credited interest.

(Added by Stats.1994, c. 933 (A.B.3171), § 3, eff. Sept. 28, 1994.)

Historical and Statutory Notes

Former § 22101, added by Stats.1993, c. 893 (A.B.1796), § 2, relating to accumulated annuity deposit contributions, was repealed by Stats. 1994, c. 933 (A.B.3171), § 2, eff. Sept. 28, 1994. See this section.

Former § 22101, enacted by Stats.1976, c. 1010, § 2, amended by Stats.1986, c. 717, § 1, defining "accumulated retirement contributions", was repealed by Stats.1993, c. 893 (A.B. 1796), § 1. See Education Code § 22102.

Derivation: Former § 22101, added by Stats. 1993, c. 893, § 2.

Former § 22102, enacted by Stats.1976, c. 1010, § 2.

Educ.C.1959, § 13822, added by Stats.1969, c. 896, p. 1738, § 2, amended by Stats.1971, c. 407, p. 776, § 2; Stats.1974, c. 1293, p. 2806, § 11.

Educ.C.1959, § 13814 (Stats.1959, c. 2, p. 983, § 13814).

Educ.C.1943, § 14263, added by Stats.1944, 4th Ex.Sess., c. 13, p. 116, § 2.

Educ.C.1943, § 14261 (Stats.1943, c. 71, p. 590).

School C. § 5.801, added by Stats.1937, c. 626, p. 1717, § 4.

Code of Regulations References

Deposit of retirement annuity fund contributions, see 5 Cal. Code of Regs. § 20534.

§ 22101.5. Accumulated defined benefit supplement account balance

Text of section as added by Stats.2000, c. 74 (A.B.1509), § 3.

"Accumulated Defined Benefit Supplement account balance" means an amount equal to the sum of member contributions, the member contributions picked up by an employer, employer contributions, and interest credited on those contributions pursuant to Section 25005, that are credited by the system to the member's Defined Benefit Supplement account.

(Added by Stats.2000, c. 1021 (A.B.2700), § 1.)

For another section of the same number, added by Stats.2000, c. 1021 (A.B.2700), § 1, see Education Code § 22101.5, post.

Historical and Statutory Notes

Section 1 of Stats.2000, c. 1021 (A.B.2700), also added a § 22101.5, related to the same subject matter.

§ 22101.5.   Accumulated defined benefit supplement account balance

Text of section as added by Stats.2000, c. 1021 (A.B.2700), § 1.

"Accumulated Defined Benefit Supplement account balance" means credits equal to the sum of member contributions, the member contributions picked up by an employer, employer contributions, interest credited pursuant to Section 25005 and additional earnings credited pursuant to Section 25006.

(Added by Stats.2000, c. 1021 (A.B.2700), § 1.)

For another section of the same number, added by Stats.2000, c. 74 (A.B.1509), § 3, see Education Code § 22101.5, ante.

Historical and Statutory Notes

Section 3 of Stats.2000, c. 74 (A.B.1509), also added a § 22101.5, related to the same subject matter.

Section 69 of Stats.2000, c. 1021 (A.B.2700), provides:

"The provisions of this act, other than Sections 3, 4, 8, 13, 27, 30, 31, 34, 35, 36, 37, and 68, shall become operative only if Chapter 74 of the Statutes of 2000 becomes effective on or before January 1, 2001." [Stats.2000, c. 74 became effective Jan. 1, 2001.]

§ 22102.   Accumulated retirement contributions

"Accumulated retirement contributions" means the sum of the member contributions, the member contributions picked up by an employer pursuant to Sections 22903 and 22904, and credited interest on those contributions. Accumulated retirement contributions shall not include accumulated annuity deposit contributions, accumulated tax-sheltered annuity contributions, accumulated Defined Benefit Supplement account balance, or additional earnings credit.

(Added by Stats.1994, c. 933 (A.B.3171), § 3, eff. Sept. 28, 1994. Amended by Stats. 2000, c. 74 (A.B.1509), § 2; Stats.2000, c. 1021 (A.B.2700), § 2.)

Historical and Statutory Notes

Operative effect of Stats.2000, c. 1021 (A.B. 2700), see Historical and Statutory Notes following Education Code § 22101.5.

Section affected by two or more acts at the same session of the legislature, see Government Code § 9605.

Former § 22102, added by Stats.1993, c. 893 (A.B.1796), § 2, relating to accumulated retirement contributions, was repealed by Stats.1994, c. 933 (A.B.3171), § 2, eff. Sept. 28, 1994. See this section.

Former § 22102, enacted by Stats.1976, c. 1010, § 2, defining "accumulated annuity deposit contributions'', was repealed by Stats. 1993, c. 893 (A.B.1796), § 1. See Education Code § 22101.

Derivation: Former § 22102, added by Stats. 1993, c. 893, § 2.

Former § 22101, enacted by Stats.1976, c. 1010, § 2, amended by Stats.1986, c. 717, § 1.

Educ.C.1959, § 13821, added by Stats.1971, c. 1305, p. 2569, § 9, amended by Stats.1974, c. 1293, p. 2806, § 10.

Educ.C.1959, § 13821, added by Stats.1969, c. 896, p. 1738, § 2, amended by Stats.1971, c. 407, p. 776, § 1.

Educ.C.1959, § 13816 (Stats.1959, c. 2, p. 984, § 13816).

Educ.C.1943, § 14263.7, added by Stats.1944, 4th Ex.Sess., c. 13, p. 116, § 2.

Code of Regulations References

Deposit of retirement annuity fund contributions, see 5 Cal. Code of Regs. § 20534.

§ 22103.   Accumulated tax-sheltered annuity contributions

"Accumulated tax-sheltered annuity contributions" means the tax-sheltered contributions made by a member and standing to the credit of the member's account, together with credited interest.

(Added by Stats.1994, c. 933 (A.B.3171), § 3, eff. Sept. 28, 1994.)

Historical and Statutory Notes

Former § 22103, added by Stats.1993, c. 893 (A.B.1796), § 2, relating to accumulated tax-sheltered annuity contributions, was repealed by Stats.1994, c. 933 (A.B.3171), § 2, eff. Sept. 28, 1994. See this section.

Former § 22103, enacted by Stats.1976, c. 1010, § 2, defining "accumulated tax-sheltered annuity contributions", was repealed by Stats. 1993, c. 893 (A.B.1796), § 1. See this section.

Derivation: Former § 22103, added by Stats. 1993, c. 893, § 2.

Former § 22103, enacted by Stats.1976, c. 1010, § 2.

Educ.C.1959, § 13823, added by Stats.1969, c. 896, p. 1738, § 2, amended by Stats.1971, c. 407, p. 776, § 3; Stats.1974, c. 1293, p. 2806, § 12.

Educ.C.1959, § 13817.1, added by Stats.1963, c. 2170, p. 4552, § 2.

Cross References

Death benefit, payment, see Education Code § 23800.
Disability retirement allowance, see Education Code § 24100.
Records and accounts, see Education Code § 22218.

§ 22104.   Actuarial equivalent

"Actuarial equivalent" means an allowance of equal value when computed upon the basis of such tables and interest rates that are adopted by the board.

(Added by Stats.1994, c. 933 (A.B.3171), § 3, eff. Sept. 28, 1994.)

Historical and Statutory Notes

Former § 22104, added by Stats.1993, c. 893 (A.B.1796), § 2, defining actuarial equivalent, was repealed by Stats.1994, c. 933 (A.B.3171), § 2, eff. Sept. 28, 1994. See this section.

Former § 22104, enacted by Stats.1976, c. 1010, § 2, amended by Stats.1982, c. 5, § 4, defining "actuarial equivalent", was repealed by Stats.1993, c. 893 (A.B.1796), § 1. See this section.

Derivation: Former § 22104, added by Stats. 1993, c. 893, § 2.

Former § 22104, enacted by Stats.1976, c. 1010, § 2, amended by Stats.1982, c. 5, § 4.

Educ.C.1959, § 13824, added by Stats.1969, c. 896, p. 1738, § 2, amended by Stats.1971, c. 407, p. 776, § 4.

Educ.C.1959, § 13823 (Stats.1959, c. 2, p. 984, § 13823).

Educ.C.1943, § 14270, added by Stats.1944, 4th Ex.Sess., c. 13, p. 116, § 2.

Educ.C.1943, § 14268 (Stats.1943, c. 71, p. 591).

School C. § 5.801, added by Stats.1937, c. 626, p. 1717, § 4.

§ 22104.5. Actuary

"Actuary" means a person professionally trained in the technical and mathematical aspects of insurance, pensions, and related fields who has been appointed by the board for the purpose of actuarial services required under this part.

(Added by Stats.1999, c. 939 (S.B.1074), § 4.)

§ 22104.7. Additional earnings credit

"Additional earnings credit" means an amount derived from investment income for the plan year as determined by the board by plan amendment and added to members' Defined Benefit Supplement accounts in addition to the amount credited at the minimum interest rate for that plan year.

(Added by Stats.2000, c. 74 (A.B.1509), § 4.)

§ 22104.9. Annuitant reserve

"Annuitant Reserve" means a segregated account within the retirement fund established and maintained for expenditure on annuities payable under the Defined Benefit Supplement Program.

(Added by Stats.2000, c. 74 (A.B.1509), § 5.)

§ 22105. Annuity

(a) "Annuity," with respect to the Defined Benefit Program, means payments for life derived from the "accumulated annuity deposit contributions" of a member.

(b) "Annuity," with respect to the Defined Benefit Supplement Program, means an alternative payment arrangement wherein a benefit based on the balance of credits in a member's Defined Benefit Supplement account is paid monthly rather than in a lump-sum.

(Added by Stats.1994, c. 933 (A.B.3171) § 3, eff. Sept. 28, 1994. Amended by Stats. 2000, c. 74 (A.B.1509), § 6.)

Historical and Statutory Notes

Former § 22105, added by Stats.1993, c. 893 (A.B.1796), § 2, defining annuity, was repealed by Stats.1994, c. 933 (A.B.3171), § 2, eff. Sept. 28, 1994. See this section.

Former § 22105, enacted by Stats.1976, c. 1010, § 2, derived from Educ.C.1959, § 13824.5, added by Stats.1971, c. 1305, § 10, amended by Stats.1972, c. 1010, § 1.5; Stats. 1974, c. 545, § 13; Stats.1974, c. 1293, § 13, defining "annual salary", was repealed by Stats. 1981, c. 124, § 3.

Derivation: Former § 22105, added by Stats. 1993, c. 893, § 2.

Former § 22106, enacted by Stats.1976, c. 1010, § 2, amended by Stats.1981, c. 124, § 4.

Educ.C.1959, § 13825, added by Stats.1969, c. 896, p. 1738, § 2, amended by Stats.1971, c. 1305, p. 2569, § 11; Stats.1974, c. 1293, § 14.

Educ.C.1959, § 13818 (Stats.1959, c. 2, p. 984, § 13818).

Educ.C.1943, § 14265, added by Stats.1944, 4th Ex.Sess., c. 13, p. 116, § 2, amended by Stats.1955, c. 1395, p. 2491, § 1.1.

Educ.C.1943, § 14263 (Stats.1943, c. 71, p. 590).

School C. § 5.801, added by Stats.1937, c. 626, p. 1717, § 4.

§ 22105.5. Annuity beneficiary

"Annuity beneficiary" means the person or persons designated by a member pursuant to Section 25011 or 25018 to receive an annuity under the Defined Benefit Supplement Program upon the member's death.

(Added by Stats.2000, c. 74 (A.B.1509), § 7.)

§ 22106. Annuity deposit contributions

"Annuity deposit contributions" means additional contributions made by a member prior to July 1, 1972, above those required for credited service for the purpose of providing additional retirement income.

(Added by Stats.1994, c. 933 (A.B.3171), § 3, eff. Sept. 28, 1994. Amended by Stats. 2000, c. 1025 (A.B.816), § 1.)

Historical and Statutory Notes

Stats.2000, c. 1025 (A.B.816), § 41, provides:

"SEC. 41. Any section of any act enacted by the Legislature during the 2000 calendar year that takes effect on or before January 1, 2001, and that amends, amends and renumbers, adds, repeals and adds, or repeals a section that is amended, amended and renumbered, repealed and added, or repealed by this act, shall prevail over this act, whether that act is enacted prior to, or subsequent to, the enactment of this act. The repeal, or repeal and addition, of any article, chapter, part, title, or division of any code by this act shall not become operative if any section of any other act that is enacted by the Legislature during the 2000 calendar year and takes effect on or before January 1, 2001, amends, amends and renumbers, adds, repeals and adds, or repeals any section contained in that article, chapter, part, title, or division."

Section affected by two or more acts at the same session of the legislature, see Government Code § 9605.

Former § 22106, added by Stats.1993, c. 893 (A.B.1796), § 2, defining annuity deposit contributions, was repealed by Stats.1994, c. 933

(A.B.3171), § 2, eff. Sept. 28, 1994. See this section.

Former § 22106, enacted by Stats.1976, c. 1010, § 2, amended by Stats.1978, c. 870, § 1, defining "annuity", was repealed by Stats.1993, c. 893 (A.B.1796), § 1. See Education Code § 22105.

Derivation: Former § 22106, added by Stats. 1993, c. 893, § 2.

Former § 22107, enacted by Stats.1976, c. 1010, § 2.

Educ.C.1959, § 13827, added by Stats.1969, c. 896, p. 1738, § 2, amended by Stats.1974, c. 1293, p. 2807, § 15.

Educ.C.1959, § 13813, (Stats.1959, c. 2, p. 983, § 13813).

Educ.C.1943, § 14262, added by Stats.1944, 4th Ex.Sess., c. 13, p. 116, § 2, amended by Stats.1955, c. 1395, p. 2491, § 1.

Educ.C.1943, § 14260 (Stats.1943, c. 71, p. 590).

School C. § 5.801, added by Stats.1937, c. 626, p. 1717, § 4.

§ 22106.1. Base days

"Base days" means the number of days of creditable service required to earn one year of service credit.

(Added by Stats.1999, c. 939 (S.B.1074), § 5.)

§ 22106.2. Base hours

"Base hours" means the number of hours of creditable service required to earn one year of service credit.

(Added by Stats.1999, c. 939 (S.B.1074), § 6.)

§ 22106.5. Definitions

"Basis of employment" means the standard of time over which the employer expects service to be performed by an employee in the position during the school year.

(a) "Full-time basis" means a basis of employment that is full time.

(b) "Part-time basis" means a basis of employment that is less than full time.

(Added by Stats.1995, c. 390 (A.B.1122), § 1, operative July 1, 1996.)

§ 22107. Beneficiary

(a) "Beneficiary," with respect to the Defined Benefit Program, means any person or entity receiving or entitled to receive an allowance or lump-sum payment under the Defined Benefit Program because of the disability or death of a member.

(b) "Beneficiary," with respect to the Defined Benefit Supplement Program, means any person or entity receiving or entitled to receive a final benefit under the Defined Benefit Supplement Program upon the death of a member.

(Added by Stats.1994, c. 933 (A.B.3171), § 3, eff. Sept. 28, 1994. Amended by Stats. 1996, c. 634 (S.B.2041), § 4; Stats.2000, c. 74 (A.B.1509), § 8.)

Historical and Statutory Notes

Former § 22107, added by Stats.1993, c. 893 (A.B.1796), § 2, defining beneficiary, was repealed by Stats.1994, c. 933 (A.B.3171), § 2, eff. Sept. 28, 1994. See this section.

Former § 22107, enacted by Stats.1976, c. 1010, § 2, defining "annuity deposit contributions", was repealed by Stats.1993, c. 893 (A.B. 1796), § 1. See Education Code § 22106.

Derivation: Former § 22107, added by Stats. 1993, c. 893, § 2.

Former § 22108, enacted by Stats.1976, c. 1010, § 2, amended by Stats.1981, c. 124, § 4.

Educ.C.1959, § 13828, added by Stats.1969, c. 896, p. 1738, § 2, amended by Stats.1971, c. 1004, p. 1921, § 3; Stats.1974, c. 1153, p. 2445, § 1; Stats.1975, c. 806, p. 1838, § 1.

Educ.C.1959, § 13810 (Stats.1959, c. 2, p. 983, § 13810).

Educ.C.1943, § 14259, added by Stats.1944, 4th Ex.Sess., c. 13, p. 115, § 2.

Educ.C.1943, § 14257 (Stats.1943, c. 71, p. 590).

School C. § 5.801, added by Stats.1937, c. 626, p. 1717, § 4.

Cross References

Beneficiary designation, see Education Code § 23300 et seq.

Library References

Legal Jurisprudences
Am Jur 2d (Rev) Pensions and Retirement Funds §§ 1651 et seq.

§ 22108. Benefits

(a) "Benefit" or "benefits ," with respect to the Defined Benefit Program, means any monthly payment due a retired member, disabled member, or beneficiary, and includes lump-sum payments due on account of death.

(b) "Benefit" and "benefits," with respect to the Defined Benefit Supplement Program, means an amount equal to the balance of credits in a member's Defined Benefit Supplement account.

(Added by Stats.1994, c. 933 (A.B.3171), § 3, eff. Sept. 28, 1994. Amended by Stats. 1996, c. 634 (S.B.2041), § 5; Stats.2000, c. 74 (A.B.1509), § 9.)

Historical and Statutory Notes

Former § 22108, added by Stats.1993, c. 893 (A.B.1796, § 2, defining benefits, was repealed by Stats.1994, c. 933 (A.B.3171), § 2, eff. Sept. 28, 1994. See this section.

Former § 22108, enacted by Stats.1976, c. 1010, § 2, amended by Stats.1981, c. 124, § 4, defining "beneficiary", was repealed by Stats. 1993, c. 893 (A.B.1796), § 1. See Education Code § 22107.

Derivation: Former § 22108, added by Stats. 1993, c. 893, § 2.

Former § 22109, enacted by Stats.1976, c. 101, § 2.

Educ.C.1959, § 13828.4, added by Stats.1971, c. 1305, p. 2569, § 13, amended by Stats.1972, c. 1010, p. 1858, § 2.

§ 22109. Board

"Board" means the Teachers' Retirement Board.

(Added by Stats.1994, c. 933 (A.B.3171), § 3, eff. Sept. 28, 1994.)

Historical and Statutory Notes

Former § 22109, added by Stats.1993, c. 893 (A.B.1796, § 2, defining board, was repealed by Stats.1994, c. 933 (A.B.3171), § 2, eff. Sept. 28, 1994. See this section.

Former § 22109, enacted by Stats.1976, c. 1010, § 2, defining "benefits", was repealed by Stats.1993, c. 893 (A.B.1796), § 1. See Education Code § 22108.

Derivation: Former § 22109, added by Stats. 1993, c. 893, § 2.

Former § 22110, enacted by Stats.1976, c. 1010, § 2.

Educ.C.1959, § 13829, added by Stats.1969, c. 896, p. 1738, § 2.

Cross References

Retirement Board, see Education Code § 22000 et seq.

§ 22109.5. Break in service; final compensation determination

"Break in service," for purposes of determining a member's final compensation, means:

(a) With respect to service of a member employed as a full-time employee and service performed by a member employed as a part-time employee, any period of time covering a pay period during which a member is on an unpaid leave or absence or a pay period in which a member has not performed any creditable service.

(b) For a member who has been employed in a substitute position:

(1) And has a change in assignment during a school year to a full-time or part-time position, a break in service is determined on the same basis as for the full-time or part-time employment during the same school year.

(2) For less than 50 percent of their teaching career for which service is credited, a break in service is determined on the same basis as full-time employment.

(3) For more than 50 percent of their teaching career for which service is credited, a break in service is any period of time within a school year for which compensation is not paid and service is not credited.

(c) If a member commenced performing service at the beginning of a school term, July and August of the school year are not a break in service; however, if the member commenced performing service after the school term begins, the previous July and August are a break in service.

325

(d) Earnable salaries for a full pay period, but not beyond the effective date of retirement, shall be used in determining final compensation when the member performed service within that pay period.

(Added by Stats.1999, c. 939 (S.B.1074), § 7.)

§ 22110. California service

"California service" means service performed in California for which credit may be given.

(Added by Stats.1994, c. 933 (A.B.3171), § 3, eff. Sept. 28, 1994.)

Historical and Statutory Notes

Former § 22110, added by Stats.1993, c. 893 (A.B.1796, § 2, defining California service, was repealed by Stats.1994, c. 933 (A.B.3171), § 2, eff. Sept. 28, 1994. See this section.

Former § 22110, enacted by Stats.1976, c. 1010, § 2, defining "board", was repealed by Stats.1993, c. 893 (A.B.1796), § 1. See Education Code § 22109.

Derivation: Former § 22110, added by Stats. 1993, c. 893, § 2.

Former § 22111, enacted by Stats.1976, c. 1010, § 2.

Educ.C.1959, § 13829.5, added by Stats.1971, c. 1305, p. 2569, § 14.

§ 22110.1. Cash balance benefit program

"Cash Balance Benefit Program" means the benefit program of the State Teachers' Retirement Plan as set forth in Part 14 (commencing with Section 26000).

(Added by Stats.1996, c. 634 (S.B.2041), § 6. Amended by Stats.1998, c. 1048 (S.B. 2085), § 2.)

§ 22110.2. Credentials; certificate

"Credential," "credentials," and "certificate" mean any life diploma, credential, certificate, or other document provided for, by, and issued pursuant to the laws of the state that authorize service in the public school system of this state.

(Added by Stats.1996, c. 634 (S.B.2041), § 6.5.)

Cross References

Diplomas and certificates, generally, see Education Code § 51400 et seq.

§ 22110.5. Certificated

"Certificated" means the holding by a person of a credential that is required by the laws of the state to be held as a condition to valid employment in the position in which the person is employed.

(Added by Stats.1996, c. 634 (S.B.2041), § 7.)

Cross References

Certificated and certified, defined, see Education Code § 90.
Certificated employees, generally, see Education Code § 44420 et seq.

§ 22111. Child's portion; children's portion

"Child's portion" or "children's portion" means the amount of a disability allowance, disability retirement allowance, family allowance, or survivor benefit allowance payable for a dependent child or dependent children.

(Added by Stats.1996, c. 1165 (A.B.3032), § 3.)

Historical and Statutory Notes

Former § 22111, added by Stats.1994, c. 933 (A.B.3171), § 3, relating to the definition of "child" or "children" under the disability allowance and family allowance programs, was repealed by Stats.1996, c. 1165 (A.B.3032), § 2. See Education Code § 22123.

Former § 22111, added by Stats.1993, c. 893 (A.B.1796, § 2, defining child or children under the disability allowance and family allowance programs, was repealed by Stats.1994, c. 933 (A.B.3171), § 2, eff. Sept. 28, 1994. See this section.

Former § 22111, enacted by Stats.1976, c. 1010, § 2, defining "California service", was repealed by Stats.1993, c. 893 (A.B.1796), § 1. See Education Code § 22110.

§ 22112. Repealed by Stats.1996, c. 1165 (A.B.3032), § 4

Historical and Statutory Notes

The repealed section, added by Stats.1994, c. 933 (A.B.3171), § 3, derived from former § 22111, added by Stats.1993, c. 893, § 2, related to the definition of "child" or "children" under the disability retirement and survivor benefits programs. See Education Code § 22123.

Former § 22112, added by Stats.1993, c. 893 (A.B.1796), § 2, derived from former § 22112.5, added by Stats.1992, c. 1166 (S.B.1885), § 1.5,

defining child or children under the disability retirement and survivor benefits program, was repealed by Stats.1994, c. 933 (A.B.3171), § 2, eff. Sept. 28, 1994. See this section.

Former § 22112, enacted by Stats.1976, c. 1010, § 2, amended by Stats.1977, c. 36, § 93; Stats.1986, c. 717, § 2; Stats.1992, c. 1167 (S.B.1886), § 1, defining "child" and "children", was repealed by Stats.1993, c. 893 (A.B. 1796), § 1. See Education Code § 22111.

§ 22112.5. Class of employees

(a) "Class of employees" means a number of employees considered as a group because they are employed to perform similar duties, are employed in the same type of program, or share other similarities related to the nature of the work being performed.

(b) A class of employees may be comprised of one person if no other person employed by the employer performs similar duties, is employed in the same type of program, or shares other similarities related to the nature of the work being performed and that same class is in common use among other employers.

(c) The board shall have the right to override the determination by an employer as to whether or not a group or an individual constitutes a "class of employees" within the meaning of this section.

(d) The amendments to this section during the 1995–96 Regular Session of the Legislature shall be deemed to have become operative on July 1, 1996.

(Added by Stats.1995, c. 390 (A.B.1122), § 2, operative July 1, 1996. Amended by Stats.1996, c. 1165 (A.B.3032), § 5, operative July 1, 1996.)

Historical and Statutory Notes

Former § 22112.5, added by Stats.1992, c. 1166 (S.B.1885), § 1.5, related to children un-

der the disability retirement and survivor benefits programs and was repealed by Stats.1993,

c. 893 (A.B.1796), § 1. See Education Code § 22112.

§ 22112.6. Special education programs; change to regular school year; days of service; election

Notwithstanding Section 22112.5, any county office of education that, prior to January 1, 1997, operated a special education program for up to 225 days, and changes that program to a regular school year of not less than 180 school days with an extended year of not more than 45 days effective July 1, 1998, may consider days of service in defining not more than two classes of employees, subject to the following:

(a) Members employed in the 225–day program prior to October 1, 1997, may remain in a class of employees for whom full-time service is 216 days per year.

(b) Any of those members may elect to belong to a second class of employees for whom full-time service is fewer than 216 days per year, but not less than the minimum standard specified in paragraph (1) of subdivision (b) of Section 22138.5, if both of the following conditions exist:

(1) The election is made on or before June 30, 1998, and is effective July 1, 1998.

(2) The election is nonrevocable.

(c) All certificated employees hired on or after October 1, 1997, shall belong to the class of employees specified in subdivision (b).

(d) This section shall not apply to certificated employees whose base year is determined pursuant to subparagraph (A) or (B) of paragraph (2) of subdivision (b) of Section 22138.5.

(Added by Stats.1997, c. 572 (A.B.686), § 1.)

Cross References

Certificated and certified, defined, see Education Code § 90.
Certificated employees, generally, see Education Code § 44420 et seq.
Special education programs, generally, see Education Code § 56000 et seq.
State, defined, see Education Code § 77.

§ 22112.8. Repealed by Stats.1993, c. 893 (A.B.1796), § 1

Historical and Statutory Notes

The repealed section, added by Stats.1992, c. 1167 (S.B.1886), § 2, defined comparable level position. See Education Code § 22113.

Legislative intent regarding Stats.1993, c. 893 (A.B.1796), including possible continuing appli-

cation of provisions of repealed State Teachers' Retirement Law, see Historical and Statutory Notes under Education Code § 22000.

§ 22113. Comparable level position

"Comparable level position" means any job in which the member can earn 66⅔ percent or more of indexed final compensation.

(Added by Stats.1994, c. 933 (A.B.3171), § 3, eff. Sept. 28, 1994.)

Historical and Statutory Notes

Former § 22113, added by Stats.1993, c. 893 (A.B.1796, § 2, defining comparable level position, was repealed by Stats.1994, c. 933 (A.B. 3171), § 2, eff. Sept. 28, 1994. See this section.

Former § 22113, enacted by Stats.1976, c. 1010, § 2, amended by Stats.1979, c. 430, § 1; Stats.1987, c. 76, § 1, defining "compensation

earnable", was repealed by Stats.1993, c. 893 (A.B.1796), § 1. See Education Code § 22115.

Derivation: Former § 22113, added by Stats. 1993, c. 893, § 2.

Former § 22112.8, added by Stats.1992, c. 1167 (S.B.1886), § 2.

§ 22113.1. Repealed by Stats.1993, c. 893 (A.B.1796), § 1

Historical and Statutory Notes

The repealed section, added by Stats.1979, c. 430, § 2, defined compensation earnable. See Education Code § 22116.

Legislative intent regarding Stats.1993, c. 893 (A.B.1796), including possible continuing appli-

cation of provisions of repealed State Teachers' Retirement Law, see Historical and Statutory Notes under Education Code § 22000.

§ 22114. Repealed by Stats.1996, c. 1165 (A.B.3032), § 6

Historical and Statutory Notes

The repealed section, added by Stats.1994, c. 933 (A.B.3171), § 3, defined compensation and salary. See Education Code § 22119.2.

Former § 22114, added by Stats.1993, c. 893 (A.B.1796), § 2, relating to compensation and salary, was repealed by Stats.1994, c. 933 (A.B. 3171), § 2, eff. Sept. 28, 1994. See this section.

Former § 22114, enacted by Stats.1976, c. 1010, § 2, amended by Stats.1977, c. 36, § 94; Stats.1981, c. 124, § 5; Stats.1985, c. 1497, § 1; Stats.1986, c. 717, § 3; Stats.1987, c. 76, § 2; Stats.1991, c. 543, § 2; Stats.1993, c. 468,

§ 1, relating to compensation and salary, was repealed by Stats.1994, c. 933 (A.B.3171), § 4, eff. Sept. 28, 1994. See this section.

Stats.1993, c. 893, § 1, provided for the repeal of § 22114, which was also amended by Stats.1993, c. 468. Stats.1993, c. 893, § 2, provided for the addition of another § 22114. Subordination of legislation by Stats.1993, c. 893, see Historical and Statutory Notes under Education Code § 22000. Section affected by two or more acts at the same session of the legislature, see Government Code § 9605.

§ 22114.5. Repealed by Stats.1993, c. 893 (A.B.1796), § 1

Historical and Statutory Notes

The repealed section, added by Stats.1982, c. 279, § 1, defined contribution rate for additional service credit. See Education Code § 22117.

Legislative intent regarding Stats.1993, c. 893 (A.B.1796), including possible continuing appli-

cation of provisions of repealed State Teachers' Retirement Law, see Historical and Statutory Notes under Education Code § 22000.

§ 22115. Compensation earnable

Text of section prior to amendment by Stats.2000, c. 1021 (A.B.2700), § 3.

(a) "Compensation earnable" means the annual creditable compensation that a person would earn in a school year if he or she were employed on a full-time basis and if that person worked full time in that position.

(b) The board may determine compensation earnable for persons employed on a part-time basis.

(c) For purposes of determining final compensation for persons employed on a part-time basis, compensation earnable shall be determined by dividing the creditable compensation earned by the service credit.

(Added by Stats.1994, c. 933 (A.B.3171), § 5, eff. Sept. 28, 1994; Stats.1994, c. 933 (A.B.3171) § 5.5, eff. Sept. 28, 1994, operative Jan. 1, 1995. Amended by Stats.1995, c. 390 (A.B.1122), § 3, operative July 1, 1996; Stats.1996, c. 634 (S.B.2041), § 8; Stats. 1997, c. 482 (S.B.471), § 2.)

> *For text of section as amended by Stats.2000, c. 1021 (A.B.2700), § 3, see Education Code § 22115, post.*

§ 22115. Compensation earnable

> *Text of section as amended by Stats.2000, c. 1021 (A.B.2700), § 3.*

(a) "Compensation earnable" means the creditable compensation a person could earn in a school year for creditable service performed on a full-time basis, excluding service for which contributions are credited by the system to the Defined Benefit Supplement Program.

(b) The board may determine compensation earnable for persons employed on a part-time basis.

(c) When service credit for a school year is less than 1.000, compensation earnable shall be the product obtained when creditable compensation paid in that year is divided by the service credit for that year, except as provided in subdivision (d).

(d) When a member earns creditable compensation at multiple pay rates during a school year and service credit at the highest pay rate is at least .900 of a year, compensation earnable shall be determined as if all service credit for that year had been earned at the highest pay rate. This subdivision shall be applicable only for purposes of determining final compensation. When a member earns creditable compensation at multiple pay rates during a school year and service credit at the highest pay rate is less than .900 of a year, compensation earnable shall be determined pursuant to subdivision (c).

(e) The amendments to this section made during the second year of the 1999–2000 Regular Session shall become operative on July 1, 2002, if the revenue limit cost-of-living adjustment computed by the Superintendent of Public Instruction for the 2001–02 fiscal year is equal to or greater than 3.5 percent. Otherwise the amendments to this section made during the second year of the 1999–2000 Regular Session shall become operative on July 1, 2003 .

(Added by Stats.1994, c. 933 (A.B.3171), § 5, eff. Sept. 28, 1994; Stats.1994, c. 933 (A.B.3171) § 5.5, eff. Sept. 28, 1994, operative Jan. 1, 1995. Amended by Stats.1995, c. 390 (A.B.1122), § 3, operative July 1, 1996; Stats.1996, c. 634 (S.B.2041), § 8; Stats. 1997, c. 482 (S.B.471), § 2; Stats.2000, c. 1021 (A.B.2700), § 3.)

Operative Effect

> *This section becomes operative upon the earlier of the events specified in subd. (e), or July 1, 2003.*

> *For text of section prior to amendment by Stats.2000, c. 1021 (A.B. 2700), § 3, see Education Code § 22115, ante.*

Historical and Statutory Notes

Section 108 of Stats.1994, c. 933 (A.B.3171), provides:

"Sections 5.5 and 6.5 of this act incorporate changes in the State Teachers' Retirement Law proposed by AB 3832 (Chapter 193 of the Statutes of 1994), and shall become operative on January 1, 1995, the date on which AB 3832 takes effect, at which time Section 5 of this act shall cease to be operative."

Section affected by two or more acts at the same session of the legislature, see Government Code § 9605.

Operative effect of Stats.2000, c. 1021 (A.B. 2700), see Historical and Statutory Notes following Education Code § 22101.5.

Section 70 of Stats.2000, c. 1021 (A.B.2700), provides:

"The Teachers' Retirement Board shall promptly notify the Secretary of State if and when the condition specified in Sections 3, 4, 5, 27, 30, and 31 of this act has been satisfied to cause those sections to become operative on July 1, 2002."

Former § 22115, added by Stats.1993, c. 893 (A.B.1796, § 2, amended by Stats.1994, c. 193 (A.B.3832), § 1, defining compensation earnable and full time, was repealed by Stats.1994, c. 933 (A.B.3171), § 2, eff. Sept. 28, 1994. See this section.

Former § 22115, enacted by Stats.1976, c. 1010, § 2, defining "county", was repealed by Stats.1993, c. 893 (A.B.1796), § 1. See Education Code § 22118.

Derivation: Former § 22115, added by Stats. 1993, c. 893, § 2, amended by Stats.1994, c. 193, c. 1.

Former § 22113, enacted by Stats.1976, c. 1010, § 2, amended by Stats.1979, c. 430, § 1; Stats.1987, c. 76, § 1.

Educ.C.1959, § 13831, added by Stats.1969, c. 896, p. 1738, § 2.

Educ.C.1959, § 13831 (Stats.1959, c. 2, p. 985, § 13831).

Educ.C.1943, § 14276.5 added by Stats.1953, c. 1779, p. 3556, § 2.

Notes of Decisions

Full-time positions   1

---

1. Full-time positions

State teachers' retirement law required that retirement allowance of employees who held two full-time teaching positions during four-year periods prior to their retirements be based on aggregate of each teacher's salaries up to equivalent of single, full-time position; law limited total amount of service credit a member could earn, doing so by utilizing one full-time position as yardstick, and member could earn no more than one year of credited service in any academic year, regardless of amount of work actually performed and number of jobs actually held. O'Connor v. State Teachers' Retirement System (App. 2 Dist. 1996) 51 Cal.Rptr.2d 540, 43 Cal.App.4th 1610, rehearing denied, review denied.

Teacher who held two full-time teaching positions prior to retirement was not denied due process or equal protection by ruling of State Teachers' Retirement Board that his retirement allowance would be based on single, full-time position; same calculation was employed for all teachers falling under same category. O'Connor v. State Teachers' Retirement System (App. 2 Dist. 1996) 51 Cal.Rptr.2d 540, 43 Cal. App.4th 1610, rehearing denied, review denied.

§ 22115.2. Concurrent membership; rights of members

"Concurrent membership" means membership in the Defined Benefit Program by an individual who is credited with service that is not used as a basis for benefits under any other public retirement system and is also a member of the California Public Employees' Retirement System, the Legislators' Retirement System, the University of California Retirement System, county retirement systems established under Chapter 3 (commencing with Section 31450) of Part 3 of Division 4 of Title 3 of the Government Code, or the San Francisco City and County Employees' Retirement System. A member with concurrent membership shall have the right to the following:

(a) Have final compensation determined pursuant to subdivision (c) of Section 22134.

(b) Redeposit accumulated retirement contributions pursuant to Section 23201.

331

(c) Apply for retirement pursuant to paragraph (2) of subdivision (a) of Section 24201.

(Added by Stats.1999, c. 939 (S.B.1074), § 8.)

§ 22115.5. Concurrent retirement; eligibility

(a) "Concurrent retirement" entitles a member of the Defined Benefit Program to retire for service from the State Teachers' Retirement System and from at least one of the retirement systems with which the member has concurrent membership, as defined in Section 22115.2, on the same date or on different dates provided that the member does not perform creditable service subject to coverage under the other system or the Defined Benefit Program between the two retirement dates.

(b) A retired member who is subsequently employed in a position subject to membership in a public retirement system, specified in Section 22115.2, shall not be eligible for concurrent retirement.

(Added by Stats.1999, c. 939 (S.B.1074), § 9.)

§ 22116. Repealed by Stats.1995, c. 390 (A.B.1122), § 4, operative July 1, 1996

Historical and Statutory Notes

The repealed section, added by Stats.1994, c. 933 (A.B.3171), § 3, derived from former § 22116, added by Stats.1993, c. 893, § 2, defined compensation earnable for part-time employees, and was repealed by its own terms.

Former § 22116, added by Stats.1993, c. 893 (A.B.1796, § 2, defining compensation earnable,

was repealed by Stats.1994, c. 933 (A.B.3171), § 2, eff. Sept. 28, 1994. See this section.

Former § 22116, enacted by Stats.1976, c. 1010, § 2, defining "county superintendent", was repealed by Stats.1993, c. 893 (A.B.1796), § 1. See Education Code § 22119.

§ 22117. Contribution rate for additional service credit

"Contribution rate for additional service credit" means the contribution rate adopted by the board as a plan amendment with respect to the Defined Benefit Program for the purchase of service credit. This rate shall be based upon the most recent valuation of the plan with respect to the Defined Benefit Program and increased to include any subsequently required contribution rates designated for funding subsequent allowance increases.

(Added by Stats.1994, c. 933 (A.B.3171), § 3, eff. Sept. 28, 1994. Amended by Stats. 1996, c. 634 (S.B.2041), § 9; Stats.1998, c. 965 (A.B.2765), § 2.)

Historical and Statutory Notes

Former § 22117, added by Stats.1993, c. 893 (A.B.1796, § 2, defining contribution rate for additional service credit, was repealed by Stats. 1994, c. 933 (A.B.3171), § 2, eff. Sept. 28, 1994. See this section.

Former § 22117, enacted by Stats.1976, c. 1010, § 2, amended by Stats.1981, c. 124, § 6,

defining "credit service", was repealed by Stats. 1993, c. 893 (A.B.1796), § 1. See Education Code § 22120.

Derivation: Former § 22117, added by Stats. 1993, c. 893, § 2.

Former § 22114.5, added by Stats.1982, c. 279, § 1.

§ 22117.5. Repealed by Stats.1993, c. 893 (A.B.1796), § 1

Historical and Statutory Notes

The repealed section, formerly § 22132.7, added by Stats.1987, c. 330, § 3, renumbered § 22117.5 and amended by Stats.1988, c. 382, § 2, defined custodian. See Education Code § 22121.

Legislative intent regarding Stats.1993, c. 893 (A.B.1796), including possible continuing application of provisions of repealed State Teachers' Retirement Law, see Historical and Statutory Notes under Education Code § 22000.

§ 22118. County

"County" includes "city and county."

(Added by Stats.1994, c. 933 (A.B.3171), § 3, eff. Sept. 28, 1994.)

Historical and Statutory Notes

Former § 22118, added by Stats.1993, c. 893 (A.B.1796, § 2, defining county, was repealed by Stats.1994, c. 933 (A.B.3171), § 2, eff. Sept. 28, 1994. See this section.

Former § 22118, enacted by Stats.1976, c. 1010, § 2, derived from Educ.C.1959, § 13834, added by Stats.1969, c. 896, § 2, amended by Stats.1974, c. 1293, § 16; Educ.C.1959, § 13824.3, added by Stats.1959, c. 1604, § 4, defining "death benefits", was repealed by Stats.1992, c. 1166 (S.B.1885), § 2.

Derivation: Former § 22118, added by Stats. 1993, c. 893, § 2.

Former § 22115, enacted by Stats.1976, c. 1010, § 2.

Educ.C.1959, § 13833, added by Stats.1969, c. 896 p. 1738, § 2.

Educ.C.1959, § 13826 (Stats.1959, c. 2, p. 984, § 13826).

Educ.C.1943, § 14273, added by Stats.1944, 4th Ex.Sess., c. 13, p. 116, § 2.

Educ.C.1943, § 14271 (Stats.1943, c. 71, p. 591).

School C. § 5.801, added by Stats.1937, c. 626, p. 1717, § 4.

§ 22118.5. Repealed by Stats.1993, c. 893 (A.B.1796), § 1

Historical and Statutory Notes

The repealed section, added by Stats.1992, c. 1167 (S.B.1886), § 3, defined dependent child. See Education Code § 22122.

Legislative intent regarding Stats.1993, c. 893 (A.B.1796), including possible continuing appli-

cation of provisions of repealed State Teachers' Retirement Law, see Historical and Statutory Notes under Education Code § 22000.

§ 22119. County superintendent

"County superintendent" means the county superintendent of schools.

(Added by Stats.1994, c. 933 (A.B.3171), § 3, eff. Sept. 28, 1994.)

Historical and Statutory Notes

Former § 22119, added by Stats.1993, c. 893 (A.B.1796, § 2, defining county superintendent, was repealed by Stats.1994, c. 933 (A.B.3171), § 2, eff. Sept. 28, 1994. See this section.

Former § 22119, enacted by Stats.1976, c. 1010, § 2, defining "dependent parent", was repealed by Stats.1993, c. 893 (A.B.1796), § 1. See Education Code § 22123.

Derivation: Former § 22119, added by Stats. 1993, c. 893, § 2.

Former § 22116, enacted by Stats.1976, c. 1010, § 2.

Educ.C.1959, § 13833.5, added by Stats.1969, c. 896, p. 1738, § 2.

Educ.C.1959, § 13828 (Stats.1959, c. 2, p. 984, § 13828).

Educ.C.1943, § 14275, added by Stats.1944, 4th Ex.Sess., c. 13, p. 117, § 2.

Educ.C.1943, § 14273 (Stats.1943, c. 71, p. 591).

School C. § 5.801, added by Stats.1937, c. 626, p. 1717, § 4.

Cross References

County superintendents of schools,
    Generally, see Education Code § 1200 et seq.
    Election or appointment and salaries, see Const. Art. 9, § 3 et seq.

§ 22119.2.   Creditable compensation; violation of reporting requirements

Text of section operative until July 1, 2002, or
July 2, 2003, as set forth in subd. (f).

(a) "Creditable compensation" means salary and other remuneration payable in cash by an employer to a member for creditable service. Creditable compensation shall include:

(1) Money paid in accordance with a salary schedule based on years of training and years of experience for creditable service performed up to and including the full-time equivalent for the position in which the service is performed.

(2) For members not paid according to a salary schedule, money paid for creditable service performed up to and including the full-time equivalent for the position in which the service is performed.

(3) Money paid for the member's absence from performance of creditable service as approved by the employer, except as provided in paragraph (7) of subdivision (b).

(4) Member contributions picked up by an employer pursuant to Section 22903 or 22904.

(5) Amounts deducted by an employer from the member's salary, including deductions for participation in a deferred compensation plan; deductions for the purchase of annuity contracts, tax-deferred retirement plans, or other insurance programs; and deductions for participation in a plan that meets the requirements of Section 125, 401(k), or 403(b) of Title 26 of the United States Code.

(6) Money paid by an employer in addition to salary paid under paragraph (1) or (2) if paid to all employees in a class in the same dollar amount, the same percentage of salary, or the same percentage of the amount being distributed.

(7) Money paid in accordance with a salary schedule by an employer to an employee for achieving certification from a national board based, in part, on years of training or years of experience in teaching service, if the compensation is paid by the employer to all employees who achieved this certification.

(8) Any other payments the board determines to be "creditable compensation."

(b) "Creditable compensation" does not mean and shall not include:

(1) Money paid for service performed in excess of the full-time equivalent for the position.

(2) Money paid for overtime or summer school service, or money paid for the aggregate service performed as a member of the Defined Benefit Program in excess of one year of service credit for any one school year.

(3) Money paid for service that is not creditable service pursuant to Section 22119.5.

(4) Money paid by an employer in addition to salary paid under paragraph (1) or (2) of subdivision (a) if not paid to all employees in a class in the same dollar amount, the same percentage of salary, or the same percentage of the amount being distributed, except as provided in paragraph (7) of subdivision (a).

(5) Fringe benefits provided by an employer.

(6) Job-related expenses paid or reimbursed by an employer.

(7) Money paid for unused accumulated leave.

(8) Severance pay or compensatory damages or money paid to a member in excess of salary as a compromise settlement.

(9) Annuity contracts, tax-deferred retirement programs, or other insurance programs, including, but not limited to, plans that meet the requirements of Section 125, 401(k), or 403(b) of Title 26 of the United States Code that are purchased by an employer for the member and are not deducted from the member's salary.

(10) Any payments determined by the board to have been made by an employer for the principal purpose of enhancing a member's benefits under the Defined Benefit Program. An increase in the salary of a member who is the only employee in a class pursuant to subdivision (b) of Section 22112.5 that arises out of an employer's restructuring of compensation during the member's final compensation period shall be presumed to have been granted for the principal purpose of enhancing benefits under the Defined Benefit Program and shall not be creditable compensation. If the board determines sufficient evidence is provided to the system to rebut this presumption, the increase in salary shall be deemed creditable compensation.

(11) Any other payments the board determines not to be "creditable compensation."

(c) Any employer or person who knowingly or willfully reports compensation in a manner inconsistent with subdivision (a) or (b) shall reimburse the plan for any overpayment of benefits that occurs because of that inconsistent reporting and may be subject to prosecution for fraud, theft, or embezzlement in accordance with the Penal Code. The system may establish procedures to ensure that compensation reported by an employer is in compliance with this section.

(d) The definition of "creditable compensation" in this section is designed in accordance with sound funding principles that support the integrity of the retirement fund. These principles include, but are not limited to, consistent treatment of compensation throughout the career of the individual member, consistent treatment of compensation for an entire class of employees, the prevention of adverse selection, and the exclusion of adjustments to, or increases in, compensation for the principal purpose of enhancing benefits.

(e) This section shall be deemed to have become operative on July 1, 1996.

(f) This section shall become inoperative on July 1, 2002, if the revenue limit cost-of-living adjustment computed by the Superintendent of Public Instruction for the 2001–02 fiscal year is equal to or greater than 3.5 percent. Otherwise this section shall become inoperative on July 1, 2003 and as of January 1, 2004, this section is repealed, unless a later enacted statute, that becomes operative on or before January 1, 2004, deletes or extends the dates on which it becomes inoperative and is repealed.

(Added by Stats.1996, c. 1165 (A.B.3032), § 7, operative July 1, 1996. Amended by Stats.1997, c. 482 (S.B.471), § 3; Stats.1999, c. 939 (S.B.1074), § 10; Stats.2000, c. 1021 (A.B.2700), § 4; Stats.2001, c. 803 (S.B.501), § 1.)

Inoperative Date and Repeal

This section becomes inoperative on the earlier of the events specified in subd. (f), or July 1, 2003, and is repealed Jan. 1, 2004, under its own terms.

For text of section operative July 1, 2002, or July 1, 2003, as set forth in subd. (f) of this section, see Education Code § 22119.2, post.

Historical and Statutory Notes

Section 70 of Stats.2000, c. 1021 (A.B.2700), provides:

"The Teachers' Retirement Board shall promptly notify the Secretary of State if and when the condition specified in Sections 3, 4, 5, 27, 30, and 31 of this act has been satisfied to cause those sections to become operative on July 1, 2002."

Operative effect of Stats.2000, c. 1021 (A.B. 2700), see Historical and Statutory Notes following Education Code § 22101.5.

Section 52 of Stats.2001, c. 803 (S.B.501), provides:

"SEC. 52. Any section of any act enacted by the Legislature during the 2001 calendar year that takes effect on or before January 1, 2002, and that amends, amends and renumbers, adds, repeals and adds, or repeals a section that is amended, amended and renumbered, added, repealed and added, or repealed by this act, shall prevail over this act, whether that act is enacted prior to, or subsequent to, the enactment of this act."

Section affected by two or more acts at the same session of the legislature, see Government Code § 9605.

Derivation: Former § 22114, added by Stats. 1994, c. 933 (A.B.3171), § 3.

Former § 22114, added by Stats.1993, c. 893, 2.

Former § 22114, enacted by Stats.1976, c. 1010, § 2, amended by Stats.1977, c. 36, § 94; Stats.1981, c. 124, § 5; Stats.1985, c. 1497, § 1; Stats.1986, c. 717, § 3; Stats.1987, c. 76, § 2; Stats.1991, c. 543, § 2; Stats.1993, c. 468, § 1.

Educ.C.1959, § 13832, added by Stats.1969, c. 896, p. 1738, § 2, amended by Stats.1971, c. 931, § 1; Stats.1972, c. 1370, § 1; Stats.1973, c. 976, § 3; Stats.1975, c. 809, § 1; Stats.1976, c. 1308, § 1.

Educ.C.1959, § 13830 (Stats.1959, c. 2, p. 985, § 13830, amended by Stats.1963, c. 1541, § 1).

Educ.C.1943, § 14276, added by Stats.1944, 4th Ex.Sess., c. 13, p. 117, § 2, amended by Stats.1955, c. 1395, § 2.

Educ.C.1943, § 14274 (Stats.1943, c. 71, p. 591).

School C. § 5.801, added by Stats.1937, c. 626, p. 1717, § 4.

Cross References

Presumptions, see Evidence Code § 600 et seq.

§ 22119.2. Creditable compensation; violation of reporting requirements

Text of section operative July 1, 2002, or July 1, 2003, as set forth in subd. (g) of this section.

(a) "Creditable compensation" means remuneration that is payable in cash by an employer to all persons in the same class of employees and is paid to an employee for performing creditable service. Creditable compensation shall include:

(1) Salary paid in accordance with a salary schedule or employment agreement.

(2) Remuneration that is paid in addition to salary, providing it is payable to all persons who are in the same class of employees in the same dollar amount, the same percentage of salary, or the same percentage of the amount being distributed.

(3) Remuneration that is paid for the use of sick leave, vacation, and other employer-approved leave, except as provided in paragraph (4) of subdivision (c).

(4) Member contributions that are picked up by an employer pursuant to Section 22903 or 22904.

(5) Amounts that are deducted from a member's compensation, including, but not limited to, salary deductions for participation in a deferred compensation plan; deductions to purchase an annuity contract, tax- deferred retirement plan, or insurance program; and contributions to a plan that meets the requirements of Section 125, 401(k), or 403(b) of Title 26 of the United States Code.

(6) Any other payments the board determines to be "creditable compensation."

(b) Any salary or other remuneration determined by the board to have been paid for the principal purpose of enhancing a member's benefits under the plan shall not be credited under the Defined Benefit Program. Contributions on that compensation shall be credited to the Defined Benefit Supplement Program. A presumption by the board that salary or other remuneration was paid for the principal purpose of enhancing the member's benefits under the plan may be rebutted by the member or by the employer on behalf of the member. Upon receipt of sufficient evidence to the contrary, a presumption by the board that salary or other remuneration was paid for the principal purpose of enhancing the member's benefits under the plan may be reversed.

(c) "Creditable compensation" does not mean and shall not include:

(1) Remuneration that is not payable in cash or is not payable to all persons who are in the same class of employees.

(2) Remuneration that is paid for service that is not creditable service pursuant to Section 22119.5.

(3) Remuneration that is paid in addition to salary if it is not payable to all persons in the same class of employees in the same dollar amount, the same percentage of salary, or the same percentage of the amount being distributed pursuant to paragraph (2) of subdivision (a).

(4) Remuneration that is paid for unused accumulated leave.

(5) Annuity contracts, tax-deferred retirement plans, or insurance programs and contributions to plans that meet the requirements of Section 125, 401(k), or

403(b) of Title 26 of the United States Code when the cost is covered by an employer and is not deducted from the member's salary.

(6) Fringe benefits provided by an employer.

(7) Job-related expenses paid or reimbursed by an employer.

(8) Severance pay or compensatory damages or money paid to a member in excess of salary as a compromise settlement.

(9) Any other payments the board determines not to be "creditable compensation."

(d) An employer or individual who knowingly or willfully reports compensation in a manner inconsistent with subdivision (a) or (c) shall reimburse the plan for benefit overpayments that occur because of that inconsistent reporting and may be subject to prosecution for fraud, theft, or embezzlement in accordance with the Penal Code. The system may establish procedures to ensure that compensation reported by an employer is in compliance with this section.

(e) For purposes of this section, remuneration shall be considered payable if it would be paid to any person who meets the qualifications or requirements specified in a collective bargaining agreement or an employment agreement as a condition of receiving the remuneration.

(f) This definition of "creditable compensation" reflects sound principles that support the integrity of the retirement fund. Those principles include, but are not limited to, consistent treatment of compensation throughout a member's career, consistent treatment of compensation among an entire class of employees, preventing adverse selection, and excluding from compensation earnable remuneration that is paid for the principal purpose of enhancing a member's benefits under the plan. The board shall determine the appropriate crediting of contributions between the Defined Benefit Program and the Defined Benefit Supplement Program according to these principles, to the extent not otherwise specified pursuant to this part.

(g) The section shall become operative on July 1, 2002, if the revenue limit cost-of-living adjustment computed by the Superintendent of Public Instruction for the 2001–02 fiscal year is equal to or greater than 3.5 percent. Otherwise this section shall become operative on July 1, 2003.

(Added by Stats.2000, c. 1021 (A.B.2700), § 5.)

For text of section operative until July 1, 2002, or July 1, 2003, as set forth in subd. (g) of this section, see Education Code § 22119.2, ante.

Cross References

Presumptions, see Evidence Code § 600 et seq.

Library References

Schools ⊕146(6).
Westlaw Topic No. 345.

C.J.S. Schools and School Districts §§ 340, 342, 345.

§ 22119.5. Creditable service

(a) "Creditable service" means any of the following activities performed for an employer in a position requiring a credential, certificate, or permit pursuant to this code or under the appropriate minimum standards adopted by the Board of Governors of the California Community Colleges or under the provisions of an approved charter for the operation of a charter school for which the employer is eligible to receive state apportionment or pursuant to a contract between a community college district and the United States Department of Defense to provide vocational training:

(1) The work of teachers, instructors, district interns, and academic employees employed in the instructional program for pupils, including special programs such as adult education, regional occupation programs, child care centers, and prekindergarten programs pursuant to Section 22161.

(2) Education or vocational counseling, guidance, and placement services.

(3) The work of directors, coordinators, and assistant administrators who plan courses of study to be used in California public schools, or research connected with the evaluation or efficiency of the instructional program.

(4) The selection, collection, preparation, classification, demonstration, or evaluation of instructional materials of any course of study for use in the development of the instructional program in California public schools, or other services related to school curriculum.

(5) The examination, selection, in-service training, or assignment of teachers, principals or other similar personnel involved in the instructional program.

(6) School activities related to, and an outgrowth of, the instructional and guidance program of the school when performed in addition to other activities described in this section within the hours considered normal on a full-time basis for full-time employees of the employer.

(7) The work of nurses, physicians, speech therapists, psychologists, audiometrists, audiologists, and other school health professionals.

(8) Services as a school librarian.

(9) The work of employees who are responsible for the supervision of persons or administration of the duties described in this section.

(b) "Creditable service" also means the work of superintendents of California public schools.

(c) The board shall have final authority for determining creditable service to cover any activities not already specified.

(Added by Stats.1995, c. 394 (A.B.948), § 1, eff. Aug. 11, 1995; Stats.1995, c. 592 (A.B.1298), § 1. Amended by Stats.1996, c. 608 (A.B.2673), § 1, eff. Sept. 19, 1996, operative July 1, 1996.)

Historical and Statutory Notes

Section affected by two or more acts at the same session of the legislature, see Government Code § 9605.

Cross References

Adult education, education programs, state master plans, see Education Code § 8500 et seq.
Charter schools, generally, see Education Code § 47600 et seq.
Diplomas and certificates, generally, see Education Code § 51400 et seq.
State teachers' retirement system, reinstatement, service retirement allowance, see Education Code § 24209.3.

§ 22120. Credited interest

"Credited interest" means interest that is credited to active members' and inactive members', accumulated retirement contributions, and accumulated annuity deposit contributions at a rate set annually by the board as a plan amendment with respect to the Defined Benefit Program.

(Added by Stats.1994, c. 933 (A.B.3171), § 3, eff. Sept. 28, 1994. Amended by Stats. 1996, c. 634 (S.B.2041), § 10; Stats.1998, c. 965 (A.B.2765), § 3.)

Historical and Statutory Notes

Former § 22120, added by Stats.1993, c. 893 (A.B.1796, § 2, defining credited service, was repealed by Stats.1994, c. 933 (A.B.3171), § 2, eff. Sept. 28, 1994. See Education Code § 22121.

Former § 22120, enacted by Stats.1976, c. 1010, § 2, amended by Stats.1981, c. 124, § 10, defining "disabilitant", was repealed by Stats.

1993, c. 893 (A.B.1796), § 1. See Education Code § 22124.

Derivation: Former § 22141, added by Stats. 1993, c. 893, § 2.

Former § 22146, enacted by Stats.1976, c. 1010, § 2.

Educ.C.1959, § 13848.1, added by Stats.1971, c. 407, § 7.

§ 22121. Credited service

"Credited service" means service for which the required contributions have been paid.

(Added by Stats.1994, c. 933 (A.B.3171), § 3, eff. Sept. 28, 1994. Amended by Stats. 1998, c. 965 (A.B.2765), § 4.)

Historical and Statutory Notes

Former § 22121, added by Stats.1993, c. 893 (A.B.1796), § 2, defining custodian, was repealed by Stats.1994, c. 933 (A.B.3171), § 2, eff. Sept. 28, 1994. See Education Code § 22122.

Former § 22121, enacted by Stats.1976, c. 1010, § 2, amended by Stats.1981, c. 124, § 11, defining "disability allowance", was repealed by Stats.1993, c. 893 (A.B.1796), § 1. See Education Code § 22126.

Derivation: Former § 22120, added by Stats. 1993, c. 893, § 2.

Former § 22117, enacted by Stats.1976, c. 1010, § 2, amended by Stats.1981, c. 124, § 6.

Educ.C.1959, § 13833.7, added by Stats.1971, c. 1305, p. 2570, § 16.

§ 22122. Custodian

"Custodian" as used in Section 22359, means any bank or trust company that serves as custodian for safekeeping, delivery, securities valuation, investment performance reporting, and other services in connection with investment of the fund.

(Added by Stats.1994, c. 933 (A.B.3171), § 3, eff. Sept. 28, 1994. Amended by Stats. 1996, c. 634 (S.B.2041), § 11.)

Historical and Statutory Notes

Former § 22122, added by Stats.1993, c. 893 (A.B.1796), § 2, defining dependent child, was repealed by Stats.1994, c. 933 (A.B.3171), § 2, eff. Sept. 28, 1994. See Education Code § 22123.

Former § 22122, enacted by Stats.1976, c. 1010, § 2, amended by Stats.1977, c. 36, § 95; Stats.1978, c. 502, § 1; Stats.1980, c. 757, § 1; Stats.1992, c. 1167 (S.B.1886), § 4, defining "disability" or "disabled", was repealed by Stats.1993, c. 893 (A.B.1796), § 1. See Education Code § 22125.

Derivation: Former § 22121, added by Stats. 1993, c. 893, § 2.

Former § 22117.5, formerly § 22132.7, added by Stats.1987, c. 330, § 3, renumbered § 22117.5 and amended by Stats.1988, c. 382, § 2.

Cross References

Custodian services, retention of bank or trust company, see Education Code § 22359.

Library References

Legal Jurisprudences
Cal Jur 3d Sch § 368.

§ 22122.4. Death payment

"Death payment" means the amount payable upon the death of a member pursuant to Section 23801, 23851, or 23880.

(Added by Stats.1996, c. 634 (S.B.2041), § 12.)

§ 22122.5. Defined benefit program

"Defined Benefit Program" means the Defined Benefit Program provided in the State Teachers' Retirement Plan as set forth in this part.

(Added by Stats.1996, c. 634 (S.B.2041), § 13. Amended by Stats.1998, c. 1048 (S.B.2085), § 3.)

Library References

Legal Jurisprudences
Cal Jur 3d Fam Law § 819; Sch § 368.

§ 22122.7. Defined benefit supplement contributions

"Defined Benefit Supplement contributions" means member contributions and employer contributions that are credited by the system to the member's Defined Benefit Supplement account pursuant to Section 25004.

(Added by Stats.2000, c. 74 (A.B.1509), § 10.)

§ 22123. Dependent child or dependent children under disability allowance and family allowance programs; offspring; financially dependent; member

(a) "Dependent child" or "dependent children" under the disability allowance and family allowance programs means a member's unmarried offspring or stepchild who is not older than 22 years of age and who is financially dependent upon the member on the effective date of the member's disability allowance or the date of the member's death.

(b) "Offspring" shall include the member's child who is born within the 10–month period commencing on the earlier of the member's disability allowance effective date or the date of the member's death.

(c) "Offspring" shall include a child adopted by the member.

(d) "Dependent child" shall not include the member's offspring or stepchild who is adopted by a person other than the member's spouse.

(e) "Dependent child" under the family allowance program shall not include:

(1) The member's offspring or stepchild who was financially dependent on the member on the date of the member's death if a disability allowance was payable to the member prior to his or her death and the disability allowance did not include an amount payable for that offspring or stepchild.

(2) A stepchild or adopted child acquired subsequent to the death of the member.

(f) "Financially dependent" for purposes of this section means that at least one-half of the child's support was being provided by the member on the member's disability allowance effective date or the date of the member's death. The system may require that income tax records or other data be submitted to substantiate the child's financial dependence. In the absence of substantiating documentation, the system may determine that the child was not dependent on the effective date of the member's disability allowance or the date of the member's death.

(g) "Member" as used in this section shall have the same meaning specified in Section 23800.

(Added by Stats.1996, c. 1165 (A.B.3032), § 9. Amended by Stats.2001, c. 802 (S.B. 499), § 1.)

Historical and Statutory Notes

Another § 22123, added by Stats.1996, c. 1165 (A.B.3032), § 9.5, to become operative Jan. 1, 2002, relating to definitions, was repealed by Stats.2001, c. 802 (S.B.499), § 2. See this section.

Former § 22123, added by Stats.1994, c. 1994 (A.B.2171), § 3, derived from former § 22122, added by Stats.1993, c. 893, § 2, relating to the definition of "dependent child", was repealed by Stats.1996, c. 1165 (A.B.3032), § 8. See this section.

Former § 22123, added by Stats.1993, c. 893 (A.B.1796, § 2, defining dependent parent, was repealed by Stats.1994, c. 933 (A.B.3171), § 2, eff. Sept. 28, 1994. See Education Code § 22124.

Former § 22123, enacted by Stats.1976, c. 1010, § 2, defining "effective date", was repealed by Stats.1993, c. 893 (A.B.1796), § 1. See Education Code § 22129.

Derivation: Former § 22123, added by Stats. 1994, c. 533, § 3.

Former § 22111, added by Stats.1994, c. 938 (A.B.3171), § 3.

Former § 22111, added by Stats.1993, c. 893 (A.B.1796), § 2.

Former § 22112, added by Stats.1994, c. 933 (A.B.3171), § 3.

Former § 22112, added by Stats.1993, c. 893 (A.B.1796), § 2.

Former § 22112, enacted by Stats.1976, c. 1010, § 2, amended by Stats.1977, c. 36, § 93; Stats.1986, c. 717, § 2; Stats.1992, c. 1167 (S.B.1886), § 1.

Former § 22112.5, added by Stats.1992, c. 1166 (S.B.1885), § 1.5.

Former § 22118.5, added by Stats.1992, c. 1167 (S.B.1886), § 3.

Former § 22122, added by Stats.1993, c. 893 (A.B.1796), § 2.

Educ.C.1959, § 13830, added by Stats.1974, c. 1153, p. 2445, § 2.5; amended by Stats.1976, c. 1322, § 1.

Educ.C.1959, § 13830, added by Stats.1971, c. 1305, p. 2569, § 15.

Cross References

Computation of time,
Generally, see Code of Civil Procedure §§ 12 and 12a and Government Code § 6800 et seq.
Time in which any act provided by the Education Code is to be done, see Education Code § 9.
Continuation of statutes relating to subjects covered by provisions of this Code, see Education Code
§ 3.

§ 22123.5. Dependent child or dependent children under disability retirement and survivor benefit allowance programs; offspring; financially dependent; member

(a) "Dependent child" or "dependent children" under the disability retirement and survivor benefit allowance programs means a member's offspring or stepchild who is not older than 21 years of age and who is financially dependent upon the member on the effective date of the member's disability retirement or the date of the member's death.

(b) "Offspring" shall include the member's child who is born within the 10–month period commencing on the earlier of the member's disability retirement effective date or the date of the member's death.

(c) "Offspring" shall include a child adopted by the member.

(d) "Dependent child" shall not include the member's offspring or stepchild who is adopted by a person other than the member's spouse.

(e) "Dependent child" under the survivor benefit allowance program shall not include a stepchild or adopted child acquired subsequent to the death of the member.

(f) "Financially dependent" for purposes of this section means that at least one-half of the child's support was being provided by the member on the member's disability retirement effective date or the date of the member's death. The system may require that income tax records or other data be submitted to substantiate the child's financial dependence. In the absence of substantiating documentation, the system may determine that the child was not dependent on the effective date of the member's disability retirement or the date of the member's death.

(g) "Member" as used in this section shall have the same meaning specified in Section 23850.

(Added by Stats.1996, c. 1165 (A.B.3032), § 10.)

Cross References

Computation of time,
Generally, see Code of Civil Procedure §§ 12 and 12a and Government Code § 6800 et seq.
Time in which any act provided by the Education Code is to be done, see Education Code § 9.
Continuation of statutes relating to subjects covered by provisions of this Code, see Education Code
§ 3.

Library References

Legal Jurisprudences

Am Jur 2d (Rev) Pension and Retirement
Funds §§ 1651 et seq.

§ 22124. Dependent parent

"Dependent parent" means a natural parent of a member, or a parent who adopted the member prior to the earlier of the occurrence of the member's marriage or his or her attaining 18 years of age, and who was receiving one-half or more of his or her support from the member at the time of the member's death.

(Added by Stats.1994, c. 933 (A.B.3171), § 3, eff. Sept. 28, 1994. Amended by Stats. 1996, c. 634 (S.B.2041), § 14.)

Historical and Statutory Notes

Former § 22124, added by Stats.1993, c. 893 (A.B.1796, § 2, defining disabilitant, was repealed by Stats.1994, c. 933 (A.B.3171), § 2, eff. Sept. 28, 1994. See Education Code § 22125.

Former § 22124, enacted by Stats.1976, c. 1010, § 2, defining "employer" and "employing agency", was repealed by Stats.1993, c. 893 (A.B.1796), § 1. See Education Code § 22130.

Derivation: Former § 22123, added by Stats. 1993, c. 893, § 2.

Former § 22119, enacted by Stats.1976, c. 1010, § 2.

Educ.C.1959, § 13834.5, added by Stats.1971, c. 1305, § 18.

§ 22125. Repealed by Stats.1996, c. 634 (S.B.2041), § 15

Historical and Statutory Notes

The repealed section, added by Stats.1994, c. 933 (A.B.3171), § 3, derived from former § 22124, added by Stats.1993, c. 893, § 2; former § 22120, enacted by Stats.1976, c. 1010, § 2; Educ.C.1959, § 13835, added by Stats. 1972, c. 1010, p. 1858, § 4, amended by Stats. 1974, c. 1153, p. 2446, § 3, defined disabilitant.

Former § 22125, added by Stats.1993, c. 893 (A.B.1796, § 2, defining disability or disabled,

was repealed by Stats.1994, c. 933 (A.B.3171), § 2, eff. Sept. 28, 1994. See Education Code § 22126.

Former § 22125, enacted by Stats.1976, c. 1010, § 2, defining "employment", was repealed by Stats.1993, c. 893 (A.B.1796), § 1. See Education Code § 22131.

§ 22126. Disability; disabled

"Disability" or "disabled" means any medically determinable physical or mental impairment that is permanent or that can be expected to last continuously for at least 12 months, measured from the onset of the disability, but no earlier than the day following the last day of service that prevents a member from performing the member's usual duties for the member's employer, the member's usual duties for the member's employer with reasonable modifications, or the duties of a comparable level position for which the member is qualified or can become qualified within a reasonable period of time by education, training, or experience. Any impairment from a willful self-inflicted injury shall not constitute a disability.

(Added by Stats.1994, c. 933 (A.B.3171), § 3, eff. Sept. 28, 1994. Amended by Stats. 1996, c. 634 (S.B.2041), § 16.)

Historical and Statutory Notes

Former § 22126, added by Stats.1993, c. 893 (A.B.1796, § 2, defining disability allowance, was repealed by Stats.1994, c. 933 (A.B.3171), § 2, eff. Sept. 28, 1994. See Education Code § 22127.

Former § 22126, enacted by Stats.1976, c. 1010, § 2, amended by Stats.1981, c. 124, § 12; Stats.1992, c. 1166 (S.B.1885), § 3, defining "family benefits", was repealed by Stats.1993, c.

893 (A.B.1796), § 1. See Education Code § 22132.

Derivation: Former § 22125, added by Stats. 1993, c. 893, § 2.

Former § 22122, enacted by Stats.1976, c. 1010, § 2, amended by Stats.1977, c. 36, § 95; Stats.1978, c. 502, § 1; Stats.1980, c. 757, § 1; Stats.1992, c. 1167 (S.B.1886), § 4.

Educ.C.1959, § 13835.2, added as § 13835 by Stats.1969, c. 896, § 2, amended by Stats.1971, c. 1305, § 19, renumbered § 13835.2 and amended by 1972, c. 1010, § 3; Stats.1976, c. 1412, § 1.

Educ.C.1959, § 13838, added by Stats.1959, c. 2060, § 2.

Cross References

Disability allowance, see Education Code § 24001 et seq.
Disability retirement, see Education Code § 24100 et seq.

Library References

Legal Jurisprudences
Am Jur 2d (Rev) Pensions and Retirement Funds §§ 1661 et seq.

§ 22127. Disability allowance

"Disability allowance" means the amount payable to a disabled member on a monthly basis.

(Added by Stats.1994, c. 933 (A.B.3171), § 3, eff. Sept. 28, 1994. Amended by Stats. 1996, c. 634 (S.B.2041), § 17.)

Historical and Statutory Notes

Former § 22127, added by Stats.1993, c. 893 (A.B.1796, § 2, defining early retirement and early retirement age, was repealed by Stats. 1994, c. 933 (A.B.3171), § 2, eff. Sept. 28, 1994. See Education Code § 22128.

Former § 22127, enacted by Stats.1976, c. 1010, § 2, amended by Stats.1977, c. 36, § 96; Stats.1979, c. 430, § 3; Stats.1982, c. 782, § 1; Stats.1992, c. 1166 (S.B.1885), § 4, defining "final compensation", was repealed by Stats.

1993, c. 893 (A.B.1796), § 1. See Education Code § 22133.

Derivation: Former § 22126, added by Stats. 1993, c. 893, § 2.

Former § 22121, enacted by Stats.1976, c. 1010, § 2, amended by Stats.1981, c. 124, § 11.

Educ.C.1959, § 13835.1, added by Stats.1972, c. 1010, p. 1859, § 5, amended by Stats.1974, c. 1293, p. 2807, § 17.

Cross References

Disability allowance, see Education Code § 24001 et seq.
Disability retirement, see Education Code § 24100 et seq.

Notes of Decisions

Aggravation of condition 3
Mental impairments 2
Usual duties 1

1. Usual duties

Substantial evidence supported court's conclusion that physical education teacher sustaining knee injury which kept her from continuing in that position was entitled to a disability benefit, even though the Teachers' Retirement Board claimed that she could continue as a classroom teacher; ability to do classroom teaching was based on credits earned 20 to 30 years previously, and Board itself had admitted that district would be required to give priority to more qual-

ified applicants if she were to seek a classroom position. Abshear v. Teachers' Retirement Board (App. 2 Dist. 1991) 282 Cal.Rptr. 833, 231 Cal.App.3d 1629.

2. Mental impairments

Evidence supported finding that junior high teacher, who suffered from passive-aggressive personality disorder, was not "disabled," within meaning of this section, which requires finding of physical or mental impairment as prerequisite to disability allowance; psychiatrist testified that teacher's personality disorder did not prevent teacher from performing his job, and evidence supported conclusion that teacher's failure to return to teaching was due to teacher's own lack of motivation. Swehla v. Teachers'

Retirement Bd. (App. 5 Dist. 1987) 237 Cal. Rptr. 789, 192 Cal.App.3d 1088.

3. Aggravation of condition

Elementary school teacher was physically impaired and prevented from performing her usual duties for her employer, and thus entitled to disability allowance, where she suffered from severe bronchial asthma which was aggravated due to her proximity to small children and their rampant infectious agents and where she had received competent medical advice that it would be dangerous for her to return to teaching. Wolfman v. Board of Trustees of State Teachers System (App. 4 Dist. 1983) 196 Cal.Rptr. 395, 148 Cal.App.3d 787.

§ 22127.1. Repealed by Stats.1993, c. 893 (A.B.1796), § 1

Historical and Statutory Notes

The repealed section, added by Stats.1989, c. 1184, § 1, amended by Stats.1990, c. 83 (A.B.54), § 1; Stats.1991, c. 543 (S.B.1171), § 3, defined final compensation and classroom teacher. See Education Code § 22135.

Legislative intent regarding Stats.1993, ·c. 893 (A.B.1796), including possible continuing application of provisions of repealed State Teachers' Retirement Law, see Historical and Statutory Notes under Education Code § 22000.

§ 22127.2. Disability benefit

"Disability benefit" means the amount payable under the Defined Benefit Supplement Program based on the balance of credits in a member's Defined Benefit Supplement account to either a disabled member pursuant to Section 24005 or to a member who retired for disability pursuant to Section 24105.

(Added by Stats.2000, c. 74 (A.B.1509), § 11.)

§ 22127.3. Repealed by Stats.1993, c. 893 (A.B.1796), § 1

Historical and Statutory Notes

The repealed section, added by Stats.1992, c. 1372 (S.B.1887), § 6, related to higher final compensation. See Education Code § 22137.

Legislative intent regarding Stats.1993, c. 893 (A.B.1796), including possible continuing appli-

cation of provisions of repealed State Teachers' Retirement Law, see Historical and Statutory Notes under Education Code § 22000.

§ 22128. Early retirement; early retirement age

"Early retirement" and "early retirement age" mean the age of 55 years, which is the age upon attainment of which the member becomes eligible under the Defined Benefit Program for a service retirement allowance with reduction because of age and without special qualifications.

(Added by Stats.1994, c. 933 (A.B.3171), § 3, eff. Sept. 28, 1994. Amended by Stats. 1996, c. 634 (S.B.2041), § 18; Stats.1999, c. 939 (S.B.1074), § 11; Stats.2000, c. 1025 (A.B.816), § 2.)

Historical and Statutory Notes

Former § 22128, added by Stats.1993, c. 893 (A.B.1796, § 2, defining educational institution, was repealed by Stats.1994, c. 933 (A.B.3171), § 2, eff. Sept. 28, 1994. See Education Code § 22129.

Former § 22128, added by Stats.1977, c. 199, § 1, defining "full-time student", was repealed by Stats.1993, c. 893 (A.B.1796), § 1. See Education Code § 22138.

Former § 22128, enacted by Stats.1976, c. 1010, § 2, defining "full-time student", was repealed by Stats.1977, c. 199, § 1.

Derivation: Former § 22127, added by Stats. 1993, c. 893, § 2.

Former § 22134.6, added by Stats.1987, c. 330, § 5.

§ 22129. Educational institution

"Educational institution" means any accredited public or private institution whose primary purpose is to provide classroom teaching and includes a high school, trade or vocational school or college, community college, or other college or university.

(Added by Stats.1994, c. 933 (A.B.3171), § 3, eff. Sept. 28, 1994. Amended by Stats. 1996, c. 634 (S.B.2041), § 19.)

Historical and Statutory Notes

Former § 22129, added by Stats.1993, c. 893 (A.B.1796), § 2, providing a definition of effective date, was repealed by Stats.1994, c. 933 (A.B.3171), § 2, eff. Sept. 28, 1994. See Education Code § 22130.

Former § 22129, enacted by Stats.1976, c. 1010, § 2, amended by Stats.1993, c. 860, § 1, defining final compensation for members incurring a salary reduction, was repealed by Stats. 1994, c. 933 (A.B.3171), § 6, eff. Sept. 28, 1994. See Education Code § 22136.

Repeal of former § 22129, by Stats.1993, c. 893 (A.B.1796), § 1, failed to become operative. See Historical and Statutory Notes relating to Stats.1993, c. 893 (A.B.1796), § 4, under Education Code § 22000, and Government Code § 9605.

Legislative intent regarding Stats.1993, c. 893 (A.B.1796), including possible continuing application of provisions of repealed State Teachers' Retirement Law, see Historical and Statutory Notes under Education Code § 22000.

Derivation: Former § 22128, added by Stats. 1993, c. 893, § 2.

Former § 22130, enacted by Stats.1976, c. 1010, § 2.

Educ.C.1959, § 13838.2, added by Stats.1974, c. 1153, p. 2447, § 6.

Cross References

Community colleges, generally, see Education Code § 70900 et seq.
Registration of sex offenders, residents enrolled in any educational institution in California, see Penal Code § 290.

§ 22130. Effective date

"Effective date" means the date upon which the benefit becomes payable.

(Added by Stats.1994, c. 933 (A.B.3171), § 3, eff. Sept. 28, 1994. Amended by Stats. 1996, c. 634 (S.B.2041), § 20.)

Historical and Statutory Notes

Former § 22130, added by Stats.1993, c. 893 (A.B.1796, § 2, defining employment, was repealed by Stats.1994, c. 933 (A.B.3171), § 2, eff. Sept. 28, 1994. See Education Code § 22131.

Former § 22130, enacted by Stats.1976, c. 1010, § 2, defining "educational institutions", was repealed by Stats.1993, c. 893 (A.B.1796), § 1. See Education Code § 22128.

Derivation: Former § 22129, added by Stats. 1993, c. 893, § 2.

Former § 22123, enacted by Stats.1976, c. 1010, § 2.

Educ.C.1959, § 13835.3, added by Stats.1974, c. 1153, p. 2446, § 4.

§ 22131. Employer; employing agency

"Employer" or "employing agency" means the state or any agency or political subdivision thereof for which creditable service subject to coverage by the plan is performed.

(Added by Stats.1994, c. 933 (A.B.3171), § 3, eff. Sept. 28, 1994. Amended by Stats. 1996, c. 634 (S.B.2041), § 21.)

Historical and Statutory Notes

Former § 22131, added by Stats.1993, c. 893 (A.B.1796, § 2, defining employment, was repealed by Stats.1994, c. 933 (A.B.3171), § 2, eff. Sept. 28, 1994. See Education Code § 22132.

Former § 22131, enacted by Stats.1976, c. 1010, § 2, defining "improvement factor", was repealed by Stats.1993, c. 893 (A.B.1796), § 1. See Education Code § 22139.

Derivation: Former § 22130, added by Stats. 1993, c. 893, § 2.

Former § 22124, enacted by Stats.1976, c. 1010, § 2.

Educ.C.1959, § 13836, added by Stats.1969, c. 896, p. 1738, § 2.

Educ.C.1959, § 13807 (Stats.1959, c. 2, p. 983, § 13807).

Educ.C.1943, § 14257, added by Stats.1944, 4th Ex.Sess., c. 13, p. 115, § 2.

Educ.C.1943, § 14255 (Stats.1943, c. 71, p. 590).

School C. § 5.801, added by Stats.1937, c. 626, p. 1717, § 4.

§§ 22131.1 to 22131.8.   Repealed by Stats.1993, c. 893 (A.B.1796), § 1

Historical and Statutory Notes

Section 22131.1, added by Stats.1981, c. 1089, § 1, defined improvement factor. See Education Code § 22140.

Section 22131.5, added by Stats.1982, c. 1314, § 1, amended by Stats.1992, c. 1166 (S.B. 1885), § 4.5, defined indexed final compensation. See Education Code § 22134.

Section 22131.7, added by Stats.1987, c. 330, § 1, defined investment manager and investment adviser. See Education Code § 22143.

Section 22131.8, added by Stats.1987, c. 330, § 2, defined investment transactions. See Education Code § 22144.

Legislative intent regarding Stats.1993, c. 893 (A.B.1796), including possible continuing application of provisions of repealed State Teachers' Retirement Law, see Historical and Statutory Notes under Education Code § 22000.

§ 22132.   Employed; employment

"Employed" or "employment" means employment to perform creditable service subject to coverage under the Defined Benefit Program or the Defined Benefit Supplement Program, except as otherwise specifically provided under this part.

(Added by Stats.1994, c. 933 (A.B.3171), § 3, eff. Sept. 28, 1994.   Amended by Stats. 1996, c. 634 (S.B.2041), § 21.5; Stats.1998, c. 965 (A.B.2765), § 5; Stats.2000, c. 74 (A.B.1509), § 12.)

Historical and Statutory Notes

Former § 22132, added by Stats.1993, c. 893 (A.B.1796, § 2, defining family allowance, was repealed by Stats.1994, c. 933 (A.B.3171), § 2, eff. Sept. 28, 1994. See Education Code § 22133.

Former § 22132, enacted by Stats.1976, c. 1010, § 2, defining "local system", was repealed by Stats.1993, c. 893 (A.B.1796), § 1. See Education Code § 22145.

Derivation: Former § 22131, added by Stats. 1993, c. 893, § 2.

Former § 22125, enacted by Stats.1976, c. 1010, § 2.

Educ.C.1959, § 13837, added by Stats.1969, c. 896, p. 1738, § 2, amended by Stats.1974, c. 1293, § 18.

Educ.C.1959, § 13808 (Stats.1959, c. 2, p. 983, § 13808).

Educ.C.1943, § 14258, added by Stats.1944, 4th Ex.Sess., c. 13, p. 115, § 2, amended by Stats.1956, 1st Ex.Sess., c. 55, p. 430, § 1.

Educ.C.1943, § 14256 (Stats.1943, c. 71, p. 590).

School C. § 5.801, added by Stats.1937, c. 626, p. 1717, § 4.

§ 22132.7. Renumbered § 22117.5 and amended by Stats.1988, c. 382, § 2

§ 22133. Family allowance

"Family allowance" means amounts payable to eligible survivors provided pursuant to Chapter 22 (commencing with Section 23800) after June 30, 1972.

(Added by Stats.1994, c. 933 (A.B.3171), § 3, eff. Sept. 28, 1994.)

· Historical and Statutory Notes

Former § 22133, added by Stats.1993, c. 893 (A.B.1796), § 2, defining final compensation, was repealed by Stats.1994, c. 933 (A.B.3171), § 2, eff. Sept. 28, 1994. See Education Code § 22134.

Former § 22133, enacted by Stats.1976, c. 1010, § 2, defining "member", was repealed by Stats.1993, c. 893 (A.B.1796), § 1. See Education Code § 22146.

Derivation: Former § 22132, added by Stats. 1993, c. 893, § 2.

Former § 22126, enacted by Stats.1976, c. 1010, § 2.

Educ.C.1959, § 13837.5, added by Stats.1971, c. 1305, p. 2570, § 20.

Cross References

Death benefits, family allowance, see Education Code § 23804.

§ 22133.5. Final benefit

"Final benefit" means the amount payable to a beneficiary under the Defined Benefit Supplement Program upon the death of the member.

(Added by Stats.2000, c. 74 (A.B.1509), § 13.)

§ 22134. Final compensation

(a) "Final compensation" means the highest average annual compensation earnable by a member during any period of three consecutive school years while an active member of the Defined Benefit Program or time during which he or she was not a member but for which the member has received credit under the Defined Benefit Program, except time that was so credited for service performed outside this state prior to July 1, 1944. The last three consecutive years of employment shall be used by the system in determining final compensation unless designated to the contrary in writing by the member.

(b) For purposes of this section, periods of service separated by breaks in service may be aggregated to constitute a period of three consecutive years, if the periods of service are consecutive except for the breaks.

(c) The determination of final compensation of a member who has concurrent membership in another retirement system pursuant to Section 22115.2 shall take into consideration the compensation earnable while a member of the other system, provided that all of the following exist:

(1) The member was in state service or in the employment of a local school district or a county superintendent of schools.

(2) Service under the other system was not performed concurrently with service under the Defined Benefit Program.

(3) Retirement under the Defined Benefit Program is concurrent with the member's retirement under the other system.

(d) The compensation earnable for the first position in which California service was credited shall be used when additional compensation earnable is required to accumulate three consecutive years for the purpose of determining final compensation under Section 23805.

(e) If a member has received service credit for part-time service performed prior to July 1, 1956, the member's final compensation shall be adjusted for that service in excess of one year by the ratio that part-time service bears to full-time service.

(f) The board may specify a different final compensation with respect to disability allowances, disability retirement allowances, family allowances, and children's portions of survivor benefit allowances payable on and after January 1, 1978. The compensation earnable for periods of part-time service shall be adjusted by the ratio that part-time service bears to full-time service.

(g) The amendment of former Section 22127 made by Chapter 782 of the Statutes of 1982 does not constitute a change in, but is declaratory of, the existing law.

(Added by Stats.1994, c. 933 (A.B.3171), § 3, eff. Sept. 28, 1994. Amended by Stats. 1996, c. 1165 (A.B.3032), § 11; Stats.1997, c. 482 (S.B.471), § 4; Stats.1998, c. 1077 (S.B.610), § 1; Stats.1999, c. 939 (S.B.1074), § 12.)

Historical and Statutory Notes

An amendment of this section by § 1.5 of Stats.1998, c. 1077 (S.B.610), failed to become operative under the provisions of § 6 of that Act.

Former § 22134, added by Stats.1993, c. 893 (A.B.1796, § 2, defining indexed final compensation, was repealed by Stats.1994, c. 933 (A.B. 3171), § 2, eff. Sept. 28, 1994. See Education Code § 22142.

Former § 22134, enacted by Stats.1976, c. 1010, § 2, defining "month", was repealed by Stats.1993, c. 893 (A.B.1796), § 1. See Education Code § 22147.

Derivation: Former § 22133, added by Stats. 1993, c. 893, § 2.

Former § 22127, enacted by Stats.1976, c. 1010, § 2, amended by Stats.1977, c. 36, § 96; Stats.1979, c. 430, § 3; Stats.1982, c. 782, § 1; Stats.1992, c. 1166 (S.B. 1885), § 4.

Educ.C.1959, § 13838, added by Stats.1969, c. 896, p. 1738, § 2, amended by Stats.1970, c. 466, p. 922, § 1; Stats.1970, c. 1263, p. 2281, § 1; Stats.1971, c. 1305, p. 2570, § 21; Stats. 1976, c. 1308, § 2.

Educ.C.1959, § 13832, (Stats.1959, c. 2, p. 985, § 13832, amended by Stats.1959, c. 2004, p. 4645, § 1).

Educ.C.1943, § 14276.6, added by Stats.1955, c. 1395, p. 2492, § 3, amended by Stats.1956, 1st Ex.Sess., c. 55, p. 430, § 2; Stats.1957, c. 2118, p. 3751, § 1.

Cross References

County superintendents of schools,
    Generally, see Education Code § 1200 et seq.
    Election or appointment and salaries, see Const. Art. 9, § 3 et seq.

Library References

Schools ⟊146(5).
Westlaw Topic No. 345.

C.J.S. Schools and School Districts §§ 340, 342 to 343, 345 to 346.

Notes of Decisions

Computation of service 1
Local retirement systems 2

Cummings v. California State Teachers' Retirement Bd. (App. 1 Dist. 1966) 50 Cal.Rptr. 391, 241 Cal.App.2d 149.

1. Computation of service

Record established that construction placed by defendant teachers' retirement board on statutory provisions, including 1957 amendments, governing computation of part-time teaching service was warranted as opposed to plaintiff teacher's construction that her retirement allowance should be computed on basis of years of service to which she was entitled to be credited under law existing prior to July 1, 1956.

2. Local retirement systems

Compensation received by a member of the state employees' retirement system while a member of a local school district retirement system should be taken into consideration in fixing final compensation under the state employees' retirement law where it is also used in fixing final compensation under state teachers' retirement law. 50 Ops.Atty.Gen. 92, 10–31–67.

§ 22134.5. Final compensation; periods of service separated by breaks; application of section

(a) Notwithstanding Section 22134, "final compensation" means the highest average annual compensation earnable by a member during any period of 12 consecutive months while an active member of the Defined Benefit Program or time during which he or she was not a member but for which the member has received credit under the Defined Benefit Program, except time that was so credited for service performed outside this state prior to July 1, 1944. The last consecutive 12–month period of employment shall be used by the system in determining final compensation unless designated to the contrary in writing by the member.

(b) For purposes of this section, periods of service separated by breaks in service may be aggregated to constitute a period of 12 consecutive months, if the periods of service are consecutive except for the breaks.

(c) The determination of final compensation of a member who has concurrent membership in another retirement system pursuant to Section 22115.2 shall take into consideration the compensation earnable while a member of the other system, provided that all of the following exist:

(1) The member was in state service or in the employment of a local school district or a county superintendent of schools.

(2) Service under the other system was not performed concurrently with service under the Defined Benefit Program.

(3) Retirement under the Defined Benefit Program is concurrent with the member's retirement under the other system.

(d) The compensation earnable for the first position in which California service was credited shall be used when additional compensation earnable is required to accumulate three consecutive years for the purpose of determining final compensation under Section 23805.

(e) If a member has received service credit for part-time service performed prior to July 1, 1956, the member's final compensation shall be adjusted for that service in excess of one year by the ratio that part-time service bears to full-time service.

(f) The board may specify a different final compensation with respect to disability allowances, disability retirement allowances, family allowances, and children's portions of survivor benefit allowances payable on and after January 1, 1978. The compensation earnable for periods of part-time service shall be adjusted by the ratio that part-time service bears to full-time service.

(g) This section shall only apply to a member who has 25 or more years of credited service, excluding service credited pursuant to Section 22714, 22715, 22717, or 22826, but including any credited service that a court has ordered be awarded to a nonmember spouse pursuant to Section 22652. This section also shall apply to a nonmember spouse, if the member had at least 25 years of credited service, excluding service credited pursuant to Section 22714, 22715, 22717, or 22826, on the date the parties separated, as established in the judgment or court order pursuant to Section 22652.

(Added by Stats.2000, c. 1028 (A.B.821), § 1.)

Historical and Statutory Notes

Former § 22134.5, added by Stats.1977, c. 659, § 3, amended by Stats.1987, c. 330, § 4, defined normal retirement and normal retire- ment age, and was repealed by Stats.1993, c. 893 (A.B.1796), § 1. See Education Code § 22148.

Cross References

County superintendents of schools,
    Generally, see Education Code § 1200 et seq.
    Election or appointment and salaries, see Const. Art. 9, § 3 et seq.
State teachers' retirement system, reinstatement, service retirement allowance, see Education Code § 24209.3.

§§ 22134.6, 22134.7. Repealed by Stats.1993, c. 893 (A.B.1796), § 1

Historical and Statutory Notes

Section 22134.6, added by Stats.1987, c. 330, § 5, defined early retirement and early retirement age. See Education Code § 22127.

Section 22134.7, added by Stats.1981, c. 124, § 13, defined option beneficiary. See Education Code § 22149.

Legislative intent regarding Stats.1993, c. 893 (A.B.1796), including possible continuing application of provisions of repealed State Teachers' Retirement Law, see Historical and Statutory Notes under Education Code § 22000.

§ 22135. Final compensation; classroom teacher

(a) Notwithstanding subdivisions (a) and (b) of Section 22134, "final compensation" means the highest annual compensation earnable by an active member who is a classroom teacher who retires, becomes disabled, or dies, after June 30, 1990, during any period of 12 consecutive months during his or her membership in the plan's Defined Benefit Program. The last 12 consecutive months of employment shall be used by the system in determining final compensation unless designated to the contrary in writing by the member.

(b) Section 22134, except subdivision (a) of that section, shall apply to classroom teachers who retire after June 30, 1990, and any statutory reference to Section 22134 or "final compensation" with respect to a classroom teacher who retires, becomes disabled, or dies, after June 30, 1990, shall be deemed to be a reference to this section.

(c) As used in this section, "classroom teacher" means any of the following:

(1) All teachers and substitute teachers in positions requiring certification qualifications who spend, during the last 10 years of their employment with the same employer which immediately precedes their retirement, 60 percent or more of their contract time each year providing direct instruction. For the purpose of determining continuity of employment within the meaning of this subdivision, an authorized leave of absence for sabbatical or illness or other collectively bargained or employer-approved leaves shall not constitute a break in service.

(2) Other certificated personnel who spend, during the last 10 years of their employment with the same employer that immediately precedes their retirement, 60 percent or more of their contract time each year providing direct services to pupils, including, but not limited to, librarians, counselors, nurses, speech therapists, resource specialists, audiologists, audiometrists, hygienists, optometrists, psychologists, driver safety instructors, and personnel on special assignment to perform school attendance and adjustment services.

(d) As used in this section, "classroom teacher" does not include any of the following:

(1) Certificated employees whose job descriptions require an administrative credential.

(2) Certificated employees whose job descriptions include responsibility for supervision of certificated staff.

(3) Certificated employees who serve as advisers, coordinators, consultants, or developers or planners of curricula, instructional materials, or programs, who spend, during the last 10 years of their employment with the same employer that immediately precedes their retirement, less than 60 percent of their contract time in direct instruction.

(4) Certificated employees whose job descriptions require provision of direct instruction or services, but who are functioning in nonteaching assignments.

(5) Classified employees.

(e) This section shall apply only to teachers employed by an employer that has, pursuant to Chapter 10.7 (commencing with Section 3540) of Division 4 of Title 1 of the Government Code, entered into a written agreement with an exclusive representative, that makes this section applicable to all of its classroom teachers, as defined in subdivision (c).

(f) The written agreement shall include a mechanism to pay for all increases in allowances provided for by this section through employer contributions or employee contributions or both, which shall be collected and retained by the employer in a trust fund to be used solely and exclusively to pay the system for all increases in allowances provided by this section and related administrative costs; and a mechanism for disposition of the employee's contributions if employment is terminated before retirement, and for the establishment of a trust fund board. The trust fund board shall administer the trust fund and shall be composed of an equal number of members representing classroom teachers chosen by the bargaining agent and the employer. If the employer agrees to pay the total cost of increases in allowances, the establishment of a trust fund and a trust fund board shall be optional to the employer. The employer, within 30 days of receiving an invoice from the system, shall reimburse the retirement fund the amount determined by the Teachers' Retirement Board to be the actuarial equivalent of the difference between the allowance the member or beneficiary receives pursuant to this section and the allowance the member or beneficiary would have received if the member's final compensation had been computed under Section 22134 and the proportionate share of the cost to the plan's Defined Benefit Program, as determined by the Teachers' Retirement Board, of administering this section. The payment shall include the cost of all increases in allowances provided for by this section for all years of service credited to the member as of the benefit effective date. Interest shall be charged at the regular interest rate for any payment not received within 30 days of receipt of the invoice. Payments not received within 30 days after receipt of the invoice may be collected pursuant to Section 23007.

(g) Upon the execution of the agreement, the employer shall notify all certificated employees of the agreement and any certificated employee of the employer, who is a member of the Public Employees' Retirement System pursuant to Section 22508, that he or she may, within 60 days following the date of notification, elect to terminate his or her membership in the Public Employees' Retirement System and become a member of this plan's Defined Benefit Program. However, only service credited under the Defined Benefit Program subsequent to the date of that election shall be subject to this section.

(h) An employer that agrees to become subject to this section, shall, on a form and within the timeframes prescribed by the system, certify the applicability of this section to a member pursuant to the criteria set forth in this section when a retirement, disability, or family allowance becomes payable.

(i) For a nonmember spouse, final compensation shall be determined pursuant to paragraph (2) of subdivision (c) of Section 22664. The employer, within 30 days of receiving an invoice from the system, shall reimburse the retirement fund pursuant to subdivision (f). Interest shall be charged at the regular interest rate for payments not received within the prescribed timeframe. Payments not received within 30 days of invoicing may be collected pursuant to Section 23007.

(Added by Stats.1994, c. 933 (A.B.3171), § 3, eff. Sept. 28, 1994. Amended by Stats. 1996, c. 383 (A.B.3221), § 1; Stats.1999, c. 939 (S.B.1074), § 13.)

Historical and Statutory Notes

Former § 22135, added by Stats.1993, c. 893 (A.B.1796, § 2, defining final compensation, was repealed by Stats.1994, c. 933 (A.B.3171), § 2, eff. Sept. 28, 1994. See this section.

Former § 22135, enacted by Stats.1976, c. 1010, § 2, defining "overtime", was repealed by Stats.1993, c. 893 (A.B.1796), § 1. See Education Code § 22151.

Derivation: Former § 22135, added by Stats. 1993, c. 893, § 2.

Former § 22127.1, added by Stats.1989, c. 1184, § 1, amended by Stats.1990, c. 83 (A.B.54), § 1; Stats.1990, c. 543 (S.B.1171), § 3.

Cross References

Certificated and certified, defined, see Education Code § 90.
Certificated employees, generally, see Education Code § 44420 et seq.

Computation of time,
    Generally, see Code of Civil Procedure §§ 12 and 12a and Government Code § 6800 et seq.
    Time in which any act provided by the Education Code is to be done, see Education Code § 9.
Continuation of statutes relating to subjects covered by provisions of this Code, see Education Code
    § 3.

§ 22136. Final compensation; members with salary reduction

(a) "Final compensation" with respect to a member whose salary while an active member was reduced because of a reduction in school funds means the highest average annual compensation earnable by the member during any three years while employed to perform creditable service subject to coverage by the Defined Benefit Program if the member elects to be subject to this section.

(b) For the purposes of this section, a year shall be considered to be a period of 12 consecutive months.

(Added by Stats.1994, c. 933 (A.B.3171), § 3, eff. Sept. 28, 1994. Amended by Stats. 1996, c. 634 (S.B.2041), § 22; Stats.1999, c. 939 (S.B.1074), § 14.)

Historical and Statutory Notes

Former § 22136, added by Stats.1993, c. 893 (A.B.1796, § 2, defining final compensation, was repealed by Stats.1994, c. 933 (A.B.3171), § 2, eff. Sept. 28, 1994. See this section.

Former § 22136, enacted by Stats.1976, c. 1010, § 2, amended by Stats.1978, c. 502, § 2; Stats.1981, c. 124, § 14, defining "other public systems", was repealed by Stats.1993, c. 893 (A.B.1796), § 1. See Education Code § 22150.

Derivation: Former § 22136, added by Stats. 1993, c. 893, § 2.

Former § 22129, enacted by Stats.1976, c. 1010, § 2, amended by Stats.1993, c. 860, § 1.

Educ.C.1959,   § 13838.15,   formerly § 13838.1, added by Stats.1974, c. 298, § 1, renumbered § 13838.15 and amended by Stats. 1974, c. 1293, § 18.5.

Educ.C.1959, § 13832 (Stats.1959, c. 2, § 13832, amended by Stats.1959, c. 2004, § 1).

Library References

§ 22136.5. Repealed by Stats.2001, c. 803 (S.B.501), § 2

Historical and Statutory Notes

The repealed section, added by Stats.2000, c. 1028 (A.B.821), § 2, defined final compensation with respect to a member whose salary was reduced due to a reduction in school funds.

§ 22137. Higher final compensation; certain managerial or supervisory employees subjected to salary range reductions

With respect to a state employee member who dies or retires on or after July 1, 1991, and who was a managerial or supervisory employee, as defined by subdivisions (e) and (g) of Section 3513 of the Government Code, whose monthly salary range was administratively reduced by 5 percent because of the salary range reductions administratively imposed upon managers and supervisors during the 1991–92 fiscal year, "final compensation" means the highest annual compensation the state employee member would have earned had his or her salary range not been reduced by the 5-percent reduction. This section shall only apply if the period during which the state member's salary was reduced would have otherwise been included in determining his or her final compensation for retirement purposes. The costs, if any, that may result from the use of the higher final compensation shall be paid for by the employer at the time of retirement in a manner prescribed by the system.

(Added by Stats.1994, c. 933 (A.B.3171), § 3, eff. Sept. 28, 1994.)

Historical and Statutory Notes

Former § 22137, added by Stats.1993, c. 893 (A.B.1796, § 2, relating to higher final compensation, was repealed by Stats.1994, c. 933 (A.B. 3171), § 2, eff. Sept. 28, 1994. See this section.

Former § 22137, enacted by Stats.1976, c. 1010, § 2, defining "parent", was repealed by Stats.1993, c. 893 (A.B.1796), § 1. See Education Code § 22152.

Derivation: Former § 22137, added by Stats. 1993, c. 893, § 2.

Former § 22127.3, added by Stats.1992, c. 1372 (S.B.1887), § 6.

§ 22137.5. Renumbered § 22138.5 and amended by Stats. 1994, c. 933 (A.B.3171), § 6.5, eff. Sept. 28, 1994, operative Jan. 1, 1995.

Historical and Statutory Notes

Section 108 of Stats.1994, c. 933 (A.B.3171), provides:

"Sections 5.5 and 6.5 of this act incorporate changes in the State Teachers' Retirement Law proposed by AB 3832 (Chapter 193 of the Stat-utes of 1994), and shall become operative on January 1, 1995, the date on which AB 3832 takes effect, at which time Section 5 of this act shall cease to be operative."

§ 22138. Final vesting

"Final vesting" means the right of a member or a beneficiary to receive a monthly retirement allowance, disability allowance, a family benefit, or survivor benefits when the member has completed the minimum number of years of credited service, has attained the minimum specified age, has formally terminated his or her active service, has made application for retirement, or has been formally retired in accordance with Section 24201, after which the kind and amount of the retirement allowance is fixed and cannot thereafter be changed except as provided in this part.

(Added by Stats.1994, c. 933 (A.B.3171), § 3, eff. Sept. 28, 1994.)

Historical and Statutory Notes

Former § 22138, added by Stats.1993, c. 893 (A.B.1796, § 2, defining full-time student, was repealed by Stats.1994, c. 933 (A.B.3171), § 2, eff. Sept. 28, 1994. See Education Code § 22139.

Former § 22138, enacted by Stats.1976, c. 1010, § 2, defining "part-time basis with respect to service", was repealed by Stats.1993, c. 893 (A.B.1796), § 1. See Education Code § 22153.

Derivation: Former § 22172, added by Stats. 1993, c. 893, § 2.

Former § 22159, enacted by Stats.1976, c. 1010, § 2.

Educ.C.1959, § 13864, added by Stats.1972, c. 1010, § 10.

§ 22138.5. Full time

(a) "Full time" means the days or hours of creditable service the employer requires to be performed by a class of employees in a school year in order to earn the compensation earnable as defined in Section 22115 and specified under the terms of a collective bargaining agreement or employment agreement. For the purpose of crediting service under this part, "full time" shall not be less than the minimum standards specified in this section.

(b) The minimum standard for full time in kindergarten through grade 12 shall be:

(1) One hundred seventy-five days per year or 1,050 hours per year, except as provided in paragraphs (2) and (3).

(2)(A) One hundred ninety days per year or 1,520 hours per year for all principals and program managers, including advisers, coordinators, consultants, and developers or planners of curricula, instructional materials, or programs, and for administrators, except as provided in subparagraph (B).

(B) Two hundred fifteen days per year or 1,720 hours per year including school and legal holidays pursuant to the policy adopted by the employer's governing board for administrators at a county office of education.

(3) One thousand fifty hours per year for teachers in adult education programs.

(c) The minimum standard for full time in community colleges shall be:

(1) One hundred seventy-five days per year or 1,050 hours per year, except as provided in paragraphs (2), (3), (4), (5), and (6). Full time shall include time for duties the employer requires to be performed as part of the full-time assignment for a particular class of employees.

(2) One hundred ninety days per year or 1,520 hours per year for all program managers and for administrators, except as provided in paragraph (3).

(3) Two hundred fifteen days per year or 1,720 hours per year including school and legal holidays pursuant to the policy adopted by the employer's governing board for administrators at a district office.

(4) One hundred seventy-five days per year or 1,050 hours per year for all counselors and librarians.

(5) Five hundred twenty-five instructional hours per school year for all instructors employed on a part-time basis, except instructors specified in paragraph (6). If an instructor receives compensation for office hours pursuant to Article 10 (commencing with Section 87880) of Chapter 3 of Part 51, then the minimum standard established herein shall be increased appropriately by the number of office hours required annually for the class of employees.

(6) Eight hundred seventy-five instructional hours per school year for all instructors employed in adult education programs. If an instructor receives compensation for office hours pursuant to Article 10 (commencing with Section 87880) of Chapter 3 of Part 51, then the minimum standard established herein shall be increased appropriately by the number of office hours required annually for the class of employees.

(d) The board shall have final authority to determine full time for purposes of crediting service under this part if full time is not otherwise specified herein.

(Added by Stats.1995, c. 390 (A.B.1122), § 6, operative July 1, 1996. Amended by Stats.1996, c. 634 (S.B.2041), § 23; Stats.1998, c. 678 (A.B.1166), § 1; Stats.1999, c. 939 (S.B.1074), § 15; Stats.2000, c. 1025 (A.B.816), § 3.)

Historical and Statutory Notes

Section 108 of Stats.1994, c. 933 (A.B.3171), provides:

"Sections 5.5 and 6.5 of this act incorporate changes in the State Teachers' Retirement Law proposed by AB 3832 (Chapter 193 of the Statutes of 1994), and shall become operative on January 1, 1995, the date on which AB 3832 takes effect, at which time Section 5 of this act shall cease to be operative."

Former § 22138.5, formerly § 22137.5, added by Stats.1994, c. 193, § 2, renumbered

§ 22138.5 and amended by Stats.1994, c. 933 (A.B.3171), § 6.5, defining "full-time", was repealed by Stats.1995, c. 390 (A.B.1122), § 5, operative July 1, 1996. See this section.

Derivation: Former § 22138.5, formerly § 22137.5, added by Stats.1994, c. 193, § 2, renumbered § 22138.5 and amended by Stats. 1994, c. 933, § 6.5.

Cross References

Adult education, education programs, state master plans, see Education Code § 8500 et seq.
Community colleges, generally, see Education Code § 70900 et seq.

§ 22138.6. Full-time equivalent

"Full–time equivalent" means the days or hours of creditable service that a person who is employed on a part-time basis would be required to perform in a school year if he or she were employed full time in that part-time position.

(Added by Stats.1995, c. 390 (A.B.1122), § 7, operative July 1, 1996. Amended by Stats.1998, c. 965 (A.B.2765), § 6; Stats.2001, c. 803 (S.B.501), § 3.)

§ 22139. Repealed by Stats.1996, c. 1165 (A.B.3032), § 12, operative Jan. 1, 2002

Historical and Statutory Notes

The repealed section, added by Stats.1994, c. 933 (A.B.3171), § 3, amended by Stats.1996, c. 1165 (A.B.3032), § 12, derived from former § 22138, added by Stats.1993, c. 893, § 2; former § 22128, added by Stats.1977, c. 199, § 1; former § 22128, enacted by Stats.1976, c. 1010, § 2; Educ.C.1959, § 13838.1, added by Stats. 1974, c. 1153, p. 2446, § 5; and Educ.C.1959, § 13830, added by Stats.1971, c. 1305, p. 2569, § 15, defined "full-time student".

Another § 22139, added by Stats.1996, c. 1165 (A.B.3032), § 12.5, to become operative Jan. 1, 2002, which defined "full-time student", was repealed by Stats.2001, c. 802 (S.B.499), § 3.

Former § 22139, added by Stats.1993, c. 893 (A.B.1796), § 2, derived from former § 22131, enacted by Stats.1976, c. 1010, § 2; Educ.C. 1959, § 13838.5, added by Stats.1971, c. 1305, § 22, amended by Stats.1974, c. 545, § 14; Stats.1974, c. 1293, § 19, defining "improvement factor", was repealed by Stats.1994, c. 933 (A.B.3171), § 2. See Education Code § 22140.

Former § 22139, enacted by Stats.1976, c. 1010, § 2, defining "pay period", was repealed by Stats.1993, c. 893 (A.B.1796), § 1. See Education Code § 22154.

§ 22139.5. Gain and loss reserve

"Gain and Loss Reserve" means a segregated account within the retirement fund that is established and maintained to do either of the following:

(a) Credit interest to members' Defined Benefit Supplement accounts at the minimum interest rate for plan years in which the board determines that the obligation cannot be met from the plan's investment earnings with respect to the Defined Benefit Supplement Program.

(b) Provide additions to the Annuitant Reserve to meet the plan's obligation for annuities payable under the Defined Benefit Supplement Program.

(Added by Stats.2000, c. 74 (A.B.1509), § 14.)

§ 22140. Improvement factor

(a) "Improvement factor," with respect to the Defined Benefit Program, means an increase of 2 percent in monthly allowances. The improvement factor shall be added to a monthly allowance each year on September 1, commencing on September 1 following the first anniversary of the effective date of retirement, or the date on which the monthly allowance commenced to accrue to any beneficiary, or other periods specifically stated in this part.

(b) "Improvement factor," with respect to the Defined Benefit Supplement Program, means an increase of 2 percent in monthly annuities. The improvement factor shall be added to a monthly annuity each year on September 1, commencing on the September 1 following the first anniversary of the date the annuity first became payable.

(c) The improvement factor shall not be compounded nor shall it be applicable to annuities payable from the accumulated annuity deposit contributions or the accumulated tax-sheltered annuity contributions. The Legislature reserves the right to adjust the amount of the improvement factor up or down as economic conditions dictate. No adjustments of the improvement factor shall reduce the monthly retirement allowance or annuity below that which would be payable to the recipient under this part had this section not been enacted.

(Added by Stats.1994, c. 933 (A.B.3171), § 3, eff. Sept. 28, 1994. Amended by Stats. 1996, c. 634 (S.B.2041), § 23.5; Stats.2000, c. 74 (A.B.1509), § 15.)

Historical and Statutory Notes

Former § 22140, added by Stats.1993, c. 893 (A.B.1796, § 2, providing an exception to the definition of improvement factor, was repealed by Stats.1994, c. 933 (A.B.3171), § 2, eff. Sept. 28, 1994. See Education Code § 22141.

Former § 22140, enacted by Stats.1976, c. 1010, § 2, defining "payroll", was repealed by Stats.1993, c. 893 (A.B.1796), § 1. See Education Code § 22155.

Derivation: Former § 22139, added by Stats. 1993, c. 893 (A.B.1796, § 2.

Former § 22131, enacted by Stats.1976, c. 1010, § 2.

Educ.C.1959, § 13838.5, added by Stats.1971, c. 1305, § 22, amended by Stats.1974, c. 545, § 14; Stats.1974, c. 1293, § 19.

§ 22141. Improvement factor; increase in benefits; commencement dates

Notwithstanding Section 22140, "improvement factor" means an increase of 2 percent in benefits provided under Sections 24408 and 24409 for each year commencing on September 1, 1981, and under Section 24410.5 for each year commencing September 1, 2001, and under Sections 24410.6 and 24110.7 for each year commencing September 1, 2002. The factor shall not be compounded nor shall it be applicable to annuities payable from the accumulated annuity deposit contributions or the accumulated tax-sheltered annuity contributions. The Legislature reserves the right to adjust the amount of the improvement factor up or down as the economic conditions dictate. No adjustments of the improvement factor shall reduce the monthly retirement allowance or benefit below that which would be payable to the recipient under this part had this section not been enacted.

(Added by Stats.1994, c. 933 (A.B.3171), § 3, eff. Sept. 28, 1994. Amended by Stats. 2000, c. 1025 (A.B.816), § 4; Stats.2000, c. 1026 (S.B.1505), § 1; Stats.2000, c. 1027 (A.B.429), § 1.)

Historical and Statutory Notes

Section affected by two or more acts at the same session of the legislature, see Government Code § 9605.

Former § 22141, added by Stats.1993, c. 893 (A.B.1796), § 2, defining credited interest, was repealed by Stats.1994, c. 933 (A.B.3171), § 2, eff. Sept. 28, 1994. See Education Code § 22120.

Former § 22141, added as § 22141.5 by Stats.1977, c. 36, § 411, renumbered § 22141 and amended by Stats.1977, c. 37, § 5; Stats. 1981, c. 124, § 15; Stats.1992, c. 1166 (S.B. 1885), § 5; Stats.1992, c. 1167 (S.B.1886), § 4.4, defining "projected salary", was repealed

by Stats.1993, c. 893 (A.B.1796), § 1. See Education Code § 22156.

Former § 22141, added by Stats.1977, c. 36, § 410.5, defining "projected salary", was repealed by Stats.1977, c. 37, § 4, eff. April 29, 1977, operative April 30, 1977.

Former § 22141, enacted by Stats.1976, c. 1010, § 2, defining "projected earned salary", was repealed by Stats.1977, c. 36, § 556, eff. April 29, 1977.

Derivation: Former § 22140, added by Stats. 1993, c. 893, § 2.

Former § 22131.1, added by Stats.1981, c. 1089, § 1.

§ 22141.5. Renumbered § 22141 and amended by Stats.1977, c. 37, § 5, eff. April 29, 1977, operative April 30, 1977

§ 22142. Indexed final compensation

"Indexed final compensation" means final compensation upon which a disability allowance or disability retirement allowance was based, adjusted annually from the school year in which an allowance begins to accrue by the rate of change in the average compensation earnable as determined by the board.

(Added by Stats.1994, c. 933 (A.B.3171), § 3, eff. Sept. 28, 1994.)

Historical and Statutory Notes

Former § 22142, added by Stats.1993, c. 893 (A.B.1796), § 2, defining regular interest, was repealed by Stats.1994, c. 933 (A.B.3171), § 2, eff. Sept. 28, 1994. See Education Code § 22162.

Former § 22142, enacted by Stats.1976, c. 1010, § 2, amended by Stats.1977, c. 36, § 97; Stats.1981, c. 124, § 16; Stats.1992, c. 1167

(S.B.1886), § 4.5, defining "projected service", was repealed by Stats.1993, c. 893 (A.B.1796), § 1. See Education Code § 22157.

Derivation: Former § 22134, added by Stats. 1993, c. 893, § 2.

Former § 22131.5, added by Stats.1982, c. 1314, § 1, amended by Stats.1992, c. 1166 (S.B. 1885), § 4.5.

§ 22143. Investment manager; investment adviser

"Investment manager" and "investment adviser" mean any person, firm, or custodian referred to in Section 22359, either appointed by or under contract with the board to engage in investment transactions or to manage or advise in the management of the assets of the Teachers' Retirement Fund with respect to the Defined Benefit Program under this part and the Cash Balance Benefit Program under Part 14 (commencing with Section 26000).

(Added by Stats.1994, c. 933 (A.B.3171), § 3, eff. Sept. 28, 1994. Amended by Stats. 1996, c. 634 (S.B.2041), § 24; Stats.1998, c. 965 (A.B.2765), § 6.5.)

Historical and Statutory Notes

Former § 22143, added by Stats.1993, c. 893 (A.B.1796), § 2, defining investment manager and investment adviser, was repealed by Stats.

1994, c. 933 (A.B.3171), § 2, eff. Sept. 28, 1994. See this section.

Former § 22143, enacted by Stats.1976, c. 1010, § 2, amended by Stats.1993, c. 920 (A.B. 1631), § 1, defining proof of death, was repealed by Stats.1994, c. 933 (A.B.3171), § 7, eff. Sept. 28, 1994. See Education Code § 22158.

Derivation: Former § 22143, added by Stats. 1993, c. 893, § 2.

Former § 22131.7, added by Stats.1987, c. 330, § 1.

Cross References

Investments, see Education Code § 22350 et seq.

§ 22144. Investment transactions

"Investment transactions" means investment services of an asset management or investment advisory nature and may include advisory services, research material, trading assistance, trading expenses, discretionary management of funds of the plan upon approval by the board, acquisition of equipment to be used as part of the investment function, services that provide a recommended course of action or personal expertise, investment-related legal expenses, investment-related contracting expenses, or custodian services referred to in Section 22359.

(Added by Stats.1994, c. 933 (A.B.3171), § 3, eff. Sept. 28, 1994. Amended by Stats. 1996, c. 634 (S.B.2041), § 25.)

Historical and Statutory Notes

Former § 22144, added by Stats.1993, c. 893 (A.B.1796, § 2, defining investment transactions, was repealed by Stats.1994, c. 933 (A.B. 3171), § 2, eff. Sept. 28, 1994. See this section.

Former § 22144, enacted by Stats.1976, c. 1010, § 2, defining public school, was repealed

by Stats.1993, c. 893 (A.B.1796), § 1. See Education Code § 22159.

Derivation: Former § 22144, added by Stats. 1993, c. 893, § 2.

Former § 22131.8, added by Stats.1987, c. 330, § 2.

Cross References

Investments, see Education Code § 22350 et seq.

§ 22144.5. Liability gains and losses

"Liability gains and losses" means the difference between actual noninvestment related experience and the experience expected based upon a set of noninvestment related actuarial assumptions during the period between two actuarial valuation dates, as determined in accordance with assumptions adopted by the board pursuant to Section 22311.5.

(Added by Stats.2000, c. 1021 (A.B.2700), § 6.)

Historical and Statutory Notes

Operative effect of Stats.2000, c. 1021 (A.B. 2700), see Historical and Statutory Notes following Education Code § 22101.5.

§ 22145. Local system

"Local system" means any retirement system, exclusive of this system, in which public school teachers are members, operated by a city, county, or other political subdivision of the state.

(Added by Stats.1994, c. 933 (A.B.3171), § 3, eff. Sept. 28, 1994.)

Historical and Statutory Notes

Former § 22145, added by Stats.1993, c. 893 (A.B.1796, § 2, defining local system, was repealed by Stats.1994, c. 933 (A.B.3171), § 2, eff. Sept. 28, 1994. See this section.

Former § 22145, enacted by Stats.1976, c. 1010, § 2, amended by Stats.1982, c. 279, § 2, defining regular interest, was repealed by Stats. 1993, c. 893 (A.B.1796), § 1. See Education Code § 22142.

Derivation: Former § 22145, added by Stats. 1993, c. 893, § 2.

Former § 22132, enacted by Stats.1976, c. 1010, § 2.

Educ.C.1959, § 13840, added by Stats.1969, c. 896, p. 1738, § 2, amended by Stats.1972, c. 1010, p. 1859, § 6; Stats.1974, c. 1293, p. 2807, § 21.

Educ.C.1959, § 13824 (Stats.1959, c. 2, p. 984, § 13824, amended by Stats.1959, c. 1604, p. 3976, § 1).

Educ.C.1943, § 14271, added by Stats.1944, 4th Ex.Sess., c. 13, p. 116, § 2.

§ 22145.5. Repealed by Stats.1994, c. 933 (A.B.3171), § 2, eff. Sept. 28, 1994

Historical and Statutory Notes

The repealed section, added by Stats.1993, c. 893 (A.B.1796), § 2, defined reinstatement. See Education Code § 22163.

§ 22146. Member

"Member" means any person, unless excluded under other provisions of this part, who has performed creditable service as defined in Section 22119.5 and has earned creditable compensation for that service and has not received a refund for that service and, as a result, is subject to the Defined Benefit Program. A member's rights and obligations under this part with respect to the Defined Benefit Program shall be determined by the applicability of subdivision (a), (b), (c), or (d), and subject to any applicable exceptions under other provisions of this part.

(a) An active member is a member who is not retired or disabled and who earns creditable compensation during the school year.

(b) An inactive member is a member who is not retired or disabled and who has not earned creditable compensation during the school year immediately prior to and the school year during which the member retires for service.

(c) A disabled member is a member to whom a disability allowance is payable under Chapter 25 (commencing with Section 24001).

(d) A retired member is a member who has terminated employment and has retired for service under the provisions of Chapter 27 (commencing with Section 24201), or has retired for disability under the provisions of Chapter 26 (commencing with Section 24100) or retired for service or disability under the provisions of Chapter 21 (commencing with Section 23400), and to whom a retirement allowance is therefore payable.

(Added by Stats.1995, c. 592 (A.B.1298), § 3. Amended by Stats.1996, c. 634 (S.B. 2041), § 26; Stats.1998, c. 965 (A.B.2765), § 7; Stats.2000, c. 1025 (A.B.816), § 5.)

Historical and Statutory Notes

Section 17 of Stats.1995, c. 592 (A.B.1298), provides:

"It is the intent of the Legislature in adding Section 22146 to the Education Code in Section

3 of this act and in repealing Sections 22502, 22503, 22505, 22506, 22507, 22602, 22603, 22604, 22605, 22606, 22607, and 22608 of the Education Code in Sections 4 to 15, inclusive, of this act to clarify the status of the active, inactive, disabled, and retired members of the State Teachers' Retirement System. Those provisions are intended to be technical and nonsubstantive and shall not be construed to affect in any manner the eligibility or rights of any person to any benefits under the State Teachers' Retirement Law."

Former § 22146, added by Stats.1994, c. 933 (A.B.3171), § 3, defining member, was repealed by Stats.1995, c. 592 (A.B.1298), § 2. See this section.

Former § 22146, added by Stats.1993, c. 893 (A.B.1796, § 2, defining member, was repealed by Stats.1994, c. 933 (A.B.3171), § 2, eff. Sept. 28, 1994. See this section.

Former § 22146, enacted by Stats.1976, c. 1010, § 2, defining "credited interest", was repealed by Stats.1993, c. 893 (A.B.1796), § 1. See Education Code § 22141.

Derivation: Former § 22146, added by Stats. 1994, c. 933, § 3.

Former § 22146, added by Stats.1993, c. 893, § 2.

Former § 22133, enacted by Stats.1976, c. 1010, § 2.

Educ.C.1959, § 13842, added by Stats.1969, c. 896, p. 1738, § 2.

Educ.C.1959, § 13806 (Stats.1959, c. 2, p. 983, § 13806).

Educ.C.1943, § 14256, added by Stats.1944, 4th Ex.Sess., c. 13, p. 115, § 2.

Educ.C.1943, § 14254 (Stats.1943, c. 71, p. 590).

School C. § 5.801, added by Stats.1937, c. 626, p. 1717, § 4.

Library References

Schools ⚖146(3).
Westlaw Topic No. 345.

C.J.S. Schools and School Districts §§ 340 to 346.

§ 22146.5. Membership

"Membership" means membership in the Defined Benefit Program, except as otherwise specifically provided in this part.

(Added by Stats.1996, c. 634 (S.B.2041), § 27. Amended by Stats.1998, c. 965 (A.B. 2765), § 8.)

§ 22146.7. Minimum interest rate

"Minimum interest rate" means the annual interest rate determined by the board by plan amendment at which interest shall be credited to Defined Benefit Supplement accounts for a plan year.

(Added by Stats.2000, c. 74 (A.B.1509), § 16; Stats.2000, c. 1021 (A.B.2700), § 7.)

Historical and Statutory Notes

Operative effect of Stats.2000, c. 1021 (A.B. 2700), see Historical and Statutory Notes following Education Code § 22101.5.

Section affected by two or more acts at the same session of the legislature, see Government Code § 9605.

§ 22147. Month

(a) "Month" means 20 working days or four weeks of five working days each, including legal holidays, with respect to the computation and crediting of service.

(b) "Month," for all other purposes, means a period commencing on any day of a calendar month and extending through the day preceding the corresponding day of the succeeding calendar month, if there is any such corresponding day, and if not, through the last day of the succeeding calendar month.

(Added by Stats.1994, c. 933 (A.B.3171), § 3, eff. Sept. 28, 1994. Amended by Stats. 1998, c. 965 (A.B.2765), § 9.)

Historical and Statutory Notes

Former § 22147, added by Stats.1993, c. 893 (A.B.1796, § 2, defining month, was repealed by Stats.1994, c. 933 (A.B.3171), § 2, eff. Sept. 28, 1994. See this section.

Former § 22147, enacted by Stats.1976, c. 1010, § 2, amended by Stats.1981, c. 124, § 17, defining "return on investments", was repealed by Stats.1993, c. 893 (A.B.1796), § 1. See Education Code § 22165.

Derivation: Former § 22147, added by Stats. 1993, c. 893, § 2.

Former § 22134, enacted by Stats.1976, c. 1010, § 2.

Educ.C.1959, § 13843, added by Stats.1969, c. 896, p. 1738, § 2.

Educ.C.1959, § 13829 (Stats.1959, c. 2, p. 984, § 13829).

Educ.C.1943, § 14275.5, added by Stats.1953, c. 907, p. 2262, § 1.

Cross References

Month defined, generally, see Civil Code § 14 and Code of Civil Procedure § 17.
School month, see Education Code § 37201.

§ 22147.5.　Nonqualified service

"Nonqualified service" means any time during which a member did not perform creditable service subject to coverage by the plan. Nonqualified service shall not include time for which the member is eligible to purchase credit pursuant to Chapter 14 (commencing with Section 22800), Chapter 14.2 (commencing with Section 22820), or Chapter 14.5 (commencing with Section 22850).

(Added by Stats.1998, c. 1076 (S.B.2126), § 3.　Amended by Stats.1999, c. 939 (S.B. 1074), § 16;　Stats.2000, c. 1025 (A.B.816), § 6.)

§ 22148.　Normal retirement; normal retirement age

"Normal retirement" and "normal retirement age" mean the age of 60 years, which is the age upon attainment of which the member becomes eligible under the Defined Benefit Program for a service retirement allowance without reduction because of age and without special qualifications.

(Added by Stats.1994, c. 933 (A.B.3171), § 3, eff. Sept. 28, 1994.　Amended by Stats. 1996, c. 634 (S.B.2041), § 28;　Stats.1999, c. 939 (S.B.1074), § 17;　Stats.2000, c. 1025 (A.B.816), § 7.)

Historical and Statutory Notes

Former § 22148, added by Stats.1993, c. 893 (A.B.1796, § 2, defining normal retirement and normal retirement age, was repealed by Stats. 1994, c. 933 (A.B.3171), § 2, eff. Sept. 28, 1994. See this section.

Former § 22148, enacted by Stats.1976, c. 1010, § 2, amended by Stats.1977, c. 659, § 3.5; Stats.1978, c. 502, § 3; Stats.1981, c. 124, § 18,

defining retirement, was repealed by Stats.1993, c. 893 (A.B.1796), § 1.　See Education Code § 22162.

Derivation: Former § 22148, added by Stats. 1993, c. 893, § 2.

Former § 22134.5, added by Stats.1977, c. 659, § 3, amended by Stats.1987, c. 330, § 4.

Library References

Legal Jurisprudences

Am Jur 2d (Rev) Pensions and Retirement
　Funds §§ 1647 et seq.

§ 22149. Option beneficiary

"Option beneficiary" means the person designated by a member to receive a retirement allowance under the Defined Benefit Program upon the member's death.

(Added by Stats.1994, c. 933 (A.B.3171), § 3, eff. Sept. 28, 1994. Amended by Stats. 1996, c. 634 (S.B.2041), § 29; Stats.2000, c. 1025 (A.B.816), § 8.)

Historical and Statutory Notes

Former § 22149, added by Stats.1993, c. 893 (A.B.1796, § 2, defining option beneficiary, was repealed by Stats.1994, c. 933 (A.B.3171), § 2, eff. Sept. 28, 1994. See this section.

Former § 22149, enacted by Stats.1976, c. 1010, § 2, defining retirant, was repealed by

Stats.1993, c. 893 (A.B.1796), § 1. See Education Code § 22161.

Derivation: Former § 22149, added by Stats. 1993, c. 893, § 2.

Former § 22134.7, added by Stats.1981, c. 124, § 13.

§ 22150. Other public systems

"Other public systems" means any of the following:

(a) Old age, survivors, disability, and health insurance program, other than the lump-sum death payment, provided by the Social Security Act (42 U.S.C.A. Sec. 300 and following).

(b) The federal civil service retirement program.

(c) Federal military disability.

(d) Railroad retirement.

(e) A workers' compensation program.

(f) Federal railroad retirement.

(g) Any other public retirement system, including, but not limited to, any disability programs financed from public funds.

(Added by Stats.1994, c. 933 (A.B.3171), § 3, eff. Sept. 28, 1994.)

Historical and Statutory Notes

Former § 22150, added by Stats.1993, c. 893 (A.B.1796, § 2, defining other public systems, was repealed by Stats.1994, c. 933 (A.B.3171), § 2, eff. Sept. 28, 1994. See this section.

Former § 22150, enacted by Stats.1976, c. 1010, § 2, amended by Stats.1981, c. 124, § 19, defining retirement allowance, was repealed by Stats.1993, c. 893 (A.B.1796), § 1. See Education Code § 22163.

Derivation: Former § 22150, added by Stats. 1993, c. 893, § 2.

Former § 22136, enacted by Stats.1976, c. 1010, § 2, amended by Stats.1978, c. 502, § 2; Stats.1981, c. 124, § 14.

Educ.C.1959, § 13844.2, added by Stats.1971, c. 1305, p. 2571, § 23, amended by Stats.1972, c. 1089, p. 2029, § 1.

Cross References

Workers' compensation, see Labor Code § 3200 et seq.
Writings, authentication and proof of, see Evidence Code § 1400 et seq.

Notes of Decisions

Construction and application   1

___

1. Construction and application

Date on which school district's employee's disability commenced, which was prior to operative date of statute allowing state teachers' retirement system to integrate benefits payable under other policies financed from public funds, rather than date of filing of claim, which was after operative date of statute was controlling

with regard to insurer's accrual of right to integrate benefits under its contract because its obligation to provide disability benefits vested the moment disability commenced, and thus retroactivity problem arose and barred application of statute given lack of indication that legislature intended it to alter obligations already vested.   Industrial Indem. Co. v. Teachers' Retirement Bd. (App. 1 Dist. 1978) 150 Cal.Rptr. 47, 86 Cal.App.3d 92.

§§ 22150.5, 22150.7.   Repealed by Stats.1993, c. 893 (A.B.1796), § 1

Historical and Statutory Notes

Section 22150.5, added by Stats.1981, c. 124, § 19.5, defined retirement fund.   See Education Code § 22164.

Section 22150.7, added by Stats.1990, c. 560 (A.B.4129), § 1, defined school year.   See Education Code § 22166.

Legislative intent regarding Stats.1993, c. 893 (A.B.1796), including possible continuing application of provisions of repealed State Teachers' Retirement Law, see Historical and Statutory Notes under Education Code § 22000.

§ 22151.   Overtime

"Overtime" means the aggregate creditable service in excess of one year (1.000) of creditable service that is performed by a member in a school year.

(Added by Stats.1994, c. 933 (A.B.3171), § 3, eff. Sept. 28, 1994.   Amended by Stats. 1998, c. 965 (A.B.2765), § 10; Stats.2000, c. 1025 (A.B.816), § 9; Stats.2001, c. 803 (S.B.501), § 4.)

Historical and Statutory Notes

Former § 22151, added by Stats.1993, c. 893 (A.B.1796, § 2, defining overtime, was repealed by Stats.1994, c. 933 (A.B.3171), § 2, eff. Sept. 28, 1994.   See this section.

Former § 22151, enacted by Stats.1976, c. 1010, § 2, amended by Stats.1980, c. 244, § 1, defining service, was repealed by Stats.1993, c. 893 (A.B.1796), § 1.   See Education Code § 22167.

Derivation: Former § 22151, added by Stats. 1993, c. 893, § 2.

Former § 22135, enacted by Stats.1976, c. 1010, § 2.

Educ.C.1959, § 13844, added by Stats.1969, c. 896, p. 1738, § 2.

Educ.C.1959, § 13833 (Stats.1959, c. 2, p. 986, § 13833).

Educ.C.1943, § 14276.7, added by Stats.1955, c. 1395, p. 2492, § 4, amended by Stats.1956, 1st Ex.Sess., c. 55, p. 430, § 3.

Library References

Legal Jurisprudences
Cal Jur 3d Sch § 368.

Notes of Decisions

Definitions   1

___

1. Definitions

"Overtime," for purposes of state teachers' retirement law, is defined as excess of all work performed in all jobs which contribute to system, not just excess pay from one single job.

O'Connor v. State Teachers' Retirement System (App. 2 Dist. 1996) 51 Cal.Rptr.2d 540, 43 Cal. App.4th 1610, rehearing denied, review denied.

Overtime, for purposes of state teachers' retirement law, is not defined as that which employer considers overtime; it is province of State Teachers' Retirement Board to determine what pay is creditable to retirement.   O'Connor v.

State Teachers' Retirement System (App. 2 Dist.
1996) 51 Cal.Rptr.2d 540, 43 Cal.App.4th 1610,
rehearing denied, review denied.

§ 22152. Parent

"Parent" means a natural parent of a member or a parent who adopted the
member prior to his or her attainment of 18 years of age or to the member's
marriage, whichever occurs earlier.

(Added by Stats.1994, c. 933 (A.B.3171), § 3, eff. Sept. 28, 1994.)

Historical and Statutory Notes

Former § 22152, added by Stats.1993, c. 893
(A.B.1796, § 2, defining parent, was repealed by
Stats.1994, c. 933 (A.B.3171), § 2, eff. Sept. 28,
1994. See this section.

Former § 22152, enacted by Stats.1976, c.
1010, § 2, defining spouse, was repealed by
Stats.1993, c. 893 (A.B.1796), § 1. See Education Code § 22168.

Derivation: Former § 22152, added by Stats.
1993, c. 893, § 2.

Former § 22137, enacted by Stats.1976, c.
1010, § 2.

Educ.C.1959, § 13844.4, added by Stats.1971,
c. 1305, p. 2571, § 24.

§ 22153. Repealed by Stats.1995, c. 390 (A.B.1122), § 8, operative July 1, 1996

Historical and Statutory Notes

The repealed section, added by Stats.1994, c.
933 (A.B.3171), § 3, derived from former
§ 22153, added by Stats.1993, c. 893, § 2, defined part-time basis with respect to service,
and was repealed by its own terms.

Former § 22153, added by Stats.1993, c. 893
(A.B.1796), § 2, defining part-time basis with
respect to service, was repealed by Stats.1994,
c. 933 (A.B.3171), § 2, eff. Sept. 28, 1994. See
this section.

Former § 22153, enacted by Stats.1976, c.
1010, § 1, derived from Educ.C.1959, § 13854,
added by Stats.1969, c. 896, p. 1738, § 2,
amended by Stats.1971, c. 407, p. 777, § 9;
Stats.1974, c. 1293, p. 2808, § 27; and Educ.C.
1959, § 13818.1, added by Stats.1963, c. 2170,
p. 4552, § 3, defining tax-sheltered annuity, was
repealed by Stats.1978, c. 870, § 2, operative
July 1, 1979.

§ 22154. Pay period

"Pay period" means a payroll period of not less than four weeks or more
than one calendar month.

(Added by Stats.1994, c. 933 (A.B.3171), § 3, eff. Sept. 28, 1994. Amended by Stats.
1998, c. 965 (A.B.2765), § 11.)

Historical and Statutory Notes

Former § 22154, added by Stats.1993, c. 893
(A.B.1796), § 2, defining pay period, was re-
pealed by Stats.1994, c. 933 (A.B.3171), § 2, eff.
Sept. 28, 1994. See this section.

Former § 22154, enacted by Stats.1976, c.
1010, § 2, derived from Educ.C.1959, § 13855,
added by Stats.1969, c. 896, p. 1738, § 2,
amended by Stats.1971, c. 407, p. 777, § 10;
Stats.1974, c. 1293, p. 2808, § 28; and Educ.C.
1959, § 13814.1, added by Stats.1963, c. 2170,

p. 4551, § 1, defining "tax-sheltered annuity
contributions", was repealed by Stats.1978, c.
870, § 3, operative July 1, 1979.

Derivation: Former § 22154, added by Stats.
1993, c. 893, § 2.

Former § 22139, enacted by Stats.1976, c.
1010, § 2.

Educ.C.1959, § 13844.8, added by Stats.1970,
c. 466, p. 923, § 2.

§ 22155. Payroll

"Payroll" includes registers, warrants, and any other documents upon which the employer identifies persons to whom compensation is paid.

(Added by Stats.1994, c. 933 (A.B.3171), § 3, eff. Sept. 28, 1994. Amended by Stats. 1997, c. 482 (S.B.471), § 5.)

Historical and Statutory Notes

Former § 22155, added by Stats.1993, c. 893 (A.B.1796), § 2, defining payroll, was repealed by Stats.1994, c. 933 (A.B.3171), § 2, eff. Sept. 28, 1994. See this section.

Former § 22155, enacted by Stats.1976, c. 1010, § 2, defining survivor allowance, was repealed by Stats.1993, c. 893 (A.B.1796), § 1. See Education Code § 22169.

Derivation: Former § 22155, added by Stats. 1993, c. 893, § 2.

Former § 22140, enacted by Stats.1976, c. 1010, § 2.

Educ.C.1959, § 13845, added by Stats.1969, c. 896, p. 1738, § 2.

Educ.C.1959, § 13821 (Stats.1959, c. 2, p. 984, § 13821).

Educ.C.1943, § 14268, added by Stats.1944, 4th Ex.Sess., c. 13, p. 116, § 2.

Educ.C.1943, § 14266 (Stats.1943, c. 71, p. 590).

School C. § 5.801, added by Stats.1937, c. 626, p. 1717, § 4.

§ 22155.5. Plan

"Plan" means the State Teachers' Retirement Plan.

(Added by Stats.1996, c. 634 (S.B.2041), § 18. Amended by Stats.1998, c. 1048 (S.B.2085), § 4.)

Historical and Statutory Notes

Former § 22155.5, added by Stats.1992, c. 1166 (S.B.1885), § 6, defined survivor benefit allowance and was repealed by Stats.1993, c. 893 (A.B.1796), 1. See Education Code § 22170.

Library References

Legal Jurisprudences
Cal Jur 3d Fam Law § 819; Sch § 368.

§ 22156. Plan vesting

"Plan vesting," with respect to benefits payable under the Defined Benefit Program, means the member has met the credited service requirement for receipt of a benefit, and has a right to receive the benefit at a future date provided all other conditions required to receive the benefit are also met.

(Added by Stats.1994, c. 933 (A.B.3171), § 3, eff. Sept. 28, 1994. Amended by Stats. 1996, c. 634 (S.B.2041), § 32; Stats.1998, c. 965 (A.B.2765), § 12; Stats.2000, c. 1025 (A.B.816), § 10.)

Historical and Statutory Notes

Former § 22156, added by Stats.1993, c. 893 (A.B.1796), § 2, defining projected final compensation, was repealed by Stats.1994, c. 933 (A.B. 3171), § 2, eff. Sept. 28, 1994. See Education Code § 22157.

Former § 22156, enacted by Stats.1976, c. 1010, § 2, defining system, was repealed by Stats.1993, c. 893 (A.B.1796), § 1. See Education Code § 22171.

Derivation: Former § 22173, added by Stats. 1993, c. 893, § 2.

Former § 22157, enacted by Stats.1976, c. 1010, § 2.

Educ.C.1959, § 13862, added by Stats.1972, c. 1010, p. 1859, § 8.

Cross References

Final vesting, see Education Code § 22138.

§ 22156.05. Plan year

"Plan year" means the period of time beginning on July 1 of one calendar year and ending on June 30 of the following calendar year. For purposes of the Defined Benefit Supplement Program, the board shall designate by plan amendment the initial plan year.

(Added by Stats.2000, c. 74 (A.B.1509), § 17.)

§ 22156.1. Present value

"Present value," for purposes of Section 22718, means the amount of money needed on the effective date of retirement to reimburse the system for the actuarially determined cost of the portion of a member's retirement allowance attributable to unused excess sick leave days. The present value on the effective date of retirement shall equal the number of unused excess sick leave days divided by the number of base days, multiplied by the prior year's compensation earnable multiplied by the present value factor.

(Added by Stats.1999, c. 939 (S.B.1074), § 18. Amended by Stats.2000, c. 1025 (A.B.816), § 11.)

Historical and Statutory Notes

Subordination of legislation by Stats.1999, c. 939 (S.B.1074), to other 1999 legislation, see Historical and Statutory Notes under Education Code § 22000.

Subordination of legislation by Stats.2000, c. 1025 (A.B.816), to other 2000 legislation, see Historical and Statutory Notes under Education Code § 22106.

§ 22156.2. Present value factor

"Present value factor," for purposes of Section 22156.1, means an overall average rate based upon the demographics of members who recently retired under the Defined Benefit Program and regular interest that shall determine present value on the effective date of retirement.

(Added by Stats.1999, c. 939 (S.B.1074), § 19.)

Historical and Statutory Notes

Subordination of legislation by Stats.1999, c. 939 (S.B.1074), to other 1999 legislation, see

Historical and Statutory Notes under Education Code § 22000.

§ 22156.5. Prior year's compensation earnable

"Prior year's compensation earnable" means the compensation earnable for the most recent school year in which the member earned service credit that precedes the last school year in which the member earned service credit.

(Added by Stats.1999, c. 939 (S.B.1074), § 20.)

Historical and Statutory Notes

Subordination of legislation by Stats.1999, c. 939 (S.B.1074), to other 1999 legislation, see Historical and Statutory Notes under Education Code § 22000.

§ 22157. Projected final compensation

"Projected final compensation" means the final compensation used in computing the disability or family allowance increased by 2 percent, compounded annually to the earlier of normal retirement age or the date the disability allowance is terminated.

(Added by Stats.1994, c. 933 (A.B.3171), § 3, eff. Sept. 28, 1994.)

Historical and Statutory Notes

Former § 22157, added by Stats.1993, c. 893 (A.B.1796, § 2, defining projected final compensation, was repealed by Stats.1994, c. 933 (A.B. 3171), § 2, eff. Sept. 28, 1994. See Education Code § 22158.

Former § 22157, enacted by Stats.1976, c. 1010, § 2, defining plan vesting, was repealed by Stats.1993, c. 893 (A.B.1796), § 1. See Education Code § 22173.

Derivation: Former § 22156, added by Stats. 1993, c. 893, § 2.

Former § 22141, formerly § 22141.5, added by Stats.1977, c. 36, § 411, renumbered § 22141 and amended by Stats.1977, c. 37, § 5, amended by Stats.1981, c. 124, § 15; Stats.

1992, c. 1166 (S.B.1885), § 5; Stats.1992, c. 1167 (S.B.1886), § 4.4.

Former § 22141, enacted by Stats.1977, c. 36, § 410.5.

Former §§ 22141, enacted by Stats.1976, c. 1010, § 2.

Educ.C.1959, § 13846.5, added by Stats.1976, c. 1308, § 4.

Educ.C.1959, § 13846.5, added by Stats.1976, c. 1412, § 3.

Educ.C.1959, § 13846.5, added by Stats.1971, c. 1305, p. 2571, § 2.5, amended by Stats.1972, c. 1010, p. 2030, § 7.

Cross References

Final compensation, classroom teacher, see Education Code § 22135.
Final compensation, members with salary reduction, see Education Code § 22136.
Higher final compensation, certain managerial or supervisory employees subjected to salary range reductions, see Education Code § 22137.
Indexed final compensation, see Education Code § 22142.

§ 22158. Projected service

(a) "Projected service" means the sum of credited service plus the credited service that would have been earned for the school years during which a disability allowance was payable if the member had performed creditable service during that time.

(b) Projected service for a school year shall be determined on the basis of the highest credited service earned by the member during any one of the three school years immediately preceding the member's death or the date the disability allowance began to accrue.

(c) Projected service shall not include credited service for which contributions have been credited to the Defined Benefit Supplement Program.

(Added by Stats.2000, c. 1021 (A.B.2700), § 9.)

Historical and Statutory Notes

Operative effect of Stats.2000, c. 1021 (A.B. 2700), see Historical and Statutory Notes following Education Code § 22101.5.

Former § 22158, added by Stats.1994, c. 933 (A.B.3171), § 3, amended by Stats.1993, c. 634 (S.B.2041), § 33, defining projected service, was repealed by Stats.2000, c. 1021 (A.B.2700), § 8. See this section.

Former § 22158, added by Stats.1993, c. 893 (A.B.1796), § 2, defining proof of death, was repealed by Stats.1994, c. 933 (A.B.3171), § 2, eff. Sept. 28, 1994. See Education Code § 22159.

Stats.1993, c. 893, provided for addition of this section, similar to § 22143, as well as for repeal of § 22143. Stats.1993, c. 920, amended § 22143. Subordination of legislation by Stats. 1993, c. 893, and legislative intent regarding that act, including possible continuing application of provisions of repealed State Teachers' Retirement Law, see Historical and Statutory

Notes under Education Code § 22000. Section affected by two or more acts at the same session of the legislature, see Government Code § 9605.

Former § 22158, enacted by Stats.1976, c. 1010, § 2, defining provisional vesting, was repealed by Stats.1993, c. 893 (A.B.1796), § 1. See Education Code § 22174.

Derivation: Former § 22158, added by Stats. 1994, c. 933 (A.B.3171), § 3, amended by Stats. 1993, c. 634 (S.B.2041), § 33.

Former § 22157, added by Stats.1993, c. 893, § 2.

Former § 22142, enacted by Stats.1976, c. 1010, § 2, amended by Stats.1977, c. 36, § 97; Stats.1981, c. 124, § 16; Stats.1992, c. 1167 (S.B.1886), § 4.5.

Educ.C.1959, § 13846.8, added by Stats.1971, c. 1305, p. 2572, § 26, amended by Stats.1976, c. 1308, § 5; Stats.1976, c. 1412, § 4.

§ 22159. Proof of death

"Proof of death" means providing to the system any evidence of death required by the system.

(Added by Stats.1994, c. 933 (A.B.3171), § 3, eff. Sept. 28, 1994.)

Historical and Statutory Notes

Former § 22159, added by Stats.1993, c. 893 (A.B.1796, § 2, defining public school, was repealed by Stats.1994, c. 933 (A.B.3171), § 2, eff. Sept. 28, 1994. See Education Code § 22161.

Former § 22159, enacted by Stats.1976, c. 1010, § 2, defining final vesting, was repealed by Stats.1993, c. 893 (A.B.1796), § 1. See Education Code § 22172.

Derivation: Former § 22158, added by Stats. 1993, c. 893, § 2.

Former § 22143, added by Stats.1976, c. 1010, § 2, amended by Stats.1993, c. 920, § 1.

Educ.C.1959, § 13846.9, added by Stats.1974, c. 1153, § 7.

§ 22160. Provisional vesting

"Provisional vesting" means the member has reached the minimum age requirement and has attained the credited service required under the Defined Benefit Program for eligibility to receive a retirement allowance, and the member is entitled to terminate employment and retire at any time to receive a retirement allowance.

(Added by Stats.1994, c. 933 (A.B.3171), § 3, eff. Sept. 28, 1994. Amended by Stats. 2000, c. 1025 (A.B.816), § 12.)

Historical and Statutory Notes

Derivation: Former § 22174, added by Stats. 1993, c. 893, § 2.

Former § 22158, enacted by Stats.1976, c. 1010, § 2.

Educ.C.1959, § 13863, added by Stats.1972, c. 1010, p. 1859, § 9.

Cross References

Final vesting, see Education Code § 22138.

Plan vesting, see Education Code § 22156.

§ 22161. Public school

"Public school" means any day or evening elementary school, any day or evening secondary school, community college, technical school, kindergarten school, and prekindergarten school established by the Legislature, or by municipal or district authority.

(Added by Stats.1994, c. 933 (A.B.3171), § 3, eff. Sept. 28, 1994. Amended by Stats. 1998, c. 965 (A.B.2765), § 13; Stats.1999, c. 939 (S.B.1074), § 21.)

Historical and Statutory Notes

Former § 22161, added by Stats.1993, c. 893 (A.B.1796, § 2, defining retirant, was repealed by Stats.1994, c. 933 (A.B.3171), § 2, eff. Sept. 28, 1994. See Education Code § 22164.

Derivation: Former § 22159, added by Stats. 1993, c. 893, § 2.

Former § 22144, enacted by Stats.1976, c. 1010, § 2.

Educ.C.1959, § 13847, added by Stats.1969, c. 896, p. 1738, § 2, amended by Stats.1971, c. 1004, p. 1921, § 4.

Educ.C.1959, § 13805 (Stats.1959, c. 2, p. 983, § 13805).

Educ.C.1943, § 14255, added by Stats.1944, 4th Ex.Sess., c. 13, p. 115, § 2.

Educ.C.1943, § 14253 (Stats.1943, c. 71, p. 590).

School C. § 5.801, added by Stats.1937, c. 626, p. 1717, § 4.

Cross References

Community colleges, generally, see Education Code § 70900 et seq.

§ 22161.5. Refund

"Refund" means the lump-sum return of a member's accumulated retirement contributions under the Defined Benefit Program and does not include the balance of credits in the member's Defined Benefit Supplement account.

(Added by Stats.1996, c. 634 (S.B.2041), § 34. Amended by Stats.2000, c. 74 (A.B. 1509), § 18; Stats.2000, c. 1021 (A.B.2700), § 10.)

Historical and Statutory Notes

Operative effect of Stats.2000, c. 1021 (A.B. 2700), see Historical and Statutory Notes following Education Code § 22101.5.

Section affected by two or more acts at the same session of the legislature, see Government Code § 9605.

§ 22162. Regular interest

"Regular interest" means interest that is compounded annually based on the annual equivalent of the prior year's average yield to maturity on the investment-grade fixed income securities attributable to the Defined Benefit Program, but not on assets attributable to the Defined Benefit Supplement Program. The regular interest rate shall be adopted annually by the board as a plan amendment with respect to the Defined Benefit Program.

(Added by Stats.2000, c. 74 (A.B.1509), § 20.)

Historical and Statutory Notes

Former § 22162, added by Stats.1994, c. 933 (A.B.3171), § 3, amended by Stats.1998, c. 965

(A.B.2765), § 14, defining regular interest, was

repealed by Stats.2000, c. 74 (A.B.1509), § 19. See this section.

Former § 22162, added by Stats.1993, c. 893 (A.B.1796, § 2, defining retirement, was repealed by Stats.1994, c. 933 (A.B.3171), § 2, eff. Sept. 28, 1994. See Education Code § 22165.

Derivation: Former § 22162, added by Stats. 1994, c. 933 (A.B.3171), § 3, amended by Stats. 1998, c. 965 (A.B.2765), § 14.

Former § 22142, added by Stats.1993, c. 893, § 2.

Former § 22145, enacted by Stats.1976, c. 1010, § 2, amended by Stats.1982, c. 278, § 2.

Educ.C.1959, § 13848, added by Stats.1971, c. 407, p. 776, § 6.

Educ.C.1959, § 13848, added by Stats.1969, c. 896, p. 1738, § 2.

Educ.C.1959, § 13811 (Stats.1959, c. 2, p. 983, § 13811).

Educ.C.1943, § 14260, added by Stats.1944, 4th Ex.Sess., c. 13, p. 115, § 2.

Educ.C.1943, § 14258 (Stats.1943, c. 71, p. 590).

School C. § 5.801 added by Stats.1937, c. 626, p. 1717, § 4.

Cross References

Credited interest, see Education Code § 22120.

§ 22162.5. Regular meeting

"Regular meeting" means a meeting of the board held in accordance with a schedule of meetings that states the dates and places of the meetings and that is adopted by the board.

(Added by Stats.1996, c. 634 (S.B.2041), § 35.)

§ 22163. Reinstatement

"Reinstatement" means the change in status with respect to the Defined Benefit Program under this part from a disabled or retired member to an active or inactive member and termination of one of the following:

(a) A service retirement allowance pursuant to Section 24208.

(b) A disability retirement allowance pursuant to Section 24117.

(c) A disability allowance pursuant to Section 24004, 24006, or 24015.

(d) A service retirement allowance or disability retirement allowance pursuant to Section 23404.

(Added by Stats.1996, c. 634 (S.B.2041), § 37. Amended by Stats.1998, c. 965 (A.B. 2765), § 15; Stats.1999, c. 939 (S.B.1074), § 22; Stats.2000, c. 1025 (A.B.816), § 13.)

Historical and Statutory Notes

Former § 22163, added by Stats.1994, c. 933 (A.B.3171), § 3, defining reinstatement, was repealed by Stats.1996, c. 634 (S.B.2041), § 36. See this section.

Former § 22163, added by Stats.1993, c. 893 (A.B.1796, § 2, defining retirement allowance, was repealed by Stats.1994, c. 933 (A.B.3171),

§ 2, eff. Sept. 28, 1994. See Education Code § 22166.

Derivation: Former § 22163, added by Stats. 1994, c. 933, § 3.

Former § 22145.5, added by Stats.1993, c. 861 (A.B.447), § 1.

Library References

Legal Jurisprudences

Am Jur 2d (Rev) Pensions and Retirement Funds §§ 1637 et seq.

§ 22164. Replacement benefits program

"Replacement benefits program" means the program established pursuant to Chapter 27.5 (commencing with Section 24250) in compliance with the provisions of Section 415(m) of the Internal Revenue Code of 1986 (26 U.S.C. Sec. 415(m)) as applicable to a governmental plan, as defined in Section 414(d) of the Internal Revenue Code of 1986 (26 U.S.C. Sec. 414(d)).

(Added by Stats.1999, c. 465 (A.B.819), § 1.)

Historical and Statutory Notes

Former § 22164, added by Stats.1994, c. 993 (A.B.3171), § 3, derived from former § 22161, added by Stats.1993, c. 893, § 2; former § 22149, enacted by Stats.1976, c. 1010, § 2; Educ.C.1959, § 13849.1, added by Stats.1969, c. 896, p. 1738, § 2, defining retirant, was repealed by Stats.1996, c. 634 (S.B.2041), § 38.

Former § 22164, added by Stats.1993, c. 893 (A.B.1796, § 2, defining retirement fund, was repealed by Stats.1994, c. 933 (A.B.3171), § 2, eff. Sept. 28, 1994. See Education Code § 22167.

§ 22165. Retirement

"Retirement" means termination of employment subject to coverage by the plan and a change in status from an inactive member, an active member, or a disabled member to a retired member.

(Added by Stats.1994, c. 933 (A.B.3171), § 3, eff. Sept. 28, 1994. Amended by Stats. 1996, c. 634 (S.B.2041), § 39; Stats.1998, c. 965 (A.B.2765), § 16; Stats.2000, c. 1025 (A.B.816), § 14.)

Historical and Statutory Notes

Former § 22165, added by Stats.1993, c. 893 (A.B.1796, § 2, defining return on investments, was repealed by Stats.1994, c. 933 (A.B.3171), § 2, eff. Sept. 28, 1994. See Education Code § 22168.

Derivation: Former § 22162, added by Stats. 1993, c. 893, § 2.

Former § 22148, enacted by Stats.1976, c. 1010, § 2, amended by Stats.1977, c. 659, § 3.5; Stats.1978, c. 502, § 3; Stats.1981, c. 124, § 18.

Educ.C.1959, § 13849, added by Stats.1969, c. 896, p. 1738, § 2, amended by Stats.1971, c.

1004, p. 1921, § 5; Stats.1974, c. 1293, p. 2808, § 23.

Educ.C.1959, § 13822 (Stats.1959, c. 2, p. 984, § 13822).

Educ.C.1943, § 14269, added by Stats.1944, 4th Ex.Sess., c. 13, p. 116, § 2.

Educ.C.1943, § 14267 (Stats.1943, c. 71, p. 590).

School C. § 5.801, added by Stats.1937, c. 626, p. 1717, § 4.

§ 22166. Retirement allowance

"Retirement allowance" means the amount payable to a retired member or an option beneficiary on a monthly basis.

(Added by Stats.1994, c. 933 (A.B.3171), § 3, eff. Sept. 28, 1994. Amended by Stats. 1996, c. 634 (S.B.2041), § 40.)

Historical and Statutory Notes

Former § 22166, added by Stats.1993, c. 893 (A.B.1796, § 2, defining school year, was repealed by Stats.1994, c. 933 (A.B.3171), § 2, eff. Sept. 28, 1994. See Education Code § 22169.

Derivation: Former § 22163, added by Stats. 1993, c. 893, § 2.

Former § 22150, enacted by Stats.1976, c. 1010, § 2, amended by Stats.1981, c. 124, § 19.

Educ.C.1959, § 13850, added by Stats.1969, c. 896, p. 1738, § 2, amended by Stats.1974, c. 1293, p. 2808, § 24.

Educ.C.1959, § 13820 (Stats.1959, c. 2, p. 984, § 13820).

Educ.C.1943, § 14267, added by Stats.1944, 4th Ex.Sess., c. 13, p. 116, § 2, amended by Stats.1949, c. 1158, p. 2073, § 1.

Educ.C.1943, § 14265 (Stats.1943, c. 71, p. 590).

School C. § 5.801, added by Stats.1937, c. 626, p. 1717, § 4.

§ 22166.5. Retirement benefit

"Retirement benefit" means the amount payable under the Defined Benefit Supplement Program, based on the balance of credits in the member's Defined Benefit Supplement account, to a member who has retired for service under the Defined Benefit Program.

(Added by Stats.2000, c. 74 (A.B.1509), § 21.)

§ 22167. Retirement fund

"Retirement fund" means the Teachers' Retirement Fund.

(Added by Stats.1994, c. 933 (A.B.3171), § 3, eff. Sept. 28, 1994.)

Historical and Statutory Notes

Former § 22167, added by Stats.1993, c. 893 (A.B.1796, § 2, defining service, was repealed by Stats.1994, c. 933 (A.B.3171), § 2, eff. Sept. 28, 1994. See Education Code § 22170.

Derivation: Former § 22164, added by Stats. 1993, c. 893, § 2.

Former § 22150.5, added by Stats.1981, c. 124, § 19.5.

§ 22168. Return on investments

"Return on investments" means income received or receivable from the system's investments.

(Added by Stats.1994, c. 933 (A.B.3171), § 3, eff. Sept. 28, 1994.)

Historical and Statutory Notes

Former § 22168, added by Stats.1993, c. 893 (A.B.1796, § 2, defining spouse, was repealed by Stats.1994, c. 933 (A.B.3171), § 2, eff. Sept. 28, 1994. See Education Code § 22171.

Derivation: Former § 22165, added by Stats. 1993, c. 893, § 2.

Former § 22147, enacted by Stats.1976, c. 1010, § 2, amended by Stats.1981, c. 124, § 17.

Educ.C.1959, § 13848.2, added by Stats.1971, c. 407, p. 777, § 8.

Cross References

Investments, generally, see Education Code § 22350 et seq.

§ 22169. School year

"School year" means the fiscal year or the academic year.

(Added by Stats.1994, c. 933 (A.B.3171), § 3, eff. Sept. 28, 1994.)

Historical and Statutory Notes

Former § 22169, added by Stats.1993, c. 893 (A.B.1796, § 2, defining survivor allowance, was repealed by Stats.1994, c. 933 (A.B.3171), § 2, eff. Sept. 28, 1994. See Education Code § 22172.

Derivation: Former § 22166, added by Stats. 1993, c. 893, § 2.

Former § 22150.7, added by Stats.1990, c. 560 (A.B.4129), § 1.

§ 22170. Service

"Service" means work performed for compensation in a position subject to coverage under the Defined Benefit Program, except as otherwise specifically provided in this part, providing the contributions on compensation for that work are not credited to the Defined Benefit Supplement Program.

(Added by Stats.1994, c. 933 (A.B.3171), § 3, eff. Sept. 28, 1994. Amended by Stats. 1998, c. 965 (A.B.2765), § 17; Stats.2000, c. 1021 (A.B.2700), § 11.)

Historical and Statutory Notes

Operative effect of Stats.2000, c. 1021 (A.B. 2700), see Historical and Statutory Notes following Education Code § 22101.5.

Former § 22170, added by Stats.1993, c. 893 (A.B.1796, § 2, defining survivor benefit allowance, was repealed by Stats.1994, c. 933 (A.B. 3171), § 2, eff. Sept. 28, 1994. See Education Code § 22173.

Derivation: Former § 22167, added by Stats. 1993, c. 893, § 2.

Former § 22151, enacted by Stats.1976, c. 1010, § 2, amended by Stats.1980, c. 244, § 1.

Educ.C.1959, § 13852, added by Stats.1969, c. 896, p. 1738, § 2, amended by Stats.1974, c. 1293, p. 2808, § 26.

Educ.C.1959, § 13808 (Stats.1959, c. 2, p. 983, § 13808).

Educ.C.1943, § 14258, added by Stats.1944, 4th Ex.Sess., c. 13, p. 115, § 2, amended by Stats.1956, 1st Ex.Sess., c. 55, p. 430, § 1.

Educ.C.1943, § 14256 (Stats.1943, c. 71, p. 590).

School C. § 5.801, added by Stats.1937, c. 626, p. 1717, § 4.

Library References

Schools ⟜146(6).
Westlaw Topic No. 345.
C.J.S. Schools and School Districts §§ 340, 342, 345.

Legal Jurisprudences

Am Jur 2d (Rev) Pensions and Retirement Funds §§ 1643 et seq.

§ 22170.5. Sick leave days; basic sick leave day; excess sick leave days

(a) "Sick leave days" means the number of days of accumulated and unused leave of absence for illness or injury.

(b) "Basic sick leave day" means the equivalent of one day's paid leave of absence per pay period due to illness or injury.

(c) "Excess sick leave days" means the day or total number of days, granted by an employer in a pay period as defined in Section 22154 after June 30, 1986, for paid leave of absence due to illness or injury, in excess of a basic sick leave day.

(Added by Stats.1999, c. 939 (S.B.1074), § 23.)

§ 22171. Spouse

"Spouse" means a person who was married to the member for a continuous period beginning at least 12 months prior to the death of the member unless a child is born to the member and his or her spouse within the 12–month period or unless the spouse is carrying the member's unborn child.

(Added by Stats.1994, c. 933 (A.B.3171), § 3, eff. Sept. 28, 1994. Amended by Stats. 1996, c. 634 (S.B.2041), § 41.)

Historical and Statutory Notes

Former § 22171, added by Stats.1993, c. 893 (A.B.1796, § 2, defining system, was repealed by Stats.1994, c. 933 (A.B.3171), § 2, eff. Sept. 28, 1994. See Education Code § 22174.

Derivation: Former § 22168, added by Stats. 1993, c. 893, § 2.

Former § 22152, enacted by Stats.1976, c. 1010, § 2.

Educ.C.1959, § 13852.5, added by Stats.1971, c. 1305, p. 2572, § 27, amended by Stats.1974, c. 1153, p. 2447, § 8.

Cross References

Computation of time,
Generally, see Code of Civil Procedure §§ 12 and 12a and Government Code § 6800 et seq.
Time in which any act provided by the Education Code is to be done, see Education Code § 9.
Continuation of statutes relating to subjects covered by provisions of this Code, see Education Code § 3.

Library References

Legal Jurisprudences

Am Jur 2d (Rev) Pensions and Retirement Funds §§ 1643 et seq.; 1655 et seq.

§ 22172. Survivor allowance

"Survivor allowance" means the allowance provided for in Section 23804 as it read under the law in effect on June 30, 1972.

(Added by Stats.1994, c. 933 (A.B.3171), § 3, eff. Sept. 28, 1994.)

Historical and Statutory Notes

Former § 22172, added by Stats.1993, c. 893 (A.B.1796, § 2, defining final vesting, was repealed by Stats.1994, c. 933 (A.B.3171), § 2, eff. Sept. 28, 1994. See Education Code § 22138.

Derivation: Former § 22169, added by Stats. 1993, c. 893, § 2.

Former § 22155, enacted by Stats.1976, c. 1010, § 2.

Educ.C.1959, § 13857, added by Stats.1969, c. 896, p. 1738, § 2, amended by Stats.1971, c. 1305, p. 2572, § 28.

Educ.C.1959, § 13837, added by Stats.1959, c. 2060, p. 4764, § 1.

Cross References

Family allowance, conditions, termination, see Education Code § 23804.

§ 22173. Survivor benefit allowance

"Survivor benefit allowance" means the monthly allowance that a surviving spouse may elect to receive pursuant to Chapter 23 (commencing with Section 23850).

(Added by Stats.1994, c. 933 (A.B.3171), § 3, eff. Sept. 28, 1994.)

Historical and Statutory Notes

Former § 22173, added by Stats.1993, c. 893 (A.B.1796, § 2, defining plan vesting, was repealed by Stats.1994, c. 933 (A.B.3171), § 2, eff. Sept. 28, 1994. See Education Code § 22156.

Derivation: Former § 22170, added by Stats. 1993, c. 893, § 2.

Former § 22155.5, added by Stats.1992, c. 1166 (S.B.1885), § 6.

Cross References

Family allowance, conditions, termination, see Education Code § 23804.

§ 22174. System

"System" means the State Teachers' Retirement System.

(Added by Stats.1994, c. 933 (A.B.3171), § 3, eff. Sept. 28, 1994.)

Historical and Statutory Notes

Former § 22174, added by Stats.1993, c. 893 (A.B.1796, § 2, defining provisional vesting, was repealed by Stats.1994, c. 933 (A.B.3171), § 2, eff. Sept. 28, 1994. See Education Code § 22160.

Derivation: Former § 22171, added by Stats. 1993, c. 893, § 2.

Former § 22156, enacted by Stats.1976, c. 1010, § 2.

Educ.C.1959, § 13859, added by Stats.1969, c. 896, p. 1738, § 2.

Educ.C.1959, § 13804 (Stats.1959, c. 2, p. 983, § 13804).

Educ.C.1943, § 14254, added by Stats.1944, 4th Ex.Sess., c. 13, p. 115, § 2.

Educ.C.1943, § 14252 (Stats.1943, c. 71, p. 590).

School C. § 5.801, added by Stats.1937, c. 626, p. 1717, § 4.

§ 22175. Repealed by Stats.1998, c. 678 (A.B.1166), § 2; Stats.1998, c. 965 (A.B.2765), § 18

Historical and Statutory Notes

The repealed section, added by Stats.1995, c. 390 (A.B.1122), § 9, defined "teaching units".

Section affected by two or more acts at the same session of the legislature, see Government Code § 9605.

§ 22176. Termination benefit

"Termination benefit" means a benefit equal in amount to the balance of credits in the member's Defined Benefit Supplement account that is payable to the member in a lump-sum when the member has terminated all employment to perform creditable service subject to coverage by the plan.

(Added by Stats.2000, c. 74 (A.B.1509), § 22.)

§ 22177. Unfunded actuarial obligation

(a) "Unfunded actuarial obligation," with respect to the Defined Benefit Program, means that portion of the actuarial present value of benefits that is not provided for by future, normal costs or covered by the actuarial value of assets attributable to the Defined Benefit Program, based on assumptions adopted by the board pursuant to Section 22311.5.

(b) "Unfunded actuarial obligation," with respect to the Defined Benefit Supplement Program, means that portion of the actuarial present value of benefits that is not provided for by future, normal costs or covered by the actuarial value of assets attributable to the Defined Benefit Supplement Program, based on assumptions adopted by the board pursuant to Section 22311.5.

(Added by Stats.2000, c. 1021 (A.B.2700), § 12.)

Historical and Statutory Notes

Operative effect of Stats.2000, c. 1021 (A.B. 2700), see Historical and Statutory Notes following Education Code § 22101.5.

Chapter 3

RETIREMENT BOARD

Chapter 3 added by Stats.1993, c. 893 (A.B.1796), § 2.

Cross References

Public pension and retirement plans, see Government Code § 7500 et seq.

§ 22200. Administration by board; membership

(a) The plan and the system are administered by the Teachers' Retirement Board. The members of the board are as follows:

(1) The Superintendent of Public Instruction.

(2) The Controller.

(3) The Treasurer.

(4) The Director of Finance.

(5) One person who, at the time of appointment, is a member of the governing board of a school district or a community college district.

(6) Three persons who are either members of the Defined Benefit Program or participants in the Cash Balance Benefit Program, as follows:

(A) Two persons who, at the time of appointment, are classroom teachers in kindergarten or grades 1 through 12.

(B) One person who, at the time of appointment, is a community college instructor with expertise in the areas of business or economics or both business and economics and who shall be appointed by the Governor for a term of four years from a list submitted by the Board of Governors of the California Community Colleges.

(7) One person who is either a retired member under this part or a retired participant under Part 14 (commencing with Section 26000).

(8) One officer of a life insurance company appointed by the Governor for a term of four years, subject to confirmation by the Senate.

(9) One officer of a bank or a savings and loan institution who has had at least five years of broad professional investment experience handling various asset classes such as stocks, bonds, and mortgage investments and who shall be appointed by the Governor for a term of four years, subject to confirmation by the Senate.

(10) One person representing the public, appointed by the Governor for a term of four years, subject to confirmation by the Senate.

(b) The members of the board described in paragraphs (5) and (7) and subparagraph (A) of paragraph (6) of subdivision (a) shall be appointed by the Governor for four-year terms from a list submitted by the Superintendent of Public Instruction.

(c) The members of the board shall annually elect a chairperson and vice chairperson.

(Added by Stats.1993, c. 893 (A.B.1796), § 2. Amended by Stats.1994, c. 933 (A.B. 3171), § 7.5, eff. Sept. 28, 1994; Stats.1996, c. 634 (S.B.2041), § 42; Stats.1998, c. 1048 (S.B.2085), § 5.)

Historical and Statutory Notes

Legislative intent regarding Stats.1993, c. 893 (A.B.1796), including possible continuing application of provisions of repealed State Teachers' Retirement Law, see Historical and Statutory Notes under Education Code § 22000.

The 1994 amendment of this section by c. 933 explicitly amended the 1993 addition of this section by c. 893.

Former § 22200, enacted by Stats.1976, c. 1010, § 2, amended by Stats.1977, c. 26, § 1; Stats.1981, c. 124, § 20; Stats.1981, c. 868, § 1; Stats.1983-84, 1st Ex.Sess., c. 5, § 1; Stats.1983, c. 558, § 1; Stats.1986, c. 56, § 1; Stats.1990, c. 1372 (S.B. 1854), § 174, relating to management of the retirement system by a board, was repealed by Stats.1993, c. 893 (A.B. 1796), § 1. See this section.

Derivation: Former § 22200, enacted by Stats.1976, c. 1010, § 2, amended by Stats. 1977, c. 26, § 1; Stats.1981, c. 124, § 20; Stats. 1981, c. 868, § 1; Stats.1983-84, 1st Ex.Sess., c.

5, § 1; Stats.1983, c. 588, § 1; Stats.1986, c. 56, § 1; Stats.1990, c. 1372 (S.B.1854) § 174.

Educ.C.1959, § 13870, added by Stats.1969, c. 896, p. 1738, § 2.

Educ.C.1959, § 13851 (Stats.1959, c. 2, p. 986, § 13851, amended by Stats.1963, c. 2135, p. 4444, § 1; Stats.1965, c. 800, p. 2394, § 2).

Educ.C.1943, § 14321 (Stats.1943, c. 71, p. 592).

Educ.C.1943, § 14301, added by Stats.1944, 4th Ex.Sess., c. 13, p. 117, § 2.

School C. § 5.820, added by Stats.1937, c. 626, p. 1720, § 4.

Cross References

Appointments by Governor, public officers and employees, see Government Code § 1300 et seq.
Superintendent of Public Instruction, election or appointment and powers, deputies and associate
superintendents, see Const. Art. 9, § 2 et seq., and Education Code § 33100 et seq.

Law Review and Journal Commentaries

Public piggy bank goes to market: Public pension fund investment in common stock and fund trustees' social agenda. Deborah J. Martin, 29 San Diego L.Rev. 39 (1992).

Library References

Schools ⬖146(1).
Westlaw Topic No. 345.

C.J.S. Schools and School Districts §§ 338, 340 to 343, 346.

Notes of Decisions

Deputies 1

_____

1. Deputies

Deputies of ex officio members of state teachers' retirement board may participate in board meetings to same extent that ex officio members themselves could, and both superintendent of public instructions and controller may be represented by deputies at same meeting. No special designation or authorization is necessary to entitle deputy of ex officio member to participate in meeting, but when deputies for both constitutional officers who are ex officio members appear at meeting, chairman may recognize one deputy who will have full powers and the unrecognized deputy may participate in meeting to same extent as member of general public but may not vote nor be counted in determining a quorum, and should such officer vote, his vote may be disregarded unless it was necessary for passage of measure, in which case vote will void the board action. 50 Ops.Atty.Gen. 120, 11-28-67.

§ 22201. Powers of board; meetings

(a) The board shall set policy and shall have the sole power and authority to hear and determine all facts pertaining to application for benefits under the plan or any matters pertaining to administration of the plan and the system.

(b) The board shall meet at least once every calendar quarter at such times as it may determine. The meetings shall be presided over by the chairperson. In the event of the chairperson's absence from a meeting the vice chairperson shall act as presiding officer and perform all other duties of the chairperson.

(Added by Stats.1993, c. 893 (A.B.1796), § 2. Amended by Stats.1996, c. 634 (S.B. 2041), § 43; Stats.1998, c. 965 (A.B.2765), § 19.)

Historical and Statutory Notes

Legislative intent regarding Stats.1993, c. 893 (A.B.1796), including possible continuing application of provisions of repealed State Teachers'

Retirement Law, see Historical and Statutory Notes under Education Code § 22000.

Former § 22201, enacted by Stats.1976, c. 1010, § 2, describing the chief executive officer of the system, was repealed by Stats.1993, c. 893 (A.B.1796), § 1. See Education Code §§ 22209, 22300.

Derivation: Former § 22202, enacted by Stats.1976, c. 1010, § 2.

Educ.C.1959, § 13872, added by Stats.1969, c. 896, p. 1738, § 2.

Educ.C.1959, § 13853 (Stats.1959, c. 2, p. 987, § 13853, amended by Stats.1959, c. 731, p. 2719, § 1; Stats.1963, c. 2135, p. 4444, § 3; Stats.1965, c. 800, p. 2395, § 3).

Educ.C.1943, § 14322 (Stats.1943, c. 71, p. 592).

Educ.C.1943, § 14302, added by Stats.1944, 4th Ex.Sess., c. 13, p. 117, § 2, amended by Stats.1957, c. 1584, p. 2938, § 2.

School C. § 5.820, added by Stats.1937, c. 626, p. 1720, § 4.

Library References

Legal Jurisprudences

Am Jur 2d (Rev) Administrative Law §§ 52 et seq.

Notes of Decisions

Hearing officers 1

─────────

1. Hearing officers

If proceeding to retire a teacher for mental or physical disability is contested, teachers' retirement board may hear the case itself with a hearing officer or it may refer the case to a hearing officer to hear alone, in which latter event, he shall submit to the board findings and a proposed decision for final determination. 25 Ops.Atty.Gen. 326 (1955).

§ 22201.2. Quorum

A quorum of the board shall consist of the majority of the board members. In determining whether or not a quorum is present, vacant positions on the board shall not be considered. The concurrence of the majority of the board members present shall be necessary to the validity of any action taken by the board.

(Added by Stats.1996, c. 634 (S.B.2041), § 44.)

§ 22201.3. Board secretary

The chief executive officer of the system shall act as secretary of the board and shall have charge of all board correspondence and shall keep a record of board proceedings.

(Added by Stats.1996, c. 634 (S.B.2041), § 45.)

§ 22202. Control of funds by board

The board has exclusive control of the administration of the funds. No transfers or disbursements of any amount from the funds shall be made except upon the authorization of the board for the purpose of carrying into effect the provisions of this part and Part 14 (commencing with Section 26000).

(Added by Stats.1993, c. 893 (A.B.1796), § 2. Amended by Stats.1998, c. 1048 (S.B. 2085), § 6.)

Historical and Statutory Notes

Legislative intent regarding Stats.1993, c. 893 (A.B.1796), including possible continuing appli- cation of provisions of repealed State Teachers'

Retirement Law, see Historical and Statutory Notes under Education Code § 22000.

Former § 22202, enacted by Stats.1976, c. 1010, § 2, relating to the policy setting and rule making authority of the board, was repealed by Stats.1993, c. 893 (A.B.1796), § 1. See Education Code § 22201.

Derivation: Former § 22224, enacted by Stats.1976, c. 1010, § 2.

Educ.C.1959, § 13896, added by Stats.1969, c. 896, p. 1738, § 2.

Educ.C.1959, § 13853.2 (Stats.1959, c. 2, p. 992, § 13912, renumbered 13853.2 and amended by Stats.1965, c. 800, p. 2396, § 8).

Educ.C.1943, § 14342, added by Stats.1944, 4th Ex.Sess., c. 13, p. 122, § 2.

Educ.C.1943, § 14370 (Stats.1943, c. 71, p. 597).

School C. § 5.832, added by Stats.1937, c. 626, p. 1725, § 4.

Library References

Legal Jurisprudences
Cal Jur 3d Pens § 34.

Am Jur 2d (Rev) Administrative Law §§ 52 et seq.

§ 22203. Investment powers of the board

The board has exclusive control of the investment of the Teachers' Retirement Fund. Except as otherwise restricted by the California Constitution and by law, the board may in its discretion invest the assets of the fund through the purchase, holding, or sale thereof of any investment, financial instrument, or financial transaction when the investment, financial instrument, or financial transaction is prudent in the informed opinion of the board.

(Added by Stats.1993, c. 893 (A.B.1796), § 2.)

Historical and Statutory Notes

Legislative intent regarding Stats.1993, c. 893 (A.B.1796), including possible continuing application of provisions of repealed State Teachers' Retirement Law, see Historical and Statutory Notes under Education Code § 22000.

Former § 22203, enacted by Stats.1976, c. 1010, § 2, relating to the power of the board to delegate, was repealed by Stats.1993, c. 893 (A.B.1796), § 1. See Education Code § 22208.

Derivation: Former § 22222, enacted by Stats.1976, c. 1010, § 2.

Educ.C.1959, § 13894, added by Stats.1969, c. 896, p. 1738, § 2, amended by Stats.1971, c. 870, p. 1710, § 1.

Educ.C.1959, § 13909 (Stats.1959, c. 2, p. 992, § 13909. Renumbered § 13853.1 and amended by Stats.1965, c. 800, p. 2395, § 5).

Educ.C.1943, § 14340, added by Stats.1944, 4th Ex.Sess., c. 13, p. 121, § 2, amended Stats. 1957, c. 1583, p. 2936, § 9.

Educ.C.1943, § 14368 (Stats.1943, c. 71, p. 597).

School C. § 5.831, added by Stats.1937, c. 626, p. 1724, § 4.

Cross References

Investments, generally, see Education Code § 22350 et seq.

Library References

Legal Jurisprudences
Am Jur 2d (Rev) Administrative Law §§ 52 et seq.

Notes of Decisions

Investment advisors   1   Repurchase agreements   2

1. Investment advisors

State Teachers' Retirement Board generally is not authorized to enter into contracts with investment advisers without approval by the Department of General Services. 68 Ops.Atty. Gen. 79, 4–18–85.

2. Repurchase agreements

State treasurer and state agencies with investing authority may invest surplus money under repurchase agreements and are not limited to dealing with banks or to purchasing United States securities. 44 Ops.Atty.Gen. 140, 11–17–64.

§ 22203.5. Investment transaction decisions; rollcall vote; disclosure

(a) All investment transaction decisions made during a closed session pursuant to paragraph (16) of subdivision (c) of Section 11126 of the Government Code shall be by rollcall vote entered into the minutes of that meeting.

(b) The board, within 12 months of the close of an investment transaction or the transfer of system assets for an investment transaction, whichever occurs first, shall disclose and report the investment at a public meeting.

(Added by Stats.1998, c. 923 (S.B.1753), § 1.)

Historical and Statutory Notes

Section 13 of Stats.1998, c. 923, provides:

"SEC. 13. The Legislature finds and declares that the provisions of this act further the purposes of the Political Reform Act of 1974 within the meaning of subdivision (a) of Section 81012 of the Government Code."

The Senate Daily Journal for the 1997-98 Regular Session, page 6542, contained the following letter dated August 31, 1998, from Senator Schiff, regarding S.B. 1753 (Stats.1998, c. 923):

"The Honorable John Burton

"President pro Tempore

"California State Senate

"Dear Senator Burton: I would like to clarify, for the record, provisions within SB 1753 applicable to the State Teachers' Retirement System (STRS) and the Public Employees' Retirement System (PERS).

"Under specified circumstances, SB 1753 would prohibit any matter involving any vendor or contractor from being considered during a closed session on any transaction involving the System. The bill would also require the governing boards of STRS and PERS to make these decisions by rollcall vote, disclose investments and report at public meetings within 12 months of the close of an investment transaction or the transfer of system assets, and specify procedures and prohibitions applicable to communications during any award of a contract and investment transaction evaluation.

"On May 27, 1998, SB 1753 was amended to provide additional flexibility in board and staff communications during the process leading to the award of a contract or the evaluation of a prospective investment transaction

"It is my intent that the bill, as amended, permit retirement system staff to communicate with existing contractors and vendors in exercising due diligence. The restrictions which SB 1753 would impose on communications with existing contractors and vendors would apply only with respect to matters concerning contracts which are currently being solicited.

"Sincerely,

"Adam B. Schiff"

Cross References

Computation of time,
    Generally, see Code of Civil Procedure §§ 12 and 12a and Government Code § 6800 et seq.
    Time in which any act provided by the Education Code is to be done, see Education Code § 9.
Continuation of statutes relating to subjects covered by provisions of this Code, see Education Code
    § 3.

§ 22204. Oaths and affirmations

Each member of the board may administer oaths and affirmations to witnesses and others transacting the business of the system.

(Added by Stats.1993, c. 893 (A.B.1796), § 2.)

Historical and Statutory Notes

Legislative intent regarding Stats.1993, c. 893 (A.B.1796), including possible continuing application of provisions of repealed State Teachers' Retirement Law, see Historical and Statutory Notes under Education Code § 22000.

Former § 22204, enacted by Stats.1976, c. 1010, § 2, relating to the power of the chief executive officer, was repealed by Stats.1993, c. 893 (A.B.1796), § 1. See Education Code § 22301.

Derivation: Former § 22207, enacted by Stats.1976, c. 1010, § 2.

Educ.C.1959, § 13877, added by Stats.1969, c. 896, p. 1738, § 2.

Educ.C.1959, § 13862 (Stats.1959, c. 2, p. 989, § 13862, amended by Stats.1967, c. 1093, p. 2728, § 1).

Educ.C.1943, § 14311, added by Stats.1944, 4th Ex.Sess., c. 13, p. 119, § 2.

Educ.C.1943, § 14330 (Stats.1943, c. 71, p. 593).

School C. § 5.821, added by Stats.1937, c. 626, p. 1721, § 4.

Cross References

Oath,
 Administration and certification of oaths, see Education Code § 60.
 Defined, see Education Code § 76.
 Oath of office, public officers and employees, see Const. Art. 20, § 3 and Government Code § 1360 et seq.

Library References

Legal Jurisprudences
 Am Jur 2d (Rev) Administrative Law §§ 52 et seq.

§§ 22204.5, 22204.6. Repealed by Stats.1993, c. 893 (A.B.1796), § 1

Historical and Statutory Notes

Section 22204.5, added by Stats.1984, c. 88, § 1, related to establishment of an ombudsman position. See Education Code § 22211, 22302.

Section 22204.6, added by Stats.1986, c. 369, § 1, authorized contracts with county superintendents or other employing agencies to provide retirement counseling. See Education Code § 22303.

Legislative intent regarding Stats.1993, c. 893 (A.B.1796), including possible continuing application of provisions of repealed State Teachers' Retirement Law, see Historical and Statutory Notes under Education Code § 22000.

§ 22205. Authority of retirement board to enter into agreements with retirement systems of other states

The board has the authority to negotiate, and enter into agreements with other states of the United States on the subject of the transfer of members' contributions and regular interest between the retirement systems of California and other states.

(Added by Stats.1993, c. 893 (A.B.1796), § 2.)

Historical and Statutory Notes

Legislative intent regarding Stats.1993, c. 893 (A.B.1796), including possible continuing application of provisions of repealed State Teachers' Retirement Law, see Historical and Statutory Notes under Education Code § 22000.

Former § 22205, enacted by Stats.1976, c. 1010, § 2, relating to employees of the board,

was repealed by Stats.1993, c. 893 (A.B.1796), § 1. See Education Code § 22212.

Derivation: Former § 22012, enacted by Stats.1976, c. 1010, § 2.

Educ.C.1959, § 13816, added by Stats.1974, c. 1293, p. 2806, § 9.

§§ 22205.1 to 22205.5. Repealed by Stats.1993, c. 893 (A.B.1796), § 1

Historical and Statutory Notes

Section 22205.1, added by Stats.1982, c. 1433, § 1, amended by Stats.1986, c. 230, § 1, related to legislative findings and declarations concerning investment expertise. See Education Code § 22350.

Section 22205.2, added by Stats.1982, c. 1433, § 2, amended by Stats.1986, c. 230, § 2; Stats.1987, c. 330, § 6, authorized the board to contract with qualified investment managers and provided for report on the nature, duration and costs of investments contracts services used. See Education Code § 22352.

Section 22205.5, added by Stats.1982, c. 1434, § 1, amended by Stats.1983, c. 426, § 1; Stats.1987, c. 330, § 7 related to employment of investment personnel on staff of PERS board. See Education Code § 22355.

Legislative intent regarding Stats.1993, c. 893 (A.B.1796), including possible continuing application of provisions of repealed State Teachers' Retirement Law, see Historical and Statutory Notes under Education Code § 22000.

§ 22206. Audits; excuse of audit findings

(a) As often as the board determines necessary, it may audit or cause to be audited the records of any public agency.

(b) The board may excuse any audit finding provided all of the following conditions are met:

(1) The audit finding relates to a period of time prior to July 1, 2002.

(2) The audit finding identifies an issue that is not in compliance with the provisions of this part with respect to creditable service or creditable compensation.

(3) The noncompliance would not have existed if the service and compensation crediting changes that shall become operative on July 1, 2002, as a result of legislation enacted during the second year of the 1999–2000 Regular Session, had been operative during the period of time investigated in the audit.

(4) The audit finding was included in an audit report issued on or after January 1, 2001.

(5) Excusing the audit finding will not have an adverse effect on the integrity of the retirement fund.

(c) The board's authority pursuant to subdivision (b) shall extend to service and compensation issues identified through activities outside the audit function that address compliance with the provisions of this part.

(Added by Stats.1993, c. 893 (A.B.1796), § 2. Amended by Stats.2000, c. 1021 (A.B. 2700), § 13.)

Historical and Statutory Notes

Legislative intent regarding Stats.1993, c. 893 (A.B.1796), including possible continuing application of provisions of repealed State Teachers' Retirement Law, see Historical and Statutory Notes under Education Code § 22000.

Operative effect of Stats.2000, c. 1021 (A.B. 2700), see Historical and Statutory Notes following Education Code § 22101.5.

Former § 22206, enacted by Stats.1976, c. 1010, § 2, amended by Stats.1981, c. 124, § 21; Stats.1983, c. 603, § 1, relating to the authority of the board to transfer and disburse funds, was repealed by Stats.1993, c. 893 (A.B.1796), § 1. See Education Code § 22307.

Derivation: Former § 22208, enacted by Stats. 1976, c. 1010, § 2.

Educ.C.1959, § 13877.5, added by Stats.1970, c. 466, p. 923, § 3.

Library References

Legal Jurisprudences

Am Jur 2d (Rev) Administrative Law §§ 52 et seq.

§ 22206.5. Repealed by Stats.1993, c. 893 (A.B.1796), § 1

Historical and Statutory Notes

Legislative intent regarding Stats.1993, c. 893 (A.B.1796), including possible continuing application of provisions of repealed State Teachers' Retirement Law, see Historical and Statutory Notes under Education Code § 22000.

The repealed section, added by Stats.1989, c. 115, § 1, amended by Stats.1990, c. 996 (A.B. 2609), § 1, related to transfer of funds for purchasing power protection payments. See Education Code § 24414.

§ 22207. Power of board to perform other necessary acts

The board shall perform any other acts necessary for the administration of the system and the plan in carrying into effect the provisions of this part and Part 14 (commencing with Section 26000).

(Added by Stats.1993, c. 893 (A.B.1796), § 2. Amended by Stats.1996, c. 634 (S.B. 2041), § 46; Stats.1998, c. 965 (A.B.2765), § 20.)

Historical and Statutory Notes

Legislative intent regarding Stats.1993, c. 893 (A.B.1796), including possible continuing application of provisions of repealed State Teachers' Retirement Law, see Historical and Statutory Notes under Education Code § 22000.

Former § 22207, enacted by Stats.1976, c. 1010, § 2, relating to administration of oaths by board members, was repealed by Stats.1993, c. 893 (A.B.1796), § 1. See Education Code, § 22204.

Derivation: Former § 22209, enacted by Stats.1976, c. 1010, § 2.

Educ.C.1959, § 13878, added by Stats.1969, c. 896, p. 1738, § 2.

Educ.C.1959, § 13864 (Stats.1959, c. 2, p. 990, § 13864).

Educ.C.1943, § 14313, added by Stats.1944, 4th Ex.Sess., c. 13, p. 119, § 2.

Educ.C.1943, § 14332 (Stats.1943, c. 71, p. 594).

School C. § 5.821, added by Stats.1937, c. 626, p. 1721, § 4.

Library References

Legal Jurisprudences

Am Jur 2d (Rev) Administrative Law §§ 52 et seq.

§ 22208. Power of board to delegate

The board may appoint a committee of two or more of its members to perform any act within the power of the board itself to perform. The board may also delegate authority to the chief executive officer to perform any such act. Except where the board, in delegating that authority, provides that the committee or the chief executive officer may act finally, all acts of the committee or the chief executive officer shall be reported to the board at its next regular meeting and shall be subject to review, ratification, or reversal by the board.

(Added by Stats.1993, c. 893 (A.B.1796), § 2.)

Historical and Statutory Notes

Legislative intent regarding Stats.1993, c. 893 (A.B.1796), including possible continuing application of provisions of repealed State Teachers' Retirement Law, see Historical and Statutory Notes under Education Code § 22000.

Former § 22208, enacted by Stats.1976, c. 1010, § 2, relating to audits by the board, was repealed by Stat.1993, c. 893 (A.B.1796), § 1. See Education Code § 22206.

Derivation: Former § 22203, enacted by Stats.1976, c. 1010, § 2.

Educ.C.1959, § 13873, added by Stats.1969, c. 896, p. 1738, § 2.

Educ.C.1959, § 13853 (Stats.1959, c. 2, p. 987, § 13853, amended by Stats.1959, c. 731, p. 2719, § 1; Stats.1963, c. 2135, p. 4444, § 3; Stats.1965, c. 800, p. 2395, § 3).

Cross References

Delegation of powers, authority to delegate grant of power to or duty imposed upon a public officer, see Education Code § 7.

Library References

Legal Jurisprudences

Am Jur 2d (Rev) Administrative Law §§ 52 et seq.

§ 22209. Chief executive officer; appointment

The office of chief executive officer shall be filled by appointment by the board and the appointee shall serve at the pleasure of the board.

(Added by Stats.1993, c. 893 (A.B.1796), § 2.)

Historical and Statutory Notes

Legislative intent regarding Stats.1993, c. 893 (A.B.1796), including possible continuing application of provisions of repealed State Teachers' Retirement Law, see Historical and Statutory Notes under Education Code § 22000.

Former § 22209, enacted by Stats.1976, c. 1010, § 2, relating to the power of the board to perform other necessary acts, was repealed by Stats.1993, c. 893 (A.B.1796), § 1. See Education Code § 22207.

Derivation: Former § 22201, enacted by Stats.1976, c. 1010, § 2.

Educ.C.1959, § 13871, added by Stats.1969, c. 896, p. 1783, § 2.

Educ.C.1959, § 13852.1 (Stats.1967, c. 1527, p. 3637, § 3).

Educ.C.1959, § 13852 (Stats.1959, c. 2, p. 987, § 13852, amended by Stats.1963, c. 2135, p. 4444, § 2).

Educ.C.1943, § 14301.1, added by Stats.1957, c. 1584, p. 2938, § 1.

§ 22210. Review by board of acts of committee or chief executive officer

(a) Reversal by the board of any act of the committee or the chief executive officer shall be effective on the date fixed by the board.

(b) Payment of benefits prior to the board's action of reversal may not be affected by such an action, except for the recovery of the amounts paid, from the beneficiary receiving the amounts, as the board may direct.

(Added by Stats.1993, c. 893 (A.B.1796), § 2.)

Historical and Statutory Notes

Legislative intent regarding Stats.1993, c. 893 (A.B.1796), including possible continuing application of provisions of repealed State Teachers' Retirement Law, see Historical and Statutory Notes under Education Code § 22000.

Former § 22210, enacted by Stats.1976, c. 1010, § 2, relating to rules and regulations adopted by the board, was repealed by Stats. 1993, c. 893 (A.B.1796), § 1. See Education Code § 22305.

Derivation: Former § 22212, enacted by Stats.1976, c. 1010, § 2.

Educ.C.1959, § 13881, added by Stats.1969, c. 896, p. 1738, § 2.

Educ.C.1959, § 13854 (Stats.1959, c. 2, p. 987, § 13854, amended by Stats.1959, c. 731, p. 2719, § 2).

Educ.C.1943, § 14303, added by Stats.1944, 4th Ex.Sess., c. 13, p. 117, § 2, amended by Stats.1957, c. 1584, p. 2939, § 3.

Educ.C.1943, § 14323 (Stats.1943, c. 71, p. 592).

School C. § 5.820, added by Stats.1937, c. 626, p. 1720, § 4.

Library References

Legal Jurisprudences

Am Jur 2d (Rev) Administrative Law §§ 52 et seq.

§ 22211. Repealed by Stats.1994, c. 933 (A.B.3171), § 8, eff. Sept. 28, 1994

Historical and Statutory Notes

The repealed section, added by Stats.1993, c. 893 (A.B.1796), § 2, establishing an ombudsman position. See Education Code § 22302.

Former § 22211, enacted by Stats.1976, c. 1010, § 2, relating to the duty of the board to

regulate employing agencies and other public authorities, was repealed by Stats.1993, c. 893 (A.B.1796), § 1. See Education Code § 22213.

§ 22212. Employees; appointment

The board shall appoint such employees as are necessary to administer the plan and the system.

(Added by Stats.1993, c. 893 (A.B.1796), § 2. Amended by Stats.1998, c. 965 (A.B. 2765), § 21.)

Historical and Statutory Notes

Legislative intent regarding Stats.1993, c. 893 (A.B.1796), including possible continuing application of provisions of repealed State Teachers' Retirement Law, see Historical and Statutory Notes under Education Code § 22000.

Former § 22212, enacted by Stats.1976, c. 1010, § 2, relating to review by the board of acts of a committee or chief executive officer, was repealed by Stats.1993, c. 893 (A.B.1796), § 1. See Education Code § 22210.

Derivation: Former § 22205, enacted by Stats.1976, c. 1010, § 2.

Educ.C.1959, § 13875, added by Stats.1969, c. 896, p. 1738, § 2.

Educ.C.1959, § 13852.2, added by Stats.1967, c. 1527, p. 3637, § 4.

Educ.C.1959, § 13852 (Stats.1959, c. 2, p. 987, § 13852, amended by Stats.1963, c. 2135, p. 4444, § 2).

Educ.C.1943, § 14301.1, added by Stats.1957, c. 1584, p. 2938, § 1.

Library References

Legal Jurisprudences

Am Jur 2d (Rev) Administrative Law §§ 52 et seq.

§ 22213. Regulatory duty of board

The board shall regulate the duties of employers and employing agencies and other public authorities, imposed upon them by this part, and shall require reports from employers, employing agencies and other public authorities as it deems advisable in connection with the performance of its duties.

(Added by Stats.1993, c. 893 (A.B.1796), § 2. Amended by Stats.1996, c. 634 (S.B. 2041), § 47.)

Historical and Statutory Notes

Legislative intent regarding Stats.1993, c. 893 (A.B.1796), including possible continuing application of provisions of repealed State Teachers' Retirement Law, see Historical and Statutory Notes under Education Code § 22000.

Former § 22213, enacted by Stats.1976, c. 1010, § 2, relating to the board's power to subpoena witnesses, was repealed by Stats.1993, c. 893 (A.B.1796), § 1. See Education Code § 22220.

Derivation: Former § 22211, enacted by Stats.1976, c. 1010, § 2.

Educ.C.1959, § 13880, added by Stats.1969, c. 896, p. 1738, § 2.

Educ.C.1959, § 13863 (Stats.1959, c. 2, p. 989, § 13863).

Educ.C.1943, § 14312, added by Stats.1944, 4th Ex.Sess., c. 13, p. 119, § 2.

Educ.C.1943, § 14331 (Stats.1943, c. 71, p. 594).

School C. § 5.821, added by Stats.1937, c. 626, p. 1721, § 4.

Library References

Legal Jurisprudences

Am Jur 2d (Rev) Administrative Law §§ 52 et seq.

§ 22214. Action to protect rights to allowances

The board may take any action it deems necessary to ensure the continued right of members or beneficiaries to receive monthly payments.

(Added by Stats.1993, c. 893 (A.B.1796), § 2. Amended by Stats.1996, c. 634 (S.B. 2041), § 48.)

Historical and Statutory Notes

Legislative intent regarding Stats.1993, c. 893 (A.B.1796), including possible continuing application of provisions of repealed State Teachers' Retirement Law, see Historical and Statutory Notes under Education Code § 22000.

Former § 22214, enacted by Stats.1976, c. 1010, § 2, relating to service credited to retirement and retirement allowances, was repealed by Stats.1993, c. 893 (A.B.1796), § 1. See Education Code § 22215.

Derivation: Former § 22216, enacted by Stats.1976, c. 1010, § 2.

Educ.C.1959, § 13885, added by Stats.1969, c. 896, p. 1738, § 2, amended by Stats.1972, c. 1010, p. 1859, § 11.

Educ.C.1959, § 13864.1, added by Stats.1963, c. 929, p. 2182, § 1.

Library References

Legal Jurisprudences

Am Jur 2d (Rev) Administrative Law §§ 52 et seq.

§ 22215. Determination of service; fixing and modifying allowance

The board shall determine the service performed by members to be credited toward qualification for retirement, and shall fix and modify allowances provided under this part.

(Added by Stats.1993, c. 893 (A.B.1796), § 2. Amended by Stats.1996, c. 634 (S.B. 2041), § 49.)

Historical and Statutory Notes

Legislative intent regarding Stats.1993, c. 893 (A.B.1796), including possible continuing application of provisions of repealed State Teachers' Retirement Law, see Historical and Statutory Notes under Education Code § 22000.

Former § 22215, enacted by Stats.1976, c. 1010, § 2, relating to mortality tables and interest tables, was repealed by Stats.1993, c. 893 (A.B.1796), § 1. See Education Code § 22221.

Derivation: Former § 22214, enacted by Stats.1976, c. 1010, § 2.

Educ.C.1959, § 13883, added by Stats.1969, c. 896, p. 1738, § 2, amended by Stats.1974, c. 1293, p. 2808, § 31.

Educ.C.1959, § 13860 (Stats.1959, c. 2, p. 989, § 13860).

Educ.C.1943, § 14309, added by Stats.1944, 4th Ex.Sess., c. 13, p. 119, § 2.

Educ.C.1943, § 14328 (Stats.1943, c. 71, p. 593).

School C. § 5.821, added by Stats.1937, c. 626, p. 1721, § 4.

Library References

Legal Jurisprudences

Am Jur 2d (Rev) Administrative Law §§ 52 et seq., Pensions and Retirement Funds § 1693.

Notes of Decisions

Overtime 2
Part-time teaching 1

_____

1. **Part-time teaching**

Record established that construction placed by defendant teachers' retirement board on former statutory provisions, including 1957 amendments, governing computation of part-time teaching service was warranted as opposed to plaintiff teacher's construction that her retirement allowance should be computed on basis of years of service to which she was entitled to be credited under law existing prior to July 1,

1956. Cummings v. California State Teachers' Retirement Bd. (App. 1 Dist. 1966) 50 Cal.Rptr. 391, 241 Cal.App.2d 149.

2. **Overtime**

Overtime, for purposes of state teachers' retirement law, is not defined as that which employer considers overtime; it is province of State Teachers' Retirement Board to determine what pay is creditable to retirement. O'Connor v. State Teachers' Retirement System (App. 2 Dist. 1996) 51 Cal.Rptr.2d 540, 43 Cal.App.4th 1610, rehearing denied, review denied.

§ 22216. Credit of contributions; interest rates

(a) The board shall annually adopt as a plan amendment with respect to the Defined Benefit Program the rate of credited interest to be credited to members' accumulated retirement contributions for service performed after June 30, 1935, and the accumulated annuity deposit contributions excluding all accumulated contributions while being paid as disability allowances, family allowances, and retirement allowances.

(b) The board shall credit interest to all other accumulated reserves at the actuarially assumed interest rate.

(Added by Stats.1993, c. 893 (A.B.1796), § 2. Amended by Stats.1998, c. 965 (A.B. 2765), § 22.)

Historical and Statutory Notes

Legislative intent regarding Stats.1993, c. 893 (A.B.1796), including possible continuing application of provisions of repealed State Teachers' Retirement Law, see Historical and Statutory Notes under Education Code § 22000.

Former § 22216, enacted by Stats.1976, c. 1010, § 2, relating to board actions to protect the right to allowances, was repealed by Stats. 1993, c. 893 (A.B. 1796), § 1. See Education Code § 22214.

Derivation: Former § 22302, enacted by Stat. 1976, c. 1010, § 2, amended by Stat.1978, c. 870, § 5; Stat.1984, c. 53, § 1.

Educ.C.1959, § 13917, added by Stats.1974, c. 795, p. 1739, § 11.

Educ.C.1959, § 13917, added by Stats.1969, c. 896, p. 1738, § 2, amended by Stats.1971, c. 407, p. 778, § 15.

Educ.C.1959, § 13856 (Stats.1959, c. 2, p. 987, § 13856, amended by Stats.1961, c. 583, p. 1723, § 1).

Educ.C.1943, § 14305, added by Stats.1944, 4th Ex.Sess., c. 13, p. 118, § 2, amended by Stats.1945, c. 1207, p. 2289, § 1; Stats.1949, c. 1157, p. 2066, § 1; Stats.1957, c. 2118, p. 3752, § 3.

Educ.C.1943, § 14324 (Stats.1943, c. 71, p. 592).

School C. § 5.821, added by Stats.1937, c. 626, p. 1721, § 4.

§ 22217. Audit by public accountant

(a) The board shall employ a certified public accountant or public accountant, who is not in public employment, to audit the financial statements of the system. The costs of the audit shall be paid from the income of the retirement fund. The audit shall be made annually commencing with the fiscal year ending June 30, 1974. The board shall file a copy of the audit report with the Governor, the Secretary of the Senate, and the Chief Clerk of the Assembly.

(b) These audits shall not be duplicated by the Department of Finance or the Auditor General. The system shall be exempt from a pro rata general administrative charge for auditing.

(Added by Stats.1993, c. 893 (A.B.1796), § 2.)

Historical and Statutory Notes

Legislative intent regarding Stats.1993, c. 893 (A.B.1796), including possible continuing application of provisions of repealed State Teachers' Retirement Law, see Historical and Statutory Notes under Education Code § 22000.

Former § 22217, enacted by Stats.1976, c. 1010, § 2, relating to the right of the board to

hold hearings, was repealed by Stats.1993, c. 893 (A.B.1796), § 1. See Education Code § 22219.

Derivation: Former § 22220, enacted by Stats.1976, c. 1010, § 2.

Educ.C.1959, § 13891.5, added by Stats.1972, c. 1436, p. 3147, § 1.

Cross References

Department of Finance, generally, see Government Code § 13000 et seq.

Library References

Legal Jurisprudences

Cal Jur 3d Pens § 35.

§ 22218. Records and accounts; establishment and maintenance

The board shall establish and maintain records and accounts following recognized accounting principles and controls.

(Added by Stats.1993, c. 893 (A.B.1796), § 2. Amended by Stats.1996, c. 634 (S.B. 2041), § 50.)

Historical and Statutory Notes

Legislative intent regarding Stats.1993, c. 893 (A.B.1796), including possible continuing application of provisions of repealed State Teachers' Retirement Law, see Historical and Statutory Notes under Education Code § 22000.

Former § 22218, enacted by Stats.1976, c. 1010, § 2, relating to an annual report by the board, was repealed by Stats.1993, c. 893 (A.B. 1796), § 1. See Education Code § 22324.

Derivation: Former § 22219, enacted by Stats.1976, c. 1010, § 2.

Educ.C.1959, § 13891, added by Stats.1969, c. 896, p. 1738, § 2, amended by Stats.1971, c.

407, p. 777, § 11; Stats.1972, c. 1010, p. 1860, § 13; Stats.1974, c. 795, p. 1739, § 3.

Educ.C.1959, § 13859 (Stats.1959, c. 2, p. 988, § 13859, amended by Stats.1963, c. 782, p. 1810, § 1; Stats.1963, c. 2170, p. 4552, § 4).

Educ.C.1943, § 14308, added by Stats.1944, 4th Ex.Sess., c. 13, p. 118, § 2.

Educ.C.1943, § 14327 (Stats.1943, c. 71, p. 593).

School C. § 5.821, added by Stats.1937, c. 626, p. 1721, § 4.

§ 22218.5. Return on investment; payroll subject to system; reports

The board, on March 1, 1995, and annually thereafter, shall report to the fiscal committees of the Legislature and to the Director of Finance the return on investments and actual payroll subject to the system for the prior fiscal year.

(Added by Stats.1994, c. 858 (S.B.586), § 1. Amended by Stats.1995, c. 91 (S.B.975), § 26.)

Historical and Statutory Notes

Former § 22218.5, added by Stats.1982, c. 1314, § 1.5, related to a summary of costs or saving to be included in an annual report, and

was repealed by Stats.1993, c. 893 (A.B.1796), § 1. See Education Code § 22326.

§§ 22218.6, 22218.7. Repealed by Stats.1993, c. 893 (A.B.1796), § 1

Historical and Statutory Notes

Section 22218.6, added by Stats.1984, c. 1503, § 1, amended by Stats.1989, c. 1004, § 3, related to the contents of an annual report to be submitted to the legislature. See Education Code § 22357.

Section 22218.7, added by Stats.1984, c. 1503, § 2, related to a quarterly report to be

submitted to the legislature reviewing the system's assets. See Education Code § 22358.

Legislative intent regarding Stats.1993, c. 893 (A.B.1796), including possible continuing application of provisions of repealed State Teachers' Retirement Law, see Historical and Statutory Notes under Education Code § 22000.

§ 22219. Right of board to hold hearings; procedures

(a) The board may in its discretion hold a hearing for the purpose of determining any question presented to it involving any right, benefit, or obligation of a person under this part.

(b) When a hearing is held, the proceedings shall be conducted in accordance with Chapter 5 (commencing with Section 11500) of Part 1 of Division 3 of Title 2 of the Government Code, relating to administrative adjudication, and the board shall have all of the powers granted in that chapter. However, the provisions of Section 11508 of the Government Code relating to the location of the hearing shall not apply, and the hearing shall be held at the time and place determined by the board.

(Added by Stats.1993, c. 893 (A.B.1796), § 2.)

Historical and Statutory Notes

Legislative intent regarding Stats.1993, c. 893 (A.B.1796), including possible continuing application of provisions of repealed State Teachers' Retirement Law, see Historical and Statutory Notes under Education Code § 22000.

Former § 22219, enacted by Stats.1976, c. 1010, § 2, relating to the board's records and accounts, was repealed by Stats.1993, c. 893 (A.B. 1796), § 1. See Education Code § 22218.

Derivation: Former § 22217, enacted by Stat. 1976, c. 1010, § 2.

Educ.C.1959, § 13886, added by Stats.1969, c. 896, p. 1738, § 2, amended by Stats.1972, c. 1010, p. 1859, § 12.

Educ.C.1959, § 13855 (Stats.1959, c. 2, p. 987, § 13855, amended by Stats.1959, c. 1149, p. 3242, § 1).

Educ.C.1943, § 14304, added by Stats.1944, 4th Ex.Sess., c. 13, p. 117, § 2, amended by Stats.1947, c. 1481, p. 3063, § 2.

Library References

Legal Jurisprudences
Cal Jur 3d Pens § 35.

Am Jur 2d (Rev) Pensions and Retirement Funds § 1716.

Notes of Decisions

Hearing officers   1

_____

1. Hearing officers

If proceeding to retire a teacher for mental or physical disability is contested, teachers' retire-ment board may hear the case itself with a hearing officer or it may refer the case to a hearing officer to hear alone, in which latter event, he shall submit to the board findings and a proposed decision for final determination. 25 Ops.Atty.Gen. 326 (1955).

§ 22220. Witnesses; subpoena power

The board may subpoena witnesses and compel their attendance to testify before it.

(Added by Stats.1993, c. 893 (A.B.1796), § 2. Amended by Stats.1996, c. 634 (S.B. 2041), § 51.)

Historical and Statutory Notes

Legislative intent regarding Stats.1993, c. 893 (A.B.1796), including possible continuing application of provisions of repealed State Teachers' Retirement Law, see Historical and Statutory Notes under Education Code § 22000.

Former § 22220, enacted by Stats.1976, c. 1010, § 2, relating to an annual audit by an accountant, was repealed by Stats.1993, c. 893 (A.B.1796), § 1. See Education Code § 22217.

Derivation: Former § 22213, enacted by Stats.1976, c. 1010, § 2.

Educ.C.1959, § 13882, added by Stats.1969, c. 896, p. 1738, § 2.

Educ.C.1959, § 13862 (Stats.1959, c. 2, p. 989, § 13862, amended by Stats.1967, c. 1093, § 1).

Cross References

Subpoenas, see Code of Civil Procedure § 1985 et seq.

Library References

Schools ☜146(7).
Westlaw Topic No. 345.

C.J.S. Schools and School Districts §§ 347 to 350.

§ 22221. Tables and interest rates; adoption

The board shall adopt, upon the recommendation of the actuary of the system, any mortality and other tables and interest rates necessary to do the following:

(a) Permit valuation of the assets and liabilities of the system.

(b) Make any determination or calculation necessary to carry out this part.

(Added by Stats.1993, c. 893 (A.B.1796), § 2. Amended by Stats.1994, c. 933 (A.B. 3171), § 9, eff. Sept. 28, 1994; Stats.1996, c. 634 (S.B.2041), § 52.)

Historical and Statutory Notes

The 1994 amendment of this section by c. 933 explicitly amended the 1993 addition of this section by c. 893.

Another § 22221, added by Stats.1976, c. 1010, § 2, amended by Stats.1993, c. 920 (A.B. 1631), § 2, relating to confidentiality of data filed by members, retirants or beneficiaries, was repealed by Stats.1994, c. 933 (A.B.3171), § 10, eff. Sept. 28, 1994. See Education Code § 22306.

Repeal of § 22221 by Stats.1993, c. 893 (A.B. 1796), § 1, failed to become operative. See Historical and Statutory Notes relating to Stats. 1993, c. 893 (A.B.1796), § 4, under Education Code § 22000, and Government Code § 9605.

Similar provisions were added by Stats.1993, c. 893, § 2, as Education Code § 22306.

Derivation: Former § 22215, enacted by Stats.1976, c. 1010, § 2.

Educ.C.1959, § 13884, added by Stats.1969, c. 896, p. 1738, § 2.

Educ.C.1959, § 13857 (Stats.1959, c. 2, p. 988, § 13857).

Educ.C.1943, § 14306, added by Stats.1944, 4th Ex.Sess., c. 13, p. 118, § 2, amended by Stats.1957, c. 1584, p. 2939, § 4.

Educ.C.1943, § 14325 (Stats.1943, c. 71, p. 592).

School C. § 5.821, added by Stats.1937, c. 626, p. 1721, § 4.

Cross References

Inspection of public records, information filed with Teachers' Retirement Board, see Government Code § 6276.44.

§ 22222. Death payments; adjustment

The board may adjust the amounts of the death payments based on changes in the All Urban California Consumer Price Index, and shall adopt as a plan amendment with respect to the Defined Benefit Program any adjusted amount, provided that the most recent actuarial valuation report indicates that the adjustment would not increase the normal cost.

(Added by Stats.1993, c. 893 (A.B.1796), § 2. Amended by Stats.1996, c. 634 (S.B. 2041), § 53; Stats.1998, c. 965 (A.B.2765), § 23.)

Historical and Statutory Notes

Legislative intent regarding Stats.1993, c. 893 (A.B.1796), including possible continuing application of provisions of repealed State Teachers' Retirement Law, see Historical and Statutory Notes under Education Code § 22000.

Former § 22222, enacted by Stats.1976, c. 1010, § 2, amended by Stats.1983, c. 1043, § 1,

relating to investment powers of the board, was repealed by Stats.1993, c. 893 (A.B.1796), § 1. See Education Code § 22203.

Derivation: Former § 22256, added by Stats. 1992, c. 1166 (S.B.1885), § 7.

Cross References

Active death benefits, family allowance, see Education Code § 23800 et seq.
Active death benefits, survivor benefits, see Education Code § 23850 et seq.

§ 22223. Compensation for board members who are not plan members or participants; travel expenses

The members of the board who are not members of the Defined Benefit Program or participants of the Cash Balance Benefit Program and who are appointed by the Governor pursuant to Section 22200 shall receive one hundred dollars ($100) for every day of actual attendance at meetings of the board or any meeting of any committee of the board of which the person is a member, and that is conducted for the purpose of carrying out the powers and duties of the board, together with their necessary traveling expenses incurred in connection with performance of their official duties.

(Added by Stats.1993, c. 893 (A.B.1796), § 2. Amended by Stats.1996, c. 634 (S.B. 2041), § 53.5; Stats.1998, c. 965 (A.B.2765), § 24.)

Historical and Statutory Notes

Legislative intent regarding Stats.1993, c. 893 (A.B.1796), including possible continuing application of provisions of repealed State Teachers' Retirement Law, see Historical and Statutory Notes under Education Code § 22000.

Former § 22223, added by Stats.1987, c. 416, § 1, amended by Stats.1992, c. 540 (A.B.1957), § 2, relating to investment priorities, was repealed by Stats.1993, c. 893 (A.B.1796), § 1. See Education Code § 22362.

Former § 22223, enacted by Stats.1976, c. 1010, § 2, derived from Educ.C.1959, § 13895,

added by Stats.1969, c. 896, p. 1738, § 2; Educ. C.1959, § 13853.3 (Stats.1959, c. 2, p. 992, § 13910, renumbered 13853.1 and amended by Stats.1965, c. 800, p. 2395, § 6); and Educ.C. 1943, § 14340.1, added by Stats.1957, c. 659, p. 1858, § 5, relating to investments in bonds, was repealed by Stats.1983, c. 1043, § 2.

Derivation: Former § 22229, added by Stats. 1977, c. 36, § 412, amended by Stats.1982, c. 701, § 1.

Educ.C.1959, § 13870.2, added by Stats.1976, c. 818, § 1.

Cross References

Appointments by Governor, public officers and employees, see Government Code § 1300 et seq.
Traveling expenses, state agency officers and employees, see Government Code § 11030 et seq.

§ 22224. Plan members appointed to board, committee, or panel; leave to attend meetings

Members of the Defined Benefit Program and participants of the Cash Balance Benefit Program, who are either appointed to the board by the Governor pursuant to Section 22200, or who are appointed by the board to serve on a committee or subcommittee of the board or a panel of the system, shall be granted, by his or her employer, sufficient time away from regular duties, without loss of compensation or other benefits to which the person is entitled by reason of employment, to attend meetings of the board or any of its committees or subcommittees of which the person is a member, or to serve as a member of a panel of the system, and to attend to the duties expected to be performed by the person.

(Added by Stats.1993, c. 893 (A.B.1796), § 2. Amended by Stats.1996, c. 634 (S.B. 2041), § 54; Stats.1998, c. 965 (A.B.2765), § 25.)

Historical and Statutory Notes

Legislative intent regarding Stats.1993, c. 893 (A.B.1796), including possible continuing application of provisions of repealed State Teachers' Retirement Law, see Historical and Statutory Notes under Education Code § 22000.

Former § 22224, enacted by Stats.1976, c. 1010, § 2, relating to control of funds by the

board, was repealed by Stats.1993, c. 893 (A.B. 1796), § 1. See Education Code § 22202.

Derivation: Former § 22229.1, added by Stats.1979, c. 287, § 1.

§ 22225. Maintenance of compensation of board, committee or panel appointees; reimbursements to employers for replacement expenses

(a) The compensation of the members of the Defined Benefit Program and participants of the Cash Balance Benefit Program who are appointed to the board, or by the board to a committee or subcommittee, or to a panel of the system, shall not be reduced by his or her employer for any absence from service occasioned by attendance upon the business of the board, pursuant to Section 22224.

(b) Each employer that employs either a member of the Defined Benefit Program or a participant of the Cash Balance Benefit Program appointed pursuant to Section 22224 and that employs a person to replace the member or participant during attendance at meetings of the board, its committees or subcommittees, or when serving as a member of a panel of the system, or when carrying out other duties approved by the board, shall be reimbursed from the retirement fund for the cost incurred by employing a replacement.

(Added by Stats.1993, c. 893 (A.B.1796), § 2. Amended by Stats.1996, c. 634 (S.B. 2041), § 55; Stats.1998, c. 965 (A.B.2765), § 26.)

Historical and Statutory Notes

Legislative intent regarding Stats.1993, c. 893 (A.B.1796), including possible continuing application of provisions of repealed State Teachers' Retirement Law, see Historical and Statutory Notes under Education Code § 22000.

Addition of another section of this number by Stats.1982, c. 1200, p. 4334, § 1, contingent upon adoption of Senate Constitutional Amendment No. 21, (1982), failed to become operative upon the rejection of S.C.A. No. 21 at the general election Nov. 2, 1982.

Former § 22225, enacted by Stats.1976, c. 1010, § 2, authorizing membership of the system in the National Council on Teacher Retirement, was derived from Educ.C.1959, § 13898, added by Stats.1969, c. 896, p. 1738, § 2; Educ. C.1959, § 13865, enacted by Stats.1959, c. 2, p. 990, § 13865; and Educ.C.1943, § 14314, added by Stats.1951, c. 389, p. 1187, § 1, was repealed by Stats.1977, c. 659, § 4.

Derivation: Former § 22229.2, added by Stats.1979, c. 287, § 2, amended by Stats.1985, c. 1532, § 1; Stats.1987, c. 1395, § 1.

§ 22226. Study on providing health insurance benefits

(a) The board shall conduct a study on providing health insurance benefits, including vision and dental care benefits, for active, disabled, and retired members, beneficiaries, children, and dependent parents. The health insurance may include vision and dental care.

(b) The study shall include, but not be limited to, assessing the lack of access of health insurance benefits for retired teachers and shall evaluate the following:

(1) The demand for health insurance benefits.

(2) The integration of health insurance benefits and Medicare coverage.

(3) The manner in which health insurance benefits would be administered and provided.

(c) There is hereby appropriated from the Teachers' Retirement Fund to the State Teachers' Retirement Board the sum of two hundred thousand dollars ($200,000) conduct a study for the purposes identified in this section. If this study results in the implementation of health insurance benefits as described in subdivision (a), the State Teachers' Retirement Board shall reimburse the sum of two hundred thousand dollars ($200,000) to the Teachers' Retirement Fund from administrative fees charged to recipients of the health insurance benefits. (Added by Stats.1998, c. 968 (S.B.1528), § 1.)

§§ 22225.5 to 22227.   Repealed by Stats.1993, c. 893 (A.B.1796), § 1

Historical and Statutory Notes

Section 22225.5, added by Stats.1982, c. 1200, § 2, amended by Stats.1989, c. 542, § 2, related to the purpose and standard of care the board and its officers and employees were to use in discharging their duties. See Education Code § 22250.

Section 22225.51, added by Stats.1989, c. 542, § 3, related to the exclusive purpose of assets and return of mistaken contributions. See Education Code § 22251.

Section 22225.52, added by Stats.1989, c. 542, § 4, related to prohibited transactions. See Education Code § 22252.

Section 22225.53, added by Stats.1989, c. 542, § 5, related to conflicts of interest. See Education Code § 22253.

Section 22225.6, added by Stats.1982, c. 1200, § 3, amended by Stats.1989, c. 542, § 6, related to liability for breach of duties, obligations and responsibilities. See Education Code § 22254.

Section 22225.65, added by Stats.1989, c. 542, § 7, related to personal liability for breach of fiduciary duties. See Education Code § 22255.

Section 22225.7, added by Stats.1982, c. 1200, § 4, amended by Stats.1989, c. 542, § 8, related to circumstances giving rise to liability for breach of fiduciary responsibility. See Education Code § 22256.

Section 22225.75, added by Stats.1984, c. 1503, § 3, related to appropriations for liability insurance for fiduciaries. See Education Code § 22258.

Section 22225.8, added by Stats.1983, c. 1043, § 3, amended by Stats.1989, c. 542, § 9, related to liability of board members for selection and monitoring of investment managers. See Education Code § 22257.

Section 22225.9, added by Stats.1984, c. 1504, § 1, related to execution of fidelity bond. See Education Code § 22259.

Section 22226, enacted by Stats.1976, c. 1010, § 2, amended by Stats.1987, c. 416, § 2, related to board duties regarding actuarial data. See Education Code § 22311.

Section 22227, enacted by Stats.1976, c. 1010, § 2, prohibited retroactive adjustment of rates. See Education Code § 22313.

Legislative intent regarding Stats.1993, c. 893 (A.B.1796), including possible continuing application of provisions of repealed State Teachers' Retirement Law, see Historical and Statutory Notes under Education Code § 22000.

§ 22228.   Repealed by Stats.1994, c. 933 (A.B.3171), § 11, eff. Sept. 28, 1994

Historical and Statutory Notes

The repealed section, enacted by Stats.1976, c. 1010, § 2, amended by Stats.1993, c. 861 (A.B.447), § 2, related to individual account statements. See Education Code § 22309.

Repeal of this section by Stats.1993, c. 893 (A.B.1796), § 1, failed to become operative.

See Stats.1993, c. 893 (A.B.1796), § 4, in the Historical and Statutory Notes under Education Code § 22000, and Government Code § 9605.

§§ 22229 to 22229.2.   Repealed by Stats.1993, c. 893 (A.B.1796), § 1

Historical and Statutory Notes

Legislative intent regarding Stats.1993, c. 893 (A.B.1796), including possible continuing application of provisions of repealed State Teachers' Retirement Law, see Historical and Statutory Notes under Education Code § 22000.

Section 22229, added by Stats.1977, c. 36, § 412, amended by Stats.1982, c. 701, § 1, related to compensation and travel expenses for board members. See Education Code § 22223.

Section 22229.1, added by Stats.1979, c. 287, § 1, related to leave time to attend meetings for members of system appointed board, committee or panel. See Education Code § 22224.

Section 22229.2, added by Stats.1979, c. 287, § 2, amended by Stats.1985, c. 1532, § 1; Stats.

1987, c. 1395, § 1, related to maintenance of compensation of board, committee or panel appointees and to reimbursement of employers for replacement expenses. See Education Code § 22225.

§§ 22230, 22230.1. Repealed by Stats.1990, c. 560 (A.B.4129), §§ 2, 3

Historical and Statutory Notes

Section 22230, added by Stats.1977, c. 130, § 1, related to transmittal of a member's payment directly to a bank, savings and loan association, or credit union. See Education Code § 24600.1.

Section 22230.1, added by Stats.1988, c. 792, § 1, required the board to send a copy of benefit payment information to retirants, disabilitants, or beneficiaries who had payments transmitted directly to a financial institution.

§ 22231. Repealed by Stats.1993, c. 893 (A.B.1796), § 1

Historical and Statutory Notes

Legislative intent regarding Stats.1993, c. 893 (A.B.1796), including possible continuing application of provisions of repealed State Teachers' Retirement Law, see Historical and Statutory Notes under Education Code § 22000.

The repealed section, added by Stats.1978, c. 870, § 4, amended by Stats.1990, c. 831 (A.B.

2552), § 1, related to offers, operation of and application of tax and insurance provisions to tax sheltered annuity plans. See Education Code § 22331.

§ 22232. Repealed by Stats.1993, c. 893 (A.B.1796), § 1

Historical and Statutory Notes

Legislative intent regarding Stats.1993, c. 893 (A.B.1796), including possible continuing application of provisions of repealed State Teachers' Retirement Law, see Historical and Statutory Notes under Education Code § 22000.

The repealed section, added by Stats.1988, c. 1089, § 2, related to correction of errors and omissions. See Education Code § 22333.

§§ 22233 to 22242. Repealed by Stats.1993, c. 893 (A.B.1796), § 1

Historical and Statutory Notes

Section 22233 added by Stats.1988, c. 1089, § 2, related to correction of errors and omissions. See Education Code § 22308.

Former § 22233, added by Stats.1987, c. 376, § 1, relating to action not taken due to inadvertence, oversight, mistake of fact or law or other cause, was repealed by Stats.1988, c. 1089, § 1.

Section 22235, added by Stats.1984, c. 683, § 2, related to installation of a toll-free telephone assistance line. See Education Code § 22329.

Section 22236, added by Stats.1984, c. 1502, § 1, related to analysis of pending legislation. See Education Code § 22330.

Section 22238, added by Stats.1984, c. 392, § 1, amended by Stats.1986, c. 69, § 1; Stats. 1986, c. 369, § 2; Stats.1988, c. 408, § 1; Stats. 1990, c. 11 (A.B.1972), § 1; Stats.1991, c. 543 (S.B.1171), § 4, related to home loan programs. See Education Code § 22360.

Section 22238.1, added by Stats.1989-90, 1st Ex.Sess., c. 35 (A.B.53), § 1, related to use of retirement funds for natural disaster relief loans. See Education Code § 22361.

Section 22239, added by Stats.1984, c. 1105, § 1, amended by Stats.1987, c. 330, § 8; Stats. 1988, c. 382, § 3, related to monitoring and advice by investment managers on all matters of corporate governance. See Education Code § 22354.

Section 22240, added by Stats.1988, c. 743, § 1, related to development of Plan II retirement plan. See Education Code § 22334.

Section 22242, formerly § 23910.3, added by Stats.1985, c. 543, § 1, renumbered § 22242 and amended by Stats.1992, c. 1167 (S.B.1886), § 2, related to disclosure of earnings informa-tion of recipients of disability allowances. See Education Code § 22327.

Legislative intent regarding Stats.1993, c. 893 (A.B.1796), including possible continuing application of provisions of repealed State Teachers' Retirement Law, see Historical and Statutory Notes under Education Code § 22000.

Chapter 4

FIDUCIARY DUTIES

Chapter 4 was added by Stats.1993, c. 893 (A.B.1796), § 2.

§ 22250. Discharge of duties; purpose; standard of care

The board and its officers and employees of the system shall discharge their duties with respect to the system and the plan solely in the interest of the members and beneficiaries of the Defined Benefit Program as well as the participants and beneficiaries of the Cash Balance Benefit Program as follows:

(a) For the exclusive purpose of the following:

(1) Providing benefits to members and beneficiaries of the Defined Benefit Program as well as the participants and beneficiaries of the Cash Balance Benefit Program.

(2) Defraying reasonable expenses of administering the plan.

(b) With the care, skill, prudence, and diligence under the circumstances then prevailing that a prudent person acting in a like capacity and familiar with those matters would use in the conduct of an enterprise of a like character and with like aims.

(c) By diversifying the investments of the plan so as to minimize the risk of large losses, unless under the circumstances it is clearly prudent not to do so.

(d) In accordance with the documents and instruments governing the plan and the system insofar as those documents and instruments are consistent with this part and Part 14 (commencing with Section 26000).

(Added by Stats.1993, c. 893 (A.B.1796), § 2. Amended by Stats.1996, c. 634 (S.B. 2041), § 56; Stats.1998, c. 965 (A.B.2765), § 27.)

Historical and Statutory Notes

Legislative intent regarding Stats.1993, c. 893 (A.B.1796), including possible continuing application of provisions of repealed State Teachers' Retirement Law, see Historical and Statutory Notes under Education Code § 22000.

Former § 22250, added by Stats.1992, c. 1166 (A.B.1885), § 7, relating to effective date

of new programs and purpose of law, was repealed by Stats.1993, c. 893 (A.B.1796), § 1. See Education Code § 23700.

Derivation: Former § 22225.5, added by Stats.1982, c. 1200, § 2, amended by Stats. 1989, c. 542, § 2.

Library References

Schools ☞146(1).
Westlaw Topic No. 345.

C.J.S. Schools and School Districts §§ 338, 340 to 343, 346.

§ 22251. Exclusive purpose of assets; mistaken contributions

(a) Except as provided in subdivision (b), the assets of the plan shall never inure to the benefit of an employer and shall be held for the exclusive purposes of providing benefits to members and beneficiaries of the Defined Benefit Program as well as the participants and beneficiaries of the Cash Balance Benefit Program and defraying reasonable expenses of administering the plan and the system.

(b) In the case of a contribution that is made by an employer by a mistake of fact, subdivision (a) shall not prohibit the return of that contribution within one year after the system knows, or should know in the ordinary course of business, that the contribution was made by a mistake of fact.

(Added by Stats.1993, c. 893 (A.B.1796), § 2. Amended by Stats.1996, c. 634 (S.B. 2041), § 57; Stats.1998, c. 965 (A.B.2765), § 28.)

Historical and Statutory Notes

Legislative intent regarding Stats.1993, c. 893 (A.B.1796), including possible continuing application of provisions of repealed State Teachers' Retirement Law, see Historical and Statutory Notes under Education Code § 22000.

Former § 22251, added by Stats.1992, c. 1166 (S.B.1885), § 7, relating to the time period

for elections, was repealed by Stats.1993, c. 893 (A.B.1796), § 1. See Education Code § 23701.

Derivation: Former § 22225.51, added by Stats.1989, c. 542, § 3.

Cross References

Computation of time,
    Generally, see Code of Civil Procedure §§ 12 and 12a and Government Code § 6800 et seq.
    Time in which any act provided by the Education Code is to be done, see Education Code § 9.
Continuation of statutes relating to subjects covered by provisions of this Code, see Education Code
    § 3.

§ 22252. Prohibited transactions

Except as otherwise provided by law, the board and its officers and employees of the system shall not cause the system to engage in a transaction if they know or should know that the transaction constitutes a direct or indirect:

(a) Sale or exchange, or leasing, of any property from the system to a member or beneficiary of the Defined Benefit Program, as well as a participant or beneficiary of the Cash Balance Benefit Program, for less than adequate consideration, or from a member or beneficiary of the Defined Benefit Program, as well as a participant or beneficiary of the Cash Balance Benefit Program, to the system for more than adequate consideration.

(b) Lending of money or other extension of credit from the system to a member or beneficiary of the Defined Benefit Program, as well as a participant or beneficiary of the Cash Balance Benefit Program, without the receipt of adequate security and a reasonable rate of interest, or from a member or beneficiary of the Defined Benefit Program, as well as a participant or beneficiary of the Cash Balance Benefit Program, with the provision of excessive security or an unreasonably high rate of interest.

(c) Furnishing of goods, services, or facilities from the system to a member or beneficiary of the Defined Benefit Program, as well as a participant or beneficiary of the Cash Balance Benefit Program, for less than adequate consideration, or from a member, or beneficiary of the Defined Benefit Program, as well as a participant or beneficiary of the Cash Balance Benefit Program, to the system for more than adequate consideration.

(d) Transfer to, or use by or for the benefit of, a member or beneficiary of the Defined Benefit Program, as well as a participant or beneficiary of the Cash Balance Benefit Program, of any assets of the plan for less than adequate consideration.

(e) Acquisition, on behalf of the system, of any employer security, real property, or loan.

(Added by Stats.1993, c. 893 (A.B.1796), § 2. Amended by Stats.1996, c. 634 (S.B. 2041), § 58; Stats.1998, c. 965 (A.B.2765), § 29.)

Historical and Statutory Notes

Legislative intent regarding Stats.1993, c. 893 (A.B.1796), including possible continuing application of provisions of repealed State Teachers' Retirement Law, see Historical and Statutory Notes under Education Code § 22000.

Another § 22252, added by Stats.1992, c. 1166 (S.B.1885), § 7, amended by Stats.1993, c. 1144 (S.B.857), § 1, relating to eligibility to make an irrevocable election, was repealed by Stats.1994, c. 933 (A.B.31717), § 12, eff. Sept. 28, 1994. See Education Code § 23702.

Repeal of former § 22252 by Stats.1993, c. 893 (A.B.1796), § 1, failed to become operative. See Historical and Statutory Notes relating to Stats.1993, c. 893 (A.B.1796), § 4, under Education Code § 22000. Section affected by two or more acts at the same session of the legislature, see Government Code § 9605.

Section 35 of Stats.1992, c. 1166 (S.B.1885), provides:

"This act shall not become operative unless both Senate Bill 1884 [Stats.1992, c. 1165] and Senate Bill 1886 [Stats.1992, c. 1167] of the 1992–92 [sic] Regular Session of the Legislature are chaptered."

Derivation: Former § 22225.52, added by Stats.1989, c. 542, § 4.

§ 22253. Prohibited activities; conflicts of interest

The board and its officers and employees of the system shall not do any of the following:

(a) Deal with the assets of the plan and the system in their own interest or for their own account.

(b) In their individual or in any other capacity, act in any transaction involving the system on behalf of a party, or represent a party, whose interests are adverse to the interests of the plan or the interests of the members and beneficiaries of the Defined Benefit Program, as well as participants and beneficiaries of the Cash Balance Benefit Program.

(c) Receive any consideration for their personal account from any party conducting business with the system in connection with a transaction involving the assets of the plan.

(Added by Stats.1993, c. 893 (A.B.1796), § 2.   Amended by Stats.1996, c. 634 (S.B. 2041), § 59; Stats.1998, c. 965 (A.B.2765), § 30.)

Historical and Statutory Notes

Legislative intent regarding Stats.1993, c. 893 (A.B.1796), including possible continuing application of provisions of repealed State Teachers' Retirement Law, see Historical and Statutory Notes under Education Code § 22000.

Another § 22253, added by Stats.1992, c. 1166 (S.B.1885), § 7, amended by Stats.1993, c. 219 (A.B.1500), § 72, relating to requirements for election of coverage, was repealed by Stats. 1994, c. 933 (A.B.31717), § 13, eff. Sept. 28, 1994. See Education Code § 23703.

Repeal of former § 22252 by Stats.1993, c. 893 (A.B.1796), § 1, failed to become operative. See Historical and Statutory Notes relating to

Stats.1993, c. 893 (A.B.1796), § 4, under Education Code § 22000. Section affected by two or more acts at the same session of the legislature, see Government Code § 9605.

Section 35 of Stats.1992, c. 1166 (S.B.1885), provides:

"This act shall not become operative unless both Senate Bill 1884 [Stats.1992, c. 1165] and Senate Bill 1886 [Stats.1992, c. 1167] of the 1992–92 [sic] Regular Session of the Legislature are chaptered."

Derivation: Former § 22225.53, added by Stats.1989, c. 542, § 5.

§ 22253.5. Repealed by Stats.1994, c. 933 (A.B.3171), § 14, eff. Sept. 28, 1994

Historical and Statutory Notes

The repealed section, added by Stats.1992, c. 1166 (S.B.1885), § 7, amended by Stats.1993, c. 219 (A.B.1500), § 73, related to a spouse's refusal to sign. See Education Code § 23704.

Repeal of this section by Stats.1993, c. 893 (A.B.1796), § 1, failed to become operative. Similar provisions were added by Stats.1993, c. 893, § 2, as Education Code § 23704. See Historical and Statutory Notes relating to Stats. 1993, c. 893 (A.B.1796), § 4, under Education

Code § 22000. Section affected by two or more acts at the same session of the legislature, see Government Code § 9605.

Section 35 of Stats.1992, c. 1166 (S.B.1885), provides:

"This act shall not become operative unless both Senate Bill 1884 [Stats.1992, c. 1165] and Senate Bill 1886 [Stats.1992, c. 1167] of the 1992–92 [sic] Regular Session of the Legislature are chaptered."

§ 22254. Breach of duties, obligations and responsibilities; liability; restoration of profits; equitable or remedial relief

(a) Any board member or officer who breaches any of the responsibilities, obligations, or duties imposed upon them by Section 22251, 22252, or 22253 shall be personally liable to make restitution to the retirement fund for any losses to it resulting from each breach, and to restore any profits that have been made through use of assets of the fund and shall be subject to any other equitable or remedial relief the court may deem appropriate, including removal from the board.

(b) No board member or officer shall be liable with respect to a breach of fiduciary duty under this part if the breach was committed before the board member or officer became one, or ceased to be one.

(Added by Stats.1993, c. 893 (A.B.1796), § 2.   Amended by Stats.1996, c. 634 (S.B. 2041), § 60.)

Historical and Statutory Notes

Legislative intent regarding Stats.1993, c. 893 (A.B.1796), including possible continuing application of provisions of repealed State Teachers' Retirement Law, see Historical and Statutory Notes under Education Code § 22000.

The 1996 amendment, at the beginning of subd. (a), substituted "Any board member or officer" for "Any member of the board or its officers"; in subd. (a) substituted "to make restitution" for "to make good"; in subd. (a) following "to the retirement fund" inserted "for";

and, in subd. (a) following "including removal", substituted "from the board" for "of the board member or officer".

Former § 22254, added by Stats.1992, c. 1166 (S.B.1885), § 7, relating to acknowledgment notices, was repealed by Stats.1993, c. 893 (A.B.1796), § 1. See Education Code § 23705.

Derivation: Former § 22225.6, added by Stats.1982, c. 1200, § 3, amended by Stats. 1989, c. 542, § 6.

§ 22255. Fiduciary duties; personal liability

(a) No board member or officer shall be personally liable for the breach of a fiduciary duty except as set forth in Section 22254 or 22256. This subdivision shall apply only to causes of actions arising on or after January 1, 1990.

(b) Nothing in this section shall be interpreted to lessen the scope of liability of board members or employees of the system for gross negligence or fraud in the investment of the retirement fund assets, nor to lessen the scope of liability of the board or system for breach of fiduciary duty pertaining to the administration of the plan.

(Added by Stats.1993, c. 893 (A.B.1796), § 2. Amended by Stats.1996, c. 634 (S.B. 2041), § 61.)

Historical and Statutory Notes

Legislative intent regarding Stats.1993, c. 893 (A.B.1796), including possible continuing application of provisions of repealed State Teachers' Retirement Law, see Historical and Statutory Notes under Education Code § 22000.

The 1996 amendment, in subd. (b) following the second occurrence of "lessen the scope of liability of the" inserted "board or"; at the end of subd. (b) substituted "administration of the plan" for "administration of retirement benefits,

including the granting, denial, or withdrawal of benefits"; and made another, nonsubstantive change.

Former § 22255, added by Stats.1992, c. 1166 (S.B.1885), § 7, relating to failure to file election, was repealed by Stats.1993, c. 893 (A.B.1796), § 1. See Education Code § 23706.

Derivation: Former § 22225.65, added by Stats.1989, c. 542, § 7.

§ 22256. Breach of fiduciary responsibilities; circumstances giving rise to liability

A board member or officer shall be liable for a breach of fiduciary responsibility of another board member or officer with respect to the system in the following circumstances:

(a) If the board member or officer knowingly participates in, or knowingly undertakes to conceal an act or omission of the other board member or officer knowing that the act or omission is a breach.

(b) If the board member's or officer's failure to comply with his or her responsibilities as set forth in Section 22251, 22252, or 22253 has enabled another board member or officer to commit a breach.

(c) If the board member or officer has knowledge of a breach unless the board member or officer makes reasonable efforts under the circumstances to remedy the breach.

(Added by Stats.1993, c. 893 (A.B.1796), § 2.)

Historical and Statutory Notes

Legislative intent regarding Stats.1993, c. 893 (A.B.1796), including possible continuing application of provisions of repealed State Teachers' Retirement Law, see Historical and Statutory Notes under Education Code § 22000.

Former § 22256, added by Stats.1992, c. 1166 (S.B.1885), § 7, relating to adjustment of death benefits, was repealed by Stats.1993, c. 893 (A.B.1796), § 1. See Education Code § 22222.

Derivation: Former § 22225.7, added by Stats.1982, c. 1200, § 4, amended by Stats. 1989, c. 542, § 8.

§ 22257. Investment managers; management contracts or appointments; liability of board members

(a) Notwithstanding Section 22203, the board may contract with or appoint one or more investment managers to manage the assets of the retirement fund. If the board has acted with care, skill, prudence, and diligence in meeting the requirements of Sections 22252 and 22253 in selecting and monitoring the investment managers, then, notwithstanding Sections 22250, 22252, 22253, 22254, and 22256, no board member shall be liable for the acts or omissions of the investment managers or be under any obligation to invest or otherwise manage any assets of the retirement fund that are subject to the management of the investment managers.

(b) Incorporation of the fiduciary duty set forth in Section 22250 into the terms of a contract between the system and an investment manager shall be admissible as evidence that the board has acted with care, skill, prudence, and diligence in the selection of the investment manager.

(Added by Stats.1993, c. 893 (A.B.1796), § 2.)

Historical and Statutory Notes

Legislative intent regarding Stats.1993, c. 893 (A.B.1796), including possible continuing application of provisions of repealed State Teachers' Retirement Law, see Historical and Statutory Notes under Education Code § 22000.

Former § 22257, added by Stats.1992, c. 1166 (S.B.1885), § 7, relating to periodic actu-arial valuation reports, was repealed by Stats. 1993, c. 893 (A.B.1796), § 1. See Education Code § 22312.

Derivation: Former § 22225.8, added by Stats.1983, c. 1043, § 3, amended by Stats. 1989, c. 542, § 9.

Cross References

Contracts, generally, see Civil Code § 1549 et seq.
Investments, generally, see Education Code § 22350 et seq.

§ 22258. Appropriations; liability insurance for fiduciaries

Notwithstanding Section 13340 of the Government Code, there is hereby continuously appropriated, without regard to fiscal years, from the retirement fund to the board, the amount necessary to pay for any insurance obtained pursuant to Section 7511 of the Government Code. These payments shall be made upon warrants drawn by the Controller upon demands made by the board.

(Added by Stats.1993, c. 893 (A.B.1796), § 2.)

Historical and Statutory Notes

Legislative intent regarding Stats.1993, c. 893 (A.B.1796), including possible continuing application of provisions of repealed State Teachers' Retirement Law, see Historical and Statutory Notes under Education Code § 22000.

Derivation: Former § 22225.75, added by Stats.1984, c. 1503, § 3.

Cross References

Liability, insurance, fiduciaries, see Government Code § 7511.

§ 22259. Fidelity bonds; fiduciary liability insurance

(a) All board members and officers and employees of the system shall execute a fidelity bond, in an amount determined by the board to be prudent, conditioned upon the faithful performance of the duties of the board member or employee.

(b) All board members and officers and all staff of the investment division who are authorized to invest funds shall be covered with fiduciary liability insurance in an amount determined by the board to be prudent.

(Added by Stats.1993, c. 893 (A.B.1796), § 2. Amended by Stats.1996, c. 634 (S.B. 2041), § 62.)

Historical and Statutory Notes

Legislative intent regarding Stats.1993, c. 893 (A.B.1796), including possible continuing application of provisions of repealed State Teachers' Retirement Law, see Historical and Statutory Notes under Education Code § 22000.

Derivation: Former § 22225.9, added by Stats.1984, c. 1504, § 1.

Cross References

Liability, insurance, fiduciaries, see Government Code § 7511.

§ 22260. Evidences of indebtedness; credit enhancement

Notwithstanding any other provision of law, the system may provide credit enhancement for bonds, notes, certificates of participation, or other evidences of indebtedness of an employer, provided that any credit enhancement transaction satisfies the requirement of Section 22250 and does not constitute a prohibited transaction for purposes of Section 503 of the United States Internal Revenue Code.

(Added by Stats.1998, c. 1076 (S.B.2126), § 4.)

Chapter 5

ADMINISTRATION

Chapter 5 was added by Stats.1993, c. 893 (A.B.1796), § 2.

§ 22300. Chief executive officer

The chief executive officer is the chief administrative officer of the system. The chief executive officer may administer oaths.

(Added by Stats.1993, c. 893 (A.B.1796), § 2.)

Historical and Statutory Notes

Legislative intent regarding Stats.1993, c. 893 (A.B.1796), including possible continuing application of provisions of repealed State Teachers' Retirement Law, see Historical and Statutory Notes under Education Code § 22000.

Former § 22300, enacted by Stats.1976, c. 1010, § 2, amended by Stats.1977, c. 659, § 5; Stats.1989, c. 115, § 2, related to establishment of the Teachers' Retirement Fund, and repealed by Stats.1993, c. 893 (A.B.1796), § 1. See Education Code § 22400.

Derivation: Former § 22201, enacted by Stats.1976, c. 1010, § 2.

Educ.C.1959, § 13871, added by Stats.1969, c. 896, p. 1783, § 2.

Educ.C.1959, § 13852 (Stats.1959, c. 2, p. 987, § 13852, amended by Stats.1963, c. 2135, p. 4444, § 2).

Educ.C.1959, § 13852.1 (Stats.1967, c. 1527, p. 3637, § 3).

Educ.C.1943, § 14301.1, added by Stats.1957, c. 1584, p. 2938, § 1.

Cross References

Chief executive officer, appointment, see Education Code § 22209.
Oath,
    Administration and certification of oaths, see Education Code § 60.
    Defined, see Education Code § 76.
    Oath of office, public officers and employees, see Const. Art. 20, § 3 and Government Code
        § 1360 et seq.
Officers authorized to administer oaths or affirmations, see Code of Civil Procedure § 2093.

§ 22301. Powers and duties of chief executive officer

The chief executive officer has the authority and responsibility for the administration of the system and the plan pursuant to the policies and rules adopted by the board. The chief executive officer may delegate to his or her subordinates any act or duty unless the board by motion or resolution recorded in its minutes has required the chief executive officer to act personally.

(Added by Stats.1993, c. 893 (A.B.1796), § 2. Amended by Stats.1996, c. 634 (S.B. 2041), § 63.)

Historical and Statutory Notes

Legislative intent regarding Stats.1993, c. 893 (A.B.1796), including possible continuing application of provisions of repealed State Teachers' Retirement Law, see Historical and Statutory Notes under Education Code § 22000.

Former § 22301, enacted by Stats.1976, c. 1010, § 2, relating to collection and deposit of receipts, was repealed by Stats.1993, c. 893 (A.B.1796), § 1. See Education Code § 22401.

Derivation: Former § 22204, enacted by Stats.1976 Cal. 1010, § 2.

Educ.C.1959, § 13874, added by Stats.1969, c. 896, p. 1738, § 2.

Educ.C.1959, § 13853 (Stats.1959, c. 2, p. 987, § 13853, amended by Stats.1959, c. 731, p. 2719, § 1; Stats.1963, c. 2135, p. 4444, § 3; Stats.1965, c. 800, p. 2395, § 3).

Cross References

Administrative regulations and rulemaking, see Government Code § 11340 et seq.
Delegation of powers, authority to delegate grant of power to or duty imposed upon a public officer, see Education Code § 7.

§ 22302. Ombudsman; duties; salary

(a) The board shall establish an ombudsman position to serve as an advocate for the members of the Defined Benefit Program and participants of the Cash Balance Benefit Program. The duties of the ombudsman position shall include reviewing and making recommendations to the chief executive officer regarding complaints by school employees, members, employee organizations, the Legislature, or the public regarding actions of the employees of the system.

(b) It is the intent of the Legislature that the salary of the position of ombudsman be offset, as much as possible, through savings realized from a reduction in interest payments on delinquent benefits to members, and through a more efficient and improved public relations program.

(Added by Stats.1993, c. 893 (A.B.1796), § 2. Amended by Stats.1994, c. 933 (A.B. 3171), § 15, eff. Sept. 28, 1994; Stats.1996, c. 634 (S.B.2041), § 64; Stats.1998, c. 965 (A.B.2765), § 31.)

Historical and Statutory Notes

Legislative intent regarding Stats.1993, c. 893 (A.B.1796), including possible continuing application of provisions of repealed State Teachers' Retirement Law, see Historical and Statutory Notes under Education Code § 22000.

Another § 22302, added by Stats.2000, c. 74 (A.B.1509), § 23, was renumbered Education Code § 22302.5 by Stats.2000, c. 1021 (A.B. 2700), § 13.5.

Former § 22302, enacted by Stats.1976, c. 1010, § 2, amended by Stats.1978, c. 870, § 5; Stats.1984, c. 53, § 1, related to credit of contributions and rates of interest, and repealed by Stats.1993, c. 893 (A.B.1796), § 1. See Education Code § 22216.

Derivation: Former § 22204.5, added by Stats.1984, c. 88, § 1.

Cross References

Statutes,
    Construction and legislative intent, see Code of Civil Procedure §§ 1858 and 1859.
    Liberal construction of Education Code, see Education Code § 3.
    Rules of construction and definition for the Education Code, see Education Code § 10.

§ 22302.5. Custodial, record keeping, and other administrative services; contracts with third-parties

The board may contract with a qualified third-party administrator for custodial, record keeping, or other administrative services necessary to carry into effect the provisions of Chapter 38 (commencing with Section 25000) of this part or Part 14.

(Formerly § 22302, added by Stats.2000, c. 74 (A.B.1509), § 23. Renumbered § 22302.5, and amended by Stats.2000, c. 1021 (A.B.2700), § 13.5.)

Historical and Statutory Notes

The 2000 amendment of this section by c. 1021 (A.B.2700) explicitly amended and renumbered the 2000 addition of this section by c. 74 (A.B.1509), without change in the text.

Operative effect of Stats.2000, c. 1021 (A.B. 2700), see Historical and Statutory Notes following Education Code § 22101.5.

Cross References

Contracts, generally, see Civil Code § 1549 et seq.

§ 22303. Retirement counseling; part-time employment of retired public employees

Due to an increase in the demand for retirement counseling services, the system, notwithstanding any other provision of law, may contract with a county superintendent or other employer to provide retirement counseling. Retired public employees may be employed on a part-time basis for that purpose, unless and until the study required by subdivision (b) of Section 7 of Chapter 1532 of the Statutes of 1985 recommends against the employment of retired public employees for these purposes. This authorization is subject to the availability of funds appropriated for that purpose in the annual Budget Act.

(Added by Stats.1993, c. 893 (A.B.1796), § 2. Amended by Stats.1996, c. 634 (S.B. 2041), § 65.)

Historical and Statutory Notes

Legislative intent regarding Stats.1993, c. 893 (A.B.1796), including possible continuing application of provisions of repealed State Teachers' Retirement Law, see Historical and Statutory Notes under Education Code § 22000.

Former § 22303, enacted by Stats.1976, c. 1010, § 2, relating to disposition of earned income, was repealed by Stats.1993, c. 893 (A.B. 1796), § 1. See Education Code § 22402.

Derivation: Former § 22204.6, added by Stats.1986, c. 369, § 1.

Cross References

Contracts, generally, see Civil Code § 1549 et seq.

§ 22303.5.   Midcareer retirement information program

(a) Notwithstanding any other provision of law, the board shall offer a midcareer retirement information program for the benefit of all members.

(b) In implementing this section, the board shall develop plans for the development and delivery of information to enhance awareness of the features and benefits of the Defined Benefit Program, and services of the system, federal Social Security Act programs and benefits as they apply to members, and awareness of personal planning responsibilities. This information shall be provided to assist members in understanding the importance of financial, legal, estate, and personal planning, and how choices and options offered by the system may impact retirement.

(c) The board, at a public meeting, may assess a participation fee for the recovery of all startup and ongoing expenses of the midcareer information program.

(d) The board shall provide both active and retired members with notice pertaining to paragraph (1) of subdivision (c) of Section 44830 and pertaining to Section 44252.5, making all members aware of the time constraints and possible requirement for passing the state basic skills proficiency test if an individual wants to return to the classroom after 39 months. The methods for providing the notice may include, but are not limited to, any of the following:

(1) Inclusion in annual member publications.

(2) Inclusion within packets of information provided to members upon or prior to retirement.

(3) Inclusion as an attachment to any warrants issued to members.

(Added by Stats.1994, c. 656 (A.B.3407), § 1. Amended by Stats.1996, c. 634 (S.B. 2041), § 66; Stats.1998, c. 965 (A.B.2765), § 32; Stats.2001, c. 734 (A.B.804), § 14, eff. Oct. 11, 2001.)

§ 22304. Administrative costs

(a) The costs of administration of the plan shall be paid from the retirement fund and those costs may not exceed the amount made available by law during any fiscal period.

(b) The administrative costs of the plan shall be divided proportionately in accordance with the assets of the Defined Benefit Program, the Defined Benefit Supplement Program, and the Cash Balance Benefit Program.

(Added by Stats.1993, c. 893 (A.B.1796), § 2. Amended by Stats.1996, c. 634 (S.B. 2041), § 67; Stats.1998, c. 1048 (S.B.2085), § 7.5; Stats.2000, c. 74 (A.B.1509), § 24.)

Historical and Statutory Notes

Legislative intent regarding Stats.1993, c. 893 (A.B.1796), including possible continuing application of provisions of repealed State Teachers' Retirement Law, see Historical and Statutory Notes under Education Code § 22000.

Former § 22304, enacted by Stats.1976, c. 1010, § 2, relating to applications to reduce the book value of securities, was repealed by Stats. 1993, c. 893 (A.B.1796), § 1. See Education Code § 22356.

Derivation: Former § 22003, enacted by Stats.1976, c. 1010, § 2.

Educ.C.1959, § 13805, added by Stats.1971, c. 1305, p. 2568, § 4, amended by Stats.1974, c. 1293, p. 2805, § 1.

Educ.C.1959, § 13805, added by Stats.1969, c. 896, p. 1738, § 2.

Educ.C.1959, § 13907, enacted by Stats.1959, c. 2, p. 991, § 13907.

Educ.C.1959, § 13907.1, added by Stats.1967, c. 1476, p. 3456, § 3.

Educ.C.1959, § 14215.1, added by Stats.1967, c. 1476, p. 3457, § 5.

Educ.C.1943, § 14338, added by Stats.1944, 4th Ex.Sess., c. 13, p. 121, § 2.

Educ.C.1943, § 14302 (Stats.1943, c. 71, p. 591).

School C. § 5.811, added by Stats.1937, c. 626, p. 1720, § 4.

§ 22305. Adoption of rules and regulations

Any rules and regulations adopted by the board for the purpose of the administration of this part and Part 14 (commencing with Section 26000), and not inconsistent with this part and Part 14 (commencing with Section 26000), have the force and effect of law.

(Added by Stats.1993, c. 893 (A.B.1796), § 2. Amended by Stats.1994, c. 933 (A.B. 3171), § 16, eff. Sept. 28, 1994; Stats.1998, c. 965 (A.B.2765), § 33.)

Historical and Statutory Notes

Legislative intent regarding Stats.1993, c. 893 (A.B.1796), including possible continuing application of provisions of repealed State Teachers' Retirement Law, see Historical and Statutory Notes under Education Code § 22000.

Former § 22305, enacted by Stats.1976, c. 1010, § 2, amended by Stats.1983, c. 1043, § 4, relating to additional authorized investments, was repealed by Stats.1984, c. 1043, § 5, operative June 5, 1984.

Derivation: Former § 22210, enacted by Stats.1976, c. 1010, § 2.

Educ.C.1959, § 13879, added by Stats.1969, c. 896, p. 1738, § 2.

Educ.C.1959, § 14024 (Stats.1959, c. 2, p. 997, § 14024).

Educ.C.1959, § 13864 (Stats.1959, c. 2, p. 990, § 13864).

Educ.C.1943, § 14424, added by Stats.1944, 4th Ex.Sess., c. 13, p. 125, § 2.

Educ.C.1943, § 14424 (Stats.1943, c. 71, p. 600).

School C. § 5.843, added by Stats.1937, c. 626, p. 1727, § 4.

Cross References

Administrative regulations and rulemaking, see Government Code § 11340 et seq.

Notes of Decisions

Validity of regulations   1

---

1. Validity of regulations

Regulation adopted by the teachers retirement board requiring that all revocations or designations of any beneficiary of the fund to be valid must be received at the system's office prior to the member's death was arbitrary and invalid. Lyles v. Teachers Retirement Bd. (App. 5 Dist. 1963) 33 Cal.Rptr. 328, 219 Cal.App.2d 523.

§ 22306.   Confidentiality of information

(a) Information filed with the system by a member, participant, or beneficiary of the plan is confidential and shall be used by the system for the sole purpose of carrying into effect the provisions of this part. No official or employee of the system who has access to the individual records of a member, participant, or beneficiary shall divulge any confidential information concerning those records to any person except in the following instances:

(1) To the member, participant, or beneficiary to whom the information relates.

(2) To the authorized representative of the member, participant, or beneficiary.

(3) To the governing board of the member's or participant's current or former employer.

(4) To any department, agency, or political subdivision of this state.

(5) To other individuals as necessary to locate a person to whom a benefit may be payable.

(6) Pursuant to subpoena.

(b) Information filed with the system in a beneficiary designation form may be released after the death of the member or participant to those persons who may provide information necessary for the distribution of benefits.

(c) The information is not open to inspection by anyone except the board and its officers and employees of the system, and any person authorized by the Legislature to make inspections.

(Added by Stats.1996, c. 634 (S.B.2041), § 69. Amended by Stats.1998, c. 965 (A.B. 2765), § 34; Stats.1999, c. 939 (S.B.1074), § 24.)

Historical and Statutory Notes

Former § 22306, added by Stats.1993, c. 893 (A.B.1796, § 2, amended by Stats.1994, c. 933 (A.B.3171), § 17, relating to confidentiality of data filed by members or beneficiaries, was repealed by Stats.1996, c. 634 (S.B.2041), § 68. See this section.

Stats.1993, c. 893, provided for addition of this section, similar to Education Code § 22221, as well as for repeal of Education Code § 22221. Stats.1993, c. 920, amended Education Code § 22221. Subordination of legislation by Stats.1993, c. 893, see Historical and Statutory Notes under Education Code § 22000. Section affected by two or more acts at the same session of the legislature, see Government Code § 9605.

Subordination of legislation by Stats.1993, c. 893, and legislative intent regarding that act, including possible continuing application of provisions of repealed State Teachers' Retirement Law,.

Former § 22306, enacted by Stats.1976, c. 1010, § 2, relating to stocks and shares as additional authorized investments, was repealed by Stats.1984, c. 1043, § 6, operative June 5, 1994.

Derivation: Former § 22306, added by Stats. 1993, c. 893, § 2, amended by Stats.1994, c. 933, § 17.

Former § 22221, enacted by Stats.1976, c. 1010, § 2, amended by Stats.1993, c. 920 (A.B. 1631), § 2.

Educ.C.1959, § 13892, added by Stats.1969, c. 896, p. 1738, § 2.

Educ.C.1959, § 14026 (Stats.1959, c. 2, p. 997, § 14026).

Educ.C.1943, § 14426, added by Stats.1944, 4th Ex.Sess., c. 13, p. 125, § 2, amended by Stats.1957, c. 2118, p. 3752, § 4.

Educ.C.1943, § 14426 (Stats.1943, c. 71, p. 600).

School C. § 5.843, added by Stats.1937, c. 626, p. 1727, § 4.

Notes of Decisions

Addresses 1

_____

1. Addresses

Addresses filed with the state teachers' retirement board by beneficiaries under the state teachers' retirement system, are data required to be filed with the board and are therefore confidential under Educ.C.1943, § 14426 (repealed). 20 Ops.Atty.Gen. 76 (1952).

§ 22307. Transfer and disbursement of funds

(a) The board may authorize the transfer and disbursement of funds from the retirement fund for the purpose of carrying into effect this part and Part 14 (commencing with Section 26000). That action shall require signatures of either the board chairperson and vice chairperson, or the signatures of the board chairperson or vice chairperson and the chief executive officer or any employee of the system designated by the chief executive officer.

(b) Notwithstanding Section 13340 of the Government Code, the board may disburse funds for benefits payable under this part and Part 14 (commencing with Section 26000), for the payment of refunds and for investment transactions. Funds for these purposes shall not require appropriation by the annual Budget Act.

(c) Funds for the payment of administrative expenses are not continuously appropriated, and funds for that purpose shall be appropriated by the annual Budget Act.

(Added by Stats.1993, c. 893 (A.B.1796), § 2. Amended by Stats.1996, c. 634 (S.B. 2041), § 70; Stats.1998, c. 1048 (S.B.2085), § 7; Stats.2000, c. 1025 (A.B.816), § 15.)

Historical and Statutory Notes

Legislative intent regarding Stats.1993, c. 893 (A.B.1796), including possible continuing application of provisions of repealed State Teachers' Retirement Law, see Historical and Statutory Notes under Education Code § 22000.

Former § 22307, enacted by Stats.1976, c. 1010, § 2, amended by Stats.1979, c. 327, § 1, relating to investment counsel, was repealed by Stats.1982, c. 1434, § 2.

Derivation: Former § 22206, enacted by Stats.1976, c. 1010, § 2, amended by Stats. 1981, c. 124, § 21; Stats.1983, c. 603, § 1.

Educ.C.1959, § 13876, added by Stats.1969, c. 896, p. 1738, § 2, amended by Stats.1974, c. 795, p. 1739, § 2.

Educ.C.1959, § 13904 (Stats.1959, c. 2, p. 991, § 13904, amended by Stats.1967, c. 1093, p. 2729, § 2).

Educ.C.1943, § 14334, added by Stats.1944, 4th Ex.Sess., c. 13, p. 120, § 2.

Educ.C.1943, § 14364 (Stats.1943, c. 71, p. 596).

School C. § 5.830, added by Stats.1937, c. 626, p. 1723, § 4, amended by Stats.1939, c. 1040, p. 2855, § 2.

§ 22308. Correction of errors and omissions

(a) Subject to subdivision (d), the board may, in its discretion and upon any terms it deems just, correct the errors or omissions of any member or beneficiary of the Defined Benefit Program, and of any participant or beneficiary of the Cash Balance Benefit Program, if all of the following facts exist:

(1) The error or omission was the result of mistake, inadvertence, surprise, or excusable neglect, as each of those terms is used in Section 473 of the Code of Civil Procedure.

(2) The correction will not provide the party seeking correction with a status, right, or obligation not otherwise available under this part.

(b) Failure by a member, participant or beneficiary to make the inquiry that would be made by a reasonable person in like or similar circumstances does not constitute an "error or omission" correctable under this section.

(c) Subject to subdivision (d), the board may correct all actions taken as a result of errors or omissions of the employer or this system.

(d) The duty and power of the board to correct errors and omissions, as provided in this section, shall terminate upon the expiration of obligations of the board, system, and plan to the party seeking correction of the error or omission, as those obligations are defined by Section 22008.

(e) Corrections of errors or omissions pursuant to this section shall be such that the status, rights, and obligations of all parties described in subdivisions (a), (b), and (c) are adjusted to be the same that they would have been if the act that was taken or would have been taken, but for the error or omission, was taken at the proper time. However, notwithstanding any of the other provisions of this section, corrections made pursuant to this section shall adjust the status, rights, and obligations of all parties described in subdivisions (a), (b), and (c) as of the time that the correction actually takes place if the board finds any of the following:

(1) That the correction cannot be performed in a retroactive manner.

(2) That even if the correction can be performed in a retroactive manner, the status, rights, and obligations of all of the parties described in subdivisions (a), (b), and (c) cannot be adjusted to be the same as they would have been if the error or omission had not occurred.

(Added by Stats.1993, c. 893 (A.B.1796), § 2. Amended by Stats.1996, c. 634 (S.B. 2041), § 71; Stats.1998, c. 965 (A.B.2765), § 35.)

Historical and Statutory Notes

Legislative intent regarding Stats.1993, c. 893 (A.B.1796), including possible continuing application of provisions of repealed State Teachers' Retirement Law, see Historical and Statutory Notes under Education Code § 22000.

Former § 22308, enacted by Stats.1976, c. 1010, § 2, relating to an annual report, was amended by Stats.1988, c. 902, § 1, and repealed by Stats.1993, c. 893 (A.B.1796), § 1. See Education Code § 22325.

Derivation: Former § 22233, added by Stats. 1988, c. 1089, § 2.

§ 22309. Individual account statements; locating inactive members

(a) The board shall issue to each active and inactive member, no less frequently than annually after the close of the school year, a statement of the member's individual Defined Benefit Program and Defined Benefit Supplement accounts, provided the employer or member has informed the system of the member's current mailing address.

(b) The board shall periodically make a good faith effort to locate inactive members to provide these members with information concerning any benefit for which they may be eligible.

(Added by Stats.1993, c. 893 (A.B.1796), § 2. Amended by Stats.1994, c. 933 (A.B. 3171), § 18, eff. Sept. 28, 1994; Stats.1996, c. 634 (S.B.2041), § 72; Stats.2000, c. 74 (A.B.1509), § 25.)

Historical and Statutory Notes

Stats.1993, c. 893, provided for addition of this section, similar to Education Code § 22228, as well as for repeal of § 22228. Stats.1993, c. 861, amended § 22228. Subordination of legislation by Stats.1993, c. 893, see Historical and Statutory Notes relating to Stats.1993, c. 893 (A.B.1796), under Education Code § 22000. Section affected by two or more acts at the same session of the legislature, see Government Code § 9605. Provisions similar to this section were formerly contained in Education Code former § 22228.

Former § 22309, added by Stats.1986, c. 900, § 1, relating to retention of a bank or trust company to serve as custodian of the teachers' retirement fund, was repealed by Stats.1993, c. 893 (A.B.1796), § 1. See Education Code § 22359.

Derivation: Educ.C.1959, § 13901, added by Stats.1971, c. 1004, § 6.

§ 22310. Unpaid benefits or refunds

(a) If a benefit or refund cannot be paid because, after a good faith effort, the member or beneficiary cannot be located, the amount payable shall be returned to the retirement fund until the time the party entitled to payment is located.

(b) Interest shall continue to accrue on the accumulated contributions pursuant to this part.

(Added by Stats.1993, c. 893 (A.B.1796), § 2. Amended by Stats.1994, c. 933 (A.B. 3171), § 19, eff. Sept. 28, 1994; Stats.1996, c. 634 (S.B.2041), § 73.)

Historical and Statutory Notes

Stats.1993, c. 893, provided for addition of this section, similar to former § 24609, as well as for repeal of § 24609. Former § 24609 was repealed by Stats.1993, c. 920, and a new § 24609 was added by that same act. Subordination of legislation by Stats.1993, c. 893, see Stats.1993, c. 893 (A.B.1796), § 4. Section affected by two or more acts at the same session of the legislature, see Government Code § 9605.

Subordination of legislation by Stats.1993, c. 893, and legislative intent regarding that act, including possible continuing application of provisions of repealed State Teachers' Retirement Law, see Historical and Statutory Notes under Education Code § 22000.

Provisions similar to this section were formerly contained in Education Code § 24609.

Former § 22310, added by Stats.1978, c. 870, § 6, amended by Stats.1990, c. 831 (A.B.2552), § 3, relating to creation of a teacher tax-sheltered annuity fund, was repealed by Stats.1993, c. 893 (A.B.1796), § 1. See Education Code § 22332.

§ 22311. Actuarial data

The board shall maintain all data necessary to perform an actuarial investigation of the demographic and economic experience of the plan and for the actuarial valuation of the assets and liabilities of the plan.

(Added by Stats.2000, c. 74 (A.B.1509), § 27.)

Historical and Statutory Notes

Former § 22311, added by Stats.1993, c. 893 (A.B.1796), § 2, amended by Stats.1994, c. 933 (A.B.3171), § 20; Stats.1996, c. 634 (S.B.2041), § 74; Stats.1998, c. 1048 (S.B.2085), § 8, relating to actuarial data and investigations, was repealed by Stats.2000, c. 74 (A.B.1509), § 26. See this section.

Legislative intent regarding Stats.1993, c. 893 (A.B.1796), including possible continuing application of provisions of repealed State Teachers' Retirement Law, see Historical and Statutory Notes under Education Code § 22000.

Derivation: Former § 22311, added by Stats. 1993, c. 893 (A.B.1796), § 2, amended by Stats. 1994, c. 933 (A.B.3171), § 20; Stats.1996, c. 634 (S.B.2041), § 74; Stats.1998, c. 1048 (S.B. 2085), § 8.

Former § 22226, enacted by Stats.1976, c. 1010, § 2, amended by Stats.1987, c. 416, § 2.

Educ.C.1959, § 13899, added by Stats.1969, c. 896, p. 1738, § 2, amended by Stats.1971, c. 407, p. 777, § 12; Stats.1974, c. 1293, p. 2808, § 32.

Educ.C.1959, § 13858 (Stats.1959, c. 2, p. 988, § 13858).

Educ.C.1943, § 14307, added by Stats.1944, 4th Ex.Sess., c. 13, p. 118, § 2, amended by Stats.1949, c. 1157, p. 2066, § 2.

Educ.C.1943, § 14326 (Stats.1943, c. 71, amended by Stats.1943, c. 364, p. 593).

School C. § 5.821, added by Stats.1937, c. 626, p. 1721, § 4.

§ 22311.5. Actuarial services

Text of section as added by Stats.2000, c. 74 (A.B.1509), § 28.

The board shall acquire the services of an actuary to do all of the following:

(a) Make recommendations to the board for the adoption of actuarial assumptions that, in the aggregate, are reasonably related to the past experience of the plan and reflect the actuary's informed estimate of the future experience.

(b) Make an actuarial investigation of the demographic and economic experience, including the mortality, service, and other experience, of the plan with respect to members and beneficiaries of the Defined Benefit Programs; members, beneficiaries, and annuity beneficiaries of the Defined Benefit Supplement Program; and participants and beneficiaries of the Cash Balance Benefit Program.

(c) Make an annual actuarial review of the goals regarding the sufficiency of the Gain and Loss Reserves with respect to the Defined Benefit Supplement Program and the Cash Balance Benefit Program and recommend to the board the goal for maintaining a sufficient Gain and Loss Reserves for the Defined Benefit Supplement Program and the Cash Balance Benefit Program.

(d) Recommend to the board the amount, if any, to be transferred to the separate Gain and Loss Reserves from the investment earnings of the plan with respect to the Defined Benefit Supplement Program and the Cash Balance Benefit Program.

(e) At least once every six years with respect to the Defined Benefit Program and annually with respect to the Defined Benefit Supplement Program and the Cash Balance Benefit Program, using actuarial assumptions adopted by the board, perform an actuarial valuation of the plan that identifies the assets and liabilities of the plan, and report the findings to the board. The report of the actuary on the results of the actuarial valuation shall identify and include the components of normal cost and adequate information to determine the effects of changes in actuarial assumptions. Copies of the report on the actuarial valuation shall be transmitted to the Governor and the Legislature.

(f) Recommend to the board all rates and factors necessary to administer the plan, including, but not limited to, mortality tables, annuity factors, interest rates, and additional earnings credits.

(g) Recommend to the board a strategy for amortizing any unfunded actuarial obligation.

(h) As requested by the board, perform any other actuarial services that may be required for administration of the plan.

(Added by Stats.2000, c. 74 (A.B.1509), § 28.)

For another section of the same number, added by Stats.2000, c. 1021 (A.B.2700), § 14, see Education Code § 22311.5, post.

§ 22311.5. Actuarial services

Text of section as added by Stats.2000, c. 1021 (A.B.2700), § 14.

The board shall acquire the services of an actuary to do all of the following:

(a) Make recommendations to the board for the adoption of actuarial assumptions that, in the aggregate, are reasonably related to the past experience of the plan and reflect the actuary's informed estimate of the future experience.

(b) Make an actuarial investigation of the demographic and economic experience, including the mortality, service, and other experience, of the plan with respect to members and beneficiaries of the Defined Benefit Programs; members, beneficiaries, and annuity beneficiaries of the Defined Benefit Supplement Program; and participants and beneficiaries of the Cash Balance Benefit Program.

(c) Make an annual actuarial review of the goals regarding the sufficiency of the Gain and Loss Reserves with respect to the Defined Benefit Supplement Program and the Cash Balance Benefit Program and make recommendations to the board for maintaining a sufficient Gain and Loss Reserves for the Defined Benefit Supplement Program and the Cash Balance Benefit Program.

(d) Recommend to the board the amount, if any, to be transferred to the separate Gain and Loss Reserves from the investment earnings of the plan with respect to the Defined Benefit Supplement Program and the Cash Balance Benefit Program.

(e) At least once every six years with respect to the Defined Benefit Program and annually with respect to the Defined Benefit Supplement Program and the Cash Balance Benefit Program, using actuarial assumptions adopted by the board, perform an actuarial valuation of each program that identifies the assets and liabilities, and report the findings to the board. The report of the actuary on the results of each actuarial valuation shall identify and include the components of normal cost, if applicable, and adequate information to determine the effects of changes in actuarial assumptions. Copies of the report on each actuarial valuation shall be transmitted to the Governor and the Legislature.

(f) Recommend to the board all rates and factors necessary to administer the plan, including, but not limited to, mortality tables, annuity factors, interest rates, and additional earnings credits.

(g) Recommend to the board a strategy for amortizing any unfunded actuarial obligation.

(h) As requested by the board, perform any other actuarial services that may be required for administration of the plan.

(Added by Stats.2000, c. 1021 (A.B.2700), § 14.)

For another section of the same number, added by Stats.2000, c. 74 (A.B.1509), § 28, see Education Code § 22311.5, ante.

Historical and Statutory Notes

Operative effect of Stats.2000, c. 1021 (A.B. 2700), see Historical and Statutory Notes following Education Code § 22101.5.

§ 22311.7. Actuarial assumptions, rates, factors, and tables

Upon the basis of the actuarial investigation and actuarial valuation pursuant to Section 22311.5, or any part thereof, the board shall adopt by plan amendment actuarial assumptions, rates, factors, and tables as the board determines are necessary for administration of the plan and its programs.

(Added by Stats.2000, c. 74 (A.B.1509), § 29.)

§ 22312. Repealed by Stats.1993, c. 893 (A.B.1796), § 2, operative Jan. 1, 1997

Historical and Statutory Notes

The repealed section, added by Stats.1993, c. 893 (A.B.1796), § 2, derived from former § 22257, added by Stats.1992, c. 1166, § 7, related to a periodic actuarial valuation report, and was repealed by its own terms, operative on Jan. 1, 1997.

Former § 22312, added by Stats.1982, c. 1432, § 1, relating to legislative intent to secure investment advisers, was repealed by Stats. 1993, c. 893 (A.B.1796), § 1. See Education Code § 22351.

Former § 22312, added by Stats.1982, c. 1194, p. 4261, § 2, relating to security loan agreements and purchase and sale of exchange-traded call options on common stock by the board, was repealed by Stats.1985, c. 54, § 1.

§ 22312.5. Repealed by Stats.1993, c. 893 (A.B.1796), § 1

Historical and Statutory Notes

The repealed section, added by Stats.1982, c. 1432, § 2, related to investment advisors to the board and appropriations. See Education Code § 22353.

Legislative intent regarding Stats.1993, c. 893 (A.B.1796), including possible continuing appli-

cation of provisions of repealed State Teachers' Retirement Law, see Historical and Statutory Notes under Education Code § 22000.

§ 22313. Retroactive adjustment of rates prohibited

(a) No adjustment shall be included in new rates of contribution adopted by the board on the basis of an investigation, valuation, and determination or because of amendment to the Teachers' Retirement Law with respect to the Defined Benefit Program, for time prior to the effective date of the adoption or amendment, as the case may be.

(b) No action of the board, other than correction of errors in calculating the allowance or annuity at the time of retirement, disability or death of a member shall change the allowance or annuity payable to a retired member or beneficiary prior to the date the action is taken.

(Added by Stats.1993, c. 893 (A.B.1796), § 2. Amended by Stats.1996, c. 634 (S.B. 2041), § 75; Stats.1998, c. 965 (A.B.2765), § 36.)

Historical and Statutory Notes

Legislative intent regarding Stats.1993, c. 893 (A.B.1796), including possible continuing application of provisions of repealed State Teachers' Retirement Law, see Historical and Statutory Notes under Education Code § 22000.

Former § 22313, added by Stats.1982, c. 24, § 1, relating to additional authorized investments of assets from the Teachers' Retirement Fund in real property by the board, was repealed by Stats.1985, c. 54, § 2.

Derivation: Former § 22227, enacted by Stats.1976, c. 1010, § 2.

Educ.C.1959, § 13900, added by Stats.1969, c. 896, p. 1738, § 2.

Educ.C.1959, § 13858 (Stats.1959, c. 2, p. 988, § 13858).

Educ.C.1943, § 14307, added by Stats.1944, 4th Ex.Sess., c. 13, § 2, amended by Stats.1949, c. 1157, § 2.

Educ.C.1943, § 14326 (Stats.1943, c. 71, amended by Stats.1943, c. 364).

School C. § 5.821, added by Stats.1937, c. 626, § 4.

§ 22314. Future tax liabilities; duty to inform member

The system shall inform a member, upon retirement, that future tax liabilities may occur as the result of the pending retirement allowance.

(Added by Stats.1993, c. 893 (A.B.1796), § 2.)

Historical and Statutory Notes

Legislative intent regarding Stats.1993, c. 893 (A.B.1796), including possible continuing application of provisions of repealed State Teachers' Retirement Law, see Historical and Statutory Notes under Education Code § 22000.

Former § 22314, added by Stats.1982, c. 72, § 1, authorizing the board to enter into security loan agreements with broker-dealers and California or national banks, was repealed by Stats. 1985 Cal. 54, § 3.

Derivation: Former § 22004.1, added by Stats.1984, c. 683, § 1, amended by Stats.1988, c. 382, § 1.

§§ 22315 to 22317. Repealed by Stats.1999, c. 465 (A.B.819), §§ 2 to 4

Historical and Statutory Notes

Section 22315, added by Stats.1993, c. 893 (A.B.1796), § 2, amended by Stats.1996, c. 634 (S.B.2041), § 76; Stats.1998, c. 965 (A.B.2765), § 37, derived from former § 22514, added by Stats.1989, c. 1004, § 1, related to legislative intent regarding the impact of the application of 26 U.S.C.A. § 415.

Section 22316, added by Stats.1993, c. 893 (A.B.1796), § 2, amended by Stats.1996, c. 634 (S.B.2041), § 77; Stats.1998, c. 965 (A.B.2765), § 38, derived from former § 22515, added by Stats.1989, c. 1004, § 2, related to benefits payable in regards to the limitations set forth in 26 U.S.C.A. § 415.

Section 22317, added by Stats.1993, c. 893 (A.B.1796), § 2, amended by Stats.1994, c. 933 (A.B.3171), § 21; Stats.1996, c. 634 (S.B.2041),

§ 78; Stats.1998, c. 965 (A.B.2765), § 39, related to benefit enhancements in regards to the limitations imposed in 26 U.S.C.A. § 415.

Stats.1993, c. 893, provided for addition of § 22317, similar to § 22004.2, as well as for repeal of § 22004.2. Stats.1993, c. 1082, amended § 22004.2. Subordination of legislation by Stats.1993, c. 893, see Historical and Statutory Notes under Education code § 22000. Section affected by two or more acts at the same session of the legislature, see Government Code § 9605.

Legislative intent relating to Stats.1993, c. 893, including possible continuing application of provisions of repealed State Teachers' Retirement Law, see Historical and Statutory Notes under Education Code § 22000.

§ 22317.5. Benefit computation; amount of compensation considered in determination; member contributions

The amount of compensation that is taken into account in computing benefits payable under this part to any person who first becomes a member of the Defined Benefit Program on or after July 1, 1996, shall not exceed the annual compensation limitations prescribed by Section 401(a)(17) of Title 26 of the United States Code upon public retirement systems, as that section may be amended from time to time and as that limit may be adjusted by the Commissioner of Internal Revenue for increases in cost of living. The determination of compensation for each 12–month period shall be subject to the annual compensation limit in effect for the calendar year in which the 12–month period begins. In a determination of average annual compensation over more than one 12–month period, the amount of compensation taken into account for each 12–month period, shall be subject to the annual compensation limit applicable to that period.

Notwithstanding any other provision of this part, no member contribution shall be paid upon any compensation in excess of the annual compensation limitations prescribed by Section 401(a)(17) of Title 26 of the United States Code.

(Added by Stats.1995, c. 829 (S.B.791), § 1. Amended by Stats.1998, c. 965 (A.B.2765), § 40.)

Library References

Schools ⊕146(5).
Westlaw Topic No. 345.
C.J.S. Schools and School Districts §§ 340, 342 to 343, 345 to 346.

Legal Jurisprudences

Cal Jur 3d Inc Tax § 28.

§ 22318. Disability payments; time of payment

(a) The initial payment to a disabled member or member retired for disability shall be paid within 45 days following the date the disability is approved, the effective date of the disability retirement or disability allowance, or receipt of all necessary information, whichever occurs last. Monthly payments shall continue thereafter. Initial payments may be based on a good faith estimated amount pending receipt by the system of all necessary employment, dependent, and other public benefit information.

(b) The allowance payable to a disabled member or member retired for disability shall be finalized and a retroactive payment, if one is due, shall be issued within 45 days of receipt by the system of all necessary information.

(Added by Stats.1993, c. 893 (A.B.1796), § 2. Amended by Stats.1996, c. 634 (S.B. 2041), § 79.)

Historical and Statutory Notes

Legislative intent regarding Stats.1993, c. 893 (A.B.1796), including possible continuing application of provisions of repealed State Teachers' Retirement Law, see Historical and Statutory Notes under Education Code § 22000.

Derivation: Former § 24612.1, added by Stats.1982, c. 1428, § 2, amended by Stats. 1990, c. 560, § 12; Stats.1992, c. 1167, § 14.

Cross References

Computation of time,
  Generally, see Code of Civil Procedure §§ 12 and 12a and Government Code § 6800 et seq.
  Time in which any act provided by the Education Code is to be done, see Education Code § 9.
Continuation of statutes relating to subjects covered by provisions of this Code, see Education Code
  § 3.
Disability retirement, see Education Code § 24100 et seq.

§ 22319. Members retired for service; payment times

(a) The initial payment to a member retired for service shall be issued within 45 days of either the effective date of retirement or receipt by the system of a completed application for retirement, whichever is later. The initial payment to an option beneficiary shall be issued within 45 days following receipt by the system of a completed application for death benefits and proof of death of the member. Monthly payments shall continue thereafter. Payments may be based on a good faith estimate pending receipt by the system of all necessary employment information.

(b) The allowance payable to a member retired for service or option beneficiary shall be finalized and a retroactive payment, if one is due, shall be issued within 45 days of receipt by the system of all necessary information.

(Added by Stats.1993, c. 893 (A.B.1796), § 2. Amended by Stats.1994, c. 933 (A.B. 3171), § 22, eff. Sept. 28, 1994; Stats.1996, c. 634 (S.B.2041), § 80.)

Historical and Statutory Notes

Stats.1993, c. 893, provided for addition of this section, similar to § 24612, as well as for repeal of § 24612. Stats.1993, c. 920 (A.B. 1631), amended § 24612. Subordination of legislation by Stats.1993, c. 893, see Stats.1993, c. 893 (A.B.1796), § 4. Section affected by two or more acts at the same session of the legislature, see Government Code § 9605.

Subordination of legislation by Stats.1993, c. 893, and legislative intent regarding that act, including possible continuing application of provisions of repealed State Teachers' Retirement Law, see Historical and Statutory Notes under Education Code § 22000.

Provisions similar to this section were formerly contained in Education Code § 24612.

Cross References

Computation of time,
  Generally, see Code of Civil Procedure §§ 12 and 12a and Government Code § 6800 et seq.
  Time in which any act provided by the Education Code is to be done, see Education Code § 9.
Continuation of statutes relating to subjects covered by provisions of this Code, see Education Code
  § 3.

§ 22320. Death benefits; timely payment

The death benefits provided pursuant to Chapter 22 (commencing with Section 23800), Chapter 23 (commencing with Section 23850), and Chapter 24 (commencing with Section 23880) shall be paid to the beneficiary or estate within 45 days of receipt by the system of all necessary information.

(Added by Stats.1993, c. 893 (A.B.1796), § 2.)

Historical and Statutory Notes

Legislative intent regarding Stats.1993, c. 893 (A.B.1796), including possible continuing application of provisions of repealed State Teachers'

Retirement Law, see Historical and Statutory Notes under Education Code § 22000.

Former § 22320, added by Stats.1982, c. 1429, § 1, relating to authority to establish permanent headquarters, was repealed by Stats. 1993, c. 893 (A.B.1796), § 1. See Education Code § 22375.

Derivation: Former § 24612.2, added by Stats.1992, c. 1167, § 16.

Cross References

Active death benefits, family allowance, see Education Code § 23800 et seq.
Active death benefits, survivor benefits, see Education Code § 23850 et seq.
Computation of time,
　Generally, see Code of Civil Procedure §§ 12 and 12a and Government Code § 6800 et seq.
　Time in which any act provided by the Education Code is to be done, see Education Code § 9.
Continuation of statutes relating to subjects covered by provisions of this Code, see Education Code
　§ 3.

Library References

Schools ⟲146(4).
Westlaw Topic No. 345.

C.J.S. Schools and School Districts §§ 340 to 342, 344.

§ 22321.　Delayed payments; interest

The system shall pay interest for delays in excess of the allowable days specified in Sections 22318 to 22320, inclusive. The interest rate for late payments shall be the regular interest rate. Interest payments shall be deemed to be interest earned in the calendar year in which paid. All interest payments under this section shall be paid in addition to any credited interest that is paid.

(Added by Stats.1993, c. 893 (A.B.1796), § 2. Amended by Stats.1996, c. 634 (S.B. 2041), § 81.)

Historical and Statutory Notes

Legislative intent regarding Stats.1993, c. 893 (A.B.1796), including possible continuing application of provisions of repealed State Teachers' Retirement Law, see Historical and Statutory Notes under Education Code § 22000.

Former § 22321, added by Stats.1982, c. 1429, § 1, relating to rental of excess space, was repealed by Stats.1993, c. 893 (A.B.1796), § 1. See Education Code § 22376.

Derivation: Former § 24612.5, added by Stats.1982, c. 1428, § 4, amended by Stats. 1989, c. 327, § 2; Stats.1990, c. 560, § 14.

§ 22322.　Report of late payments

The system shall report monthly to the board on all late payments.

(Added by Stats.1993, c. 893 (A.B.1796), § 2. Amended by Stats.1996, c. 634 (S.B. 2041), § 81.)

Historical and Statutory Notes

Legislative intent regarding Stats.1993, c. 893 (A.B.1796), including possible continuing application of provisions of repealed State Teachers' Retirement Law, see Historical and Statutory Notes under Education Code § 22000.

Former § 22322, added by Stats.1982, c. 1429, § 1, relating to assistance of department of general services, was repealed by Stats.1993, c. 893 (A.B.1796), § 1. See Education Code § 22377.

Derivation: Former § 24613, added by Stats. 1982, c. 1428, § 5.

§ 22323. Report of outstanding death benefits

The system shall report monthly to the board concerning outstanding death benefits payable that have not been paid within six months of the notification of the death of the member.

(Added by Stats.1993, c. 893 (A.B.1796), § 2. Amended by Stats.1996, c. 634 (S.B. 2041), § 82.)

Historical and Statutory Notes

Legislative intent regarding Stats.1993, c. 893 (A.B.1796), including possible continuing application of provisions of repealed State Teachers' Retirement Law, see Historical and Statutory Notes under Education Code § 22000.

Former § 22323, added by Stats.1982, c. 1429, § 1, relating to deposit of funds to pur-

chase condemned property, was repealed by Stats.1993, c. 893 (A.B.1796), § 1. See Education Code § 22378.

Derivation: Former § 24618, added by Stats. 1986, c. 1006, § 3.

Cross References

Active death benefits, family allowance, see Education Code § 23800 et seq.
Active death benefits, survivor benefits, see Education Code § 23850 et seq.
Computation of time,
    Generally, see Code of Civil Procedure §§ 12 and 12a and Government Code § 6800 et seq.
    Time in which any act provided by the Education Code is to be done, see Education Code § 9.
Continuation of statutes relating to subjects covered by provisions of this Code, see Education Code
    § 3.

§ 22324. Report; need for public contributions; content

The board shall file an annual report with the Governor and the Legislature by March 1 of each year on all phases of its work that could affect the need for public contributions for costs of administration of the system, including the subjects of benefits, programs, practices, procedures, comments on trends and developments in the field of retirement, and the following information on the assets of the plan:

(a) A copy of the annual audit performed pursuant to Section 22217.

(b) A certification letter from the system's consulting actuary concerning the findings of the most recent actuarial valuation, accompanied by summaries of the actuarial cost method, assumptions, and demographic data and analysis of funding progress.

(c) A review of the system's asset mix strategy, a market review or the economic and financial environment in which investments were made, and a summary of the system's general investment strategy.

(d) A description of the investments of the system at cost and market value, and a summary of major changes that occurred since the previous year.

(e) The following information regarding the rate of return of the system by asset type:

(1) Time-weighted market value rate of return on a five-year, three-year, and one-year basis.

(2) Time-weighted book value rate of return on a five-year, three-year, and one-year basis.

(3) Portfolio return comparisons that compare investment returns with universes and indexes.

(f) A report on the use of outside investment advisers and managers.

(g) A report on shareholder voting.

(Added by Stats.1995, c. 829 (S.B.791) § 3. Amended by Stats.1996, c. 634 (S.B.2041), § 83.)

Historical and Statutory Notes

Former § 22324, added by Stats.1993, c. 893 (A.B.1796, § 2, relating to a report by the board regarding work that could affect the need for public contributions for administrative costs of the system, was repealed by Stats.1995, c. 829 (S.B.791), § 2. See this section.

Former § 22324, added by Stats.1982, c. 1429, § 1, relating to bidding procedures, was repealed by Stats.1993, c. 893 (A.B.1796), § 1. See Education Code § 22379.

Derivation: Former § 22324, added by Stats. 1993, c. 893, § 2.

Former § 22218, enacted by Stats.1976, c. 1010, § 2.

Former § 22218.6, added by Stats.1984, c. 1503, § 1, amended by Stats.1989, c. 1004, § 3.

Former § 22357, added by Stats.1993, c. 893, § 2, amended by Stats.1994, c. 933, § 24.

Educ.C.1959, § 13890, added by Stats.1969, c. 896, p. 1738, § 2.

Educ.C.1959, § 13868, added by Stats.1966, 1st Ex.Sess., c. 141, p. 638, § 1.

§ 22325. Repealed by Stats.1995, c. 829 (S.B.791), § 4

Historical and Statutory Notes

The repealed section, added by Stats.1993, c. 893 (A.B.1796), § 2, derived from former § 22308, enacted by Stats.1976, c. 1010, § 2, amended by Stats.1988, c. 902, § 1; Educ.C. 1959, § 13923, added by Stats.1971, c. 870, § 5, related to additional inclusions to the annual report.

Former § 22325, added by Stats.1982, c. 1429, § 1, relating to a building account for construction and improvements and purchase of insurance, was repealed by Stats.1993, c. 893 (A.B.1796), § 1. See Education Code § 22380.

§ 22326. Repealed by Stats.1994, c. 840 (A.B.3562), § 3

Historical and Statutory Notes

The repealed section, added by Stats.1993, c. 893 (A.B.1796), § 2, derived from former § 22218.5, added by Stats.1982, c. 1314, § 1.5, related to a summary of costs or savings to be included in the annual report.

Legislative findings, declarations and intent relating to Stats.1994, c. 840 (A.B.3562), see Historical and Statutory Notes under Education Code § 10020.

§ 22327. Disability benefit recipients; disclosure of earnings

Notwithstanding any other provision of law, the Employment Development Department shall disclose to the board information in its possession relating to the earnings of any person who is receiving a disability benefit under the Defined Benefit Program. The earnings information shall be released to the board only upon written request from the board specifying that the person is receiving disability benefits under the Defined Benefit Program. The request may be made by the chief executive officer of the system or by an employee of the system so authorized and identified by name and title by the chief executive officer in writing. The board shall notify recipients of disability benefits that earnings information shall be obtained from the Employment Development

Department upon request by the board. The board shall not release any earnings information received from the Employment Development Department to any person, agency, or other entity. The system shall reimburse the Employment Development Department for all reasonable administrative expenses incurred pursuant to this section.

(Added by Stats.1993, c. 893 (A.B.1796), § 2. Amended by Stats.1996, c. 634 (S.B. 2041), § 84; Stats.1998, c. 965 (A.B.2765), § 41; Stats.1999, c. 939 (S.B.1074), § 25.)

Historical and Statutory Notes

Legislative intent regarding Stats.1993, c. 893 (A.B.1796), including possible continuing application of provisions of repealed State Teachers' Retirement Law, see Historical and Statutory Notes under Education Code § 22000.

Derivation: Former § 22242, added as § 23910.3 by Stats.1985, c. 543, § 1, renumbered § 22242 and amended by Stats.1992, c. 1167, § 12.

§ 22328. Credits to individual account upon termination of retirement or disability allowance

(a) Upon termination of a retirement allowance or disability allowance that began to accrue on or after July 1, 1972, the person's individual account shall be credited with the amount of his or her accumulated retirement contributions as they were on the effective date of retirement or disability, less the sum of all payments made under paragraph (1) of subdivision (a) of Section 24202, and under Sections 24006 and 24007. The reduction shall not be greater than the total of the accumulated retirement contributions.

(b) Upon the termination of a retirement allowance, the person's accumulated annuity deposit contribution accounts shall be credited with the amounts of the contributions as they were on the date the annuity became payable because of the retirement less the sum of all payments made under paragraph (2) of subdivision (a) of Section 24202.

(Added by Stats.1993, c. 893 (A.B.1796), § 2. Amended by Stats.1996, c. 634 (S.B. 2041), § 85.)

Historical and Statutory Notes

Legislative intent regarding Stats.1993, c. 893 (A.B.1796), including possible continuing application of provisions of repealed State Teachers' Retirement Law, see Historical and Statutory Notes under Education Code § 22000.

Derivation: Former § 23914, enacted by Stats.1976, c. 1010, § 2, amended by Stats. 1978, c. 870, § 15; Stats.1984, c. 53, § 4.

Educ.C.1959, § 14223, added by Stats.1972, c. 1010, p. 1868, § 48, amended by Stats.1974, c. 1293, p. 2816, § 79.

Educ.C.1959, § 14223, added by Stats.1969, c. 896, p. 1738, § 2, amended by Stats.1971, c. 1305, p. 2584, § 107.

Educ.C.1959, § 14312, enacted by Stats.1959, c. 2, p. 1021, § 14312.

Educ.C.1943, § 14534 (Stats.1943, c. 71, p. 615).

Educ.C.1943, § 14613, added by Stats.1944, 4th Ex.Sess., c. 13, p. 138, § 2, amended by Stats.1949, c. 1157, p. 2069, § 11; Stats.1957, c. 2118, p. 3754, § 10.

School C. § 5.874, added by Stats.1937, c. 626, p. 1738, § 4, amended by Stats.1939, c. 1040, p. 2867, § 12.

§ 22329. Telephone assistance; toll-free line

In order to provide equitable telephone assistance to all members and beneficiaries, regardless of their location in California, the system shall install a toll-free, "800" prefix, line.

(Added by Stats.1993, c. 893 (A.B.1796), § 2. Amended by Stats.1996, c. 634 (S.B. 2041), § 86.)

Historical and Statutory Notes

Legislative intent regarding Stats.1993, c. 893 (A.B.1796), including possible continuing application of provisions of repealed State Teachers' Retirement Law, see Historical and Statutory Notes under Education Code § 22000.

Derivation: Former § 22235, added by Stats. 1984, c. 683, § 2.

§ 22330. Legislation pending; analysis; submission to legislature; appropriations

(a) The board shall provide the Legislature with an analysis of the asset and liability implications of each bill that would affect the investment strategy of the system, the funding of the plan, or the benefit structure of the plan. The analysis shall include an explanation of the methodology employed and the assumptions used in its preparation. Neither fiscal committee of the Legislature shall hear any such bill until the analysis has been provided to the committee.

(b) There is hereby continuously appropriated, without regard to fiscal years, from the retirement fund, an amount sufficient to pay all costs arising from subdivision (a), but not to exceed fifty thousand dollars ($50,000) in any one fiscal year.

(Added by Stats.1993, c. 893 (A.B.1796), § 2. Amended by Stats.1996, c. 634 (S.B. 2041), § 87.)

Historical and Statutory Notes

Legislative intent regarding Stats.1993, c. 893 (A.B.1796), including possible continuing application of provisions of repealed State Teachers' Retirement Law, see Historical and Statutory Notes under Education Code § 22000.

Derivation: Former § 22236, added by Stats. 1984, c. 1502, § 1.

§§ 22331 to 22333. Repealed by Stats.1994, c. 291 (A.B.3064), §§ 1 to 3

Historical and Statutory Notes

Section 22331, added by Stats.1993, c. 893 (A.B.1796), § 2, derived from former § 22231, added by Stats.1978, c. 870, § 4, amended by Stats.1990, c. 831, § 1, related to a tax-sheltered annuity plan.

Section 22332, added by Stats.1993, c. 893 (A.B.1796), § 2, derived from former § 22310, added by Stats.1978, c. 870, § 6, amended by

Stats.1990, c. 831, § 3, related to a tax-sheltered annuity plan.

Section 22333, added by Stats.1993, c. 893 (A.B.1796), § 2, derived from former § 22232, added by Stats.1987, c. 1419, § 1, amended by Stats.1990, c. 831, § 2, related to a tax-sheltered annuity plan.

§ 22334. Repealed by Stats.1996, c. 634 (S.B.2041), § 88

Historical and Statutory Notes

The repealed section, added by Stats.1993, c. 893 (A.B.1796), § 2, derived from former § 22240, added by Stats.1988, c. 743, § 1, related to an alternative retirement plan to be known as Plan II.

§ 22335. Teacher Tax-Sheltered Annuity Fund; continuous appropriation; purpose; payment form rules; fund existence

(a) All moneys in the Teachers Tax–Sheltered Annuity Fund are continuously appropriated to the board for disbursement for the purposes of the tax-sheltered annuity plan previously provided under this part.

(b) The board may provide by board rule for optional forms of payment from the Teachers Tax–Sheltered Annuity Fund.

(c) The Teachers Tax–Sheltered Annuity Fund as it existed on December 31, 1994, shall continue to exist for purposes of this section.

(d) This section shall cease to be operative 180 days after the date that an annuity contract and custodial account established pursuant to Chapter 36 (commencing with Section 24950) becomes operative. On the date this section ceases to be operative this section is repealed unless a statute that is enacted before that date deletes or extends that date.

(Added by Stats.1994, c. 489 (A.B.3705), § 1. Amended by Stats.1996, c. 634 (S.B. 2041), § 89.)

Repeal

Operative effect and repeal of this section, see subd. (d).

Chapter 6

INVESTMENTS

Section

22364.   Award of contract or prospective investment transaction; prohibited communications by board members; notice; application.

Chapter 6 was added by Stats.1993, c. 893 (A.B.1796), § 2.

§ 22350. Legislative findings and declarations; investment expertise

The Legislature finds and declares that changing economic conditions and increasing complexity in the investment market make it necessary and desirable that the system obtain the best possible investment expertise.

(Added by Stats.1993, c. 893 (A.B.1796), § 2.)

Historical and Statutory Notes

Legislative intent regarding Stats.1993, c. 893 (A.B.1796), including possible continuing application of provisions of repealed State Teachers' Retirement Law, see Historical and Statutory Notes under Education Code § 22000.

Derivation: Former § 22205.1, added by Stats.1982, c. 1433, § 1, amended by Stats. 1986, c. 230, § 1.

Library References

Schools ⟜146(1).
Westlaw Topic No. 345.

C.J.S. Schools and School Districts §§ 338, 340 to 343, 346.

§ 22351. Legislative intent; qualified investment advisors

It is the intent of the Legislature that the board secure investment advisors with the composite expertise necessary for the investment of the retirement fund portfolio.

(Added by Stats.1993, c. 893 (A.B.1796), § 2.)

Historical and Statutory Notes

Legislative intent regarding Stats.1993, c. 893 (A.B.1796), including possible continuing application of provisions of repealed State Teachers' Retirement Law, see Historical and Statutory Notes under Education Code § 22000.

Derivation: Former § 22312, added by Stats. 1982, c. 1432, § 1.

Cross References

Investment managers and advisers, see Education Code § 22143.
Investment transactions, see Education Code § 22144.
Statutes,
    Construction and legislative intent, see Code of Civil Procedure §§ 1858 and 1859.
    Liberal construction of Education Code, see Education Code § 3.
    Rules of construction and definition for the Education Code, see Education Code § 10.

§ 22352. Contracts with qualified investment managers as alternatives; reports

(a) Upon a finding by the board that necessary investment expertise is not available within existing civil service classifications, and with the approval of the State Personnel Board, the board may contract with qualified investment managers having demonstrated expertise in the management of large and diverse investment portfolios to render service in connection with the investment program of the board.

(b) The board shall report to the Governor, the Legislature, and the Joint Legislative Budget Committee on the nature, duration, and cost of investment contract services used. The report shall first be submitted in April 1987, and annually in April of every year thereafter.

(Added by Stats.1993, c. 893 (A.B.1796), § 2. Amended by Stats.2001, c. 803 (S.B.501), § 5.)

Historical and Statutory Notes

Legislative intent regarding Stats.1993, c. 893 (A.B.1796), including possible continuing application of provisions of repealed State Teachers' Retirement Law, see Historical and Statutory Notes under Education Code § 22000.

Derivation: Former § 22205.2, added by Stats.1982, c. 1433, § 2, amended by Stats. 1986, c. 230, § 2; Stats.1987, c. 330, § 6.

Cross References

Contracts, generally, see Civil Code § 1549 et seq.
Investment managers and advisers, see Education Code § 22143.
Investment transactions, see Education Code § 22144.
State Personnel Board, see Const. Art. 7, § 2 et seq. and Government Code § 18710 et seq.

§ 22353. Contracts with individual investment advisors; payment of costs

(a) Notwithstanding any other provision of law, the board shall by contract retain not less than two separate individual investment advisers.

(b) Notwithstanding Section 13340 of the Government Code, there is hereby continuously appropriated without regard to fiscal years, from the retirement fund, an amount sufficient to pay all costs arising from this section.

(c) No costs arising from this section shall be paid from the General Fund.

(Added by Stats.1993, c. 893 (A.B.1796), § 2.)

Historical and Statutory Notes

Legislative intent regarding Stats.1993, c. 893 (A.B.1796), including possible continuing application of provisions of repealed State Teachers' Retirement Law, see Historical and Statutory Notes under Education Code § 22000.

Derivation: Former § 22312.5, added by Stats.1982, c. 1432, § 2.

Cross References

Contracts, generally, see Civil Code § 1549 et seq.
Investment managers and advisers, see Education Code § 22143.
Investment transactions, see Education Code § 22144.

§ 22354. Corporate investments; investment managers to monitor and advise

(a) The board shall, pursuant to the state civil service statutes, either contract with, or establish and fill full-time positions for, investment managers who are experienced and knowledgeable in corporate management issues to monitor each corporation any of whose shares are owned by the plan and to advise the board on the voting of the shares owned by the plan and on the responses of the system to merger proposals and tender offers and all other matters pertaining to corporate governance.

(b) Notwithstanding Section 13340 of the Government Code, there is hereby continuously appropriated, without regard to fiscal years, from the retirement fund, an amount sufficient to pay all costs arising from this section.

(Added by Stats.1993, c. 893 (A.B.1796), § 2. Amended by Stats.1994, c. 933 (A.B. 3171), § 23, eff. Sept. 28, 1994; Stats.1998, c. 965 (A.B.2765), § 42.)

Historical and Statutory Notes

Legislative intent regarding Stats.1993, c. 893 (A.B.1796), including possible continuing application of provisions of repealed State Teachers' Retirement Law, see Historical and Statutory Notes under Education Code § 22000.

Derivation: Former § 22239, added by Stats. 1984, c. 1105, § 1, amended by Stats.1987, c. 330, § 8; Stats.1988, c. 382, § 3.

Cross References

Contracts, generally, see Civil Code § 1549 et seq.
Investment managers and advisers, see Education Code § 22143.
Investment transactions, see Education Code § 22144.

§ 22355. Employment of investment personnel also serving PERS board

In no event shall the board employ through interagency agreement any investment personnel who would also serve during the term of the agreement as investment staff to the Board of Administration of the Public Employees' Retirement System.

(Added by Stats.1993, c. 893 (A.B.1796), § 2.)

Historical and Statutory Notes

Legislative intent regarding Stats.1993, c. 893 (A.B.1796), including possible continuing application of provisions of repealed State Teachers' Retirement Law, see Historical and Statutory Notes under Education Code § 22000.

Derivation: Former § 22205.5, added by Stats.1982, c. 1434, § 1, amended by Stats. 1983, c. 426, § 1; Stats.1987, c. 330, § 7.

Former § 22307, enacted by Stats.1976, c. 1010, § 2, amended by Stats.1979, c. 327, § 1.

Educ.C.1959, § 13922, added by Stats.1971, c. 870, p. 1712, § 4.

Cross References

Investment managers and advisers, see Education Code § 22143.
Investment transactions, see Education Code § 22144.

§ 22356. Reduction of book value of securities; excess proceeds

The board may apply to reduce the book value of securities purchased, all or part of the excess of the proceeds of the sale or redemption prior to maturity of securities over the book value of the securities sold or redeemed provided the purchase of securities is made with those proceeds and provided that the terms of both securities from the date of sale, redemption, or purchase, as the case may be, to the respective dates of maturity, do not differ by more than five years. All applications of excess of sales or redemption proceeds, even with greater difference in terms, made by the board before October 1, 1949, are hereby validated and confirmed.

(Added by Stats.1993, c. 893 (A.B.1796), § 2.)

Historical and Statutory Notes

Legislative intent regarding Stats.1993, c. 893 (A.B.1796), including possible continuing application of provisions of repealed State Teachers' Retirement Law, see Historical and Statutory Notes under Education Code § 22000.

Derivation: Former § 22304, enacted by Stats.1976, c. 1010, § 2.

Educ.C.1959, § 13919, added by Stats.1969, c. 896, p. 1738, § 2.

Educ.C.1959, § 13856 (Stats.1959, c. 2, p. 987, § 13856, amended by Stats.1961, c. 583, § 1).

Educ.C.1943, § 14305, added by Stats.1944, 4th Ex.Sess., c. 13, § 2, amended by Stats.1945, c. 1207, § 1; Stats.1949, c. 1157, § 1; Stats. 1957, c. 2118, § 3.

Educ.C.1943, § 14324 (Stats.1943, c. 71).

School C. § 5.821, added by Stats.1937, c. 626, § 4.

§ 22357.   Repealed by Stats.1995, c. 829 (S.B.791), § 5

Historical and Statutory Notes

The repealed section, added by Stats.1993, c. 893 (a.B.1796), § 2, amended by Stats.1994, c. 933 (A.B.3171), § 24, related to the contents of an annual report.   See Education Code § 22324.

Legislative intent regarding Stats.1993, c. 893 (A.B.1796), including possible continuing application of provisions of repealed State Teachers' Retirement Law, see Historical and Statutory Notes under Education Code § 22000.

§ 22358.   Repealed by Stats.1998, c. 965 (A.B.2765), § 43

Historical and Statutory Notes

The repealed section, added by Stats.1995, c. 829 (S.B.791), § 7, amended by Stats.1996, c. 634 (S.B.2041), § 90, derived from former § 22358, added by Stats.1993, c. 893, § 2; former § 22218.7, added by Stats.1984, c. 1503, § 2, related to submission of the plan assets to the legislature.

Former § 22358, added by Stats.1993, c. 893 (A.B.1796, § 2, requiring a review of the sys-

tem's assets, was repealed by Stats.1995, c. 829 (S.B.791), § 6. See this section.

Legislative intent regarding Stats.1993, c. 893 (A.B.1796), including possible continuing application of provisions of repealed State Teachers' Retirement Law, see Historical and Statutory Notes under Education Code § 22000.

§ 22359.   Custodian services; retention of bank or trust company

Notwithstanding any other provision of law, the board may retain a bank or trust company to serve as custodian for safekeeping, delivery, securities valuation, investment performance reporting, and other services in connection with investment of the retirement fund.

(Added by Stats.1993, c. 893 (A.B.1796), § 2.)

Historical and Statutory Notes

Legislative intent regarding Stats.1993, c. 893 (A.B.1796), including possible continuing application of provisions of repealed State Teachers' Retirement Law, see Historical and Statutory Notes under Education Code § 22000.

Derivation: Former § 22309, added by Stats. 1986, c. 900, § 1.

§ 22360.   The Dave Elder State Teachers' Retirement System Home Loan Program Act.

(a) Notwithstanding any other provision of law, the board may pursuant to Section 22203 and in conformance with its fiduciary duty set forth in Section

22250, enter into correspondent agreements with private lending institutions in this state to utilize the retirement fund to invest in residential mortgages, including assisting borrowers, through financing, to obtain homes in this state.

(b) The program shall, among other things, provide:

(1) That home loans be made available to borrowers for the purchase of single-family dwellings, two-family dwellings, three-family dwellings, four-family dwellings, single-family cooperative apartments, and single-family condominiums.

(2) That the recipients of the loans occupy the homes as their principal residences in accordance with policies established by the board.

(3) That the home loans shall be available only for the purchase or refinance of homes in this state.

(4) That the amount and length of the loans shall be pursuant to a schedule periodically established by the board that shall provide a loan of up to 100 percent of the appraised value. In no event shall the loan amount exceed 200 percent of the conforming loan limit set by the Federal National Mortgage Association (FNMA) or 200 percent of the conforming loan limit set by the Federal Home Loan Mortgage Corporation (FHLMC), whichever is greater. The portion of any loan exceeding 80 percent of value shall be insured by an admitted mortgage guaranty insurer conforming to Chapter 2A (commencing with Section 12640.01) of Part 6 of Division 2 of the Insurance Code, in an amount so that the unguaranteed portion of the loan does not exceed 75 percent of the market value of the property together with improvements thereon.

(5) That there may be prepayment penalties assessed on the loans in accordance with policies established by the board.

(6) That the criteria and terms for its loans shall be consistent with the financial integrity of the program and the sound investment of the retirement fund.

(7) Any other terms and conditions as the board shall deem appropriate.

(c) It is the intent of the Legislature that the provisions of this section be used to establish an investment program for residential mortgages, including assisting borrowers in purchasing homes in this state, or refinancing a mortgage loan. The Legislature intends that home loans made pursuant to this section shall be secured primarily by the property purchased or refinanced and shall not exceed the appraised value of that property.

(d) Appropriate administrative costs of implementing this section and Section 22360.5 shall be paid by the participating borrowers. Those costs may be included in the loan amount.

(e) Appropriate interest rates shall be periodically reviewed and adjusted to provide loans to borrowers consistent with the financial integrity of the home loan program and the sound and prudent investment of the retirement fund. Under no circumstances, however, shall the interest rates offered to borrowers be below current market rate.

(f) The board shall administer this section and Section 22360.5 under other terms and conditions it deems appropriate and in keeping with the investment standard. The board may adopt policies as necessary for its administration of this section and Section 22360.5 and to assure compliance with applicable state and federal laws.

(g) This section and Section 22360.5 shall be known as, and may be cited as, the Dave Elder State Teachers' Retirement System Home Loan Program Act.

(Added by Stats.1998, c. 419 (S.B.1945), § 2. Amended by Stats.1999, c. 939 (S.B. 1074), § 26; Stats.2001, c. 802 (S.B.499), § 4.)

Historical and Statutory Notes

Former § 22360, added by Stats.1993, c. 893 (A.B.1796), § 2, amended by Stats.1994, c. 933 (A.B.3171), § 25; Stats.1996, c. 634 (S.B.2041), § 91, relating to home loan programs, was repealed by Stats.1998, c. 419 (S.B.1945), § 1. See this section.

Derivation: Former § 22360, added by Stats. 1993, c. 893 (A.B.1796), § 2, amended by Stats.

1994, c. 933 (A.B.3171), § 25; Stats.1996, c. 634 (S.B.2041), § 91.

Former § 22238, added by Stats.1984, c. 392, § 1, amended by Stats.1986, c. 69, § 1; Stats. 1986, c. 369, § 2; Stats.1988, c. 408, § 1; Stats. 1990, c. 11, § 1; Stats.1991, c. 543, § 4.

§ 22360.5. Financing for single-family dwelling units; inclusion in investment program under § 22360; criteria

(a) The board may include in any investment program established pursuant to Section 22360 a procedure whereby a member may obtain 100 percent financing for the purchase for a single-family dwelling unit in accordance with the following criteria:

(1) The member shall obtain one loan secured by the purchased home, pursuant to Section 22360, and a second personal loan secured by a portion of the accumulated retirement contributions in the member's individual account. The personal loan shall only be used for the purchase of the member's principal residence and not for a loan to refinance the member's existing mortgage.

(2) The loan secured by the purchased home shall be consistent with the requirements imposed by Section 22360.

(3) In no event may the personal loan secured by the accumulated retirement contributions in the member's individual account exceed the lesser of 50 percent of the current value amount of the accumulated retirement contributions or fifty thousand dollars ($50,000).

(4) If two members are married, the personal loan secured by the sum total of accumulated retirement contributions in both members' accounts shall not exceed 5 percent of the loan.

(5) The pledge of security under this section shall remain in effect until the personal loan is paid in full.

(b) The pledge of security under this section shall take binding effect. In the event of a default on the personal loan secured by the member's retirement contributions as authorized by this section, the board shall deduct an amount from the member's accumulated retirement contributions on deposit and adjust the member's accumulated retirement contributions as necessary to recover any outstanding loan balance prior to making any disbursement of a refund or a lump-sum distribution.

(c) In the event of a default on the personal loan by a member, the board shall deduct the monthly principal plus appropriate interest from the member's benefit, when the member begins receiving a benefit, until the loan is paid in full.

(d) In the event of a default on the personal loan by a member receiving a benefit, the board shall deduct the monthly principal and interest from the member's benefit until the personal loan is paid in full.

(e) The secured personal loan permitted under this section shall be made available only to members who meet eligibility criteria as determined by the board.

(f) In the event of a refund or lump-sum distribution of the accumulated retirement contributions, the member's account shall be adjusted as necessary to recover any outstanding loan balance.

(g) If the member is married at the time the home is purchased with a personal loan secured by the member's accumulated retirement contributions as authorized by this section, then the member's spouse shall agree in writing to the pledge of security, as to his or her community interest in the amount pledged, regardless of whether title to the home is held in joint tenancy.

(h) For purposes of the section only, "member" means any person who is entitled to receive an allowance funded by the system pursuant to this part or Part 14, notwithstanding any vesting requirement and without regard to present eligibility to retire, and who is not retired or disabled.

(Added by Stats.1999, c. 939 (S.B.1074), § 27.)

§ 22361. Natural disaster relief; loans from retirement funds; terms and conditions

(a) The board may, subject to and consistent with its fiduciary duty, establish a program utilizing the retirement fund to assist currently employed members and retired members who are victims of a natural disaster to obtain loans from the retirement fund for the sole purpose of repairing or rebuilding their homes that have been damaged by a natural disaster. In order to qualify for such a loan, the home of the currently employed member or retired member shall have been damaged by a natural disaster and the home shall have been in an area that has been declared a disaster area in a proclamation of the Governor of a state of emergency affecting the area in which the currently employed member or retired member resides.

(b) The board may loan any amount of money, up to and including 100 percent of the current appraised value of a home of a currently employed member or retired member. However, 5 percent of the loan may, at the discretion of the board, be secured by the contributions of the member who requests the loan.

(c) The board may, under such conditions as it may deem prudent, require that a currently employed member or retired member pledge other assets as collateral for a loan.

(d) The board shall establish terms for the termination of loans made pursuant to this section upon the separation of members from service, to ensure, in the case of any default, that the fund shall not suffer any loss and to provide, as a condition of retirement, for alternative security. The board may impose any other terms and conditions the board may determine appropriate.

(e) The Legislature hereby reserves full power and authority to change, revise, limit, expand, or repeal the loan program authorized by this section.

(Added by Stats.1993, c. 893 (A.B.1796), § 2. Amended by Stats.1996, c. 634 (S.B. 2041), § 92.)

Historical and Statutory Notes

Legislative intent regarding Stats.1993, c. 893 (A.B.1796), including possible continuing application of provisions of repealed State Teachers' Retirement Law, see Historical and Statutory Notes under Education Code § 22000.

Derivation: Former § 22238.1, added by Stats.1989–90, 1st Ex.Sess., c. 35, § 1.

§ 22362. Investments

(a) Notwithstanding any other provision of law, the board shall give first priority to investing not less than 25 percent of all funds of the plan that become available in a fiscal year for new investments, in any of the following:

(1) Obligations secured by a lien or charge solely on residential realty, including rental housing, located in the state and on the security of which, commercial banks are permitted to make loans pursuant to Article 2 (commencing with Section 1220) of Chapter 10 of Division 1 of the Financial Code.

(2) Securities representing a beneficial interest in a pool of obligations secured by a lien or charge solely on residential realty located in the state.

(3) Certificates of deposit issued by savings and loan associations, if the savings and loan associations agree to make loans, or to fund tax-exempt notes or bonds issued by housing authorities, cities, or counties, on residential realty located in the state, including rental housing, in an amount equal to the amount of the deposit.

(b) Funds subject to investment pursuant to this section include all moneys received as employer and member contributions, investment income, and the proceeds from all net gains and losses from securities, reduced by the amount of benefit payments and withdrawals occurring during the fiscal year. In computing the amount of investment pursuant to this section, a dollar-for-dollar credit shall be given for residential realty investments described in this section that are contractually agreed to be made by a financial institution from which the board, in consideration thereof, purchases other such investments. In computing the amount of investment pursuant to this section, the board may elect to include the dollar amount of commitments to purchase mortgages from public revenue bond programs in the year the commitment is given. However, that election may not exceed one-fifth of the total guideline amount.

(c) Nothing in this section shall be construed to require the acquisition of any instrument or security at less than the market rate.

(d) If the board determines during any fiscal year that compliance with this section will result in lower overall earnings for the retirement fund than obtainable from alternative investment opportunities that would provide equal or superior security, including guarantee of yield, the board may substitute those higher yielding investments, to the extent actually available for acquisition, for the investments otherwise specified by this section. Additionally, if, and to the extent that, adherence to the diversification guideline specified in this section would conflict with its fiduciary obligations in violation of Section 9 of Article I of the California Constitution or Section 10 of Article I of the United States Constitution, or would conflict with the standard for prudent investment of the fund as set forth in Section 17 of Article XVI of the California Constitution, the board may substitute alternative investments. In that case, the board shall estimate the amount of funds available in substitute alternative investments and the amount of funds invested pursuant to subdivision (a) and shall submit its resolution of findings and determinations, together with a description of the type, quantity, and yield of the investments substituted, to the Governor and to the Joint Legislative Audit Committee within 20 days following the conclusion of the fiscal year. Within 30 days thereafter, the Joint Legislative Audit Committee shall transmit the Auditor General's report to the Speaker of the Assembly and to the Senate Committee on Rules for transmittal to affected policy committees.

(e) The board, upon determining the final amount of funds available for investment in substitute alternative investments and the estimated amount of funds invested pursuant to subdivision (a), shall submit that information to the Governor and the Joint Legislative Audit Committee. Thereafter, the Joint Legislative Audit Committee shall transmit the report of the Auditor General to the Speaker of the Assembly and the Senate Committee on Rules for transmittal to the affected policy committees.

(Added by Stats.1993, c. 893 (A.B.1796), § 2. Amended by Stats.1996, c. 634 (S.B. 2041), § 92.5.)

Historical and Statutory Notes

Legislative intent regarding Stats.1993, c. 893 (A.B.1796), including possible continuing application of provisions of repealed State Teachers' Retirement Law, see Historical and Statutory Notes under Education Code § 22000.

Derivation: Former § 22223, added by Stats. 1987, c. 416, § 1, amended by Stats.1992, c. 540, § 2.

Cross References

Computation of time,
    Generally, see Code of Civil Procedure §§ 12 and 12a and Government Code § 6800 et seq.
    Time in which any act provided by the Education Code is to be done, see Education Code § 9.
Continuation of statutes relating to subjects covered by provisions of this Code, see Education Code
    § 3.

Library References

Schools ⬅146(1).
Westlaw Topic No. 345.

C.J.S. Schools and School Districts §§ 338, 340 to 343, 346.

§ **22363.** **Matter involving vendor or contractor; closed session; disclosure of campaign contribution**

No matter involving any vendor or contractor, in their individual or any other capacity, shall be considered during a closed session on any transaction involving the system unless, prior to the closed session, a written disclosure has been submitted by the vendor or contractor of any campaign contributions aggregating two hundred fifty dollars ($250) or more and any gifts aggregating fifty dollars ($50) or more in value that the vendor or contractor has made during the preceding calendar year to any member of the board or any officer or employee of the system. Failure to disclose the campaign contributions and gifts shall provide the basis for disqualification of the contractor or the vendor.

(Added by Stats.1998, c. 923 (S.B.1753), § 2.)

Historical and Statutory Notes

Section 13 of Stats.1998, c. 923, provides:

"SEC. 13. The Legislature finds and declares that the provisions of this act further the purposes of the Political Reform Act of 1974 within the meaning of subdivision (a) of Section 81012 of the Government Code."

For letter of intent from Senator Schiff regarding Stats.1998, c. 923 (S.B.1753), see Historical and Statutory Notes under Education Code § 22203.5.

§ **22364.** **Award of contract or prospective investment transaction; prohibited communications by board members; notice; application**

(a) During the process leading to an award of any contract by the system, no member of the board or its staff shall knowingly communicate concerning any matter relating to the contract or selection process with any party financially interested in the contract, or an officer or employee of that party, unless the communication is (1) part of the process expressly described in the request for proposal or other solicitation invitation, or (2) part of a noticed board meeting, or (3) as provided in subdivision (c). Any applicant or bidder who knowingly participates in a communication that is prohibited by this paragraph shall be disqualified from the contract award.

(b) During the evaluation of any prospective investment transaction, no party who is financially interested in the transaction, or an officer or employee of that party, may knowingly communicate with any board member concerning any matter relating to the transaction or its evaluation, unless the financially interested party discloses the content of the communication in a writing addressed and submitted to the executive officer and the board prior to the board's action on the prospective transaction. This subdivision shall not apply to communications that are part of a noticed board meeting, or as provided in subdivision (c).

(1) The writing shall disclose the date and location of the communication, and the substance of the matters discussed. The board shall prescribe other procedures concerning this disclosure.

(2) Any board member who participates in a communication subject to this subdivision shall also have the obligation to disclose the communication to the executive officer and board, prior to the board's action on the prospective

transaction. The board shall prescribe procedures for this disclosure, including procedures to apply to board members who fail to disclose communications as required by this subdivision.

(3) Consistent with its fiduciary duties, the board shall determine the appropriate remedy for any knowing failure of a financially interested party to comply with this subdivision including, but not limited to, outright rejection of the prospective investment transaction, reduction in fee income, or any other sanction.

(4) The communications disclosed under this subdivision shall be made public, either at the open meeting of the board in which the transaction is considered, or if in closed session, upon public disclosure of any closed session votes concerning the investment transaction.

(c) The procedures and prohibitions prescribed by this section shall not apply to:

(1) Communications that are incidental, exclusively social, and do not involve the system or its business, or the board or staff member's role as a system official.

(2) Communications that do not involve the system or its business and that are within the scope of the board or staff member's private business or public office wholly unrelated to the system.

(Added by Stats.1998, c. 923 (S.B.1753), § 3.)

Historical and Statutory Notes

Section 13 of Stats.1998, c. 923, provides:

"SEC. 13. The Legislature finds and declares that the provisions of this act further the purposes of the Political Reform Act of 1974 within the meaning of subdivision (a) of Section 81012 of the Government Code."

For letter of intent from Senator Schiff regarding Stats.1998, c. 923 (S.B.1753), see Historical and Statutory Notes under Education Code § 22203.5.

Cross References

Contracts, generally, see Civil Code § 1549 et seq.
Open meetings,
    Bagley-Keene, actions of public agencies, see Government Code § 11120.
    Ralph M. Brown Act, meetings of public commissions, boards and councils and other public
    agencies, see Government Code § 54950 et seq.

Chapter 7

SYSTEM HEADQUARTERS

Chapter 7 was added by Stats.1993, c. 893 (A.B.1796), § 2.

§ 22375. Authority to establish permanent headquarters

Notwithstanding Section 20205.9 or Part 11 (commencing with Section 15850) of Division 3 of Title 2 of the Government Code, the board may select, purchase, or acquire in the name of the plan, the fee or any lesser interest in real property, improved or unimproved, and may remodel and equip, or construct an office building in the County of Sacramento for the purposes of establishing a permanent headquarters facility for the system.

(Added by Stats.1993, c. 893 (A.B.1796), § 2.   Amended by Stats.1996, c. 634 (S.B. 2041), § 93.)

Historical and Statutory Notes

Legislative intent regarding Stats.1993, c. 893 (A.B.1796), including possible continuing application of provisions of repealed State Teachers' Retirement Law, see Historical and Statutory Notes under Education Code § 22000.

Derivation: Former § 22320, added by Stats. 1982, c. 1429, § 1.

§ 22376. Excess; rentals

All buildings acquired or improvements constructed by the board under the provisions of this chapter may contain space in excess of immediate requirements. The board may contract with the Department of General Services to handle the rentals of any excess space over and above that required by the board and to furnish general supervision and maintenance of buildings and improvements constructed under the provisions of this chapter.

(Added by Stats.1993, c. 893 (A.B.1796), § 2.)

Historical and Statutory Notes

Legislative intent regarding Stats.1993, c. 893 (A.B.1796), including possible continuing application of provisions of repealed State Teachers' Retirement Law, see Historical and Statutory Notes under Education Code § 22000.

Derivation: Former § 22321, added by Stats. 1982, c. 1429, § 1.

Cross References

Contracts, generally, see Civil Code § 1549 et seq.

§ 22377. Assistance of department of general services

The board may contract with the Department of General Services or any other state agency for assistance in the acquisition of real property and any construction thereon of buildings or improvements authorized by this chapter.

(Added by Stats.1993, c. 893 (A.B.1796), § 2.)

Historical and Statutory Notes

Legislative intent regarding Stats.1993, c. 893 (A.B.1796), including possible continuing application of provisions of repealed State Teachers' Retirement Law, see Historical and Statutory Notes under Education Code § 22000.

Derivation: Former § 22322, added by Stats. 1982, c. 1429, § 1.

Cross References

Contracts, generally, see Civil Code § 1549 et seq.

§ 22378.   Eminent domain; deposit of purchase funds

In the event that condemnation of the property selected is necessary, the board may elect to deposit with the treasurer funds it deems necessary, and that are appropriated, for purchase of the selected property subject to the Property Acquisition Law (Part 11 (commencing with Section 15850) of Division 3 of Title 2 of the Government Code).

(Added by Stats.1993, c. 893 (A.B.1796), § 2.)

Historical and Statutory Notes

Legislative intent regarding Stats.1993, c. 893 (A.B.1796), including possible continuing application of provisions of repealed State Teachers' Retirement Law, see Historical and Statutory Notes under Education Code § 22000.

Derivation: Former § 22323, added by Stats. 1982, c. 1429, § 1.

§ 22379.   Bidding procedures

Work on all projects shall be done under contract awarded to the lowest responsible bidder pursuant to bidding procedures set forth in the State Contract Act (Chapter 1 (commencing with Section 10100) of Division 2 of the Public Contract Code).

(Added by Stats.1993, c. 893 (A.B.1796), § 2.)

Historical and Statutory Notes

Legislative intent regarding Stats.1993, c. 893 (A.B.1796), including possible continuing application of provisions of repealed State Teachers' Retirement Law, see Historical and Statutory Notes under Education Code § 22000.

Derivation: Former § 22324, added by Stats. 1982, c. 1429, § 1.

Cross References

Contracts, generally, see Civil Code § 1549 et seq.

Library References

States ☞98.
Westlaw Topic No. 360.
C.J.S. States §§ 160 to 167.

§ 22380.   Building account; insurance; investment in lieu of facilities operation cost

(a) The board shall establish a building account for the transfer of money appropriated for that purpose from the retirement fund for the construction or remodeling of buildings and improvements thereon, maintenance, repair, and improvement thereof. For accounting purposes, the board shall pay rental to the building account in an amount sufficient to repay all costs of acquisition, construction, and maintenance of space used by the board plus interest to the retirement fund.

(b) The board may contract with the Department of General Services for the purchase of insurance against loss of, or damage to, the property or the loss of use or occupancy of the building, liability insurance, and other insurance that is customarily carried on state office buildings.   Premiums for this insurance shall be paid from the building account.

(c) The land, building, equipment, and improvements thereon, shall constitute an investment, in lieu of facilities operations cost, in the retirement fund and shall be carried on the books thereof as such in accordance with generally accepted accounting practices.

(Added by Stats.1993, c. 893 (A.B.1796), § 2.)

Historical and Statutory Notes

Legislative intent regarding Stats.1993, c. 893 (A.B.1796), including possible continuing application of provisions of repealed State Teachers' Retirement Law, see Historical and Statutory Notes under Education Code § 22000.

Derivation: Former § 22325, added by Stats. 1982, c. 1429, § 1.

Cross References

Contracts, generally, see Civil Code § 1549 et seq.

Chapter 8

ESTABLISHMENT AND CONTROL OF FUNDS

Chapter 8 was added by Stats.1993, c. 893 (A.B.1796), § 2.

§ 22400.   Teachers' Retirement Fund; deposit; disbursements

(a) There is in the State Treasury a special trust fund to be known as the Teachers' Retirement Fund.   There shall be deposited in that fund the assets of the plan and its predecessors, consisting of employee contributions, employer contributions, state contributions, appropriations made to it by the Legislature, income on investments, other interest income, income from fees and penalties, donations, legacies, bequests made to it and accepted by the board, and any other amounts provided by this part and Part 14.   General Fund transfers pursuant to Section 22954 shall be placed in a segregated account known as the Supplemental Benefit Maintenance Account within the retirement fund, which is continuously appropriated without regard to fiscal years, notwithstanding Section 13340 of the Government Code, for expenditure for the purposes of Section 24415.

(b) Disbursement of money from the retirement fund of whatever nature shall be made upon claims duly audited in the manner prescribed for the disbursement of other public funds except that notwithstanding the foregoing disbursements may be made to return funds deposited in the fund in error.

(Added by Stats.1993, c. 893 (A.B.1796), § 2. Amended by Stats.1996, c. 634 (S.B. 2041), § 94; Stats.1999, c. 939 (S.B.1074), § 28.)

Historical and Statutory Notes

Another § 22400, enacted by Stats.1976, c. 1010, § 2, amended by Stats.1993, c. 861 (A.B. 447), § 3, amended by Stats.1993, c. 861 (A.B. 447), § 1, relating to information affecting the status of a member or beneficiary, was repealed by Stats.1994, c. 933 (A.B.3171), § 26, eff. Sept. 28, 1994. See Education Code § 22450.

Repeal of § 22400 by Stats.1993, c. 893 (A.B. 1796), § 1, failed to become operative. See Stats.1993, c. 893 (A.B.1796), § 4, in the Historical and Statutory Notes under Education Code § 22000, and Government Code § 9605.

Similar provisions were added by Stats.1993, c. 893, § 2 as Education Code § 22450.

Derivation: Former § 22300, enacted by Stats.1976, c. 1010, § 2, amended by Stats. 1977, c. 659, § 5; Stats.1989, c. 115, § 2.

Educ.C.1959, § 13910, added by Stats.1969, c. 896, p. 1738, § 2, amended by Stats.1974, c. 795, p. 1739, § 4.

Educ.C.1959, § 13901 (Stats.1959, c. 2, p. 990, § 13901, amended by Stats.1963, c. 782, p. 1811, § 2).

Educ.C.1943, § 14331, added by Stats.1957, c. 1583, p. 2935, § 3.

Cross References

State treasury, generally, see Government Code § 16300 et seq.

Library References

Schools ⬭146(1).
States ⬭127.
Westlaw Topic Nos. 345, 360.

C.J.S. Schools and School Districts §§ 338, 340 to 343, 346.
C.J.S. States § 228.

Notes of Decisions

Interest 2
Transfers to fund 1

1. Transfers to fund

Transfer of funds from general fund to teachers' retirement fund was compelled by continuing appropriation statutes, notwithstanding appropriations for payments of lesser amounts in annual budget bills enacted subsequently, in view of principles prohibiting impairment of contract. California Teachers Ass'n v. Cory (Teachers' Retirement Bd. of State Teachers' Retirement Ass'n) (App. 3 Dist. 1984) 202 Cal. Rptr. 611, 155 Cal.App.3d 494.

2. Interest

Interest earned on investment of outstanding balance of warrants drawn against the State Teachers Retirement Fund should be credited to that Fund. 71 Op.Atty.Gen. 89, March 9, 1988.

§ 22401. Collection and deposit of return on investments and other receipts

Return on investments shall be collected by the Treasurer, and together with any other moneys received for the retirement fund shall be immediately deposited to the credit of that fund and reported immediately to the system. Money in whatever form received directly by the system shall be deposited immediately in the State Treasury to the credit of that fund.

(Added by Stats.1993, c. 893 (A.B.1796), § 2.)

Historical and Statutory Notes

Legislative intent regarding Stats.1993, c. 893 (A.B.1796), including possible continuing application of provisions of repealed State Teachers' Retirement Law, see Historical and Statutory Notes under Education Code § 22000.

Former § 22401, enacted by Stats.1976, c. 1010, § 2, amended by Stats.1977, c. 36, § 98; Stats.1982, c. 1314, § 2, relating to required information, was repealed by Stats.1993, c. 893 (A.B.1796), § 1. See Education Code § 22451.

Derivation: Former § 22301, enacted by Stats.1976, c. 1010, § 2.

Educ.C.1959, § 13915, added by Stats.1969, c. 896, p. 1738, § 2, amended by Stats.1971, c. 407, p. 778, § 14; Stats.1974, c. 795, p. 1739, § 9.

Educ.C.1959, § 13905 (Stats.1959, c. 2, p. 991, § 13905).

Educ.C.1943, § 14335, added by Stats.1944, 4th Ex.Sess., c. 13, p. 120, § 2, amended by Stats.1957, c. 1583, p. 2936, § 7.

Educ.C.1943, § 14366 (Stats.1943, c. 71, p. 597).

School C. § 5.830, added by Stats.1937, c. 626, p. 1723, § 4, amended by Stats.1939, c. 1040, p. 2855, § 2.

Cross References

State treasury, generally, see Government Code § 16300 et seq.

§ 22401.1. Renumbered § 22451.5 and amended by Stats.1994, c. 933 (A.B.3171), § 27, eff. Sept. 28, 1994

Historical and Statutory Notes

Stats.1993, c. 920 provided for addition of this section, similar to Education Code § 22801, as well as for the repeal of § 22801. Stats. 1993, c. 893 also repealed § 22801 and added Education Code § 22452. Subordination of legislation by Stats.1993, c. 893 (A.B.1796), see Stats.1993, c. 893, § 4. Section affected by two or more acts at the same session of the legislature, see Government Code § 9605.

§ 22401.2. Renumbered § 22451.7 and amended by Stats.1994, c. 933 (A.B.3171), § 28, eff. Sept. 28, 1994

Historical and Statutory Notes

Stats.1993, c. 920 provided for addition of this section, similar to Education Code § 22801, as well as for the repeal of § 22801. Stats. 1993, c. 893 also repealed § 22801 and added Education Code § 22452. Subordination of legislation by Stats.1993, c. 893 (A.B.1796), see Stats.1993, c. 893, § 4. Section affected by two or more acts at the same session of the legislature, see Government Code § 9605.

§ 22401.5. Repealed by Stats.1991, c. 543 (S.B.1171), § 5

Historical and Statutory Notes

The repealed section, which related to spousal notification of selection of specified benefits made by a member, was added by Stats.1986, c. 235, § 2, and was amended by Stats.1989, c. 270, § 1. Similar provisions were added by Stats.1991, c. 543 (S.B.1171), § 6 as Education Code § 22401.6.

§ 22401.6. Repealed by Stats.1994, c. 933 (A.B.3171), § 29, eff. Sept. 28, 1994

Historical and Statutory Notes

The repealed section, added by Stats.1992, c. 1166 (S.B.1885), § 8.4, amended by Stats.1993, c. 219 (A.B.1500), § 74, related to applications for benefits. See Education Code § 22453.

Stats.1993, c. 893, § 1, provided for the repeal of this section, which was also amended by Stats.1993, c. 219. Stats.1993, c. 893, § 2, provided for the addition of § 22453, which is similar to this section. Subordination of legislation by Stats.1993, c. 893, see Historical and Statutory Notes under Education Code § 22000. Section affected by two or more acts at the same session of the legislature, see Government Code § 9605.

Former § 22401.6 added by Stats.1990, c. 1390, § 1, amended by Stats.1991, c. 543, § 6; Stats.1992, c. 163, § 67, relating to spousal signature, was repealed by Stats.1992, c. 1166 (S.B.1885), § 8, eff. Sept. 30, 1992.

Subordination of legislation by Stats.1992, c. 163 (A.B.2641), see Historical and Statutory Notes under Business and Professions Code § 1320.

Section affected by two or more acts at the same session of the legislature, see Government Code § 9605.

§ 22401.7. Repealed by Stats.1994, c. 933 (A.B.3171), § 30, eff. Sept. 28, 1994

Historical and Statutory Notes

The repealed section, added by Stats.1992, c. 1166 (S.B.1885), § 8.5, amended by Stats.1993, c. 219 (A.B.1500), § 75, related to a spouse's refusal to sign. See Education Code § 22454.

Repeal of this section by Stats.1993, c. 893 (A.B.1796), § 1, failed to become operative.

See Stats.1993, c. 893 (A.B.1796), § 4, in the Historical and Statutory Notes under Education Code § 22000 and Government Code § 9605.

Similar provisions were added by Stats.1993, c. 893, § 2 as Education Code § 22454.

§ 22402. Defined Benefit Program; interest and other income; allocation

Earned interest on plan assets with respect to the Defined Benefit Program that is not credited to member accounts under the Defined Benefit Program and the plan's other income with respect to the Defined Benefit Program shall be allocated to provide benefits payable under the Defined Benefit Program.

(Added by Stats.1993, c. 893 (A.B.1796), § 2. Amended by Stats.1998, c. 1048 (S.B. 2085), § 9; Stats.2000, c. 1025 (A.B.816), § 16.)

Historical and Statutory Notes

Legislative intent regarding Stats.1993, c. 893 (A.B.1796), including possible continuing application of provisions of repealed State Teachers' Retirement Law, see Historical and Statutory Notes under Education Code § 22000.

Former § 22402, enacted by Stats.1976, c. 1010, § 2, relating to notice of employment, death, resignation or discharge, was repealed by Stats.1993, c. 893 (A.B.1796), § 1. See Education Code § 22457.

Derivation: Former § 22303, enacted by Stats.1976, c. 1010, § 2.

Educ.C.1959, § 13918, added by Stats.1969, c. 896, p. 1738, § 2, amended by Stats.1971, c.

407, p. 778, § 16; Stats.1971, c. 1305, p. 2572, § 32.

Educ.C.1959, § 13856 (Stats.1959, c. 2, p. 987, § 13856, amended by Stats.1961, c. 583, § 1).

Educ.C.1959, § 13856.1, added by Stats.1967, c. 1476, p. 3456, § 1.

Educ.C.1943, § 14305, added by Stats.1944, 4th Ex.Sess., c. 13, § 2, amended by Stats.1945, c. 1207, § 1; Stats.1949, c. 1157, § 1; Stats. 1957, c. 2118, § 3.

Educ.C.1943, § 14324 (Stats.1943, c. 71).

School C. § 5.821, added by Stats.1937, c. 626, § 4.

§ 22403. Finding and declaration; discharge of loan

The Legislature hereby finds and declares that pursuant to the authorizing legislation creating and establishing the Cash Balance Plan, the board transferred one million dollars ($1,000,000) in the form of a loan from the retirement fund holding assets at that time exclusively for the State Teachers' Retirement System Defined Benefit Plan to the newly created Cash Balance Plan. That loan represented an asset receivable to the State Teachers' Retirement System Defined Benefit Plan and a liability obligation to the State Teachers' Retirement System Cash Balance Plan. As a result of the merger of these two plans authorized under this part, the assets held in the retirement fund shall hereby reflect the combined assets of the State Teachers' Retirement

Plan. That loan shall be discharged by the creation and establishment of the State Teachers' Retirement Plan pursuant to the merger.

(Added by Stats.1998, c. 1048 (S.B.2085), § 10.)

Historical and Statutory Notes

Former § 22403, enacted by Stats.1976, c. 1010, § 2, related to information to be supplied by the county superintendent and was repealed by Stats.1993, c. 893 (A.B.1796), § 1. See Education Code § 22455.

§§ 22403.1, 22404. Repealed by Stats.1993, c. 893 (A.B.1796), § 1

Historical and Statutory Notes

Section 22403.1, added by Stats.1991, c. 543 (S.B.1171), § 7, related to contents of copies of documents respecting compensation paid employees. See Education Code § 22458.

Section 22404, enacted by Stats.1976, c. 1010, § 2, related to withholding of salary for failure to file information or pay an amount due. See Education Code § 22459.

Legislative intent regarding Stats.1993, c. 893 (A.B.1796), including possible continuing application of provisions of repealed State Teachers' Retirement Law, see Historical and Statutory Notes under Education Code § 22000.

Chapter 9

MEMBER AND EMPLOYER DUTIES

Chapter 9 was added by Stats.1993, c. 893 (A.B.1796), § 2.

§ 22450. Information affecting status of members or beneficiaries; current mailing address and information

(a) Each member and beneficiary shall furnish to the board any information affecting his or her status as a member or beneficiary of the Defined Benefit Program as the board requires.

(b) A member who has not had any creditable service reported during the prior school year shall provide the system with his or her current mailing address and beneficiary information.

(Added by Stats.1993, c. 893 (A.B.1796), § 2. Amended by Stats.1994, c. 933 (A.B. 3171), § 31, eff. Sept. 28, 1994; Stats.1996, c. 634 (S.B.2041), § 95; Stats.1998, c. 965 (A.B.2765), § 44.)

Historical and Statutory Notes

Stats.1993, c. 893, provided for addition of this section, similar to Education Code § 22400, as well as for repeal of § 22400. Stats.1993, c. 861, amended § 22400. Subordination of legislation by Stats.1993, c. 893, see Stats.1993, c. 893 (A.B.1796), § 4. Section affected by two or more acts at the same session of the legislature, see Government Code § 9605.

Provisions similar to this section were formerly contained in Education Code § 22400.

Derivation: Educ.C.1959, § 13930, added by Stats.1969, c. 896, p. 1738, § 2.

Educ.C.1959, § 14025 (Stats.1959, c. 2, p. 997, § 14025, amended by Stats.1959, c. 870, p. 2903, § 1).

Educ.C.1943, § 14425, added by Stats.1944, 4th Ex.Sess., c. 13, p. 125, § 2.

Educ.C.1943, § 14425 (Stats.1943, c. 71, p. 600).

School C. § 5.843, added by Stats.1937, c. 626, p. 1727, § 4.

§ 22451. Statements by members; information required

(a) Each member shall file a statement with the board, at the option of, and upon the form furnished by, the system, giving the following information:

(1) Date of birth.

(2) All service previously performed subject to coverage by the plan or its predecessors.

(b) Each person becoming a member on or after January 1, 1983, shall include in the health résumé required by the teacher preparation and licensing agency all information that shall verify any and all handicaps and disabling conditions at the time of application. Upon request by the system this information shall be made available when an application for disability benefits is received.

(Added by Stats.1993, c. 893 (A.B.1796), § 2. Amended by Stats.1996, c. 634 (S.B. 2041), § 96.)

Historical and Statutory Notes

Legislative intent regarding Stats.1993, c. 893 (A.B.1796), including possible continuing application of provisions of repealed State Teachers' Retirement Law, see Historical and Statutory Notes under Education Code § 22000.

Derivation: Former § 22401, enacted by Stats.1976, c. 1010, § 2, amended by Stats. 1977, c. 36, § 98; Stats.1982, c. 1314, § 2.

Educ.C.1959, § 13931, added by Stats.1969, c. 896, p. 1738, § 2, amended by Stats.1974, c. 1293, p. 2808, § 33; Stats.1976, c. 560, § 1.

Educ.C.1959, § 14025 (Stats.1959, c. 2, p. 997, § 14025, amended by Stats.1959, c. 870, § 1).

Educ.C.1943, § 14425, added by Stats.1944, 4th Ex.Sess., c. 13, § 2.

Educ.C.1943, § 14425 (Stats.1943, c. 71).

School C. § 5.843, added by Stats.1937, c. 626, § 4.

§ 22451.5. Proof of date of birth; duty to provide

(a) Upon request by the system, a member shall provide proof of his or her date of birth to resolve any discrepancy between the member's date of birth as originally documented on the records of the system and the member's date of birth as subsequently submitted.

(b) A member shall provide proof of the date of birth of a person designated by the member as beneficiary under an option selected pursuant to Chapter 28 (commencing with Section 24300) if the beneficiary is not also a member of the plan.

(c) Documentation substantiating the date of birth of a member's dependent child shall be provided if an allowance payable under this part will include an amount for that dependent child.

(d) At the time application is made for payment of a family allowance or survivor benefit allowance to a surviving spouse or dependent parent, a member's surviving spouse or dependent parent shall provide proof of his or her date of birth.

(e) At the discretion of the board, an original document, a certified copy of the original, or a photocopy shall be acceptable to establish proof of the date of birth.

(Formerly § 22401.1, added by Stats.1993, c. 920 (A.B.1631), § 3. Renumbered § 22451.5 and amended by Stats.1994, c. 933 (A.B.3171), § 27, eff. Sept. 28, 1994. Amended by Stats.1996, c. 1165 (A.B.3032), § 13.)

Historical and Statutory Notes

Derivation: Former § 22801, enacted by Stats.1976, c. 1010, § 2.

Educ.C.1959, § 14021.5, added by Stats.1974, c. 342, p. 673, § 1.

§ 22451.7. Proof of date of birth; benefit payments withheld

The system may withhold benefit payments until proof of the date of birth of a member, beneficiary under an option selected pursuant to Chapter 28 (commencing with Section 24300), surviving spouse, dependent child or dependent parent has been received and accepted by the system.

(Formerly § 22401.2, added by Stats.1993, c. 920 (A.B.1631), § 4. Renumbered § 22451.7 and amended by Stats.1994, c. 933 (A.B.3171), § 28, eff. Sept. 28, 1994. Amended by Stats.1996, c. 1165 (A.B.3032), § 14.)

§ 22452. Repealed by Stats.1994, c. 933 (A.B.3171), § 32, eff. Sept. 28, 1994

Historical and Statutory Notes

The repealed section, added by Stats.1993, c. 893 (A.B.1796), § 2, derived from former § 22801, enacted by Stats.1976, c. 1010, § 2; Educ.C.1959, § 14021.5, added by Stats.1974, c. 342, p. 673, § 1, required proof of date of birth. See Education Code §§ 22401.1, 22401.2.

Stats.1993, c. 893 provided for addition of this section, similar to Education Code § 22801,

as well as for repeal of § 22801. Stats.1993, c. 920 also repealed § 22801 and added Education Code §§ 22401.1 and 22401.2. Subordination of legislation by Stats.1993, c. 893 (A.B.1796), see Historical and Statutory Notes under Education Code § 22000. Section affected by two or more acts at the same session of the legislature, see Government Code § 9605.

§ 22453. Applications for benefits; spousal signature; exceptions

(a) Except as provided in Section 22454, the signature of the spouse of a member shall be required under the Defined Benefit Program on any application for, or cancellation of, an unmodified allowance; the election, change, or cancellation of an option; or any request for a refund of the member's accumulated retirement contributions or accumulated annuity deposit contributions; and under the Defined Benefit Supplement Program on any application for, or cancellation of, a retirement benefit, disability benefit, or termination benefit; and under either the Defined Benefit Program or the Defined Benefit Supplement Program on any other requests related to the selection of benefits by a member in which a spousal interest may be present, unless the member declares, in writing, under penalty of perjury, that one of the following conditions exists:

(1) The member is not married.

(2) The current spouse has no identifiable community property interest in the benefit.

(3) The member and spouse have executed a marriage settlement agreement pursuant to Part 5 (commencing with Section 1500) of Division 4 of the Family Code that makes the community property law inapplicable to the marriage.

(4) The spouse is incapable of executing the acknowledgment because of an incapacitating mental or physical condition.

(5) The member does not know, and has taken all reasonable steps to determine, the whereabouts of the spouse.

(b) This section shall not be applicable to an application for a disability allowance under the Defined Benefit Program.

(c) The sole purpose of this section is to provide for spousal protection in the selection of specified benefits made by a member.

(Added by Stats.1993, c. 893 (A.B.1796), § 2. Amended by Stats.1994, c. 933 (A.B. 3171), § 33, eff. Sept. 28, 1994; Stats.1996, c. 634 (S.B.2041), § 96.5; Stats.2000, c. 74 (A.B.1509), § 30; Stats.2000, c. 1021 (A.B.2700), § 15.)

Historical and Statutory Notes

Stats.1993, c. 893, provided for addition of this section, similar to Education Code § 22401.6, as well as for repeal of § 22401.6. Stats.1993, c. 219, amended § 22401.6. Subordination of legislation by Stats.1993, c. 893, see Stats.1993, c. 893 (A.B.1796), § 4. Section affected by two or more acts at the same session of the legislature, see Government Code § 9605.

Subordination of legislation by Stats.1993, c. 893, and legislative intent regarding that act, including possible continuing application of

provisions of repealed State Teachers' Retirement Law, see Historical and Statutory Notes under Education Code § 22000.

Provisions similar to this section were formerly contained in Education Code § 22401.6.

Operative effect of Stats.2000, c. 1021 (A.B. 2700), see Historical and Statutory Notes following Education Code § 22101.5.

Section affected by two or more acts at the same session of the legislature, see Government Code § 9605.

Cross References

Community property, see Family Code §§ 65 and 760.

Library References

Schools ⚎146(7).
Westlaw Topic No. 345.

C.J.S. Schools and School Districts §§ 347 to 350.

§ 22454.   Spouse's refusal to sign application; right to action

If a spouse refuses to sign an application, as set forth in Section 22453, the member may bring an action in court to enforce the spousal signature requirement or to waive the spousal signature requirement.   Either party may bring an action pursuant to Section 1101 of the Family Code to determine the rights of the party.

(Added by Stats.1993, c. 893 (A.B.1796), § 2.   Amended by Stats.1994, c. 933 (A.B. 3171), § 34, eff. Sept. 28, 1994; Stats.1994, c. 1269 (A.B.2208), § 4; Stats.1996, c. 634 (S.B.2041), § 97.)

Law Revision Commission Comment

1994 Amendment

Section 22454 is amended to correct a typographical error made in 1993 Cal. Stat. ch. 893 (AB 1796). This is a technical, nonsubstantive change.   [24 Cal.L.Rev.Comm. Reports 621 (1994)]

Historical and Statutory Notes

Stats.1993, c. 893, provided for addition of this section, similar to Education Code § 22401.7, as well as for repeal of § 22401.7. Stats.1993, c. 219, amended § 22401.7. Subordination of legislation by Stats.1993, c. 893, see Stats.1993, c. 893 (A.B.1796), § 4. Section affected by two or more acts at the same session of the legislature, see Government Code § 9605.

Subordination of legislation by Stats.1993, c. 893, and legislative intent regarding that act, including possible continuing application of provisions of repealed State Teachers' Retirement Law, see Historical and Statutory Notes under Education Code § 22000.

Provisions similar to this section were formerly contained in Education Code § 22401.7.

The 1994 amendment by c. 933 substituted "Section 1101 of the Family Code" for "Section 11101 of the Family Code".

The 1994 amendment by c. 1269 incorporated the changes made by c. 933.

The 1996 amendment substituted "the member" for "the member or retirant".

§ 22455.   Information required to be furnished by county superintendents and other employing agencies

The county superintendent and other employing agencies shall furnish any further information concerning any member or beneficiary the board may require.

(Added by Stats.1993, c. 893 (A.B.1796), § 2.)

Historical and Statutory Notes

Legislative intent regarding Stats.1993, c. 893 (A.B.1796), including possible continuing application of provisions of repealed State Teachers' Retirement Law, see Historical and Statutory Notes under Education Code § 22000.

Derivation: Former § 22403, enacted by Stats.1976, c. 1010, § 2.

Educ.C.1959, § 13933, added by Stats.1969, c. 896, p. 1738, § 2.

Educ.C.1959, § 14021, enacted by Stats.1959, c. 2, p. 996, § 14021.

Educ.C.1943, § 14421, added by Stats.1944, 4th Ex.Sess., c. 13, p. 124, § 2.

Educ.C.1943, § 14421 (Stats.1943, c. 71, p. 600).

School C. § 584.2, added by Stats.1937, c. 626, p. 1727, § 4, amended by Stats.1939, c. 1040, p. 2856, § 3.

§ 22455.5.   Legislative findings and declarations; public employers; social security coverage or qualified retirement plan membership

(a) The Legislature finds and declares that the federal Omnibus Budget Reconciliation Act of 1990 (P.L. 101–508) requires all public employers to provide their employees with either social security coverage or membership in a qualified retirement plan.

(b) Employers shall make available criteria for membership, including optional membership, in a timely manner to all persons employed to perform creditable service subject to coverage by the Defined Benefit Program, and shall inform part-time and substitute employees, within 30 days of the date of hire, or by March 1, 1995, whichever is later, that they may elect membership in the plan's Defined Benefit Program at any time while employed. Written acknowledgment by the employee shall be maintained in employer files on a form provided by this system.

(c) Employers shall be liable to the plan for employee and employer contributions and interest with respect to the Defined Benefit Program from the date of hire, or March 1, 1995, whichever is later, in addition to system administrative and audit costs, if an audit or a member's complaint reveals noncompliance. However, no employer shall be liable for employee contributions for service performed prior to January 1, 1995.

(Added by Stats.1994, c. 603 (A.B.2554), § 1. Amended by Stats.1996, c. 634 (S.B. 2041), § 98; Stats.1999, c. 939 (S.B.1074), § 29.)

Historical and Statutory Notes

Governor Wilson issued the following signature message, dated Sept. 15, 1994, regarding A.B. 2554 (Stats.1994, c. 603):

"I have signed this date Assembly Bill No. 2554.

"This bill would require school districts under the State Teachers Retirement System to provide information on STRS membership criteria to all their certificated employees. This bill would also make the districts liable for the employee and employer contributions and interest for noncompliance beginning March 1, 1995.

"The Department of Finance is concerned that this bill may impose a state-mandated program on local public employers. Legislative Counsel has issued an opinion to the contrary. However, unlike a similar bill I considered in the 1991–1992 legislative session this bill does not contain express language declaring that any costs are not state-reimbursable. The sponsor has agreed to work for passage of clean-up legislation next year which contains this express declaration."

Cross References

Computation of time,
    Generally, see Code of Civil Procedure §§ 12 and 12a and Government Code § 6800 et seq.
    Time in which any act provided by the Education Code is to be done, see Education Code § 9.
Continuation of statutes relating to subjects covered by provisions of this Code, see Education Code
    § 3.

§ 22456. Information to be furnished by employer

At any time upon the request of the system, the employer shall furnish a statement of the amount of contributions deducted from the compensation of any member, the service performed and the compensation earned by the member since the end of the period covered by the last report of the employer. The system may use the information shown in the statement in determining contributions to be paid by or to the member or to a beneficiary, or use it in determining the member's status upon retirement, even though the member's and employer's contributions will not be received by the board until after the payment or determination.

(Added by Stats.1993, c. 893 (A.B.1796), § 2. Amended by Stats.1996, c. 634 (S.B. 2041), § 99; Stats.1997, c. 482 (S.B.471), § 6.)

Historical and Statutory Notes

Legislative intent regarding Stats.1993, c. 893 (A.B.1796), including possible continuing application of provisions of repealed State Teachers' Retirement Law, see Historical and Statutory Notes under Education Code § 22000.

Derivation: Former § 23012, enacted by Stats.1976, c. 1010, § 2.

Educ.C.1959, § 14062, added by Stats.1973, c. 742, p. 1391, § 4.

Educ.C.1959, § 14059, added by Stats.1969, c. 896, p. 1738, § 2.

Educ.C.1959, § 14125 (Stats.1959, c. 2, p. 1007, § 14125).

Educ.C.1943, § 14492, added by Stats.1944, 4th Ex.Sess., c. 13, p. 131, § 2.

Educ.C.1943, § 14454 (Stats.1943, c. 71, p. 606).

School C. § 5.852, added by Stats.1937, c. 626, p. 1730, § 4, amended by Stats.1939, c. 1040, p. 2859, § 6.

§ 22457. Notice of employment, death, resignation or discharge

(a) Each county superintendent shall give immediate notice in writing to the board of the employment, death, resignation, or discharge of any person employed by the county or by a school district or community college district in the county to perform creditable service subject to coverage by the Defined Benefit Program.

(b) Every other employing agency shall give similar notice with respect to each person it employs to perform creditable service subject to coverage by the Defined Benefit Program.

(Added by Stats.1993, c. 893 (A.B.1796), § 2. Amended by Stats.1996, c. 634 (S.B. 2041), § 100; Stats.1999, c. 939 (S.B.1074), § 30.)

Historical and Statutory Notes

Legislative intent regarding Stats.1993, c. 893 (A.B.1796), including possible continuing application of provisions of repealed State Teachers' Retirement Law, see Historical and Statutory Notes under Education Code § 22000.

Derivation: Former § 22402, enacted by Stats.1976, c. 1010, § 2.

Educ.C.1959, § 13932, added by Stats.1969, c. 896, p. 1738, § 2, amended by Stats.1974, c. 1293, p. 2809, § 34.

Educ.C.1959, § 14021 (Stats.1959, c. 2, p. 996, § 14021).

Educ.C.1943, § 14421, added by Stats.1944, 4th Ex.Sess., c. 13, p. 124, § 2.

Educ.C.1943, § 14421 (Stats.1943, c. 71, p. 600).

School C. § 584.2, added by Stats.1937, c. 626, p. 1727, § 4, amended by Stats.1939, c. 1040, p. 2856, § 3.

§ 22458. Compensation of employees; documentation

Each employer shall provide the system with information regarding the compensation to be paid to employees subject to the Defined Benefit Program in that school year. The information shall be submitted annually as determined by the board and may include, but shall not be limited to, employment contracts, salary schedules, and local board minutes.

(Added by Stats.1993, c. 893 (A.B.1796), § 2. Amended by Stats.1996, c. 634 (S.B. 2041), § 101; Stats.1999, c. 939 (S.B.1074), § 31.)

Historical and Statutory Notes

Legislative intent regarding Stats.1993, c. 893 (A.B.1796), including possible continuing application of provisions of repealed State Teachers' Retirement Law, see Historical and Statutory Notes under Education Code § 22000.

Derivation: Former § 22403.1, added by Stats.1991, c. 543 (S.B.1171), § 7.

§ 22459. Withholding salary on failure to file information or to pay amount due

(a) The county superintendent or other employing agency shall withhold the salary of any member who fails to file information required by the board in the administration of the Defined Benefit Program, or to pay amounts due from the members to the fund with respect to the Defined Benefit Program.

(b) The salary shall be withheld by the county superintendent or employing agency upon his or her own knowledge, if any, of the failure or upon notice from the board of the failure of the member to file or pay.

(c) The salary shall be withheld and not released until notice is given by the board to the county superintendent or employing agency, or until the county superintendent or agency knows otherwise, that the information has been filed or the payment has been made.

(Added by Stats.1993, c. 893 (A.B.1796), § 2. Amended by Stats.1996, c. 634 (S.B. 2041), § 102; Stats.1999, c. 939 (S.B.1074), § 32.)

Historical and Statutory Notes

Legislative intent regarding Stats.1993, c. 893 (A.B.1796), including possible continuing application of provisions of repealed State Teachers' Retirement Law, see Historical and Statutory Notes under Education Code § 22000.

The 1996 amendment, in subd. (a), substituted "plan" for "system" in two places; and in subd. (b) following "failure of the", substituted "member" for "teacher".

Derivation: Former § 22404, enacted by Stats.1976, c. 1010, § 2.

Educ.C.1959, § 13934, added by Stats.1969, c. 896, p. 1738, § 2.

Educ.C.1959, § 14022 (Stats.1959, c. 2, p. 996, § 14022).

Educ.C.1943, § 14422, added by Stats.1944, 4th Ex.Sess., c. 13, p. 124, § 2.

Educ.C.1943, § 14422 (Stats.1943, c. 71, p. 600).

School C. § 5.842, added by Stats.1937, c. 626, p. 1727, § 4, amended by Stats.1939, c. 1040, p. 2856, § 3.

§ 22460. Notification to terminating employee of benefits

(a) If a member terminates employment with less than five years of credited service, the employer shall notify the member of the following:

(1) That unless the member is eligible, or becomes eligible in the future, for concurrent retirement pursuant to paragraph (2) of subdivision (a) of Section 24201, the member is eligible only for a refund of accumulated retirement contributions under the Defined Benefit Program and the return of the member's accumulated Defined Benefit Supplement account balance.

(2) The current rate of interest that shall be earned on accumulated retirement contributions that are not refunded and the current minimum interest rate that shall be applied to the member's Defined Benefit Supplement account.

(3) Actions that may be taken by the board if accumulated retirement contributions are not refunded under the Defined Benefit Program and the member's Defined Benefit Supplement account balance is not returned.

(b) Employers shall transmit to a member who terminates employment with less than five years of credited service the information specified in subdivision (a) as part of the usual separation documents.

(Added by Stats.2000, c. 1021 (A.B.2700), § 17.)

Historical and Statutory Notes

Section 32 of Stats.2000, c. 74 (A.B.1509), also added a § 22640, related to the same subject matter.

Section affected by two or more acts at the same session of the legislature, see Government Code § 9605.

Operative effect of Stats.2000, c. 1021 (A.B. 2700), see Historical and Statutory Notes following Education Code § 22101.5.

Former § 22460, added by Stats.1993, c. 893 (A.B.1796), § 2, amended by Stats.1996, c. 634 (S.B.2041), § 103, relating to notification to ter-

minating members, was repealed by Stats.2000, c. 74 (A.B.1509), § 31 and Stats.2000, c. 1021 (A.B.2700), § 16. See this section.

Derivation: Former § 22460, added by Stats. 1993, c. 893 (A.B.1796), § 2, amended by Stats. 1996, c. 634 (S.B.2041), § 103.

Former § 23108, enacted by Stats.1976, c. 1010, § 2, amended by Stats.1977, c. 36, § 104.

Educ.C.1959, § 14076, added by Stats.1975, c. 729, p. 1718, § 1, amended by Stats.1976, c. 605, § 1.

§ 22461. Notice of earnings limitation; maintenance of earnings records and reports; liability of employer

(a) Upon retaining the services of a retired member under Section 24116, 24214, or 24215, the school district, community college district, county superintendent of schools, California State University, or other employing agency shall do both of the following regardless of whether the retired member performs the services as an employee of the employer, an employee of a third party, or an independent contractor:

(1) Advise the retired member of the earnings limitation set forth in Sections 24116, 24214, and 24215.

(2) Maintain accurate records of the retired member's earnings and report those earnings monthly to the system and the retired member regardless of the method of payment or the fund from which the payments were made.

(b) This section shall not be construed to make any school district, community college district, county superintendent of schools, the California State University, or other employing agency liable for any amount paid to the retired member in excess of the earnings limitation under any circumstance, including the failure to inform the retired member that continuation of service would exceed the limitations.

(Added by Stats.1993, c. 893 (A.B.1796), § 2. Amended by Stats.1996, c. 634 (S.B. 2041), § 104.)

Historical and Statutory Notes

Legislative intent regarding Stats.1993, c. 893 (A.B.1796), including possible continuing application of provisions of repealed State Teachers' Retirement Law, see Historical and Statutory Notes under Education Code § 22000.

Derivation: Former § 23921, added by Stats. 1979, c. 796, § 12, amended by Stats.1983, c. 143, § 15.

Educ.C.1959, § 14228, added by Stats.1974, c. 873, p. 1862, § 4, amended by Stats.1976, c. 697, § 4.

Cross References

"Any school district", "all school districts", defined, see Education Code § 80.
California State University, generally, see Education Code § 89000 et seq.
County superintendents of schools,
    Generally, see Education Code § 1200 et seq.
    Election or appointment and salaries, see Const. Art. 9, § 3 et seq.

Chapter 10

MEMBERSHIP

Chapter 10 was added by Stats.1993, c. 893 (A.B.1796), § 2.

§ 22500. Membership eligibility

All persons who were members of the California State Teachers' Retirement System on June 30, 1996, are members of the Defined Benefit Program under the plan, in accordance with Section 401(a) of the Internal Revenue Code of 1986, as amended.

(Added by Stats.1993, c. 893 (A.B.1796), § 2. Amended by Stats.1996, c. 634 (S.B. 2041), § 105; Stats.1998, c. 965 (A.B.2765), § 45; Stats.2000, c. 1025 (A.B.816), § 17.)

Historical and Statutory Notes

Legislative intent regarding Stats.1993, c. 893 (A.B.1796), including possible continuing application of provisions of repealed State Teachers' Retirement Law, see Historical and Statutory Notes under Education Code § 22000.

Former § 22500, enacted by Stats.1976, c. 1010, § 2, relating to membership eligibility, was repealed by Stats.1993, c. 893 (A.B.1796), § 1. See this section.

Derivation: Former § 22500, enacted by Stats.1976, c. 1010, § 2.

Educ.C.1959, § 13940, added by Stats.1969, c. 896, p. 1738, § 2, amended by Stats.1972, c. 1010, p. 1860, § 14.

Educ.C.1959, § 13952 (Stats.1959, c. 2, p. 993, § 13952).

Educ.C.1943, § 14372, added by Stats.1944, 4th Ex.Sess., c. 13, p. 122, § 2, amended by Stats.1945, c. 1207, p. 2289, § 2.

Educ.C.1943, § 14391 (Stats.1943, c. 71, p. 598).

School C. § 5.840, added by Stats.1937, c. 626, p. 1725, § 4.

Library References

Schools ☞146(3).
Westlaw Topic No. 345.
C.J.S. Schools and School Districts §§ 340 to 346.

Legal Jurisprudences

Cal Jur 3d Fam Law § 819; Sch § 368.

Notes of Decisions

Cafeteria employees 3
Implied rights 1
Rules and regulations 2

1. Implied rights

Legislative intent to grant contractual rights can be implied from statute if it contains unambiguous element of exchange of consideration by private party for consideration offered by the state. California Teachers Ass'n v. Cory (Teachers' Retirement Bd. of State Teachers' Retirement Ass'n) (App. 3 Dist. 1984) 202 Cal.Rptr. 611, 155 Cal.App.3d 494.

2. Rules and regulations

A rule adopted by the state board of education concerning the right of teachers to a retirement salary is of no effect if it conflicts with an act of the legislature. Dean v. Clarke (App. 2 Dist. 1921) 53 Cal.App. 30, 199 P. 857.

3. Cafeteria employees

Under Educ.C.1943, § 14372 et seq. and Gov.C. ch. 4 of Part 3, §§ 20491, 20532 and specifically Educ.C.1943, § 14725 where a school participated in the state employees' retirement system on behalf of its cafeteria employees, the district may have made contributions from school district funds. 12 Ops.Atty. Gen. 72 (1948).

§ 22501. Membership eligibility; full time

(a) Any person employed to perform creditable service on a full-time basis who is not already a member of the Defined Benefit Program under the plan shall become a member as of the first day of employment, unless excluded from membership pursuant to Section 22601.

(b) Creditable service in more than one position shall not be aggregated for the purpose of determining mandatory membership under this section.

(c) This section shall be deemed to have become operative on July 1, 1996.

(Added by Stats.1996, c. 634 (S.B.2041), § 107, operative July 1, 1996. Amended by Stats.1998, c. 965 (A.B.2765), § 46.)

Historical and Statutory Notes

Former § 22501, added by Stats.1993, c. 893 (A.B.1796, § 2, relating to teachers' membership eligibility, was repealed by Stats.1996, c. 634 (S.B.2041), § 106. See this section.

Former § 22501, enacted by Stats.1976, c. 1010, § 2, relating to membership of teachers in the retirement system, was repealed by Stats. 1993, c. 893 (A.B.1796), § 1. See this section.

Derivation: Former § 22501, added by Stats. 1993, c. 893, § 2.

Former § 22501, enacted by Stats.1976, c. 1010, § 2.

Educ.C.1959, § 13941, added by Stats.1969, c. 896, p. 1738, § 2, amended by Stats.1970, c. 466, p. 923, § 4.

Educ.C.1959, § 13953 (Stats.1959, c. 2, p. 993, § 13593).

Educ.C.1943, § 14373, added by Stats.1944, 4th Ex.Sess., c. 13, p. 122, § 2.

Educ.C.1943, § 14392 (Stats.1943, c. 71, p. 598).

School C. § 5.840, added by Stats.1937, c. 626, p. 1725, § 4.

Cross References

San Francisco teachers as members, see Education Code § 24700.

Library References

Legal Jurisprudences
  Cal Jur 3d Sch § 368.

Notes of Decisions

Local systems 1

_____

1. Local systems

  All salaries received for service for which a teacher was entitled to retirement benefits un-der a local retirement system were to be excluded in assessing contribution to or allowing benefits from the retirement annuity fund of the state teachers retirement system, under Educ.C. 1943, §§ 14373, 14401, 14479. 12 Ops.Atty. Gen. 235 (1948).

§ 22502. Membership eligibility; part time; 50 percent or more of full time

  (a) Any person employed to perform creditable service on a part-time basis who is not already a member of the Defined Benefit Program shall become a member as of the first day of subsequent employment to perform creditable service for 50 percent or more of the full-time equivalent for the position, unless excluded from membership pursuant to Section 22601.

  (b) This section shall apply to persons who perform service subject to coverage under this part and to persons who are employed by employers who provide benefits for their employees under Part 14 (commencing with Section 26000).

  (c) This section shall be deemed to have become operative on July 1, 1996.

(Added by Stats.1998, c. 965 (A.B.2765), § 47. Amended by Stats.1999, c. 939 (S.B. 1074), § 33.)

Historical and Statutory Notes

  Former § 22502, added by Stats.1993, c. 893 (A.B.1796, § 2, derived from former § 22502, enacted by Stats.1976, c. 1010, § 2; Educ.C. 1959, § 13943, added by Stats.1969, c. 896, § 2; Educ.C.1959, § 13955 (Stats.1959, c. 2, § 13955, amended by Stats.1961, c. 878, § 1); Educ.C.1943, § 14375, added by Stats.1944, 4th Ex.Sess., c. 13, § 2, amended by Stats.1947, c. 1481, § 3; Educ.C.1943, § 14394 (Stats.1943, c. 71, p. 598; School C. § 5.840., added by Stats.1937, c. 626, § 4, relating to membership of librarians, was repealed by Stats.1995, c. 592 (A.B.1298), § 4.

  Former § 22502, enacted by Stats.1976, c. 1010, § 2, relating to membership by librarians in the retirement system, was repealed by Stats. 1993, c. 893 (A.B.1796), § 1. See this section.

§ 22503. Membership eligibility; substitute teacher

  (a) Any person employed to perform creditable service as a substitute teacher who is not already a member of the Defined Benefit Program shall become a member as of the first day of the pay period following the pay period in which the person performed 100 or more complete days of creditable service during the school year in one school district, community college district, or county superintendent's office, unless excluded from membership pursuant to Section 22601.

  (b) This section shall not apply to persons who are employed by employers who provide benefits for their employees under Part 14 (commencing with Section 26000).

(c) This section shall be deemed to have become operative on July 1, 1996.

(Added by Stats.1998, c. 965 (A.B.2765), § 48. Amended by Stats.1999, c. 939 (S.B. 1074), § 34.)

Historical and Statutory Notes

Former § 22503, added by Stats.1993, c. 893 (A.B.1796, § 2, derived from former § 22503, enacted by Stats.1976, c. 1010, § 2, amended by Stats.1990, c. 1392 (S.B.2298), § 1; Educ.C. 1959, § 13944, added by Stats.1969, c. 896, § 2, amended by Stats.1970, c. 557, § 80; Educ.C. 1959, § 13956 (Stats.1959, c. 2, § 13956); Educ.C.1943, § 14376, added by Stats.1944, 4th Ex.Sess., c. 13, § 2; Educ.C.1943, § 14395 (Stats.1943, c. 71, p. 598; School C. § 5.840., added by Stats.1937, c. 626, § 4, relating to membership of other employees, was repealed by Stats.1995, c. 592 (A.B.1298), § 5.

Former § 22503, enacted by Stats.1976, c. 1010, § 2, amended by Stats.1990, c. 1302 (S.B. 2298), § 1, relating to membership by other employees in the retirement system, was repealed by Stats.1993, c. 893 (A.B.1796), § 1. See, now, this section.

§ 22504. Membership eligibility; part time; hourly or daily basis

(a) Any person employed to perform creditable service on a part-time basis who is not already a member of the Defined Benefit Program shall become a member as of the first day of the pay period following the pay period in which the person performed at least 60 hours of creditable service, if employed on an hourly basis, or 10 days of creditable service, if employed on a daily basis, during the school year, in one school district, community college district, or county superintendent's office, unless excluded from membership pursuant to Section 22601.

(b) This section shall not apply to persons who are employed by employers who provide benefits for their employees under Part 14 (commencing with Section 26000).

(c) This section shall be deemed to have become operative on July 1, 1996.

(Added by Stats.1998, c. 965 (A.B.2765), § 49. Amended by Stats.1999, c. 939 (S.B. 1074), § 35.)

Historical and Statutory Notes

Former § 22504, added by Stats.1977, c. 36, § 413, amended by Stats.1990, c. 1372 (S.B. 1854), § 176, related to membership in the system on change of employment, and was repealed by Stats.1993, c. 893 (A.B.1796), § 1. See Education Code § 22508.

§§ 22505 to 22507. Repealed by Stats.1995, c. 592 (A.B.1298), §§ 6 to 8

Historical and Statutory Notes

Section 22505, added by Stats.1993, c. 893 (A.B.1796, § 2, derived from former § 22505, enacted by Stats.1976, c. 1010, § 2; Educ.C. 1959, § 13947, added by Stats.1969, c. 896, § 2; Educ.C.1959, § 13958 (Stats.1959, c. 2, § 13958); Educ.C.1943, § 14376.2, added by Stats.1947, c. 1481, § 5, related to employees performing duties and counselors.

Former § 22505, enacted by Stats.1976, c. 1010, § 2, relating to membership by counselors or coordinators in the system, was repealed by Stats.1993, c. 893 (A.B.1796), § 1. See this section.

Section § 22506, added by Stats.1993, c. 893 (A.B.1796, § 2, derived from former § 22506, enacted by Stats.1976, c. 1010, § 2; Educ.C. 1959, § 13950, added by Stats.1969, c. 896, § 2; Educ.C.1959, § 13961 (Stats.1959, c. 2, § 13961); Educ.C.1943, § 14377, added by Stats.1944, 4th Ex.Sess., c. 13, § 2; Educ.C. 1943, § 14396 (Stats.1943, c. 71, p. 598; School C. § 5.840, added by Stats.1937, c. 626, § 4, relating to superintendents, deputies and certificated employees.

Former § 22506, enacted by Stats.1976, c. 1010, § 2, relating to membership by county superintendents, deputies, and certificated employees in the system, was repealed by Stats. 1993, c. 893 (A.B.1796), § 1. See this section.

Section 22507, added by Stats.1993, c. 893 (A.B.1796, § 2, derived from former § 22507.1, added by Stats.1977, c. 213, § 5, related to independent data-processing center employees.

Former § 22507, enacted by Stats.1976, c. 1010, § 2, derived from Educ.C.1959, § 13951,

added by Stats.1969, c. 896, § 2, and Educ.C. 1959, § 13970, added by Stats.1967, c. 912, § 1, relating to specified employees who were later employed in exempt positions, was repealed by Stats.1981, c. 124, § 22.

Legislative intent relating to Stats.1995, c. 592 (A.B.1298), see Historical and Statutory Notes under Education Code § 22146.

§ 22507.1. Repealed by Stats.1993, c. 893 (A.B.1796), § 1

Historical and Statutory Notes

The repealed section, added by Stats.1977, c. 213, § 5, related to membership in the system by independent data-processing center employees. See Education Code § 22507.

Legislative intent regarding Stats.1993, c. 893 (A.B.1796), including possible continuing appli-

cation of provisions of repealed State Teachers' Retirement Law, see Historical and Statutory Notes under Education Code § 22000.

§ 22508. Membership in another public retirement system; election to continue; creditable service

(a) A member who becomes employed by the same or a different school district or community college district, or a county superintendent, or who becomes employed by the state in a position described in subdivision (b), to perform service that requires membership in a different public retirement system, and who is not excluded from membership in that public retirement system, may elect to have that service subject to coverage by the Defined Benefit Program of this plan and excluded from coverage by the other public retirement system. The election shall be made in writing on a form prescribed by this system within 60 days from the date of hire in the position requiring membership in the other public retirement system. If that election is made, the service performed for the employer after the date of hire shall be considered creditable service for purposes of this part.

(b) Subdivision (a) shall apply to a member who becomes employed by the state only if the member is also one of the following:

(1) Represented by a state bargaining unit that represents educational consultants, professional educators, or librarians employed by the state.

(2) Excluded from the definition of "state employee" in subdivision (c) of Section 3513 of the Government Code, but performing, supervising, or managing work similar to work performed by employees described in paragraph (1).

(3) In a position not covered by civil service and in the executive branch of government, but performing, supervising, or managing work similar to work performed by employees described in paragraph (1).

(c)(1) A member of the Public Employees' Retirement System described in paragraph (2) who is subsequently employed to perform creditable service subject to coverage by the Defined Benefit Program of this plan may elect to have that subsequent service subject to coverage by the Public Employees' Retirement System and excluded from coverage by the Defined Benefit Program pursuant to Section 20309 of the Government Code. If the election is made, creditable service performed for the employer after the date of hire shall be subject to coverage by the Public Employees' Retirement System.

(2) This subdivision shall apply to a member of the Public Employees' Retirement System who either (A) is employed by a school district, community college district, a county superintendent, or the State Department of Education or (B) has at least five years of credited service under the system.

(d) An election made by a member pursuant to this section shall be irrevocable.

(Added by Stats.1996, c. 383 (A.B.3221), § 3. Amended by Stats.1998, c. 965 (A.B. 2765), § 50; Stats.1999, c. 939 (S.B.1074), § 36; Stats.2000, c. 1025 (A.B.816), § 18; Stats.2000, c. 880 (S.B.1694), § 1; Stats.2001, c. 77 (S.B.165), § 1.)

Historical and Statutory Notes

Subordination of legislation by Stats.2000, c. 1025 (A.B.816), to other 2000 legislation, see Historical and Statutory Notes under Education Code § 22106.

Former § 22508, added by Stats.1993, c. 893 (A.B.1796), § 2, relating to membership upon change of employment, was repealed by Stats. 1996, c. 383 (A.B.3221), § 2. See this section.

Former § 22508, enacted by Stats.1976, c. 1010, § 2, relating to termination of membership and mailing of warrants, was repealed by Stats.1981, c. 124, § 23. See Education Code § 23101.5.

Derivation: Former §§ 22508 and 22509, added by Stats.1993, c. 893, § 2.

Former § 22504, added by Stats.1977, c. 36, § 413, amended by Stats.1990, c. 1372 (S.B. 1854), § 176.

Former § 22608, added by Stats.1977, c. 36, § 414.

Educ.C.1959, § 13946, added by Stats.1969, c. 896, p. 1738, § 2, amended by Stats.1974, c. 1293, p. 2809, § 35.

Educ.C.1959, § 13956.1, added by Stats.1961, c. 878, p. 2300, § 2.

Educ.C.1959, § 13969, added by Stats.1969, c. 896, p. 1738, § 2, amended by Stats.1974, c. 1293, p. 2810, § 41.

Educ.C.1959, § 14001.4, added by Stats.1961, c. 878, p. 2302, § 11.5.

Cross References

Computation of time,
    Generally, see Code of Civil Procedure §§ 12 and 12a and Government Code § 6800 et seq.
    Time in which any act provided by the Education Code is to be done, see Education Code § 9.
Continuation of statutes relating to subjects covered by provisions of this Code, see Education Code
    § 3.

Library References

Legal Jurisprudences
    Cal Jur 3d Sch § 368.

§ 22508.5. Performance of duties requiring membership in a different public retirement system; exclusion from membership; election

(a) Any person who is a member of the Defined Benefit Program of the State Teachers' Retirement Plan employed by a community college district who subsequently is employed by the Board of Governors of the California Community Colleges to perform duties that are subject to membership in a different public retirement system, shall be excluded from membership in that different system if he or she elects, in writing, and files that election in the office of the State Teachers' Retirement System within 60 days after the person's entry into the new position, to continue as a member of the Defined Benefit Program. Only a person who has achieved plan vesting is eligible to elect to continue as a member of the program.

(b) A member of the Public Employees' Retirement System who is employed by the Board of Governors of the California Community Colleges who subsequently is employed by a community college district to perform creditable service subject to coverage under the Defined Benefit Program, may elect to have that service subject to coverage by the Public Employees' Retirement System and excluded from coverage under the Defined Benefit Program pursuant to Section 20309 of the Government Code.

(c) This section shall apply to changes in employment effective on or after January 1, 1998.

(Added by Stats.1997, c. 838 (S.B.227), § 1. Amended by Stats.1998, c. 965 (A.B.2765), § 51; Stats.1999, c. 939 (S.B.1074), § 37.)

Cross References

Computation of time,
  Generally, see Code of Civil Procedure §§ 12 and 12a and Government Code § 6800 et seq.
  Time in which any act provided by the Education Code is to be done, see Education Code § 9.
Continuation of statutes relating to subjects covered by provisions of this Code, see Education Code § 3.

§ 22508.6. Defined Benefit Program members; membership in Public Employees' Retirement System; coverage exclusions

(a) Any person who is a member of the Defined Benefit Program and who subsequently became employed and continues to be employed by the state to perform service that requires membership in the Public Employees' Retirement System and who meets the requirements of subdivision (b) may elect to have that state service subject to coverage by the Defined Benefit Program and excluded from coverage by the Public Employees' Retirement System.

(b)(1) Only a person who has achieved program vesting shall be eligible to make the election under this section.

(2) A person is eligible to make the election if he or she left employment with a school district, county superintendent of schools, or community college district and began employment with the state within 30 days without any intervening employment and that change in employment occurred on or after July 1, 1991, and prior to the effective date of this section.

(3) A person is eligible to make the election if, at the time of the election, he or she is a member of the Public Employees' Retirement System subject to Second Tier benefits and is one of the following:

(A) Represented by a State Bargaining Unit that has agreed by a memorandum of understanding to become subject to Section 20309.5 of the Government Code.

(B) Excluded from the definition of "state employee" in subdivision (c) of Section 3513 of the Government Code, but performing, supervising, or managing work similar to work performed by employees described in subparagraph (A).

(C) In a position not covered by civil service and in the executive branch of government, but performing, supervising, or managing work similar to work performed by employees described in subparagraph (A).

(c) The election under this section shall be made in writing to each system within 90 days after the effective date of this section or within 60 days after the eligible member is notified by the system of his or her right to make the election, whichever is later. The member's election shall be effective on the day following the date on which the election is received by the Public Employees' Retirement System.

(d) If the election is made, the state service performed from and after the date of the election shall be considered creditable service for purposes of this part and the provisions of Section 22801.5 shall be applicable with respect to service performed prior to that date.

(Added by Stats.2000, c. 402 (A.B.649), § 2, eff. Sept. 11, 2000.)

Cross References

Computation of time,
    Generally, see Code of Civil Procedure §§ 12 and 12a and Government Code § 6800 et seq.
    Time in which any act provided by the Education Code is to be done, see Education Code § 9.
Continuation of statutes relating to subjects covered by provisions of this Code, see Education Code
    § 3.
County superintendents of schools,
    Generally, see Education Code § 1200 et seq.
    Election or appointment and salaries, see Const. Art. 9, § 3 et seq.
Defined benefit program of the State Teachers' Retirement Plan members, see Government Code
    § 20309.5.

§ 22509. Election to continue membership; forms; filing; effective date

(a) Within 10 working days of the date of hire of an employee who has the right to make an election pursuant to Section 22508 or 22508.5, the employer shall inform the employee of the right to make an election and shall make available to the employee written information provided by each retirement system concerning the benefits provided under that retirement system to assist the employee in making an election.

(b) Any election made pursuant to subdivision (a) of Section 22508 or subdivision (a) of Section 22508.5 shall be filed with the office of the State Teachers' Retirement System and a copy of the election shall be filed with the other public retirement system. Any election made pursuant to subdivision (b) of Section 22508 or subdivision (b) of Section 22508.5 shall be filed with the office of the Public Employees' Retirement System and a copy of the election shall be filed with the office of this system.

(c) Any election made pursuant to Section 22508 or Section 22508.5 shall become effective as of the first day of employment in the position that qualified the employee to make an election.

(Added by Stats.1996, c. 383 (A.B.3221), § 5. Amended by Stats.1997, c. 838 (S.B.227), § 2.)

Historical and Statutory Notes

Former § 22509, added by Stats.1993, c. 893 (A.B.1796, § 2, relating to election to remain in system, was repealed by Stats.1996, c. 383 (A.B. 3221), § 4. See Education Code § 22508.

Former § 22509, enacted by Stats.1976, c. 1010, § 2, amended by Stats.1981, c. 714, § 80;

Stats.1983, c. 143, § 13, relating to election to transfer to the Public Employees Retirement System, was repealed by Stats.1993, c. 893 (A.B.1796), § 1. See Education Code § 22510.

Cross References

Computation of time,
     Generally, see Code of Civil Procedure §§ 12 and 12a and Government Code § 6800 et seq.
     Time in which any act provided by the Education Code is to be done, see Education Code § 9.
Continuation of statutes relating to subjects covered by provisions of this Code, see Education Code
     § 3.

Library References

Legal Jurisprudences

Cal Jur 3d Sch § 368.

§ 22510. Election to retain membership; effect

Members who on January 1, 1976, are in state service positions according to former Section 13948 as it read on December 31, 1975, or who are employees of the Trustees of the California State University, may elect in writing prior to July 1, 1976, not to continue as members of this system and to transfer membership to the Public Employees' Retirement System. Failure to execute and file the election, which shall be received in the office of this system by the close of business on June 30, 1976, shall be deemed a decision to remain a member of the plan.

(Added by Stats.1993, c. 893 (A.B.1796), § 2. Amended by Stats.1996, c. 634 (S.B. 2041), § 108.)

Historical and Statutory Notes

Legislative intent regarding Stats.1993, c. 893 (A.B.1796), including possible continuing application of provisions of repealed State Teachers' Retirement Law, see Historical and Statutory Notes under Education Code § 22000.

Former § 22510, enacted by Stats.1976, c. 1010, § 2, relating to limitation of benefits for certain members who elect to remain in the system, was repealed by Stats.1993, c. 893 (A.B. 1796), § 1. See Education Code § 22511.

Derivation: Former § 22509, enacted by Stats.1976, c. 1010, § 2, amended by Stats. 1981, c. 714, § 80; Stats.1983, c. 143, § 13.

Educ.C.1959, § 13948, added by Stats.1975, c. 954, p. 2131, § 3.

Educ.C.1959, § 13948, added by Stats.1969, c. 896, p. 1751, § 2, amended by Stats.1970, c. 557, p. 1126, § 81, Stats.1970, c. 1401, p. 2663, § 1; Stats.1970, c. 1450, p. 2838, § 6.5; Stats. 1974, c. 1293, p. 2809, § 36.

Educ.C.1959, §§ 13957, 13959 (Stats.1959, c. 2, p. 993, §§ 13957, 13959, amended by Stats. 1961, c. 878, p. 2300, § 4).

Educ.C.1943, §§ 14376.1, 14376.3, added by Stats.1947, c. 1481, p. 3064, §§ 4, 6, amended by Stats.1951, c. 1454, p. 3432, § 1.

Cross References

California State University, generally, see Education Code § 89000 et seq.

Notes of Decisions

Compulsory retirement   1

1. Compulsory retirement

Civil service employees of the department of education who are not members of the state employees' retirement system are not subject to compulsory retirement at age 70. 46 Ops.Atty. Gen. 32, 9–8–65.

§ 22511. Eligibility for benefits

Members eligible to elect under Section 22510 and who elect to retain membership in the plan shall be eligible only for those benefits available for all other members and shall not be eligible for the benefits of the Berryhill Total Compensation Act, as amended, except for the reduced hospitalization insurance premiums. These members shall not be considered eligible for any additional benefits that may accrue to other state employees.

(Added by Stats.1993, c. 893 (A.B.1796), § 2. Amended by Stats.1996, c. 634 (S.B. 2041), § 109.)

Historical and Statutory Notes

Legislative intent regarding Stats.1993, c. 893 (A.B.1796), including possible continuing application of provisions of repealed State Teachers' Retirement Law, see Historical and Statutory Notes under Education Code § 22000.

Former § 22511, enacted by Stats.1976, c. 1010, § 2, relating to the effect of election of membership in the Public Employees' Retirement System, was repealed by Stats.1993, c. 893 (A.B.1796), § 1. See Education Code § 22512.

Derivation: Former § 22510, enacted by Stats.1976, c. 1010, § 2.

Educ.C.1959, § 13948.1, added by Stats.1975, c. 954, p. 2131, § 4.

Library References

Schools ⊕146(3).
Westlaw Topic No. 345.

C.J.S. Schools and School Districts §§ 340 to 346.

§ 22512. Election counted as break in service

If a member elects membership in the Public Employees' Retirement System under Section 22510, this election shall not be counted as a break in service if employment is continuous.

(Added by Stats.1993, c. 893 (A.B.1796), § 2.)

Historical and Statutory Notes

Legislative intent regarding Stats.1993, c. 893 (A.B.1796), including possible continuing application of provisions of repealed State Teachers' Retirement Law, see Historical and Statutory Notes under Education Code § 22000.

Former § 22512, enacted by Stats.1976, c. 1010, § 2, amended by Stats.1988, c. 382, § 4, relating to retention of survivor and disability benefits for persons who have achieved planned vesting, was repealed by Stats.1993, c. 893 (A.B. 1796), § 1. See Education Code § 22513.

Derivation: Former § 22511, enacted by Stats.1976, c. 1010, § 2.

Educ.C.1959, § 13948.2, added by Stats.1975, c. 954, p. 2132, § 5.

§ 22513. Retention of survivor and disability benefits; plan vesting

Members of the Defined Benefit Program who elect membership in the Public Employees' Retirement System and have achieved plan vesting according to Section 22156 shall retain the vested rights to survivor and disability benefits under this part until they qualify for the similar benefits in the Public Employees' Retirement System.

(Added by Stats.1993, c. 893 (A.B.1796), § 2. Amended by Stats.1996, c. 634 (S.B. 2041), § 110; Stats.1998, c. 965 (A.B.2765), § 52.)

Historical and Statutory Notes

Legislative intent regarding Stats.1993, c. 893 (A.B.1796), including possible continuing application of provisions of repealed State Teachers' Retirement Law, see Historical and Statutory Notes under Education Code § 22000.

Another § 22513, enacted by Stats.1976, c. 1010, § 2, amended by Stats.1988, c. 382, § 5; Stats.1989, c. 118, § 2; Stats.1993, c. 1144 (S.B.857), § 2; Stats.1993, c. 1144 (S.B.857), § 2, derived from Educ.C.1959, § 13948.4, added by Stats.1975, c. 954, § 7, relating to qualifi-

cations when planned vesting not achieved, was repealed by Stats.1994, c. 933 (A.B.3171), § 35, eff. Sept. 28, 1994. Similar provisions were added by Stats.1994, c. 933 (A.B.3171), § 36 at Education Code § 22514.

Derivation: Former § 22512, enacted by Stats.1976, c. 1010, § 2, amended by Stats. 1988, c. 382, § 4.

Educ.C.1959, § 13948.3, added by Stats.1975, c. 954, p. 2132, § 6.

Cross References

Disability allowance, see Education Code § 22127.
Disability benefit, see Education Code § 22127.2.
Disability or disabled, see Education Code § 22126.
Final vesting, see Education Code § 22138.

§ 22514. Qualifications when plan vesting not achieved

Members who have not achieved plan vesting shall become eligible for benefits under the Defined Benefit Program when total service under the Defined Benefit Program and the Public Employees' Retirement System equals the minimum required under Sections 23801 and 23804. These members shall retain vested rights to survivor and disability benefits under this plan until they qualify for the similar benefits under the Public Employees' Retirement System.

(Added by Stats.1993, c. 893 (A.B.1796), § 2. Amended by Stats.1994, c. 933 (A.B. 3171), § 36, eff. Sept. 28, 1994; Stats.1996, c. 634 (S.B.2041), § 111; Stats.1999, c. 939 (S.B.1074), § 38.)

Historical and Statutory Notes

Stats.1993, c. 389, provided for addition of this section, similar to Education Code § 22513, as well as for repeal of § 22513. Stats.1993, c. 1144, amended § 22513. Subordination of legislation by Stats.1993, c. 893, see Stats.1993, c. 893 (A.B.1796), § 4. Section affected by two or more acts at the same session of the legislature, see Government Code § 9605.

Subordination of legislation by Stats.1993, c. 893, and legislative intent regarding that act, including possible continuing application of

provisions of repealed State Teachers' Retirement Law, see Historical and Statutory Notes under Education Code § 22000.

Provisions similar to this section were formerly contained in Education Code § 22513.

Former § 22514, added by Stats.1989, c. 1004, § 1, relating to legislative findings and declarations concerning the state teachers' retirement system, was repealed by Stats.1993, c. 893 (A.B.1796), § 1. See Education Code § 22315.

Cross References

Final vesting, see Education Code § 22138.

§ 22515. Persons excluded under §§ 22601.5, 22602, and 22604; irrevocable election to join plan

Persons excluded from membership pursuant to Sections 22601.5, 22602, and 22604 may elect membership in the Defined Benefit Program at any time while employed to perform creditable service subject to coverage under that program. The election shall be in writing on a form prescribed by this system, and shall be filed in the office of this system prior to submission of contributions. The election is irrevocable, and shall remain in effect until the member terminates employment and receives a refund of accumulated retirement contributions. The amendments to this section enacted during the 1995–96 Regular Session shall be deemed to have become operative on July 1, 1996.

(Added by Stats.1993, c. 893 (A.B.1796), § 2. Amended by Stats.1994, c. 507 (A.B. 2647), § 2; Stats.1996, c. 634 (S.B.2041), § 112, operative July 1, 1996; Stats.1998, c. 965 (A.B.2765), § 53.)

Historical and Statutory Notes

Legislative intent regarding Stats.1993, c. 893 (A.B.1796), including possible continuing application of provisions of repealed State Teachers' Retirement Law, see Historical and Statutory Notes under Education Code § 22000.

Section 1 of Stats.1994, c. 507 (A.B.2647), provides:

"It is the intent of the Legislature that the State Teachers' Retirement System address the issue of compensation and service credit equity for adult school teachers and make recommen-

dations to the Legislature during the 1995 Regular Session of the Legislature."

Former § 22515, added by Stats.1989, c. 1004, § 2, relating to benefits payable to members who became members on or after January 1, 1990, was repealed by Stats.1993, c. 893 (A.B.1796), § 1. See Education Code § 22316.

Derivation: Former § 22603.1, enacted by Stats.1976, c. 1010, § 2.

Educ.C.1959, § 13964.1, added by Stats.1975, c. 604, p. 1325, § 2.

Library References

Treatises and Practice Aids

Witkin, Summary (9th ed) Agency § 467.

§ 22516. Persons not excluded from membership

(a) Nothing in this chapter shall be construed or applied to exclude from membership in the Defined Benefit Program any person employed to perform creditable service at a level that requires mandatory membership in the program for which he or she has the right to elect membership in the program or another retirement system and who elects membership in the other retirement system, or who is employed to perform creditable service at a level that does not require mandatory membership in the Defined Benefit Program.

(b) Service performed after becoming a member of another retirement system shall not be credited to the member under this part, nor shall contributions or benefits under this part be based upon that service or the compensation received by the member during that period of service, except as provided in the definition of "final compensation" contained in Section 22134.

(Added by Stats.1993, c. 893 (A.B.1796), § 2. Amended by Stats.1996, c. 634 (S.B. 2041), § 113; Stats.1998, c. 965 (A.B.2765), § 54; Stats.1999, c. 939 (S.B.1074), § 39.)

Historical and Statutory Notes

Legislative intent regarding Stats.1993, c. 893 (A.B.1796), including possible continuing application of provisions of repealed State Teachers' Retirement Law, see Historical and Statutory Notes under Education Code § 22000.

Derivation: Former § 22610, enacted by Stats.1976, c. 1010, § 2.

Educ.C.1959, § 13971, added by Stats.1969, c. 896, p. 1738, § 2, amended by Stats.1974, c. 1293, p. 2810, § 43.

Educ.C.1959, § 14002 (Stats.1959, c. 2, p. 996, § 14002).

Educ.C.1943, § 14402, added by Stats.1945, c. 1207, p. 2289, § 4, amended by Stats.1949, c. 1157, p. 2068, § 6; Stats.1956, 1st Ex.Sess., c. 55, p. 431, § 5.

Chapter 11

EXCLUSIONS FROM MEMBERSHIP

Chapter 11 was added by Stats.1993, c. 893 (A.B.1796), § 2.

§ 22600.   Repealed by Stats.1998, c. 965 (A.B.2765), § 55

Historical and Statutory Notes

The repealed section, added by Stats.1993, c. 893 (A.B.1796, § 2, amended by Stats.1996, c. 608 (A.B.2673), § 1.3, related to membership in local system or county retirement systems.

The repealed section was derived from:

Former § 22600, enacted by Stats.1976, c. 1010, § 2.

Educ.C.1959, § 13961, added by Stats.1969, c. 896, p. 1738, § 2, amended by Stats.1970, c. 466, p. 923, § 7.5; Stats.1971, c. 1305, p. 2572, § 33; Stats.1972, c. 239, p. 479, § 2.

Educ.C.1959, § 14001 (Stats.1959, c. 2, p. 995, § 14001, amended by Stats.1959, c. 1271, p. 3418, § 2; Stats.1961, c. 878, p. 2301, § 11; Stats.1963, c. 1126, p. 2605, § 2; Stats.1965, c. 25, p. 901, § 2, eff. March 30, 1965; Stats.1965,

c. 348, p. 1453, § 2; Stats.1967, c. 1057, p. 2683, § 2; Stats.1968, c. 99, p. 309, § 2; Stats. 1968, c. 1447, p. 2857, § 2).

Educ.C.1943, § 14401, added by Stats.1944, 4th Ex.Sess., c. 13, p. 123, § 2, amended by Stats.1949, c. 1157, p. 2067, § 5.

Educ.C.1943, § 14411 (Stats.1943, c. 71, p. 599, amended by Stats.1943, c. 364, p. 1600).

School C. § 5.841, added by Stats.1937, c. 626, p. 1726, § 4.

Former § 22600, enacted by Stats.1976, c. 1010, § 2, relating to exclusion of persons who are members of a local system or county retirement system, was repealed by Stats.1993, c. 893 (A.B.1796), § 1. See this section.

§ 22601.   Exchange or sojourn teachers

Persons serving as exchange teachers or sojourn teachers from outside of this state are excluded from membership in the plan.

(Added by Stats.1993, c. 893 (A.B.1796), § 2.   Amended by Stats.1996, c. 634 (S.B. 2041), § 114.)

Historical and Statutory Notes

Legislative intent regarding Stats.1993, c. 893 (A.B.1796), including possible continuing application of provisions of repealed State Teachers' Retirement Law, see Historical and Statutory Notes under Education Code § 22000.

Former § 22601, enacted by Stats.1976, c. 1010, § 2, relating to membership by exchange or sojourn teachers in the retirement system, was repealed by Stats.1993, c. 893 (A.B.1796), § 1. See this section.

Derivation: Former § 22601, enacted by Stats.1976, c. 1010, § 2.

Educ.C.1959, § 13962, added by Stats.1969, c. 896, p. 1738, § 2.

Educ.C.1959, § 14001 (Stats.1959, c. 2, p. 995, § 14001, amended by Stats.1959, c. 1271, p. 3418, § 2; Stats.1961, c. 878, p. 2301, § 11; Stats.1963, c. 1126, p. 2605, § 2; Stats.1965, c. 25, p. 901, § 2, eff. March 30, 1965; Stats.1965, c. 348, p. 1453, § 2; Stats.1967, c. 1057, p. 2683, § 2; Stats.1968, c. 99, p. 309, § 2; Stats. 1968, c. 1447, p. 2857, § 2).

Educ.C.1943, § 14401, added by Stats.1944, 4th Ex.Sess., c. 13, p. 123, § 2, amended by Stats.1949, c. 1157, p. 2067, § 5.

Educ.C.1943, § 14411 (Stats.1943, c. 71, p. 599, amended by Stats.1943, c. 364, p. 1600).

School C. § 5.841, added by Stats.1937, c. 626, p. 1726, § 4.

§ 22601.5. Employment basis of less than 50 percent full-time equivalent for position

(a) Any person employed to perform creditable service who is not already a member in the Defined Benefit Program and whose basis of employment is less than 50 percent of the full-time equivalent for the position is excluded from mandatory membership in the Defined Benefit Program.

(b) This section shall apply to persons who perform service subject to coverage under this part and to persons who are employed by employers who provide benefits for their employees under Part 14 (commencing with Section 26000).

(c) This section shall be deemed to have become operative on July 1, 1996.

(Added by Stats.1996, c. 634 (S.B.2041), § 115, operative July 1, 1996. Amended by Stats.1998, c. 965 (A.B.2765), § 56; Stats.1999, c. 939 (S.B.1074), § 40.)

Historical and Statutory Notes

Section 329 of Stats.1998, c. 965 (A.B.2765), provides:

"SEC. 329. Sections 56, 57, 58, 256, 262, 263, 266, 312, and 319 of this act shall not become operative if SB 2085 of the 1997–98 Regular Session [Stats.1998, c. 1048] is enacted prior to this act and amends Sections 22601.5, 22602, 22604, 26301, 26400, 26401, 26504, 27410, and 28100 of the Education Code, in which case Sections 11, 12, 13, 40, 42, 43, 50, 51, 64, and 66 of SB 2085 of the 1997–98 Regular Session shall be given effect and Sections 56, 57, 58, 256, 263, 266, 312, and 319 of this act shall be repealed on January 1, 1999."

§ 22602. Substitute teachers; application

(a) Any person employed to perform creditable service as a substitute teacher who is not already a member in the Defined Benefit Program and who performs less than 100 complete days of creditable service in one school district, community college district, or county superintendent's office during the school year is excluded from mandatory membership in the Defined Benefit Program.

(b) This section shall not apply to persons who perform service for employers who provide benefits for their employees under Part 14 (commencing with Section 26000).

(c) The amendments to this section enacted during the 1995–96 Regular Session shall be deemed to have become operative on July 1, 1996.

(Added by Stats.1993, c. 893 (A.B.1796), § 2. Amended by Stats.1995, c. 592 (A.B. 1298), § 9; Stats.1996, c. 634 (S.B.2041), § 116, operative July 1, 1996; Stats.1998, c. 965 (A.B.2765), § 57; Stats.1999, c. 939 (S.B.1074), § 41.)

Historical and Statutory Notes

Section 329 of Stats.1998, c. 965 (A.B.2765), provides:

"SEC. 329. Sections 56, 57, 58, 256, 262, 263, 266, 312, and 319 of this act shall not become operative if SB 2085 of the 1997–98 Regular Session [Stats.1998, c. 1048] is enacted prior to this act and amends Sections 22601.5, 22602, 22604, 26301, 26400, 26401, 26504, 27410, and 28100 of the Education Code, in which case Sections 11, 12, 13, 40, 42, 43, 50, 51, 64, and 66 of SB 2085 of the 1997–98 Regular Session shall be given effect and Sections 56, 57, 58, 256, 263, 266, 312, and 319 of this act shall be repealed on January 1, 1999."

Former § 22602, enacted by Stats.1976, c. 1010, § 2, amended by Stats.1988, c. 497, § 1, relating to membership of substitute teachers in the retirement system, was repealed by Stats. 1993, c. 893 (A.B.1796), § 1. See, now, this section.

Derivation: Former § 22602, enacted by Stats.1976, c. 1010, § 2, amended by Stats. 1988, c. 497, § 1.

Educ.C.1959, § 13963, added by Stats.1969, c. 896, p. 1738, § 2, amended by Stats.1974, c. 1293, p. 2809, § 37.

Educ.C.1959, § 14001 (Stats.1959, c. 2, p. 995, § 14001, amended by Stats.1959, c. 1271, p. 3418, § 2; Stats.1961, c. 878, p. 2301, § 11; Stats.1963, c. 1126, p. 2605, § 2; Stats.1965, c. 25, p. 901, § 2, eff. March 30, 1965; Stats.1965, c. 348, p. 1453, § 2; Stats.1967, c. 1057, p. 2683, § 2; Stats.1968, c. 99, p. 309, § 2; Stats. 1968, c. 1447, p. 2857, § 2).

Educ.C.1943, § 14401, added by Stats.1944, 4th Ex.Sess., c. 13, p. 123, § 2, amended by Stats.1949, c. 1157, p. 2067, § 5.

Educ.C.1943, § 14411 (Stats.1943, c. 71, p. 599, amended by Stats.1943, c. 364, p. 1600).

School C. § 5.841, added by Stats.1937, c. 626, p. 1726, § 4.

Notes of Decisions

Military service   2
Substitute status   1

—————

1. Substitute status

Where teacher reported for work on May 1, 1944, to fill a vacancy caused by resignation of former substitute teacher and did not fill position of person absent from service, and school board made no formal classification as to status of teacher at time of employment, but classified teacher as substitute at next meeting and teacher was paid on a day to day basis for a period of six weeks, teacher was a substitute teacher and not a probationary teacher within teachers' retirement system and hence upon retirement was not entitled to credit for out-of-state service. 34 Ops.Atty.Gen. 142 (1959).

2. Military service

A member of the teachers' retirement system was entitled to military service credit pursuant to Educ.C.1959, § 13994 where his only employment prior to entering military service was as a substitute teacher for less than 100 days. 55 Ops.Atty.Gen. 390, 10–25–72.

§ 22603.   Repealed by Stats.1995, c. 592 (A.B.1298), § 10

Historical and Statutory Notes

The repealed section, added by Stats.1993, c. 893 (a.B.1796), § 2, related to instructors in adult education.

The repealed section was derived from:

Former § 22604, enacted by Stats.1976, c. 1010, § 2.

Educ.C.1959, § 13965, added by Stats.1969, c. 896, p. 1738, § 2.

Educ.C.1959, § 14001 (Stats.1959, c. 2, p. 995, § 14001, amended by Stats.1959, c. 1271,

p. 3418, § 2; Stats.1961, c. 878, p. 2301, § 11; Stats.1963, c. 1126, p. 2605, § 2; Stats.1965, c. 25, p. 901, § 2, eff. March 30, 1965; Stats.1965, c. 348, p. 1453, § 2; Stats.1967, c. 1057, p. 2683, § 2; Stats.1968, c. 99, p. 309, § 2; Stats. 1968, c. 1447, p. 2857, § 2).

Educ.C.1943, § 14401, added by Stats.1944, 4th Ex.Sess., c. 13, p. 123, § 2, amended by Stats.1949, c. 1157, p. 2067, § 5.

Educ.C.1943, § 14411 (Stats.1943, c. 71, p. 599, amended by Stats.1943, c. 364, p. 1600).

School C. § 5.841, added by Stats.1937, c. 626, p. 1726, § 4.

Legislative intent relating to Stats.1995, c. 592 (A.B.1298), see Historical and Statutory Notes under Education Code § 22146.

Former § 22603, enacted by Stats.1976, c. 1010, § 2, amended by Stats.1988, c. 497, § 2,

relating to membership by part-time employees in the system, was repealed by Stats.1993, c. 893 (A.B.1796), § 1. See Education Code § 22604.

§ 22603.1. Repealed by Stats.1993, c. 893 (A.B.1796), § 1

Historical and Statutory Notes

The repealed section, enacted by Stats.1976, c. 1010, § 2, related to the irrevocable election to join the system by substitute teachers and part-time employees. See Education Code § 22515.

Legislative intent regarding Stats.1993, c. 893 (A.B.1796), including possible continuing application of provisions of repealed State Teachers' Retirement Law, see Historical and Statutory Notes under Education Code § 22000.

§§ 22603.2, 22603.3. Repealed by Stats.1979, c. 787, p. 2681, §§ 1, 2

Historical and Statutory Notes

The repealed sections, enacted by Stats.1976, c. 1010, § 2, related to credits for persons who had been excluded from membership and who subsequently became members in the system.

Section 22603.3 was amended by Stats.1977, c. 242, § 10.5.

See Education Code § 22802.

Section 37 of Stats.1979, c. 787, provided:

"The provisions of this act shall not be applicable to persons who are members of the State Teachers' Retirement System on December 31, 1979, until on and after July 1, 1980. It shall be applicable to persons who become members on and after January 1, 1980, on the effective date of their membership."

§ 22604. Part-time employees; application

(a) Any person employed to perform creditable service on a part-time basis who is not already a member in the Defined Benefit Program and who performs less than 60 hours of creditable service in a pay period if employed on an hourly basis, or less than 10 days of creditable service in a pay period if employed on a daily basis, during the school year in one school district, community college district, or county superintendent's office is excluded from mandatory membership in the Defined Benefit Program.

(b) This section shall not apply to persons who are employed by employers who provide benefits for their employees under Part 14 (commencing with Section 26000).

(c) The amendments to this section enacted during the 1995–96 Regular Session shall be deemed to have become operative on July 1, 1996.

(Added by Stats.1993, c. 893 (A.B.1796), § 2. Amended by Stats.1995, c. 592 (A.B. 1298), § 11; Stats.1996, c. 634 (S.B.2041), § 117, operative July 1, 1996; Stats.1998, c. 965 (A.B.2765), § 58; Stats.1999, c. 939 (S.B.1074), § 42.)

Historical and Statutory Notes

Section 329 of Stats.1998, c. 965 (A.B.2765), provides:

"SEC. 329. Sections 56, 57, 58, 256, 262, 263, 266, 312, and 319 of this act shall not become operative if SB 2085 of the 1997–98

Regular Session [Stats.1998, c. 1048] is enacted prior to this act and amends Sections 22601.5, 22602, 22604, 26301, 26400, 26401, 26504, 27410, and 28100 of the Education Code, in which case Sections 11, 12, 13, 40, 42, 43, 50,

51, 64, and 66 of SB 2085 of the 1997–98 Regular Session shall be given effect and Sections 56, 57, 58, 256, 263, 266, 312, and 319 of this act shall be repealed on January 1, 1999."

Former § 22604, enacted by Stats.1976, c. 1010, § 2, relating to membership of adult education instructors in the retirement system, was repealed by Stats.1993, c. 893 (A.B.1796), § 1. See Education Code § 22603.

Derivation: Former § 22603, enacted by Stats.1976, c. 1010, § 2, amended by Stats. 1988, c. 497, § 2.

Educ.C.1959, § 13964, added by Stats.1969, c. 896, p. 1738, § 2, amended by Stats.1974, c. 1293, p. 2810, § 38; Stats.1975, c. 604, p. 1325, § 1.

Educ.C.1959, § 14001 (Stats.1959, c. 2, p. 995, § 14001, amended by Stats.1959, c. 1271, p. 3418, § 2; Stats.1961, c. 878, p. 2301, § 11; Stats.1963, c. 1126, p. 2605, § 2; Stats.1965, c. 25, p. 901, § 2, eff. March 30, 1965; Stats.1965, c. 348, p. 1453, § 2; Stats.1967, c. 1057, p. 2683, § 2; Stats.1968, c. 99, p. 309, § 2; Stats. 1968, c. 1447, p. 2857, § 2).

Educ.C.1943, § 14401, added by Stats.1944, 4th Ex.Sess., c. 13, p. 123, § 2, amended by Stats.1949, c. 1157, p. 2067, § 5.

Educ.C.1943, § 14411 (Stats.1943, c. 71, p. 599, amended by Stats.1943, c. 364, p. 1600).

School C. § 5.841, added by Stats.1937, c. 626, p. 1726, § 4.

Cross References

Members previously excluded, election to receive credit for part-time service, see Education Code § 22802.

Library References

Legal Jurisprudences

Am Jur 2d (Rev) Pensions and Retirement Funds § 1632.

§§ 22605 to 22608. Repealed by Stats.1995, c. 592 (A.B.1298), §§ 12 to 15

Historical and Statutory Notes

Section 22605, added by Stats.1993, c. 893 (A.B.1796), § 2, related to part-time employees who are members of another system. Section 22605 was derived from:

Former § 22605, enacted by Stats.1976, c. 1010, § 2.

Educ.C.1959, § 13966, added by Stats.1969, c. 896, p. 1738, § 2, amended by stats.1974, c. 1293, § 39.

Educ.C.1959, § 14001 (Stats.1959, c. 2, p. 995, § 14001, amended by Stats.1959, c. 1271, p. 3418, § 2; Stats.1961, c. 878, p. 2301, § 11; Stats.1963, c. 1126, p. 2605, § 2; Stats.1965, c. 25, p. 901, § 2, eff. March 30, 1965; Stats.1965, c. 348, p. 1453, § 2; Stats.1967, c. 1057, p. 2683, § 2; Stats.1968, c. 99, p. 309, § 2; Stats. 1968, c. 1447, p. 2857, § 2).

Educ.C.1943, § 14401, added by Stats.1944, 4th Ex.Sess., c. 13, p. 123, § 2, amended by Stats.1949, c. 1157, p. 2067, § 5.

Educ.C.1943, § 14411 (Stats.1943, c. 71, p. 599, amended by Stats.1943, c. 364, p. 1600).

School C. § 5.841, added by Stats.1937, c. 626, p. 1726, § 4.

Former § 22605, enacted by Stats.1976, c. 1010, § 2, relating to membership by part-time employees who are members of another system,

was repealed by Stats.1993, c. 893 (A.B.1796), § 1. See this section.

Section 22606, added by Stats.1993, c. 893 (A.B.1796), § 2, related to employment in health positions. Section 22606 was derived from:

Former § 22606, enacted by Stats.1976, c. 1010, § 2.

Educ.C.1959, § 13968, added by Stats.1969, c. 896, p. 1738, § 2, amended by Stats.1970, c. 466, § 9; Stats.1970, c. 557, § 82.

Educ.C.1959, § 14001 (Stats.1959, c. 2, p. 995, § 14001, amended by Stats.1959, c. 1271, p. 3418, § 2; Stats.1961, c. 878, p. 2301, § 11; Stats.1963, c. 1126, p. 2605, § 2; Stats.1965, c. 25, p. 901, § 2, eff. March 30, 1965; Stats.1965, c. 348, p. 1453, § 2; Stats.1967, c. 1057, p. 2683, § 2; Stats.1968, c. 99, p. 309, § 2; Stats. 1968, c. 1447, p. 2857, § 2).

Educ.C.1943, § 14401, added by Stats.1944, 4th Ex.Sess., c. 13, p. 123, § 2, amended by Stats.1949, c. 1157, p. 2067, § 5.

Educ.C.1943, § 14411 (Stats.1943, c. 71, p. 599, amended by Stats.1943, c. 364, p. 1600).

School C. § 5.841, added by Stats.1937, c. 626, p. 1726, § 4.

Former § 22606, enacted by Stats.1976, c. 1010, § 2, relating to membership by persons with health and development credentials, was repealed by Stats.1993, c. 893 (A.B.1796), § 1. See this section.

Section 22607, added by Stats.1993, c. 893 (A.B.1796), § 2, related to student teachers' membership. Section 22607 was derived from:

Former § 22609, enacted by Stats.1976, c. 1010, § 2, amended by Stats.1987, c. 1452, § 136.

Educ.C.1959, § 13970, added by Stats.1969, c. 896, p. 1738, § 2, amended by Stats.1971, c. 1032, § 1.

Educ.C.1959, § 14001.5, added by Stats.1961, c. 1383, § 3.

Former § 22607, enacted by Stats.1976, c. 1010, § 2, defining "pay period", was repealed by Stats.1993, c. 893 (A.B.1796), § 1.

Former § 22607 was derived from Educ.C. 1959, § 13968.5, added by Stats.1969, c. 896, p. 1738, § 2, amended by Stats.1974, c. 1293, p.

2810, § 40; Educ.C.1959, § 14001 (Stats.1959, c. 2, p. 995, § 14001, amended by Stats.1959, c. 1271, p. 3418, § 2; Stats.1961, c. 878, p. 2301, § 11; Stats.1963, c. 1126, p. 2605, § 2; Stats. 1965, c. 25, p. 901, § 2, eff. March 30, 1965; Stats.1965, c. 348, p. 1453, § 2; Stats.1967, c. 1057, p. 2683, § 2; Stats.1968, c. 99, p. 309, § 2; Stats.1968, c. 1447, p. 2857, § 2); Educ.C. 1943, § 14401, added by Stats.1944, 4th Ex. Sess., c. 13, p. 123, § 2, amended by Stats.1949, c. 1157, p. 2067, § 5; Educ.C.1943, § 14411 (Stats.1943, c. 71, p. 599, amended by Stats. 1943, c. 364, p. 1600); and School C. § 5.841, added by Stats.1937, c. 626, p. 1726, § 4.

Former § 22608, added by Stats.1977, c. 36, § 414, relating to election to remain in the Public Employees' Retirement System, was repealed by Stats.1993, c. 893 (A.B.1796), § 1. See Education Code § 22509.

Legislative intent relating to Stats.1995, c. 592 (A.B.1298), see Historical and Statutory Notes under Education Code § 22146.

§§ 22609 to 22610. Repealed by Stats.1993, c. 893 (A.B.1796), § 1

Historical and Statutory Notes

Legislative intent regarding Stats.1993, c. 893 (A.B.1796), including possible continuing application of provisions of repealed State Teachers' Retirement Law, see Historical and Statutory Notes under Education Code § 22000.

Section 22609, enacted by Stats.1976, c. 1010, § 2, amended by Stats.1987, c. 1452, § 136, related to membership by certificated teacher-assistants. See Education Code § 22607.

Section 22609.1, added by Stats.1987, c. 373, § 1, related to additional classifications for exclusions from membership. See Education Code § 22608.

Section 22610, enacted by Stats.1976, c. 1010, § 2, related to persons not excluded from membership. See Education Code § 22516.

Chapter 12

COMMUNITY PROPERTY

Section
22661. Accumulated retirement contributions; nonmember spouse's right to refund; lump-sum payment.
22662. Accumulated retirement contributions refunded to members; redeposit by nonmember spouse.
22663. Additional service credit; purchased by nonmember spouse.
22664. Service retirement allowance for nonmember spouse; conditions for retirement for service; limitations; calculation of allowance; increases.
22665. Service credit awarded in judgment or court order; calculation of retirement or disability allowance.
22666. Terminable interest doctrine; legislative intent.

Chapter 12 was added by Stats.1993, c. 893 (A.B.1796), § 2.

Cross References

Community property, see Family Code §§ 65 and 760.
Division of accumulated community property contributions and service credit, see Family Code § 2610.

§ 22650. Marriage dissolutions or legal separations; community property rights

This chapter establishes the power of a court in a dissolution of marriage or legal separation action with respect to community property rights in accounts with the plan under this part and establishes and defines the rights of nonmember spouses in the plan under this part.

(Added by Stats.1993, c. 893 (A.B.1796), § 2. Amended by Stats.1996, c. 634 (S.B. 2041), § 118; Stats.1998, c. 965 (A.B.2765), § 59.)

Historical and Statutory Notes

Legislative intent regarding Stats.1993, c. 893 (A.B.1796), including possible continuing application of provisions of repealed State Teachers' Retirement Law, see Historical and Statutory Notes under Education Code § 22000.

Former § 22650, added by Stats.1988, c. 542, § 2, relating to the power of the court in marriage dissolution and legal separation actions, was repealed by Stats.1993, c. 893 (A.B.1796), § 1. See this section.

Derivation: Former § 22650, added by Stats. 1988, c. 542, § 2.

Cross References

Community property, see Family Code §§ 65 and 760.

Library References

Legal Jurisprudences
Cal Jur 3d Fam Law § 784.
Am Jur 2d (Rev) Pensions and Retirement Funds §§ 1655 et seq.

Treatises and Practice Aids
Witkin, Summary (9th ed) Com Prop §§ 43, 47, 266.

The Rutter Group, Family Law (Hogoboom & King) §§ 3:447, 8:150, 8:1212, 9:268, 9:385.

§ 22651. Nonmember spouse

For purposes of this chapter and Section 23300, "nonmember spouse" means a member's spouse or former spouse who is being or has been awarded a community property interest in the service credit, accumulated retirement contributions, accumulated Defined Benefit Supplement account balance, or benefits of the member under this part. A nonmember spouse shall not be considered a member based upon his or her receipt of any of the following being awarded to the nonmember spouse as a result of legal separation or dissolution of marriage: a separate account of service credit and accumulated retirement contributions, a retirement allowance, or an interest in the member's retirement allowance under the Defined Benefit Program; or a separate account based on the member's Defined Benefit Supplement account balance, a retirement benefit, or an interest in the member's retirement benefit under the Defined Benefit Supplement Program.

(Added by Stats.1993, c. 893 (A.B.1796), § 2. Amended by Stats.1996, c. 634 (S.B. 2041), § 119; Stats.1998, c. 965 (A.B.2765), § 60; Stats.2000, c. 74 (A.B.1509), § 33; Stats.2000, c. 1021 (A.B.2700), § 18.)

Historical and Statutory Notes

Legislative intent regarding Stats.1993, c. 893 (A.B.1796), including possible continuing application of provisions of repealed State Teachers' Retirement Law, see Historical and Statutory Notes under Education Code § 22000.

Operative effect of Stats.2000, c. 1021 (A.B. 2700), see Historical and Statutory Notes following Education Code § 22101.5.

Section affected by two or more acts at the same session of the legislature, see Government Code § 9605.

Former § 22651, added by Stats.1988, c. 542, § 2, relating to nonmember spouses, was repealed by Stats.1993, c. 893 (A.B.1796), § 1. See, now, this section.

Derivation: Former § 22651, added by Stats. 1988, c. 542, § 2.

Former § 22651.5, added by Stats.1990, c. 1390, § 2.

Cross References

Community property, see Family Code §§ 65 and 760.

Library References

Treatises and Practice Aids

The Rutter Group, Family Law (Hogoboom & King) § 8:1212.

§ 22651.5. Repealed by Stats.1993, c. 893 (A.B.1796), § 1

Historical and Statutory Notes

The repealed section, added by Stats.1990, c. 1390 (A.B.3042), § 2, related to the definition of a nonmember spouse. See Education Code § 22651.

Legislative intent regarding Stats.1993, c. 893 (A.B.1796), including possible continuing application of provisions of repealed State Teachers' Retirement Law, see Historical and Statutory Notes under Education Code § 22000.

§ 22652. Court orders; division of contributions and service credits; community property rights

(a) Upon the legal separation or dissolution of marriage of a member, other than a retired member, the court shall include in the judgment or a court order the date on which the parties separated.

(b) The court may order in the judgment or court order that the member's accumulated retirement contributions and service credit under the Defined

Benefit Program, or the member's Defined Benefit Supplement account balance, or both, under this part that are attributable to periods of service during the marriage be divided into two separate and distinct accounts in the name of the member and the nonmember spouse, respectively. Any service credit and accumulated retirement contributions under the Defined Benefit Program and any accumulated Defined Benefit Supplement account balance under this part that are not explicitly awarded by the judgment or court order shall be deemed the exclusive property of the member under the Defined Benefit Program or the Defined Benefit Supplement Program, as applicable.

(c) The determination of the court of community property rights pursuant to this section shall be consistent with this chapter and shall address the rights of the nonmember spouse under this part, including, but not limited to, the following:

(1) The right to a retirement allowance under the Defined Benefit Program and, if applicable, a retirement benefit under the Defined Benefit Supplement Program.

(2) The right to a refund of accumulated retirement contributions under the Defined Benefit Program and the return of the accumulated Defined Benefit Supplement account balance that were awarded to the nonmember spouse.

(3) The right to redeposit all or a portion of accumulated retirement contributions previously refunded to the member which the member is eligible to redeposit pursuant to Sections 23200 to 23203, inclusive, and shall specify the shares of the redeposit amount awarded to the member and the nonmember spouse.

(4) The right to purchase additional service credit that the member is eligible to purchase pursuant to Sections 22800 to 22810, inclusive, and shall specify the shares of the additional service credit awarded to the member and the nonmember spouse.

(Added by Stats.1993, c. 893 (A.B.1796), § 2. Amended by Stats.1998, c. 965 (A.B. 2765), § 61; Stats.2000, c. 74 (A.B.1509), § 34; Stats.2000, c. 1020 (A.B.820), § 1, operative July 1, 2001; Stats.2000, c. 1021 (A.B.2700), § 19.5.)

Historical and Statutory Notes

Legislative intent regarding Stats.1993, c. 893 (A.B.1796), including possible continuing application of provisions of repealed State Teachers' Retirement Law, see Historical and Statutory Notes under Education Code § 22000.

Section 16 of Stats.2000, c. 1020 (A.B.820), provides:

"Sections 1, 2, 5, 6, 7, 8, 9, and 10 of this act shall become operative July 1, 2001."

Under the provisions of § 65 of Stats.2000, c. 1021 (A.B.2700), the 2000 amendments of this section by c. 1020 (A.B.820) and c. 1021 (A.B. 2700) were given effect and incorporated in the form set forth in § 19.5 of c. 1021 (A.B.2700).

An amendment of this section by § 19 of Stats.2000, c. 1021 (A.B.2700), failed to become

operative under the provisions of § 65 of that Act.

Section affected by two or more acts at the same session of the legislature, see Government Code § 9605.

Operative effect of Stats.2000, c. 1021 (A.B. 2700), see Historical and Statutory Notes following Education Code § 22101.5.

Former § 22652, added by Stats.1988, c. 542, § 2, relating to court orders upon the legal separation or dissolution of marriage of a member and the rights of nonmember spouses, was repealed by Stats.1993, c. 893 (A.B.1796), § 1. See this section.

Derivation: Former § 22652, added by Stats. 1988, c. 542, § 2.

Cross References

Community property, see Family Code §§ 65 and 760.

Library References

Treatises and Practice Aids
  Witkin, Summary (9th ed) Com Prop § 47.

The Rutter Group, Family Law (Hogoboom & King) §§ 8:1213, 8:1214, 9:385.

§ 22653. Status of nonmember spouse; limitation of rights and benefits

(a) The nonmember spouse who is awarded a separate account under this part pursuant to Section 22652 is not a member of the Defined Benefit Program based on that award. The nonmember spouse is entitled only to rights and benefits based on that award explicitly established by this chapter.

(b) This section shall not be construed to limit any right arising from the account of a nonmember spouse under this part that exists because the nonmember spouse is or was employed to perform creditable service subject to coverage by the Defined Benefit Program.

(Added by Stats.1993, c. 893 (A.B.1796), § 2. Amended by Stats.1996, c. 634 (S.B. 2041), § 120; Stats.1998, c. 965 (A.B.2765), § 62.)

Historical and Statutory Notes

Legislative intent regarding Stats.1993, c. 893 (A.B.1796), including possible continuing application of provisions of repealed State Teachers' Retirement Law, see Historical and Statutory Notes under Education Code § 22000.

Former § 22653, added by Stats.1988, c. 542, § 2, relating to the status and rights of a non-

member spouse, was repealed by Stats.1993, c. 893 (A.B.1796), § 1. See this section.

Derivation: Former § 22653, added by Stats. 1988, c. 542, § 2.

Library References

Treatises and Practice Aids
  The Rutter Group, Family Law (Hogoboom & King) § 8:1212.

§ 22654. Repealed by Stats.1996, c. 634 (S.B.2041), § 121

Historical and Statutory Notes

The repealed section, added by Stats.1993, c. 893 (A.B.1796), § 2, derived from former § 22661, added by Stats.1988, c. 542, § 2, related to benefits and rights of a nonmember spouse.

Former § 22654, added by Stats.1988, c. 542, § 2, relating to a nonmember spouse's right to designate a beneficiary, was repealed by Stats. 1993, c. 893 (A.B.1796), § 1. See Education Code § 22660.

§ 22655. Retirement allowance or retirement annuity; community property rights of nonmember spouse; rights upon death

(a) Upon the legal separation or dissolution of marriage of a retired member, the court may include in the judgment or court order a determination of the community property rights of the parties in the retired member's retirement allowance and, if applicable, retirement benefit under this part consistent with this section. Upon election under subparagraph (B) of paragraph (3) of subdivision (a) of Section 2610 of the Family Code, the court order awarding the nonmember spouse a community property share in the retirement allowance or retirement benefit, or both, of a retired member shall be consistent with this section.

(b) If the court does not award the entire retirement allowance or retirement annuity under this part to the retired member and the retired member is receiving a retirement allowance that has not been modified pursuant to Section 24300, or a single life annuity pursuant to Section 25011 or 25018, the court shall require only that the system pay the nonmember spouse, by separate warrant, his or her community property share of the retired member's retirement allowance or retirement benefit, or both, under this part.

(c) If the court does not award the entire retirement allowance or retirement benefit under this part to the retired member and the retired member is receiving an allowance that has been actuarially modified pursuant to Section 24300, or a joint and survivor retirement benefit pursuant to Section 25011 or 25018, the court shall order only one of the following:

(1) The retired member shall maintain the retirement allowance or retirement benefit, or both, under this part without change.

(2) The retired member shall cancel the option that modified the retirement allowance under this part pursuant to Section 24305 and select a new joint and survivor option or a new beneficiary or both, and the system shall pay the nonmember spouse, by separate warrant, his or her community property share of the retirement allowance under this part of the retired member, the option beneficiary, or both.

(3) The retired member shall cancel the joint and survivor annuity under which the annuity is being paid pursuant to Section 24305.3, and select a new joint and survivor annuity or a new annuity beneficiary or both, based on the actuarial equivalent of the member's canceled annuity, and the system shall pay the nonmember spouse, by separate warrant, his or her community property share of the retirement annuity payable to the retired member, the annuity beneficiary, or both.

(4) The retired member shall take the action specified in both paragraphs (2) and (3).

(5) The retired member shall cancel the option that modified the retirement allowance under this part pursuant to Section 24305 and select an unmodified retirement allowance and the system shall pay the nonmember spouse, by separate warrant, his or her community property share of the retired member's retirement allowance under this part.

(6) The retired member shall cancel, pursuant to Section 24305.3, the joint and survivor annuity under which the retirement benefit is being paid, and select a single life annuity, and the system shall pay the nonmember spouse, by separate warrant, his or her community property share of the retirement benefit payable benefit to the retired member.

(7) The retired member shall take the action specified in both paragraphs (5) and (6).

(d) If the option beneficiary or annuity beneficiary or both under this part, other than the nonmember spouse, predeceases the retired member, the court shall order the retired member to select a new option beneficiary pursuant to Section 24306, or a new annuity beneficiary pursuant to Section 24305.3 and shall order the system to pay the nonmember spouse, by separate warrant, his or her share of the community property interest in the retirement allowance or retirement benefit or both under this part of the retired member or the new option beneficiary or annuity beneficiary or each of them.

(e) The right of the nonmember spouse to receive his or her community property share of the retired member's retirement allowance or retirement benefit or both under this section shall terminate upon the death of the nonmember spouse. However, the nonmember spouse may designate a beneficiary under the Defined Benefit Program and a payee under the Defined Benefit Supplement Program to receive his or her community property share of the retired member's accumulated retirement contributions and accumulated Defined Benefit Supplement account balance under this part in the event that there are remaining accumulated retirement contributions and a balance of credits in the member's Defined Benefit Supplement account to be paid upon the death of the nonmember spouse.

(Added by Stats.1993, c. 893 (A.B.1796), § 2. Amended by Stats.1994, c. 1269 (A.B. 2208), § 5; Stats.1996, c. 634 (S.B.2041), § 122; Stats.1998, c. 965 (A.B.2765), § 63; Stats.2000, c. 74 (A.B.1509), § 35; Stats.2000, c. 1021 (A.B.2700), § 20.)

Law Revision Commission Comment

1994 Amendment

Section 22655 is amended to correct a cross-reference to Family Code Section 2610. This is a technical, nonsubstantive change. [24

Cal.L.Rev.Comm.Reports ___ (1994), Annual Report for 1994, App. 5]

Historical and Statutory Notes

Stats.1993, c. 893, § 1, provided for the repeal of § 22655, which was also amended by Stats.1993, c. 1082. Stats.1993, c. 893, § 2, provided for the addition of another § 22661. Subordination of legislation by Stats.1993, c. 893, see Historical and Statutory Notes under Education Code § 22000. Section affected by two or more acts at the same session of the legislature, see Government Code § 9605.

Subordination of legislation by Stats.1993, c. 893, and legislative intent regarding that act, including possible continuing application of provisions of repealed State Teachers' Retirement Law, see Historical and Statutory Notes under Education Code § 22000.

Stats.1993, c. 893, § 2, provided for addition of this section, similar to § 22662, as well as for repeal of § 22662. Stats.1993, c. 1082 (A.B. 2278) amended § 22662. Subordination of legislation by Stats.1993, c. 893, see Stats.1993, c. 893 (A.B.1796), § 4. Section affected by two or more acts at the same session of the legislature, see Government Code § 9605.

Similar provisions were formerly contained at Education Code § 22662, added by Stats.1988, c. 542, § 2, amended by Stats.1992, c. 163, § 68; Stats.1993, c. 1082 (A.B.2278), § 3.

Operative effect of Stats.2000, c. 1021 (A.B. 2700), see Historical and Statutory Notes following Education Code § 22101.5.

Section affected by two or more acts at the same session of the legislature, see Government Code § 9605.

Another § 22655, added by Stats.1988, c. 542, § 2, amended by Stats.1993, c. 1082 (A.B.2278), § 2; Stats.1993, c. 1082 (A.B.2278), § 2, relating to refund of accumulated retirement contributions, was repealed by Stats.1994, c. 933 (A.B.3171), § 37, eff. Sept. 28, 1994. See Education Code § 22661.

Sections 8 to 10 of Stats.1988, c. 542, provide:

"Sec. 8. It is the intent of the Legislature that this act apply to all public retirement benefits in which there is an undivided community property interest and in all dissolution of marriage or legal separation cases which are pending on the effective date of this act or in which the court has reserved jurisdiction over the benefit or not yet awarded the benefit. Entitlements and benefits for which the nonmember spouse is not eligible shall include, but not be limited to, health benefits, dental benefits, and vision care.

"Sec. 9. This act shall be deemed to be retroactive to June 1, 1988.

"Sec. 10. Nothing in this act shall be construed to create or vest in the nonmember spouse, as defined in Sections 22651 of the Education Code and 21215.1 of the Government Code, any class of entitlement or benefits that would not be available to the nonmember spouse had he or she been a member of the system for the same time and upon the same terms as the member spouse. Additionally, nothing in this act shall be construed to make the nonmember spouse a member of the Public Employees' Retirement System or the State Teachers' Retirement System."

Cross References

Community property, see Family Code §§ 65 and 760.

§ 22656. Judgments or orders; conditions for binding effect

No judgment or court order issued pursuant to this chapter is binding on the system with respect to the Defined Benefit Program or the Defined Benefit Supplement Program until the system has been joined as a party to the action and has been served with a certified copy of the judgment or court order.

(Added by Stats.1993, c. 893 (A.B.1796), § 2. Amended by Stats.1996, c. 634 (S.B. 2041), § 122.5; Stats.1998, c. 965 (A.B.2765), § 64; Stats.2000, c. 74 (A.B.1509), § 36; Stats.2000, c. 1021 (A.B.2700), § 21.)

Historical and Statutory Notes

Legislative intent regarding Stats.1993, c. 893 (A.B.1796), including possible continuing application of provisions of repealed State Teachers' Retirement Law, see Historical and Statutory Notes under Education Code § 22000.

Operative effect of Stats.2000, c. 1021 (A.B. 2700), see Historical and Statutory Notes following Education Code § 22101.5.

Section affected by two or more acts at the same session of the legislature, see Government Code § 9605.

Former § 22656, added by Stats.1988, c. 542, § 2, relating to a nonmember spouse's right to redeposit accumulated retirement contributions previously refunded to the member, was repealed by Stats.1993, c. 893 (A.B.1796), § 1. See Education Code § 22662.

Derivation: Former § 22664, added by Stats. 1988, c. 542, § 2.

Library References

Treatises and Practice Aids
Witkin, Summary (9th ed) Com Prop § 47.
The Rutter Group, Family Law (Hogoboom & King) § 8:1219.

Forms

B-W Cal Civil Practice: Family Law Litigation § 6:67.

§ 22657. Nonmember spouse; applicable statutory provisions

(a) The following provisions shall apply to a nonmember spouse as if he or she were a member under this part: Sections 22107, 22306, 22906, 23802, subdivisions (a) and (b) of Section 24600, 24601, 24602, 24603, 24605, 24606, 24607, 24608, 24611, 24612, 24613, 24616, and 24617.

(b) Notwithstanding subdivision (a), this section shall not be construed to establish any right for the nonmember spouse under this part that is not explicitly established in Sections 22650 to 22655, inclusive, and Sections 22658 to 22665, inclusive.

(Added by Stats.1993, c. 893 (A.B.1796), § 2. Amended by Stats.1996, c. 634 (S.B. 2041), § 123; Stats.1998. c. 965 (A.B.2765), § 65.)

Historical and Statutory Notes

Legislative intent regarding Stats.1993, c. 893 (A.B.1796), including possible continuing application of provisions of repealed State Teachers' Retirement Law, see Historical and Statutory Notes under Education Code § 22000.

Former § 22657, added by Stats.1988, c. 542, § 2, relating to a nonmember spouse's right to purchase additional service credit, was repealed by Stats.1993, c. 893 (A.B.1796), § 1. See Education Code § 22663.

Derivation: Former § 22665, added by Stats. 1988, c. 542, § 2, amended by Stats.1992, c. 1166, § 11.

Library References

Treatises and Practice Aids

Witkin, Summary (9th ed) Com Prop § 47.

§ 22658. Accounts of nonmember spouse; administration; separation

(a) A separate account awarded to a nonmember spouse pursuant to Section 22652 shall be administered independently of the member's account.

(b) An accumulated [1] Defined Benefit Supplement account balance, accumulated retirement contributions, service credit, and final compensation attributable to a separate account of a nonmember spouse under this part shall not be combined in any way or for any purpose with the accumulated Defined Benefit Supplement account balance, accumulated retirement contributions, service credit, and final compensation of any other separate account of the nonmember spouse.

(c) An accumulated [1] Defined Benefit Supplement account balance, accumulated retirement contributions, service credit, and final compensation attributable to the separate account of a nonmember spouse shall not be combined in any way or for any purpose with the accumulated Defined Benefit Supplement account balance, accumulated retirement contributions, service credit, and final compensation of an account that exists under this part because the nonmember spouse is employed or has been employed to perform creditable service subject to coverage under the Defined Benefit Program or the Defined Benefit Supplement Program.

(Added by Stats.1993, c. 893 (A.B.1796), § 2. Amended by Stats.1996, c. 634 (S.B. 2041), § 123.5; Stats.1998. c. 965 (A.B.2765), § 66; Stats.2000, c. 74 (A.B.1509), § 37.)

[1] So in enrolled bill.

Historical and Statutory Notes

Legislative intent regarding Stats.1993, c. 893 (A.B.1796), including possible continuing application of provisions of repealed State Teachers' Retirement Law, see Historical and Statutory Notes under Education Code § 22000.

Former § 22658, added by Stats.1988, c. 542, § 2, amended by Stats.1990, c. 83 (A.B.54), § 2; Stats.1992, c. 1166 (S.B.1885), § 9, relating to a nonmember spouse's right to a service retirement allowance, was repealed by Stats.1993, c. 893 (A.B.1796), § 1. See Education Code § 22664.

Derivation: Former § 22660, added by Stats. 1988, c. 542, § 2.

Treatises and Practice Aids
   Witkin, Summary (9th ed) Com Prop § 47.

§ 22659.   Information from nonmember spouse

   Upon being awarded a separate account or an interest in the retirement
allowance or retirement benefit of a retired member under this part, a nonmember spouse shall provide the system with proof of his or her date of birth,
social security number, and any other information requested by the system, in
the form and manner requested by the system.

(Added by Stats.1993, c. 893 (A.B.1796), § 2. Amended by Stats.1996, c. 634 (S.B.
2041), § 124; Stats.1998, c. 965 (A.B.2765), § 67; Stats.2000, c. 74 (A.B.1509), § 38;
Stats.2000, c. 1021 (A.B.2700), § 22.)

Historical and Statutory Notes

   Legislative intent regarding Stats.1993, c. 893
(A.B.1796), including possible continuing appli-
cation of provisions of repealed State Teachers'
Retirement Law, see Historical and Statutory
Notes under Education Code § 22000.
   Operative effect of Stats.2000, c. 1021 (A.B.
2700), see Historical and Statutory Notes fol-
lowing Education Code § 22101.5.
   Section affected by two or more acts at the
same session of the legislature, see Government
Code § 9605.

   Former § 22659, added by Stats.1988, c. 542,
§ 2, amended by Stats.1992, c. 1166 (S.B.1885),
§ 10, relating to a member's eligibility for service retirement, disability retirement or disability allowance, was repealed by Stats.1993, c. 893
(A.B.1796), § 1. See Education Code § 22665.
   Derivation: Former § 22663, added by Stats.
1988, c. 542, § 2.

§ 22660.   Beneficiary of nonmember spouse; modification of allowance

   (a) The nonmember spouse who is awarded a separate account under this
part shall have the right to designate, pursuant to Sections 23300 to 23304,
inclusive, a beneficiary or beneficiaries to receive the accumulated retirement
contributions under the Defined Benefit Program and to designate a payee to
receive the accumulated Defined Benefit Supplement account balance under
the Defined Benefit Supplement Program remaining in the separate account of
the nonmember spouse on his or her date of death, and any accrued allowance
or accrued benefit under the Defined Benefit Supplement Program that is
attributable to the separate account of the nonmember spouse and that is
unpaid on the date of the death of the nonmember spouse.

   (b) This section shall not be construed to provide the nonmember spouse
with any right to elect to modify a retirement allowance under Section 24300
or to elect a joint and survivor annuity under the Defined Benefit Supplement
Program.

(Added by Stats.1993, c. 893 (A.B.1796), § 2. Amended by Stats.1998, c. 965 (A.B.
2765), § 68; Stats.2000, c. 74 (A.B.1509), § 39; Stats.2000, c. 1021 (A.B.2700), § 23;
Stats.2001, c. 159 (S.B.662), § 59.)

Historical and Statutory Notes

   Legislative intent regarding Stats.1993, c. 893
(A.B.1796), including possible continuing application of provisions of repealed State Teachers'

Retirement Law, see Historical and Statutory
Notes under Education Code § 22000.

Operative effect of Stats.2000, c. 1021 (A.B. 2700), see Historical and Statutory Notes following Education Code § 22101.5.

Section affected by two or more acts at the same session of the legislature, see Government Code § 9605.

Former § 22660, added by Stats.1988, c. 542, § 2, relating to separate administration of sepa-

rate accounts of a nonmember spouse, was repealed by Stats.1993, c. 893 (A.B.1796), § 1. See Education Code § 22658.

Derivation: Former § 22654, added by Stats. 1988, c. 542, § 2.

Library References

Treatises and Practice Aids

The Rutter Group, Family Law (Hogoboom & King) § 8:1213.

§ 22661. Accumulated retirement contributions; nonmember spouse's right to refund; lump-sum payment

(a) The nonmember spouse who is awarded a separate account under this part shall have the right to a refund of the accumulated retirement contributions in the account under the Defined Benefit Program, and a return of the Defined Benefit Supplement account balance, of the nonmember spouse under this part.

(b) The nonmember spouse shall file an application on a form provided by the system to obtain a refund or lump-sum payment.

(c) The refund of accumulated retirement contributions and the return of the accumulated Defined Benefit Supplement account balance under this part are effective when the system deposits in the United States mail an initial warrant drawn in favor of the nonmember spouse and addressed to the latest address for the nonmember spouse on file with the system. If the nonmember spouse has elected on a form provided by the system to transfer all or a specified portion of the accumulated retirement contributions or accumulated Defined Benefit Supplement account balance that are eligible for direct trustee-to-trustee transfer to the trustee of a qualified plan under Section 402 of the Internal Revenue Code of 1986 (26 U.S.C.A. Sec. 402), deposit in the United States mail of a notice that the requested transfer has been made constitutes a refund of the nonmember spouse's accumulated retirement contributions or accumulated Defined Benefit Supplement account balance.

(d) The nonmember spouse is deemed to have permanently waived all rights and benefits pertaining to the service credit, accumulated retirement contributions, and accumulated Defined Benefit Supplement account balance under this part when the refund and lump-sum payment become effective.

(e) The nonmember spouse may not cancel a refund or lump-sum payment under this part after it is effective.

(f) The nonmember spouse shall not have a right to elect to redeposit the refunded accumulated retirement contributions under this part after the refund is effective, to redeposit under Section 22662 or purchase additional service credit under Section 22663 after the refund becomes effective, or to redeposit the accumulated Defined Benefit Supplement account balance after the lump-sum payment becomes effective.

(g) If the total service credit in the separate account of the nonmember spouse under the Defined Benefit Program, including service credit purchased under Sections 22662 and 22663, is less than two and one-half years, the board shall refund the accumulated retirement contributions in the account.

(Added by Stats.1993, c. 893 (A.B.1796), § 2. Amended by Stats.1994, c. 933 (A.B. 3171), § 38, eff. Sept. 28, 1994; Stats.1996, c. 634 (S.B.2041), § 125; Stats.1998, c. 965 (A.B.2765), § 69; Stats.2000, c. 74 (A.B.1509), § 40; Stats.2000, c. 1021 (A.B.2700), § 24.)

Historical and Statutory Notes

Stats.1993, c. 893, provided for addition of this section, similar to § 22655, as well as for repeal of § 22655. Stats.1993, c. 1082, amended § 22655. Subordination of legislation by Stats.1993, c. 893, see Stats.1993, c. 893 (A.B. 1796), § 4. Section affected by two or more acts at the same session of the legislature, see Government Code § 9605.

Subordination of legislation by Stats.1993, c. 893, and legislative intent regarding that act, including possible continuing application of provisions of repealed State Teachers' Retirement Law, see Historical and Statutory Notes under Education Code § 22000.

Provisions similar to this section were formerly contained in Education Code § 22655.

Operative effect of Stats.2000, c. 1021 (A.B. 2700), see Historical and Statutory Notes following Education Code § 22101.5.

Section affected by two or more acts at the same session of the legislature, see Government Code § 9605.

Former § 22661, added by Stats.1988, c. 542, § 2, relating to a nonmember spouse's rights and benefits from a separate account, was repealed by Stats.1993, c. 893 (A.B.1796), § 1. See Education Code § 22654.

Library References

Legal Jurisprudences
    Am Jur 2d (Rev) Pensions and Retirement
        Funds §§ 1641 et seq.

Treatises and Practice Aids
    Witkin, Summary (9th ed) Com Prop § 47.

The Rutter Group, Family Law (Hogoboom & King) § 8:1214.

§ 22662. Accumulated retirement contributions refunded to members; redeposit by nonmember spouse

The nonmember spouse who is awarded a separate account under the Defined Benefit Program may redeposit accumulated retirement contributions previously refunded to the member in accordance with the determination of the court pursuant to Section 22652.

(a) The nonmember spouse may redeposit under the Defined Benefit Program only those accumulated retirement contributions that were previously refunded to the member and in which the court has determined the nonmember spouse has a community property interest.

(b) The nonmember spouse shall inform the system in writing of his or her intent to redeposit within 180 days after the judgment or court order that specifies the redeposit rights of the nonmember spouse is entered. The nonmember spouses' election to redeposit shall be made on a form provided by the system within 30 days after the system mails an election form and the billing.

(c) If the nonmember spouse elects to redeposit under the Defined Benefit Program, he or she shall repay all or a portion of the member's refunded accumulated retirement contributions that were awarded to the nonmember spouse and shall pay regular interest from the date of the refund to the date payment of the redeposit is completed.

(d) All payments shall be received by the system before the effective date of the nonmember spouse's retirement under this part. If any payment due because of the election is not received at the system's office in Sacramento within 120 days of its due date, the election shall be canceled and any payments made under the election shall be returned to the nonmember spouse.

(e) The right of the nonmember spouse to redeposit shall be subject to Section 23203.

(f) The member shall not have a right to redeposit the share of the nonmember spouse in the previously refunded accumulated retirement contributions under this part whether or not the nonmember spouse elects to redeposit. However, any accumulated retirement contributions previously refunded under this part and not explicitly awarded to the nonmember spouse under this part by the judgment or court order shall be deemed the exclusive property of the member.

(Added by Stats.1993, c. 893 (A.B.1796), § 2. Amended by Stats.1996, c. 634 (S.B. 2041), § 126; Stats.1998, c. 965 (A.B.2765), § 70; Stats.2000, c. 74 (A.B.1509), § 41; Stats.2000, c; 1020 (A.B.820), § 2, operative July 1, 2001; Stats.2000, c. 1021 (A.B. 2700), § 25.5.)

Historical and Statutory Notes

Legislative intent regarding Stats.1993, c. 893, including possible continuing application of provisions of repealed State Teachers' Retirement Law, see Historical and Statutory Notes under Education Code § 22000.

Section 16 of Stats.2000, c. 1020 (A.B.820), provides:

"Sections 1, 2, 5, 6, 7, 8, 9, and 10 of this act shall become operative July 1, 2001."

Under the provisions of § 66 of Stats.2000, c. 1021 (A.B.2700), the 2000 amendments of this section by c. 1020 (A.B.820) and c. 1021 (A.B. 2700) were given effect and incorporated in the form set forth in § 25.5 of c. 1021 (A.B.2700).

An amendment of this section by § 25 of Stats.2000, c. 1021 (A.B.2700), failed to become operative under the provisions of § 66 of that Act.

Section affected by two or more acts at the same session of the legislature, see Government Code § 9605.

Operative effect of Stats.2000, c. 1021 (A.B. 2700), see Historical and Statutory Notes following Education Code § 22101.5.

Another § 22662, added by Stats.1988, c. 542, § 2, amended by Stats.1992, c. 163 (A.B.2641), § 68; Stats.1993, c. 1082 (A.B.2278), § 3, was repealed by Stats.1994, c. 933 (A.B.3171), § 39, eff. Sept. 28, 1994. See Education Code § 22655.

Stats.1994, c. 1269 (A.B.2208), § 6, provided for amendment of § 22662 without specifying which § 22662 was to be amended. Based on the text of the amendment and the Legislative Counsel's Digest in c. 1269, and based on the Law Revision Commission's Report on c. 1269 (see 24 Cal.L.Rev.Comm.Reports 621 (1994), Annual Report for 1994, App. 5), it appears that the intent was to amend the text as amended by Stats.1993, c. 1082 (A.B.2278), § 3. Amendment of repealed section, see Government Code § 9609.

Derivation: Former § 22656, added by Stats. 1988, c. 542, § 2.

Cross References

Community property, see Family Code §§ 65 and 760.
Computation of time,
    Generally, see Code of Civil Procedure §§ 12 and 12a and Government Code § 6800 et seq.
    Time in which any act provided by the Education Code is to be done, see Education Code § 9.
Continuation of statutes relating to subjects covered by provisions of this Code, see Education Code
    § 3.

§ 22663. Additional service credit; purchased by nonmember spouse

The nonmember spouse who is awarded a separate account under this part shall have the right to purchase additional service credit in accordance with the determination of the court pursuant to Section 22652.

(a) The nonmember spouse may purchase only the service credit that the court, pursuant to Section 22652, has determined to be the community property interest of the nonmember spouse.

(b) The nonmember spouse shall inform the system in writing of his or her intent to purchase additional service credit within 180 days after the date the judgment or court order addressing the right of the nonmember spouse to purchase additional service credit is entered. The nonmember spouse shall elect to purchase additional service credit on a form provided by the system within 30 days after the system mails an election form and billing.

(c) If the nonmember spouse elects to purchase additional service credit, he or she shall pay, prior to retirement under this part, all contributions with respect to the additional service at the contribution rate for additional service credit in effect at the time of election and regular interest from July 1 of the year following the year upon which contributions are based.

(1)(A) The nonmember spouse shall purchase additional service credit by paying the required contributions and interest in one lump sum, or in not more than 60 monthly installments, provided that no installment, except the final installment, shall be less than twenty-five dollars ($25). Regular interest shall be charged on the monthly unpaid balance if the nonmember spouse pays in installments.

(B) If any payment due because of the election is not received at the system's office in Sacramento within 120 days of its due date, the election shall be canceled and any payments made under the election shall be returned to the nonmember spouse.

(2) The contributions shall be based on the member's compensation earnable in the most recent school year during which the member was employed, preceding the date of separation established by the court pursuant to Section 22652.

(3) All payments of contributions and interest shall be received by the system before the effective date of the retirement of the nonmember.

(d) The nonmember spouse shall not have a right to purchase additional service credit under this part after the effective date of a refund of the accumulated retirement contributions in the separate account of the nonmember spouse.

(e) The member shall not have a right to purchase the community property interest of the nonmember spouse of additional service credit under this part whether or not the nonmember spouse elects to purchase the additional service credit. However, any additional service credit eligible for purchase that is not explicitly awarded to the nonmember spouse by the judgment or court order shall be deemed the exclusive property of the member.

(Added by Stats.1993, c. 893 (A.B.1796), § 2. Amended by Stats.1996, c. 634 (S.B. 2041), § 127; Stats.1998, c. 965 (A.B.2765), § 71.)

Historical and Statutory Notes

Legislative intent regarding Stats.1993, c. 893 (A.B.1796), including possible continuing application of provisions of repealed State Teachers' Retirement Law, see Historical and Statutory Notes under Education Code § 22000.

Former § 22663, added by Stats.1988, c. 542, § 2, relating to information required of a non-

member spouse acquiring a separate account or an interest, was repealed by Stats.1993, c. 893 (A.B.1796), § 1. See Education Code § 22659.

Derivation: Former § 22657, added by Stats. 1988, c. 542, § 2.

Cross References

Community property, see Family Code §§ 65 and 760.
Computation of time,
    Generally, see Code of Civil Procedure §§ 12 and 12a and Government Code § 6800 et seq.
    Time in which any act provided by the Education Code is to be done, see Education Code § 9.
Continuation of statutes relating to subjects covered by provisions of this Code, see Education Code
    § 3.

Library References

Legal Jurisprudences
Am Jur 2d (Rev) Pensions and Retirement Funds §§ 1643 et seq.

Treatises and Practice Aids
Witkin, Summary (9th ed) Com Prop § 47.

The Rutter Group, Family Law (Hogoboom & King) § 8:1214.

§ 22664. Service retirement allowance for nonmember spouse; conditions for retirement for service; limitations; calculation of allowance; increases

The nonmember spouse who is awarded a separate account shall have the right to a service retirement allowance and, if applicable, a retirement benefit under this part.

(a) The nonmember spouse shall be eligible to retire for service under this part if the following conditions are satisfied:

(1) The member had at least five years of credited service during the period of marriage, at least one year of which had been performed subsequent to the most recent refund to the member of accumulated retirement contributions. The credited service may include service credited to the account of the member as of the date of the dissolution or legal separation, previously refunded service, out-of-state service, and permissive service credit that the member is eligible to purchase at the time of the dissolution or legal separation.

(2) The nonmember spouse has at least two and one-half years of credited service in his or her separate account.

(3) The nonmember spouse has attained the age of 55 years or more.

(b) A service retirement allowance of a nonmember spouse under this part shall become effective upon any date designated by the nonmember spouse, provided:

(1) The requirements of subdivision (a) are satisfied.

(2) The nonmember spouse has filed an application for service retirement on a form provided by the system, that is executed no earlier than six months before the effective date of the retirement allowance.

(3) The effective date is no earlier than the first day of the month in which the application is received at the system's office in Sacramento and the effective date is after the date the judgment or court order pursuant to Section 22652 was entered.

(c)(1) Upon service retirement at normal retirement age under this part, the nonmember spouse shall receive a retirement allowance that shall consist of an annual allowance payable in monthly installments equal to 2 percent of final compensation for each year of credited service.

(2) If the nonmember spouse's retirement is effective at less than normal retirement age and between early retirement age under this part and normal retirement age, the retirement allowance shall be reduced by one-half of 1 percent for each full month, or fraction of a month, that will elapse until the nonmember spouse would have reached normal retirement age.

(3) If the nonmember spouse's service retirement is effective at an age greater than normal retirement age and is effective on or after January 1, 1999, the percentage of final compensation for each year of credited service shall be determined pursuant to the following table:

Age at Retirement	Percentage
60¼	2.033
60½	2.067
60¾	2.10
61	2.133
61¼	2.167
61½	2.20
61¾	2.233
62	2.267
62¼	2.30
62½	2.333
62¾	2.367
63 and over	2.40

(4) In computing the retirement allowance of the nonmember spouse, the age of the nonmember spouse on the last day of the month in which the retirement allowance begins to accrue shall be used.

(5) Final compensation, for purposes of calculating the service retirement allowance of the nonmember spouse under this subdivision, shall be calculated according to the definition of final compensation in Section 22134, 22134.5, 22135, or 22136, whichever is applicable, and shall be based on the member's compensation earnable up to the date the parties separated, as established in the judgment or court order pursuant to Section 22652. The nonmember spouse shall not be entitled to use any other calculation of final compensation.

(d) If the member is or was receiving a disability allowance under this part with an effective date before or on the date the parties separated as established in the judgment or court order pursuant to Section 22652, or at any time applies for and receives a disability allowance with an effective date that is before or coincides with the date the parties separated as established in the judgment or court order pursuant to Section 22652, the nonmember spouse shall not be eligible to retire until after the disability allowance of the member terminates.   If the member who is or was receiving a disability allowance returns to employment to perform creditable service subject to coverage under the Defined Benefit Program or has his or her allowance terminated under Section 24015, the nonmember spouse may not be paid a retirement allowance until at least six months after termination of the disability allowance and the return of the member to employment to perform creditable service subject to coverage under the Defined Benefit Program, or the termination of the disability allowance and the employment or self-employment of the member in any capacity, notwithstanding Section 22132.   If at the end of the six-month period, the member has not had a recurrence of the original disability or has not had his or her earnings fall below the amounts described in Section 24015, the nonmember spouse may be paid a retirement allowance if all other eligibility requirements are met.

(1) The retirement allowance of the nonmember spouse under this subdivision shall be calculated as follows: the disability allowance the member was receiving, exclusive of the portion for dependent children, shall be divided between the share of the member and the share of the nonmember spouse.   The share of the nonmember spouse shall be the amount obtained by multiplying the disability allowance, exclusive of the portion for dependent children, by the years of service credited to the separate account of the nonmember spouse, including service projected to the date of separation, and dividing by the projected service of the member.   The nonmember spouse's retirement allowance shall be the lesser of the share of the nonmember spouse under this subdivision or the retirement allowance under subdivision (c).

(2) The share of the member shall be the total disability allowance reduced by the share of the nonmember spouse.   The share of the member shall be considered the disability allowance of the member for purposes of Section 24213.

(e) The nonmember spouse who receives a retirement allowance is not a retired member under this part.   However, the allowance of the nonmember spouse shall be increased by application of the improvement factor and shall be eligible for the application of supplemental increases and other benefit maintenance provisions under this part, including, but not limited to, Sections 24411, 24412, and 24415 based on the same criteria used for the application of these benefit maintenance increases to the service retirement allowances of members.

(Added by Stats.1993, c. 893 (A.B.1796), § 2.   Amended by Stats.1996, c. 634 (S.B. 2041), § 128; Stats.1998, c. 965 (A.B.2765), § 72.5; Stats.1999, c. 939 (S.B.1074), § 43; Stats.2000, c. 74 (A.B.1509), § 42; Stats.2000, c. 1021 (A.B.2700), § 26; Stats.2001, c. 803 (S.B.501), § 6.)

Historical and Statutory Notes

Legislative intent regarding Stats.1993, c. 893 (A.B.1796), including possible continuing application of provisions of repealed State Teachers' Retirement Law, see Historical and Statutory Notes under Education Code § 22000.

Section 330 of Stats.1998, c. 965 (A.B.2765), provides:

"SEC. 330. Section 72.5 of this act shall only become operative if SB 2126 of the 1997–98 Regular Session [Stats.1998, c. 1076] is enacted, in which case Section 72 of this act shall not become operative and shall be repealed on January 1, 1999. If SB 2126 of the 1997–98 Regular Session is not enacted, then Section 72.5 shall not become operative and shall be repealed on January 1, 1999 and Section 72 shall become operative."

Subordination of legislation by Stats.1999, c. 939 (S.B.1074), to other 1999 legislation, see

Historical and Statutory Notes under Education Code § 22000.

Operative effect of Stats.2000, c. 1021 (A.B. 2700), see Historical and Statutory Notes following Education Code § 22101.5.

Section affected by two or more acts at the same session of the legislature, see Government Code § 9605.

Former § 22664, added by Stats.1988, c. 542, § 2, relating to conditions before a judgment or order is binding in the system, was repealed by Stats.1993, c. 893 (A.B.1796), § 1. See Education Code § 22656.

Derivation: Former § 22658, added by Stats. 1988, c. 542, § 2, amended by Stats.1990, c. 83, § 2; Stats.1992, c. 1166, § 9.

§ 22665. Service credit awarded in judgment or court order; calculation of retirement or disability allowance

The system shall include the service credit awarded to a nonmember spouse in the judgment or court order to determine the eligibility of a member for a retirement or disability allowance under this part. That portion of awarded service credit based on previously refunded accumulated retirement contributions or on permissive service credit may not be used by the member for eligibility requirements until the member has redeposited or purchased his or her portion of the service credit. The member's service retirement allowance shall be calculated based on the service credit in the member's account on the effective date of service retirement.

(Added by Stats.1993, c. 893 (A.B.1796), § 2. Amended by Stats.1996, c. 634 (S.B. 2041), § 129; Stats.1998, c. 965 (A.B.2765), § 73; Stats.2000, c. 74 (A.B.1509), § 43.)

Historical and Statutory Notes

Legislative intent regarding Stats.1993, c. 893 (A.B.1796), including possible continuing application of provisions of repealed State Teachers' Retirement Law, see Historical and Statutory Notes under Education Code § 22000.

Former § 22665, added by Stats.1988, c. 542, § 2, relating to statutory provisions applicable

to a nonmember spouse, was repealed by Stats. 1993, c. 893 (A.B.1796), § 1. See Education Code § 22657.

Derivation: Former § 22659, added by Stats. 1988, c. 542, § 2, amended by Stats.1992, c. 1166, § 10.

§ 22666. Terminable interest doctrine; legislative intent

It is the intent of the Legislature to abolish any remaining application of the terminable interest doctrine in California relating to the division of public retirement benefits of a member in the event of dissolution of marriage or death if the division is made under this chapter.

(Added by Stats.1993, c. 893 (A.B.1796), § 2.)

Historical and Statutory Notes

Legislative intent regarding Stats.1993, c. 893 (A.B.1796), including possible continuing application of provisions of repealed State Teachers' Retirement Law, see Historical and Statutory Notes under Education Code § 22000.

Former § 22666, added by Stats.1988, c. 542, § 2, amended by Stats.1990, c. 560 (A.B.4129),

§ 4, relating to legislative intent regarding the terminable interest doctrine, was repealed by Stats.1993, c. 893 (A.B.1796), § 1. See, now, this section.

Derivation: Former § 22666, added by Stats. 1988, c. 542, § 2, amended by Stats.1990, c. 560, § 4.

Cross References

Statutes,
   Construction and legislative intent, see Code of Civil Procedure §§ 1858 and 1859.
   Liberal construction of Education Code, see Education Code § 3.
   Rules of construction and definition for the Education Code, see Education Code § 10.

Library References

Treatises and Practice Aids
   Witkin, Summary (9th ed) Com Prop § 43.

INDEX TO

EDUCATION CODE

See last volume of Code

END OF VOLUME